THE LETTERS OF RUDYARD KIPLING

Kipling standing before the statue of Joan of Arc in the cathedral square of
Rheims, 16 August 1915, during his tour of the French front. The photograph was
probably taken by his travelling companion, Perceval Landon

The Letters of Rudyard Kipling

Volume 4
1911–19

Edited by

THOMAS PINNEY

University of Iowa Press, Iowa City

Contents

List of Illustrations

Frontispiece: Kipling standing before the statue of Joan of Arc in the cathedral square of Rheims, 16 August 1915, during his tour of the French front. The photograph was probably taken by his travelling companion, Perceval Landon (University of Sussex).

Plates

In-text illustrations

Preface and Acknowledgements

To the list of abbreviations and short titles in the first volume of this edition the following item is added:

Clinical History   A typescript calendar, evidently drawn from Mrs Kipling's diaries, recording the dates of RK's illnesses and giving a detailed, sometimes daily, account of his sufferings, treatments, recoveries and relapses between 1915 and 1936. It includes a list of the doctors who attended Kipling and a summary of the different diagnoses they offered in those years (Kipling Papers, University of Sussex).

I should like to acknowledge here the assistance I have received from Mr John Dagger towards the identification of the many officers and men of the armed forces who are mentioned in Kipling's letters from the war years. I am also grateful to Jessica Berets, Pomona College, 1997, who was indispensable in the long work of collating the transcripts of Kipling's letters with the manuscripts.

Chronology of Rudyard Kipling's Life, 1911–19

1911	26 January	Death of John Lockwood Kipling.
	18 February– 25 March	Vernet-les-Bains.
	25 March–8 April	Return to England by car through France.
	July	*A History of England*, with C. R. L. Fletcher.
	4–18 August	Tour in France with Mr and Mrs Max Aitken.
	21 September	John Kipling enters Wellington College.
	17–24 October	Tour in Ireland with CK: Dublin, Belfast.
	28 December	To Engelberg.
1912	14 February– 20 March	In Florence and Venice.
	20–27 March	Return to England via Paris.
	September	Motor tour in west of England.
	18 October	Election speech at Ashton-under-Lyne.
	October	*Songs from Books*.
	26 December	To Engelberg.
1913	7 February– 15 March	Voyage to Egypt and up the Nile.
	15 March–7 April	Return to France; by car across France on return journey to England.
	April	RK's play *The Harbour Watch* produced.
	24 August– 10 September	At Kessingland Grange, Norfolk.
	22 December	To Engelberg.
1914	4–7 February	Return to England via Paris.
	22 February– 18 March	Vernet-les-Bains.
	March	Helps promote "British Covenant" against Irish Home Rule.
	18 March–17 April	Return to England by car through France.
	16 May	Speech on Ulster at Tunbridge Wells.
	23 July–10 August	At Kessingland Grange.
	10 September	Secures commission in Irish Guards for John Kipling from Lord Roberts.

1915   February   *The New Army in Training.*
         April   Bath.
         12–26 August   Visits French front.
         27 September   John Kipling reported wounded and missing.
         29 September   RK has gastritis: onset of permanent illness
                                     (duodenal ulcer).
         October   *France at War.*
         December   *The Fringes of the Fleet.*

1916   February   Bath.
         December   *Sea Warfare.*

1917   29 January   Resigns from Society of Authors.
         February   Bath.
         17 April   *A Diversity of Creatures.*
         May   Visits Italian front.
         17–30 August   Trip to Edinburgh.
         27 August   Accepts appointment as Rhodes Trustee.
         September   Joins War Graves Commission.

1918   February–March   Bath.
         c. April   *The Eyes of Asia.*
         10–23 September   Visit to Newquay, Cornwall.

1919   10 February–   Bath.
           early March
         April   *The Years Between.*
         3–29 September   Motor tour to Scotland.

Part One
Towards Armageddon

1911–July 1914

INTRODUCTION

The war dominates the years covered in this volume, but even before the war things were hardly peaceful for Kipling, caught up as he was in the often bitter and violent social and political conflicts of the time. The idea that the Edwardian age was a long, golden afternoon of Imperial repose has now passed into established myth, but for Kipling it was anything but that: he saw change and decay all around.

There were severe industrial disturbances: a railway strike in 1911, a coal strike and a dock strike in 1912 – events that Kipling took to mean that "there is no law in England save the whim of the unions" (9 June 1912). The women were restless too. The Suffragettes had become visible and troubling by 1909 and, by 1911, increasingly difficult to laugh away. Kipling's public response was "The Female of the Species", begun some time before July 1910 and published in, of all places, the *Ladies' Home Journal* in 1911. Caroline Kipling was, if anything, even more resolutely opposed to the aims of the Suffragettes than was her husband, and they confirmed each other in their disapproval. It was a sign of the foolishness of the times when their daughter Elsie's presention at Court was "spoilt by a demonstration by a suffragette" (CK diary, 4 June 1914).

In official politics, the constitutional crisis that arose over the Liberal budgets made political observers and prophets such as Kipling very anxious indeed. When the Lords rejected the budget at the end of 1909, they provoked legislation aimed at curbing their power to obstruct. This Parliament Bill, as it was called, in turn elicited the most determined reactionary defences from the so-called "Die-hard" Tories. Kipling, without being exactly a "Die-hard", saw things in sufficiently melodramatic terms: when, at the end of 1912, the Lords had been shorn of their power, the unions indulged, the schemes of national unemployment and national health insurance passed, he could write that "There is no particular law of any kind in England at present."

The bitterness of party feeling, developed over the years following the great Liberal victory in 1906, broke out on many occasions, but never more violently, perhaps, than on the occasion of the Marconi scandal in 1912. Kipling's response was the poem called "Gehazi", an attack on Sir Rufus Isaacs, one of the principals in the Marconi affair, so unmeasured that no one, not even Kipling's political friends, dared publish it at the time.

3

From 1912 on, however, the whole foreground of politics, so far as RK was concerned, was occupied by Home Rule and the fate of Ulster. The Home Rule bill, twice passed and twice rejected, would finally come into force in 1914. The prospect that Protestant Ulster would then become part of a Catholic Ireland seemed so likely that it raised serious threats of civil war. Kipling's "Ulster" (1912) expressed the mood of the Unionists:

> The dark eleventh hour
> Draws on and sees us sold
> To every evil power
> We fought against of old.

Thousands signed an "Oath of the Covenant", pledging themselves to resist any form of Home Rule. Kipling himself was active in promoting a "League of British Covenanters" vowed to oppose any use of British troops in Ulster, and in May of 1914 he made a speech at Tunbridge Wells attacking the government's Ulster policy and concluding that civil war was "inevitable". Acting on this belief, he and his wife were busy in making preparations for the refugees that would stream across the Irish Sea to England when the fighting began.

The degree to which passions had been heated is measured by Kipling's utterances in his verses on "Ulster" and "The Covenant", and in his speech at Tunbridge Wells: "betrayal", "conspiracy", "lies", "poison", "treason", "rapine" crowd together in them. All this agitation, passionately intense and utterly absorbing at the time, was at once overwhelmed when the war in Europe broke out. For the general public, it was as though the Ulster crisis had never been. Yet the question at issue was only postponed, and it remained as unresolved as ever. Nor did Kipling himself forget. In the middle of the war, when Lord Selborne resigned from the government in protest against a move to grant immediate home rule, Kipling wrote at once to congratulate Selborne on the integrity of his stand (29 June 1916).

The one new book that Kipling published in this time was also an exercise in partisan politics. This was the collaboration with the Oxford historian C. R. L. Fletcher on *A History of England*, a small book intended for use in the schools, with a text by Fletcher and illustrative verses by Kipling – including such things as "The River's Tale", "The Dutch in the Medway", and "The Glory of the Garden". The book is very readable, and, for those who feel no personal interest in the questions treated, often amusing. But it outraged many readers at the time, particularly among the Irish: a question was raised in Parliament, asking whether the President of the Board of Education would proscribe the book for its libels on the Irish? Kipling affected to be indifferent or amused, but the reception rankled. He perhaps learned something from the experience. Fletcher repeatedly asked him to collaborate on new, extended editions of the book, both during the war and after, but Kipling steadily refused.

The only other book that Kipling published in these years was called *Songs from Books* (1912), a nearly-complete harvest of the verse scattered through the collections of his stories and miscellaneous publications and not included in any volume of his poems. It was in fact something more than a compilation, for Kipling took a number of poems that had originally appeared only as a few lines or stanzas and wrote them out at greater length. He also planned the publication of a new collection of his stories, the volume later published as *A Diversity of Creatures*, but this plan was for a time shelved by the war. So too was the plan to publish *Letters of Travel (1892–1913)*, which was scheduled for the autumn of 1914 but did not come out until 1920. Thus the years 1911–14 are not marked by any notable new book by Kipling, the first time that such a thing could have been said since the beginning of his fame in 1890.

In his private life, 1911 was marked by the death of Kipling's father in January, just two months after the death of his mother. That ending was set off by a hopeful beginning when John Kipling entered Wellington College in September 1911. John's career there, however, was undistinguished and a disappointment to his father. He did not rise beyond the Middle Second form and left, "superannuated", in 1914, when he was sent to an Army crammer's in Bournemouth. The uncertainty of John's prospects was resolved at a stroke on the outbreak of the war.

There seems to have been no thought of sending Elsie, John's sister and elder, to school. She remained at home, with a governess, but frequently travelled with her parents and had at least two stays in Paris for her finishing.

One new friend appears suddenly and prominently in Kipling's life: the young and irrepressible Canadian, Max Aitken, soon to be Sir Max and, not long after, Lord Beaverbrook. They met in 1910, shortly after Aitken arrived in England, and almost at once the Kipling family and the Aitken family were on terms of close friendship: Kipling advised Aitken on the purchase of a home, made a speech on the hustings for him, consulted him (as did all Aitken's friends) on financial matters, was godfather to Aitken's second son; the two families spent a Christmas together, and travelled together on the Continent. At some time after the war, however, the friendship ended on Kipling's motion. Aitken (now Beaverbrook) was unsound on the Irish question, so Kipling thought: probably that was only one issue among many on which Kipling would have seen Beaverbrook as unreliable and untrustworthy. Beaverbrook made several attempts to restore the friendship, unsuccessfully.

After he had made the Swiss Alps at Engelberg his regular winter destination, Kipling did more travelling in Europe and around the Mediterranean than he had before – a pattern that was to remain largely unchanged until his death. There were trips to Rome in 1909, to Florence and Venice in 1912. In 1913, after the usual stay at Engelberg, Kipling and his wife, leaving the children behind, travelled up the Nile as far as Wady Halfa, a trip that they were twice to repeat in later years.

To John Lockwood Kipling, 4 January 1911

ALS: University of Sussex

Hotels Cattani / Engelberg / Jan. 4. 1911:

Dear Man –

Your last two in – notably the second with the news about the Nurse who seems to be satisfactory; and the still more satisfactory news that there seems to be reasonable hope of a good place for T[rix]. to meditate in, at Andover;[1] and the *most* satisfactory account of your arteries by Cecil Ensor.[2] All these three things (since 'tis not *I* who have to bear the brunt of carking Jack!)[3] make me more cheered. But I can imagine the desolation of daily letters (such men leak daily) from that sleeplessly cantankerous invalid. Blowed if I see, though, what can be done. There's no law to forbid a man writing, or advising, about his wife: all one can be thankful for is that he don't assert all his rights. But I conceive that a reasoned plan, such as T. going to Andover, plainly set forth, ought to ease him and for a while keep him quiet. He must have some sort of idea that he ought to do something and since worrying comes easiest why he worries the nearest thing in sight!

When T. is away he might be led, by medical advice, to look after his own precious health in the south of Europe for three or four months. I don't know whether Cecil wouldn't assist him to that idea.

As you say, there's no restraint needed. It's change and firm sympathy that the poor child wants but above all change, and – low be it spoken – the assurance that J. will not descend on her and tell her to "pull herself together." Here's hoping and praying that the new nurse will secure her confidence. But – Oh Lord – what a job for a man to turn to in his later days. I always knew you were a man of size but I didn't know what a bigness of man you were.

"Silky" as a term of approbation for an artery is new to me and I find myself murmuring it over several times.

We've had no sun since Sunday – only snow to three feet almost – and low straight roofs of cloud a thousand feet up the mountain, with here and there, as the light from the sky strove to fight through, great semi-luminous patches of *solid* blue atmosphere. On this the Head Waiter Tschoppf (him who writes me odes on going and coming) delivered his poetic soul at breakfast. An artist has an exhibition of pictures for sale in one of the corridors –attempts to render this blue snow effect. Said Tschoppf, pointing out of window to the luminous shadow of the Joch Pass,[4] "*That* is what you see. It's air. Air, you understand. But that is not what he (the artist) can paint. *Why* is that. Because he has no *Sowl* in his pictures." The voice was exactly like Alma Tadema's.[5]

And yesterday, monologing on hotel management in which by the way Tschoppf lectures at Lucerne in the slack season. The Swiss, I believe, have classes if not colleges of hotel-keeping. "*As* I tell my pupils at Lucerne, Mistare Kipling, when I speak of hotels. I say to them there is only three things in a hotel – cleanness, you understand? and *then* cleanness. And then cleanness more! I suppose (this [   ][6]) I walk thirty forty kilometres a day looking at cleanliness!"

Was out this morn for an hour on skis with the professor but my damned boot-fastenings kept getting loose and I finished each glissade thus: – [sketch of RK with one ski on and one ski off]. So I gave it up and skated with the kids. Net result not much done but no end of a sweat which I take it is why one comes here.

C. I am rejoiced to say is keeping well – albeit she sat out on the rink too long and I fear must have got chilled. She pads about on snow-shoes which give her all the exercise she needs.

Now I will finish up the letter and add it to your already-haggis-like envelope.

Dearest love
Rud.

Notes
1. Trix suffered a nervous breakdown after the death of her mother; following JLK's death she was put into the care of J. F. Williams-Freeman of Weyhill House, Andover, where she remained for at least two years.
2. The Tisbury doctor, son of the Tisbury doctor Arthur John Ensor (see 2 August 1894).
3. Colonel Fleming: JLK wrote of Fleming at this time that he "would give a brass monkey depression" (to Edith Plowden, 23 December 1910: ALS, Sussex).
4. South of Engelberg, 7,000 feet high.
5. Sir Lawrence Alma-Tadema (1836–1912), Dutch painter resident in London from 1870, specialising in "classical" subjects with great popular success.
6. Word illegible.

To John Lockwood Kipling, [*c.* 7–8 January 1911]
ALS: University of Sussex

Hotels Cattani / Engelberg

Dear Man,

Another day – the third – of bright blazing blue sunshine closing with deep purple twilight lights high up among the snows. We were out skating all the morn and on our *skis* this afternoon – the packed snow a shade too hard for comfortable falling down upon and the trodden paths like ice – insomuch that I got out of my skis in the village street and pushed 'em home before me. John, who had been in gross difficulties with his straps etc., we turned out on a snow slope and left alone. Whereat he announced that the trick of it was "coming back to him" and did an hour's experiments by himself to his own great satisfaction.

The other day he had another experience – on a sleigh this time. He was fascinated by a new patent *luge* – called an "auto-bob" – a luge with a wheel-steering tiller like a motor, thus [sketch of sleigh with steering wheel]. I warned him that the steering gear was apt to be tricky but he *would* have it: and he and E. went out on the village run – a double-twisting hillside path ending at right angles to the main street – between a fence and a house front thus [sketch of fence, path, and house front]. Natural result. The run was *very* bumpy; the bumps knocked the wheel out of his hand and he ran sideways along the shop-front, scraping his foot between the luge and the stone wall, and bending it backwards. Equally naturally – hot water, bandages, and iodine and a day's meditation with a lame foot. But it was a great gain. They don't teach English schoolboys to think for themselves or to look after themselves and a knock now and again wakes 'em up. He is great fun, and, I make bold to think, genuinely amusing – He and E. capping each other's quotation as quickly as fencers at work and the two together preferring to be with us two in all things.

Thank goodness, the first wild new year rush is abating. Twenty people or more leave each day and only 12 or 15 take their places, so that we have more room and tis possible to get baths without fighting for 'em.

I have not been altogether idle for I've done an additional set of verses for my history book – a metrical version of the life, death and adventures of the old Tower musket which from 1710 to 1835 or 40 was *the* arm of England and won for us all the main blocks of Empire. Naturally the refrain is "Brown Bess."

> "At Blenheim and Ramillies fops 'ud confess
> They were pierced to the heart by the charms of Brown Bess –

and

> Kings as they danced had no reason to bless
> The figures they cut – by command of Brown Bess![1]

And so on, till the Battle of Waterloo when: –

> Later, near Brussels, Napoleon no less –
> Arranged for a Waterloo Ball with Brown Bess."

B.B. dances him down of course and

> "When his gilt carriage wheeled off in the press
> 'I have danced my last dance for the world' said Brown Bess."

A conceit somewhat elaborately beaten out but it amused me in the doing – sign that may be t'will amuse other folks to read.

Your last letter seems cheerier but do you think 'twould be well to let T[rix]. go direct to the Tennants[2] or even to Stan's with her nurse before she had gone through a thought out cure at Andover such as you proposed. It seems to me that the excitement of meeting people, the fear that she might not keep hold of herself might pre-dispose her to further trouble. And again – Don't think I'm like J[ack]. F[leming] – don't she need a lot of exercise? You see she has never had much occupation on the physical side – and if she needs being well nourished, would need, I imagine, corresponding bodily work. Maybe, a cure with a nurse would contemplate that better at Andover than, at present at any rate, as a guest in a county house. And, perhaps, isn't there something in the notion that when T. has her balance again she would not like to think that she had been among friends, however sympathetic, when she was off it. Your notion of Andover, with the nurse, in the family of a doctor, seems to me *the* thing. I don't like journeys and meetings with sympathetic acquaintances, just now.

Sorry for your bother with folk who ask questions but I expect they mean well. The Doubledays are coming over in March – leaving N.Y. per *Lusitania* Mar. 1. I think they'd like to come down and see you if you'd give 'em a sign.

With love as ever

Rud.

Notes
1. This couplet does not appear in the published poem.
2. Probably Edward Tennant (1859–1920), 2nd Baronet and 1st Baron Glenconner, and his wife, who was the daughter of the Wyndhams of Clouds.

To Colonel H. W. Feilden, 13 January 1911
ALS: Syracuse University

Hotels Cattani / Engelberg / Jan. 13. 1911

To the Illustrious Fireworker
      The Colonel Sahib
The Destroyer of Winged Birds
Greeting!
And the first thing C. said when she read of your success with the stove was: – "*Why* did he burn his fingers if he didn't try to feed the thing from in front?" I've done that myself – shoved in a coal at a time through those awkward bars. But it isn't the proper way at all! However, we're rejoiced that

the old thing functions and 60° for a steady indoors temperature is all right. Our temperature has varied between 15°F. and 0°F. with generally a clean blue sky and sunshine. There have been two heavy falls of snow – one accompanied by an N.W. wind which cut through all wrapping. E. and I went out in it for an hour and felt that Arctic exploration had no terror for us. Glory be to Allah C. keeps *very* well. Hasn't had any cold and skates daily. *Exempli gratia*. She came out on the rink yesterday at 11: 45: had lunch, on skates on the rink at 1. and went on skating till 3: 30, which I call a fair day's work.

Last night was a Bioscope show in the Theatre. The usual comic French rot; ending, quite unexpectedly, with the most beautiful nature coloured studies of Birds feeding their young. The return of a wild-duck to its nest, its uncovering of the eggs and, when it departed, recovering them with weeds was perhaps the most marvellous: though a missel-thrush feeding its young was almost as good. I suppose 'tis telephoto work but I never saw anything to touch it. Films said to be American. D'you know anything about 'em?

There's no one very interesting here – except a fat Lieutenant of sub-marines, and the Engineer of the *Bonaventure* that is mother ship to a whole hatching of subm's at Portsmouth. Says the Engineer to me last night: – "We're taking half a dozen submarines to Malta in February. The *Bonaventure* will chaperone 'em. Come along!" I wish to goodness that I could! The Lieutenant tells me yarns about sighting and judging distance under water – i.e. when you have only the periscope for guide. Also, a queer yarn of one of his own practise torpedoes, fired under water, which turned tail over tip and returned and smote the submarine on the side. A nice sensation! Likewise a practical hint. "If you ever find the next man to you fall over or sink down as you're cleaning the engines it's a sign he has been overcome by C.O. (Carbon Monoxide I suppose). *Don't* take him into the fresh air. He'll probably snuff out if you do. Just carry him into the bows and let him lie beside the torpedo, and he'll recover." So now you know the etiquette of submarines. And that reminds me. The fat Lieutenant is a bit of an ornitholo-gist. Spent his childhood near Seaford where, he swears, the Raven is not extinct. Tells me of a battle he saw on the edge of the cliffs 'twixt a nesting peregrine and an inquisitive buck raven lazily flapping along the edge of the chalk. Mrs. P. routed Dr. R. Says further that you'll find Ravens at Birling Gap *today*.

I get good news of my Father's health for which I'm grateful. He talks of visiting the Wyndhams at Clouds – comes to us, all being well, in April. Yes, I wept over the Winston business for the same reason as you and my father did.[1] Three hours small-arm fire and devil a shot where it would have done some good to the nation. However I suppose the Scots Guards will be "Winston's Own" in the next Army List.

I have done, for the history book, a new set of verses called "Brown Bess". Not bad. They describe the old lady as

"An outspoken, flinty-lipped, brazen faced jade
With a habit of looking men straight in the eyes"

They deal with her career from 1709 to 1815 when Napoleon arranges for "a Waterloo Ball with Brown Bess" and

"Before her set squares his battalions gave way
And her last fierce quadrille put his lancers to flight"

ending with

"If you go to Museums (there's one near Whitehall)
    Where old weapons are shown, with their names writ beneath,
You'll find her upstanding, her back to the wall,
    As stiff as a ramrod, the flint in her teeth.
And if ever we English have reason to bless
    Any arm save our Mothers', that arm is Brown Bess!"

Dear love from us all. Keep your two selves well.

> Affectionately
> Rudyard.

P.S. A man here, evidently opulent tradesman, named Johnson or Johnston, rents a big shoot at Bulksteep, Dallington.[2] Who is he?

Notes
1. At the end of December a gang of armed robbers were besieged by the police in a building in Stepney. The police requested aid from the Scots Guards in the Tower, and Winston Churchill, as Home Secretary, authorised their use. Churchill then went to the scene, and was afterwards much ridiculed by the press for seeming to direct the "battle".
2. The Village of Dallington is a few miles south of Bateman's.

To Louisa Baldwin, 31 January 1911
ALS: Dalhousie University

> The Gables / Tisbury / Jan. 31. 1911

Dear Aunt Louie
    Thank you for your so kind note.[1]
    I am having the house kept on for a while in order as I hope to connect the children with it. It has been emptied of papers[2] and for the rest will stand

exactly as it did, except for Trixie's things which I have passed over to Colonel Fleming.

We hope to return to Engelberg tomorrow.[3] There I greatly look forward to being with Stan.[4]

All our love
Ruddy.

Notes
1. JLK died on 26 January, at Clouds, where he was visiting the Wyndhams. RK and CK left for England from Engelberg on 27 January (Rees extracts).
2. It was at this time, according to Trix, that RK destroyed a great many family papers: see, e.g., Birkenhead, *Rudyard Kipling*, p. 253.
3. They left on the afternoon of the 31st and reached Engelberg on 2 February (Rees extracts).
4. The Baldwins were at Engelberg sometime after the middle of January; probably they arrived after RK and CK had been summoned back to England.

To Edmonia Hill, 10 February 1911
ALS: Library of Congress

Grand Hotel and Kuranstalt / Engelberg Feb. 10. 1911

My dear Mrs Hill

Thank you so much for both your kind letters, the second of which reached me today. Believe me I value your sympathy very greatly. My mother died of heart-failure on November 23rd. It was not, mercifully, a long illness and we were all with her, but the shock of her death was so severe on my sister that her health gave way, and she is now in a doctor's house near Andover. It was after my mother's death that my father judged it best to have my sister with him and, to a great extent, looking after her blunted the edge of his loneliness or at least prevented him from realizing it. When she went away, on the 16th of last month, he went on a visit to some dear friends close by Tisbury. His last letter to me was full of pleasure at his visit and his relief at escaping for a while from the little house that was so full of sadness for him.

He died, quickly, without pain, of heart-failure on the 26th of January and I was told by wire while I was here where my son was very ill.[1] I went over at once and arranged matters: keeping the little house that had covered nearly 20 years of their lives together. Then I came back here to find my son better and here I have been ever since. So you see that I have suffered a little. Dear as my mother was, my father was more to me than most men are to their sons: and now that I have no one to talk or write to I find myself desolate. But I am glad he died with his powers unbroken and his interest in life keen till the end. I saw him just before Xmas, when he promised me that he would not go away and we had arranged he was to spend the summer with us in Sussex.

I know that you who loved your father so keenly will realize what his loss means to me: and you are *very* good to write to me so kindly. I have had a heavy time with business and correspondence for life goes on just the same whatever happens.

Very sincerely and gratefully yours
Rudyard Kipling

Note
1. John had a "severe touch of influenza" (RK to Stanley Baldwin, 19 January 1911: ALS, Sussex). On 13 February he left Engelberg to return to school (CK *Diary*).

To Colonel H. W. Feilden, 23 February 1911
ALS: Syracuse University

Hôtel du Parc / *Vernet-les-Bains*[1] / Feb. 23. 1911

Dear Colonel Sahib –

I had been meditating a letter to you for days: and the burden of my meditation was, once again, the ease and comfort and celerity with which Mrs Fielden could come down here and be washed, and rewashed and yet again washed; and what a pleasant English Club, with all papers, was waiting for you; and what comfortable rooms could be obtained.

The process is simplicity. Bag a *closed* motor from the Duke; roll down to Folkestone in time for the 4:10. p.m. Boulogne* Boat. Thence Paris. Thence at 7. p.m. – the next day for you may need a night's rest – leave the Quai D'Orsay in the one direct through carriage for Vernet. Occupy two *lits-toilettes* which are vastly superior to wagons-lits: and at 12:30 (it is seventeen hours) arrive at Ville Franche to be met in a motor by us, and taken to lunch here. Tired, yes Mrs. Fielden will be: but I think, somehow, when the tire is out of her, she'd feel better: and she could really be comfy and happy for six weeks.

---

*No. Better the morning train because of climbing up into that d—d Paris express in the twilight. It's the only climb up en route as the Vernet carriage at the Quai D'Orsay lies almost level with the platform.

Lady Bobs (and the Chief) who to put it mildly is twice as incapacitated as Mrs Fielden comes here next week.[2] And how *you'd* revel in the land! But I can quite appreciate her point of view – which used to be my Mother's. "Why – oh *why* when I am at ease, more or less, in my own Zion, must I upstick and travel!"

I feel great yearnings for Bateman's – which strengthen as the flowers appear.

And now I want you to do me a favour – several in fact. When next you go down the hill, go in (mind the steps) to Bateman's and in C's room and you will find, among several other Bædekers, two Bædekers – one of North and one of South France. Please send us them *both*: for we meditate a motor-tour back,[3] and they are our guides and friends for Hotels etc. They are on the left hand side bookshelves at the top of the steps (oh be careful of those same steps!) as you go up.

When you have found the books, return home and with care and prayer choose me half a dozen trout-flies of a kind guaranteed to allure the Catalan trout. For some unexplained reason – I suppose all dynamite has gone to Barcelona for political uses[4] – the Cadi is full of rude little trout who make faces at me and I don't think I can put up with it much longer. Some are between $\frac{1}{4}$ and $\frac{1}{2}$ lb. and the water is beautiful but colder than anything out of Switzerland. It has been a late winter, with lots of snow which is still lying all about in patches. But the sun is Spanish and stabs through the gorges like a knife; the hellebore is out and peacock and brimstone butterflies sit on the rocks. Haven't seen any lizards yet. The almonds were in bloom round Cette and Narbonne: but up here, nearly 2000 feet, Nature is merely lying low, except for the Laurustines.[5] Nothing'll keep a laurustine from flowering.

By the way, I don't suppose you know that you are already here! Elsie discovered you the other day as she was looking out of window and shouted: – "There's the Colonel." Naturally we ran and behold it was you in your lighter suit and knicks! – a most curious likeness and now it is the plain duty of any member of the family who is at the window and sees you passing to warn the others. I haven't talked to the "colonel" yet because in that respect I *know* he'll be a lamentable failure.

Why did Bassett say "statesmen"?[6] was it ironical or dialect? Surely "statesmen" in the sense of land holders is *Cumberland* and Cumberland only. Please enlighten me.

And talking of ethnology I met at Lucerne a professor Corning[7] (an American continentalized) from Zurich. To him I addressed enquiries as to where I could get anything about Swiss lacustrine villages. Result – he sent me a complete bibliography of the subject – some of which I want to get hold of. He, talking of ethnology, spoke of the Neanderthal skull and it's probable antiquity. "But you can never be sure about anything" said he. "I've got the double of it in my collection." "And where did you get it?" says I. "Round the corner" said he. "It was the skull of a Bâsle concierge who had been killed in a lift accident – but, for all that, it was practically identical in measurements etc. with the Neanderthal one." Come to think of it, a concierge with a Neanderthal skull would naturally find some difficulty in dealing with modern lifts. Thus does Nature – kind thing! – ensure the survival of the fittest.

Our news is naught. We came to Vernet, *not* because Carrie was bad with rheumatism but because it did her so much good last year and, meeting Osler on the boat from Folkestone to Boulogne, he said that, if that was so we couldn't do better than repeat the dose. She hadn't a twinge all the time we were at Engelberg but, within the past few days she has had a regular siege of it and says things not to be written down. Moreover, it's a very good place for nerves, and having come here last year we knew the road and the ropes which saved exertion. You see, we've both been a bit strained. John was horrid ill at Engelberg – I had fifteen broken nights on and before I went to my father's funeral – and altogether rest is what we need. It's the quietest life under the sun. Elsie and I went swimming in the big sulphur bath this afternoon and are now slack and lazy. C. takes sulphur baths in her own room but has not yet begun the drastic course of massage sous l'eau that makes her swear yet makes her better. Oh! I forgot to say that C. has invited our old Mademoiselle who was four years with us at Bateman's to come down and teach Elsie French and German. The old Lady came and is now enraptured at the sight of the southern end of her own country.

I've done my proofs of the English History verses – but there's always a temptation to add odds and ends to it. I am trying to resist it.

Thank you for what you said about my Dad. He was a man and besides being all he was to me, I'd worked with him for the better part of 30 years and he with me. So I feel a bit desolate. But *he* was in luck. He died quick, among friends, in pleasant quarters and fit to the last.

Our best love to both of you.

Ever affectionately
Rudyard.

Damn all traction engines! They used to break the hedge on the Uckfield side. I've written Martin about fencing the new Forest. I know Malpass's hungry sheep!

Notes
1. They left for Vernet-les-Bains via Paris on 16 February and arrived on the 18th (CK diary).
2. Lord Roberts, his wife, and daughter arrived in Vernet on 27 February (CK diary).
3. See 7 April 1911.
4. There had been an Anarchist bombing in Barcelona in 1910.
5. Laurustinus, a winter-flowering evergreen shrub, *Viburnum Tinus*.

6. I cannot identify Bassett. "Statesman", meaning an independent farmer, is northern usage, found in Cumberland and elsewhere.
7. Hanson Kelly Corning (1861–1951), an American educated in Zurich and Heidelberg, was Professor of Anatomy at the University of Basel, 1898–1929.

To Claude Johnson, [*c.* early March 1911]
ALS: Cornell University

Hôtel du Parc / Vernet-les-Bains

Dear Johnson

I've been thinking a lot what to do with the car.[1] This place which was reasonably quiet last year simply stinks and fizzles with every make of car except R[olls]. R[oyce]. It's a Christian duty to raise the tone of the community.

So when you're ready, send it along. We shall be ready any day after the 20th March.

I want to do two or three runs that I can do from here (always with Fleck[2] *bien entendu*) with one night out. Barcelona and Carcasonne are among 'em.

But I'm badly stuck about new routes to Paris. I've got all Taride[3] but it only makes it worse as I don't know the mountains. Do you know anything, or any book that would help me. Bædeker is an anachronism.[4]

I've just had the last report on my man. The company finds him "competent to drive a privately owned Rolls Royce."

I did *not* write them the story of the tramp who turned up with one button in his hand and requested the mistress of the house to sew a shirt on to it. Your kindness in sewing, so to speak, your shirt to my button, put that retort out of the question but my wrath against Barker[5] is still unquenched. *He's* not fit to conduct a privately-owned workshop.

Lord and Lady Roberts are here with, I regret to say, a Silent Knight.[6] Rather low, don't you think.

And there is also a man of wealth[7] much oppressed by his servants who has come from Paris en automobile with a French chauffeur with a passion for breaking down in large towns, and an English valet who sits gibbering with terror beside the chauffeur with whom he cannot converse. Said the valet to his master this evening, tentatively: – "Don't you think travelling by rail Sir, is much preferable to travelling by motor?" Incidentally the master is but newly married and the valet opened the honeymoon by losing as much as was entrusted to him, of *their* baggage at Calais!

After all, it is a nice world. Come out and enjoy it.

Ever sincerely
Rudyard Kipling

P.S. This year I do really hope to do something descriptive (perhaps even truthful) about motoring in France.

Notes
1. RK appears to have bought a new Rolls-Royce before the end of 1910 (CK diary, 2 November 1910) but had not yet taken possession of it. It was then damaged by a fire at the premises of the coachbuilder: see note 5, below, and [*c*. mid-March 1911]. The car in question in this letter must be one on loan from Rolls-Royce.
2. The chauffeur supplied by Rolls-Royce. He has been described as "Rolls-Royce's best chauffeur" (*Kipling Journal*, March 1986, p. 57).
3. The road maps and guides published by the Paris firm of Taride.
4. The Baedeker itineraries were still based on the railways.
5. Barker and Co., a noted firm of coachbuilders in London. See [*c*. mid-March 1911].
6. An American five-seater touring car in production from 1906 to 1909, priced at $3,500 (G. N. Georgano, ed., *The Complete Encyclopedia of Motorcars 1885–1968*, New York, 1968, p. 515).
7. Chauncey Mitchell Depew, Jr, the son of the Vanderbilt lawyer and railroad president, Chauncey Depew, Sr; he and his wife, the former Julia Catlin (see [16 April 1894], had arrived in Vernet at the end of February (CK diary).

To Colonel H. W. Feilden, [15–19 March 1911][1]
ALS: Syracuse University

Hôtel du Parc / Vernet-les-Bains

Dear Colonel Sahib

Your long and most delightful letter greeted me on my return from a day-long excursion to Port Vendrees and Banyuls sur Mer (you can't get further south in France than B. Sur M. because there the road to Spain stops). We went with some friends[2] in a huge loose-limbed long-bodied 75 h.p. De Dietrich via Vernet, Prades (of course), Millas, Thuir, Elsne (or isn't it Elne?), Argeles sur Mer and so along the coast line passing eventually a most casually situated dynamite factory which if it blew up – and there don't seem any special reason why it shouldn't! – would infallibly wreck both the road *and* the main line to Barcelona. But Lord what a journey! A divine blue day with a keen wind – the tail end, I suppose, of the mistral – but yet quite warm when we stopped which we had to for a punctured tyre. This was on the edge of Thuir and among the crowd turned up a youth on a bicycle to whom Depew the owner of the car presented the badly split tyre. We left the boy staring at the huge floppy thing on the ground. The chauffeur told him that the iron studs on the rim would be excellent for boots. I had a vision of him and all his family (except the toothless grandmother) sitting down after our departure to worry out the studs with their teeth. What the dooce *ought* one to do with a tyre suddenly presented to one.

Then the Mediterranean hove up, all sapphire, with a shark's fin of a lateen sail here and there and a rip or two of white wave tops before the wind, and forty foot palms (they looked like date palms) waving in the hollows of the hills against the coast. We lunched at Port Vendrees – a large Catalan lunch – but I made my meal chiefly of Bouillabaisse. Never met it before: never knew it could be so perfect – specially the sauce of pale yellow with slices of bread soaked in it. And the fish seemed to have been out of the water less than an hour.* I noted the local fishing boats, that they are fully decked and the deck has a camber more steep than that of the old fashioned torpedo boats. Tremendous timbers too for their size, knees and deck beams out of all proportion: so that they can stand unlimited hammering and with the hatches closed should be as tight as the bottle that they resemble in section [sketch of cross-section of fishing boat with caption: "A regular nest of timbers" and labels: "hatch", "washboards", "bilge pieces"]. The sail stuff *very* poor – like cotton. I think the system of painting 'em makes it easy for every family to spot its own boat coming in, at the extreme limit of vision. Also the head of the mast with the pulley in it is this shape and painted as gaily as a fishing float [sketch of mast head with caption: "painted to taste"]. All thoroughly effective and workmanlike and evolved by the attrition of wind, water and rock. I take it Marryatt's *Speronares*[3] are pretty much the same as the Gulf of Lyons fishing boat. You probably know all this but 'tis new to me.

Sunday.   Another lunch – a most tremendous lunch, but this time at Perpignan. One of the three brothers who run this hotel – his name is Emile Kiesler – finds in us, and specially in Carrie, sympathetic listeners to his woes, his ambitions and his plans for the hotel's future. C. talks to him about pigsties, rubbish destructors, sanitation, finance etc. Well the result was that he insisted on us coming for a motor drive. His plans were varied and mutable. His idea was first of a picnic in the open air on the top of a mountain where hares lived by the million (he said) and could be caught by lighting fires. Some form of "jacking" I suppose – suitable for jack hares. And we were to have our chicken roasted in the open. But today the weather was overcast and threatening. Emile promptly jettisoned all his plans, but kept the lunch on top of the motor, in case of accidents; telephoned to Perpignan to a friend who keeps the Lion d'Or and, gay as a child, set out to show us Perpignan. We ran through drifts of pink peach-blossom, with white touches of almond blossom here and there, and the hills were just brushed at their tips and edges with gorse in bloom. Then we went to the Lion D'Or – small, filthy and hidden. Imagine Perpignan – on a Sunday – all the garrison out in

---

*Likewise there were anchovies – caught at Port Vendrees!

the big streets with their girls, the stone-cobbled, brick centred streets all deserted; and one small voluble intensely funny little Franco-German (Kiesler seems to be a mixture of at least three nationalities) explaining the history of illustrious families in the wine trade who lived behind the shuttered doors. Then he produced a lunch of a beauty and a succulence which made one weep.

item: a locally made pate de foie gras (fresh and lovely)
Oysters from Arcachon (weeping bitterly I had to pass them).
Omelette with tips of wild asparagus! (a dream)
Grilled sole (a revelation!)
Tripes a la mode de Caen. (a delight!)
fresh peas from the Spanish frontier with a tournedos sitting on a crust of
     bread soaked in some magic sauce!!! (Indescribable!)

Then a soufflé unlike any soufflé that ever souffled, with strawberry jam of whole strawberries. C. says I didn't play the game: but shirked while she gorged herself to the edge of apoplexy. I deny this. I stuffed me to the limit of rotundity. After which we went to see the cathedral and thence by a natural transition the Bishop – a delightful old man with an ivory face sitting in a room lined with books and no piece of furniture less than 150 years old. There was the untouched Church Itself! A charming talker, a mountaineer, no mean archaeologist and an authority on Catalan poems and traditions. You'd have rejoiced in him. Thence to the Citadel occupied by a line regiment and a colonial one – both equally filthy but the latter a splendid set of ruffians. Why, oh *why* are the French so incurably foul in their habits? Yet, all the standpipes in the barrack yard were neatly labelled as capable of giving the drinker typhoid fever and it was "punition" to drink from 'em. The "adjutant of the week" was in mufti – looked like a prosperous grocer. They tell me that the French officer nowadays skins out of his uniform as fast and as often as he can.

Then a walk under the giant plane-trees where all Perpignan walks of a Sunday – and our host explaining everything as we went along. They're *not* French down here but equally *not* Spanish and except now and then I didn't catch a word of French. So home in the grey misty evening light with the clouds banking heavily over Canigou. Then I went downstairs to interview Lady Roberts on the subject of the Pulsator.[4] Yes, said she, it had done her sciatica a great deal of good. Removed it althogether for a while and thereafter had kept it under control. But it had *not* cured the stiffness of her knees. How had it been applied? The man himself had come down and worked it twenty times but she had no doubt that if one knew what and where the malady was, one could apply it with unskilled labour. This I take it means that only one who knows the trajet of the nerves – and the sciatic nerve explains its course *quite* clearly – one could get a maid or someone to apply the pulsator.[5] She spoke of it also with approval for face-ache and neuralgia.

So there you are! Incidentally, she, aged 73 and almost shapelessly fat, has benefited hugely by the treatment here – pulse stronger, pains fewer and capable of walking both on the flat and up and down stairs. More and more do I lament that Mrs F. and you didn't try a turn down here. I have written to Martin twice urging him to protect the trees in the New Forest (it will never be called anything else) from bunnies *and* sheep: but I pray you fervently see that his grey hairs do not go down untroubled etc.[6] when you pass that way. Couldn't old Istead[7] go in and wire – or would all the village follow his example?

I've heard the expression "the moon is on her back" many times. Surely it's a well known one. I also watch the rising of the sun from the south day by day; for *never* have I *so* keenly wished to return to Bateman's.

Affectionately
Rudyard.

Haven't seen Gurney[8] since you wrote. I'll do what you suggest about M. Westell.[9] If you don't know him – I hæ my doots about the gentleman.

Notes

1. Dated from postmark.
2. The Depews.
3. A "speronara" is "a large rowing and sailing boat used in southern Italy and Malta" (*OED*). See Marryat, *Mr Midshipman Easy*, ch. 18: "Of all the varieties of vessels which float upon the wave, there is not, perhaps, one that bounds over the water so gracefully or so lightly as a speronare, or any one so picturesque and beautiful to the eye of those who watch its progress."
4. I have not succeeded in finding any account of this machine.
5. Thus in text. RK seems to be writing for the sake of Feilden or Mrs Feilden, but he had himself just endured a bout of sciatica. On 27 February he was "lamed – crippled" (CK diary), and on 1 March he was still unable to walk (Rees extracts). On 6 March he wrote to Feilden that "for five days I had a hellish time" (ALS, Syracuse).
6. Cf. Genesis 42:38; 44:29, 31.
7. William Isted (or Istead), Sr, one of RK's Sussex neighbours and occasional employee. On 10 June 1912 RK wrote a note for Isted thus: "William Isted (snr) is hereby authorized to catch ground game – hares and rabbits – on all land owned by me in the parish of Burwash" (ALS, Texas A&M University). In the next year we hear that "Old Istead (who has been a poacher all his life) is horrid indisposed because some damned gipsy has stole a dozen of his wires that he set out for rabbits in my quarry field" (to John Kipling, [7 October 1913?]: ALS, Sussex).
8. John Henry Gurney (1848–1922), ornithologist. RK reported meeting him at Vernet, where Gurney was "cataloguing the birds of these parts" (to Feilden, 6 March 1911: ALS, Syracuse).
9. William Percival Westell (1874–1943), writer and lecturer on natural history and curator of the Letchworth Museum.

To Frank N. Doubleday, [*c.* mid-March 1911]
AL: Princeton University

Hôtel du Parc / Vernet-les-Bains

Dear Frank

Yours of the 26th Feb just in and filled us with the wildest excitement – specially the Brett part.[1] Herewith unfinished design for allegorical statue of Doubleday enlightening the world – or the Frankish conquest of the U.S. Observe base of completely flattened publishers. Decorative, *I* think. We shall be sorry to miss seeing you here – because this is a lovely place but if you come to Bateman's in the summer *do* plan to have a little leisure and, above all, *do* bring Dorothy.[2] Elsie is clamouring for her. You shall have a room to sleep in at Bateman's *all* day after you have digested Macmillan's western end. One of the Macs is fat.

You ask about the history book.[3] It is *the* History book of all time; embellished with about four and twenty elegant verses, all hand made, by me; also, the text is very good – done by an expert – C. R. L. Fletcher who knows more about history than is wholesome for any man to know. You may know his Introductory history of England which reads like a novel. Likewise there are pictures and maps. I've just passed the proofs of the verses.

We are getting on all right here: and mean to motor home via Paris: tho' our body has been burned to ashes. Me and the King we trusted Barker the coach-builder who has been in business for two hundred years to build a body for my new car and to regilt George's coronation coach which was 200 years old. Barker upset a lamp or something and his whole place took light. George is awfully put out about his coronation coach – so much so that he hasn't sent me any message of condolence about the loss of my body. And yet the meanest of his subjects is entitled to the benefit of habeas corpus. George is getting a new coach and I can't get a new body out of Barker till he has finished.[4] Otherwise there is no particular news. C. will add her version.

[no closing or signature]

Notes
1. George Brett was president of the American Macmillan Company (see 8 February 1895). Doubleday evidently had designs on the company, but whatever the scheme might have been it does not seem to have been carried out. A note on the letter reads: "This letter was written by R.K. in 1910 when certain plans of consolidation were discussed." The date, however, must be 1911.
2. The Doubledays were at Bateman's, 7–10 July (Bateman's Visitors Book).
3. RK and Fletcher's *History of England*.
4. Later this year, in June, RK wrote to Claude Johnson of Rolls-Royce refusing to accept his car as it came from the hands of Barker and asking to have the matter arbitrated (24 June 1911: copy, House of Lords Record Office).

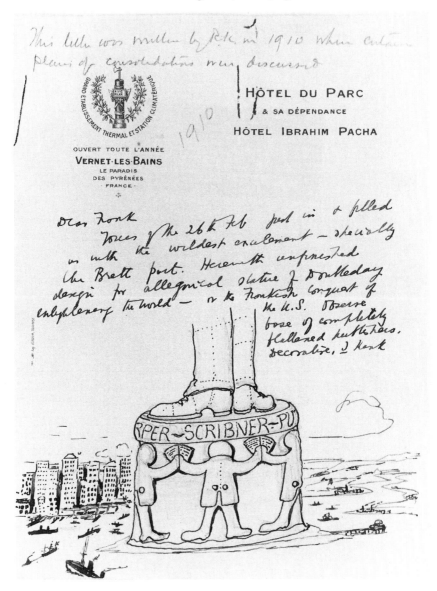

1. Kipling's sketch for an "allegorical statue of Doubleday enlightening the world", *c.* mid-March 1911.

To Stanley Baldwin, 18 March 1911
ALS: Dalhousie University

Hôtel du Parc / Vernet-les-Bains / Mar. 18. 1911:

Dear Stan,

I quite see the local etiquette of Bewdley Forest. After all a bashed man is *pro tem* out of comission and shouldn't be used to hurt horses with. Pity the same argument don't work in politics where a drunken premier[1] is not laid aside.

This place here is a cheerful sort of place – a pool of Bethesda plus a casino and streaks of snow on the mountains. When we came on the 20th Feb the snow lay in two foot thick patches beside the roads. Then we had a fortnight's glorious weather and it left. Then it snowed again and thawed.[2] Since which the weather has had worms.

C. has gone in for baths religiously – hot ones with massage and still hotter ones without. That lasted till Monday when she took to her bed and has been there ever since. She is a little better now but she has been very far from well. Now the local sponge-doctor thinks that "she is delicate for baths." She was far better (afterwards) for having come last year; so I hope she will be better this year – if she lives to pull through. She is next door, still in bed knitting and arguing that such drastic results must lead to something. I agree with her. Roberts is here with his family – wife and one daughter. He's as tough an old nut as was ever made: walks about at unearthly hours of the morning and looks as fit as a flea. She is being washed – on the instalment plan I should imagine – for she is enormous. There is also a Reb. peer here – Lord Sheffield[3] with a wife whose niece Winston married.[4] She is some kin to the Lowthian Bells[5] and has a wildly offensive sister[6] here of cheap Radical tendencies and a lofty air of patronizing Religion. The others have legs or backs or guts or something wrong with 'em. A fortnight ago, to our great joy, came Mrs. De Pew – own sister to Tommy Catlin of the old days at Creich[7] – remarried a few weeks before and very happy; she having been widow of a wealthy New Yorker who drank. Likewise she had a sixteen year old daughter[8] with whom Elsie plays about – badminton, tennis and such; *and* a 75 h.p. de Dietrich with which C. and I played. There was with 'em a chauffeur Jules who one evening at 6 p.m. fled, saying that he had heard they were going on into Spain and he did not wish to go there. So he e'en left 'em planted here, without tyres. I wondered why he was in such haste but it is coming out, day by day, that he has received many monies for the purchase of tyres, accessories etc. all of which he has diverted – up to date his little "earnings" amount to between 7 and 10,000 francs! Seems a profitable job chauffering. Doubtless he was driven to theft by his employer's parsimony; they allowing him only 400 fr. a month wages + 13 fr. a day allowance while on tour. To him has succeeded one Etienne ex-driver for a Vanderbilt, accustomed to a

140 h.p. stink cart. By simple proportion St. Stephen should steal 20,000 fr. She (Mrs. De P) reminds me pleasantly now and again of Tommy who by the way may be coming over this year, as Mrs. Phelps.

Mrs. De Pew suffers from severe wealth of an unregulated description, up to £30,000 a year. She has a chateau in Compiègne – a flat in Paris – and a general hankering (but this was before her marriage) to live anywhere between Nice and Copenhagen. But – *un autre homme autres mœurs* – now she is just happy and peaceful. The wretched daughter (who is a delightful maiden) is even worse off than her mother inasmuch as she *begins* her majority with £40,000 per ann: and other small sums accrue thereafter. The principal is absolutely at her own disposition. She and E. are now downstairs dressing paper dolls. She is restricted just now to a beggarly £4,000 per ann: or I suppose the dolls would be wax ones.

All of which is a very funny study. The American is curious. Money being with him plentiful, it don't in the least affect his or her heart or head and I find much to say for their way of dealing with cash *as* cash – mentioning it slam out in dollars and cents, instead of trying, as we English do, to spread a general air of gilded opulence inferentially, through our talk.

C. pleased herself t'other day by saying to a haughty dame who wanted to know "who these people were": – "Oh you'll know 'em well in a few years. A girl with her money simply can't escape an English title in these days of Lloyd-George." And there the conversation stopped.

And talking of cash (this letter reeks of it) by all means let me play with your tare-and-tret-wagon,[9] to the extent of £200 (two hundred pounds). Sometimes such things pay dividends. Even the Chicago cash register must have been a babe once! Tell me when you want it paid.

Glad to learn that Mrs. Ambrose Poynter[10] has called upon you. The extent to which cherry-blossom does *not* appear in the domestic interior of Bateman's cannot be measured by geographical degrees. Moreover, I don't feel easy in my mind – somehow. Let us with all our demerits, and other peoples' demerits, thank God that we did our marrying *young*, Mr. Baldwin. We are expecting, when C. gets better, to go away from here by car about the 25th but how we get to Paris I don't (in spite or because of 21 large maps) yet know. They say the passes of the Auvergne are still blocked with snow.

Now I have no more news except that we have seen an Archbishop out of an Anthony Hope novel, and eaten tripes à la mode de Caen (which is sublime) *and* bouillabaisse (which is sublimer) *and* snails which are like chopped rubberworms – I have three tales for you which I grieve I cannot write.

I never wanted to get home more than I do this year. I assume, sir, your Whitsuntide arrangements for coming to Bateman's still hold good.[11] I gather from Miss Norton[12] that Cissie is taking lessons at Princes.

This for the post. Bless you for writing, old man.

Rud.

P.S.   When Haldane's[13] Hound upon Haldane's hobbies
                Writes a book which is full of lies
                Then we find out what a first class job is
                And how Inspector-Generals rise.

                              I think Swinburne wrote this.[14]

Notes

1. Herbert Henry Asquith (1852–1928), 1st Earl of Oxford and Asquith, succeeded Campbell-Bannerman as Liberal Prime Minister in 1908 and held office until 1916. Among RK's *bêtes noires* his standing was perhaps only a little below that of Lloyd George. His drinking – or his character as a bon-vivant, in politer speech – was well known.
2. The weather perhaps suggested RK's "Why Snow Falls at Vernet", a fable about the weather and the English. It was published in the April 1911 number of a magazine called *The Merry Thought*, conducted by a Mrs Whidborne for the guests at Vernet, and was reprinted in a booklet entitled *Pages from "The Merry Thought"* in May 1911 (uncollected). One of the heroes of the story is afflicted with sciatica, as RK had just been (see [15–19 March 1911]).
3. Edward Lyulph Stanley (1839–1925), 4th Baron Sheffield, had been a Liberal MP and was long active on the London School Board.
4. Winston Churchill married Clementine Ogilvy Hozier in 1908. I do not find any connection with Lady Sheffield (see next note).
5. Lady Sheffield was the daughter of Sir Isaac Lowthian Bell (1816–1904), 1st Baronet, wealthy ironmaster and mine owner of Newcastle.
6. Lady Sheffield was one of three sisters: I do not know which sister is meant here.
7. See 8 August 1899. "Tommy" is Edith Catlin.
8. Francis Park (1895–1937), afterwards Mrs Gerald Stanley. Her husband was an English doctor practising in Paris, where RK and CK frequently stayed with the Stanleys and their children.
9. "Tare and tret" are commercial terms for allowable deductions of weight in the measurement of commodities.
10. Poynter married Cherry Margaret Burnett (d. 1959) in 1907. He was then thirty-nine.
11. The Baldwins were at Batemans from 3 to 7 June (Bateman's Visitors Book).
12. Sally Norton.
13. Richard Burdon Haldane (1856–1928), 1st Viscount Haldane, was Secretary of State for War, 1905–12, and incurred RK's wrath by his reorganisation of the army, by which the regular army was reduced but the reserve greatly augmented.
14. Cf. *Atalanta in Calydon*, beginning of the first chorus. Ian Hamilton (see 29 July [1911]) published late in 1910, at Haldane's instance, a book called *Compulsory Service*, with a long introduction by Haldane. The book was a defence of the voluntary system of military service, in opposition to the campaign carried on by Roberts and the National Service League. Since Hamilton had been a special protégé of Roberts his book was seen by Roberts' circle as a betrayal. It was also suspected, as in RK's verses, that Hamilton's promotion in 1910 to the position of General Officer Commanding in the Mediterranean and Inspector General of Overseas Forces was payment for the book, even though the promotion antedated the publication of the book.

To C. R. L. Fletcher, [*c.* 22 March 1911]

ALS: University of Sussex

Hôtel du Parc / Vernet-les-Bains

Dear Fletcher,

Yours of the 18th. Following fashionable precedents of the day I submitted the case to the arbitration of one Horace (you may have heard of him at the Press?). I took three dips at random. The first oracle gave: – *Cur me querellis*[1] etc. with which I quite agreed. I think he meant Chapman[2] – but not the one who translated Homer. Second oracle said: – *i, pedes quo te rapiunt et auræ;*[3] obviously referring to my tour; *auræ*, I take it being indicated horse power of car. You may urge that "*pedes*" means metrical feet. But no matter. Third oracle said: – *Musis amicus.*[4] Again my tour! But I can't leave grief behind me so I write in haste to say that you can ring my bells and stop my engines as you Clarendamn-well think best.

The wife who has been very ill is better; spring seems to have come here at last; and in a day or two the car will come too to carry us clean away into the ruins of a decent and honourable past – the more awful because of the untidy, deboshed surroundings. I hope you'll have a good time in Germany with your son. I'll be back on the 8th of April at Bateman's.

Ever sincerely
Rudyard Kipling.

Notes
1. *Odes*, II, xvii, 1: "Why do you crush out my life by your complaints?"
2. Robert William Chapman (1881–1960), assistant to the Secretary to the Delegates of the Clarendon Press from 1906 and Secretary from 1920, a distinguished publisher and scholar. Chapman presumably had raised difficulties about the *History of England*, which, though RK had reviewed the proofs of it in February (see 23 February 1911), had not yet been approved for publication by the Delegates of the Press (Peter Sutcliffe, *The Oxford University Press*, pp. 158–9).
3. *Odes*, III, xi, 49: "Go whither your feet and the breezes hurry you."
4. *Odes*, I, xxvi, 1: "Dear to the Muses, I will banish grief and fear."

To George Auriol,[1] [*c.* March? 1911]

Text: C. Scott O'Connor, *Travels in the Pyrenees*, 1913, p. 123

I came here in search of nothing more than a little sunshine. But I found Canigou,[2] whom I discovered to be a magician among mountains, and I submitted myself to his power. At first he could reproduce for me, according to the thought or the desire of the moment, either a peak of the Himalayas or the outlines of certain hills in South Africa which are dear to me; transporting me, for example, to the still heat and the unforgettable smell of the pines behind my house under Table Mountain, at the instant when I expected to hear the horns of some Hindu temple upon his upper slopes.

But this year he has taken to himself his own place in my mind and heart, and I watch him with wonder and delight. Nothing that he could do or give birth to would now surprise me, whether I met Don Quixote himself riding in from the Spanish side, or all the chivalry of ancient France watering their horses at his streams, or saw (which each twilight seems quite possible) gnomes and kobbolds swarming out of the mines and tunnels of his flanks.

That is the reason, my dear Monsieur Auriol, that I venture to subscribe myself among the number of the loyal subjects of Canigou.

Notes
1. Identified only as "of Perpignan" in O'Connor's *Travels in the Pyrenees*.
2. The mountain, nearly 9,000 feet high, on whose north-west slopes Vernet-les-Bains lies.

To Herman Moroney,[1] 7 April 1911
ALS: Princeton University

Tete de Boeuf Hotel / Abbeville. / Ap. 7. 1911

To Herman Moroney Esq.
Dear Sir,

I have just finished a tour of eleven days[2] based very largely on the excellent information which you were kind enough to supply to Mr Claude Johnson for me: and thanks to your notes etc. we have come through it with great enjoyment.

I am forwarding with this for the Touring Dept. a few notes of the various Hotels at which I stopped and one or two road notes. If it is of any use to you to check my accounts against any others I shall be glad to send in our bills for a party of four and mechanician.[3]

Our route covered Nimes: Arles: Aigues Mortes: Montpelier: Carcasonne: Toulouse: Bergerac: Angouleme: Poitiers: Tours: Blois: Chartres: Rouen, Beauvais: Amiens – approximately 1200 miles.

Very sincerely and gratefully yours
Rudyard Kipling.

[sketch map of route between Béziers and Carcassonne]

Direct Road from Béziers to Carcasonne via Capestang needs clear posting at right hand fork to Laredorte (Taride 21) as there is a new bridge being built over Aude between Homps and Laredorte fork which is confusing.

  In point of view scenery this road is better than via Narbonne Lezignon Capendu and I think not quite so much cut up by heavy traffic.

Towns		*Hotels*
	Grand Hotel de la Dorade (Albert Montal Proprietor) *Narbonne*	Food very good and specially excellent lunch for party can be prepared on giving a few hours notice. Suggest Hotel worthy of further investigation.
	Hotel Metropole *Montpelier*	Bad, dear and greedy. They try the old trick of charging extra franc on wine ordered from wine-list in restaurant hoping guest will not notice on paying bill. Should be spoken to severely. They try on too much. Beds comfortable and clean.
		Rudyard Kipling Mar. 28. 1911. Carcassone.
Carcasonne	Hotel Bernard –	Needs a little overhauling to become fair hotel. Sanitary arrangements good, but no possible baths. High stone staircase with no lift. Indifferent

food. Charges high and they are a little given to cheating over minor items. *Note*. Letter-box in hall unsatisfactory being small and casual.

Mar. 29.th

| Bergerac | De Londres et des Voyageurs – | *Not* over clean; food only fair reasonable charges and obliging. Sanitary arrangements old fashioned and dirty impossible for ladies until cleaned. No baths. |

Mar. 30th.
Rudyard Kipling

Poitiers:	Hotel du Palais.	Certainly up to date for baths heating and cleanliness but food and dining room service very bad for so large a town.
Angoulème –	Hotel de France.	Lunch only – *very* good food and sanitary arrangements clean.
Tours.	Hotel de L'Univers	I found this hotel exceptionally good and not at all expensive for accomodation provided.
Blois –	Grand Hotel de Blois	One very bad lunch here: bad service bad food and even bad butter. Charges high.
Chartres	Hotel de Grand Monarque	– Very good and not expensive:
Rouen	" de la Poste.	Fair lunch only.

Beauvais:	" de France et D'Angleterre:	Not modern but comfortable and moderate in price.
Amiens.	Hotel de l'Univers	Have raised prices of dej[euner]. from 3. to 3.50 on account, they say, of general scarcity of provisions. Service slow. Poor.
Abbeville	Hotel Tete de Boeuf.	Not over clean. Obliging, speak English

Ap. 7.

Note   We were a party of four – two men and two ladies. I have kept my bills at the different hotels I have quoted and if comparisons will be of any advantage shall be glad to send them in.

Rudyard Kipling

Notes
1. Not identified; he was presumably an official of the Royal Automobile Club, though the Club has not been able to provide any information about him.
2. They left Vernet on 25 March with Perceval Landon and arrived in Paris on 3 April (ten days, not eleven). For the itinerary, see note 4.
3. The fourth was presumably CK's maid.
4. The notes that follow are written on printed forms supplied by the Royal Automobile Club. RK has signed the bottom of each form. The sequence and the dates of the itinerary are as follows: Narbonne, 25 March; Montpellier, 26 March; Carcassonne, 28 March; Bergerac, 29 March; Angoulême, 30 March; Poitiers, 30 March; Tours, 31 March; Blois, 1 April; Chartres, 1 April; Rouen, 2 April; Beauvais, 2 April; Amiens, 3 April; [Paris, 3–7 April]; Abbeville, 7 April (Motor Tours, 1911). They reached Bateman's via Boulogne on 8 April (CK diary).

To Claude Johnson, [7 April 1911]
Text: *Kipling Journal*, September 1985, pp. 73–5

Hotel Tete de Boeuf / Abbeville / Friday evening

Dear Johnson

Here we are, at the end of our 1200 mile trip in the Spectre: hoping to get to Boulogne tomorrow and cross to England. Fleck wants to put our valves right after he arrives, and to see that everything is clean and in good order. This he proposes to do on Monday and Tuesday: after which I hope to hand over to my own man.

It has been a wonderful run but she has been a Terror on tyres. She busted four – all in the same place – the wall: so I imagine that she must roll on them. Fleck put in new springs at Paris and she has ridden easier since though this doesn't mean she was anything to complain of at any time. She carried us from the South to the North without a slip. I don't count the bog into which she sank for three hours at Marsillargues and was hauled out by horses.[1] More of this later.

The weather has *not* been good and we were profoundly thankful for the top – heavy as it undoubtedly is. It didn't rattle much till just at the end. That big front window is almost impossible to plug.

I am sorry we couldn't come round to see you and Montague[2] but that would have meant missing our connections in the North. From what I read in the papers you don't seem to have been much of a flower garden either. Our route was Nimes: Arles: Les Baux: Aigues Mortes: Montpelier: this because we had Perceval Landon with us who hadn't seen any of it: then Carcassonne: Toulouse: Bergerac (325 k. in one day): Poitiers: Angouleme: Tours: Blois: Chartres: Rouen [?Bloisois]: Amiens; Beauvais; Paris: Beauvais: Abbeville.

Paris is a bad city inhabited by lunatics. We had a bit of an onset with a Choisy-le-Roi tram which for no known reason suddenly crosses the boulevard diagonally: the rails being sunk one can't see when the d—d thing swerves. The tram never made a sign or warning but simply charged us. Fleck got us out of it with nothing worse than a bent axle.[3] It was a glorious bit of driving but I'm only sorry we didn't harm the tram. I never saw such a death-trap of a line in my life. You can imagine the rest! We were all going to port together and she touched us just before Fleck could jump the curb. (Note: F had not curled his moustache that morn!)

I wish you had been with us for some of our trip. However I think that I shall be able to describe a piece or two of it. When are you coming back to England and how are you?

Do you believe in the Resurrection of the Body? If so, do you believe that my body will be ever resurrected?[4]

Now here is a Serious Tale – a contribution to social science.

You know of course that the automobile is spreading civilization through the South – in no respect more markedly than in the Sanitary line – what you and me would call the Rear. That is to say the Northern or civilized seat [sketch of toilet] is rapidly superseding the Southern slipper seat or stand [sketch of slipper stand]. Where the two civilizations meet – i.e. at Carcassonne – there is a prayer on the back of the W.C. door urging messieurs les voyagers not to "mount upon" the seat of the modern W.C. and since evidently that prayer has not always been attended to, they have rigged up a board projecting from the wall to prevent the devotees of the old or slipper civilization from mounting on the modern, oval or ovoid polished seat. Heaven knows how they *could* squat on such a basis but they've done it because I saw the scrapes of boot nails on the varnish. I give diagram on 4th page of apparatus to prevent 'em mounting.

Projecting board [sketch of toilet bowl, with dotted-outline figure seated, board on brackets fixed on wall above], to prevent MM les voyageurs from [sketch of figure squatting above toilet bowl] misusing the glorious gifts of civilization. Selah!

Now I can't report this to the R.A.C. but I've sent in a less serious review of the various hotels I've been in.

Ever sincerely yours
Rudyard Kipling.

Notes
1. Marsillargues is on the road to Aigues Mortes, where they were on 26 March. RK describes it thus in Motor Tours: "Took an accursed short cut through little street at Marsillargues. Got stuck for 3 hours. Saved by Joseph Coste Electrician and Cyprien with 4 horses" (26 March 1911).
2. Lord Montagu of Beaulieu: see 3 March 1910.
3. The accident occurred on 5 April, south of Paris. RK describes it in detail in a letter to the Legal and Commercial Insurance Company of Leeds, 12 April 1911 (TLS, Syracuse University).
4. The body of his Rolls-Royce: see [*c.* early March 1911] and [*c.* mid-March 1911].

To Brander Matthews, 8 May 1911
ALS: Columbia University

Bateman's / Burwash / Sussex / May. 8. 1911.

Dear Brander:
I can't say I like "economic approaches" as a phrase.[1] Likewise I believe Dryden, in any case, would have done pretty much what Dryden did.[2] Certain

sure Charles Reade would have. He was a didactic bard from the first – *Masks and Faces* notwithstanding; and no play writing could have contained him.[3]

Hooker's article[4] is very kind indeed but I'm a bit sorry that he has got on to my game – or, rather, that he is calling attention to it.[5] I want it left very much alone for the next few years, if I live, so that it can soak in quietly. Of course the Frenchman has been on to it for some time. Hooker's writing is *very* good and well made. All here is standing on its head for Coronation affairs but I hope to see you in July at the club.

Ever sincerely
Rudyard.

Notes
1. Matthews' "Economic Interpretation of Literary History", originally given as the presidential address to the Modern Language Association, 1910; it is collected in *Gateways to Literature*, 1912.
2. Matthews argues that Dryden was corrupted by his dependence on the court ("Economic Interpretation of Literary History", in *Publications of the Modern Language Association*, XXVI [1911], Appendix, lxvii).
3. "Charles Reade … used to assert that he had been intended by nature for a dramatist, and that he had been forced into fiction by bad laws" (*ibid.*, p. lxx). Reade's play *Masks and Faces* (with Tom Taylor) was produced in 1852.
4. Brian Hooker, "The Later Work of Mr. Kipling", *North American Review*, CXCIII (May 1911), 721–32. Hooker (1880–1946) was a teacher, editor, song writer, opera librettist, and novelist.
5. Hooker writes that the connecting link in RK's work is the idea of "the victory of organization over anarchy" (p. 725). He also comments at length on the greater complexity of the later stories, perceptively calling them "palimpsests of implication" (p. 732).

To Brander Matthews, 31 May 1911

ALS: Columbia University

Bateman's / Burwash / May. 31. 1911.

Dear Brander,

Ever so many thanks for your "Study of Versification."[1] It's useful to me in my job – like the rest of your books – so I don't mind betting that your own public across the water hasn't any idea of the value of the work you've been doing. There isn't to my knowledge another set of workman's books like yours.

By the way have you got Hood's *"How I taught a youngster to write verse?"*[2] It was written serially ages ago for a boy's magazine in England and I remember reading it again and again. Maybe I've rhymed "abroad" with Lord more than once[3] but I think, the only time I did it consciously I corrected in another edition – if so be the rhyme you allude to was in *White Horses*. But this yere poeting is a strange and baffling business. All the same I'm glad I wasn't born an Alexandrine Frenchman.

p. 104. "*Seventeen hundred and thirty nine* etc. etc."[4] "Beau Brocade" came out originally in *Hood's Comic Annual* and has been greatly changed by Austin Dobson. I speak from memory.

I'd like to war over the sonnet idea with you. A sonnet is much more lawless than you'd have it[5] – inside the 14 line limit. I can't write sonnets but I'm persuaded of that.

Ever sincerely
Rudyard Kipling.

Notes
1. *A Study of Versification*, Boston, 1911.
2. Tom Hood, *The Rules of Rhyme: A Guide to English Versification*, 1869, originally published as "The Young Poet's Guide". RK must not have read Matthews' "Prefatory Note" to *A Study of Versification*, which begins by saying that Matthews "about thirty years since" had "prepared an American edition of a little book by the younger Tom Hood, which purported to set forth the rules of rime (the 'Rhymester,' Appleton & Co., 1882)" (p. v).
3. As an instance of the fact that "many poets of high distinction" employ imperfect rhyme Matthews notes that "Kipling weds *abroad* and *lord*" (p. 53). "White Horses" originally concluded thus: "To mill your foeman's armies – / To bray his camps abroad – / Trust ye the wild white horses / The Horses of the Lord!" (*Literature*, 23 October 1897, p. 16). In the poem as collected in *The Five Nations* the first two of these lines have been altered thus: "To bray your foeman's armies – / To chill and snap his sword –".
4. The beginning of Austin Dobson's "The Ballad of 'Beau Brocade'", *Hood's Comic Annual*, 1877, quoted by Matthews on p. 104 of his book in a discussion of the couplet form.
5. "It is best to follow the rules without cavil and without claiming any license to depart from them. ... It is in the rigidity of its skeleton that the charm of the sonnet is solidly rooted" (*A Study of Versification*, p. 139).

To Lady Bathurst, 15 June 1911
ALS: Leeds University

Bateman's / Burwash: / June. 15. 1911

Dear Lady Bathurst

I see that Fabian Ware has resigned the *Morning Post* and that Gwynne has resigned the *Standard*.[1] Have you ever thought of Gwynne as a successor to

Ware?[2] I ask because I am keenly anxious that the one really independent paper we have on our side should be captained by the best man I know.

Forgive me for bothering you. I am in a tiny way interested in a tiny little paper,[3] and *I* know how all the world joyfully assists one in one's own business. But Gwynne is good – good all through. I've seen him serene and adequate under fire in the war where it was difficult to edit and be shot at at the same time.

Very sincerely yours
Rudyard Kipling

Notes
1. Gwynne resigned the editorship of the *Standard* on 9 June, owing to differences with his new proprietor; in the next week Ware was dismissed from the editorship of the *Morning Post* by Lady Bathurst (Stephen Koss, *The Rise and Fall of the Political Press in Britain: The Twentieth Century*, 1984, pp. 177–8).
2. Gwynne succeeded Ware: see 24 June 1911.
3. Perhaps the *Civil and Military Gazette*. At his death RK owned 1,100 shares in the *CMG*, but how early he had acquired an interest in the paper is not known.

To C. Hooper,[1] 16 June 1911

TLS: University of Kansas

Bateman's / Burwash / Sussex / 16th June 1911.

My dear Hooper,

I am tremendously obliged to you for sending me those proofs of my D.D. prefaces[2] which I had clean forgotten. I fear Ramsay Macdonald[3] will always be with us.

Best congratulations and all good wishes on your approaching marriage.

Yours very truly,
Rudyard Kipling

C. Hooper Esq.,
> Messrs Thacker, Spink and Co.
>> Calcutta.

Notes
1. Not identified, but perhaps connected with George Hooper (see 3–25 December 1899).
2. Hooper had evidently turned up in the offices of Thacker, Spink and Co. and had sent to RK the cancelled proofs of two prefaces that RK had written for the fourth

edition (first English) of *Departmental Ditties*, one evidently aimed at his readers in India and the other at those in England. On the first leaf has been written in an unknown hand "Both prefaces *cancelled* by author preserve this copy JHP." The note is confirmed by an undated letter from RK to Spink ([c.January 1890]: ALS, Yale) saying: "I've taken Eminent Advice about those prefaces. No. They won't do, so I've cut 'em out and I think I'm on the safe side. No use telling the public you think 'em a damned ass." The proofs have been inserted in a copy of *Departmental Ditties and Other Verses*, 4th edn (Calcutta: Thacker, Spink and Co.; London: W. Thacker and Co., 1890), in the collection of books from RK's own library now in the British Library. On the half-title page preceding the two inserted proofs RK has written – presumably at a later date – "This is *all* faked and a lie. R.K." In annotating bibliographies and other lists and records in his later years RK often denied authorship of early work known to be his. The two prefaces have now been published in Sandra Kemp and Lisa Lewis, eds, *Writings on Writing by Rudyard Kipling* (Cambridge, 1996), pp. 25–6.

3. Macdonald (1866–1937), Labour leader, at this time MP for Leicester and chairman of the Labour group in Parliament; in 1924 he became the first Labour Prime Minister.

To Stanley Baldwin, [23 June 1911]

Text: Copy, University of Sussex

[Bateman's] The day after / 9 a.m.

Dear Stan,

Thanks to your hospitality in every way and at every turn the Coronation was for Carrie and me made most delightfully easy.[1] Only, where were you? We got into our route and were at Dean's Yard in fifteen minutes. Then a kindly usher passed us direct through the Abbey, all among early peeresses looking rather yellow, to the Poets Corner end, and so into the House where we found your name opened all doors and led us directly to a very nice breakfast, which we ate and for which we gave you thanks, *in absentia*. Two of the ushers immediately in front of us, and we were in the second row on the floor of the S. aisle, were Landon and Montgomery[2] whom we knew; and we found ourselves all among acquaintances. So when the show was ended and the peeresses were still locked up behind grills, a door was opened in what looked like an impossible barrier and we were taken across the Abbey again to the covered way, went straight to Westminster Hall, breathed your name, were affectionately led to a cold collation of the best; heard that "a gentleman and two young ladies" – who I take it were Phil and your maidens – had had lunch there about one o'clock; we ate and drank in great comfort and ease – but devil a sign of you or Ciss. So we left a message and walked out round the Abbey, much pitying the Lords and Ladies who were ramping furiously for their carriages. At the west door an aged harridan shouted at me, apropos to a gilt and brazen chariot which was thunderously announcing itself as "The Russian Ambassador" – "*Is* this Lady Hood?" "No", says I and went on, quite quiet and comfy, round the corner into Deans Yard where the first person I saw was Moore. That was four o'clock. We got into the car. In five minutes were down Victoria Street and then – a queer experience! – broke into an absolute vacuum of deserted streets, populated by one or two empty tram cars. We might have gone forty miles an hour and done no hurt, but we were not pressed and got home in *two hours and one quarter*! C. was dead and is now in bed but she hasn't taken as much harm as I feared. If it hadn't been for the comfort and rest of Queen's Gate, and the rest and repairs at the House, there would have been an unrevived corpse at the end, for which my thanks and blessings to you both.

But where were you? Let's have a word of your doings.

Ever affectionately
Rud.

Notes
1. The coronation of George V, 22 June. They spent the night before with the Baldwins in Queen's Gate (CK diary). The invitation came to them from the Duchess of Connaught; as CK wrote, "it's an invitation that can't be refused though Rud would have greatly liked to do so and we spent a few hours doing what we could by wire to arrange with tailors and dress makers. It means court dress for us both" (to [Mrs Balestier, 3 June 1911]: ALS, Dunham Papers).
2. Possibly Sir Charles Hubert Montgomery (1876–1942) of the Foreign Office. He was secretary of the Earl Marshal's Office for the Coronation of King George in 1911.

To H. A. Gwynne, 24 June 1911
ALS: Dalhousie University

Bateman's / June. 24. 1911

Dear Old Man –

No! I don't think, nor does Carrie, that there is any try-on in that letter.[1] It doesn't seem to me it would be like the lady.

There may be one man or more in the field. The wife, with no more than instinct to back her, suggests that Geoffrey Robinson,[2] whose place on the *Times* is none too pleasant, may be one of 'em – and Garvin[3] may be another. Anyway there is but one plan and that seems to be to write the lady somewhat after this fashion: – acknowledge her kind letter, say that you quite understand that there must be other applicants for the post and also that the matter can't be settled in a single interview. But unless you hear from her to the contrary before the 8th, you will be very happy to call upon her.

Embroider it as much as you like but I think the plainer it is put the better.

I never supposed you were the only man who was trying for the billet. Fleet Street alone is paved with chaps who would think themselves competent to run the *Times* at a minute's notice. Let alone all the young amateurs who think they are "gifted."

But our best wishes are with you.[4]

Ever thine
Rud.

Notes
1. Presumably a response by Lady Bathurst to Gwynne's candidacy for the editorship of the *Morning Post*.
2. Geoffrey Robinson (1874–1944), who assumed the name of Dawson in 1917, had served as Milner's private secretary in South Africa, 1901–5; he then edited the Johannesburg *Star*, 1905–10, at the same time serving as South African correspondent for *The Times*. He had now joined *The Times*, which he edited, 1912–19. He resigned the editorship in disagreement with Lord Northcliffe but returned in 1923 after Northcliffe's death and remained editor until 1941.
3. James Louis Garvin (1868–1947), editor of the *Observer*, 1908–42.
4. Gwynne was appointed editor of the *Morning Post* on 8 July and held the position until the paper was absorbed by the *Daily Telegraph* in 1937.

To George Earle Buckle, 27 June [1911]
ALS: The Times

[Bateman's] June. 27th

private
Dear Buckle –

I was away when your note came but I sent you a wire to say that I couldn't do anything about the Coronation. My place gave me a good view of the processions but nothing of the actual ceremonies. Of course the essential note of the thing was precisely what we are trying to throw away – the oneness of the people and the ease and intimacy that goes with it. For example French's[1] (?) tone and bearing to his gentlemen at arms was identical with the carriage and temper of the Bobby outside and Mr Rice the Abbey Beadle who set the time for the processions was as much part of the fabric as His Majesty.

This must be so with a democracy of aristocrats which, at bottom, is what the English are – specially the "lower classes," and that is where your alien or semi alien politician is going to trip up.

Haldane looked like a Toby dog strayed from a Punch and Judy show as he scuttled up the aisle in his unadjusted peer's robes,[2] and all the Winstonism of Churchill simply blazed up against that background of decent ritual. *He* looked like an obscene paper backed French novel in the Bodleian.

But these are obviously matters one can't bore the public with.

> Ever sincerely
> Rudyard Kipling.

Notes

1. General John Denton Pinkstone French (1852–1925), afterwards Field Marshal and 1st Earl of Ypres, held commands in the Boer War and was Commander-in-Chief of the British Expeditionary Force in the Great War from the beginning until the end of 1915. He was now Inspector-General of the Forces, and was present at the coronation in that capacity. The Captain of the Gentlemen-at-Arms in the procession was not French but Lord Denman.
2. Haldane's peerage had been conferred in March 1911.

To Colonel Lionel Charles Dunsterville, 29 July [1911]

ALS: University of Sussex

Bateman's: / Burwash: / July. 29. (about as hot as Multān)

Dear Old Man,

Yours of June 22nd. Oddly enough, the day before it arrived I was browzing through Whittaker and adding up the number of O.U.S.C.'s commanding Native Regiments. I made it you, Prendergast, Buck (who used to train hawks) C. H. U. Price; Jones and Mardall.[1] There must be more. How d'you make it eight? I haven't seen an O.U.S.C. for ever so long, and was almost beginning to imagine that the breed was extinct but the other day I went over to Lydd[2] where they are playing with a new 10″ Howitzer (an Austrian bitch of a thing with a weak and complicated breech-block) and there I met the soldier man and his officer pretty much the same as before. I expect he'll be needed before long. The politicians have tied things into the very devil of a knot and are now much surprised to find that they can't make revolutions without making counter-revolutions. But our people aren't yet ready for business. You've seen all about the riot in the House.[3] That was only a flash in the pan.

I've been down in France this spring visiting with French troops of sorts and seeing Roberts and French generals on the bukh[4] together. The French guns are very good – their handling is quicker than ours – and the average horsemanship of their cavalry is higher but I can't yet make up my mind as to what the Linesman may be worth. He is a filthy looking brute and I gather that he does pretty much as he pleases. Maybe we shall know more in the next few months.

We're all well here – barring our most wonderful summer. We've had practically three months in Sussex without rain and one month of good, solid, still heat – the kind of heat I'd forgotten – that amazed me. We go out into the garden after dinner and gasp for breath. There's no sign of it breaking.

I most earnestly pray (as the Babu says) that your honour's ladyship will be blessed with a daughter.[5] They are great joys and an abiding delight to the mother. Likewise they boss the Father which is very good for him.

I've been socking your merits (quite non-existent I dare say) into [   ][6] big brass-hats within the last two years but as things stand now, one has got to be a different sort of a liar from what you are, to get on. I hope to goodness you won't be landed with Ian Hamilton[7] as C. in C. one of these days. One can't help liking him but he ain't my notion of a straight person. Half our Generals here spend their time in backing up Haldane's nonsense: and the state of the territorials would make you sick. I want you when you come over to interest yourself in that game. It's dangerous and deadly and as long as it lasts grows more dangerous every year.

As to what you say about your new boys, read the August *Pearson's* in which I've made free with your name again.[8] But I know what you mean about the new chaps: They are too hide-bound for men so young.

Send us another letter when you can and specially let us know when there's any chance of your coming over.

Gwynne resigned the *Standard* because he took on the *Morning-Post* which is a much bigger billet and *is a free paper* that says what it likes.

Give my love to Buck, and Tuppeny and Potiphar;[9] and any other of the old crowd.

Bless you.

Ever yours
Gigger

Notes

1. Brigadier-General Charles Gordon Prendergast (1864–1942), commanded the 28th Punjabis, 1909–14; "Buck" is possibly K. J. Buchanan of the 54th Sikhs, who was at USC, 1875–82; Brigadier-General Charles Henry Uvedale Price (1862–1942), commanding the 129th Baluchis in 1911; W. S. Mardall, commanding the 31st Lancers. According to *Whitaker's Almanack*, H. J. Jones commanded the Zepore Sikhs, but he was never at USC. The USC *Register* does not list any eligible Jones.

2. Near Dungeness in Kent. I have no information about this occasion.
3. In the struggle over the Parliament Bill the Unionist "Die-hards" in the Commons shouted down the Prime Minister on 24 July.
4. Talk, chatter.
5. Dunsterville's daughter Susanna, afterwards Mrs van Doorninck.
6. Word illegible.
7. General Sir Ian Hamilton (1853–1947), whom RK first knew as aide-de-camp to Lord Roberts in India. Writing in 1944, Trix Fleming called Hamilton "one of my oldest friends in every sense of the word – ever since 1885! Ruddy and I made friends with him at once" (to J. H. C. Brooking, 8 October 1944: ALS, Texas A&M University). Hamilton served throughout the war in South Africa, and was now commanding in the Mediterranean. RK associated Hamilton with Haldane (see 18 March 1911) and so disapproved of him, though liking him personally. Hamilton is now remembered especially as the army commander in the Gallipoli campaign.
8. "The Honours of War", not in *Pearson's* but in the *Windsor Magazine*, August 1911 (*A Diversity of Creatures*).
9. Potiphar is possibly J. C. Rimington (see 9 May 1896), who is identified with Potiphar Mullins in "Regulus" and "The United Idolators".

To Lieutenant W. H. Lewis,[1] [29 July 1911]
ALS: University of Sussex

[Bateman's] Sat.

Dear Lewis

Loud and earnest congratulations! A mountain-battery is Some Guns and what I know of No 5 battery is that it's about as smart as they make 'em. It will be a quick change from petting the 10" howitzer to consorting with the 14.3. Govt mule. As I remember it the 1st M.B. was at Jutogh last year commanded by F. R. Drake[2] a man I knew when he was about your age. I think H. R. Cook[3] is major of the 5th.

Well: Here's luck! Wear a flannel band next your skin and always have one dry one in reserve, no matter how wet you get elsewhere. *Never* drink water; never touch any fizzy-water outside a regimental mess whose mineral-water machines are above reproach; take boiling hot tea in hot weather. (This will make you sweat but will cool you and keep you from heat apoplexy.) Bet not on the interesting but evasive pony; least of all when the "gentleman rider" is up; and strictly avoid the innocent looking man who makes half his living by playing bridge. As for females – you probably have your own information on that head.

There's no *shikar* worth a dam round Jutogh but if you can get back into the hills behind Mashobra there's an occasional bear and some birds, if you get off the beaten tracks.

When do you sail? I do hope we will be able to have a glimpse of you before your departure.

You evidently had a cheery time with your car. We're just off in a R.R. for the wilds of Gloucestershire[4] and by the feel of the weather that means at least *one* tyre going pop. With all our best wishes

Very sincerely
Rudyard Kipling

P.S.   If you ever get into a hole and need advice ask Colonel L. C. Dunsterville commanding Brownlow's Punjabis (20th) at Jhelum. Tell him I sent you.

Notes
1.   William Herbert Lewis (b. 1884), MC, DSO, was a Second Lieutenant in the Royal Artillery who had just been assigned to Number 5 Mountain Battery in India. He served in the World War and retired as a Lieutenant-Colonel. I do not know the history of his acquaintance with RK, but perhaps he was RK's host at Lydd, where RK saw the "10" Howitzer" (see preceding letter). Lewis was a guest at Bateman's on 6–8 May 1911 (Bateman's Visitors Book).
2.   Lieutenant-Colonel Francis Richard Drake (1862–1935).
3.   Brigadier-General Henry Rex Cook (1863–1950).
4.   They visited Lord and Lady Bathurst at Cirencester, 29–31 July (Rees extracts).

To H. A. Gwynne, 16 August 1911
ALS: Dalhousie University

Château d'Annel[1] / *Longueil-Annel (Oise)* / Aug. 16. 1911.

Dear Old Man –

We've been off since Aug. 4. with the kids and the motor, touring through Normandy in the fiercest heat I've ever known outside of India.[2] Now we are staying with friends here about 30 miles from Paris among the woods of Compiègne. Our only source of news is the Paris Edition of the *Daily Mail* and from that I see that things are moving a little abruptly in England.

The latest news is that a general railway strike is to be proclaimed in a day or two. Now I don't want to go to Folkestone and to be hung up there with the motor and the family, unable to get to Bateman's, either for lack of petrol or because the dockers won't handle stuff out of the steamers and I *do* want to get home if I can.

I'm going to ask you to send me *on receipt of this* a wire to say how things stand at the moment of receipt: so that I may know whether to leave here

Friday morn with the idea of getting to Folkestone Friday evening: by the boat leaving Boulogne at 7: p.m.: as I didn't intend to stay away more than a fortnight and all sort of work is piling up for me.[3] But I distinctly do *not* want to be held up on the pier-side at Folkestone with the motor aboard. The telegraphic address as you will note is

Kipling: care of Depew:
Longeuil-Annel Oise

Send it in French as less likely to be mistaken this end: there's no knowledge of English anywhere about here.

You might turn up the *Morning Post* files and re-read my "City of Brass" and see if there aren't a few quotations now fairly apposite which were considered extreme and pessimistic when the verses appeared. Seriously, the whole thing is set out there in black and white: but even I did not guess it would come so soon.

Love from us all.

Ever thine
Rud

Notes
1. The home of Mr and Mrs Depew.
2. They left on 4 August with Mr and Mrs Max Aitken (see 6 September 1911) and in the next two days visited Rouen and Le Havre. The Aitkens then returned to England, while RK's party went on to Caen, Bayeux, Mont St Michel, Mortain, and Falaise before going to the Château d'Annel on 13 August (Motor Tours). The summer of 1911 was the hottest since 1868.
3. A railway strike – an episode in the great series of strikes that ran from 1910 through 1912 in England – was scheduled for this day. The union leaders, however, agreed to meet the Prime Minister on the 17th. RK, on Gwynne's advice, crossed the channel that day and was back at Bateman's on the 18th, when the strike in fact began (CK diary).

To William R. S. Bathurst,[1] 26 August 1911
ALS: Boston Public Library

Bateman's, / Aug. 26. 1911.

Dear Billy

Here is a map of one of my Islands which Sihan-Skalla the Head-Governor has just had made for me. It is not a bad little island and the people, specially

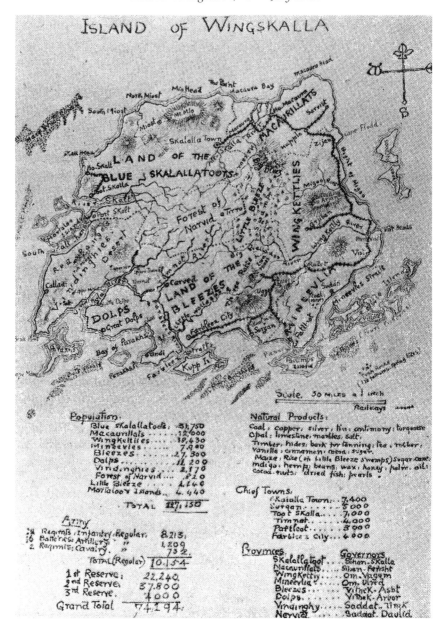

2. Kipling's map of the Island of Wingskalla, country of the Blue Skalallatoots, 26 August 1911.

the Blue Skalallatoots, are very nice but I find that I am so busy just now that I cannot look after it properly.[2] Would you and Ralphie[3] take care of it for me? You will find Sihan-Skalla the Head Governor a very good man indeed. He wants to build a railway from Skalalla Town direct to Farbleez through the Forest of Narvid which is all swampy and full of rivers; and he wants new lighthouses and lightships to be put up to mark the shoals and rocks on the South Coast.

I think you had better take the *Flutter*, the Lighthouse Steamer at Undi, and make a trip yourself and see what is really wanted. Vithek Arbor Governor of Dolpo will take you round and show you anything you want to see. I know that a lighthouse is wanted at Cape Mave and there ought to be a red flashing light at the End of the Belt Shoals but I have not been along the Kupp and Passimpo coast for some time. You will want a coast-guard steamer to look after the pearl fisheries off the Mineerles because the Vindinghy fishermen, who are rather a rough lot, come over in the pearl fishery season and fight with the Mineerlia people. However you can trust Om-Ulred to keep them in order *if* you give him a steamer. Even an armed steam launch would be enough if it moved about regularly. A new pier and stone built dock is wanted at Port Skalt where the river brings down sand and mud. Two steam dredgers are at work there already and there is a third dredger at Toot-Skalla across the river which could be used also, after the autumn rains.

It is not the least good trying to make a harbour at Vist Heads. I have spoken to Om-Vagon Governor of the Wingkettlies about this. The sand is always shifting at the mouth of the Wingkettly and nothing you can do will keep the river open. It is just the same thing at Macaura in the North. *Don't* waste money and men in trying to make harbours there, for the North and East coasts are open to all the bad weather.

There ought to be a narrow-guage railway to link up the Vindinghy salt and copper mines and you might, later on, run a railway from Callad through the gap in the Red range to the copper mines. Saddat-Tirak the Governor of the Vindinghies has the plans of the proposed railway in his office. There is no use in putting railways into the Forest of Narvid. All that country is full of rivers and you will find it easier to float your timber down by water. The people at Tirro are excellent foresters and woodmen but they must be governed by some one who understands them. Ask Saddat-Daulid their governor to take you elephant hunting through Narvid and get to know the Tirro hunters.

Little Bleeze is full of swamps but the Macaurillats go there every year to plant rice. They come away again in the autumn and generally catch fever and colds. There ought to be a hospital and a doctor *and plenty of quinine* on Big Bleez – about 3,000 feet above the level of the swamp. Sihon-Feresht, Governor of the Macaurillats, should build it, as his people own all the land in Little Bleez.

But you must decide for yourself. If I were you I should go on tour for six months through the Island before I did anything. Then I should call a council of Governors and ask them what was most wanted. They will always ask for twice as much as they want. The Government treasury is at Skalalla Town: where most of the artillery is. Sihan-Allat-al-Darogh commands the Army. He is a good man with one eye and a squint but very amusing to talk to. Ask him about his war against the Vindinghies in 1907. –

Very sincerely yours
Rudyard Kipling

Notes
1. Bathurst (1903–70) was the second son of Lord and Lady Bathurst. This letter perhaps follows up a line of discussion begun when RK visited the Bathursts at the end of July (see [29 July 1911]). It was accompanied by a map of the country, but the map is not in the Boston Public Library with the letter, and its present whereabouts are unknown. The map is reproduced here from the *Kipling Journal*, March 1968.
2. The Blue Skalallatoots are found in an introductory paragraph to the first of the *Just So Stories* as it appeared in *St Nicholas*, December 1897: "Some stories are only proper for rainy mornings, and some for long hot afternoons, when one is lying in the open, and some stories are bedtime stories. All the Blue Skalallatoot stories are morning tales." The paragraph was not reprinted in the volume of *Just So Stories*.
3. Ralph Henry Bathurst (b. 1904), the third son.

To Sir Max Aitken,[1] 6 September 1911

TLS and ALS: Harvard University

Bateman's / Burwash / Sussex / Sept. 6th, 1911.

private

Montreal Star[2]

Dear Sir,

I do not understand how nine million people can enter into such arrangements as are proposed with ninety million strangers on an open frontier of four thousand miles, and at the same time preserve their national integrity. Ten to one is too heavy odds. No single Canadian would accept such odds in any private matter that was as vital to him personally, as this issue is to the nation. It is her own soul that Canada risks today. Once that soul is pawned, for any consideration, Canada must inevitably conform to the commercial, legal, financial, social and ethical standards which will be imposed upon her by the sheer admitted weight of the United States. She might, for example, be compelled later on to admit reciprocity in the murder-rate of the United States which at present, I believe, is something over one hundred and fifty per million per annum. If these proposals had been made a generation ago, or if the Dominion were today, poor, depressed and without hope, one would perhaps understand their being discussed. But Canada is none of these things. She is a Nation and as the lives of nations are reckoned, will, ere long, be among the great nations. Why then, when she has made herself what she is, should she throw the enormous gifts of her inheritance and her future into the hands of a people, who by haste and waste have so dissipated their own resources that even before national middle life, they are driven to seek virgin fields for cheaper food and living?

Whatever the United States gains – and I presume the U.S. proposals are not wholly altruistic – I see nothing for Canada in Reciprocity, except a little ready money which she does not need and a very long repentance.

Yours sincerely,
Rudyard Kipling.[3]

Dear Aitken

Above behold the result of a wire from the London corres. of the *Montreal Star* asking me to say something about Reciprocity. So I have! I hope it will help but it's difficult at 3000 miles range to avoid saying the wrong thing.

You've evidently interested Abe Bailey. We dined with him and Jameson before A.B.'s wedding – to cheer him up.[4] He needs it. She is 20 – and young at that and he is 46 and all of that, with a 16 year old daughter. Thus we see that even financiers have weak moments. And that reminds me. We've got £2,000 ($10,000) snatched from the burning to invest *out* of England. Can you give me an idea if there's anything coming on?

It's red hot down here and we wish we were in Scotland with you. When can you come and see us after you get back.

Ever thine
RK

Are you J. Russell and are you at Roy Bridge (R.Y.B.) under Ft. William? Some birds have come from there for which we are most grateful.

The wife begs for a line from Lady Aitken to ask where you are going after Worplesdon Place.[5] She won't be happy till she is sure you are *not* settled in a 32-bedpower house.

RK

Notes
1. Aitken (1879–1964), 1st Baron Beaverbrook, a highly successful Canadian financier, came to England in 1910 and entered politics as a Conservative; MP, Ashton-under-Lyne from 1910 to 1917, when he was created Lord Beaverbrook. Aitken was the most notable newspaper proprietor of his day, whose properties included the *Daily Express*, the *Sunday Express*, and the *Evening Standard*. RK and Aitken were introduced by H. A. Gwynne, who brought Aitken down to Bateman's on 27 October 1910; RK noted him as a "Canadian millionaire" in the Bateman's Visitors Book. They were on terms of close friendship soon after and remained so until after the war, when RK broke with Aitken because he thought him unsound on the Irish and other political questions (their wives remained good friends). As he did for many of his friends, Aitken acted as financial consultant to RK and gave him many investment opportunities. RK was godfather to Aitken's second son, christened Peter Rudyard.
2. RK, as he explains to Aitken, was responding to a request from the *Montreal Star* for an opinion on the proposed reciprocal trade agreement between Canada and the US. The proposal was backed by Laurier's government but widely opposed as opening the way to US domination of Canada. RK's letter was published in the *Star* on 7 September, headed "by Special Cable from Our Own Correspondent". In the general election of 21 September the government was badly beaten on the question. See the letter to Milner, 23 September 1911.
3. The letter, from the signature on, is in RK's holograph.
4. Bailey's first wife died in 1902; on 5 September 1911 he married Mary Westenra (1890–1960), daughter of the 5th Baron Rossmore: there were two sons and three daughters by this second marriage.
5. George Allen's house, near Guildford. Aitken had rented it (see 23 September 1911); later he bought Cherkley Court (see 16 October 1912). According to A. J. P. Taylor, it was while driving with RK that Aitken found Cherkley Court, and, with RK's approval, determined to buy it (*Beaverbrook*, New York, 1972, p. 72). RK wrote the verses called "Home" for Lady Aitken on the occasion of the Aitkens' move to Cherkley Court (uncollected: printed in, e.g., Sir George MacMunn, *Rudyard Kipling: Craftsman*, 1937).

To Lucy Baldwin, [mid-September 1911]
ALS: Dalhousie University

Bateman's

I had some notion of treating the Visit[1] in detail but it would have run to a fairly long story: and even then I couldn't have done the thing justice. It was immense – overwhelming but *not* cyclonic – rather more in the nature of a steady compelling gale sweeping through the house; or the enlargement of Natural Forces, yet they never did a thing that by any stretch could be called riotous or unseemly. Only I felt as one who had two 8 h.p. engines lightly attached to inadequate bed-plates.

That she dressed up as a ghost and pranced about in the moonlight was naught: but when she turned up with three or four pillows to enhance her charms, inside a red dressing gown her teeth in some awful way stopped out so that she resembled an obscene hag of fifty (and was *yet* the spit and image of you at 14); when she sat, most strictly in character, dribbling and sucking her teeth and dabbing her neck like a washerwoman with a handkerchief rolled into a tight damp wad, I own I *was* impressed. As a character study it beat the next night when she was a nigger in Elsie's pyjamas, with a tennis racket for banjo. *Then* we only laughed ourselves ill but the study of Dame Quickly[2] (I suppose that was what she meant it for) was Art.

We have laughed as we haven't in ages. Beyond alluding to ventriloquists as "Those stomachists" and giving us a lurid account of her canaries and three reasons why she should object to sleeping with a man, if married which she protests she will not be she said nothing specially notable but her doings—well, I'll try someday to give you an idea.

And Oliver whom I knew not, blossomed like a lotos. He acted – he acted beautifully; he acted with observation and comprehension (a) as a man buying boots at a shop and being coerced into boots he didn't want (b) as a military man telling a tale in a mess room (c) as a lounger of fashion by the sea side (d) as several people rendering comic songs of several descriptions and we sat round him and clamoured for him to go on. Do *you* know that that self-contained young imp *automatically* stores up and packs away in his mind everything that he sees? I gave him a suggestion, verbally, for a sketch. He went out into the hall for less than a minute and returned with the idea elaborated into a duologue with a beginning, a middle and a climax. And almost every gesture had been observed and reproduced: he throwing away the unessential. Elsie and John who have no imagination in these regards hung round with mouth open.

And so it went on – varied by wars in the water of the pond; attentions to a leaking dinghy and the manufacture of a pier across the pond; a bathing trip to Hastings and a loud and joyous return in the motor when they sang and passers by waved to 'em for joy, I take it, in their countenances.

But the fizz, the vitality, the genuine innocent joyous *devil* of the whole thing isn't to be described. I don't suppose (from my own experience) that any parent knows all about his children. I know uncles know nought about nephews and neices. But I'll learn. Keep on sending 'em down whenever you can – if so be they care to come – and I'll learn.

We've been running an hotel this summer for all nationalities[3] but the Visit was our only reward and recompense.

Rud.

Notes
1. Lorna and Oliver Baldwin were at Bateman's from 9 to 15 September (Bateman's Visitors Book). Lorna (Leonora) was the second of the four Baldwin daughters.
2. Hostess of the Boar's Head Tavern (*Henry IV*, 1 and 2).

3.   Their visitors in this summer included the Doubledays, the Aitkens, the de Forests, the Depews, and the Cornfords (Bateman's Visitors Book).

To Lord Milner, 23 September 1911
ALS: Bodleian Library

Bateman's / Sep. 23: 1911.

Dear Lord Milner

Yesterday I was at Sir Max Aitken's place[1] sitting in the sunshine while telegrams of the results of the Canadian elections were handed to me on a lordly dish. It's some few years – 7 or 8 I think – since I have been happy, and knowing that you also must have rejoiced a little, I write to you, to remind you

(a) that this busts the Laurier-Botha liaison in what are called our Imperial councils:
(b) that it sickens Bryce[2] which is always a work acceptable to God.
(c) that Fisher[3] of Australia will now have leisure to modify his views on the limited liability of colonies within the Empire, because Borden will explicitly repudiate Laurier's pronouncement on that subject
(d) Australia will be deprived of Big Sister's example as an excuse for nibbling after American "protection" on her own behalf.
(e) I do believe it smashes the French power for good: Borden being on his (46) majority as Independent of the nationalists as Asquith was of the Irish in the days of his 350 majority.
(f) It's the making of a new Canada because the U.S. will now lose her temper and say rude things without reserve and that will stiffen Canada's national back (see this week's U.S. papers).

These, and as many more, are points you know a hundred times better than I; but it's consoling to write them out in order. Seriously, don't you think it's the best thing that's happened to us in ten years? I was so resigned to defeat that I didn't realize what victory meant – if it should come; and I only hope now that I'm not overestimating. *Anyway* it should give us five years of breathing space and one can do three-quarters of anything in that time.

Ever sincerely
Rudyard Kipling

P.S.   Also we've worked *very* hard for it.

Notes
1. Worplesdon Place (see 6 September 1911). RK and CK spent the night there after taking John to school at Wellington College on the 21st.
2. James Bryce: see 19 April 1910. Bryce, a free-trader, was suspected by the Unionists in England to be plotting for reciprocity between Canada and the US. His biographer says that there was "not a word of truth" in the allegations made (H. A. L. Fisher, *James Bryce*, 1927, vol. II, p. 65).
3. Andrew Fisher (1862–1928), three times Australian Prime Minister between 1908 and 1915; leader of the Federal Labour Party and a staunch imperialist.

To Robert Underwood Johnson, 23 September 1911
TLS: Dalhousie University

Bateman's / Burwash / Sussex / Sept. 23rd, 1911.

private
Dear Johnson,

Thanks for the poetical underwriter's figures of the U.S. murder-rate (with reservations and exceptions).[1] They are very pretty, but I'm afraid, rather like "the flowers that bloom in the spring, tra-la."[2]

If you look up the June number of the World's Work pp. 14521, 2, 3[3] you will find a few figures that give to think otherwise. That writer makes it 115 per mil; but if you go back to *McClure's Magazine* about ten or it may be eleven years ago,[4] you will again find that the 10,000 murders per annum rate was exceeded even then on a smaller population.

It's a question that has always interested me a good deal and my own estimate, based on a study of U.S. papers, is that the murder rate today is *one per State per diem on the average.* I think if you made investigation you'd find this was under the mark.

I own the figures startled me. They work out (Territories apart) at 365×45 = 16425!! So I modified 'em – for considerations which the pious underwriter explicitly taxes me with having overlooked and took a mean between Herbert Bruce Fuller's figures (exceeded, remember, 10 years ago) and my own appalling totals; i.e. 12,000, which at 80,000,000 works out at 150 per million.

That is conservative.

I expressly omitted Judge Holt's reference[5] to the large proportion of the persons who had taken part in extra-legal executions, because if one had added the numbers of murderers (men *and* women) at large in the U.S. the figures would have been, though true, too ghastly.

It might be worth while to try to arrive, on the basis of selected large newspaper currency, the East, Centre, Middle West and West of the U.S., at an estimate of the whole butcher's bill for last year.[6]

Naturally, most of the papers that I've seen, represent me as a malignant and multitudinous liar and for the sake of great kindness in the past and great love in the present, *I'm* not going to reply. Reciprocity is finished and that's all I care for; but seriously, – and without in the least committing the Century to a muck-raking policy, I do think that the results of an investigation into the murder-rate of the U.S. would astonish you. So far as my press clippings serve me I haven't met any authoritative denial of these figures.

Sincerely yours,
Rudyard Kipling

Notes
1. Johnson had evidently sent someone's published response to RK's statement about the murder rate in the United States: see 6 September 1911.
2. Gilbert and Sullivan, *The Mikado*, II: "The flowers that bloom in the spring, / Tra la, / Have nothing to do with the case."
3. Herbert Bruce Fuller, "The Serious Absurdities of the Criminal Courts", *World's Work*, XXII (June 1911): "Today we have in the United States 115 homicides per million inhabitants" (p. 14522).
4. RK perhaps means S. S. McClure's "The Increase of Lawlessness in the United States", *McClure's Magazine*, XXIV (December 1904), 163–71 (see 27 November 1904): this reports more than 10,000 murders per annum in both 1895 and 1896.
5. Judge George Chandler Holt; in a report cited in Fuller's article, Holt states that of 300,000 people who participated in lynchings in the preceding 40 years, 100,000 were still living – "unhung murderers of that particular type" (p. 14521).
6. The sentence stands thus in the original.

To Lord Milner, 14 October 1911
ALS: Bodleian Library

Bateman's / Oct. 14. 1911.

Dear Lord Milner,
Rather a cheery and perspicuous note from Crewe, for "information and destruction." But how he at his time of ripe political iniquity can write of a Boer govt. as having "two policies" rather surprises me.

"Yet there are not two policies but one policy."
The Englishman an Uitlander and the Dutch a child of God.
The Botha incorruptible: and the Hertzog irreconcilable and the Gladstone
    irreclaimable.
Yet there is not one damned mess but a dozen damned messes, etc. etc.

Don't you somehow take pride and joy in the half-caste shamelessness of Sauer?[1] I confess I do.

The rest you will interpret with a clearer eye than I can bring to bear. I always squint when people talk of a "coalition govt." down below. It strikes me as a Dutch scheme for getting skilled (political) labour for less than nothing.

We're off to Ireland almost at once for a little change of air. Perhaps we may find Larkin[2] on the Throne.

Ever sincerely
Rudyard Kipling.

The Halsbury club[3] sounds promising and possibly tonic – like strychnine. It's too nice that everyone should belong except Balfour and Landsdowne.[4] Aren't you afraid of their joining.

(From The Stele Of Bal-Phour-Dunforusal: Circa. 1910. B.C.)

+ (1).   … said It was a matter of purely Historical Interest. … to be left to Future *agiz*. … and sat down. … in large parts surrounded by *femalz* of matured views. … not understanding he had done. … or said anything unusual *dammim*.

(2)   To which They made answer: Not *by a damsite* and took steps. … very pronouncedly. … but always with the most loyal intentions. … and. … collecting the *Vehri Worstofhem* some which had called Him every *namunder The sun* … … on the Tenth penultimo. …

(3)   made as you might say a fragrant bunch of 'em. … . a nosegay of withered loves. …

(4)   Thrust it under his nose *first* and then

(5)   in case he should *djibb* a second time cut a large and spiky *Khlub* for … the other End. … Holding it *in Terrorem* … (what you might call an … …

(6)   (*Arrière Pensée*) The most devoted of *Adherentz* so long as he kept running in front of them … in the way he should go. … sweating big drops. … without an ounce of conviction. …

(7)   but acutely concerned for his position which is

(8)   that of a Natural Leader +

Notes

1. Sauer, who had supported Merriman against Botha as the first premier of the Union of South Africa, accepted office in Botha's ministry even though Merriman declined to join it.
2. James Larkin (1876–1947) was editor of the *Irish Worker* and the organiser of the Irish Transport and General Workers' Union. His style was violent. A railway strike in Ireland under his leadership had just been settled against the strikers on 4 October.

3. Formed by Unionist members from both Houses of Parliament on 12 October to "restore a free Constitution to the United Kingdom" (*The Times*, 13 October 1911). It was named for the very old and very reactionary Tory Lord Halsbury (1823–1921), thrice Lord Chancellor. He had just led the "Die-hard" peers in their unsuccessful opposition to the Parliament Bill. Milner was among those "unavoidably prevented from attending the meeting" at which the club was formed (*ibid.*).
4. The Unionist leaders in the Commons and the Lords, both of whom were thought not to have resisted the Parliament Bill sufficiently.

To Sir James Walker, 15 October 1911
ALS: Dalhousie University

Bateman's / Burwash: / Oct. 15. 1911.

Dear Sir James

I have just received your two letters from Simla; and made haste to write at once to the London manager of the *Pioneer* to tell him that I could not undertake the commission to write verses for the Delhi Durbar.[1] He should have wired the *Pi* by now. What I did *not* tell him was that I most earnestly hope that the Durbar will not take place. The risks both of life and of plague are so heavy; and the situation both in England and on the Continent is so menacing that it seems possible that even at the eleventh hour H.M. may be led to think better of it. Anyhow I feel so strongly on the matter that I fear I could not write anything worthy of the occasion. My heart isn't in it. If it were I shouldn't charge my old paper for it.

My father died at Clouds while I was in Switzerland, of heart-disease, quickly and thank God without pain. My sister had broken down at my mother's death and was with my father and a nurse till within a few days of when he died. He wished that she should be in his care and I make no doubt that the strain of looking after her was more than his heart could endure.

She is now under a doctor's care at Andover where I go to see her in a few days.[2] She is reported to be much better – and I believe will be cured by the end of the year. These things do not make for happiness.

Father and mother have told me many times what a delight their visit to Worplesdon[3] was to them and your kindness to them made them very happy. They were rich in their friends and they loved their life as they lived it which is more than a good many people dare say.

You are greatly mistaken in thinking that I have anything against the old *Pi*. Dare[4] was a natural as well as a semi-educated brute but apart from that (and I don't recall that he ever did me any harm) I have only the kindest remembrances of all the staff. And I am not likely to forget that it was to you and Sir George Allen that I owed my start in life on the C. & M. By the way George Allen is now my best and oldest friend.

But the fact is that I am and have been for years a very busy man, much abroad every year, and concerned with all sorts of affairs that leave one but little time for one's natural inclination. I always heard of you from my folk but now that you have spoken I shall hope, all being well, to see you next summer. My boy is now at Wellington[5] and this will call me there; and I have already realized that Worplesdon is close by as we spent the night there (after leaving John at school) with your tenants Sir Max and Lady Aitken who are friends of ours. The photoes on the walls brought back old days.

Ever sincerely yours,
Ruddy.

Notes
1. The King and Queen attended a durbar at Delhi on 12 December as the climax of their visit to India, 2 December 1911–10 January 1912.
2. He went the next day (CK diary).
3. In Surrey, near Guildford, where Walker lived when in England.
4. William John Dare, manager of the *Pioneer*: see [January? 1889].
5. John entered Wellington College on 21 September; for the visit to Aitken, see 23 September 1911.

To Elsie and John Kipling, [18 October 1911][1]
ALS: University of Sussex

Shelbourne Hotel [Dublin] / 9. p.m. (written on the top of a – well, the neatly polished little cabinet they put on one side of a bed – [sketch of cabinet] because all the electric light is at one end of the room and I can't drag the table there!) –

Me daughter – O me daughter – (Likewise, since you will probably send it on to John) me son!

Mother says she wrote you last night. If she did she must have been a pretty tired mother because, even when the railway is as good as the North Western – nine or ten hours of travel do not make for peace or comfort. However, we both dropped into bed last night about 8:30: p.m. and were soothed by the noise of trams. (N.B. The Dublin tram is the noisiest machine that ever growled round corners.)

We woke at early hours – much cheered by the thought that there were no beastly little – no darling children to be considered and did not descend to breakfast till nine. a.m.!!! The food was good and recherche; the waiters were all German. It was a warm, sticky summer day with blue sky and heaps of smoke in the air. Not *quite* as black as London. Then we went out for a walk. Such a walk! We trailed all round St. Stephen's Square first, in a climate that rather reminded one of Madeira. *The* astonishing thing to us was the absence of taxis. As I wrote John the Dublin cab-driver will see himself blessed before he allows a taxi to be driven for hire. Result. Dublin is still in the horse-age and – stinks according! Then we loafed along through the pale sunshine till we reached the buildings of Trinity College – great blocks of grey stone houses and chapels and libraries, set in gardens and sheets of turf greener than emerald with youngsters and oldsters in college gowns all cutting about and now and then a girl graduate with her gown swinging coquettishly from her shoulders. Tell Miss P.[2] that girls *wear* their gowns; boys just chuck 'em on anyhow. We went to the College Library and saw *The Book of Kells* – a most wonderfully illuminated old Irish M.S.: as well as a heap of other volumes, *most* interesting to your parents. We just browsed along like camels on the loose through those heavenly still gardens for an hour or so. Then we strolled out and got into Grafton Street which is as you might say the Bond Street of these parts. At 76 Grafton Street is the Royal Irish Industries, where they sell Limerick and Irish point lace, poplins, linens, Irish tweeds and all that sort of flub-dub. Mother very kindly assisted the Royal Irish Industries. She assisted 'em from 11.50. till 1:25: p.m.! I won't tell you what she bought because she would beat me if I did – but she bought a whole floor full of things. How glad I am that I do not need collars of transparent muckings, or blouses that one can see through or hankies that one can spit through. I *never* spit through my hankies praise be to Allah! But I daresay you will be pleased with some of the things. It's much more difficult to buy things for a man than for a woman. The only thing I could get John would be a trunkful of horse-dung. It's cheap in Dublin. Another funny experience is lying in bed and hearing the pat-pat of horses' feet. One very rarely hears the hoot of a motor.

Well, as I was saying, we shopped till lunch time and after lunch went out for a drive to Phœnix park in a jaunting-car. My dears, jaunting cars were designed by the Devil thus: – [sketch of jaunting-car from rear]. This is the back view. You step on step A. which is about as big as a stirrup [sketch of stirrup]. Then you sit sideways on cushion B. Your legs hanging outside the wheels. Here is the side view – [sketch of horse and car from side]. The driver sits in front. Heaven knows how.

But (Mummy says) one thing is certain. If anything happens the passenger falls out sideways. If there is any congestion of traffic in the streets the passenger's legs are hit. We were jerked and jolted along sideways at the awe-inspiring pace of at least 6-miles per hour. Mummy on one side – me on the other [sketch of RK and CK on jaunting car]. (I'm trying to get the blessed thing right. This is almost correct).

We drove along the banks of the River Liffey which is a rich, pure black stone faced sewer that calls itself a river. Guinness' Brewery is on one bank of it. Liffey water is the same colour as Dublin porter.

Well, in due time, say half an hour, we got to Phœnix Park – which is of Enormous Extent – about 1200 acres but in a jaunting car this feels like 18 miles in circumference. We took an hour to jaunt round it so it must have been eighteen miles in pure exposure and suffering. There were hundreds and hundreds of fallow deer in the park: all slightly sooty, like everything else in Dublin: and cows and sheep – and the horse (who was really a good little horse) – lifted up one leg and put it down and lifted up the next leg and put it down, till I nearly wept with boredom. I distinctly saw the wool growing on the sheeps' backs between every stride: and Mummy got cold and silent (like Lot's wife) and I grew cold and quite voluble (which is how cold affects me) and we wrote our name in the book at Viceregal Lodge; and also at General Lyttleton's[3] house which was half an hour distant from Viceregal lodge and after two hours of jovial jaunting car-dom we got back to our hotel and urged our frozen limbs into half an hour's walk before tea to get warm. *You*, my dears, are young. When you meet a jaunting car you may ride in it if you want to. But, be warned by me, *don't* ride for fun in Dublin. It's too like a funeral with you for corpse.

Then we had tea and a man came and talked to us for an hour about farming in Ireland and somehow we weren't grateful to him. Then your letter came for which we were grateful. You'll know by this time, Elsie, that we got your telegram – many thanks for same – and you will have got John's letter. It says much for the health of Wellington that, with all we've sent him in the way of grub, the little beast isn't sick. Perhaps four swims a week keeps it down.

This is all. Mums and I both send love.

We are going to Belfast tomorrow in a *motor* – a hired one. It's a hundred miles run. We want to see Ireland. At present we have only smelt it.

Ever lovingly
Dad.

Notes
1. They left on 17 October for Dublin (CK diary).
2. Dorothy Ponton, who had just arrived as Elsie's governess and who remained until the end of 1913. In 1919 she returned to the Kiplings' employ as secretary and remained in that position until 1924. Miss Ponton published her recollections of the Kiplings in *Rudyard Kipling at Home and at Work* (Poole, Dorset, 1953).
3. General Sir Neville Lyttelton (1845–1931), Commander-in-Chief, Ireland, 1908–12.

To Andrew Macphail, 21 October 1911
ALS: Photocopy, National Archives of Canada

Northern Counties Hotel, / *Portrush.* / Oct. 21. 1911.

Dear Macphail,

I was more glad than I could tell you to get your letter written in an un-altered hand. But the baccy at first puzzled me. I thought it was mummy-dust at first (Haggard had been staying with me and our talk had been of these idols).[1] It slipped out of the envelope as I opened it. Then I saw and mixed it with some sophisticated baccy: Then I smoked a pipeful alone. It's perfectly clean bright and good: but it's a bit full for my taste. Question, I take it, of manures in the ground. They say guano or too much phosphates will load up the leaf with mineral stuffs till it fair purrs like a kettle when one smokes it. This leaf didn't purr and didn't leave any residue worth talking of. Maybe there will be something in it. After all the man who makes two blades etc. is *the* person.[2]

One realizes it in Ireland more than elsewhere. The wife and I came over at the beginning of this week, being wearied of doing lots of things; and besides she has not been well lately though she is now better. Ireland began at Euston Station where a long bright-eyed and dramatic guard, in charge of the Holyhead mail, was also, it seemed, in personal and intimate charge of all the passengers. He knew 'em all; chaffed the elderly, chaperoned the young, arranged us all in our places and spread the wings of a large vague benevo-lence over us. One felt that somehow one had already set foot in a society apart from the rest of the uncomprehending world. And there were long-limbed, loose-lipped men in hairy, loud-patterned frieze-coats who rolled their heads together in corners and whispered portentously and (I suppose) politically. Rummy atmosphere of make-believe all about us; with the guard for its centre and dispenser.

A *hot* – downright hot – passage to Dublin in front of a North East wind moving exactly as fast as we did. So we took off our coats and treated it like summer. Then Dublin in the evening – warm, soft and full of black smoke but devil a taxi at the station, only horse-drawn nuisances, with rubber tyres and a smell of horse-dung and stable blankets that took one back to the middle ages. (The car-drivers of Dublin will not permit petrol in any form). So we filed out of the station, which was also a manure pit at, at least, four miles an hour and got to an hotel which (now this *is* curious) smelt exactly like a U.S. hotel. So did all Dublin and one realized how potent is the Irish esprit de corps. The people in the streets spat joyously (after the manner of the U.S.) and were just as casual and inexact and interested-in-their-own-affairs-at-the-time-they-were-supposed-to-be-on-duty as any citizen of the U.S. Thus we saw the very egg whence the Eastern U.S. was born. (The

Pilgrim fathers don't count except for purposes of fiction. V. *Vine of Sibmah*).[3]
It was like walking in a past existence.

And the next day was hot and sunny and soft as a South Irish accent. We loafed into Trinity College quad and spent a couple of hours watching the come and go of students and professors in and out of the soft grey-black buildings: went to the library – unkempt and unswept – saw the Book of Kells and certain other M.S. that I was keen on but it was enough merely to move about the grey quad and the soft green gardens in a sub-tropical atmosphere. Everything outside that limit looked and smelt like a deboshed U.S. (truly a little leaven. . ...)

Then next day by automobile from Dublin to Belfast via Balbriggan, Drogheda, Dundalk, Newry, Lisburn through a hand-fed government-aided land of damnably inartistic cottages – for which I am taxed by the way – of expensive make and eye-blistering design. And the only return these fashionless creatures made for it to me, in a hireling motor halting at four muddy cross roads, was to erect a sign-post in *Erse* – in Gaelic – or whatever they called it. Anyhow it was a four-handed piece of self-conscious affection like this: – [sketch of four-armed signpost]. I don't know why it made me so hopping mad – but it did. To waste money on an ingrate and to have him jabber at you in an unknown tongue just when you wanted a simple direction. ... ...

And what made me madder was the land's blatant *un*loveliness wherever man had set his mark on it! They couldn't spoil the green or the sombre superb autumn colouring as we saw it through open and shut mists but their houses – their plantless gardenless, unkempt workhouse like cottages and villas – and their own personal aridity of culture! Allah must needs make them poets (and they insist on letting us know that they all are poets) for surely He has deprived them of love of line or knowledge of colour. Again a U.S. trait for village after village was but the Irish patch in a New England town. And most of the folk had new strong red-painted carts and good tools which I would have admired more had I not spent half the evening before with an official of some Govt department or other for "encouraging agriculture" and I noticed how the man was, so to speak, carried away by the lust of administration, debauched by the people he was hired to help so that it seemed to him right and holy to supply them with good houses, tools, manures and the deuce knows what else, on the easiest terms, *because* they were incompetent and had been improvident, and he "hopeth to raise them in the scale." Maybe I grow harder-hearted in my middle age but it all seemed so false and unsound.

Then we got into the North and the car literally bumped into a new country of decent folk, unadorned by Government cottages and new red carts. (Do you suppose that having a great-great grandfather buried at Ballynamallard[4] in a grim Methody churchyard has anything to do with my fine impartial outlook on Ireland?) The talk was familiar and so was the decent, unaccomodating Northern type of face; the modelling of cheek and jaw-bone and by the time we ran into the roar and rush of Belfast I was comforted. I do not think I should like to collect taxes for a Home Rule Parliament from Belfast – against her will – even with a brigade of troops – not often – or for a living.

That was a city, and it went about its job. We stayed, by error, in a big commercial caravanserai – the wife being the only woman visible in it. Those grim faced business men met without any of the graces, and none of the airs of the South, put away enormous slugs of whiskey quite unemotionally at 10. a.m.; did their job and marched out into the wet and black of the streets. Rain was falling in Belfast for the first time in months. The drouth has hit Ireland as hard as England. The Hotel bathrooms were shut from 5: p.m. to 10. a.m. on account of lack of water: it was the same thing all through our tour in Normandy this August: where we finished up at a Franco-American chateau with 23 servants 9 beautiful bathrooms and, perhaps, 50 gallons water per diem![5]

We walked about the city simply to see things by ourselves and fetched up at a cinematograph theatre (!!) where a stolid audience on red velvet chairs at 6d a-bottom sat out the moving history of Rob Roy with deep satisfaction. Have *you* ever seen Scott on a film? Then be thankful you haven't. I wanted to yell aloud against the outrage but, on considering what new worlds the cinema is giving people, very kindly forbore. Then to the docks and the City Hall and so on – just for sheer love of being alive among folks – and next day by train through a decently farmed land to Portrush which, you know, is that bit of land the Canadian liners first sight as they swing round the nose of Ireland to get to Liverpool (watched an Allen boat doing so this afternoon and blessed her). It's a huge summer-resort, now dead and boarded up, thank Heaven, till next season, with golf-links said to be second only to St. Andrews (but they all say that) and rows on rows of ghostly white damp-spotted crop-eared stucco houses: but nothing they can do, and they and the Railway company continually do their damnedest, can defile the glorious air that is soft and yet keen, or make any large mark on the sweeps of green, the pale gold of the dunes, the black-purple of the rocks and the great bronze shield of the North Atlantic. The sea strays into this quiet little bay very meekly but with a swing and a snuff to it, like an elephant breathing into a baby-carriage. We've just been walking about – the wife and I, among new things and unfeignedly glad there isn't any one to explain 'em. Here's a fine hotel, with a ball-room of about $3/4$ of an acre as near as I can judge and rows and rows of sea water baths – all at the disposal of about a dozen serious minded golfers. They don't dance but they wash.

On Monday we turn our faces home which we hope to reach on Tuesday. It has been hot and sticky ever since we left. What an awful screed I've inflicted on you. See what comes of *not* losing your eyesight![6]

This here's a small world. Lord Grey he went round this corner opposite my window yesterday in his boat: and yesterday morn we watched Lady Aberdeen[7] going to Belfast City Hall to do something or other – probably to lecture it severely. She looked grossly in earnest. We hid like Adam and Eve in the Municipal Gardens or she'd have lectured *us* because this enclosed is what appeared in the papers yesterday.[8] How hard it is to be loved.

And talking of verse that sonnet sequence you sent me seems uncommon like poetry. Will you make the maker of it my respectful compliments. You've all so warm a corner (and justly) in your hearts for Grey that you must also keep one for the Connaughts.[9] They are good straight simple folk as ever were – with the simplicity that comes from being It and having seen all the world from the inside since birth. She has all the gifts of the Hohenzollerns[10] and sees *very* straight – a capable nice *true* woman and I do hope you'll get to know her really. When you do let me know. I should like your impressions. There's a nice Irish Lady in waiting (Pelly)[11] and Lowther[12] of course is very good. Now I will really stop. With love

Ever yours
Rudyard Kipling.

Notes

1. Rider Haggard was at Bateman's from 30 September to 2 October (Bateman's Visitors Book). Haggard's diary account of the visit is in Morton Cohen, ed., *Rudyard Kipling to Rider Haggard*, pp. 69–73.
2. Swift, *Gulliver's Travels*, Book II, ch. 7. Beginning about 1910 Macphail and his brother Alexander experimented with tobacco growing on Prince Edward Island, and as a result of their work tobacco has become a significant crop in the province (information from Professor Ian Ross Robertson).
3. *The Vine of Sibmah: A Relation of the Puritans*, 1906, a historical romance by Macphail, about a Quakeress and one of Cromwell's captains in Puritan New England.
4. John Macdonald, who emigrated from Skye to Ballinamallard in the 18th century. Ballinamallard is near Lough Erne, north of Enniskillen.
5. The Château d'Annel: see 16 August 1911.
6. Macphail's eyes had been seriously injured in June 1911, by glass from an exploding soda water bottle. He lost most of the sight in his left eye.
7. Ishbel Maria Gordon (1857–1939), wife of the 1st Marquess of Aberdeen and Temair, then Lord-Lieutenant of Ireland. Lady Aberdeen was touring the north of Ireland on an official visit; when RK saw her she was on her way to the mayor's reception at city hall followed by a visit to the meeting of the Women's National Health Association (*Belfast Evening Telegraph*, 21 October 1911).
8. The enclosure does not appear to have survived.
9. The Duke of Connaught was going out to Canada as Governor-General. CK's diary, 3 October 1911, records that RK was "writing Canadian notes for guidance of the Connaughts". The Duchess responded on 6 November, thanking RK for "the most interesting paper you have been so very good as to draw up for me on Canadian people, and matters of great importance" (ALS, Sussex).
10. The Duchess was the daughter of Prince Friedrich of Prussia.
11. A Miss Pelly is among the party sailing with the Duke of Connaught to Canada listed in *The Times*, 5 October 1911.
12. Major (afterwards General) Sir Henry Cecil Lowther (1869–1940) was secretary to the Duke of Connaught as Governor-General, 1911–13.

To Colonel H. W. Feilden, 22 October 1911
ALS: Syracuse University

Northern Counties Hotel, / *Portrush.* / Oct. 22. 11.

Colonel Sahib –

I gather from Elsie's last letter that you progress favourably: "which is tidings of comfort and joy"[1] to both of us. Persevere in that path and for the Lord's sake have a care of yourself when you get better.

We have had rather an interesting time of it. We found Dublin in full possession of the Middle Ages. There isn't such a thing as a carriage at the Station there – nothing but horse-drawn nuisances smelling of their original manure. The Jarvies of Dublin won't have any dealings with Taxis and I never realized till I smelt him in bulk once more, what an odoriferous imposter the Common or Hired Horse was!

We hired a car (petrol) to take us from Dublin to Belfast, lunching at Dundalk, where I saw the young and lively subaltern of our Army – God bless him! – looking much as I used to know him. I daresay you've been quartered at Dundalk and know the Queen's Arms (or Williams's) Hotel well. The day was warm and misty. We didn't see as much of the country as I should have liked but there were a-plenty of fine new government built cottages for which you and I are taxed.

While in Dublin we went for a drive in the Phœnix, in that Devil's own sitz-bath called a jaunting-car. We went out for two chilly hours and must have gone at least 10 miles. Wrote our names in the viceroy's books and in Neville Lyttleton's book at the Royal Hospital and so did our duty. But Lord the dirt and slop and general shiftlessness of Dublin beats belief. What must it have been in Lever's day![2]

At Belfast we found a notice in our hotel that owing to scarcity of water the bathrooms would be locked from 5:p.m. till 10. a.m. But nothing about Belfast gave me the idea that anything short of The Deluge could clean the city. There was a fine mizzle of rain – the first in months I believe – that turned the streets to black slush. Lady Aberdeen was at the City Hall opening or shutting something. C. and I stood about in the gardens and watched her come in. Aberdeen is not much of a man but I am sorry for him.

We went on from Belfast to Portrush which is a delightful place at this time of year; tho' in the summer it must be a crowded, tripper-ridden Hades. We look out of our window on to the track of the Canadian boats swinging round the nose of Ireland on their way to Liverpool. 'Saw an Allen liner yesterday. They've had no rain here for months, so we didn't complain when it fell, warm and sticky, yesterday. We were out for two hours walking by the sea or plunging across sand-bunkers or walking ankle deep in sand of the shore. It's a bare, deep green treeless land of beautiful lights and shadows with a golf-course reported to be second only to St Andrews. I saw a man yesterday with compressed lips and set brows toiling across the greens as one who was fighting his way into the Heavenly City; and I thanked God *sotto voce* that you weren't given to that form of lunacy. And he played dam-bad too.

Today is a dull sky with a dry north east wind blowing in from Rathlin Island. We do *not* intend to go nine miles in a jaunting car to the Giant's Causeway.[3]

We hope to get away tomorrow for Belfast: then Dublin and leave by the 8:p.m. boat (with, I imagine, the bulk of the Irish M.P.s) for Holyhead and be at home – please Allah – on Tuesday after lunch when I propose to do myself the honour of inquiring after your health. It has been a most pleasant stand-easy for us both and I have a notion that I have learned something. But it isn't fit for publication.

With all good wishes from us both to you both.

Affectionately
Rudyard K.

Notes
1. Cf. the carol "God Rest Ye Merry Gentlemen".
2. Charles Lever (1806–72), Irish novelist.
3. But they did (Rees extracts, 22 October 1911); CK's diary (misdated entry of 19 October 1911) reports: "Giants' Causeway. Delighted, would like to come again."

To George B. Richards,[1] 24 October 1911
ALS: University of Texas

Bateman's / Burwash / Sussex / Oct 24. 1911.

private
Dear Sir

Many thanks for your most interesting letter. I know the h.p. of the *Mauretania* but I took 30,000 h.p. as a rough average of what one gets in the Atlantic trade nowadays.[2] I began the next verse with an allusion to the M. and her *nine* decks. Aren't there eleven as a matter of fact?

However, to make it all clear, I'll put the h.p. up to 70,000 in the next edition which is just being printed.[3] What am I to do if there is slackness in the stoke-hold and it drops to 54,000? She didn't develop *that* much in August?[4]

What you tell me about the new "oiler" is very interesting. I fancy we've been digging coal out of dirt, and boiling water above it, quite long enough and the Almighty is sending us rail and coal strikes as a gentle hint that we must find a new power.

How would "Keroseiner" or "parafeamer" do for an oil-driven steamer? Or seriously (I)nternal (C)ombustion ship *So and So*, or simply (p)ower-ship.

Very sincerely
Rudyard Kipling.

George B. Richards Esq.

Notes
1. Not identified. In the University of Texas catalogue this letter is described as addressed to "George Richardson". The name as RK has written it at the end of the letter might be either Richards or Richardson.
2. In "The Secret of the Machines" (*History of England*, pp. 247) RK speaks of "thirty thousand horses" as available to those who wish to cross the "Western Ocean"; the next stanza names the "Mauretania", a "monstrous nine-decked city". The Cunard liners *Mauretania* and *Lusitania* entered service in 1907; both developed 70,000 horse power.
3. So he did: later printings of the poem read "seventy thousand horses".
4. I can find no record of any accident or untoward incident involving the *Mauretania* in August 1911.

To Major-General J. B. Sterling, [*c*. October 1911]
AL: Cornell University

[Bateman's?]

Mr. Rudyard Kipling presents his compliments to the Archbishop of Canterbury and is pained and grieved to learn that His Holiness should have spent seven shillings and sixpence on Modern Licentious Literature. Mr. Kipling feels it his duty as a Christian to point out that for half the above-mentioned sum, His Holiness could have purchased two entirely Blue French Novels; thus saving three shillings and sixpence to meet the rapidly approaching menace of Disendowment.

Mr. Kipling would further add that if His Holiness had bought the latest edition of "*The Only History of England*" His Holiness would have discovered that the late "red" cliffs of Plymouth had changed their colour and are now "dear" or words to that effect.[1] Mr. Kipling reluctantly admits that there may be some substratum of justification for His Holiness's objection to sentences that end with prepositions and has the felicity to inform His Holiness that Mr. Kipling's collaborator – the Rev. Athanasius Origen Fletcher – is now knocking them out with a marlinspike. Mr. Kipling is not prepared to enter into any discussion with His Holiness on the Infallibility or otherwise of the Pope in regard to the Late Miss J. D'Arc.[2] Mr. Kipling has been brought up with a strong prejudice against all Whores – of whom Mr. Kipling considers the Whore of Babylon quite the most unladylike and he does not desire the Young to know anything about her.

If His Holiness's recollection extends to the case of Miss Cass[3] His Holiness will recognize that even Police Magistrates are sometimes fallible, and Mr. Kipling cannot too severely reprehend the narrow spirit of sectarian jealousy shown in His Holiness's wanton jibe at his brother Bishop of Rome.

Mr. Kipling hopes to be able to explain his views more fully next week, in person, at the Cathedral in Pall Mall where he trusts that his Prebendal Stall[4] will not be Disestablished before he wants his lunch.

Notes
1. In the earliest printings of *A History of England* the cliffs of Plymouth are "white" (not red); in later printings they are "the dear cliffs" (p. 133).
2. According to a note on the MS of this letter at Cornell, Sterling objected to the statement in the *History* that Joan of Arc was captured and burned by the English (p. 103); he pointed out that she had been handed over to the English by the Church of Rome. The statement was not altered.
3. Miss Cass was a respectable young working woman who, in 1887, had been wrongly arrested as a prostitute in London. The affair created a minor political crisis. RK refers to the business at the end of his article entitled "Our Change. By 'Us'" in the *CMG*, 1 August 1887 (Pinney, *Kipling's India*).
4. The table in the Athenaeum dining room where Sterling presided: see [October? 1910].

To Henry James, 4 November 1911
ALS: Harvard University

Bateman's: / Nov. 4. 1911.

Dear Henry James,

Got your letter, both Carrie and I rejoiced that you aren't going to stick in Rye through the British Winter. It's not that I should mind (so much) a certain clammy and unrelieved darkness that belongs to all small towns but the mean and measly drizzle of small society that accompanies it in the long evenings, which I'm sure kills vitality. So if one doesn't live frankly in the middle of fields – as we do – London is the best place. But *why* did you hang[1] up the taxis? 'Tisn't hospitable to those who want to see you.

C. and I expect to be up in town ere long for shopping and we'd dearly love to see you.[2] On second thoughts I don't know that *I* should be so pleased because I've read and re-read The Outcry[3] and had sat down and stolidly hated you. How do you make your dialogues solid – solid in three dimensions like a stage – with peeps and loopholes and vistas and depth and luminosity and a few trifles of that kind, which I can't? There are whole lumps of it which (without scenery) appeal directly *through the eye*, not as the drama of the persons concerned but as a whole setting of life. And the joyous thing to me is to see the other people imitating you and failing horribly!

C. hasn't been very well this summer but is now much better and our recent visit to Ireland (where Time and Affairs are not) set her up a great deal.

With dear love from us both

Affectionately yours always
Rudyard

Notes
1. Word not clear: bang?
2. CK's diary, 28 October 1911, reads: "to see Henry James", but that may be a mistaken transcription.
3. James's novel, published on 5 October.

To H. A. Gwynne, 10 November 191[1][1]
ALS: Dalhousie University

Bateman's / Nov. 10. 1910

Dear Old Man –

I *quite* admit all you say about Ian Colvin. Who has suffered more from it than I – beginning in S. Africa. He is awfully conceited but he has got conviction – after his conviction that Ian Colvin is the most important person in sight. He is an ass to say your men can't write but – good as the leaders are – they don't get home. They don't read as if they were meant. This at least is my opinion and therefore it seemed to me he'd be valuable.[2] But remember what I said I said for the paper and the game *not* for him. I'm not after any man at the present crisis. I'm after the Game. I got your betting list (most immoral). I say that Bonar Law will be leader.[3] He's dead sound on Tariff Reform and (N.B.) it's a feather in Canada's cap! And mark my words, from now on A. J. B[alfour]. will give us no end of fireworks – just to show that he can do it. His resignation speech was very fine.[4]

I do wish you could come down, take a night off and jaw, and see Elsie sew. By the way that young Lady wants your editorial blood.

As to the "Female"[5] I've been deluged with correspondence, poems etc. etc. etc. But no cheque from the *Morning Post*. Consider this. It marks an epoch.

Our best love to you.

Ever yours
Rud

Notes

1. Though RK has dated the letter 1910, internal evidence make the date 1911 certain.
2. Colvin had been on the staff of the *Morning Post* since 1909, though this letter appears to speak of him as something new on the paper.
3. Balfour having resigned the leadership of the Unionist Party, it was expected that either Austen Chamberlain or Walter Long would succeed him. In order to avoid splitting the party, both withdrew in favour of Bonar Law: see 15 November 1911.
4. Balfour announced his resignation in a speech to the City of London Conservative Association, 8 November.
5. "The Female of the Species", *Morning Post*, 20 October 1911 (*The Years Between*). This went back before 1910, when CK's diary (21 July 1910) records that RK "starts on his suffragette verses – put aside for a long time".

To Sir Max Aitken, 15 November 1911

TL: Harvard University

Bateman's / Burwash / Sussex / Nov. 15th, 1911.

Dear Aitken,

It would seem from your wires and some casual references in the local press that there has been a ripple or two of excitement in political circles.[1] But, as a very great man remarked a very short time ago, these are matters of purely historical interest, – like the authorship of Junius' letters.

It must have been a nice peaceful home coming for you. I highly approve of the choice; it has annoyed and disgruntled the Radicals, both publicly and privately. They would have loved Long most, and next to him, Austen. I confess I wonder that our Party itself did not plump for Long. He would have been more immaculately useless and genteely incompetent than anything in sight. Austen – alas! is a son of a Father and when the Father is dead, the son's stock will drop heavily. However the fact that we have chosen B.L. gives me hope, and I have promptly renewed my defaulting local political subscriptions.

I have a vision of B.L. already snowed under by good advice to which I will at once add my shovelful.

The Central Conservative Organisation needs being taken to bits and reassembled as soon as may be. It does not seem to know that there is such a thing as the Press even in London, much less in the provinces where a few thousand votes turn many elections. As far as I can make out, and I have gone into the matter pretty thoroughly, it has no efficient head working under the Leader of the Party who can turn in accurate confidential information to editors, etc., which will enable them to understand, not only what the policy of the party is, but how to lead up to, and prepare the public mind for that policy. You can't expect the Leader of a Party to be at the beck and call of every journalist outside a few big dailies, who wishes to keep abreast of the situation, and it is essential that every journalist should be kept abreast of the situation.

Further, it is not fair to anyone that a leader's instructions, views, etc., should filter down to the rank and file, through the medium of third parties. In Balfour's day his views were some one else's views, and he didn't use the papers, but now that we have a leader who proposes to lead, there must be no more room for error or misinterpretation.

To do this work you need one man directly in touch with the leader, and through him drawing the confidential political information to be given to the party editors, writers and the like. Under this man must be a staff which collects and prepares political news of all kinds; the material for campaign agitations; facts about Home Rule and the Insurance Bill; but first and foremost, *news*.

Newspapers exist for news, and editors are just as grateful for being saved trouble as are other people.

The man at the head of this work (let us call him Division 1) must know from his leader the right moment to make public the right facts; must also know the right men to start correspondence, and draw attention to the moves of the other side – we have during the last few years lost heavily by neglecting this elementary precaution. Every man has fired when he thought it was right at any mark that turned up.

But the preparation of material and the distribution of it are different matters.

So we come to this. Division 1 gives the confidential information on policy to trustworthy editors; collects the political news from all quarters; starts letters and correspondence in the Press, and should be relied on to furnish political ammunition as any campaign develops.

Division 2 distributes the news. And this is all one man's job.

For this work you want a man who knows the newspaper press of the United Kingdom from A to Z (Irish and Scotch specially valuable) and who can create and control an organisation which is in direct touch with all these papers. They are all open to free news if it is short. They are all grateful for advance summaries of speeches so that their leader writers can have time to deal with the matter adequately. In fact, you must give your own press a few hours' start of the other side.

But don't for a minute think I advocate any sort of party control over the press of the party. Give the editors the facts – give the editors news – and advance news as far as possible on big issues; keep them supplied with paras of smaller news and interesting news and let them deal with the stuff as they choose. The Radicals have debauched their press and it's going to be useless just as the Press in America is. That is why big newspaper syndicates should not be singled out for special favour in news. It is the free papers in the provinces that swing votes.

This is just my outline. If you care to go into it further, there is an organisation existing, working of course on a smaller scale, on very much these lines, and I believe you could take it over. The man in charge of one of the departments has been at work under my eyes for fifteen years – in fact I steered him into politics – and I know him to be loyal – which is the first qualification – and aggressive – which is the second. Also he knows the press and he can write.[2]

I never have, and I never intend to back any man as a man – all that has ever concerned me is a man's value in the game, and when I say I have known this man fifteen years I have known his work in and for the game [the rest is missing].

Notes

1. On 13 November Bonar Law was chosen over his rivals Walter Long and Austen Chamberlain to succeed Balfour as head of the Conservative party. Aitken had a central role in the negotiations that led to this result and had enlisted RK to play a small part: see Anne Chisholm and Michael Davie, *Lord Beaverbrook* (New York, 1993), pp. 110–12.
2. My guess is that RK means Leslie Cope Cornford, whose politics he seemed to approve of. Cope Cornford began his journalistic career as a contributor to the *National Observer* under Henley, where, it is said, his articles attracted RK's attention (*The Times*, 5 August 1927, p. 12). I have no evidence that anything came of RK's suggestion.

To Edward Bok, 4 December 1911

ALS: Syracuse University

Bateman's / Dec. 4. 1911.

private

Dear Bok:

I owe you a good laugh over the clippings you sent.[1] They were delightful: but what a quantity of spare time some people in this world have to burn!

Here's a suggestion – it hardly amounts to a theory – which maybe could be used as an editorial note.

There are in England approximately 1 1/2 million more women than men. Hence, when you dive into the matter physiologically, the desire for any movement, etc. that brings the surplus into contact with men. If suffrage[2] fails, or succeeds (and they find there is nothing in it) the same surplus will agitate for admission into the church and so on – *anything* that mentally or physically, brings 'em into contact, even dilutedly, with the male.

So much for *our* side of the question. With you in the U.S. (and here I see the L.H.J. having its windows plentifully cracked!) the U.S. female is perhaps the loneliest creature on God's earth. Man, as must be the case in the making of a new country, has for generations been fighting time, trees, bears, distance, dirt, etc. etc. He has at first been compelled to withdraw himself largely from the society of the female while he did these things. Today, distance, dirt etc. etc. being more or less subdued, the instinct still persists. He is busy over money matters and the like – matters which he has been accustomed to carry through in conjunction with or opposition to his fellow male.

But, during the time he was engaged in the first rush of the frantic *material* fight to rough-shape his country, he evolved as a labour-saving device, a theory of immense respect and deference for his (and other men's) lonely female.

In short, it was cheaper for him to kill or chastise a man who was rude to a female by herself than to sit around with the female to see that she wasn't pestered. (The West lynched men for horse-stealing because to set a man afoot in a sad barren land was equivalent to murder or attempted murder. Similarly to insult an American woman in the old days meant to imply that a man should be taken off his job to protect her, which *personal* protection, a new country could not afford.)

So we have now today, the theory – extravagantly developed, of immense theoretical devotion and deference to woman in the U.S. – a theory evolved, as I have said for labour-saving purposes, *pari passu* with the fact that the woman *qua* woman is immensely neglected by the U.S. male. *Do* you wonder that the woman given everything except the attention and companionship of the man; told and retold that she is a miraculous and superior being, worshipped, practically, in the same way as a tribal idol that everyone shoves into a corner when the tribe is out for real business – *do* you, I say, wonder that the U.S. woman is a little bit bewildered and off her base?

With us of course where men and women, as must be the case in an old country, are all inconceivably mixed up together in all the activities of life, from the lowest to the highest, the driving force of the suffrage agitation comes (a) from the surplus who, consciously or unconsciously want a man and don't care a curse for politics (b) from the women without power to hold or charm the man they've got. In fact a regular female Cave of Adullam.[3]

Summa. You won't treat women as companions of men in your new civilization. *We*, in our old civilization, treat 'em maybe too much as companions but there ain't enough men to go around. In both lands arises the cry for "comradeship." Your women *do* need being treated more as comrades. Ours (the surplus) want something else.

I've put the idea coldly: but there may be something you could work up in it.

Who is the enclosed who goes about enticing your hired men? I'm sorry to tell him that 2.50 per diem isn't enough. But I never heard of McCall.[4]

With best greetings

Yours sincerely
Rudyard Kipling

Notes

1. No doubt in response to "The Female of the Species", published in the *Ladies' Home Journal*, November 1911.
2. The women's suffrage movement was now at its height.
3. I Samuel 22:1, 2: where are gathered "every one that was in distress, and every one that was in debt, and every one that was discontented".
4. James McCall (d. 1884). *McCall's Magazine*, which grew out of an earlier periodical devoted to dress-patterns, was now a large-circulation woman's magazine competing with the *Ladies' Home Journal*.

To Andrew Macphail, 5 December 1911

ALS: Photocopy, National Archives of Canada

Batemans / Burwash: / Dec. 5. 1911

Dear Macphail

First to answer your second letter of the 23rd. November. If you sent over anything with life in it the same would be an honoured and welcome guest of mine. How much the more therefore the Angel who came to Tobit – tho' I hope Byers' materia medica was of a later edition than Raphael's![1]

But – we leave England for Switzerland as usual on the 28th of this month and return not till the middle of March. Now how can this be got round? From Dec. 29th till the middle of February our address will be Cattani's Hotels

Engelberg
Switzerland

and after that in all likelihood

> Hotel du Parc.
> Vernet-les-Bains
> Pyrenees Orientales
> France

Is there any chance of our catching him in one of his moves. He has to come to England late in January you say? Give him my geographical position at that time, which will be Engelberg – 14 miles from Lucerne which again is on the main Italian road and see if he can make connection. If he (and she) have never seen a modern winter sport resort in full blast they might be amused. That is the nearest that I can see at the present time. I shall be genuinely grieved to miss him. As to *your* coming, we should be home *not* later than the third week in March. I don't suppose you'll be facing the atrocities of an Early Saxon Spring before that date. But keep us informed and *herein fail not*. If I can show you the valley alight with primroses I'll be happy – and so'll you when you can take the boy[2] over to Germany at leisure – if indeed the German does not arrive in England to meet him. It's an odd thing to live on the edge of a volcano as we do; hearing, almost, the guns from the North Sea. No matter. When the war comes it will come. But what a splendid boy yours is! Does the mathematical side of his mind compensate itself (as often happens) with music. If so the greater need for Germany. To me π is one of the Black Arts, which view I have, alas, handed down to my babes.

Today is *very* dark, soft, moist, warm and raining like the devil. But we've had a wonderful winter. Yesterday I was up tarring new planted fir-trees against the bites of rabbits in a climate like late May; ending with moonlight and a greenish sky. Except for three days of light snow-powder every hour has been usable in the open and we've worked like beavers cutting wood, putting in great water-drains under roads, setting up fences, hauling faggots etc. etc.; always with one eye on our Rogue River – the innocent brook that has already flooded us once this year. Which things make me even more sympathetic with your battle in Prince Edward Island. I suppose God gave us superfluous energy same way he gave the Beaver incisors that have to grow; and for fear our mental incisors should end by growing on and on and curving back and piercing our brains, he invented the whole generation of stubborn, ox-eyed, mule-hearted, mud-footed farmers in lieu of the Beaver's wood stumps. So we all run about chewing and biting and carrying mud in our fore-paws ('wish you'd seen mine yesterday!) and slapping our tails to the greater glory of God and, I hope, the advantage of the land. But it's an uphill job.

As to what I said about the tobacco, by all means use it if you think it would be any help.[3] Remember tho' the baccy *qua* baccy is a bit full on the tongue. You may have to use it, as we did our Porsa tobacco in India, adulterated with milder stuff.

Did I ever tell you the yarn of the young civil servant in India – otherwise an ass – who rose to great honour and position. He had a superior officer whose mission in life was growing tobacco in his various districts. Likewise he had a palate of iron. He smoked every sample submitted to him, reported favourably on all and ended by securing enormously well paid appointments. But what I noticed about the leaf you sent was its brightness. I don't suppose you use fish-manure: but if you do, stop it. It gets into the weed.

How pleasing are your local politics! How pleasing are all politics, if it comes to that. The lunatics who vote in England are, worse luck, not certificated.

I wish you'd been here through the change of leadership and had seen the turmoil, the intrigues and general larks that followed Balfour's resignation. I went bald-headed for Bonar Law; he being a man of business, with no entangling alliances, no debts to pay, cool, a temperance man perfectly honest and straight and with a constructive mind. Incidentally he was a Canadian. The whole party has waked up now and is out for blood. They've only just realized that we've no constitution in England and, oddly enough, they don't seem to like it.

In a few years they will realize what the rest of the world is realizing, that the people are fed up with "The People" – sick, and tired and most deadly of all, bored with the solemn pump and incontinent peedle[4] of Democracy. In which connection, Honoured Sir, permit me to refer you to a yarn which will be coming out in February called "As Easy as A.B.C." I don't recall whether I read it you when you were here.

Oh, and there's a spurio-pseudo medical yarn in Harpers this Xmas[5] – based more or less (tho' that's no recommendation) on facts. I got a queer confirmation of it 'tother day. There was a woman whose husband went off his head temporarily. She being in the family way, saw him one night from behind her bedroom door, in his dressing room, with horror in his eyes and a naked razor in his hand. There was a moment's contraction of the nerves, ere she said quietly: – "Give me that razor." Which he done and the incident as the papers say, closed. Then the child was born – to a heritage of deadly night terrors. They used to find her, shaking and sweating, and hiding behind a door – always a door. And for fifty years that burden lay and was not lifted till, I suppose, the menopause.

And this mark you is the kind of animal we propose to govern by formulæ!

Bless you for the lace – It's much too good to shove under a whiskey glass. So I'll e'en keep it for Bateman's table. How lovingly and carefully it was done. Pray you convey my best thanks to the maker.

Now, having enjoyed myself, I'll get back to my job. I'm trying to collect all my odd verses that have appeared in books, into one volume.[6] It is like a low form of Patience and I sit over slips of verse, heroically resisting the temptation to amplify 'em. I have fallen several times but as Cunegonde said, my virtue is rather thereby confirmed.[7]

When next you write me address Engelberg and forgive this scrawl. I've got a single sheet of paper and it's buckling under me in the half-light.

Ever affectionately
Rudyard Kipling.

Send me a map and details – agricultural etc. – of P.E.I.

Notes
1. The angel Raphael instructs Tobit how to drive away devils with the fumes of burnt fish: see Tobit 5–8. John Roddick Byers, a physician educated at McGill, was in charge of the Laurentian Sanatorium, St Agathe-des-Monts, Quebec. I cannot explain the connection between Tobit and Byers.
2. Jeffrey Macphail (1894–1947), Macphail's only son.
3. See 21 October 1911.
4. I make out the words to be "pump" and "peedle" but I cannot supply a sense for them.
5. "In the Same Boat", *Harper's Magazine*, December 1911 (*A Diversity of Creatures*).
6. *Songs from Books*, 1912.
7. Voltaire, *Candide*, ch. 8: "Une personne d'honneur peut être violée une fois, mais sa vertu s'en affermit.'

To Bonar Law,[1] 9 December 1911
ALS: House of Lords Record Office

Bateman's / Burwash. / Dec. 9. 1911.

NO ANSWER REQUIRED.

Dear Mr. Law:

This is a line to thank you for your Wednesday speech on the Insurance Bill.[2] It meant business; it was business: and it did business, and from every source of information that is open to me it has been of the greatest possible use to our side and of immense disservice to L[loyd]. G[eorge].'s "financial" reputation.

So far as I can arrive at things the general feeling in the public mind is somewhat akin to the relief that steals over an angry and puzzled meeting of shareholders when a man who really understands figures gets up and straightens out the situation. And this of course has been what the whole land, irrespective of party, has been wanting – whether they were aware of it or not.

When the small grocer and local hardware store keeper (who also know something of accounts) begin to feel uneasy, and to question their idol's knowledge of figures, the end is in sight.

Best of all your form of attack shakes the nerves (already not too sound) of the Revolutionary Committee.[3]

Very sincerely
Rudyard Kipling.

Notes
1. (Andrew) Bonar Law (1858–1923), Canadian-born politician, brought up in Glasgow where he was a successful merchant. Unionist MP since 1900, he became leader of his party in 1911 as a compromise choice; Prime Minister, 1922–3.
2. On the third reading, 6 December 1911; the bill, which passed, was an important piece of social welfare legislation, authorising a contributory scheme of health insurance.
3. As the Unionists were now calling the Liberal Government.

To Captain R. A. Duckworth Ford, 10 December 1911
ALS: University of Sussex

Bateman's /Dec. 10. 1911.

private
Dear Captain Duckworth Ford,
Just got your typed letters before moving out for Switzerland and some winter sport.[1] The matter of the photo for His Excellency shall be attended to ere I leave.

Now can you send me any reports on sanitation? Disposal of rubbish, village water arrangements, and your methods of dealing with cholera outbreaks. Cholera don't seem to matter as much as it did in India.

Permanganate of potash down the village well, and dilute sulphuric for the villager appears to be the accepted treatment now, and they tell me they can get an outbreak under control in three days. But we don't make any head against plague.

Also I want specimen of battalion and troop orders of sorts – enough to give one an outline of what the U.S. Army on detachment is supposed to do. One set orders for detachment up country; one ditto in a big town. Likewise any figures of venereal in regiments. There must be a fair amount of it.

Things in England are as mad as usual. If there were any logic in the English we should be steering straight for at least three revolutions at the same time, so I suppose they will neutralize each other. Meantime the Teuton has his large cold eye on us and prepares to give us toko when he feels good and ready. Our chances are not so slim as they look for the reason that the Teuton knows all about war as it should be waged scientifically and my experience has been that when a man knows exactly how everything ought to be done under every conceivable contingency he is apt to be tied up by his own knowledge. But we ought to see in a few years now. Today is a typical English winter Sunday – black dark, a howling gale from the south with heavy rain. There was a lot of shooting round us yesterday and I couldn't help thinking how it would be if all the wounded birds now lying in the woods were wounded men.

We've been fighting floods in our valley – putting in pipes and drains and trying to persuade our innocent looking little brook that it isn't a Colorado river – so far without success.

Here's every good wish for the health and long life of the Family with a merry Christmas and a happy new year. It comes late but it means well.

Ever sincerely
Rudyard Kipling

Note

1. They left for Engelberg on 28 December and arrived on the afternoon of the next day; the two children of Abe Bailey were with them, accompanied by their governess, Miss Howard (CK diary, 28–9 December 1911).

To Robert Underwood Johnson, 11 December 1911

TLS: Dalhousie University

Bateman's / Burwash / Sussex / Dec. 11th, 1911.

Dear Johnson,

Many thanks for your kind letter. The same to you and many of them.

Why yes I have no objection at all to Miss Smith making pictures of my babies,[1] but she must remember that Wee Willie Winkie was an Anglo-Indian baby and didn't wear much. Also, what about Muhummad Din – small and brown and almost quite naked?

I'm following "Stover at Yale."[2] What an amazing world it opens!

Yours truly
Rudyard Kipling

R. N. Johnson Esq.,
    The Century Magazine

Notes

1. Jessie Wilcox Smith (1863–1935), of Philadelphia, specialised in painting children. A series of her drawings of Dickens' children was currently running in *Scribner's*. Her colour illustrations of "Kipling's Children" appeared in *Scribner's*, January 1915, pp. 49–51: they were taken from "Wee Willie Winkie", "Baa Baa, Black Sheep", "The Brushwood Boy", and "They".
2. By Johnson's son Owen (1878–1952). The story ran serially in *McClure's*, October 1911–May 1912; it remains a minor classic in its field.

To Albert Bigelow Paine,[1] 12 December 1911

Text: Copy, Cornell University

Bateman's / Burwash / Sussex / December 12th, 1911

I have been following your biography of Mark Twain in Harpers with very great interest and I only wish I could be of any service to you about his letters to me.[2] But I make a reprehensible habit of burning all my personal correspondence and the few letters that I had from him have long ago gone by that road.[3]

Notes

1. Paine (1861–1937), journalist, playwright, and novelist, was Twain's literary executor and wrote the authorised biography, 3 vols, 1912: it appeared serially in *Harper's*, November 1911–November 1912.
2. Paine was already at work on the edition of Twain's letters that he published in 1917.
3. One letter from Twain to RK, 23 May 1901, is in the Kipling papers at Sussex.

To R. A. Duckworth Ford, 13 December 1911

ALS: University of Sussex

Bateman's / Burwash / Sussex / Dec. 13. 1911

Dear Duckworth-Ford (I don't know what your official rating is now but I gather from your note that you've been promoted so I'm going to "damn you at a venture" as Major)

I wish to goodness you would *not* write such a letter as you have just sent. We haven't seen the sun for weeks; we are up to our eyes in mud and flood: and a grey-black sky hangs exactly 25 feet above our damp heads.

Naturally then your invitation upset us both. Says the wife: – "Why shouldn't we go to the Philippines?" and "How the dooce does one get to the Philippines?" That fairly woke me up. I dismissed the San Francisco route and the passage of the Continent at this time of year – as I did the railway run to Vladivostock but I sketched out a heavenly run to Singapore per P. & O. (touching at Colombo), thence south into Malayan archipelagoes and hot moist sunshine and bamboos etc. etc. and I saw ourselves loafing round your Islands under awnings, in white clothes, with bananas on the staunchions, and pineapples and custard apples and, perhaps, jack fruit. And I saw ourselves returning via the Barrier Reef and Australia *after* I had revenged Theodore's advice to England by telling all the functionaries of Manila how Colonies should be run![1] A seductive dream which is frankly impossible for domestic reasons (aged 13 and 15). But I don't despair. The wife is uneasy and interested and someday surely, we'll pick up our feet and pack up our trunks and get out. I haven't seen the tropics for *three* years! and I'm sure it isn't good for me.

Even your account of the typhoon only made me home-sick. But (mark this) I never knew a man with a standing bedstead aboard ship who didn't get into trouble – same as you did. They aren't intended to be used afloat. I've paid for 'em on the Atlantic and been hove out. I've seen Hebrew millionaires hire 'em on Union-Castle Liners and lament bitterly in the Bay of Biscay, where also I once saw electric light bulbs disconnected, like yours were, and flung about the saloon while a fat Dutchwoman threw fits on the saloon floor.

What a gay time you must have had at Hong Kong! They have drinks at the Club there *and* curries. But I grow maudlin.

Tell 'em that some day if I live I'll come and in the meantime with all good wishes for you and yours

believe me,

Yours enviously
Rudyard Kipling

The quotation is "Steady the Buffs!"[2]

Notes
1. The reference is to Roosevelt's speech on Egypt at the Guildhall, May 1910: see 17 June 1910.
2 Said to be traditional in the Royal East Kent Regiment – the "Buffs"; it is attributed to RK, "Poor Dear Mama" (*The Story of the Gadsbys*), by the *Oxford Dictionary of Quotations*. RK also uses it in "The Last Term" (*Stalky & Co.*), "His Brother's Keeper" (*Abaft the Funnel*) and elsewhere: see Harbord, *Readers' Guide*, I, 297.

To Anna Smith Balestier, 25 December 1911
ALS: Dunham Papers

Bateman's / Christmas Day. 1911.

Sunshine at last after unlimited rain and darkness.

Dearest Mother

I write on Carrie's behalf to thank you for all your gifts and loving kindness at this season. As usual you had hit off the postal arrangements (you really ought to have been Postmistress General) to the very hour. Your letter and the Xmas cards for the children arrived this morning for breakfast. Bless you for the *Kitten's garden of verses*.[1] I had seen a review of it in the *Spectator* and very much wanted a copy of it for my own. I read it to the family last night amid shouts of applause. We have "The Night before Xmas" as a solemn religious ceremony every Xmas eve.

We kept our own Christmas yesterday as we are off today to Sir Max Aitken's to help him and his family keep theirs.[2] As I think you know they live near Guildford, about 64 miles north of us, but what is that in a motor? Our presents yesterday were many and glorious. Elsie got an old work table of the kind that has a bag hanging from its inside, and a screen that slides up and down, something like this [sketch of work table]. She has to find material to make the bag and screen – which she much prefers. She made me a complete set of eight costume dolls – a lady and gentleman each of the Georgian period; the time of King Charles; Elizabeth; and Norman, all perfect down to their shoes and caps; all done by herself to the last stitch and out of material that she had by her. I am more pleased than I can say. They are going into a special cupboard to illustrate my *Puck* yarns. John had a gramophone with 24 records. You can imagine how lively the house has been ever since. C. gave me a magnificent *solid* gold waverley nib with which I am writing at the present moment and one of the best atlasses that is published. As we shall have been married twenty years (!) in a few days I gave her a little string of pearls. Altogether it was one of the nicest, happiest and quietest Christmases that we have ever spent. We leave for Engelberg on Thursday and C. is running about helping to pack. That is why I am writing to you. She had a little bit of a cold a few days ago which she borrowed from Elsie who had found it in town while she was visiting her Aunt Margaret Mackail for a couple of days. But she is much better now.

John has come back from school, growing like a cornstalk, with a deep cracked voice and a great taste for clothes! This is very comic. He talks about his school with the greatest love and pride – not to say swagger – and is really a humorous chap. Now and then he reminds me of Wolcott, in the speed and accuracy of his repartees. He has just discovered that his Father is a sort of public man – a fact that he didn't realize before – and he is very funny about it. They ask him at school whether he has read any of his father's books and when he, quite truthfully, says "no," they don't believe him.

There is no particular news except that we have been getting ready to go away and I hope that the next three months without house keeping will be beneficial to Carrie. She is much better than she was in the early summer.

I have cleared off the last of my work and am ahead of all my letters which gives me a feeling of great virtue and peace.

All goes well here – thanks to my most wonderful Carrie (you ought to have seen her in her coronation dress with the diamond tiara on her head) and I am as ever dearest mother

Your most affectionate son
Ruddy.

Notes
1. Oliver Herford, *The Kitten's Garden of Verses* (New York, 1911). I do not find any notice of it in the *Spectator.*
2. "The Aitkens and the Bonar Laws on Christmas Day, and many children. 22 for dinner, 17 in the house" (CK diary, 25 December 1911).

To C. R. L. Fletcher, [late December? 1911]
ALS: University of Sussex

Bateman's / Burwash / Sussex

Brother Ridley (or was it Latimer)[1]

I don't get anything half as respectable as the Widow Green[2] – with the sale of whose books I fear we are interfering somewhat. *My* little lot knowing, that as a "poet" I am not to be approached on hysterical facts, simply shove abuse at me straight. I can't yet decide whether the Nonconformist or the R.C. is the most malignant in this regard but I *do* understand why our wise ancestors impartially penalized 'em both.

But how badly, how extremely urgently the Work was needed! And how nice it is to think that anything the Sons of Wantoness produce as a counterblast will only be an imitation.

I distinctly approve of the end of your letter to the Cathcathartic Wason.[3] The front part strikes me as superfluous politesse. The game, I think, is to rasp their nerves. Then they have less energy to devote to more important matters.

Yours at the next stake
RK.

I'm sorry now I didn't write an Irish poem.

The enclosed is a most gentle Roland. Will you please answer him nicely, on these simple lines in future.

Notes
1. Nicholas Ridley, Bishop of London, and Hugh Latimer, both burnt at the stake for heresy at Oxford, 1555.
2. According to Fletcher's note on this letter, this was Mrs J. R. Green, "who abused 'RKF' fiercely for the Irish part". Alice Stopford Green (1848–1929), the widow of the historian J. R. Green, was herself a historian; she was also Irish and a Home Ruler, and later a member of the Irish parliament. She published *Irish Nationality* in 1911. I have not found any published attacks by her on the *History of England.*
3. In the House of Commons on 20 November J. Cathcart Wason asked the President of the Board of Education whether he had considered proscribing the *History of England* as a text for schools "in view of the very distinct libel on the Irish race contained in the book" (*Parliamentary Debates*, 5th Series, XXXVI: 20 November 1911). I can find no letter from Fletcher published in any of the London papers around this time on the subject; presumably it was a private letter that RK refers to.

To Frank N. Doubleday, 11 January 1912
ALS: Princeton University

Hotels Cattani Engelberg / Jan. 11. 1912

Dear Frank,

Yours of the 29th Dec. has just been sent on to us here. As to the hand-made paper edition[1] I don't know how far it has come along but as soon as we get back we'll see what "our Mr. Scribner" has sent in. I fancy that, as you say, the last two books haven't arrived but of this I can't be sure.

We've been having rather a hell of a time climatically. The bottom has dropped out of the European winter with the result that since we came here on the 29th we've been having torrents of sub-tropical rain. Imagine a bucket among mountains, filled with damp, bored, wet-footed, white-jerseyed samples of all nations at their wits end to know how to amuse themselves.

Today, glory be, we have about 12° frost and there is skating, and a sky that would do credit to New York or Cape Town.

On Sunday the Zurich hockey team plays us on the ice. It is called Zurich to disguise the fact that it is 80% American. They are a very delightful crowd and played us last year. Their captain is Burr – lineal descendant of the great Aaron and they include representatives of three at least U. S. colleges. I have just finished a serious discussion with one of the boys who wanted to know whether an English bob-team would consent to enter for the sports (there isn't snow enough yet for bobbing and they'll break their necks if they try) under the badge, on their jerseys, of the U.S. Eagle. I said they'd enter without a murmur under any one who could skip a bob, *so long as the Eagle wasn't double-headed.*

Likewise we have three or four very nice American maidens – Cleveland, Pittsburgh, New York and Philadelphia – all under the same chaperonage and each as different as the cities they hail from.

And that reminds me – just before I left I met the Colonel's neice up at the Colonel's house in Burwash. You must have given them a holy and a joyous time for they said things about you and Nellie and Dorothy that should have made your ears burn. I don't think they'd ever had such a time in their life and the Colonel sat in a corner and beamed and purred and chuckled.

From time to time Bok sends me excerpts from the surrounding news-paper press. He seems to have got more out of the "Female of the Species" than he expected: for I see, with joy, that his female subscribers are now hitting *him* on the head for having published the thing.[2] We've got a pair of suffragines here – a Mrs and Miss Ruggles-Brice with an incidental and highly docile papa Ruggles.[3] The Miss Brice rode at the head of a procession in London as Joan of Arc and by the uninviting looks of her I should say she was extremely likely to remain *la pucelle* to the end of her days.[4]

John has shot up several inches during the last few months and is now a "man" at Wellington college where I gather it is very rude to speak of "boys." He goes back to Wellington on the 25th. Carrie here interrupts to say that she has written to you of our plan to transfer the cheque for interest in plates to stock in the Company: what we should like to do would be to take up some more stock when the next cheque falls due. We have been so occupied in getting what we could out of England that we've hardly had time to turn round. It's a funny sensation – to be living in a lunatic asylum managed by maniacs who call themselves "Cabinet Ministers." And we've got to be worse before we're better.

The rest from house keeping is doing C. good. We are now going to put on our skates and go forth on the Rink for our first skates in four days. Dear love to you all from us four and every wish for a happy and prosperous new year all along the line.

Ever affectionately
Rud.

Notes
1. A special printing of the Outward Bound Edition. RK's set is now at Wimpole Hall. A printed note in the first volume states: "There have been printed two sets of the Outward Bound Edition on Dickinson's handmade paper for Rudyard Kipling and F. N. Doubleday."

2. Bok says that he published the poem on a dare by RK: "One day at Mr. Kipling's home in Sussex he read to me his latest poem, and at its conclusion said 'You can never publish that. The Journal sisters would break all your windows with the stones they would fire at you. You wouldn't have a pane left.' I agreed that this might be so. All the same, I argued, we should publish the poem" (Edward Bok, *Twice Thirty*, pp. 373–4). In another place Bok reports that "the suffragists at once took the argument in the poem as personal to themselves, and now Kipling got the full benefit of their vitriolic abuse. Bok sent a handful of these criticisms to Kipling, who was very gleeful about them. 'I owe you a good laugh over the clippings,' he wrote. 'They were delightful. But what a quantity of spare time some people in this world have to burn!'" (*The Americanization of Edward Bok*, p. 306).
3. Archibald Weyland Ruggles-Brise (1853–1939), of Spain Hall, Braintree, Essex; his wife, Mabel Coope; they had two unmarried daughters in 1912: Marjory Mabel and Octavia Florence.
4. A large procession, the most splendid of many in support of the Woman's Suffrage Bill, was held in London on 17 June 1911. The Joan of Arc who rode at its head is identified as "Miss Annan Bryce" in *The Times*, 10 June 1911. A photograph of her in the role appears in Lisa Tickner, *The Spectacle of Women: Imagery of the Suffrage Campaign 1907–14* (Chicago, 1988), p. 210, where she is identified as Joan Annan Bryce, the daughter of an MP. If the identification with Joan Annan Bryce is correct, then she must have been the daughter of John Annan Bryce, Liberal MP, 1906–18, and RK has wrongly put Miss Ruggles-Brise in the role of Joan of Arc.

To Colonel H. W. Feilden, 8 February 1912

ALS: Syracuse University

Hotels Cattani / Engelberg / Feb. 8. 1912.

Dear Colonel Sahib

Not a word from you these last six weeks – nothing but wails from Martin about the weather and Petell's ulcerated toe and Lawyer Coppard's death. We've been waiting on in hopes of a word but you keep the silence of the frozen-in woodchuck. Not, I hope, for the same reason? By all accounts the weather with you must be more than filthy. *Ours* has gone clean mad and has wound up a green and unstable winter with one of the most complete and devastating thaws that ever I've seen. There has been a three days *fohn* – the warm south wind that has simply peeled the snow off the slopes while we watched. It stinks of Africa even at this distance! Result: all sports stopped: the rink a large snipe-jhil[1] And the roads down to the pasty blue-grey stone which seems to be their original formation. I didn't know that such a break up was possible in February. None the less the hotels are roaring full, as no one seems to know where to go next and, apparently, all the continent outside Switzerland is frozen stiff. I am driven to take refuge (a) in work (b) in talking to some of the people as under: –

(1)   Cambridge man (Johns)[2] from Lagos where he is in the Southern Nigeria secretariat says that the Nigerian frontier is the only one where there is a permanent war on. Tells me interesting things about black water fever and mosquito annihilation.

(2)   Man from Lord knows where East Africa way who tells me of wars on the Abyssinian border.

(3)   Swain (Sir H)[3] But he has gone now – the man who made and loved Somaliland and saw it wrecked by the home "Government." One of the most interesting men I've ever struck. He saw the surrender of the 10,000 Italians after Adowa to the Abyssinians[4] and does not think much of the Italians' chances against the Tripolitan Arab.[5] His accounts of some of the shindies with the mad Mullah in Somaliland were wondrous. Now he is governor of British Honduras in a town built on 50 foot deposits of mahogany chips and rum-bottles hove in by generations of pirates and beach combers. There's a geological formation for you.

(4)   A big sleepy man in the Guards who has been in that mad treasure-hunt for King Soloman's treasures in Jerusalem.[6] Operations are held up at present but he hopes next year to continue 'em. His account of the siphoning of the pool of Siloam (they got into an air-chamber of sorts which they tapped – with the result that the Pool was "troubled" fifteen times in one day)[7] was amazing. Also he told me that the cypher on which they worked, and it appeared to be a perfectly accurate cypher, was discovered in the St. Petersburgh museum by one Jurisius a Finn.[8] Jurisius had his points both as a decipherer of cyphers and as an explorer but he *would* rape the local virgins. Hence trouble with the Turkish authorities and the final elimination of Jurisius the fornicating Finn. Also, this man told me that it was quite true that they struck the old main drain of Jerusalem. One of their party explored it. He came back looking white and said it was "very strong." But outside these talks there is nothing to do and we wait a letter from you with local and home news.

With all our love

Affectionately
Rudyard K.

Notes

1.   A *jhil* or *jheel* is a marsh or lagoon.
2.   F. Johns, Inspector of Works, Public Works Department, Southern Nigerian Secretariat, 1910–13; the Foreign and Commonwealth Office has no record of him after 1913.
3.   Brigadier-General Sir Eric John Eagles Swayne (1863–1929), commanded in Somaliland, 1901–4, and served as Consul-General, 1902–6. He was Governor of British Honduras, 1906–13.
4.   Adowa, in Ethiopia, was the scene of a crushing Italian defeat at the hands of the Emperor Menelek II in March 1896.

5. Italy declared a largely-unprovoked war against Turkey in September 1911; the fighting was mostly in Libya. Peace was signed in October 1912.
6. An English expedition beginning in 1909 headed by Captain Montagu Parker was excavating the site of Soloman's Temple; in connection with this the drain of the pool of Siloam had been cleaned. The "man in the Guards" is possibly Major C. Foley, who was part of the original expedition (*The Times*, 8 May 1911). It was reported that the expedition was basing its work on a cipher "supposed to indicate the exact position of a quantity of treasure buried by the ancient Jewish kings" (*The Times*, 4 May 1911).
7. Cf. John 5:4.
8. Not identified.

To C. R. L. Fletcher, 8 February 1912

ALS: University of Sussex

Hotels Cattani / Engelberg / Feb. 8. 1912.

Dear Fletcher,

This amazing season has to all appearance finished by a yet more amazing thaw – three days of riotous sickly *Föhn* which has simply skinned the snow off; turned the rink to a puddle and flooded the meadows. It's still going on; the therm 10 degrees above freezing and the hotel feeling like an orchid house. But the people are by no means flowers. You never saw such a mess.

I *don't* envy the reviewer who has to do your book;[1] unless he knows something of the subject. I've been enjoying it slowly and thoroughly and sharing it with a cousin of mine[2] who, knowing a little bit about the period, is enthusiastic. *My* pleasure in it is in the artistic lay out and handling and grouping which strike me as *very* good indeed. The dovetailing of one land's affairs into another's is beautiful. I've got through it once for the general idea and am now back again for special bits. Personally I'm most obliged thank you, for the map of the military roads and frontier details. Please let me know how it has been treated by those who know.

There's a school book (on school life: upperform) just out by Hornung who wrote Raffles.[3] I've been reading it and it strikes me as very much of a book – a sane presentment of public school life without gush or poppycock, and with, I should imagine, rather close studies of Thring and some of the housemasters of that generation. Get it and read it. It's called "Fathers of Men" and see how it strikes you. I was very delighted with it – and specially with the things and conditions it took for granted.

Talking of boys there is a child at Magdalene – they call him the Magdalene Baby – a young S. African educated Scot, Maitland Park,[4] son of my old Editor in India, whose parents are now in South Africa, where Park is editor of the *Cape Times*. He is a clever boy I imagine, cox I believe to

M's second eight and his mother's child – the only one. If you can see him and have a look at him some time I'd be grateful. He has the Colonial's somewhat wider knowledge of life (for all his years) than the average undergrad but he hasn't passed through an English school. He reports himself to me at intervals but I'd like you just to run an eye over him. Wants to get into the Army by way of the University. My own idea is he may be something of a scholar. But O Lord the Undergrad's a queer beast. He writes me letters in a slang as modern as last night.

There's a man here (John's) who is at Headquarters in Southern Nigeria – Cambridge plus West Coast Africa makes a funny mixture; also a large sleepy man who has been mixed up in the hunt for Soloman's treasures at Jerusalem – pool of Siloam and all the rest of it. Talk of fiction! Fiction isn't in it.

Ever sincerely
RK

Notes

1. Volume 1 of *The Making of Western Europe: Being an Attempt to Trace the Fortunes of the Children of the Roman Empire*, 2 vols, 1912–14.
2. Stanley Baldwin: the Baldwins were evidently with them again at Engelberg this year.
3. E. W. Hornung, *Fathers of Men*, published in January 1912.
4. Maitland Park the younger (1894–1969) entered Magdalen from the College School, Cape Town, in 1911. He survived the war as a Captain in the Black Watch in France and Mesopotamia and was awarded the DSO. His college has no further information about him. In 1926 RK helped Park to find a position but refused to lend him money (to Park, 22 and 26 June; 8 August 1926: ALS, Dalhousie University).

To John Kipling, 14 February 1912

ALS: University of Sussex

Hotels Cattani / Engelberg / Feb. 14. 1912.

Illustrissimo! (I am already practising my Italian!),

It isn't often that you might have seen as pleased a person as your parent when your letter came. I smiled – I smiled all over and then I am afraid I smiled again *not* (this time) because of your being top of the form the second week running but because of Fenn! It isn't often that a man has the chance of rubbing it into his late form-master every time he goes up in form but you've got that chance. Rub it in! Each time you hold your place it proves that the

Of(Fenn)sive One was wrong. Selah! Mother was also hugely pleased: and thus you see we start on our journey to Florence[1] in the best of spirits. (For the third time I repeat our address will be

> *Hotel Grande Bretagne et Arno*
> *Florence.*

I wrote you that Sunday, and have also written to Pompey.[2])

A foolish and feeble fall of slush arrived the night before last – just enough to make the landscape look white without making it possible for any one to do anything. Lorna and Elsie and I and Mummy went up to the Gerschni[3] in the afternoon. It was a beautiful day and not at all a bad climb up. Hundreds of people, among whom was Uncle Stan whose legs were recognizable from a mile off, were *ski*-ing all over the landscape. Then we came across Di[4] who was ski-ing about three yards at a time and then flinging herself down in the snow, in order to avoid running into some one. There wasn't any one to run into – but that made no odds to Di. Lucky for her we helped her down. She was pretty helpless *on* skis but perfectly paralytic *off* 'em! And the coming down was awful! I had Mummy who only fell once; and Elsie who fell *eight* times: and Lorna who didn't fall at all: and Di who walked like an agitated elephant leading one *ski* in the loop of her comforter while I carried the other – all these people to look after. So I hadn't time to slip. Quite a hectic trip and I felt stiff all over. Wish you'd been there!

Today we saw the joyous notice "Rink open from 8–12!" We hadn't had a sniff of a skate for over a week. Mums and I took out our boots to the rink – for the good reason that there was *no ice* on the way to the rink – nothing but blue gravel! After one look at the cut and ragged and blistered and puffy ice, Mum and I decided that it wasn't good enough. Elsie slacked all day after her tumblings up and down the Gerschni – she falls with equal ease ascending or descending. And so ends our last day! I have been packing the skis and snow boots and gloves and ski socks into the big case where they will wait till we return. *But* – oh my son – next winter we must *all* have a pair of stout local made boots to walk in, with a full supply of nails in the sole. No more fooling up Gerschni in jonties[5] for me! Also it looks to me as if you'd need a complete new set of ski-clothes. *If*, as Cattani says, they have the funicular railway to Gerschni in working order by next year, you'll be able to have all the ski-ing that your heart can desire. Likewise it will keep amateurs and toddlers off the Rink.

I was *awfully* pleased to find that old Gwynnie had been to see you. You must have had a high old time together. I should like to have seen you showing the old boy round the Coll.

Mother had a letter today from Lady Aitken[6] who wrote Mum that she was very pleased with the nice letter you wrote her. I can't say how pleased Mum was to find that you had done this. Of course it was only a bit of elementary civility but you've no notion how much a hostess likes to have her hospitality acknowledged.

(Here is a little saying (not quite proper) which I picked up in the smoking room the other night. "Behold the bounding chamois who leaps from precipice to piss and back again." I don't know why it made me laugh but it did!)

And now I'll finish. My next letter, all being well, will be from the land of Macaroni and Lazzaroni. Keep well. Be happy. You've made us very pleased and happy.

Incidentally you'll get 10/- (ten bob) refunded you by me for expenses of skates. There's a promise in writing for you.

Oscar[7] says he had 10 days skating at Eton. More than we had since you've left.

Dad

Notes
1. They left this day and remained in Florence until the 7th of March.
2. As John's house master, John Pearson, was called.
3. The Gerschnialp, south-west of Engelberg.
4. Diana Lucy Baldwin, eldest of the Baldwin sisters.
5. The word is not clear: gonties?
6. Gladys Henderson (d. 1927), Aitken's first wife; Aitken had been knighted on 20 June 1911.
7. Oscar Hornung (d. 1915), the son of the writer E. W. Hornung, was at Eton, 1908–14. The Hornung family had apparently been at Engelberg with the Kiplings this season. Lady Lorna Howard writes that Oscar Hornung, who was killed at Ypres, was John Kipling's "best friend" (*Kipling Journal*, September 1985, p. 68).

To Sir Charles P. Crewe, 14–22 February 1912

ALS: East London Museum, South Africa

Engelberg. Feb 14. 1912

Dear Crewe,

Your last undated catches me on the very edge of going to Florence this afternoon. We've had a slushy winter (very little skating and absolutely no sports) at Engelberg and are now going for a change to N. Italy. How I wish it were the U[nion]. C[astle]. L[ine]. and the Woolsack at the end of it. But with a 14 year old boy at Wellington one can't stray far.
Florence Feb. 22

Thus far had I got and then the journey – Italian railways are a complete exemplar of what State Railways will be in Hell – and a mass of work shot down on me from England. But now I'm clear for a bit.

We are both grieved about what you tell us of your health. Don't the symptoms as you describe 'em point to nothing more than poverty of the blood. To which I hear you reply:- "Yes: but dam your eyes do you know anything worse than anaemia." And truly, except toothache I know none. On the other hand there aren't any troubles that yield more easily to change of climate *and* food – specially food. You've probably got what Rhodes's lions got in the war – too much cold storage. Come and be fed! Now I wonder very much whether your holiday will be as peaceful as you think. *My* fear is that this "Government" will go out before the full result of its various sins are directly brought home to the people. In that event it will still be a power for evil in the background and not, what it ought to be, an *exposed public danger*. And what is more important I fear that if we do come in we shan't do so with a sufficiently emphatic majority. In that event if we have any trouble with Germany the Radical party will be a vastly graver danger to the Empire that it was in the Boer War. The best thing would be to have it in power for that war because the conservatives understand the elements of I won't say patriotism but of common safety – which the Soccers[1] don't.

And yet I am afraid by what I hear that the collapse of the Government may come within a few months, over (a) Home Rule and (b) Welsh Disestablishment.[2] The two work together and react on each other in a way that it would be difficult to explain. So far, the one note of reality in all the dismal pantomime comes from Ulster and the defeat (it was nothing less) of Churchill and his confinement to the Kaffir Reservation (i.e. the Celtic football club ground) has been the most serious knock that the Revolutionary Committee have experienced.[3] Now, men say, if this can be done in Ulster why not elsewhere. But behind everything else hangs the cloud of the coal-strike which in essence is Revolution and the frightened elector is saying: – "Why did we destroy the Lords to unchain these devils." On the other hand, actual violence and rapine and murder have not shown themselves visibly over large areas of England. The August troubles led, indirectly, to a great many deaths but there was no spectacular (except in Liverpool) discomfort and distress.[4] Should the coal-strike bring all these things then I believe that the "government" would be thrust out as a public danger and would be no more heard of for half a generation. Should the trouble be masked or avoided or even respectably kept under by wholesale employment of troops then the "government" though defeated might still have life enough to go on making itself a nuisance.

But the situation is further complicated. They are all (except I think Grey) desperately dependent on their salaries. Asquith, extravagant with expensive children and a not cheap wife, most dependent of all. He *must* have money and go he can't till he gets Loreburn's billet.[5] I see today that L. most obligingly has an attack of heart. This may open the road to A's retirement via a peerage, and to L[loyd]. G[eorge].'s succession. This would to some extent clarify things as L.G. by iron necessity of his temperament and position *must* lead the extremists even to naked communism. W[inston]. C[hurchill]. may probably pretend to take the middle way but not L.G. Then should come something like a crack among such few Liberals as console themselves, till now, with the thought that they follow Asquith the Whig and not L.G. the Socialist. Such a crack might make our victory at the next election more ample and more definite and if the election took place on the heels of the coal-strike the electorate could see how much sane and how much *in*sane Labour was in existence. I don't know if I make myself clear. Labour in England is on the split too – *precisely* as it is in the *U.S.* – and it may be that L.G.'s succession to Asquith and his first pronouncement thereafter, may divide Labour.

II

Now you can see how this will fit into *your* game down South? The dynamite vials in the U.S. should clear the air there;[6] the horrors of the coal strike *plus* the silently maturing revolt from within against Trade Union Tyranny should clear the air in England and given a Cons. victory here 'tis just possible that the Union party in S.A. might without imputation of unworthy motives be able to approach the sane Labour on the Rand. *But not now.* The air has to be cleared and, I fancy, some of our English strike leaders may have to go through purging experiences. This is my sketch. The next forty eight hours may knock it galley-west.

I like Bonar Law. I spent last Xmas with him[7] and the more I saw the more I respected his deadly accuracy, his absence of illusions and his *conviction*. Moreover the Soccers detest and fear him which is a good sign.

I think you'll be pretty wearied by the time you come to the end of this scrawl. Write us fully when where and how you come to England and with all our best wishes

Ever thine
Rudyard Kipling.

P.S.   Just now I'm rather a believer in Sanatogen[8] as a tonic and general lifter up. I saw it work wonderfully in Switzerland. Dose at 11.a.m. and 4:p.m. and if you like ere you go to bed. Try it.

We are going home D.V. about the third week in March. So write Bateman's.

Notes

1. Socialists.
2. Bills for Irish Home Rule and for Welsh Disestablishment were introduced on 11 and 12 April, respectively.
3. Churchill had been scheduled to speak in support of Home Rule in the Ulster hall, Belfast, on 8 February. As Churchill's father had made a famous speech against Home Rule in 1886 in the same hall, the choice of place was interpreted by the Unionists as a deliberate provocation. Churchill spoke instead at the Celtic Road football ground in a Catholic district, but even then had to face threatening crowds.

4. Two men were shot and killed in riots in connection with a dockers' strike in August 1911. The Navy was summoned to protect the docks.
5. Robert Threshie Reid (1846–1923), Earl Loreburn, Lord Chancellor, 1905–12. Loreburn had a history of heart trouble; when he resigned in June 1912 he was succeeded by R. B. Haldane.
6. The investigation and trial following the dynamiting of the *Los Angeles Times* building in 1910 was now in progress; forty union leaders in the metal trades were charged with "organising dynamite outrages in some fifty places" (*Annual Register, 1912*) in disputes over the hiring of non-union labour. All but two were convicted, and thirty-three received prison sentences. The case was regarded as a serious discrediting of organised labour.
7. See 25 December 1911.
8. A proprietary tonic wine introduced in 1897.

To John Kipling, 21 February 1912

ALS: University of Sussex

Hôtel Royal / Grande Bretagne & Arno / Florence, le 21 Feb. 1912

Dear Old Man –

Your Sunday letter (with Eno) just received. Sorry for the Eno but proud to see that in spite of it you keep well up in form. You'll never know till you have a son of your own how indecently proud parents are of their son's achievements. Of course I don't want you to be nothing but a clever swot (there isn't the least danger of that!) but every time I get news of your being top I throw a little chest and go out and smile at the world. The head waiter (who is uncommonly like Theo) will not know at lunch today why I am so dashed affable and grinsome to him. *Good* boy!

And so your little noses were rubbed in the dirt by Sandhurst – big, hairy, hard-footed young men! Well, cheer up. Perhaps if you do well and grow strong you may, some year, be strong enough to take on the Lower School Fifteen from Eton! Don't be puffed up at the prospect.

Glad you got your ten bob all right. Don't make a beast of yourself with it. Spend it on Carter's Little Liver pills and cascara-sangrada.

You ask what Florence is like. It's beautiful – miles more beautiful than Rome, and we'll send you some postcards to prove it. It lies all among low hills at the foot of the Apennines (kindly consult Dicker[1] to see if I have put in enough n's) and the hills are covered with white and pink and grey villas and cypress trees and olives, mixed up with vineyards and cultivated fields and here and there an almond tree in blossom from head to foot. You know, the grass does not wither in winter at Florence. It just stops growing for a few weeks but stays as green as before. February here comes to about the same as April at home. There are great pink and white anemones growing wild in the grass, and the rose-trees are sprouting, the lilac is in bud and yesterday we saw the first irises in full bloom, in the English cemetery. (*Note*. It may help you sometime in form. Arthur Hugh Clough,[2] English poet who wrote "The Bothy of Tober-na-Voulich" as well as some other dashed good poems died and was buried at Florence 1861: Also Elizabeth Barrett Browning poetess and wife of Robert Browning died here in the same year and was buried in the English Cemetery. That was why we went there. Also, Walter Savage Landor,[3] eminent man of letters is in same cemetery. I have a feeling that you will find all those pieces of information useful before a month has passed. But to resume.)

The air is beautifully light and springy and on a fine day with a hot sun shining one feels as though one were drinking champagne that did not give one a head. The River Arno runs through the town and the houses come slap down into the river just like the pictures of Venice. Our Hotel is on the river but separated from it by a narrow stone paved street which one does not see as one looks out of window. (We are on the first floor). So the effect is as though we were on a steamer (I can't tell you how vile this ink is. If I don't half-print every blessed letter the stuff won't leave any mark on the paper). There are no pavements worth mentioning anywhere but every street is laid down with large slabs of pale grey neatly jointed stone and as most of the streets are not as wide as Bateman's Lane and as the city is full of cats, cars and trams we all float about together in an easy good natured slow-moving crowd. Yesterday was the Carnival – the last big kick-up before Lent begins – and people had dressed up as Pierrots with masks and were driving and walking about blowing absurd tin trumpets and chucking confetti at each other. One boy about your age had painted his face various colours instead of using a mask and had finished off the general effect with – a gilt nose! I had never seen a gilt nose before and it filled me with joy. (From the change in the colour of the ink you must realize that the waiter has just come in with a pot of fresh brew. Observe the effect on my handwriting).

Of course Florence is full of the most glorious buildings – churches, cathedrals, towers, palaces and so on, each one of them crammed with horrible stories and murders. Our Hotel used to be the palace of a Cardinal who was murdered in it and one of the most awful attempts at murder on record was made a few hundred years ago in the Duomo, the Cathedral, just as the victim (he was a Medici) was going to mass.[4] The little game failed. There was a riot and before the day ended the Medici, who did not care for any one except themselves to go in for murder, hanged an Archbishop (who had been mixed up in the attempt) out of his own window and generally played Hell with the City. Every body in Florence in the Middle Ages always played Hell with everything when they could. Dante lived here till he was banished. He filled up his "Inferno" with characters whom he knew in real life in Florence and when you realize that Florence was then not much bigger than Tunbridge Wells, and when you read the list of crimes that Dante's neighbours were guilty of you can begin to imagine what a cheery little Murder-and-Torture-Society old Florence must have been.

But one forgets all that as one loafs about in the sunshine and visits the wonderful picture galleries where all the pictures one has ever read about or seen in prints are hanging on the walls *quite* real. You and I have got to see this place together, some time, old man.

Well, I won't worry you with more fine (and small writing).

We live very quietly in a suite of huge rooms. We go out sight-seeing for about two hours in the morning and an hour and a half in the afternoon and find that quite enough. Today it is raining and as you see, I'm writing letters.

Dear Love to you from us all. We are counting days till April 2:[5] thus:

$$\text{Feb. } 7 + \text{Mar } 31 + 2 \text{ Ap} = 40$$
$$31$$
$$2$$
$$7 \quad 40 \quad 5 \text{ weeks!}$$
$$35$$
$$\overline{\qquad}$$
$$5 \text{ days:}$$

> Ever your
> Dad.

Notes

1. Dictionary.
2. Clough (1819–61) was an early favourite of RK's. "The Bothy of Tober-na-Voulich" is from 1848.
3. Landor's dates are 1775–1864.
4. RK means the murder of Giuliano de Medici, 26 April 1478, and the revenge that followed, including the execution of Archbishop Salviati.
5. When John's school term ended.

To Colonel H. W. Feilden, [6 March 1912][1]

ALS: Syracuse University

Hôtel Royal / Grande Bretagne & Arno / Florence

Dear Colonel Sahib

This on the eve of our departure for Venice –

> Grand Hotel Britannia
> Venice[2]

to thank you for your kindness in writing and to beg you to send us to the address given all the news that may be.

As you can imagine we are a good deal upset about the strike[3] but from the Housemaster's letter from Wellington which arrived today the College appears to be going on absolutely normally. Of course with reasonable forethought they ought to be able to carry on for three or four weeks – but on the other hand they might have assumed that the strike was going to end and in that belief have under provisioned 'emselves.

My fear is that if this is the case we might suddenly get a wire telling us that the school was breaking up. In which case we should have to come home of course – but on the other hand how can we come home? The house is shut up: the servants are scattered: and there may be difficulty in communications and also, as we were to be away, Bateman's isn't garrisoned or victualled.

So I sometimes think that the best thing would be in event of Wellington shutting down, to send Moore[4] in the car to fetch John to Bateman's have him sleep there the night and get him over to France next day. But it is all very complicated and makes going away as much of a horror as staying at home. But I can't imagine a big school like Wellington not having taken precautions. Meantime I live on telegrams which is an unsatisfactory diet: and so shall be the more grateful for your first hand news.

The hotels here are all filling up and the foreigners are jubilant: hoping that the strike will continue and divert trade and keep their hotels full. Here (9.p.m.) comes a note from Moore telling us, among other matters, that he has seen you and I think (but he writes so damnably) Mrs Feilden out for a walk. Thus closely are your movements overseen and reported!

I can't quite make out from Moore what Wood has actually done to the road in front of our gate. Anyhow it seems both from Martin's and Moore's reports that the water don't run off as it should. *Do* have a look at it and tell us what the net result has been.

Florence is full of Americans – real ones with decent English names and faces: not the continentalized new breed. They all eat afternoon tea at Doney's.[5]

(*Note*. I arranged with Wood for the road to drain *away* from Bateman's – not towards it).

Now I must cease as there are many matters to be attended to before we leave. The town is filling up rapidly and today we have, for the first time, noticed the existence of flies! Iris, almond and stocks in full bloom and anemones all over the grass.

With all best greetings

Ever affectionately
Rudyard.

Notes
1. Dated from internal evidence.
2. They left on 7 March for Venice (CK diary).
3. The coal miners struck on 1 March; the strike was settled by minimum wage legislation in April.
4. RK's chauffeur: see [18 August 1908].
5. Doney et Neveux, 16 Via Tornabuoni: "expensive" (Baedeker's *Northern Italy*, 1909). It is still in business.

To Frank N. Doubleday, 6 March 1912
ALS: Princeton University

Hôtel Royal / Grande Bretagne & Arno / Florence, le 6 Mar. 1912:

Dear Frank –
   This is on the morrow of our departure for Venice; after a most delightful and interesting stay in Florence which by the way is apparently populated by 25% of the female population of the United States – chiefly over 50 or under 25. A few of them drag around profoundly uninterested men but the majority flock in herds of from two to six and their only companion is trusty Karl Baedeker. He is a great man. I wish I had his sales. He is even more full of facts than another author whom I could name.
   You seem to have had a lovely time in your tropics – barring the black "female of the species." But cheer up! England is still undefeated! Our suffragettes in their latest mood can give the female of any other lands a beating in all that makes for true spirit and womanliness. Isn't it curious that their energies should turn to smashing the windows of drapery stores?[1] I have been through the proofs of "Verses from Books" and will shortly return them to you.[2] They are vilely badly printed by Messrs Budd and Bliss whom I recommend to your special attention.[3] The type of the index is too small and too cramped and the Italic headings to the verses look too insignificant.
   I have added, so far, four additional sets of verses which I find I had overlooked and have duly marked their position in the index.
   Since sending you the copy I have realized ("it has been brought to my notice" is the sacramental English phrase) that there is a very strong demand for the inclusion of the chapter-headings out of Plain Tales, the Naulakha, Kim etc. (Also the pirates have been reproducing 'em). I have therefore collected together some 20 or more chapter-headings, which I should like to have printed some in the front of the book – blank page to precede – and others if possible – in the same type as the rest of the poems – not more than

three or four such chapter headings on one page. That will prevent a certain amount of criticism; and it is better to have some in front of the verses than *all* together as a sort of anti-climax at the end. I hope you agree to this or how would it be to divide the chapter headings into three sections – one at the beginning; one in the middle; and one at the end of the book?[4] In that case I suggest printing the chapter-headings in italics which will vary the monotony of the book – I *must* ask for page-proofs before I pass the thing finally as this galley stuff is so badly run up. I had no notion that there were so many odd verses flying about.

Bless you for the story about the Colonel's neice which filled us with joy. It is English – quite English, you know. There is a tale my Father (on whom be the peace!) told me which almost exactly parallels it.

Things in England are at present in a state of elaborately organized chaos — and yet, in one sense, a relief. Now we know that Demos is even more effective than King or Pope and it will be curious to see how, in the long run, mankind will quietly push him aside same as they have done Popes and Kings. The wife and Elsie (Oh that Dorothy were here to join in the shopping!) send their best love to you all and I am ever

> Your affectionate
> Rud.

Tell us more about your g.r.q. land scheme.[5] Somehow land don't seem to me as safe as once it did.

> R.

To Hotel Britannia.

Notes

1. On 1 March "some hundreds of women sallied forth, with hammers concealed in their muffs, and simultaneously broke plate-glass windows in the Strand, the Haymarket, Regent Street, Oxford Street, and Bond Street, and adjacent thoroughfares". At the same time, three women, including Mrs Emmeline Pankhurst, drive to Downing Street and broke some windows with stones. Following the arrest of large numbers of women, more windows were broken on 4 March. Mrs Pankhurst was sentenced to two months' imprisonment (*Annual Register, 1912*, p. 36).
2. The corrected proofs that RK sent were lost in the sinking of the *Titanic*, 15 April 1912; RK received a second set in May (Rees extracts, 11 May 1912).
3. Perhaps the compositors. According to the colophon of the first American edition of *Songs from Books*, 1912, the book was printed by Doubleday's Country Life Press.
4. There are three sets of "Chapter Headings" in the first American edition, a total of 43 items. They are not distinguished typographically from the rest of the text.
5. Not identified.

To Stephen Paget,[1] 12 March 1912
ALS: Syracuse University

Grand Hotel Britannia / Venise / Mar. 12. 1912

To Stephen Paget Esq.
Sir
    Your letter of Mar 5. has been forwarded to me here and I write to say that
I shall be very happy to be a Vice-president of the Research Defence Society.

Faithfully yours
Rudyard Kipling.

Notes
1.   Paget (1855–1912), a surgeon, founded the Research Defence Society in 1908 to
    defend the use of animals in scientific experiments. Paget was a prolific essayist and
    published several biographies. RK had given his view of the use of animals in
    research in his speech at the Middlesex Hospital in 1908 (see 4 October 1908), speak-
    ing of "those persons who consider their own undisciplined emotions more import-
    ant than the world's most bitter agonies – those people who would limit, and
    cripple, and hamper research because they fear research may be accompanied by a
    little pain and suffering" ("A Doctor's Work", *A Book of Words*, New York, 1928, p. 46).

To Colonel H. W. Feilden, 16 March 1912
ALS: Syracuse University

Grand Hotel Britannia / Venise / Mar. 16. 1912

Dear Colonel Sahib
    Bless you for your delightful account of Moore "in the sweat of his brow."[1]
Quite like Adam and Eve (you needn't tell Mrs Moore this!) with you in the
role of T.G.A.O.T.U.[2] walking in the cool of the evening. Moore as an earth-
mechanic fills me with joy.
    We should leave here on Wednesday Mar. 20. at noon for Paris; Hotel
Regina Place Rivoli where we should arrive on Thursday morn. 7.25. Mar. 21.
Thence we hope to get home on the 25th as and how we can – or the 26th if
the house can't be got ready before.[3] So far no sign that Wellington will close.
    The Kaiser's yacht the *Hohenzollern* came in here day before yesterday,[4]
coaled, washed herself all over, and is now painting and gilding like a public
prostitute. The harbour, under our window, is alive with German steam
launches and broad-beamed German officers.

Yesterday there was a Te Deum at San Mark's in honour of the King's escape from assasination.[5] We saw it from the Gallery – a wonderful sight. Officers, consuls, cuirassiers etc. etc. and the Patriarch of Venice (he comes next to the Pope and glowed in his robes like a rose tiger beetle under a microscope) read a speech. Here's a question. The pigeons at San Mark's have bred there for say, 700 years. They are all one stock curiously mimicking the grey, white splashed, black shadowed masonry of the square. Very good. For, say, 300 years there must have been a 12. o'c. gun fired in Venice – the easiest way of marking time. *Still* all those pigeons rise in their thousands and fly hurtling round the square when the gun fires? Why? What price hereditary instinct? Explain.

Went to the arsenal today and saw a model of the Bucentaur.[6] Likewise a Turkish flag taken at Lepanto. Not till one comes to Venice does one realize what a secular enemy is the Turk to the Italian. They are taking their war[7] very quietly and coolly but are really grieved and puzzled at the world's lack of sympathy. Weren't we rather like that during the Boer War?

The hotel is filling up – Americans and Germans mostly and up till now our weather has been divine. Today was soft, grey and cloudy after nearly a week of pale blue sky and thin mild air. It has never yet been really cold. I was thinking the other day over the *Archangel of the English*[8] and wondering how soon it would be before some angry man with cold toes started in to harness the tide.

You might write the Standard and point out that if a beneficent Tyrant of the mediæval type had wished to encourage invention he could hardly have got about the job more effectively than our Masters, Messrs Smillie and Hartshorn.[9] Only *they* proceed, on the old Papal lines, that there is one, unalterable, God-given way to horse power and before five years are gone they will get their answer from mankind:- "But *is* it necessary to use coal?"

Imagine Harun-al-Raschid[10] desirous of finding something nice to wash with, forbidding all true Believers to make ablution with sand. How long before some Muslim would have arrived at soap? (The analogy is rather weak because soap may contain the fat of swine).

I am dying to see Bateman's again. Venice is a nice place but there's only sea and paving-stones. The wife joins me in best love to you and Mrs Feilden and I am

Ever affectionately
Rudyard K.

Notes
1. Cf. Genesis 3:19.
2. The Great Architect of the Universe: a Masonic phrase.
3. They left by train for Paris on the 20th as planned, but did not return to Bateman's until 27 March (CK diary).
4. The Kaiser paid a visit to King Victor Emmanuel on 25 March in preparation for a renewal of the Triple Alliance of Germany, Austria and Italy.

5. On 14 March Antonio Dalba fired a revolver at the King and Queen of Italy.
6. The state galley of the Doges of Venice.
7. With Turkey: see 8 February 1912, to Colonel Feilden.
8. Not identified. RK, in response to the coal strike, was frequently speculating on alternative sources of power at this time, but I do not know what he means. Perhaps some labour leader?
9. Robert Smillie (1857–1940), president of the Scottish Miners' Federation; Vernon Hartshorn (1872–1931), president of the South Wales Miners' Federation.
10. The Caliph of Baghdad who figures in the *Arabian Nights*.

To H. A. Gwynne, 16 March 1912
ALS: Dalhousie University

Grand Hotel Britannia / Venise / Mar. 16. 1912:

Dear Old Man:

Many thanks for your kind note and for what you tell us about the strike.

Our plan is to leave here on Wednesday (noon. Mar. 20th) and arrive at Hotel Regina (Thursday. Mar. 21st) Paris and reach England on the 25th.

So far there has been no sign from Wellington but I have arranged, that *if* the school shuts up John is fetched by Moore to Bateman's or rather to Colonel Feilden's there to await our return which would of course be expedited if the College shut up. Burwash, so the Col. writes me, knows naught of the strike. But of course my plans like everyone else's are in the melting pot and I should be most grateful if you could snatch time even to dictate me a letter to the Hotel Regina
    Place Rivoli.
    Paris

giving me the news up to receipt of this.

It is the end of Labour either way. Cæsar has come to his triumph and will die in it. But it is also the end of coal as a prime necessity. They have made all the minds of a nation active by causing bodily discomfort and have thereby supplied the very strongest possible stimulus to invention that even a Tyrant could have conceived. Consequently, over and above the bending of thousands of men's energies towards the discovery of more oil, the development of existing supplies, the refurnacing of ships, thousands more will pick up (with the dogwhips of Pain, Fear *and* Hate behind 'em) the old unresolved but not insoluble problem of harnessing the tides. And that will be done partially, within the next few years. Side by side with oil comes in, for the present need, all patent fuels, compressed waste and neglected and chucked away by-products – *all* made possible – i.e. remunerative – by the revolt against coal. *Pari passu* or I'm mistaken, simplification of our railways; drastic cutting down of rolling stock, *full* compartments in all trains and mechanical handling of freight. So, in the long run *if* we survive, the jolt may be a blessing. Oddly enough I'd just done a yarn about it describing how the English were driven to harness the tides by a coal strike.[1]

As a side issue if and when the strike ends have you reflected on the automatic nemesis that awaits some few hundred of those miners who having spread want, disease and death above ground return to face death *under* ground. They will be excited many of them, some will be uneasy, and, as surely as night follows day, the year will not end without several hideous accidents in the pits. I've got a set of verses on the stocks for the M.P. – *quite* simple and direct. They may come off and they may not.[2]

I think you might invest a bit more on the certainty of the revolt against coal. If the Pope hadn't coerced men to *one* way of salvation, the birth of the printing press would have been delayed.

We've been having good weather here. Our hotel faces the business-end of the Grand Canal where the big steamers come in and the downstairs rooms smell like the Cape Hongkong and San Francisco mixed. Venice *is* really the edge of the East. The Kaisar is coming here on the 24th to talk to Humbert.[3] The Hohenzollern got in day before yesterday, coaled and is now painting and gilding herself no end. She lies close to our hotel and the German officers parade the town in great glory. One of 'em lunched at our hotel yesterday *in mufti!* – He dines, with his mamma and sister I think, in full uniform but this concession of mufti *at any time* rather surprised me. Oh – and one night he dined in mufti. We saw a Te Deum yesterday at St Mark's to celebrate Humbert not being assassinated. Everybody turned up. The Italians are taking their war very quietly but very seriously and it's pathetic to hear 'em calling "extras" in the street and to see the poor women letting down baskets from fifth story windows to get the list of dead and wounded. I've had a hell of a time dodging interviewers. We are the greatest (or we were, let's say) Muhammedan power in the world and taint for *me* to open my head. But, they feel the lack of the world's sympathy *very* keenly poor little devils. One don't realize till one gets to Venice and sees the Arsenal how the Turk has been Italy's "hereditary enemy" so to speak. Well I won't inflict more.

Elsie bids me to say that she is like the suffragettes and will *not* stop her attacks on the M.P. She says she is *herself* on her way to Paris where she can check your fashion statements. She smiled over your French words in your descriptions of the Court.

Ever

RK

Notes
1. "The Benefactors", *National Review*, July 1912: not collected until the Sussex Edition.
2. "Ulster", *Morning Post*, 9 April 1912 (*The Years Between*).
3. RK means Victor Emmanuel, not his father Umberto.

To Lady Edward Cecil, 16 March 1912

ALS: Syracuse University

Grand Hotel Britannia / Venise / Mar. 16. 1912

Dear Lady Edward

That was a curious experience you write of but, as it seems to me, quite in the line of the ordinary waking dream which is always more vivid than the dream of deep, or clouded, sleep. The hour is a usual one and all the rest fits in. I wonder if you remember whether you had been looking during the day – not directly perhaps but with the tail of your eye – at some picture or print of a child's figure or face. Generally when one works back through a dream one can piece it out almost like a jig-saw puzzle – a borrowed phrase here; a half-look there; a train of thought picked up idly in the day time and thrown aside and so on. But yours is evidently an unusual gift *and by just that much the more deadly*. This is a matter on which I feel very strongly indeed – so I won't say more.

We hope to come home on the 25th – to find I suppose some sort of England in existence. But hasn't it come quickly!

Mrs Kipling joins me in the kindest regards.

Very sincerely
Rudyard Kipling.

To Colonel H. W. Feilden, 24 March [1912]

ALS: Syracuse University

Château d'Annel / Longueil-Annel (Oise) / Sunday: Mar: 24.

Dear Colonel Sahib

To our surprise and delight we found in Paris our old friends the Depews whom we visited in the middle of last year's drouth.[1] They were just back from Russia and forthwith bade us come to their chateau. So we came for the week end which means we don't leave Paris till Wednesday (27th) by the 9.50 train to Dover where we should arrive at 3.20 p.m. and thence by motor to Blessed Bateman's.

Carrie is much cheered and delighted by what you tell her about her floor. I gather, incidentally, that Ellen is devoting all her time to getting a fit gloss on it.

Here's an interesting week-end crowd:-

(1) German Baron: young: marked with duelling sabre cuts: attaché at the German embassy and Captain of Hussars. *Very* keen on next war with plenty pious wishes that it won't come.
(2) *The* Millionaire of Belgium. Large, fat, tall smiling young sugar-beet King who farms and gambles and talks perfect English.
(3) Lean, hard-trained, wonderfully supple American man of fashion aged 52! Looks a late thirty. Was once one of America's best polo players: knows *all* the steps of all the modern dances – one-steps two steps etc. and *thirteen* different steps of one dance. Queer sort of game in which to shine but the result gives him a glorious figure.
(4) French, round-faced boy in a bank – talks little English and is very bored.
(5) Daughter of German ambassador to Paris.[2] U.S. father: Roumanian mother: Jewish caste of countenance: all that there is of the latest cry in *all* respects. Queer girl and don't much like her.
(4)[3] Long, sallow daughter of the richest widow in the U.S. now being finished off at a school in Paris. Thought maple-sugar came from the South!!! Spends winter in New York and summers in Maine. Dark with bad teeth but good manners.
(5) Plump, pinky-velvety 18-year old daughter of a French artist. Nice little minx with effective eyes.

Host and hostess – American millionaires parisianized and altogether delightful; but Oh Lord! what a sinful comfortable life! Luxury heaped and rampant all around. We're dying to be back to Bateman's as soon as may be.

How can the Govt go on with its Home Rule, Welsh Disestablishment piffle. It's like trying to get up a fancy-bazar in Ladysmith the day after the siege begins.

But of these things when we meet.

Ever affectionately
Rudyard Kipling.

Notes
1. See 16 August 1911. The Kiplings had left Venice on 20 March for Paris; they spent two days with the Depews at the Château d'Annel, 23 and 24 March, and on the 27th they returned on Bateman's (CK diary).
2. Presumably RK means not daughter but daughter-in-law. The German Ambassador to France at this time was Baron Wilhelm von Schoen (1851–1933); I have not found whether he had a daughter-in-law answering RK's description.
3. RK has lost his count and repeats numbers 4 and 5.

To H. A. Gwynne, [*c.* March? 1912]
ALS: Dalhousie University

Bateman's / Burwash / Sussex

Dear Old Man –

I *quite* see your point about *The Benefactors*. Even though the Pope were a Borgia of the XVIth century the pious R[oman]. C[atholic]. would throw fits.[1] But, since it came to you, an American magazine has taken it for publication on the 25th of June I believe.[2] Don't know whether they saw it or took it blind. As there are about 6,000,000 R.C.'s in the U.S. there may be a circus. Anyway I suppose it will come out then – and if I alter it here which is where I want it to do most good, there would be more of a circus. So I've got to stick to my Pope. He's the key of the position as a matter of fact. So don't you worry about taking it. I'll try it somewhere else if you send it back. If nobody takes it this side (for papal reasons) I must run it out somewhere or another in a mag. of limited circulation.[3]

This last strike is curious – and I think definitely marks the beginning of the revolution – in which (poor devils!) the machines in the long run will win.

Ever yours
RK.

Notes

1. The story is set in Hell, where a nameless Pope, "pale and intellectual-looking", explains how he ruled over material power by spiritual weapons until overcome by the printing press. He then observes that, since the invention of the press was a response to spiritual oppression, he is "in a measure responsible for the invention". Thus he, and all others who held power until displaced by new forms whose development they provoked, are "public benefactors". The latest instance of oppressive power overthrown is the coal-strike leader, "Honest Pete" Sugden, newly arrived in Hell, where the Pope explains the situation to him.
2. *American Magazine*, July 1912.
3. English publication was in Leo Maxse's *National Review*, July 1912. RK offered the story to Maxse without charge, calling it a "little loving idyll of organized Labour" (1 June 1912: ALS, West Sussex Record Office).

To H. A. Gwynne, 5 [April]¹ 1912
ALS: Dalhousie University

Bateman's / Mar. 5. 1912

Dear Old Man

I send with this the set of verses about which I wired.²

Cornford is handling the Irish side of it and, I think, will use it for all it is worth among the loyal papers.

If you take it for the M.P. you will have exclusive English use. I am not sending it to any other paper in England.

*March. 9th:*³ eve of B[onar]. L[aw].'s Belfast speech is the date.⁴

Only I must ask you to save the American copyright for me: and to do this it will be necessary for you to telegraph it in full to

Doubleday
Garden City
New York

and add "Please print and copyright for publication here March. 9th. Rudyard Kipling."

At the new night rates this I think will not be expensive.

Further I want you to back it up with as good a leader as you can.⁵ I don't want anything about myself or poetry but I want it made the excuse for a really hard blow, which will be followed up by the Bonar Law meeting.

Ever yours
R.K.

Notes
1. RK has misdated the letter, which is certainly April, not March.
2. "Ulster", RK's attack on Home Rule for Ireland.
3. That is, April, not March.
4. On 9 April Law took the salute of the Ulster Volunteers at a mass meeting in Belfast and made a speech against Home Rule.
5. A leader against the (third) Home Rule bill, which was to be introduced two days later, appears in the *Morning Post* with RK's "Ulster" on 9 April. "In the stirring lines which we publish to-day from his pen, Mr. Rudyard Kipling gives fitting expression to the feeling aroused by this attempted betrayal."

To Sir Max Aitken, 12 April 1912
TLS: Harvard University

Bateman's / Burwash / Sussex / April 12th, 1912

private

Dear Aitken,

Thank you. I write up to my knees in hectic wires and letters and do not feel any urgent need of further notoriety just now; but I would not for the world deprive your Mr. Martin of his innocent amusements.[1]

It occurs to me that his question offers an opening for something useful, because my information is that the other side are very much annoyed by the verses. I presume, though, that question time does not allow of speeches or anything but the briefest remarks.

But surely, Mr. Martin should be invited, entreated and urged to recite the offending verses. This is only justice to the author. If he does not comply with that reasonable, and audible, request, the verses or a sufficient portion of them should be recited – preferably from different parts of the house – by stalwarts told off *ad hoc*. By these means, two or four lines delivered at a time, you may be able to arrive at the precise lines Mr. Martin objects to. Should he, however, be lost enough to recite the verses, it seems to me that your obvious duty is to see that the stalwarts recite in unison with him, carrying on the quotation when he stops.

If this causes disorder, as I fear is possible, the lines

> What answer from the North
> One law, one land, one throne

spoken by all available voices and repeated again and again and again, after the manner of a Buddhist prayer would undoubtedly clarify the situation. You will readily see that in the event of a member of the Government rising to appeal for order, the simple statement

> "What need of further lies
> We are the sacrifice."

clearly and continuously delivered would do much good. Similarly if Redmond[2] is drawn into the riot; –

> "Before an Empire's eyes
> The traitor claims his price"

is obviously the proper remark.

I only indicate the outline; leaving the details to be filled in. Personally, I should be sorry if the House adjourned that night without thoroughly understanding "Ulster" from beginning to end.

(This by the way is my second offence. I wrote a poem called "Cleared" twenty years ago, after the findings of the Parnell Commission, for which the Irish of those days wanted to have me called to the Bar of the House.[3] I don't know whether this point might be used; – "Is this Mr Kipling the person who wrote 'We are not ruled by murderers but only by their friends?'"[4] The Irish might be soothed by this reminder).

Also, I think much of Ulster might be used throughout the coming Home Rule Debates. The two lines quoted above "What need of further lies" tactfully interjected, or murmured *or* shouted, whenever a member of the Government was up, might certainly enliven proceedings. And if your stalwarts look at the verses carefully they will see that almost every possible turn of a home-rule debate lends itself to a quotation which might be delivered by one, two or more voices. Redmond whenever he touched on safeguards might be met with; –

> We know when all is said
> We perish if we yield.

and any reference to the ne temere decree or the later Papal pronouncement forbidding priests to be summoned as witnesses without leave of the church[5] would equally call forth (in a distinct voice)

> We know the hells prepared
> For such as serve not Rome.

I don't know whether there is anything at all in these suggestions, but I certainly think that on Monday 15th Mr Martin should recite Ulster or the House should be kept waiting till Ulster is recited.

Ever yours
R.K.

Notes

1. Joseph Martin, Liberal MP for St Pancras, East, asked the Attorney-General in the House of Commons, 15 April, if "he intends to prosecute Mr. Rudyard Kipling for the offence of sedition for his verses entitled 'Ulster'"; the answer (by Sir Rufus Isaacs, whom RK in the next year pilloried as "Gehazi") was No (*Parliamentary Debates*, 5th Series, XXXVII, 17: 15 April 1912). RK's reply in this letter is a litany of texts from "Ulster".
2. John Redmond (1856–1918), MP for Waterford, the political heir to Parnell and the leader of the Irish Party since 1900. In the parliamentary moment described in note 1, above, Redmond added a remark about RK's "doggerel".
3. I have found no record of such a thing.
4. The last line of "Cleared".
5. The papal decree *Motu propria*, 9 October 1911, forbade, on pain of excommunication, the summoning of priests before secular tribunals without ecclesiastical

permission. The decree could operate in only a few European countries, but it was supposed that Ireland might be one of them and that the decree was aimed at stifling political liberty. See *The Times*, 22, 26, 27 December 1911.

To John Kipling, [1 May 1912]
ALS: University of Sussex

Bateman's / Burwash / Sussex / Wed.

Dear Old Man –

Behold me recovering, though still in a drenched and drabbled condition from my cold. My word! It was a beauty! Now Bird seems to have got something of the same sort and is in bed "enjoying" much the same treatment as I had. Her throat has been sore but is now better: but her nose and eyes are running no end and she lives on slops – not without protests and outcries! Poor old girl.

Well, I only hope you haven't been following the family example. The wind has gone round into the S. West and felt quite round and balmy today. I was out for nearly a couple of hours looking at the new land which Mother has decided upon buying. Otherwise I haven't done much except tried to think what sort of paper I shall read "The twelve" on the 25th May.[1]

What really bothered me most was not being able to have a last jaw with you.[2] I wanted to tell you a lot of things about keeping clear of any chap who is even suspected of beastliness. There is no limit to the trouble possible if one goes about (however innocently) with swine of that type. Give them the widest of wide berths. Whatever their merits may be in the athletic line they are at heart only sweeps and scum and *all* friendship or acquaintance with them ends in sorrow and disgrace. More on this subject when we meet. The Leonards came over yesterday: with Bargee and my small god-daughter Meriel.[3] Then came Sir F. Merrieless[4] of the Union Castle Line with his wife and two long girls in a motor – so we had a lively afternoon. There isn't any other news.

Sorry you can't look at a cricket match without feeling faint and having to lie down in a four and sixpenny chair. Yah!

Now I am going to bed.

Lovingly ever
Pater.

The Challenge Rubber Co keeps on sending me copies of the Motor Cycle (or whatever it is) which I send on to you. Dear love from us all. Landon comes tomorrow – fresh from the Persian Gulf.[5]

Notes

1. The talk that RK gave to the Literary Society of Wellington at Pearson's House on 25 May 1912, collected in *A Book of Words* as "The Uses of Reading". The Archivist of Wellington reports that the speech, then entitled "The Possible Advantages of Reading", was given to about fifty boys. The account of the event in the school magazine concludes by saying that "The Society was deeply impressed by [RK] and carried away from that meeting feelings of delight and fascination, which it is impossible to describe" (Mark Baker, "John Kipling at Wellington", *Kipling Journal*, June 1982, p. 14).
2. John had just returned to Wellington from the Easter holidays.
3. "Bargee" is presumably Charles (b. 1909), first child of the Leonards' daughter Violet, who married John Cavendish Lyttelton, 9th Viscount Cobham. Meriel (1911–30) was the second child.
4. That is, Mirrielees: see 21 June 1900.
5. Political anarchy in Persia had led to manoeuvrings between Russia and England; the Russians sent in troops at the end of 1911, but held up on the protest of their British allies, who had earlier sent troops to the Persian Gulf to protect trade.

To Stanley Baldwin, 6 May 1912

ALS: University of Sussex

Bateman's / Burwash / Sussex / May. 6. 1912 / 5:50. p.m.

Dear Stan:

Just in from Rottingdean where of course I went over to Stanford's and had a squint at Littley.[1] Waited quietly by the pavilion opposite the gate, at 2:20 for 'em to come out. Littley charged forth with a pal – no sign of any pensive steps and slow about A. Baldwin. Elsie and I hailed him and he came to anchor, legs very wide apart, the new, very new schoolboy; overlying the child now four days in the background. Looked eminently fit. Conversation short and naturally weighted with the knowledge that he was on his way to cricket. Did he like the place? *"Oh yes."* "What dormitory?" *"Finch, I think."* "What form-master?" *"Don't quite know."* "Where are you playing cricket?" *"I'm just going to ask the Master that."* (No ounce of fear about Masters, evidently). Where are you in the school? Long thought on Littley's part. *"Well, the bottom boy is called Thesiger. A very curious name. I thought it was Messenger at first. But it's Thesiger and he's bottom of the form."* "Where are you," says his uncle – "five or six places from the bottom?". ... *"I may be"* says Littley guardedly and dives off like a trout across the field in the sunshine, picks up a scarlet-headed yaffingale[2] of a kid called Buzzard (blazing red hair) and the two prance off with their arms on each other's shoulders. I follow at leisure and see Littley and a small thing in grey, amicably sparring at and squaring up to each other in the interval of waiting till sides are arranged. Then the

Master appeared and they all ran to him like young hounds – almost you could see their sterns wagging. So he set 'em to their game and the last I see of Littley is a flourish of a bat and a man-of-the-world wave of the hand. *Quite* full of beans and evidently realizing his new world with pleasure. Bless him. Love to Ciss.[3]

R.

Notes
1. Arthur W. Baldwin (1904–76), second son of Stanley Baldwin, had just entered St Aubyn's, C. E. M. Stanford's school in Rottingdean, where John Kipling had been before him. Arthur succeeded his brother Oliver as 3rd Earl Baldwin in 1958. He published a valuable family history, *The Macdonald Sisters*, in 1960.
2. Woodpecker.
3. As Lucy Baldwin was called.

To Brander Matthews, 7 May 1912

ALS: Columbia University

Bateman's / May. 7. 1912.

Dear Brander,
   I've been laid by for a bit with a cold and arrears – the result of my holiday on the continent: but Venice and Florence were worth it – so I haven't answered your letter nor acknowledged the book.[1]
   Now here's a curious thing. Over twenty years ago, I find I quoted (and I remember I quoted from memory) a quatrain from your Yankee Maiden.[2] That would be in 1889 – and the thing must have been in my head before that year. Now where and how and in what way did your verses come to me in India? An old Harper? I can't tell but it's very curious. I think you'll find 'em in a last chapter of my From Sea to Sea stuff. A lot of the other verses I know in the back of my head. Proof – if it were needed – that your verse has an adhesive quality which, when all is said and done, is more important than anything else. But *do* try and assist me as to the form in which the Yankee Maiden was first published. It's dated – excellent plan – 1880. Can you look it up.
   Also kindly identify the following – all of which I knew

The Willow. 1881
A Ballade of Midsummer. 1878
En route 1878.

This I think set me to work trying to copy it which I failed in. My very bad Ballad of Jakko Hill[3] was done about 1884 – using for rhyme reference Ballade of Midsummer. That's odd too. But *what* journals were they in. *Note*. Next time you publish an uncut vellum paper edition please send own razor to cut with. It was as tough as parchment.

As to that other man's verses you sent me,[4] about hating the U.S., I confess they wore my patience rather thin. The charge is just as true as the other which runs it close in the U.S., or did, that I ill-treat my wife. If he had considered for half a minute he would have seen that my chiefest joys *and* sorrow came out of that land. Instead of which he slops about what I wrote on Reciprocity.[5] He might have waited till his own fat President[6] confirmed and more than confirmed every word I said in that regard. Even *I* draw the line at saying that Canada would become an "adjunct" of the U.S. So please walk all over your friend several times – hard.

Meanwhile the last member of the "hated race" who has been at Bateman's is the Governor of the Phillipines[7] – a millionaire, scholar and all the rest of it, keenly enthusiastic over his job – full to the back teeth of the needs material and spiritual of his flock – roads, piers, schools etc. etc. so that I was delighted. And here a curious thing. The man's face was weirdly (that *is* the word I want tho' I admit a vile one) familiar to me. Couldn't for the life of me think why, till he told me that he was Emerson's grandson. Portrait of Emerson in my study for the past ten years; and the setting of the eyes, modelling of upper part of nose and lower part of forehead *absolutely* Emerson. His name Cameron Forbes – polo-player and administrator. I fancy there's a new type in evolution among those islands.

Now what are your chances of coming over this year? You might as well because all signs point to us reverting to a Heptarchy ere long. In which case you will be running into a separate and aggressive "nation" every time you change gear on your automobile. This is the price we pay for Demos – who is a Particularist and a Tyrant.

Moreover the country side looks simply heavenly – everything forced by sunshine a month earlier than it should be: and the fields ablaze with flowers. So come along and be hated for a bit.

Ever yours
Rudyard

Notes
1. *Fugitives from Justice*, published in 1912 in an edition of 99 copies. All of the poems mentioned in this letter are collected in the book.
2. RK quotes Matthews' "Envoy to an American Girl" as the epigraph to chapter 36 of *From Sea to Sea*, originally published in the *Pioneer*, 4 March 1890.
3. Published in the second edition of *Departmental Ditties*, 1886.
4. Not identified.

5. See 6 September 1911.
6. William Howard Taft; on 26 May, in a campaign speech, Taft read from a letter he had written to Roosevelt on 10 January 1911 in which he said that the reciprocity treaty would make Canada an "adjunct" of the US. The word raised a newspaper storm in England.
7. William Cameron Forbes (1870–1959). A Harvard graduate, he served as head football coach at Harvard before becoming a Boston investment banker. He was appointed to the Philippines Commission in 1904, was Vice-Governor, 1908, and Governor 1909–13, when he was removed by President Wilson. He was later Ambassador to Japan, 1930–2. Forbes was an ardent polo player and wrote a standard book on the subject. He was at Bateman's, 17–18 April (Bateman's Visitors Book).

To John Kipling, [8 May 1912]
ALS: University of Sussex

The White Hart Inn (or Hotel) / Andover. / Wednesday night 8.20. p.m.

Dear Old Man –
We're on tour – Mum and I at least, for the Bird is at home – for two days. I had to see my sister (Aunt Trix) at Weyhill[1] which is a few miles from Andover and Mother and I decided to have out the Green Goblin[2] and make a jaunt of it. So far it has been great fun. We left Batemans at 2:15 this afternoon, came via Cross in Hand, Hadlow Down, Buxted, Newick and Chailey, Cuckfield, Bolney, Billingshurst, Petworth, Midhurst, Petersfield and Winchester and then across the Downs to here.

A simply divine day – hot and sticky after the rain with everything rushing into flower or bud everywhere. The may was out; the horse chesnuts were out, Irises and wistarias were out in people's gardens and the whole hundred or hundred and twenty mile run looked like the English country in a picture.

We had the motor open and enjoyed ourselves awfully. We stopped for tea for half an hour at Petersfield which made our running time about 4 hours. You will be pleased to learn that nothing passed us. You will further be pleased to learn that a Rolls-Royce inspector (Hanbury) came down this morn at about $^1/_4$ to 12 to overhaul the Goblin. Moor of course opened her up and jawed like sixty. Mr. Hanbury was pleased to say that the Goblin was in excellent condition and needed nothing being done to her. We also had no complaints to make: so we gave him lunch and parted the best of friends. He told me an awful story about a friend of his who had an American car and had just climbed with it to the very top of some big French pass near the Puy de Dome. Anyway it was a ten mile climb. When he reached the top it was lighting up time so he got down and lit the lamps and – owing to a leaky carburettor or something, the car lit too. There wasn't much available earth about – only terraced walls with tiny vineyards on top. This sort of thing in fact [drawing of mountain road between terraced walls]: and *ten* smitten miles from anywhere! And the car blazed and blazed! They scooped up earth out of the gutter: they dragged the bonnet off and used it as a scoop for getting a little damp earth out of one of the terraced little vineyards. But, as you can imagine, that didn't do much good. The man's wife picked up what she thought (it was dark by that time) was a clod of clay and wildly dumped it down on the engines. It turned out to be a healthy and hard piece of rock! Result – engines went pungo! They just had to wait by the blaze till the car was burnt out. Luckily the wheels remained – so they piled into the still smoking carcass and coasted back, by gravity, ten miles down the pass to the place they had started from! That's a nice tale. *And* true. But can't you see the agitated woman in the dusk dashing a big rock into the guts of the blazing engine.

And since we are talking of motors I may as well confide to you that, when we went for a stroll around Andover while our frugal dinner was being got ready, I came on a motor garage with an 8–10 brand new Bédelia.[3] I'd never seen a Bedelia close to before. The man in charge of the garage owned it and was very communicative. She was painted a rich *dark* blue and cost 103 guineas. Cheaper makes of lower horse power cost between 60–70 guineas. *This* I consider a plain swindle. No side-doors. You step into a sort of canoe and the seats are hammock seats. But I expect you know that. The belts are apparently changed by hand or a stick. On the whole I'm glad I've seen her. I don't love her any more. A bug-trap and a rattle-trap, is my verdict Sir [drawing of Bédélia]. Nor do I like her steering gear so far aft.

Well this seems rather a motorious letter but after sitting for so long in one I expected my mind is unconsciously full of 'em. You may care to know that a few days ago coming down from town we were passed by a 6.h.p. Rex. It was all that the poor brute could do (he caught us at the foot of a hill). He kept his position for about $\frac{1}{4}$ mile and then very kindly let us go by.

I haven't anything more to say – dear man. This letter smells of petrol already. Dear love from Mum and me. Angy[4] has been staying with us and I am quite sure would send you her love too.

Ever
Dad.

Notes
1. See 4 January 1911.
2. The Rolls-Royce that RK acquired this year.
3. The Bédélia was a French light-weight car built from 1910 to 1925. It carried two passengers in tandem (the rear passenger steered), had a single cylinder engine and a belt transmission, and was named after the initials of its builders, Bourbeau et Devaux.
4. Sara Anderson was at Bateman's May 6–9 (Bateman's Visitors Book).

To John Kipling, [21 May 1912]
ALS: University of Sussex

Bateman's / Tuesday: / 3.30.p.m.

Dear Old Man –

Got your letter for which many thanks. Sorry I haven't written but this d—d lecture of yours *and* the dentist (awful excavations twice a week) + a speech at the Royal Geographical Society[1] + a lot of proofs of a book[2] have filled up my time.

Now listen and attend. Owing to the Baldwin girls (Lorna and Margot[3]) having to be met on Sat. morn and me having an engagement we can't be at Wellington for lunch. We hope to be there at 3.p.m. and I have written Pompey asking him to let you be at the Hotel at 3 where we will have a visit together and come back to Pompey's about 5.p.m. Then dinner with Pomp. At 7:30 and *then* the paper! I don't mind this plan so much because we are staying with Lord Roberts next weekend June 1. and I mean to come and have tea with you on that Saturday and to come over and spend Monday night at Wellington Hotel. Do you quite understand?

Glad to hear about your being 2nd in your form. I keep a strict eye on you (a mental one) nearly all the time and it delights me to find that *you* find this term so good. Bits of lime and cement are now rolling about in my mouth as I am just back from a hectic hour with the Brighton Dentist (D—n him!) so I will now bring my letter to a close.

Ever lovingly
Your Pater.

Notes
1. 20 May 1912, collected as "The Verdict of Equals" (*A Book of Words*). It is in the form of a toast to the president of the Society, Lord Curzon.
2. *Songs from Books.*
3. Margot (Pamela Margaret) Baldwin was the third of the Baldwin sisters. She and Lorna were at Bateman's, 25–8 May 1912 (Bateman's Visitors Book).

To Frank N. Doubleday, 27 May 1912
ALS: Princeton University

[Bateman's] Sunday. / May. 27. 1912.

Dear Frank –

My head is just above water after the pains of parturition – the metaphor is mixed but it means that I've had to make a speech (me and the Prime

Minister and the Archbishop of Canterbury[1] at the Royal Geographical dinner) *and* to read a paper on literature before the Literary Society of John's college – Wellington. I didn't mind the Geographical Society dinner but the other thing was serious and so I had to sweat big drops over it and got my reward when John told me this morning (we're just back from Wellington) that "it wasn't so bad after all." High praise, Sir, in the mouth of Youth.

John by the way is a little taller than I am and seems to be settled down to growing in earnest.[2] He is a desperate keen private in the ranks of the College training corps and is going out under canvas for a week at the beginning of the holidays. I'm glad he looks so fit.

I wish to goodness they'd let the wretched Titanic sleep in peace.[3] I can't quite make out from the report of our proceedings (yours were *quite* unintelligible) whether the Court is trying *every* survivor for being personally responsible for the loss of the boat or whether they really *do* want to find out what caused the accident. I expect the warning will last for about two years with luck. After that, passengers will swear if they are not shot across the water in record time. We are a queer breed.

What you tell me about the new land that you have spied out and covet and propose to shift to, is very interesting. I am more impressed by the calm way in which you contemplate building a house all over again. Now Carrie is building a tennis racket-court, 29 × 98, and as far as I am privileged to understand the workings of the British mind, the building of your new home on the same time scale would occupy the best half of this century.

But I don't doubt that you'll have your new place built within the year. You will not reproduce the old house. You will throw out little additions and improvements – quite tiny things: and you will run up a bill for a quarter of a million dollars and will wonder how the extra expenses crept in. I'll bet you and Nellie anything you please that that's what will happen.

Which reminds me that on a train going to Florence I met a big Buffalo publisher who told me that Roosevelt was "down and out." In return I betted him a year's subscription to any magazine I should name to one of my books that Theodore would give Taft the run of his life.[4] I'm lucky in bets. Seriously, yours is a curious political situation – almost as bad as ours which I begin to hope cannot be worse. Meantime, I agree with you, that this is a hard and an unfeeling world for any poor devil who merely asks leave to work at his own job as hard as he can. When everyone is arranging for everybody else's future wellfare, I suppose we'll have to stop for lack of food-supplies. This is the situation which we are just confronting in England. I was more grateful than I could say when Taft (whose stomach be exalted) went out of his way to confirm every last line I've written about Canadian reciprocity. I met Jack Hammond (Hays-Hammond)[5] the day that the "private" letter came out and we could not do anything for laughing. Somehow or other to hint that a lady like Miss Canada would become an "adjunct" struck me as worse than "concubine" which until then, I considered the foulest word in the language. No matter. Unless R. gets the bit very much between his teeth his last term, I fancy he won't make too bad a President. The Lord only knows what sort of government *we* are likely to get: but our people still keep up their fat and unbroken calm.

I have one or two stories that I want to write now that I have got the verses out of my light and I am deeply thankful to say that C. is much better since her three months on the Continent this spring. She seems stronger and more equable in every way. Elsie is growing and developing very prettily. She has at present two red-headed cousins staying with her. *How* I wish Dorothy were here. They are filling the whole house with piano and phonograph – not to say their own talk. I'd be sorry for Dorothy with Elsie to chaperone! Being myself but of reasonable stature I consider Nelson's 6.5$^{1}/_{2}$ of height simply indecent. Hope you put weight on him as your secretary for the purpose of keeping him down.

Now I will return to my raft of mail. Every idle son of Belial in Great Britain seems to think he has a right to ask me any fool question that comes into his head.

Dear love to you all from us all.

Ever
Rud

Notes
1. Randall Thomas Davidson (1848–1930), 1st Baron Davidson, Archbishop of Canterbury, 1903–28. The Archbishop and the Prime Minister preceded RK as speakers at the Royal Geographical Society banquet (see [21 May 1912]).
2. John measured 5ft 4in in May 1912 (Rees extracts, 2 May 1912).
3. The *Titanic* sank on the night of 14–15 April 1912. A Senate committee of inquiry in the US, whose proceedings were much criticised, published its report on 24 May, distributing blame in many directions. A special commission in England, under Lord Mersey, did not issue its report until 30 July 1912, so RK must be referring to the newspaper accounts of its sittings.
4. Roosevelt ran against Taft in the presidential election of 1912 as the candidate of the Bull Moose Party. The result was that the Republican Party was split, and the Democrat Woodrow Wilson was elected.
5. John Hays Hammond (1855–1936), American mining engineer, had been Rhodes's chief consulting engineer in South Africa. He was instrumental in the preparation of the Jameson Raid and was one of those sentenced to death after its failure. After his release and return to the US in 1899 he was associated with, among other things, the Guggenheim interests. He was a close friend and associate of Taft, and assisted in the negotiations for Canadian reciprocity.

To Colonel E. D. Ward, 4 June 1912
ALS: Bodleian Library

Bateman's / Burwash. / June 4. 1912

re. *Capt Stewart Newcombe*[1] R. E. *Longmoor*.[2]

Dear Ward:

About twelve years ago a subaltern of engineers called Stewart Newcombe got me very nearly shot at Karree Siding[3] by telling me that some scrub in front of me was "all clear" whereas it was anything but cleared and I had to lie on my tummy in great bodily and mental distress for some hours. I have owed that boy something ever since but haven't set eyes on him.

Now he has come to England a captain of Sappers with, I am sorry to say, about ten years of uncommonly good African work to his credit – central Africa, Uganda, Lado Enclave[4] and all that sort of thing. He is in the Intelligence (a branch of the service which I should not naturally connect with Sappers) and he does not seem to have intelligence enough to want to stay in England. He wants to get back to his Africa and, I believe, to Egypt for choice. He is now at Longmoor doing nothing in particular – not even recovering from fever because, I gather, the African climate has not affected his health.

I repeat I know nothing about him except his record which is a fine one – so I am not swayed by any personal bias. Isn't there any way by which you could set him on his return to Africa? If he dies there I shall be revenged for his attempt on my life at Karree Siding. If he lives I fancy the service will be richer by his work. Can you tell me any one to whom I ought to write about him?

Ever sincerely
Rudyard Kipling.

Notes
1. Captain (later Colonel) Newcombe (1878–1956) served in South Africa, 1899–1900; Egyptian Army, 1901–11. In 1913–14 he carried out the survey of the Palestine border across the Sinai Peninsula for the Palestine Exploration Fund. In the First World War he served with T. E. Lawrence in the Arab revolt against the Turks, during which he was captured. He retired in 1932.
2. A military camp in Hampshire.
3. 28 March 1900: see 24 July 1900.
4. On the Upper Nile, part of the Anglo-Egyptian Sudan.

To John Kipling, 5 June 1912

ALS: University of Sussex

Bateman's, / June. 5. 1912 / 7: p.m.

Dear Old Man,

We did have a day and three quarters yesterday! Words cannot describe the riot and confusion and crowded streets of Eton – one jam of parents, motors and georgeously attired kids. As we moved slowly through the press at 11:30. a.m. Oliver[1] in white or yellow waistcoat, huge button hole and immaculate topper suddenly appeared on the foot-board. His hawk-eye had discovered us and he piloted us to a great yard roaring full of more parents and kids and glossy toppers where they were having call over which they call Absence. Here, *longo intervallo*, we picked up Aunt Ciss with Elsie, Di and Lorna who had come from town in Uncle Stan's motor (Uncle Stan was there too, of course) and then we found Oscar Hornung and Mr and Mrs Hornung. Then (*of* course: it's always the case on the 4th of June) it began to rain. We waited till it cleared up and moved off slowly to see the great cricket match.

You never dreamed of such superb playing-grounds as those of Eton – in summer. In winter they must be ghastly damp and rheumatic and influenza-ish. It was close, and hot and sticky at first with heavy clouds and about 500 parents sat round the pitch in chairs while Eton played New College. Sir Guy Campbell's son[2] (major) was playing for Eton and I saw Sir Guy and Lady Campbell.[3] Also I saw Inigo Freeman Thomas[4] being talked to by his grandfather Lord Brassey[5] (at which I fled). Also I saw (or rather Elsie saw) a Gibbs boy.[6] I suppose I saw a lot more men but they were all so dead alike under their toppers that I could not tell t'other from which. Well, the girls sat on chairs and watched the match – Di and Lorna furiously excited. Elsie, I grieve to say, quite a heathen and unimpressed by the nobility of the game. But it was very pretty. I *might* have gone to attend speeches in the Great Hall but as the first piece spouted was "The White Man's Burden" – by R.K. – I did not. Then at 1.15 Elsie Mummy and I went to lunch at the White Hart (straw-berries and cream) while the rest of the party went to lunch with Oliver's tutor. Somehow it seemed to us we'd be the happier at the White Hart: and we were.

And *then* it began to rain and when we got back to the cricket ground things were damp and they were covering the Sacred Pitch with tarpaulin. Every one sheltered under the trees like wet-hens till it got too bad. Then there was a general break to go to the Memorial Hall and see the chapel and the schools and similar things. Oscar Hornung was our pilot. It was very interesting but the form rooms tho' old struck me as pretty frowzy and full of germs. Then we went back and had tea in Oscar's rooms with his people. A rather jolly room but, on the whole, the houses didn't strike me as being specially clean and the lavatory accomodation was not extra special.

Then the sun came out and Elsie insisted on staying on and we went to the big school yard to attend Absence – General Call Over. Every man raises his topper as he says "Here Sir!" Then, in the car, (with thousand of other cars), up a lane and across grassy fields down to the river to get a good place to see the procession of boats. We got a ripping place and saw the whole shoot – eight or nine boats; the rowers got up like ancient man'o'war's men; the cox's attired as middies with dirk and belts, and with bridal bouquets of flowers on their knees. A very ancient and sacred ceremony but not exactly what you might call impressive. They rowed past us twice. Then at 7: we made a break across the dripping fields, not waiting for the fireworks and, leaving Windsor at 7:30 p.m. arrived at Batemans at 10.30: p.m. – most of the time raining. A great day altogether and E. enjoyed it enormously.

I believe that Lorna and Margot are coming down by motor on speech-day to join our party at Wellington,[7] which I think will be rather fun. We shall make a fine and good looking crowd. I *do* hope it will be decent weather.

I can't tell you what a joy it was to me to have that time with you.[8] I hope I didn't bore you with good advice but it *is* good advice. Oscar Hornung who is only 17 is now on the edge of having a house to manage and I'd give a deal if some day I could see you head of your house. Remember my council. Keep your tongue between your teeth; don't criticize aloud (write it out all to me!) and flee from the Contaminating Swine! More later. I hear the postman.

Ever
Daddo.

Notes
1. Baldwin.
2. Edward Fitzgerald Campbell, third son of Sir Guy Campbell, on the Eton eleven, 1911–12.
3. Lt.-Colonel Sir Guy Campbell (1854–1931), 3rd Baronet, and his wife Nina; he had served in India on the staff of the Lieutenant-Governor of Bengal.
4. Freeman-Thomas (1899–1979), second son of Freeman Freeman-Thomas, 1st Marquess Willingdon; he succeeded his father in 1941.
5. Thomas Brassey (1836–1918), 1st Earl Brassey, Liberal MP, 1868–86, formerly Civil Lord of the Admiralty and Secretary to the Admiralty; publisher of *Brassey's Naval Annual*.
6. There were currently three at Eton. I have no evidence to suggest which one RK means.
7. On 15 June.
8. RK had tea with John at Wellington on 1 June and called again on 3 June: see [21 May 1912].

To Sir Charles Crewe, 9 June 1912
ALS: East London Museum, South Africa

Bateman's / Burwash / Sussex / Sunday / June. 9. 1912

Dear Crewe –

I owe you for two letters: the second of May 20th quite the most joyous I've read in many sad years. The crisis filled me with the wildest curiosity at 6,000. m. range – and it wasn't all political curiosity either. As psychologist I am profoundly interested in (a) Hull's conception of the Truth and (b) Sauer's.[1] As an ethnologist I have never till now enjoyed the privilege of watching two half-castes, in responsible positions, at war. (My proof-readers in India were Goanese half-castes and used occasionally to fall out but that gives me no line to go on). In your "Cabinet" I take it both combatants refer directly (or with one generation's interval) to the Bantu Stock. This, my de-ah Colonel Crewe encourages me to expect developments on lines which are beyond the White Man's dreams.

May I suggest a commission to enquire into the charges preferred on each side? I will be President – for nothing. Nay, I'll pay for the post.

As far as I can see it (and you say the same) this kick-up in the Kaffir Kraal or circus in Kaffirs will make no odds. All parties and preeminently Botha are without shame or knowledge: and I am more mortally sick of that bald-headed ineptitude Merriman dodging round the outskirts of your political offal-heaps, pecking and screaming like an Indian adjutant-bird, than I can well say. Before you die you must do one book (it will be a *magnum opus*) of *"Politics from Within."*

I haven't seen Jameson yet. I can only, and that rarely, get up to Town at the end of the week, by which time he is away golfing. But all reports are that he is getting steadily better.[2] I quite agree with you that as he improves he will come down South at intervals to hang on to Smartt's coat-tails. At present he talks of the Chartered[3] and Rhodesia as his only loves. Whence I draw my own conclusions. I spent Empire day, as usual, with Milner at Sturry: and he was rejoicing over the Hull–Sauer *amour*. I think that man can hear S. Africa's every word even while he sleeps. He looks very fit.

Latterly (it's a long jump from Milner) I've run across Tim Healey[4] – an unscrupulous politician, even by Irish standards, a devout and mystic Roman Catholic, and a first-class criminal lawyer, inspired with one perfect and passionate hatred for the Government which they cordially reciprocate. "Thank God" he said to me "the very sight of my face is enough to drive 'em woild." He swears – wish I could believe him – that Lloyd-George, whom he peculiarly loves, started with convictions but now has lost 'em all and is simply a political adventurer and *"the* most unscrupulous scoundhrel, I should think, that ever sat in a cabinet." Well, Tim ought to know!

Our situation here is state-aided anarchy. But it has it's good side. The Government (see McKenna's last pronouncement refusing protection to free labour[5]) has cast itself down abjectly at the feet of the Unions – so abjectly that even Labour is frightened. You see, the Unions that are making the trouble are, in effect, the three *naturally protected* ones – i.e. Power (coal) Food (transport works in London docks) and Distribution (Railways). The other Unions (speaking broadly) cannot do much because of Free Trade – as you can see.

Well, the Colliers Unions are pretty much bankrupt: the A[malgated]. S[ociety of]. R[ailway]. Servants has been heavily crippled but the dockers having little to lose and counting over much on the possibility of starving London have tried their hand and to a large extent have failed.[6] (Had they succeeded, obviously a belly strike could not have lasted more than three or four days – and they would have won with great eclat). But even slow thinking London saw, and sees, it was not safe to leave London's food supply in any one set of hands. So the dockers fought with all public opinion and a mass of their own men against 'em. *Now* comes this fool-Government with proposals to hand over control of the food-supply to two huge federations – Masters and Employees.[7] This, for commercial reasons, is impossible for the masters and (tho' they don't say it) equally impossible for the men who don't want to be ordered out by Czars of Ben Tillett's[8] type. The leaders, being well-fed, had made the mistake of forgetting that their men have been pinched not once but thrice by strikes during the past twelve months. Actually it's less than ten months since the Railway strike. The men are fed up. Their leaders are flustered and so is the Government. We shall see how the vote of censure on McKenna will be received in the House.[9] However they vote, the Liberals are angry *and* frightened at his back-down; Lloyd-George in his desire to retrieve his waning popularity, will most likely back up the cause of the Unions *but – the Unions are sick of 'emselves* and the men outside the unions are indignant. So all points, to my mind, towards the sifting out of good from bad Labour at which I hinted some letters ago. As soon as men see that there is no law in England save the whim of the unions they'll kick: but till the kick comes life will be hectic. I'll spare you more of this or you'll think I'm in politics.

Our best love to you all. I wish to goodness you'd come over here and be vetted by a posse of intelligent doctors (I can put you on to a whole covey of 'em). There's fifteen critical years ahead of you. After which you can do as you please but now I think you'll be needed.

Ever sincerely
Rudyard Kipling

Notes
1. Henry Hull (see 27 March 1906), as Finance Minister in Botha's cabinet, complained that J. W. Sauer (see 24 October 1901), the railway minister, had made Hull's position impossible by authorising heavy expenditures and by granting

reductions in railway rates, all without consulting the cabinet and all in favour of the Cape over the Transvaal. Since Sauer was politically far more powerful than Hull, Botha accepted Hull's resignation in June.
2. Jameson, for reasons of health, had retired from South African politics in April 1912 and returned to England.
3. Rhodes's British South Africa Company. Jameson had been a director since 1902 and was president from 1913; the work of the Company was now Jameson's main occupation.
4. Timothy Michael Healy (1855–1931) first came to notice as a Parnellite MP in 1880; he turned against Parnell but continued to represent the Irish cause in Parliament, though his relation to parties was always stormy. After a long career in the Irish courts, in 1910 he took up practice in London. Healy was the first Governor-General of the Irish Free State, 1922–8.
5. Reginald McKenna (1863–1943), as Home Secretary, had refused to send police to protect strike breakers unloading a ship at Purfleet (*The Times*, 7 June 1912).
6. A London dock strike at the end of May continued through July before collapsing. "This abject failure … put an end for the time being to the strike-ferment in England. It had lasted round about two years, and the workers saw that they must give it a rest" (R. C. K. Ensor, *England 1870–1914*, p. 444).
7. The proposal, made on 1 June, was for a joint conciliation board, and was rejected by the masters.
8. Tillett (1860–1943), founder and leader of the Dockers' Union, and a founder of the Labour Party.
9. Austen Chamberlain moved a vote of censure on McKenna on 12 June on the question of protecting non-union workers (see note 5, above). After a tumultuous debate the motion was defeated by a margin of 77.

To R. D. Blumenfeld,[1] 18 June 1912
ALS: University of Texas

Bateman's / Burwash / Sussex / June. 18. 1912.

private.
Dear Blumenfeld,
    The wife is much obliged for the answers to her questions and your letter.[2] But it's all bloody chaos and the curious thing is how we (she and I but specially she) are expected to hold the hands of the (a) indoor servants (b) gardeners (c) casual bricklayer (d) village nurse, (e) laundry woman etc. etc. throughout the village and explain everything to 'em. I fancy big trouble will come from the rural farmers. Have you realized that the bulk of the successful farmers – such as employ 6 or 8 hands – are of the pre-Board school stock who rarely read and *have the greatest difficulty in writing*. In addition therefore to their natural wrath, they are troubled with the fear that the bill will expose their ignorance and if there is any passive resistance shyness and sulks will be at the bottom of it. Meantime they are laying their pipes to reduce all carter's wages by 6^d per week!

I see the *News of the World* calls the date the Bill comes in "Lloyd George's *Day*."[3] They'll be "sorry for this in the morning" but were *I* an editor as thank God I am not, I would rub in that phrase.

And that reminds me the owner of *Reynolds Weekly* is a Privy Councillor.[4] *Reynolds Weekly* was high in repute among the Boers in the War – used to find its way to 'em along with the *Review of Reviews*.[5] Were I an Editor etc. etc., I would look up its back files and give half a column of selected extracts. There are things about Lord Milner in 1900–1–2 which are rather pretty. *Do* put a man on to it.

I have observed with delighted sympathy and appreciation your kindly championship of Lloyd George's sunny amiability.[6] (Protect me from having you as an editorial friend!) Now don't you think you could attend to some other member of the cabinet? I suggest Honest John Burns.[7] Tillett to whom you are so unkind[8] has not said anything much worse than Honest John did in his earlier days. Can't a correspondent point that out? For pity's sake look up the files and parallel John of Trafalgar Square with Tillett of the Tower.[9] Then you'll get some more kind letters. Tillett's only blunder is the fatal one of not seeing when people are bored. John was a tactful bird: also he was first on the field with his "penny parcels post to Heaven etc.". He ought to receive encouragement and reminders. You are attacking now the crop that John sowed.*

Later, I want Seely[10] attended to. I suggest that he be alluded to in future as "The Colonel": or, if you think Theodore[11] has pre-empted that title: "The Other Colonel." He is a man who knows it all and hates being laughed at. Were I an Editor I should call him "The Nut" and keep on calling him the Nut. It's a pretty name – suggests youth and gaiety and for some absurd reason irritates a man to whom it is applied more than much better thought out labels.

Also look up what he said when we betrayed the Somalis to the Mad Mullah.[12] S. said in the house that it would do 'em good to be knocked about a bit – or words to that effect.[13] A loyal and honourable soul is Seeley. Love him!

As to my wire about Churchill and Asquith that was given with such profligate abundance of detail that I gravely suspected. Howbeit, it served its turn as a smoke-test (same as you do on drains to see if they leak) and I'm not going to play with my informant seriously anymore.

This I think is all for today. Excuse haste and a bad pen.

Ever thine
RK.

---

*Talk about convenient shortness of the public memory! *Look up your files and remember: –*

> In the name of *Justice*
> Give to each his meed –
> Tillet is the flower
> But Burns sowed the seed!

Or, if you prefer the Basic Facts of Life: –

> Tillett is the midwife
> But Burns he got the kid!
>
> – It takes a generation
>   To show what people did –
> Tillet is the midwife etc.
>
> It takes a generation
>   Before a people learns
> Everything that Tillett says
>   Was preached – by – Burns!

Haven't you a poet on the staff to fit in the verses to that chorus?

Notes
1. Ralph David Blumenfeld (1864–1948), American-born newspaper editor. He had been head of the London office of the New York *Herald*, and after resigning that position sold linotype machines to the English trade. In 1900 he became editor of Northcliffe's *Daily Mail*, but in 1902 joined Pearson's *Daily Express*, which he edited from 1904 to 1932. The second half of that tenure was under the proprietorship of Lord Beaverbrook.
2. About the procedures to be observed under the National Insurance Act. "Hardly any one seems to know what to be at or how to conform to the innumerable legal requirements" (*The Times*, 6 July 1912).
3. The *News of the World*, 16 June 1912, prints an article instructing its readers in the procedures required by the National Insurance Act under the heading "Lloyd George's Day". The Act came into operation on 15 July.
4. James Henry Dalziel (1868–1935), afterwards 1st Baron Dalziel, Liberal MP from 1892 and owner of the popular *Reynolds' Weekly Newspaper*; a part of Lloyd George's entourage, he was knighted in 1908 and made a Privy Councillor in 1912.
5. The *Review of Reviews*, founded in 1890, belonged to the journalist W. T. Stead (1849–1912), who had strongly opposed the Boer War.
6. On 8 June the parliamentary correspondent of the *Daily Express* referred to the "amiable, sunny-spirited Chancellor of the Exchequer". When a reader objected to the terms, the *Express* noted editorially that if he were not "amiable and sunny-spirited … he could hardly have won his way to the position he has attained". There was further correspondence on the subject for some days afterwards.
7. Burns (1858–1943), Radical politician, had a seat in the cabinet as President of the Local Government Board, 1905–14. In his earlier days Burns had been a militant socialist.

8. The *Express* regularly referred to him as "Dictator Tillett".
9. In the current dock strike Tillett had addressed the strikers on Tower Hill, 11 June. The *Express* reported him as saying, in response to the threat of military force, that "if our men are to be murdered I am going to take a gun, and I will shoot Lord Devonport [chairman of the Port of London Authority]". The *Express* described this as "silly violence and sham heroics" (12 June 1918). Tillett was remembered for his addresses to strikers on Tower Hill in the great dock strike of 1889. Burns had had a prominent part in the so-called riot at Trafalgar Square in 1887 ("Bloody Sunday").
10. John Edward Seely (1868–1947), afterwards 1st Baron Mottistone, left the Conservative for the Liberal Party in 1904. As Under-Secretary for War he was called "Colonel"; he had just succeeded (10 June) Haldane as Secretary for War.
11. Roosevelt.
12. Mohammed bin Abdullah, the so-called "Mad" Mullah of Somalia, had caused constant disturbance and destruction amidst the tribes in the British protectorate in Somalia since 1899, and inconclusive campaigns had been undertaken against him in 1900–1, 1903, and 1904. In the face of renewed attacks by the Mullah's forces in 1909 the British determined to defend only the coastal regions.
13. In a debate on the government's policy of concentration in Somalia, 23 March 1910, Seely affirmed "that the fact we are abandoning these posts will, in the long run, make the lot of the people in Somaliland far happier and far better" (*Parliamentary Debates*, Commons, 5th Series, xv, 1705).

To Anna Smith Balestier, [9 July 1912]
ALS: Dunham Papers

[Bateman's]

(Here Rud takes on).[1] We only spent one night in town and by the usual luck found a small hay-stack of letters awaiting us on our return. C. and I have been racing through them together and I carry on while she finishes up cheques and things.

Our dinner last night[2] was to meet Bonar Law the leader of the Conservative party and Borden[3] the Canadian premier as well as several members of his cabinet – Hazen[4] and Foster[5] among them. There were sixty people at five round tables of twelve each – each table dressed with sweet peas of different hues. Everybody was there and as one Canadian woman said to me "I felt like walking about in bound volumes of *Punch.*" At my table – I had Mrs. F. E. Smith[6] wife of the rising star of the Conservative party, to take in – there were Arthur Balfour, *very* happy at being relieved from the yoke of leadership; Lady Londonderry[7] the big, in every sense, political hostess of the party wearing a necklace of emeralds not much smaller than a breast-plate and presenting a noble appearance; Lord Selborne, late High Commissioner of S. Africa, Lady Doreen Long,[8] wife of Walter Long who was one of the leaders of the Conservative party. She was a plain lady but liberally adorned with diamonds: – old Chaplin,[9] the war-horse of the party, McMasters[10] a Canadian M.P. and some others. Carrie was taken in by George Wyndham. Lady Roberts presided at her table – very large and fat. There were also the Dukes of Devonshire[11] and Marlboro,[12] and Lord Lansdowne; and the Salisbury's[13] and Lady Grosvenor[14] and (what every one appreciated most) Mrs. Joseph Chamberlain.[15] She by the way was at my table. She is a sweet thing and it was very pretty to see how every one deferred to and admired her both for her own as well as her husband's sake.

It was an awfully warm night and the rooms were none too big. We talked – every one talked at once – and in the crush afterwards we met Lady Bathurst who is a dear and with whom we hope to lunch on the 17th. She owns the Morning Post and looks about 25 years old with a daughter – out! We went home with Sir Max and Lady Aitken, for a chat after the dinner and did not get to our little beds at Brown's till the unholy hour of 1.30. C. was in her silvery grey dress with her tiara of swinging drop diamonds (I wish you could have seen her) and looked delightfully well. Even now I haven't given you the names of half the interesting people who were there. It was a long time since we had been out in the giddy world and we quite enjoyed it. Now I will let C. take on on her own account. She has gone upstairs to try some things on.

She is not here. It is 5: p.m. I must catch the post.

Love,
Rud

Notes

1. This letter is written at the end of one begun by CK to her mother, dated Bateman's, July 19. Internal evidence seems to point clearly to a date of 9 July.
2. At the Carlton Hotel (CK diary).
3. (Sir) Robert Borden (1854–1937), leader of the Conservative Party since 1901, Prime Minister, 1911–20. He had just arrived in England leading a Canadian mission to discuss commercial and military questions with the imperial government. The main item was Imperial Preference, and Borden's visit was part of Aitken's campaign in that cause (Chisholm and Davie, *Beaverbrook*, p. 114). On 19 July Borden was sworn a privy councillor.
4. (Sir) John Douglas Hazen (1860–1937), Conservative politician from New Brunswick, Minister of Marine and Fisheries and Naval Affairs in Borden's cabinet.
5. (Sir) George Eulas Foster (1847–1931), Conservative politician from New Brunswick, in Borden's cabinet as Minister of Trade and Commerce.
6. For Smith, see 27 September 1913. His wife was Margaret Eleanor Furneaux, who married Smith in 1901.
7. Lady Theresa Talbot (1856–1919), daughter of the 19th Earl of Shrewsbury, married the 6th Marquess of Londonderry in 1875. She was notable as a hostess in high Tory society.
8. Lady Dorothy (Doreen) Boyle (d. 1938), daughter of the 9th Earl of Cork and Orrery, married Walter Long in 1878.

9. Henry Chaplin (1840–1923), in Parliament since 1868; a life-long protectionist; created Viscount, 1916. He was best known for his interest in hunting and racing.
10. (Sir) Donald Macmaster (1846–1922), not a "Canadian M.P." but an MP from Canada. A native of Ontario, Macmaster had a successful career as a barrister in Canada before coming to England, where he had been a Unionist MP since 1910. Borden had just spend the weekend at Macmaster's home in Sunningdale.
11. Victor Christian William Cavendish (1868–1938), 9th Duke of Devonshire, afterwards Governor-General of Canada and Secretary of State for the Colonies.
12. Charles Richard John Churchill (1871–1934), 9th Duke of Marlborough.
13. James Cecil (1861–1947), 4th Marquess of Salisbury.
14. Constance Edwina Cornwallis-West, first wife of Earl Grosvenor, afterwards 2nd Duke of Westminster
15. Née Mary Endicott, an American, Chamberlain's third wife.

To Colonel [W. F.] Prideaux,[1] 15 August 1912

ALS: Harvard University

Bateman's / Burwash / Sussex / Aug. 15. 1912.

Dear Colonel Prideaux,

Thank you very much for your letter which I have delayed answering till I could thoroughly consider it.[2]

There was a bibliography done some ten or more years ago by Mr LeGallienne[3] which was not authorized and which had many inaccuracies. This bibliography was used, I gather, in a recent "Kipling Dictionary" (Routledge and Sons) compiled by Arthur Young.[4] But I feel that no serious harm was done because the book was not authoritative.

Such a book as you propose would have to be checked by me throughout – else I could not authorize it. Now I am extremely busy and have in addition a heavy correspondence and with the best will in the world could not lay upon myself the extra work which this would entail. I am sorry therefore that I cannot give you the authorization for which you ask.

Very sincerely
Rudyard Kipling

Notes
1. The envelope of the letter is addressed to "Col. N. S. Prideaux", but the recipient is certainly Colonel William Francis Prideaux (1840–1914), Indian Army Staff Corps, who was Resident in Jaipur, Udaipur, and Kashmir. He had been stationed in Lahore in the early 1890s, where he was acquainted with JLK (JLK to Col. H. Skey Muir, 11 December [1891]: ALS, Cornell).
2. Prideaux proposed to publish a bibliography of RK. He published notes on RK in *Notes and Queries*, 1897–9, and some of the material he collected towards a bibliography is now at Harvard.

3. RK means the bibliography of his work by John Lane appended to Richard Le Gallienne's *Rudyard Kipling: A Criticism*, 1900 (in which Prideaux's help is acknowledged).
4. W. Arthur Young, *A Dictionary of the Characters and Scenes in the Stories and Poems of Rudyard Kipling, 1886–1911*, 1911.

To Anna Smith Balestier, 24 September 1912
ALS: Dunham Papers

Bateman's / Burwash / Sussex / Sep. 24. 1912:

Dear Mother:

I write once more for Carrie who is in bed (but still on deck) after a rather hectic week end which I will now tell you all about.

For some time past she had been troubled by a lump low down in her back which seemed to press on the sciatic nerve and made walking painful to her. Also she always had the sensation of pain, present or waiting just round the corner. And she walked lame.

About ten days ago – John and Elsie being away on a visit to the Baldwins – she went up to town to see Sir John Bland Sutton who, besides being the best surgeon in England, is also an old friend of ours. He diagnosed it at once as a small fatty tumour (of the sort I imagine that used to take the shape of cysts in C's head. You remember Conland took one or two out of her at Brattleboro and the doctor here did one also). "You'd better have it out" he said "because otherwise it will grow and press more on the nerve. I'll do it myself."

"Can't you do it at Bateman's?" said C. "No" says he. "But you come to my nursing home the night before the operation and I'll do it bright and early in the morning of the next day."

Well. C. told me about this when our trip to the west of England by car was finished.[1] What worried me most was the extent to which C. would *not* like going to a "home" for a night. I knew pretty well what the actual trouble in the back was; and knew also that the operation, *qua* operation, would be very much like the one that Conland had undertaken on her head. We talked it over and decided that she should go up to town on Friday[2] – the day after John had gone to Wellington. We didn't tell John and only told Elsie just before we left. Sir John Bland-Sutton whom I had seen early in the week said: – "All right. I'll operate on Saturday morning at nine o'clock and she can go down to Bateman's by car on Sunday afternoon." I suppose that some day C. will tell you what her feelings were when I left her on Friday night at 16 Fitzroy Square – the nursing home where all Sir John's patients go. There are thirty rooms and, I should imagine, about as many nurses. The walls are painted a very pale pea-green in hard washable paint; the beds are of the proper height for nurses to lift patients without stooping; the elevator is big enough to take a stretcher and there is a pale faint smell of ether and such things up and down the passages. But the place is, of course, the finest and best kept of the kind.

I left C. there at 5: p.m. on Friday. It was *not* nice. She did not sleep much, she told me. Perhaps she will tell you some day how the situation struck her. Polite uniformed nurses came in and out (without knocking which C. rather resented) and gave her her dinner in bed and she had a bath and a dose of medicine. At five o'clock a.m. they brought her her tea and hoped she had slept well! You can imagine her wrath. The only truthful one among 'em was the chambermaid who came in to light her fire at 7.a.m. and (*not* being a nurse) said cheerily: – "Well I don't expect you had much of a night, had you?"

Sir John Bland Sutton himself (this was a great honour) in ordinary clothes *not* the awful white operating smock, came to conduct C. to the operating room and there the thing was done. Incidentally, to my very great joy, the anaesthetist who gave the mixture reported that her heart was "as sound as a bell." She was under the influence for ten minutes or so – the actual cut being about $3^1/_2$ or 4 inches long through fat for the most part. Nothing to do with any internal organ of any sort. Sir John found precisely what he had suspected – a small fatty tumour.

I came over from Brown's where I had spent the night at about 10.30. and found the poor little woman, as you might say, quite drunk for a few minutes. As luck would have it, some painters happened to be painting the house and their ropes hung down in front of her window swaying a little in the wind. As all her room and bed were swaying too, she had the blind drawn down to hide the sight: said it reminded her too much of a ship's side in rolling seas. I don't wonder. I didn't stay long that time but turned up again at 3: p.m. and found her quite recovered but naturally extremely stiff and sore. Then I went down by the 4:50 to Bateman's to tell Elsie (to whom I had sent a wire at 11 o'clock) how things were. On Sunday morning at 10. Elsie and I came up to town in the car with a whole lot of rugs and pillows. We weren't quite sure whether C. would really come down that afternoon so we also took our night things, in case we had to spend Sunday night in town. Saw C. at 12.45 in bed, looking very nice. We lunched with the Bland Suttons and went over to Fitzroy Square at 3: p.m. and saw C. *dressed* and sitting in a chair ready to be took home! Sir John himself helped her into the car – she walked *very* stiffly because the dressing had been painted with collodion and it naturally pulled.

Also she could only sit, lie or recline on one side of her poor little body. *She* says she could only sit on a bit of herself the size of a ten-cent piece. Consequently you can imagine that she had cramps. But she stood the 52-mile journey magnificently even when the car burst a tyre which it did with a loud report. She was quite calm and we got her home at 6. p.m. (we had been running slowly) and put her to bed *very* happy at being home again. Well, that was Sunday night. On Monday morning she sent for her secretary and began to take hold of things. She was bored by lying in bed but she was easier than the day before (she must tell you herself of a little trouble that she had – nothing to do with the operation but *very* absurd and annoying).

At night time she sat up and washed her hands and sat in a chair while her bed was being made. I sleep in the next bed. She did not have a very good night because she could only lie in one position. *She* says she didn't get back to sleep till 1. a.m. but I think she had been dozing some time before that.

She is going to spend today in bed but swears she will get up tomorrow. I hope to goodness she won't do any such thing but she is like her mother – not to held when she is sot. The stitches will be taken out on Friday by the village nurse.

I am more pleased than I can tell you that the business is put behind us because it had filled C. (quite naturally) with gloomy forebodings. Also I am delighted at the practical test of the heart. There is no getting round the verdict of ten minutes under ether and chloroform. Knowing her nature as I do I am sure she will from time to time think that she is growing more tumours inside her but I fancy that as her health gets better with the absence of pain in the hip her whole bodily tone will be raised and strengthened. She will be able to take more exercise for one thing and that always suits her.

As you know I have a moderately large admiration for your daughter but I confess that the nerve, the pluck, the grit and the cool-headedness of my little girl when she was going into what *she* believed offered her an even chance of dying, was beyond all praise. There were a few things at loose ends left over and she spent the two or three days before the operation wheeling them into line and telling me what I ought to do afterwards. The attitude of the nurses in the home when they realized what an exceedingly (from their point of view) trivial operation she was in for was very funny. In a "home" you rank by the amount of trouble that you have in your inside and though they were kindness itself it was difficult for 'em to conceal their lack of interest in – I won't say contempt for – "the patient." C. does not like being called "the patient."

Have just taken this into C's room and there being no ink around I am finishing in pencil.

She wishes me to acknowledge your letter of Sep 16th received this morning and the one preceding it which she found on her return from London. (By the way her pearl necklace is away being restrung by Tiffany – I wonder whether they could do it better in N.Y.)

She is lying in bed quite serene. She sends you her love but says there is nothing more to say. I send you my love too and am

Ever affectionately
Your Son

P.S.   In some ways John reminds us of Wolcott. His hands and feet and nose are very like and he gives promise of being long!

Notes

1.   John and RK went fishing with B. H. Walton at Cawsand, 4–8 September, while Elsie was visiting the Mackails. In their absence CK consulted Bland-Sutton on

5 September. On 8 September she joined RK and John at Exeter; next day they met Elsie at Luggershall and began their western tour: Falmouth, Tintagel, Westward Ho!, Glastonbury, and Salisbury. They returned to Bateman's on 13 September (Rees extracts).
2. 20 September; the operation was on Saturday, 21 September.

To Brander Matthews, [September? 1912]

ALS: University of Sussex

Bateman's / Burwash / Sussex

Dỳr Brandŕ

Yu no I luv yu. Hav luvìd yu for yŋrs. Yu wil sy then that I rite this out ov pūr afeckshun.

I hav got yūr Gātwaze ov Literatuer[1] and I began tu rŋd it. I did not mind "t" as a substitût for "ed". At lŋst I did not mind it mutch but I cood not stummak "thru". It was Helish even az an ordinerry wurd of yūr oone (I bet yu du not rite thru when yu ar riting yūr furst draft) but wen yu import it into a Kwotashun such as "wandered thru the ralmz of glume"[2] I hav to protezt.

Brandŕ it is WIKKID.

It is trŋzon to Leterz – trechery agãntz the Illustrius Ded – altugethr Horid! and besidz, it cutz oph Umerriker from the Komunitie of Sivlizashun and maks it a Montinŋgrin amung the nashunz. Brandr I O mutch to Ummerriker as yu no, but if Shŋ spelz "thru" the wai yu spel it shŋ wil Di ful of Jooz like Herrod or Wurmz![3] And morover no 1 will be sorri. Wen the Japanŋz and the Mexicanz mŋt over her prostrat Korps in Boston and the Germanz okkupi Hoboken with Armŋz the Wurld will onli sa "Thank God; for She was lower than the Broot Beests and we ar glad it is over." No 1 will kare a Dam exsept Me and I shal rite to the Tymz and sa "wunce I luvved her but Brandr Mathuz led her astra and Roozveld helped him".[4]

Notes

1. Matthews's *Gateways to Literature* was published in New York in September 1912. Matthews had notions about simplified spelling, and in this book adopted such forms as "approacht", "altho", "colleag", and "thru".
2. Matthews prints "wandered thru the realms of gloom" (*Gateways to Literature*, p. 16).
3. Acts 12:23.
4. This letter was apparently never sent. In a letter of [14 July 1913] to Matthews RK says that "I *did* acknowledge Gateways to Literature in a letter of fonetik design but it became so dam' scandalous and ribald that I never sent it" (ALS, Columbia University). The original of the letter is now at Sussex, instead of Columbia, where virtually all the other extant holograph letters from RK to Matthews now are.

To John Kipling, 16 October 1912
ALS: University of Sussex

Bateman's / Burwash / Sussex / Oct: 16. 1912.

Dear Sir

The Kipling family were both pleased and surprised to receive your kind letter of the 16th as they were under the impression that you had either emigrated to S. Africa or joined the Turkish Army. Mr R. Kipling suggested that you were at Broadmoor[1] – for reasons of State. As it is only ten days since you have written the wildest conjectures were naturally rife. (That's a specimen of dam bad journalese).

We are still in England. Mother is much better after her operation though she is not quite her old self yet. Phipps[2] has been having an irritated gum (it makes her furious if you call it a tooth ache). Her face swelled and she looked like a wet pillow. All the family is much set up with your news. It's splendid but I *do* hope you've been vetted by your doctor. Remember it's dead easy to overstrain oneself in a long run. Mother of course is not pleased at the idea of the skin being taken off your chest by another chap's boots. It is, when you come to think of it, a somewhat rough and ready way of performing what a mustard-plaster would do cheaper – if not as quickly. The thing to remember is *not* to overdo but to slack in between when you can and to get all the sleep you possibly can. I suppose that now you are so well up in running you haven't got to hang about and wait for a bath. If you do the work for your house take care you get its privileges as regards baths etc.

I expect by this time that you will have taken Oscar prisoner or *vice versa*. Give us full news of the bloody debacle.

By the way, are you following the war in the Balkans?[3] It will be, if the winter doesn't stop it, one of the most merciless wars that has ever been waged. The Turk is, to put it mildly, annoyed and intends to settle the question once and for all. Also there is a danger of Muhammedans throughout the world taking a hand.[4]

Went out today for 2 hours in the woods with your 20-bore. Saw (and spared) four pheasants and a covey of partridges. Heavenly afternoon. Wished you were with me. Tomorrow (if I live) I have to go and make a speech at Ashton under Lyme which is Sir M. Aitken's constituency.[5] I've been sweating blood for days just trying to think what the deuce I am to say. Pity me!

We are busy in rebuilding the little cottage at Keylands as a week end place for Mr Landon to rent.[6] Also a new tenant has come to Dudwell – Dan having moved to a farm near Mayfield. The new man is a cowman employed by a big grazier called Hyland – a huge chap with chin whiskers and a tummy – who wants all the land I can rent him. He looks and talks like a man of substance who knows how land ought to be looked after. He wants it all for grazing cattle and I think I shall let him have all the fields round the house.

Yes, we hope to be with you on the 26th. I believe we shall be at Cherkley[7] for the 25th. I feel as if we were all bursting with news to tell each other when we meet. What about sausages at the Hotel if we have tea together. We have to go on to Basingstoke afterwards.

I observe you say nowt about your work. Send us a line and let us know if your Dorothea's[8] tips have been of use to you.

Dearest love from us all.

Ever
The Pater

Notes
1. A prison for the criminally insane, less than a mile from Wellington College.
2. RK's current name for Elsie: sometimes "Fipps", or even "Fibbs".
3. Montenegro declared war on Turkey on 8 October; Turkey, after settling a peace with Italy (see 8 February 1912, to Colonel Feilden), then declared war on all the members of the Balkan League. The Turks were put on the defensive against attacks by Serbia, Bulgaria, Montenegro, and Greece; the regions fought over suffered terrible devastation. A treaty of peace was signed in 1913, by which Turkey gave up most of its European territory. This "first" Balkan War was then followed by a "second" fought among the former allies of the League.
4. A result that RK imagines in his story "A Reinforcement", *Near East*, 10 May 1912 (collected in Sussex Edition).
5. RK made the speech on 18 October; it was reported in the *Morning Post*, 19 October 1912, and in the Ashton-under-Lyne *Herald*, 26 October 1912 (uncollected). RK said, among other things, that "we are ... under the very shadow of Armageddon, for which ... we are utterly unprepared". He also attacked the National Insurance Act and Home Rule. Aitken was re-elected.
6. CK bought this property, about a mile west of Bateman's, in July. Landon did not move into the cottage as a week-end tenant until some time late in 1913.
7. Cherkley Court, Sir Max Aitken's house near Leatherhead. According to CK's diary, RK was at Lord Curzon's house, Hackwood, on 26 October, at the Aitkens on 28 October for the christening of his godson, Aitken's second son, Peter Rudyard Aitken (1912–47), and with John "to see flying machines at Aldershot" on 1 November.
8. Miss Ponton's. She had tutored John in maths over the Christmas holidays (*Rudyard Kipling at Home and at Work*, p. 16).

To Lord Roberts, 3 November 1912
ALS: National Army Museum

Bateman's / Burwash / Sussex / Nov. 3. 1912

Dear Lord Roberts,

I cannot refrain from offering you my heartiest congratulations on your Manchester speech.[1] If, as I believe, the effect of such pronouncements is to be judged by the amount of abuse elicited, it looks as if the reward of your long labours were in sight at last. I have never heard anything so taken to heart by *all* classes of society: and the fact that 105 Members of Parliament should have pledged themselves to acceptance of your principles[2] is to my mind one of the most gratifying of the results.

The feeling among the common peoples, in pubs and such places, is, so far as I know it, one of amused and rather coarsely expressed contempt for the persons who have paid themselves £400 per annum and now enquire into other people's pensions![3]

Would it not be possible now for the N.S. League to issue a very simply worded single sheet giving the ages between which the young men might be expected to come up for training and the amount of time yearly that they should devote to training. Such a sheet could, without the League being formally committed to the actual length of time and age of recruit, be discussed this winter at the pubs and conservative meetings. I may be wrong but I fancy that the general feeling among the common people now is that they would like a concrete proposal to discuss and get used to. The principle of service has been accepted to a much greater extent than our politicians imagine.

Forgive me for having taken up your time and believe me

Yours always sincerely
Rudyard Kipling

Notes
1. Roberts spoke to a mass meeting of the National Service League in the Trade Hall, Manchester, on 22 October, explaining the German menace, calling for an increased army and navy, and affirming the necessity of compulsory military service: "Arm and prepare to quit yourselves as men, for the time of your ordeal is at hand" (*The Times*, 23 October 1912). The speech provoked much protest from the Liberals.
2. A letter, dated 30 October, supporting the principles of the Manchester speech, was signed by many Unionist MPs and sent to Roberts (*The Times*, 1 November 1912).
3. A question was asked in Parliament by Sir William Byles whether Roberts's pension could be withdrawn (*Parliamentary Debates*, Commons, 5th Series, XLIII, 574: 31 October 1912).

To Frank N. Doubleday, 5 November 1912

ALS: Princeton University

Bateman's / Burwash / Sussex / Nov. 5. 1912.

Dear Frank,

The books have come. I can't tell you how pleased I am with the new Just-So's and with Kim.[1] The former particularly is a delight. I thought Gleeson's illustrations were good when I saw them in proof but in the book they look even better. The orientalized borders to Kim set him off nobly too.

I like the type and paging of Songs from Books[2] but I incline to think now that that two-tinted green cover is a bit heavy. The red leather is *very* good.

We have had rather a chequered summer. Carrie as you know has had to have an operation – not a severe one thank goodness but it pulled her down a good deal and she is only now getting abreast of herself. Elsie has not been quite fit either – just a little run down and pale looking but she, again, is better than she was.

This here business of looking after a family isn't all beer and skittles.

I see by the papers that you've got Woodrow Wilson.[3] Whatever he is and by all reports he seems to be harmless, he can't be one tenth the danger *our* political lot are – and you lucky folk haven't got a Balkans question alight and stinking under your nose. Consider a moment how swiftly Allah puts an end to Empires of which he is weary. The Turk has been in Europe lo these thousand years. He has passed in less than 1,000 hours![4] *Allah Karim*[5]

These are exciting times for Europe. We too hope (be spared) to get away to Switzerland some time in the spring – I had written Cyprus,[6] but one doesn't know whether the Meditteranean will be open.

I am middling busy with odds and ends of work: and you will be pleased to hear that Carrie is altering a cottage on one of the farms into a week-end residence.[7] This amuses us both and furnishes us with exercise for the winter. Dear love to you all – specially Dorothy. (Daughters are nice things when, as I explain to Elsie, well-behaved).

Ever affectionately
Rud.

Notes

1. *Just So Stories* (New York, 1912), extra-illustrated by Joseph M. Gleeson; *Kim* (New York, 1912), in which JLK's illustrations are surrounded by an ornamental border in colour. These were the first editions of these titles to be printed at Doubleday's new Country Life Press, opened at the end of 1910.
2. *Songs from Books* was first published in October 1912 in the US.
3. Wilson (1856–1924), a Democrat, had just been elected President of the US in the election in which Roosevelt and Taft divided the Republican vote. RK later changed his mind about Wilson's "harmlessness".
4. In the Balkan War (see 16 October 1912) the Turks had effectively been driven from their European territories by the end of October.
5. "God is merciful."
6. For "Switzerland" in this sentence RK first wrote "Cyprus" and then lined it out. The Greeks in Cyprus had rioted against the Turks on the news of Turkish defeats in the Balkan War, and the British garrison had, in consequence, been strengthened.
7. The house called Keylands: see 16 October 1912.

To Colonel Lionel Charles Dunsterville, 10 December 1912
ALS: University of Sussex

Bateman's / Burwash / Sussex / Dec. 10 / 1912.

Dear Substantial Colonel –
  'Ought to have answered your letter before this but it got itself hidden under my dawk and only emerged this morning. I'm *awfully* glad they've given you an extension and also that Nicholson (who, by the way, is some, but not all, sorts of an ass) had you up before his commission.[1] I'd like to have heard the evidence.
  It was probably incendiary and unconventional.
  Did I tell you that, the other day, I met old Johnny Baugh[2] in town. White headed but absolutely unaltered in voice and manner. I've been down at Aldershot exploring a new world – the Royal Flying Corps.[3] It's a rummy sensation to stand at the very beginning of things – as it might be with Primitive man when he first launched his canoe. They don't know a dam thing but they are finding it out by experience – such of 'em as live. It's exactly like a kid rolling down a flight of steps and discovering the laws of gravity at the age of two. But they seemed to me to have already developed a typical eye and face. I noticed also that there is a New Smell in the Service – not Infantry (hot or cold), not artillery (which is horse-sweat and leather), not motor transport, which is petrol and oil, but a fourth and indescribable stink – a rather shrill stink if you understand – like chlorine gas on top of petrol fumes plus gummy calico in a shop. That's the stink of the æroplane and (adding more gas) the dirigible. I was furiously interested and the boys were very good to me. They are all quite crazy enthusiasts. One chap is married. His three year old kid asks when he comes home of evenings: – *Did* Daddy come by motor or plane?" The present generation (your kids and mine) of course have discarded the horse from their talk long ago; but it's a bit disconcerting to see the air-generation coming along.
  This summer the wife and I went motoring into Devonshire – *and* to Westward Ho![4] If you'd been with me you and I would have done a blub together. I went into the printer's shop where the old *Chronicle* was printed. *Not a thing was changed there!*[5] Bideford High Street was the same too. But the Coll! … I'll draw a veil over that.[6] It's a line of dirty lodging houses and they seem to have turned the old gym into a private house. I wanted to go up and look at our old study but I hadn't the heart. The trees round the church are twenty foot high and – Cory's baths[7] are for sale. They were all boarded up but I looked through a crack in the door and saw 'em – the same as ever. Don't you ever go back to Westward Ho!
  And that reminds me. Did you see that Crofts has been drowned in Jersey a few weeks ago?[8]

The state of politics here is mixed and hectic beyond words – so bad that I've got a notion that it'll mend. The Balkan show has been a fine moral lesson. I had a chap here yesterday[9] who has just done two months with the Turks – Lule Burgass[10] etc. He never concerned himself about war before that. Now he has come home awfully excited – has just discovered that nothing except trained troops are any use in war! I couldn't help laughing at his conversion.

I haven't heard anything about your boy since he was sent over with one exception. I wish you'd let me know where you are going to send him to his final school. The Modern School-life, tho' different from ours, has still a certain amount of roughness in it. But what impresses me most is the amount of beastliness – elaborate and organized – that seems to exist at some of those institutions. John is now a tall slim youth who plays full-back for his house at Wellington and has rather a reputation as a runner in house-runs. (D'you remember some of our runs from the cattle gate to Coll? When I used to roll along grunting with you and Beresford). He also seems to have a turn for mathematics – which amazes me. He has managed to get himself licked by a prefect – ostensibly for breaking bounds, actually, I imagine, for cheek. The young generation ain't born with reverence in their minds. But Lord! how they are fed and warmed and cubicled and looked after in the modern house as compared to our day.

Well, here's luck and come home soon as let's have a look at you. I enclose a new photo of me out of a book.[11] It's very like – specially about the hair. The wife joins me in love and best wishes to you all and

I am as ever
Gigger.

I want to know when you're coming home, as soon as you can give me the approximate date.

Notes

1. Dunsterville's command of the 20th Punjabis had been extended for a year (Dunsterville, *Stalky's Reminiscences*, p. 239). The "commission" was that on the Indian Army presided over by Field Marshal Sir William Nicholson to consider reductions in the cost of the army. Nicholson had left for India in April and concluded taking evidence in October. RK had known him in Simla when he was still Major Nicholson: see [25–6] June 1888.
2. Mackenzie Walcott Baugh: see 30 January 1886.
3. RK was at Aldershot on 1 November and at Farnborough, 24 November, where he had "a long interesting talk with a Flying Corps Major and Lieutenant" (CK diary). He was at work at this time on his early story involving aeroplanes, "The Edge of the Evening" (*A Diversity of Creatures*).
4. See 24 September 1912.
5. "At Bideford we went to see the printing room in a shed upstairs where Rud used to correct the proofs of his school paper" (Rees extracts, 11 September 1912).

6. "Westward Ho gloomy and depressing to a degree – all going to seed and the old school low class lodging houses" (Rees extracts, 11 September 1912).
7. "Cory the bathman" is mentioned in "The Propagation of Knowledge" (*Debits and Credits*, p. 287). See also Dunsterville, *Stalky's Reminscences*, p. 33.
8. On 26 November, in Sark, not Jersey.
9. CK's diary, 8 December 1912, identifies him as "Ashmead-Bartlett", i.e. Ellis Ashmead-Bartlett (1881–1931); he had served in the Boer War, and was a war correspondent with the Japanese in 1904, the French in Morocco in 1907, the Italians in Tripoli in 1911, and the Turks in the Balkan War in 1912. He published, among other titles, *With the Turks in Thrace*, 1913. I do not know what RK can mean by saying that Ashmead-Bartlett had "never concerned himself about war".
10. Lule Burgas in Thrace was the site of the principal battle in the Balkan War at the end of October 1912.
11. The photograph, cut from a printed page, still accompanies the MS of the letter. It is by Emile Otto Hoppé; taken at Bateman's on 22 July 1912 (CK diary), it was first published in *The Bookman*, December 1912. It shows the bust of RK in profile, looking right, with a pipe in his left hand. The earliest publication of the photograph in a book that I know of is in Arthur St John Adcock, *Gods of Modern Grub Street*, but that did not appear until 1913: perhaps RK had a proof copy.

To John Kipling, 12 December 1912

ALS: University of Sussex

Bateman's / Burwash / Sussex / Dec 12. 1912

Dear Old Man,

You know Elsie's slivery voice? The mail was a bit late at breakfast this morn as the old motor that brings it down from London had smashed up again. So Mother had left the table when your letter came in. I read it out slowly to fat Bird, laying proper stress on your success in Maths which she was pleased to hear. Then I read out the P.S. announcing that you had got the Young Cup.[1] ... I do *not* say that Fipps squealed like a stuck pig or even like a locomotive but she let the house know the fact in one long clear high yell. She tore upstairs howling: – "Mother! Mother! He's got it." As if it was small-pox. A nice child that Fipps. I never saw her so pleased in my life.

I sat at table and lit a cigarette and did a private gloat. Wait till *you* have a son of your own (God help the poor little kid!) and you'll know how *you* feel when your son does well. And *you've* done a double shot – maths and the Young Cup. I don't – between ourselves – much care if you aren't high in form subjects (one can always pull up on them any time) but I am *greatly* rejoiced about your going up in maths. You'll be rather a Duke next term because your Revered masters will respect you for your maths and the Young Cup will ... never mind. I'm not an unkind man at heart so I only say I'm sorry for Roberts. It was a well-calculated and nice little revenge. *Don't* rub it in. *So* sorry you didn't enjoy your pleasant Joan of Arc evening.[2] She was a great lady but hardly the kind to interest a chap for an evening. And you didn't appreciate the company you were in! Shocking! Hope you'll like "Drake"[3] better. I'm looking forward to it no end. You know the programme. You come up *summo ingenio*,[4] by the first train (8.22 at Charing +) and get over to Browns in time for a classic feed. I shall not be at the station because I'm dining at the House of Commons with Uncle Stan on Monday night. Then we perambulate about town, doing shopping and things. In the afternoon Mother and I may go to see General Baden-Powell. In the evening Drake – and then Bateman's next morn, where there will be a lot of things to show you. We leave for Engelberg on Boxing Day – Dec. 26th and you may as well pray for snow, as I hear there isn't much at present. I simply *can't* think of any presents for you this Xmas but if we go to the Stores together I'll give you a look (that's generosity) at the motor-byke you're going to get in the Easters. I believe that Mother is getting you fine raiment and purple linen.

Dear old man we're all very pleased and proud of you and you'll get a high old welcome when we meet. It's only about 120 hours now – what *dam* folly to have a cup run in the middle of the exams.

Ever thine
Pater.

P.S.   For goodness sake tell me what books you'd like for Xmas.

Notes
1. A prize for running in a competition among the members of Pearson's House at Wellington College.
2. A lecture on Joan of Arc by the Reverend H. Bedford Pim given at Wellington on 8 December (Elliot Gilbert, ed., *O Beloved Kids*, p. 145).
3. *Drake: A Pageant Play in Three Acts*, by Louis Napoleon Parker, opened at His Majesty's Theatre, London, in September 1912.
4. Using your superlative abilities.

To Sir Charles Crewe, 22 December 1912
ALS: East London Museum, South Africa

Bateman's / Burwash / Sussex / Dec. 22. 1912

Dear Crewe,

Yours just in: but why haven't we had a line or a sign from Mrs. Crewe? And now the deuce of it is that we're off for Switzerland in a couple of days. However we're going to write to the Standard Bank and get some news of her and Ralph.[1] How about your own health: of which I observe you say naught? And do your plans hold for coming back to England next year?

Bless you for your resumé of your politics. But I want to know heaps more about Botha and Hertzog. I can't imagine Dutchmen fighting each other under any circs: and the spectacle of a Fisher, Malan, Burton, Sauer Ministry[2] labelled "Imperialist" cheers me not at all. I saw it in a paper yesterday. What *is* the truth of the present row and to what extent can Hertzog swing his following?

Our affairs are simply lovely. B[onar]. L[aw]. (whom I love because he hates) has been ass enough to speak the truth.[3] Consequently all the men our side who are intriguing against him are laboriously misunderstanding what he says. Curzon, *of* course, is the chief offender in this respect. The blessed word "Food-Tax" is the banner (sheet, rather) behind which much of the hanky-panky is being conducted.

It would take me about half an hour to give you the silliness of it verbally (How I wish I could) but I can't set it out in writing. My own notion is that our people will simmer down during the Xmas holidays. My *fear* is that they may have an election and win within the next six months – which will be about the time that the present "Government" obligations will mature and I specially want the Government to face the consequence of their own acts. This you may recall, has seldom been done by a Liberal Govt. The air stinks with Marconi and silver contract scandals *plus* navy and oil[4] and these little affairs are better handled by an alert and hungry opposition than by a busy conservative Government. The Insurance Act is still a failure and a great danger and I want it faithfully worked for the next three months. Likewise there is a human possibility of trouble on the Continent in the Spring which I would not deprive the present "Government" of for worlds.

There is no particular law of any kind in England at present. The Knox case and Mr Chester Jones[5] have disposed of *that* and we are all at sixes and sevens in every direction. But as I said my fear is that our side may win too soon and be saddled with the duty of carting away the rubbish under hot liberal fire. We hope to go on to Egypt in February so at least we still have the comfort of being at one end of the Beloved Continent. And I only wish it were 5000 miles south.

Haven't seen anything of Jameson in ages but I have been horribly busy revising a new edition of my books.[6]

With every good wish for you and yours through the new year.

Ever sincerely
Rudyard Kipling

Do let us know for sure when you are coming home.

Notes

1. Ranulph (d. 1937), Crewe's only child.
2. General Hertzog, Minister of Justice, upset Botha's cabinet by his extreme anti-English position, and Botha resigned in December. Botha was then asked to form a new cabinet; this, announced on 20 December, excluded Hertzog and included J. W. Sauer, Abraham Fischer, F. S. Malan, and Henry Burton.
3. At Ashton-under-Lyne, 16 December, in favour of tariff reform and imperial preference, or, in the terms of resolute free-traders, "food taxes". In the reaction that followed, Law had little support from his own party.
4. All three of these scandals have to do with the suspected financial misbehaviour of officials. The Marconi scandal was prolonged and bitter; it involved Lloyd George, Sir Rufus Isaacs, and Lord Murray of Elibank, who were charged with having profited from a government contract with the Marconi Company for a chain of imperial radio stations. A parliamentary commission of inquiry appointed in October 1912 presented a divided report in June 1913; the majority report acquitted the ministers of all wrong-doing, and the ministers for their part admitted having acted indiscreetly. RK's "Gehazi", a savage condemnation of Isaacs for his part in the affair, though not published until 1919 in *The Years Between*, was written while the scandal was still seething (CK diary, 25 July and 1 August 1913). It embodies the violent feeling generated by the scandal. In the "silver contract scandals" official conflict of interest was suspected in the purchase of silver for India through a banking firm with which one of the ministers was connected, but the people concerned were exonerated after debate on the question in the House of Lords in November. The subject of converting the Navy to oil fuel was assigned to a Royal Commission under Admiral Fisher in July 1912, and there was concern that the Government would be delivered into the hands of the "Oil Trust". All three episodes are instances of the intensely hostile state of parties in these years.
5. See 25 December 1912.
6. The Bombay Edition, in 31 volumes, published from 1913 to 1938. Printed in Florentine type, it was originally to be called the "Florence" edition (A. S. Watt to Sir F. Macmillan, 2 October 1912: TLS, British Library). It was sold by subscription, and contains several items not previously collected.

To Edward Lucas White, 25 December 1912

ALS: University of Texas

> *Bateman's / Burwash / Sussex /* Xmas day: 1912
> (warm; wet and windy)

Esteemed Younger Brother –

Didn't I answer your last? Then it must have been no fault of mine but – well if you saw the state of my table you'd understand. I excavated a letter t'other day to which I'd been angrily expecting an answer. It had retired gracefully under a blotter. But don't drop me from the list of your correspondents. I've been very busy over a whole lot of things which I suppose I'll have to print some day. But it's much better fun just to write 'em. Likewise I've been doing verses and revising books.

As usual we've been sitting on dynamite kegs and are now persuaded that there will be no real trouble over the Balkan Question. We shall know more, of course, in March. Ourselves, wife and both babes, are off to Switzerland tomorrow (D.V.) and in Feb. to Egypt just to look at the sun and the sky, and it may be Khartoum. There has been neither winter nor autumn for the last two months – only a sort of grey hottish glue.

Glad you liked "In the presence".[1] 'Tis neither here nor there in a question of art but the tale – both tales[2] in fact – are absolutely, and literally true. Thank Allah, action and reaction are equal and opposite. All our present lawless débacle is producing quite inevitably a harder note of patriotism and loyalty among men who ten years ago would have called themselves "open minded" and such like. Incidentally England is rather an interesting place to watch just now. We've established (under threats) the principle of the recall about which Mr. Roosevelt has been so eloquent.[3] If you want to see exactly the parting of the ways at which this land took the downward lawless plunge, pray you study the ruling of one Chester-Jones (a magistrate) sent down from London to reverse sentence duly passed by law on a drunken engine driver of the name of Knox.[4] It is one of the rare cases when one can distinctly *see* a nation turning a corner. And nobody seems to care very much either. They will in another generation.

Side by side with it, the constant mob violence in "Celtic" "Pictish" etc. nationalities, has awakened a most interesting (because ugly) "national" frame of mind among the down-trodden English who are everybody's dog. I had a simple (?) peasant ask me the other day: – "Why don't these damned nationalities go back where they belong?" And I take it that question will be asked several times in the years to come. So you see I'm not exactly optimistic over the state of affairs here but I do believe our present phrenzy is wearing itself out. It's great fun to see at close hand.

Those Baltimore pictures are more than pretty. They're beautiful – too good for blotters (By the way, U.S. blotting paper is miles superior to our English stuff. How?)

With all wishes for a good and a happy new year.

Ever sincerely
Rudyard Kipling

Notes
1. Published in *Pearson's Magazine*, March 1912 (*A Diversity of Creatures*).
2. The other tale must be "A Reinforcement", published in May: see 16 October 1912.
3. In the presidential campaign of 1912 Roosevelt had advocated the recall of judicial decisions by popular vote.
4. An engine driver on the North-Eastern Railway named Nichol Knox was convicted of drunkenness on 26 October and demoted. The railwaymen of Gateshead struck on 6 December when their demand for Knox's reinstatement was not met. Knox was then exonerated by Chester Jones, a magistrate sent down by the Home Secretary to reconsider the case. The strike was settled on 14 December.

To Colonel H. W. Feilden, 4 January 1913
ALS: Syracuse University

Grand Hotel / Engelberg / Jan. 4. 1913: 5: p.m. Temp – 5 cent.

Dear Colonel Sahib

I do not, of course, know what your experiences in Spitzbergen may have been but I assure you that in our 40 mile run from Cherkley Court[1] to Folkestone on Boxing Day, the Siberian *tundras* weren't in it. Ask Moore if you want further details. I never was out in a livelier blow in my little life and we slammed through or rather *across* it at an average 28 knots. When we reached the sea-front at Folkestone we found the road neatly paved with wet shingle in our honour – a gift from the coffee-brown, white laced channel which was behaving like a crowd of mulattoes in a fit. Never saw the sea deep *brown* before. At this our bowels turned to water – mine specially! – and I wished we might wait over at Folkestone (I *knew* in my heart that with the gale in that quarter Boulogne at $^1/_2$ ebb would be out of the question) but the wife said: – "Come on, you coward" or words to that effect, and I withdrew my objections.

Inside the pier there was an ugly hysterical cross-minded surge. Outside the channel – always brown – was standing on its head. Tide being against wind the waves didn't roll – they eructed! And so we went out – two hundred odd English, each with an offertory box on his or her knees. (I except here a voice raised ten minutes later which said reproachfully: – "Hadn't you better get one for yourself?" Then we performed – on our head for choice with circular variations and double-handed scoops into the brine, and large languid fainting motions that ended in being violently kicked *a tergo*.[2] We four had a cabin – only a beast of a man in yellow oilskins *would* lay his basin, filled, at our threshold. Elsie suffered a little but the rest of us "called upon the Prophet and thought but little of it." Meantime, outside, the basins clashed joyously like cymbals and the voyageurs and voyageuses gave up their lunches and their souls each in his or her proper key. *Most* interesting! I have a theory that the note of sickness (let us call it the vomit-note) bears a definite relation to the person's speaking voice. After an hour and three quarters we neared Boulogne and began the old game of "turn round twice and catch whom you may" (you know that weary game of trying to hit that harbour stern first.) Well, we rolled notably and joyously the first time and missed; flooding the after-cabins. The second time – we didn't hurry – we rolled a lot more, got two converging waves on us and – my own impression is that we touched ground somewhere. I heard that unmistakeable jarr, stop and crack that tells of a plate strained somewhere. Then we circled out warily into the sea again, and after a lot of babble on the Marconi, were told to go round to Calais. When the news was passed around, a voice (evidently at the end of its patience – and abdominal contents) burst out into a loud and despairing – "Oh God! Oh God! Oh my God!" But the Lord was engaged elsewhere.

I didn't care where we went so long as we were shut of Boulogne harbour *and* its environs at dead low tide – we had started nearly a quarter of an hour late anyhow and the wind had about emptied out what water we were entitled to. The only thing that bothered me was that sharp stinging crack aft – so I made casual enquiries and was told, in confidence, that we *had* started a plate. I fancied then that I heard a pump going. But it was comparative bliss to go with the gale behind us till we got round old Gris Nez – the night dead clear now and the S. Foreland looking near enough to light a cigarette at – into sheltered water. And so into Calais at 8.30 instead of Boulogne at 5:30 all our party well *and* hungry. But I wish you had been along. We arrived at Engelberg in dolorous, warm rain – the tail of a vehement thaw. But in a couple of days that passed and tho' we have been having no snow, the frost had settled and strengthened every day and the skating is superb. I am rejoiced to say that Mrs Kipling is skating, more and better, with more pleasure in it than ever before. Elsie is deep in school-figures of an abstruse order so that she may pass a certain test and be enrolled a member of *the* skating club. So far, only two of the judges themselves can pass the tests. John has bitterly lamented the absence of snow for ski-ing but has been consoled by the presence of certain boys of his own age with whom he consorts and has today been taken up, as a promising recruit, by a real, full-grown hockey player. Wherefore his heart is all hockey now.

This game, though painful, surely leads to such swift death or so much expensive mangling, as bobbing down ice-runs where there is no snow to break your fall if you upset. So we get him hockey skates and pray to Allah.

Nobody much here except a few odd men from W. Africa, Nigeria, the Argentine; Australia etc. but I haven't tapped any good tales yet. Fact is I have led the life of a hog on skates: eating, sleeping and exercising four and five hours a day. Peradventure I, even I, may learn yet to begin to skate.

And now let us know our news from our tiny corner – *ille præter omnes, Angulus ridet.*[3] Tho' I don't suppose Martin is laughing much. How goes Keylands? Does Holmes still preserve his virginity or did Boxing day (when I don't blame any man for getting drunk) defeat him? Kindly submit sketch plan with coloured elevation of actual progress of works; carefully specifying approximate soundings, in feet, of mud on the road. Also, how does Curteis[4] stand with regard to this new development of imported (workhouse) medicoes?[5] I am deeply delighted with L[loyd]. G[eorge]. He is our chief asset. But my soul at present is far from politics. We dine tonight, in state, with the proprietors of these Hotels and an Austrian professor of medicine[6] (our good friend for five years here). He tells me incidentally that there *has been no gold in Vienna for the past six months.* Incidentally, 800,000 men are mobilized in Austria.

Well, here's a happy new year to you Colonel Sahib and with all our best wishes to you and Mrs Feilden,

Affectionately ever
Rudyard.

P.S.   And in the papers later I saw that the S.S. *Invicta had* "strained" a plate.[7]

Notes

1. Aitken's house, where they spent Christmas with the Aitkens and the Bonar Laws. They left for Switzerland on 26 December and arrived in Engelberg on the 27th (CK diary).
2. From the rear.
3. Horace, *Odes*, II, vi, 13–14: "Ille terrarum mihi praeter omnes / angulus ridet" ("that corner of the world smiles for me beyond all others").
4. Dr Arthur William Statter Curteis (d. 1943), of "The Ivy", Burwash, RK's physician. He was a graduate of Yorkshire College, Leeds; MRCS and LRCP, London, 1899. His name, a Sussex one, is always spelled "Curties" in the *Medical Directory* but always "Curteis" by RK.
5. The British Medical Association was in prolonged and bitter conflict with the government over the terms of the Insurance Act. The government hinted at the establishment of a state medical service if the doctors did not agree to support the Act.
6. Dr Fröhlich: see [10? February 1909].
7. "The South-Eastern Railway Company's turbine steamer *Invicta* reported damage by the sea to shell plating and several frames" (*The Times*, 28 December 1912).

To Herbert Baker, 24 January [1913]

ALS: University of Sussex

Hotels / Cattani / Engelberg / Jan 24.

Dear Baker,

Yours of the 20th comes to us here in Switzerland where we go every year to play in the snow. If I had been at home I'd have been over to Owletts[1] with all horse-power to congratulate you – and India.[2]

If any man can hold on to Lutyens[3] you are the man: and if ever a man needs holding on to it's Lutyens before he "smarms" Delhi with his affectations. Don't you make up any part of your mind till you see Delhi laid out in the sun with her Minars and Kutubs[4] above her and her dead below. Also, for goodness sake, try to get into Rajputana – if it's only to see Jodhpur and one or two modern buildings in Ajmir.[5] Ajmir otherwise is detestable – but *do* try for Rajputana.

If you were here I'd talk your head off – so be joyful that you ain't. Accept all our best congratulations, and please send our love to the family.

Ever yours,
Rudyard Kipling

P.S.   And about ten (or eleven) years ago there was a man who said he was going to chuck S. Africa? Do you remember??

Notes
1. Baker's house in Cobham, Kent.
2. Baker had just been appointed, with Sir Edward Lutyens, as architect for the building of New Delhi.
3. (Sir) Edward Lutyens (1869–1944), the leading British architect of his generation, best known for his work as joint-architect with Baker of New Delhi. He was later on the Imperial War Graves Commission, and so a collaborator with RK.
4. A *minar* is a tower; by *kutubs* I conjecture that RK means the Kutub Minar, a great tower to the south of Delhi.
5. Both cities were visited by RK in 1887–8 and are described in *Letters of Marque*, chs 6, 12–14 (*From Sea to Sea*).

To Colonel H. W. Feilden, 29 January 1913
ALS: Syracuse University

Hotels / Cattani / Engelberg / Jan. 29. 1913.

Dear Colonel Sahib:

Bless you for your last two letters but what the Hell – that is the precise word – have Brooks & Co been doing all this past month that they have not even now begun to tile?[1] Were they swimming or taking journeys or marrying wives?[2] I expect that they took life easy – and when Burwash does *that* the hour hand of a clock is lively in comparison. Keylands is going to cost about as much as Buckingham palace after the public works dept. has restored it.[3] But you are right about the hidden significance of Keylands. 'Tis the key to the position – the key of the woods.

Landon I gather sits among precarious and agitated ambassadors each telling the other lies that no man believes[4] – no man knowing when the next stick of dynamite will explode, nor whose crowned bottom it will singe. And now I hear that the Poles are awakening to "race-consciousness" on the German side.

I told you did not of young Garnier[5] (Lt. of the 3rd Hussars) the aviator who has been staying here and how he told me that the best horsemen make the best aviators? Well, he has told me many delightsome tales of other races. Here be some.

(I.)   In Tripoli – A Regiment of Italians well entrenched, under cover of the Fleet big guns, see on the horizon a frieze of wandering Bedouins.[6] Arrives, with orders to attack, the Colonel. He takes off his helmet and shouts "Eviva l'Italia!" All the regiment follows suit. Then he shouts: – "Avanti!" "Avanti!" The entire regiment rises as one man, shouts "Avanti" and – remains where it was! Somehow it reminds me of railway travel in Italy.

II.   He (Garnier) was once at Verdun – on the frontier – a sort of receiving house for deserters of all nationalities escaping into France to join the Legion Etrangère. Among 'em was a weary footsore Russian who had slunk some 600 Kilms. on foot from far away Russia. His army service was up. He wished to enter the Legion. Did he like service in the Russian Army? Oh yes. If you are in the army you are no longer beaten by the Police – you beat other people. Why? Oh the Colonel orders it and you beat 'em. What sort of people? Oh – *chefs de gare* – station-masters for example. You beat 'em hard – five or six of you together if the Colonel gives orders. And what does the station-master say? What can he say? *The Colonel has always his cossacks!* That, as Garnier says, opens horizons.

III.   A pretty little study of Russian Regimental Life. A subaltern joins his regiment. After introductions, his Colonel looks fixedly at the boy's boots. "Who made those?" "Such and such an one," says the Sub naming no inexpert St. Petersburgh bootmaker. "Well they won't do for *our* regiment. No man can consort with *us* and wear that sort of foot-case. You must get new boots. Here's the address of my bootmaker and you'd better not parade till he's built you a pair." The sub goes to the Colonel's bootmaker who makes him the boots and charges *300 roubles!* Talk about paying your footing! There was no pretence anywhere that the bulk of the cost did not go to the Colonel and the Lieutenant who told Garnier the tale couldn't see anything out of the way in the incident. And that again, as Garnier said, opens horizons.

Also I have met a charming French Naval Captain, soon to be made Admiral – a Baron, a sailor, and a well-read sahib with a queer triangle of snowy-white hair on his grizzly head which seemed very like the souvenir of an ugly wound. Had done most of his service in the China seas – knew lots about typhoons and respected 'em.

Also, a Queensland sheep-farmer of the second generation, born and bred among the black fellows whom he liked but of whose ethnological customs he knew naught. He was with a mob of 10,000 sheep in N. Queensland, trekking 8 mile a day and wished to camp by a certain lagoon, birdless and flowerless. Said his black-fellow: – "Don't camp there. Bunyip.[7] Camp about a mile away. You won't sleep well *that* place."

But he was tired and camped. Late at night he was woke up by an infernal roaring – rushed out from under his waggon, hitting his head, en route, to find his sheep scattered and his white men as panic-stricken as the sheep.

They said: – "A roaring came up underneath 'em." Then they shifted. Next day he came back to the silent lagoon, spliced three fishing lines together, got on a log by the bank and – found no bottom. He thinks the "roaring" had something to do with steam or volcanic agencies but he says ever since, when one of his own black-fellows told him not to camp anywhere, he didn't.

Also a tale of some black trackers who tracked Ned Kelly[8] (the iron-plated bushranger: you remember?) Ned K. being caught and disposed of, the Govt. forgot the trackers, one of whom strayed into Melbourne, got tight, killed a man, and fled back to Queensland, hundreds of miles. Other black trackers were set on the murderer's trail. He had a slightly distorted big toe on the left foot – and one imprint of his foot was seen at a place called Dora-Dora, by one of the trackers who, two years later, came into my friend's employ in Queensland. They were riding together. Suddenly the black fellow reined up and pointed to the ground saying simply:– "Asinis (that was as near as they could get to my friend's Christian name) Dora-Dora black-fellow here." And it was true. They tracked him and landed him in gaol. My friend said also that an ordinary native tracker will follow a white man's booted track at a canter! But what vexed me was his absolute ignorance of native customs. Their *ideas* he understood perfectly. Loved 'em but always *slept with his face* to his black-fellows. Had been advised to do so by the black fellow who looked after him when a boy, who told him that no black-fellow kills a man facing him. Is that so?

Here's a budget of disconnected gossip but the purport of it all is to beg you to send us a letter to the Hotel Regina, Place de Rivoli, Paris. We expect to be there Monday next: and so far our arrangements to leave Feb. 7 Marseilles P & O Persia hold good.[9] Hotel in Cairo Semiramis but address for all letters etc. T. Cook.

We all send love and best wishes.

Affectionately
Rudyard.

Notes
1. The subject is the work being done on the cottage at Keylands: see 16 October 1912. Tom and Fred Brooks are mentioned in 25 December 1913 as among the workers on the cottage.
2. Cf. I Kings 18:27.
3. The east front of Buckingham Palace was reconstructed by Sir Aston Webb in 1912–13 at a cost of £60,000.
4. Possibly in connection with the peace negotiations in the Balkan War, held at St James's Palace (see 16 October 1912); they had been thrown into confusion by a coup d'état in Turkey on 23 January.
5. Not identified. No Garnier appears on the rolls of the 3rd (King's Own) Hussars. The only Lieutenant Garnier in the *Army List* for 1913 was A. P. Garnier, Northumberland Fusiliers.

6. Even after signing a peace with the Turks in Libya (see 8 February 1912, to Colonel Feilden) the Italians held only the coastal region and faced much opposition from the native tribes in the interior.
7. A monster of Aboriginal myth, said to live in swamps and water-holes.
8. Kelly (1855–80), celebrated Australian bushranger, leader of Ned Kelly's gang, long evaded the pursuit of the police. RK calls him "iron-plated" because during the gun battle in which he was captured Kelly wore metal armour.
9. See 30 January for the actual itinerary.

To H. A. Gwynne, 30 January [1913]
ALS: Dalhousie University

Hotels / Cattani / Engelberg / Jan. 30th.

Dear Old Man,

Yours of the 27th for which many thanks. I know H[ouse]. of C[ommons]. speeches are privileged all the world over but I had hopes that some Rad. journal here might take the remarks over and comment on 'em in such a manner that we could catch him.[1] But it doesn't matter and we'll let it go.

Ever so many thanks for your kindness to John.[2] He sets great store by your words and you seem to have given him a jolly send-off at the station. He writes cheerily from Coll.

Doesn't all this Suffragette racket remind you rather of Ladies Sports on ship just before a heavy gale?[3] When the men ought to be furling awnings and lashing boats they're told off to slice the potatoes, get out buckets, quoits, chalks and string for chalking the pig's eye, and the officers who ought to be on the bridge are hanging around advising their respective females how to pick up eggs with spoons – specially spoons.

We hope to go to Paris (Hotel Regina: Place de Rivoli) on the 2nd. Thence all being well from Marseilles per Persia, Feb 7th.[4]

If you see John this term which I greatly hope you will, try to draw him out on the subject of a profession. It's early, as you say, but I want to make out what is working in the boy's mind.

With love
Rud.

Notes
1. Alexander K. Maclean, Liberal MP for Halifax, Nova Scotia, in a speech on 23 January attacked the ignorant intervention of the Unionists in Canadian affairs. He alluded to RK as the "hired versifier and Poet Laureate of the Unionist party".

RK wrote to Gwynne on 25 January suggesting that, if the remark should be quoted in any one of the "Rad. papers", a libel suit should be brought. "I don't think that the Unionist Party ought to be saddled with me as their 'hired versifier and poet Laureate' and my position is that I don't in the least intend to have it said of me" (ALS, Dalhousie).

2. John left Engelberg on 21 January to return to school. RK wrote to Gwynne on 16 January asking Gwynne to meet John in London "to ask him to an early tea … and send him away with *masculine* councils… . J. has developed a good deal and is just in the state to respond to the advice of a man he looks up to and admires – and I know no man I'd sooner have him hear straight talk from than you" (ALS, Dalhousie).
3. From July 1912 the Suffragette campaign had entered a new phase of violence: arson was the main mode, but there were many forms.
4. They went to Paris on Tuesday, 4 February; Elsie remained there while RK and CK went on to Marseille on the 6th. There they sailed on 7 February aboard the S.S. *Persia* for Cairo, where they arrived on 11 February (CK diary).

To C. R. L. Fletcher, [January? 1913?]
ALS: University of Sussex

Grand Hotel / Engelberg

Dear Fletcher,

I read it[1] (and moreover the wife gave it me) as soon as it came out, read it as carefully as I did Her Letters.[2]

It beats Browning and proves that no art comes up to raw nature. I felt as you did – only I broke off at intervals to curse Stockmar[3] – the dark and deadly Stockmar: political pimp and preparer of our defeat at Germany's hands. The whole Melbourne idyll[4] moved me almost to tears – but I remembered what She said later when she had found "real happiness" in the arms of dear Albert. (It's a brutal selfish sentence worthy to be written on the hearts of those who put their trust in princes. Also it's a complete answer to all suffragettes present and to come. I forget the precise wording but in essence she wonders how she could have thought so much of M.[5])

Really, to me, the book was a study of Melbourne and a world before the flood.

Our snow is now but our frost is here nightly-becomen in great-and-greater-strength. Therefore the rink grossly-overcrowded is and daily as the trains-with-fresh-vistors-filled arrive more to be so threatens. Our percentage of Germans has increased and has affected my lambent style.

I do nothing except eat and sleep and skate – the first two superbly, the last not very well. In my leisure I admire Lloyd-George for the unswerving and fundamental truth of his ineluctable (good word that!) character which he cannot escape. Have you noticed how the Pict of Today is driven to defile the graves of his enemies? It's a mark, of course, of the lower races – even the Goths and the Balts didn't dig up dead Romans much – but if you will oblige me by studying the Welsh disendowment Bill[6] you will see the Pict harrying graves – all same his brother the wolf. No one has noticed it!

With all good wishes for the New Year

Ever sincerely
Rudyard Kipling.

Notes

1. Viscount Esher, ed., _The Girlhood of Queen Victoria: A Selection from Her Majesty's Diaries between the Years 1832 and 1840_, 2 vols, 1912.
2. _The Letters of Queen Victoria … 1837–1861_, ed. A. C. Benson and Viscount Esher, 3 vols, 1907.
3. Baron Christian von Stockmar (1787–1863), formerly physician to Victoria's uncle, King Leopold of Belgium, and now his confidential agent. RK's attack on Stockmar is not, evidently, apropos of anything in particular in the Queen's diaries. Stockmar was instrumental in bringing about the marriage of Albert and Victoria and thus in making a Germanophile of the Queen.
4. Lord Melbourne (1779–1848), Whig Prime Minister at the time of Victoria's accession, when he undertook to act as her private secretary and so saw her constantly: "He treated the Queen with unbounded consideration and respect, yet he did not hesitate to administer reproof. He consulted her tastes and her wishes, but he checked her inclination to be headstrong and arbitrary. He knew well how to chide with parental firmness, but he did so with a deference that could not fail to fascinate any young girl in a man of his age and attainments. The Queen was completely under his charm. The ease of his frank and natural manners, his quaint epigram and humourous paradox, his romantic bias and worldly shrewdness, were magnified by her into the noblest manly virtues" (Viscount Esher, _The Girlhood of Queen Victoria_, I, 35).
5. RK probably means this passage from Victoria's diary of 1842: "I cannot forbear remarking what an artificial sort of happiness _mine_ was _then_, and what a blessing it is I have now in my beloved Husband _real_ and solid happiness, which no Politics, no worldly reverses _can_ change; it could not have lasted long, as it was then, for after all, kind and excellent as Lord M. is, and kind as he was to [me], it was but in Society that I had amusement, and I was only living on that superficial resource, which I _then fancied_ was happiness! Thank God! for _me_ and others, this is changed, and I _know what_ REAL happiness is" (quoted in Lord David Cecil, _Melbourne_, Indianapolis and New York, 1954, pp. 426–7).
6. The bill, introduced in April 1912, was acrimoniously debated at the end of 1912 and the beginning of 1913: it contained a provision by which control over churchyards would pass from the Church to the separate parishes (_Annual Register, 1913_, p. 34). The bill, rejected in the House of Lords, would have become law in 1914 under the Parliament Act, but its operation was put off by the War until 1920.

To John and Elsie Kipling, 10 February 1913
ALS: University of Sussex

FORWARD TO JOHN / S.V.P.

S.S. Persia: / Feb: 10. 1913: 10:30. a.m. / Blue sky and sun – but *not* warm.

Dearest Family: –

Here am I in the smoking-room of a P & O. You'd think it wasn't any way different from a Union Castle but, as Sunshine T.[1] observed: – "There's no smell of paint – nor india-rubber." That was the first thing Sunshine noticed. Then she observed slowly: – "It smells quite different from other ships." That again is true. There is a queer faint mixture of curry, Lascars, and the East generally. It's precisely the same smell as I remember when I was a kid on the P. & O. Nothing has changed on this venerable line. The saloon decorations are all pure pale whites, the smoking room is a highly respectable arrangement in oak and pictures of mermaids; and the stewards are *very* quiet, highly respectable, soft-spoken gentlemen. Our cabin steward is called "Stevenson" but he might be Matchum. Our white haired stewardess is called Mrs. Scott – and she is like all the stewardesses one ever knew rolled into one. The Lascars – the native sailors in their blue clothes and red turbans – are the same (so it seems to me) as the ones I played with when I was five: and the big fat-stomached *Serang* (Lascar petty officer) with his chain and boatswain's whistle might have been the very man who used to carry me about on deck.

You'd be amused over the ship. To begin with, she is a single-screw and she thumps along at about 13 miles an hour.[2] The food is good – what there is of it – and it is served without any frills or flub dubs – dingy silver, table cloths not too clean – salad all dumped into a plate, glasses big and thick and like tooth glasses. *But* the cabins are big and roomy. Everything in them is dingy and battered but clean. And the passengers themselves are a quiet crowd. No rowdy dows on deck; no gambling in the smoking saloon, not even much laughing at dinner.

We left Marseilles with a strong sun, a blue sky and a calm sea. Even Elsie could not have found any excuse for being sick. But there was a Lady travelling with a small red-faced boy called "Robert." She had hired a Scotch nurse (with false front teeth) to look after him. The nurse had never been to sea before. She understood, however, that people are always sick the first night out. So she solemnly turned in and – was sick. She did it, I presume, from a sense of duty but *how* the deuce she could manage it, beats me.

Then on Saturday the sea got still calmer and calmer, till at last it oiled down and looked exactly like the Equator. But it wasn't warm. I never imagined that the terrible gulf of Lyons could behave so prettily. And we went strolling through it – we haven't got the mails aboard so it don't matter what we do – with this absurd old single screw going *wop-wop-wop* – sixty to the minute. Last night about midnight we were roused by the old ship swinging and curtseying in a stately manner. Mummy, after much thought and some words, got up and shut the porthole. But we were on the lee side and nothing happened. Some people on the weather side, however, got the top of a wave or two through their porthole – and we saw their bedding today drying in the alley ways. A familiar sight!

There isn't a thing to tell you about. You never knew or saw or heard of so quiet a ship. A lot of us are getting off at Port Said for Cairo. We expect to get into Port Said about 2: p.m. tomorrow. If there are sixty of us they will telegraph for a special train to take us to Cairo. If there aren't sixty (and, between ourselves, I don't think there will be) we shall be left to knock our heels in Port Said till the regular train goes at 7: p.m. In that case we shall arrive at Cairo about midnight. But as Mother says: – "What *does* it matter? We have only our two selves to think about. No beastly little girl who has to be fed and put to bed. No outrageous boy who demands to be amused."

Quite true: and in a way we feel free but (also between ourselves) we are lonesome – *very* lonesome. The first day we came aboard, as the luggage was being stowed in the hold, I saw – a pair of *skis* – SKIS!!! – going down. Now for what earthly purpose does a man transport skis – full size – black with white lines – to India for? It was a touching sight; and reminded me of ancient days.

Now as I write I can feel the air getting a little warmer: and a big fat gull is sailing over the smoking-room skylight. Mummy is somewhere in the music saloon doing her letters. She is *much* better, I am glad to say. She has got rid of her cough and appears to be enjoying life. If only you two were along I couldn't wish for anything jollier. We are living in the hope of getting letters from you at Port Said. I think the time when I miss you two most is when Stevenson enters with my tea and two bananas in the morning. Then I feel as if it were my duty to hunt for you and take you round the decks in bare feet.

I haven't found anybody interesting yet. There are not many young people and the small "Robert" (who calls himself "Wob") doesn't mind accepting a box of bricks (bought at the barber's) from me but he doesn't want me to help to play with 'em. I tried yesterday. "Wob" stood it as long as he could. Then he screwed up his face and pointed towards the people walking up and down on the decks and whispered: " – you – go – there!" So I went "there" and as I turned away "Wob" said "Good-bye" and went back happy to his bricks.

6: p.m. Smoking room again. Nothing more to tell except that it has got cold and rainy again. This within a day's sail of Port Said. Sunshine with a face like the butt-end of a pyramid has packed most of our things ready for going ashore (it *is* settled that we can't have a special train) and Mummy has gone down for her bath.

It remains only to subscribe myself

dear Sir and Madam

As ever

Your lovingest

Pater

P.S.   Forgot to tell you that there is a lady aboard with an eighteen-year old daughter, going out to Egypt for the first time. *And* tho' the weather is as still as a mill-pond the 18-year-old persists in feeling sick. I told her that she ought to have a brother to rag her. She groaned and went downstairs. Perhaps *she has brothers*!

Notes
1.   Evidently the servant who accompanied them on the trip.
2.   See RK's description of the ship in the first chapter of *Egypt of the Magicians*: " 'O, come and see!' they cried. 'She has *one* screw – only one screw! Hear her thump!' " (*Letters of Travel*, p. 210).

To John Kipling, [17 February 1913][1]
AL: University of Sussex

Cook's Steamer / Rameses III / Monday morning. 7.20 a.m.

running down the Nile.

Dear Old Man –

The only trouble in this letter is how and where to begin. We are in a Cook's river steamer – an elaborate house on a boat, as per picture post-card, leading a life like life on an ocean liner except that we tie up every night as we used to do on the Norfolk broads.[2]

We left Cairo by train at 8:30 a.m. last Friday morning. The train might have been going from Salt River to Johannesberg except that the dining car (International Wagon Lits Co.) was pure white and the grub was a shade better than they give you on the Cape trains. The night before we left Cook's man came to us and said that our steamer "Rameses III" had stuck on a sand-bank just off Assuit and that he didn't know when they could get her off (steamers are apt to stick on sandbanks when the Nile is low). However, some way or another they got her off and when we reached Assuit (which is about 200 miles from Cairo by rail) we found her waiting for us – all clean and swept, with big carpets, and easy chairs and writing tables on the deck and the black stewards getting tea ready. Exactly like a house-boat.

We left Assuit in her about 4: p.m. and had to make a very awkward turn in order to get out into the river where a dredger was dredging mud. While engaged in the manœvre we hit the bank an awful wop – said bank being faced with stone, thus [sketch of stone bank, steamer, and river; in background a structure labelled "this is the Assuit barrage"]. I heard a whack and a crack which were sufficiently familiar to me – reminded me of Boulogne in fact.[3] Then we paddled out across the river which is about a mile wide and in less than ten minutes ran ourselves ashore on the edge of a sand bank just at sunset. It was necessary for us to do this because we had cracked one of our plates and we were making water. A naked devil went overboard to locate the leak and, I suppose, they must have puttied it up somehow for after two or three hours we got off the bank and began our journey up the Nile by moonlight. This isn't usually done but we had a good pilot and the moon was strong enough to show us the outlines of the sand banks and the sails of the native craft. Of course they carry no lights and take a hellish joy in tacking just under the nose of Cook's steamers. One has to slow up for 'em every few minutes just like sleepy carters on the road in a car. Well we carried on till 2.30: a.m. on Friday night, or rather Saturday morning – and when we woke this was the landscape we saw [sketch of river, two sailing boats, and line of palms on bank]. It never changes – it runs for hundreds and hundreds of miles and it is always interesting.

The Nile at present is low and one can't see over the dark earthen banks – exactly like the banks of the Dudwell when there has been a slip – but magnified ten thousand times. There is always a native village of square mud huts and big towers of mud for pigeon-cots: there is always the solemn fringe of date palms behind it: there is always the vivid blue-green of young wheat, or onions or the pale goldy-green of sugar cane and behind everything else, four or five miles away is the pale pinkish grey of the utterly barren hills of the desert. One feels that one is sliding down a gutter less than ten miles wide. I had no notion Egypt was so long and so thin. It's an absolute length-without-breadth-country. *But* you never saw such cultivation. They get three and *four* crops a year off this amazing Nile mud, which again is only the silt of the Dudwell: and, *on an average* after all expenses have been paid, they make £7 (seven pound) profit per acre! At these rates our land at Burwash would fetch us in over £2000 a year. Of course all this cultivation is limited to where the water can be put on the land and where the Nile can deposit its honey coloured mud. The traffic on the River is incessant. Boats loaded with chopped wheat straw for the beasts to eat when the country is flooded, pots for pigeon-nests; pots for drinking water; lime, stone; sugar cane and all that sort of thing are always in sight. They navigate by the grace of God but they don't seem to come to any harm. At least we have only seen one wreck of a dahabeah[4] and that looked very ancient.

The rummy thing is the climate. It's – not to put too fine a point on it – rotten cold in the mornings and the evenings and today, within 2 or 3 degrees of the tropic, it hasn't got warm yet at 11: a.m. I have been wearing my thick winter things till today and only wish I'd not taken 'em off. The sky isn't S. African blue but a sort of washed out pale bluish-grey. The river is a pale brown and the banks are dark-brown and the natives are blue black with a smile on 'em like a split water-melon.

The night before we left Cairo we dined with Fitzgerald,[5] Kitchener's aide-de-camp – the man who saved K's life on the last occasion when an Egyptian tried to assassinate him. Fitzgerald is a cheery bird – all medals and decorations and hard service with a cheery brown face. He is a Wellington boy of course – Hardinge dormitory – and knew all about Pompey.[6] The man on my right was Captain Flower[7] who runs the Zoo at Cairo and is *quite* one of the most interesting men I have ever met. He can tame anything that exists from Panthers to snakes and knows more about the inner private life of snakes, bats, wolves and hyænas than any man. He was a Wellington man of course (every one out here seems to be Wellington) and *of* course knew Pompey. Spoke of him with great affection. We are going to Cairo Zoo as soon as we get back and Flower says he'll turn out all the beasts for us to play with. Did I tell you that the Hippo's name is Kitty. And he has trained her to sit up and beg! *Quite* mad but as I have said one of *the* most interesting.

And last night, sitting on the deck after dinner, an old chap called Pasley[8] who used to be in the Navy and is now Secretary of the Royal Yacht Squadron told us a story which is worth preserving. We were talking about Marryatt's novels which Pasley knew by heart and some one said something about *Snarley Yow*.[9] "Well" said Pasley, "I'll tell you a tale (you needn't believe it but it's true) about another *Snarleyow*." And he began: – "When I was in the old *Blanche* (cruiser) on the Jamaica station, our Captain who was a bit of a brute, bought (or stole) or somehow procured at Havana an awful hound as bad tempered as himself which he said was a Cuban blood-hound. He called the beast Limon: and Limon used to take a piece out of you whenever he got the chance. All the ship's crew and all the officers hated him and, after some weeks when we were lying in a harbour of one of the South American ports, a young officer of the name of Meredith, saw the back fins of at least three sharks under the counter and promptly kicked Limon overboard, in the hope he'd be eaten. Devil a shark 'ud touch him. The Captain heard the splash, saw the splutter, ordered the life boat away and Limon was rescued. Defeat no. 1. for the crew. A few weeks later, the Blanche being then at another S. American port, young Meredith went ashore with Limon under pretext of giving the brute exercise and tied him firmly to a tree with a rope. Came back and reported Limon as lost. Great hopes that the Blanche would have to sail without him. *But* half an hour before sailing *Limon* came flying aboard. He'd gnawed through the rope and escaped.

A few weeks later, at some port in British Honduras where small-pox and yellow jack were raging, the Blanche sent a boat ashore with the mail. She wasn't going to let any of her men go ashore. Limon of course flung himself into the boat as soon as it was lowered, and being the Captain's dog no one interfered with him. The instant the boat touched the jetty Limon was off, up the street and fighting with strange dogs and out of sight. The midshipman in charge of the boat came back, apparently depressed but secretly elated, with news that Limon this time really _had_ been disposed of. The Captain was pretty wrath but even _he_ couldn't take a dog aboard out of an infected port. So the Blanch went away and continued her cruise from island to island and six or eight weeks later fetched up in the harbour at Barbadoes. I don't know how far that is from British Honduras – say 800 miles. Anyhow, the Royal Mail Steamer came in as she was there and suddenly over its side, leaped the undefeated Limon. He'd recognized his own ship and plunged at once to rejoin her. The crew received him with cheers, made him as big a pet as they had made him a beast before; his nature was changed and chastened. He became the idol of the ship and after many years died and had a tombstone erected to him by his sorrowing owner.

Do you know what he had done? No mail packet touches at British Honduras. The wise beast had stowed away on a tramp steamer to Colon on the Isthmus where the British consul knew him and his owner and the consul had shipped him on the R.M.S. packet to Barbadoes, to be sent on, as occasion served, to Jamaica which was the Blanche's dockyard. But Limon as soon as he saw the Blanche made his own arrangements. How is that for a tale? Doesn't it almost equal the original Snarleyow – Limon was always a Devil – even when the Blanche's crew loved him. At least, he wouldn't bite them but he bit everything else that wasn't connected with his ship [the rest is missing].

Notes
1. This letter is published in Gilbert, _O Beloved Kids_, pp. 153–7, under date of [24 February 1913]; internal evidence makes 17 February almost certain. RK and CK left Cairo by train on 15 February for Assuit, where they began their Nile voyage; they reached Wady Halfa, the far point of their trip, on 27 February, and they were back in Cairo on 11 March. Their stops in between included Karnac, Luxor, Thebes, Assouan, and Abu Simbel.
2. In 1906: see 19 August 1906.
3. See 4 January 1913.
4. A large Nile sailing boat.
5. Lt-Colonel Oswald Arthur Gerald Fitzgerald (d. 1916) had been Kitchener's ADC since 1906 and remained on his personal staff until the end: both men drowned in the sinking of H.M.S. _Hampshire_. Fitzgerald shielded Kitchener, who had been Consul-General in Egypt since 1911, from a would-be assassin in the Cairo railway station in July 1912.
6. John's housemaster, John Pearson.
7. Captain Stanley Smyth Flower, 5th (Northumberland) Fusiliers, in Egypt since 1901.
8. Thomas Pasley (1861–1927), retired from the Navy in 1898 as Staff Paymaster and was afterwards Secretary of the Royal Yacht Squadron.
9. _Snarleyyow, or the Dog Fiend_, 1837, a novel by Captain Marryat.

To [John and Elsie Kipling], 2[5]¹ February–2 March [1913]
AL: University of Sussex

S.S. / Prince Abbas. / 160 feet long: / on the road to Wady Halfa: /
Tues: Feb. 24: 10. a.m:

Did I happen to tell you anything about the great dam at Assouan? I fancy I alluded to it casually.² It is about 100 feet high *but* it holds back the water for 120 miles! We are now sailing on a Nile without sandbanks, without any shallows – a river that runs brim full slam up to the orange and black rocks of the desert. It's exactly – to compare very wee things with enormously big ones, like the Dudwell when it's full. But the extraordinary thing is to see over a hundred miles of date-palms with only their tops sticking out of the water. You see they added sixteen feet more to the height of the dam only a year ago: and as there is less than a foot of fall per mile to this most marvellous river, the effect of that rise is felt all along. Here's a rough diagram of what I mean [sketch of Nile with drowned palm trees]. There is a line of half drowned date palms on both sides of the river showing where the actual banks of the river ran before they built the dam. Of course in the summer when they let out the water to irrigate all the cotton-crop of Lower Egypt the date palms will breathe for a few months but in the long-run they will all die. A palm can only stand being stuck in water for three months at the most – and if water gets into the crown of leaves it dies and turns white like a skeleton.

Meantime the effect of this great river being turned into what looks like a canal half a mile wide is very curious – utterly unlike the straggly shallow sandbanked Nile below Assouan. The people too are different, being black Nubians with flashing teeth – not Egyptians. The costume of the children on the banks is of extreme simplicity [sketch of five children]. One small maiden whom I saw just now was rather elaborately dressed in a Nubian confection of bootlaces and cowries – not too many of either. Here it is: – [sketch of boot-lace and cowrie necklace]. There were also a few blue beads mixed up with the cowries. From time to time our steamer stops – a bell rings: a plank is let down from the boat and we all troop ashore like a school-treat shepherded by our dragoman (he jaws more than Ibrahim of the Rameses III did) and are taken round a temple. The temples here aren't built in the open like the ones in Lower Egypt but they are cut out from the solid rock with just a portico, and the remains of an avenue of sphinxes in front of 'em – rather like this [sketch of approach to temple portico]. They are all awfully impressive in their gloom and darkness (an oxy-hydrogen lamp is employed to light the inner chambers) and they all stink of bats – which is one of the most concentrated stinks that I know.

We saw the temple of El-Sebra this morning. Lord knows how old it is. They are only just clearing away the sand that filled it up – but about

1200 years ago it was turned into a Christian church by the Copts who painted their saints and their crosses all over the hieroglyphics. The result is rather weird. There's a bad figure of St. Peter mixed up with a relief of Rameses II who seems to be offering incense to it.

Feb. 25[3]   II
Wednesday: 9.30. a.m.

I forgot to tell you that when we were ashore yesterday afternoon visiting a temple, a native came up carefully carrying a green branch and bade us look at it. In among the leaves, one eye cocked forward and t'other cocked back sat a chameleon – bright green. But he wouldn't perform as a chameleon should for, even when the man dumped him out on the yellow sand and pulled him by his tail he wouldn't change colour. None the less we blessed him because it reminded us of old days on the Union-Castle.

We tied up last night at the foot of an enormous red rock that stuck out of the edge of the desert and was crowned by an old Egyptian temple, all mixed up with a Roman fortress and a byzantine church. I wish I could give you any idea of the desolation of the place. It was one huge heap of grey, brown and black speckled stones and behind it was the absolutely desert desert. Not a breath, not a sound or a blade of grass – nothing but stones, rocks and blown sand [sketch of enormous rock with steamer at foot, captioned: "all the lower part is rose-red"]. We had to climb this place by a winding road and then we waited at the very top, all among fallen columns and dangerous-looking old walls of loose stones for the sun to set. I suppose we must have looked over 50 miles of desert with the Nile a mile wide at our feet. There were a few villages on the edge of the bank – bits of vivid green against the orange of the sands. Everything else was orange and the hills were black. But the space, the dry air and the absolute *silence* of the huge view were beyond anything I had ever seen. And when the sun went down in greens and reds and the river turned to violet and gold and a big string of pelicans began to fly into the desert, it was magnificent.

Today we are pounding on and on with the desert on each side except for a few yards – sometimes almost feet – of green crops on either hand. Now and again the cultivated strip widens to quite a hundred yards and one comes upon date palms and acacias and water wheels whining and creaking. Our steamer, too, often skirts one bank or other of the river within a few feet of the bank and we look right *into* the village across the shade of the tall palms. It's a most curious sort of existence – life on what feels like a luxuriously appointed ocean liner, on a river, *in* the middle of a desert.

But our life ain't *all* luxury. Our cabin is next the ladies' bath room: so that we know all about it when any woman bathes. They prefer to begin to wash at about 10: p.m. The baths are tin: the taps deliver a strong supply of water. It runs in like a gong and runs out like a dying pig. I need say no more.

Mummy has said it all. On the other side of our cabin live two American boys. Their mother sends 'em to bed at nine. They have had all day to jaw in but they defer the discussion of really exciting subjects till ten. Last night they argued for 20 minutes as to what was the precise colour of brown. Then they ragged over it. Then their mother came in to see that they had cleaned their teeth. Then she read 'em some verses from the bible. Then she had to kiss 'em. Then she said good night. Then she really said good night. Then they had to have some more talk. Then she said she must go. Then they argued. Then she went. Then they began to talk – and kick – and giggle. Then I beat on the wall with an angry fist. They'd been 40 minutes going to bed which is quite long enough for any one. Then I heard one say sulkily to the other – "I wonder who is in that next cabin any how." *Then* – Allah be praised – they went to sleep! If it hadn't been that I also have a boy I should have kicked up a row at the end of 20 minutes.

Our other fellow passengers don't seem to be specially amusing. A large amount of 'em are Americans – two are Californian girls and one of 'em spends all her time playing cards *and* singing. She sings as she plays which adds variety to the game.

III.   *Abu Simbel*:

Thursday. 27.th. 9. a.m.

There isn't any use trying to tell anyone about the great temple of Abu Simbel. I've sent you post-cards which pretend to give an idea of the four enormous statues of Rameses – each sixty six feet high – carved out of solid red sandstone which sit outside it. They are like a novel by Rider Haggard! Two of them are rather battered by the course of 4000 years but two are almost untouched. They sit with their hands on their knees and stare out straight across the Nile at the rising sun. You look up and up at them and feel a worm. That is all there is to it. Then you go into the heart of the temple, all cut out of solid rock and find eight enormous pillars each a full sized statue of Rameses. One of the pillars is an exact likeness of Napoleon! Rameses must have been something of a man!

Well, we were with our party and the dragoman was reeling off whole yards of guide books for our edification when suddenly a letter was brought to me by a strange Arab. It said that Mr and Mrs Newman would be very pleased if we would come to tea with them at 4.30 and Mr Newman would show me his pictures.[4] My first thought was that we had gone mad – quite mad. Then Mummy and I recollected that we had seen a striped painting-tent, very like a bathing tent on the banks of the river just outside the temple and that an old gentleman and lady had fled away in a boat just as soon as our joyous party of forty had landed from the steamer. So I wrote on a card to say we'd be happy to come. It seemed odd that we couldn't retire into the inside of Egyptian temples without getting a letter.

At four thirty there appeared round a bend in the river a boat rowed by four aged Arabs, with green weed trailing from its sides: and *then* I saw the two thin masts of a private dahabiya (don't laugh, you little beasts) still further down stream. We set off in great state and in about ten minutes were rowed to an old, old red and white dahabiya like this: – [sketch of boat with captions: "tables and chairs on hurricane deck" and "owners living rooms"]. An old gentleman, with bright eyes and very brown hands, and an old lady with silvery hair parted in the middle, both with very low voices, received us and took us into a private drawing room the full width of the boat – say 17 feet wide and perhaps 15 feet long (the full length of the dahabiya is 100 feet) and then, very quietly, the old gentleman (his name was Mr. Newman) showed us his pictures. His sole business in life was to paint the old temples – specially the temple of Abu Simbel. You never saw such pictures. They were taken in every stage of the light and season. Some showed the old coloured temples of philæ – it is all drowned now since the Assouan dam was made and well, he told us that he has come to the Nile every year for 26 years: and for 23 years in the same dahabiyah. He bought it off a consumptive and in the 23 years it has been repaired again and again and again. They have kept their servants nearly all that time – which accounted for the appearance of extreme age in the cook and the waiter. They had turned the old dahabiyah into a treasure trove of all sorts of things – Egyptian, Persian, and Italian – brocades, beads, things found in tombs and priceless bits of old china. To look at, you would say that these two frail old people needed a nurse apiece but there they were tucked away under a bank of the Nile 600 miles from Cairo, as happy as a pair of pigeons. All the villages from Assouan to Wady Halfa knew them and they bought fowls and eggs and milk from the simple peasantry. They had given up sailing long ago. The sails were stowed away somewhere in the hold, they told me. When they wanted to move from one place to another they just waited till a government steamer came along and were towed. It reminded me somehow or other of the Ancient Mariner and the Flying Dutchman and Darby and Joan all mixed. But the sight of the beautiful drawing room, and the big cabins with standing beds and all the arrangements which they had thought out for themselves in the past quarter of a century, has made mother and me dead keen on getting a dahabiyah of our own. We talked last night how we'd furnish it. If you're good you may be invited aboard.

IV

We spent about two hours there and then were rowed back in the magnificent twilight light.

Oh, I forgot to tell you that the sands round Abu Simbel are a magnificent orange and are supposed never to lose their colour. To make sure of this Mum and I got a big bottle of Evian (empty) with a cork and set out to fill it at the foot of a glorious sand slope. Of course *all* the available Nubian kids (about ten) came to assist *and* to hinder. One young devil – rather like Johann in his youth – did the hindering. He climbed up the slope and began chucking down *damp* sand with both hands till I wanted to kill him – but I had to laugh. However we got our sand and it is a rich ripe orange. Last night we made the discovery that the donkeys of these parts do the work of cocks. There was one small beast in the tiny strip of cultivation that we tied up at and that dam' little beast (perhaps he was wanting his mummy) crowed – I mean, brayed – every three hours. He woke us up at dawn – such a fiery orange dawn – and as our cabin door was exactly opposite the Four Terrible Statues – we stayed awake and saw the sunrise hit them. It was an awful sight. First the great Colossi were dim clay colour – one could hardly make out what they were meant to be. Then they got clearer and as the morning light fell on their faces, it looked as though they were alive and struggling to get up. One figure particularly seemed to be just on the point of rising up. Then the sun fell full on 'em and they seemed to freeze into stillness again. I can quite understand why there are always colossi and hideous stone images in Haggard's yarns. If I lived in Egypt long I'd believe any yarn about *any*thing.

Now we are pounding on again up the river. It has got full of sand banks once more and from time to time our boat almost stops and the men at the bows begin to sound with long red and white painted poles. The desert is close on both sides of us, squeezing in the little thin strips of cultivation – date palms, acacias, wheat and millet. There are no more kites even. There isn't anything for 'em to pick up. The dragoman has just entered the smoking room with the news that there is an interesting "*Beez*antine" fortress on the bank. This is its exact "interesting" picture [sketch of fortress, with caption: "Telegraph poles in the foreground. The 'fortress' is dark brown mud"].

Sunday: Mar. 2: 1913.
On the way back from Wady Halfa where I sent John a telegram. Wady Halfa is the last edge of desolation where the railway line starts off for Khartoum across the desert. There's no hotel, there's no bazar: there is just the strip of thin green beside the river and then comes the desert. But somehow one doesn't get tired of the desert. It is always changing. While we waited at Halfa our party went off on donkeys across the desert to look at the Second Cataract. Mums and I stayed behind and when every one had gone we went for a walk into the said desert. We climbed a stony kopje and found 25 rock cut tombs all round it. Some of the tombs were drifted up with sand but all that we could see into were full of bones and skulls as white and as thin as paper. There were moss agates on the sands and I picked up a few to have them polished when I get back to England. The steamer had to wait at

Halfa for the Khartoum train. We expected to meet all the Doubledays in it but only Mr and Mrs D. turned up.[5] The others – Dorothy and Florence Johnson etc. – were touring in Italy. Our Cook steamer was too full for them to be able to get a place in it, so, to our great regret they had to go by the Government boat which is a big steamer chock full of passengers. However in our brief talk with them we arranged for a meeting in Paris. The funny thing is that they never knew till Elsie wrote to Dorothy that we intended to go to Egypt too. If we had only known we could have arranged our dates to fit. As it was we neatly managed to miss each other at every turn. They had had a spiffing time at Khartoum and had bought snake-skins, tiger skins, assegais and no end of curios. Mr Doubleday brought me back a terrible Abyssinian knife. We were both awfully sorry that we couldn't go on to Khartoum but the weather is getting hot (104° in the shade at Khartoum already) and we want to turn our faces northward again. There is something awfully impressive in the sight of the great cool white train steaming out to Khartoum when one remembers that less than fifteen years ago the whole Soudan was just one pigstye of blood and butchery and fire. One can go on beyond Khartoum for six days in a steamer and see crocodile and pig and hippo rioting along the banks. It's so funny to hear the tourists who had done this talking casually of seeing giraffe!

Well, altogether this has been a most marvellous trip and I think it has done Mum a lot of good. We expect to get to Assouan after lunch; then we take a little railway trip of 5 miles to get below the dam and join the steamer Rameses (*not* Rameses III) which takes us to Luxor tomorrow morning. We ought to be at the Luxor Hotel on the 4 or 5th and expect to stay there a few days. But we hope immensely to get your letters at Assouan. It is ages and ages since we have had any news of you but our hearts are always with you. I will leave this sheet open so that I can just acknowledge your letters when they come, and after that, be spared, we sit down and write you at length. Dearest love, meantime, from us both.

[no signature]

Notes

1. RK dates the letter Tuesday 24 February; but Tuesday was the 25th in 1913: I conjecture that he has the day of the week right but the day of the month wrong.
2. RK describes a visit to the dam in his letter of 21–3 February [1913] (ALS: University of Sussex).
3. Presumably the 26th.
4. Henry R. Newman (1843–1917), a New Yorker originally trained as a doctor but drawn to painting by his study of Ruskin. He went to Europe in 1869 and settled in Florence. Ruskin was among his admirers, and Newman did some work as a draftsman for him. His wife, the former Mary Watson Willis, whom he married in 1883, was English. Most of Newman's paintings are now in America.
5. This was on 28 February (CK diary).

To Colonel H. W. Feilden, 27–28 February 1913
Text: Copy, University of Sussex

S.S. Prince Abbas. / Cook's Nile Service. / Feb: 27th 1913. /
Thursday, 2.45 a.m. 82°

Now where the deuce am I to begin? We're at the end of everything here, under the far off dominion of Khartoum; and the Egyptian Telegraph Office is tucked away in a corner of the Soudan Govt. offices. Even Cook takes second place and is given an anchorage far from the town while the Government steamer lies proudly in the exact centre of the landscape. The E[gyptian].S[tate].R[ailways]. of the Railway trucks was left at Assouan. We are S[oudan].G[overnment].R[ailways]. in huge brass letters on the Khartoum express which we have just been saying good-bye to. The shade-less blinding platform – with one purposeful ant hurrying off half a dead wasp whose wings flickered in the glare like mica – might have been Umballa in May: only that the carriages were Cape Govt. Railway in size, arrangements and shape *plus* one notable exception—*one Sahib one compart-ment*. Your card neatly stuck in a slot – vertically! – outside the door, a wicker chair to change into when the leather bunk became insupportable, and the things for night – *heavy* blankets – all neatly laid out beforehand. For the first time since the Cape we felt the ground hot under our feet. And yet C. and I had left the steamer thoroughly chilled, I wearing my aquascutum and she her coat. After all, Father Nile is no more than a 5000 mile gutter down which draws a most damnable draught from the North. We have not really been baked through since we started, and the chill of morning and evening send one into thick things at once.

Wady Halfa is – just Wady Halfa; a long, dirty bank of the River, speckled with donkeys, boxes, bales, coal-barges and cattle-steamers crammed with mild-eyed cattle from Khartoum going to Cairo to be beefed, Government steamers and nondescript harbour craft at the bottom of the bank. At the top against the pale blue sky a line of flat-topped, blue-washed native buildings, an acacia or two, a line of mud walls and that is all; except that the monotony is broken by the rigid corrugated iron back and dull red brick walls of the English church. Here you are: – [sketch]. The rest is sand-bars and *eau-de-nil*. There isn't any hotel: there doesn't seem to be an administrator in charge except God (and we all know how casual He is) and the Bimbashi, who asserts that he is in charge of the postal arrangements, ought to be licked to death with his own stamps. The office was frankly asleep when our horde of tourists invaded 'em. A casual native with a handful of stamps turned up and sold 'em out of his grimy fist into ours. That was the moment our American tourists (and they are in the vast majority) chose to start a collec-tion of Soudanese stamps of all values! Useful when one wants to catch a real mail. However we got off a telegram to John, after much discussion and the production of a huge book. Said the Babu in charge (he looked like a cross between Zangwill[1] and a Pharoah): – "You must send it to Wellington College Station. Otherwise they will not be able to identify". So do the ends of the earth come together in the Cable Address Book!

Then in the cool of the evening for a walk through the spacious and absolutely odourless town of Wady Halfa, where we saw the barracks of the 2nd Soudanese Regiment; the local hospital; the mosque and a crowd of youths playing football – "soccer" if you please! – in the desert. I asked a passing donkey-boy who they might be. "E-school", says he. "Yes, but what do they call the school?" says I. "Madrissah", says he, and goes on marvelling at my folly. I see the casual tourist gravely describing the "Madrissah School of Halfa".[2]

Friday morn: 10.30 Up the river a few miles above Halfa. Oh but I wish you had been with us this morn. All the rest of our crowd went either by donkey or boats to see the Second Cataract. C. and I waited till they were gone and then set off for a stroll across the desert – the unmitigated howling desert. We could hear it howl in the breeze. It's a dam sight more hopeless than anything I've ever struck in the way of desert. I fancy a lot of it must be volcanic, but the merciless wind has scoured and scrubbed and sand-blasted every ledge and boulder and rock down to bones and lace work. These rocks lie out in violet and pale French-grey beds and the coarse-grained desert sand runs into every little hollow a rich orange. Then there's a sprinkling of what looks like black basalt, bits of chert, agate, rounded nodules of rough limestone, quartz and unprofitable slag. I picked up also what I thought were moss agates. But that ain't our story. We bent our steps to a kopje of split and riven stone with ridges of bluish stuff on it like mining dumps [sketch of kopje]. Naturally we climbed it. At A. I found the entrance to a rock-hewn chamber marked in black paint I. There was much drifted sand in the doorway which was rudely thus [sketch of doorway] and only darkness behind. Then working round the kopje we found all at the same level a series of tombs marked up to 25 – all rock hewn or rather picked out of the coarse-grained rock stuff, and such of 'em as we could see into filled with neatly arranged bones and skulls. Leg and arm bones arranged by themselves – ditto skulls. Perhaps half the tombs had been drifted up again and of course nothing of any value had been left, tho' we both felt sure that if you had been along you'd have found treasures. I looked for worked flints but found none. One peculiarity I noticed in one tomb (probably all the others had it) in the shape of a portcullis entrance. The door-posts were grooved for the insertion of a sliding slab which lay by the side of the tomb. The edge of the slab had been worked down to fit into the grooves: this I suppose is the idea; width of groove approx. $2\,^1/_2$ ins. [sketch]. I believe there is some sort of ruined temple – maybe Coptic church – about here: but our dragoman is a dam fool (and one-eyed at that) and the antiquity books stop at Nubia. Anyway C. and I felt we were rewarded and lamented your absence.

We turn back to Halfa to-night where we see the Doubledays returning from Khartoum. They were to have joined us in this steamer but it is most unluckily full. So they take the Government Steamer and we all hope to meet at Assouan or Luxor.

This is the kind of trip simply made for you; a life of unlimited but dignified luxury; servants who run – run like hares – when you give an order; a perfect climate, if you can remember to change about 4 times a day; donkeys for gentle exercise and temples for information. No words of mine can give you the faintest notion of the dawn as we saw it strike the statues of Rameses outside Abu Simbel, when the statues came to life (these eyes saw 'em) and the wild duck woke up and thanked God. And then there are the little black and white Nilotic Kingfishers, and the hoopees,³ and the great skeins of heavy flying birds which men say are pelicans flying away from the river after sunset, and herons on the bank. I hope to see Whymper (Birds of Egypt) at Luxor.⁴

The stones I sent you from Denderah are rotten – only flakes and fakes but I couldn't get any others. C. and I say we won't count this trip but next year, be spared, we'll really come and see Egypt. I'm an *Upper* Egyptian now. Nothing below Assouan interests me.

With love from us both to you both,

Ever affectionately,
Rudyard.

Notes
1.   The novelist: see 24 January 1895.
2.   The Arabic word "madrissah" or "madrasa(h)" means a school, a Muslim college. "The Madrissah School of Halfa" would be simple tautology.
3.   Thus in copy, no doubt for hoopoe, a bird so called after its cry.
4.   Charles Whymper (1853–1941), an artist who specialised in illustrating books of travel, sport, and natural history, e.g., C. Dixon's *Game Birds and Wild Fowl of the British Isles*, 1900, and his own *Egyptian Birds*, 1909. There is no evidence that RK met him at Luxor.

To Lady Burne-Jones, 28 February 1913
ALS: University of Sussex

S.S. "Prince Abbas," / Feb. 28 1913

Very dear-

This is at the turning-point of our trip – a few miles above Wady Halfa where we have come to let our tourists see the Second Cataract. All the dear angels have gone, either in boats or on donkeys, and C and I are sitting alone in the boat which is just big enough for two, though it holds 40 with great comfort. We have been for a quiet walk across the desert – and it *is* quiet. We found a lonely hill and climbed it and behold it was full of tombs cut into rocks and neatly numbered from 1. to 25 with lilly-white skulls and bones disposed neatly within. But there is no explanation. Our Dragoman, a one-eyed Kalendar of inauspicious aspect, is off with the donkey-riding tourists and even afoot he knows less than nothing. Here we are at rest under a bank of the Nile just sprinkled with a thin crop of beans and castor oil bushes. The desert begins less than thirty paces away – begins without a word of apology or compromise and runs without any break for some trifle of three thousand miles. But between the desert and the river are a few huts, all apparently full of women and each woman has two babes and each babe is fat and well-looking tho' given to snuffles and begging for bakshish. Our Greek cook is sitting on the bank in his shirt-sleeves roasting coffee. Such small Ethiops as are wearied of begging for bakshish sit round him in a solemn ring. When he wants to smoke, which is often, he lets one of 'em twiddle the roaster. He had a crocodile most of the voyage – a crocodile quite eighteen inches long and every time the steamer halted he bathed his crocodile at the end of a string. He is a fat, pale perspiring earnest man. But yesterday the crocodile died and he is awfully solemn about it. Our native cook – the head scullion – is also along the banks of the river scrubbing out the copper stock-pot with sand. He will bring it back looking like gold. He does that, too, every time we stop. The rest of the crew are a little further away, washing themselves and their clothes in the river. You see, tourists ain't expected to be aboard when they ought to be on donkeys and we are watching the intimate life of the ship. Our head laundryman rigged up a clothes pole from the bows to the beach the instant we tied up and all the ship's wash is already dried and bleaching there. He is the only person the children of the soil fear. Four dogs are sitting hopefully on the bank with their eyes on every movement. Our chief steward – may Allah requite him – always puts out a big mess of scraps for the local dogs and they come down according to etiquette which is strict among dogs. If a lady-dog (such poor haggard ladies) takes a mouthful of some one else's ration she is to all appearance knocked over and severely bitten. But it's only appearance. I saw one attacked at least thrice but I noticed that no dog ever closed his jaws on her. Then she stood off and called 'em names. One shadow of a beast – a cream coloured beast – has voluntarily left the hungry watch in order to escort two small babes along the bank to the next village. They take no sort of heed of him; he, apparently, regards them not; but he keeps about three yards behind 'em with the air of one who is out for his own pleasure. The babes are quite two feet high and have two garments between them.

There is not the faintest use to try to describe the temples. All I know is that the spectacle of the dawn striking the Colossi outside the temple of Abu Simbel is the most wonderful and awe-striking thing I have ever seen. It *is* true, as many assert, that the statues come to life. I saw them do it: but, just as they are ready to burst through the stone and the centuries and to stand up, the full sunlight pins them down into their places again. When the day of judgement comes the dawn will be delayed long enough for them to escape from their bondage and they will walk about the earth shouting. So far, Abu Simbel has been more to us than all the rest. By the way we saw the Pyramids with Lady Edward Cecil,[1] in rain, under a heavy leaden sky with wisps of rain between us and Cairo all across the flat plain. I don't know what they can do in normal weather but they seemed to darken the dark sky itself. Now here's a queer tale. While we were in the temple at Abu Simbel and the Dragoman (may Allah recompense him according to his sins!) was dragging us about there came an Arab and thrust a letter into my hand. It was from a Mrs. Newman and please would we come to tea with them in their dahabiyah and Mr. Newman would show me his pictures. C. and I laughed helplessly. It *did* seem as if Abu Simbel ought to have been moderately safe against letters. But we scribbled back we'd be delighted to come. We hadn't a ghost of a notion where but we had noticed a painter's tent outside the temple and had seen a boat with two white people in its hastily pulling forth from the bank as our joyous and valiant horde landed. At four thirty came that boat again, rowed by aged servitors like Elaine's[2] and a foot of green weed hanging from her sides. They rowed us down stream to an old, old private dahabiyah (the latest dream of our lives is to do the Nile on our own ship) where we were received by an old gentleman with *very* brown hands (artist's hands) very dreamy eyes and a subdued voice; and a dear old lady with silvery slightly crimped hair parted in the middle and a delicious voice. We fell in love with both of 'em at once: and I'm sorry now I didn't kiss her. They told us, sitting in a little cream panelled, bare drawing room that for six-and-twenty years past (26 years!) they had come to the Nile – spending the summer in Florence: and had owned this dahabiyah for 23. He was a man of one job only. He painted temples. Had made as it were a complete record of many-coloured Philæ before the submersion.[3] Did nothing else; cared for nothing else and had been long enough in Egypt to say that he knew nothing. A casual commission had given him his bent and he had become enslaved to the Pharoahs. Then he showed us his pictures – just some piccys of Abu Simbel and Philæ: only I have never seen stone painted after that fashion – with such love and knowledge and joy. The things were alive and splendid – notably one picture of the statue of an Egyptian princess "low as the king's right knee" – she's only about thirty foot high. I wanted awfully to know what it's price was. The Philæ piccys were glorious too but, then, I didn't know Philæ: whereas I had fallen in love with the princess. The painter meantime said very little. That was his work: he couldn't say how he did it but 'twas his life's delight and he did not care for any thing else. He would be seventy in five days and this year for the first time found it hard to go to work twice in the day. And she – kind and tender watching him and pouring us tea, reminded me somehow of Mary de Morgan[4] and Annie Catherwood[5] (tho' Mrs N. was sanity itself) and all sorts of kindly mid-

Victorian ghosts. Evidently *she* ran the practical side of life – buys eggs and fowls and corn from the villagers who all know 'em. It was odd to think of this frail couple anchored in their old Flying Dutchman of a ship, under their chosen bank of the Nile, fleeing from Cook's tourists and when they wished to change position hailing any steamer that happened to come along. "All the river knows us" said they, and nodded.

Before we left they took us into their own little study in the stern – a long-established nest full of treasures – Florentine brocades, Persian tiles, China and Egyptian trove. Nothing crowded: nothing insisting and they themselves well-poised and content. I'm sorrier than ever now that I didn't kiss her. We stayed nigh two hours and went off in a ragged [   ]⁶ of orange and green afterglow. Wasn't that a delightful experience?

I won't tire your eyes with more.

Dear love
Your Boy.

Notes

1. Her husband was now financial advisor to the government of Egypt, where he had been since 1901 and where he remained until 1917. Lady Cecil decline to live in Egypt and visited her husband there only rarely.
2. Cf. Tennyson, "Lancelot and Elaine", lines 1135, 1146: "the dumb old servitor".
3. The island of Philæ in the Nile was submerged after the height of the Aswan dam had been raised in 1912.
4. Mary Augusta De Morgan (1850–1907), sister of the potter and novelist William De Morgan. RK recalls, in *Something of Myself*, being taken to see Mr and Miss De Morgan, who let him "play with their queer sticky paints" (p. 22). See also 22 October 1919.
5. A daughter of Frederick Catherwood (1799–1854), artist, traveller, and architect, who was connected by marriage to the Burne-Jones family; Burne-Jones always regarded her as a cousin.
6. Word illegible, cusp? rush?

To John Kipling, 12 March [1913]

AL: University of Sussex

Semiramis-Hotel / Cairo / Wed: Mar. 12. 3: p.m.

Dear Old Man:

We've been separated from our mails for a fortnight thanks to the dam stupidity of Cook: but when the last mail, up to Mar. 5th from England, came in there wasn't a word from you. Have you forgotten or weren't you fit – or what? Of course the thing may have gone astray in the post, for this is a casual land but I confess I'd have felt happier at a line from you. Elsie wrote and she seems to be working hard at her French. Evidently a superior accent is *not* enough. One must also be perfect in one's verbs.

I believe I left ourselves, in my last letter to you,[1] sitting on a sandbank in the middle of the Nile with most of Cook's fleet stuck round us. Well Sir, we stayed there for 29 hours! All that time a bitter wind blew and the temperature was 55°. Seems to me we can do that sort of game in England on dry land.

A few hours after we had got off we found two native boats anchored, or aground, in the channel. There didn't seem to be room to avoid 'em so we hit the first one on the nose and dented it. Then we scraped *all* along its side and wiped off – obliterated, ecrazed – its silly tiller. This is the size of the tiller [sketch of Nile boat]. We removed all the black part. The rudder itself was made of old packing-caseboards about $\frac{1}{2}$ in thick but was not injured. When he saw that the collision was inevitable our native pilot's behaviour was superb. He simply turned his broad back on the whole show while our paddle box went banging and scraping and crackling down the full length of the *gassiah*.[2] Their crew behaved also with noble calm, knowing well that T. Cook and son would have to repair all damage. They simply drew back a little and watched the good work much as you would watch a street accident.

But there was a small naked kid of about six aboard – probably the owner's son. It was the first time he'd seen a collision and he argued that the boat and the family fortunes were ruined and done for. He wrung his hands like a figure in a play – only no actor could have put so much feeling into it – then he threw back his head and howled and the tears ran down his inky round cheeks. Nobody took the faintest notice of him. As soon as we had extricated ourselves we sent over a boat's crew and helped 'em to make and ship a new tiller. Result – we got into Luxor on Wednesday evening instead of Monday night;[3] throwing out our arrangements altogether. The man who keeps the Winter Palace Hotel at Luxor knows the Cattanis well. It is my firm belief that *all* the Swiss without exception are cousins and hotel keepers. The Winter Palace is beautifully managed and they have dances every other night. It's just Engelberg all over again – even down to the ices on Thursdays and Sundays!

We went about five miles out on the edge of the desert to spend a night with a Mr and Mrs. Winlock.[4] He is an Egyptologist and excavates ruins (for short they call 'em diggers) on the site of old Thebes. The Metropolitan Museum in New York employs him. Everything he finds goes to the Museum in N.Y. *unless* the Cairo Museum cares to claim anything that it has not got in its own collection. At first sight the life of a digger in Egypt sounds like one perpetual and fascinating treasure-hunt. As a matter of fact it simply means, in most cases, watching a few hundred smelly men and boys digging rubbish under a hot sun, putting it in baskets and dumping it into blowy heaps. I went down to see his works. There were 450 men and boys and a light railway clearing away dust and debris from the foundations of a gigantic wall: thus [sketch of workers at excavation site].

I was nearly choked by the dust. I asked 'em to show me their finds for the past month. They showed me a large blotter with perhaps 20 small odds and ends arranged on it – an amethyst necklace, a lapis lazuli scarab, an amethyst scarab, some odd beads and a few other things. It looked like awful rubbish but they said its value was £1000. I bought some antiquities which are *real* antiquities at Luxor. Among 'em is a small god which would make a good tie pin for you. It's not more than 3000 years old. And also a lot of small charms and odds and ends in blue pottery – gods mostly. Today Mummy went to the bazars here which I believe are wonderful and has come back with the complete dress of a Bedouin of the desert for you. It's a swell affair. In this land the men's clothes are more expensive than the women's. The inner long coat is a sort of gold coloured affair, bound at the waist by a flaming waist-cloth. The outer coat is a delightful grey silk. The head gear is the *burnous* – *not* the turban but the *pukka* Arab desert dress thus: – [sketch of head wearing burnous with part marked "A"]. A is a sort of black and white fillet from which I am inclined to think our Crusaders evolved the idea of the twist under the crest [drawing of heraldic twist] in heraldry, and the cloth can be arranged on either side the neck. Red slippers complete this charming outfit. I tried it all on myself and felt very noble. There is also a heavy white scarf for use against desert-storms. I don't advise you to wear anything much under it at dances. It's awfully thick.

Mummy got a Persian dress for Elsie – an arrangement in pale green, rose and yellow – awful fine but it hasn't the barbaric effect of yours. Yes I think Mummy had a *dam* good time. With her usual forethought she loaded me up with Carters little liver pills (I don't deny I needed 'em) and left me in my private suite (bed *and* bathroom) to commune with the mysteries of nature. She had the decency to bring me back an inlaid box for cigarettes.

Now we are going out to tea at Shepheard's hotel. It only rains in Cairo on twenty days of the year. This has been repeated to me a thousand times. Altogether we have only been in Cairo five full days counting our first visit here. It has rained three of those days. This afternoon without any warning there came the deuce of a shower and it looks as though it might come down again at any minute.

I have a lot of things I'd love to tell you but I do detest "word-painting" in a letter so I'll let you off.

We are coming to Marseilles in the *Cordillere* – a 10,000 ton Messageries Maritimes boat which leaves Alexandria on the 15th and should be at Marseilles on the 19th. I will wire you ere I leave as to sending your next letters to Marseilles c/o Thomas Cook. I *am* sorry not to have had a word from you.

Dearest love from us both.

Ever
Your Pater

Does that rhyme stick in your head still? I haven't got it out of mine yet. Donkeys?[5]

Come to think of it I haven't told you about our amazing visit to the Cairo Zoo. It is run by a man called Flowers – Captain Stanley S. Flowers[6] – who is one of the most fascinating chaps I ever met. He showed us over and told us at the beginning that he wouldn't keep any beast that he couldn't pet! The Zoo isn't a *general* Zoo but confines itself chiefly to the animals and birds of Egypt and the Soudan and Arabia. It reminded me in its light and warmth rather of Groot-Schuur but, of course, it is a real Zoo with lions, leopards, ibex, gazelles, buck of all kind, wilderbeestes, giraffes and elephants all rejoicing so to speak in their natural climate. The hippo has a lake, *much* bigger than the mill pond at home, and there is a crocodile pond on the banks of which crocodile sun themselves. But that isn't anything. Flower began by taking us to the hyæna cages. You know what a mean treacherous hound a hyæna is. There were five of 'em and they each received him with roars and grunts of joy and flung themselves down on the floor for him to pat their backs; one old beast nearly nineteen years old simply fawned and slobbered. It was the same thing with the Syrian wolves and the jackals. The instant Flower appeared and called 'em by name they ran to the bars and waited for him to pet 'em. *And it was the same thing with the lions!* The whole shoot from little three month old cubs up to a great silent four year old full maned lion ran at him like so many cats – purring, rolling on the ground, rubbing against the bars and squirming. Talk of Hagenbeck and Co.[7] They weren't in it. Flower, to be sure, was not inside the cage (he doesn't go there he says, while the public are about) but he had no whip; he wasn't feeding 'em. They were simply overjoyed to see him.

Then we found a lot of pelicans on a lake. He called. They came and a man fed 'em fish in a bucket. You never saw such fielding in your born days. Then to the hippo tank. The Hippo is called "Said." He is trained to come out of water at the word of command and to beg for food and to go back to his pond quietly without splashing the audience. The Rhino rejoices in the name of "Kitty." She is a frail and slender virgin of about $1\frac{3}{4}$ tons whose pet companion is a small native goat that spends its spare time butting Kitty's enormous arrière-pensée. I don't suppose the shock ever communicates itself to Kitty's brain but she likes the goat. She too comes up to be tickled. "I'd take you inside" said Flower "only Kitty has an absent minded way of shoving her head down to be scratched and bringing it up again suddenly and *if* her nose is between your legs, you see the horn catches you in the crotch and throws you all over the place. She doesn't mean it but" – I hastily explained *I* didn't want to love Kitty. Can't you imagine the result of a rhino catching you in the fork with her horn.

There was a wild buffalo – *the* most dangerous beast in creation on account of his cunning and devilish courage. He was only two years old but stood about 16 hands already. He came up to Flower at a lumbering canter and had his cheek scratched. "Ah" said Flower pensively. "We shall have trouble with you next year, my friend. I hope the bars of your enclosure are strong enough." He (the bull-buffalo) looked like a quiet mountain of blue-grey mud but when I realized the size and sweep of his horns [sketch of buffalo head] I could see that if once he got his temper going he'd be about as safe as so much dynamite.

The baby-elephant here interrupted us begging for biscuits. He is a regular professional beggar – about 4 feet high. Looks like a pig in the face.

Then we saw tortoises – whoppers! Like the ones at Groot Schuur. Blessed if Flower didn't pat one of 'em – tickled her under the neck and she purred and scratched and sidled up to him. She is between 60 and 200 years old – from the Aldebara islands[8] – but the keepers solemnly assure the crowd that she is *much* older than the pyramids.

Then he had a lot of snakes out for us. Some he said were only semi-poisonous because their poison fangs are their *back* teeth – not their front fangs. Consequently, they have to have a good steady chew at you before they can fix their back teeth in you. Flower explained this with one of the semi-poisonous gentlemen in his hand. I think you would have enjoyed that day more than anything that Egypt could offer you. But I perceive that I grow discursive. Mother will add a few lines to this. God bless you my boy. I've a million things I want to talk over with you – about Egypt and careers and things.[9]

Notes

1. 3 March 1913 (ALS, University of Sussex).
2. The Arabic *ghaziyya* means "boat, ship, or vessel".
3. 5 March instead of 3 March.
4. Herbert Eustis Winlock (1884–1950) and his wife, the former Helen Chandler; Winlock conducted excavations for the Metropolitan Museum in Egypt from 1906 to 1931. He was director of the Metropolitan, 1932–9.
5. In his letter of 3 March RK transcribes for John "a silly rhyme that a man told me after a donkey-ride. It's hardly the thing one could write to a girl but I *couldn't* get it out of my head for days. You know, of course, that one sits right aft on a donkey. Here's the rhyme

> As I sat on my ass on the back of my ass
> This paradox came to my mind
> Two thirds of my ass was in front of my ass
> And the whole of my ass was behind."
> (ALS, Sussex)

6. Flower, not Flowers: see [17 February 1913].
7. The great German menagerie near Hamburg.
8. Aldabra Island, in the Seychelles.
9. CK adds a line at the end of the letter.

To H. A. Gwynne, 14 March 1913

ALS: Dalhousie University

Semiramis-Hotel / Cairo / Mar. 14. 1913.

private

Dear Old Man –

There is a whole lot of trouble brewing here among the commercial community on account of K[itchener]'s latest piece of legislation which, in effect, prevents anyone who holds less than 5 feddans (acres) from borrowing on the security of his land.[1] The Law came into operation on the 4th of January and, as you can see, it has already hit the Agricultural Bank of Egypt pretty hard. Now the Agricultural Bank was started by Cromer[2] precisely for the purpose of lending money to the agricultural interests. It carries a 3% state guarantee and, I believe – but see Sidney Peel[3] – there is about £7,000,000 of capital involved. The enclosed figures will show you what an enormous acreage is owned by the small holder of less than 5 feddans. The result of striking all that amount of land out of the market as a commercial security naturally depresses credit all round; knocks out a large percentage of the Bank's business (at 8%) and sends the fellah himself to the Greek money lender who can walk all round the act in half a dozen ways that a bank can't, and the Greek lends to the fellah at from 18% to 36% per cent.

The typed statement herewith enclosed, with figures of holders and acreage, came from the best authority and you need have no fear in using them.

Well, I went and saw Kay about the business yesterday afternoon: had ten minutes' talk with him specifically about the Act before we went to tea – and the net result scared me! *Qua* man, he has gone to seed awfully. *Qua* administrator he seems to be garrulously intoxicated with power. He began by telling me a yarn of how in India he had out of spite spiked some proposal of the Financial Member there because the Financial Member had refused to allow him some extra batteries. (All very proper to do of course, if necessary, but nothing to talk about). Then I opened up about his new Act and the dissatisfaction it was causing. He assured me (he's a practised liar but a bad one which is a rare combination) that he had made certain modifications and offered certain advantages to the Bank which they, the Bank, had accepted in writing as perfectly satisfactory. But there, again, he told the tale with a sort of arrogant smirk as though he had coerced 'em into it. I suggested this. He denied it with another smirk. "Anyhow they've put themselves on record as being satisfied" said he. Sidney Peel and Babington Smith[4] came out from England on behalf of the Bank some time back and I presume K. meant that *they* were satisfied. Then I asked him why he had put the Act through. He gave me a lot of guff about the poor fellahin, keeping the money in the country, dealing with Egyptian notables etc.

which didn't amount to a row of pins. I referred to the statistics (as enclosed) and hinted that there seemed to be a steady growth in small holdings if that was what he wanted. "Oh" said he. "Those figures are all wrong. I'm having 'em re-done!" Then I suggested that if you deprived a man of his borrowing powers he couldn't very well launch out and buy more land. "Quite right" says K. "That's the thing I want to prevent. They ruin 'emselves trying to buy land."

(And a man can only *just* live, with luck to help him, on two feddans!)

This struck me as fairly mediæval and primitive but the butcherly arrogance of this physical flaccid old bird struck me still more. The Law was his own idea and was to be put through by his order and he was going to make things hot for any one who interfered.

I asked him if the Law wouldn't depress credit. He rounded on me, almost like a Lloyd-George; said it would do no such thing and repeated over and over: "It's all right. I tell you it's all right." Then I said that there might be a circus about it in England. He said he thought there wouldn't and he added "The quieter the Bank keeps the better for the bank." *That* was the illuminating sentence. You know the man better than I so you must imagine the tone he said it in. He gave me to understand quite clearly that he could make life uncomfortable for the Bank. *Nota Bene.* Govt collects a proportion of the Bank's debts. Well, I'd got what I wanted to know about *him* so his finale about the fellahin didn't much interest me. Then we went up on the stoep for tea – the wife, Mrs. Elgood[5] (interested in maternity training for the Egyptians, nurses and generally raising more babies) Fitzgerald, Cecil (Finance Minister) Steward[6] his Secretary and Sir William Garstin,[7] guest staying in the house. There the comedy began; he playing to his unworthy gallery (me!) and his little court backing him up and fawning; Mrs Elgood in rapt wrapped attention (she wants more money for her nursing schools) and Carrie not daring to look at me. It reminded me of a sort of nebulous Rhodes without grip or restraint. Well, we learned what a devil of a great man he was; and how what he said to notables and pashas was respected; and how he called up a big man with much money and bade him subscribe to a fund for his tenants; and how he is going to double the population of Egypt in a few years or at least to get the ground ready to carry a doubled population. Cecil at intervals interpolating appreciative purrs and murmuring "That is a question of finance."[8] Then he lightly let fall – his note, I believe, was meant to be light but compelling – how he intended to raise the age of marriage throughout Egypt. "How?" says I. "By order" he says. "They're a biddable people and they'll do what they're told." Murmurs (Mrs E. leading) "Oh yes they'll do what they're told!"

If the place hadn't been Egypt and the year 1913 it would have been only funny. But, as things stand, it scared me! – *But* I ain't the only one. I've been going round among "business interests" and to say *they* are scared is to put it mildly. One big business man said: – "You see we don't know what he'll do next. There's a rumour now that he means to regulate all wages and house-rents." "And can't you protest?" I said. He shook his head. "No. The Government would take it out of you in some way sooner or later if you did."

II

In *that* opinion all the men I talked to were quite agreed. I know him to be unscrupulous but I didn't realize that the fact was so generally admitted and acted upon. Of course the officials can't open their heads without running the risk of having 'em chopped off.

So here's the business community, uneasy, almost panicky, and unable to say anything. I gather that K. had a down on Sir E. Cassel[9] and anything that he had anything to do with has got to be punished.

I do *not* know precisely what proposals K. has made to the Ag. Bank for the future conduct of their business but I *do* know that he's chortling at having done 'em somehow or other.

There has been a protest already in the Financial news – a letter from Sir W. Mieville[10] pub. here Mar 13th: and I expect there will be a row later after the effect of the Law becomes clearer. K. don't value local opinion one dam but I expect he don't like a row from home. Of course he is all that is useful to us in the Game but he won't be useful if he discredits or holds up the development of the country, which he is certainly doing at present.

Now you can do what you dam please. Only you ought to realize that the chap thinks himself a sort of second Rameses and – finance ain't his strong point. He didn't know what the land-settlement of Egypt was.

With love from us both

Ever
RK
F.

Check me by Babington Smith or Sydney Peel.
K. don't want English capital if he can control Egyptian notables.

RK

Notes
1. The law, passed in 1912, was designed to help small landholders; it provided that those who held less than five *feddans* of land could not be expropriated for debt, a protection that effectively made it impossible for them to obtain loans. The operation of the law was not a success (Robert L. Tignor, *Modernization and British Colonial Rule in Egypt, 1882–1914*, Princeton, NJ, 1966, pp. 237–40).
2. Evelyn Baring (1841–1917), 1st Earl of Cromer, Kitchener's predecessor as British agent and consul-general in Egypt, in effect the Imperial pro-consul from 1883 to 1907.

3. Lieutenant-Colonel Sir Sidney Peel (1870–1938), of the Bedfordshire Yeomanry; vice-president of the Morocco State Bank and a director of the Westminster Bank. He published *The Binding of the Nile and the New Soudan*, 1904.
4. Sir Henry Babington Smith (1863–1923), a civil servant with a talent for finance, was appointed administrator of the newly-created National Bank of Turkey in 1909.
5. The former Bonte Amos, wife of Lieutenant-Colonel Percival George Elgood (1883–1941), in the financial ministry of Egypt. She was made a CBE in 1939.
6. Perhaps Colum Edmund Crichton-Stuart (1886–1957), third son of the 3rd Marquess of Bute, an attaché on Kitchener's staff at Cairo. He resigned from the diplomatic service in 1920 and was Unionist MP for the Norwich division of Cheshire, 1922–45.
7. Garstin (1849–1925) presided over the development of irrigation in Egypt from 1892 to 1908.
8. Cecil "had little technical experience of finance but could be trusted unquestioningly to carry out the Consul-General's orders and generally to act as his Chief of Staff" (Lord Lloyd, *Egypt Since Cromer*, I [1933], p. 148).
9. Sir Ernest Cassel (1852–1921), German-born English financier, underwrote the construction of the Aswan dam and helped to found the Agricultural Bank of Egypt.
10. Sir Walter Mieville (1855–1929), in the consular service and Foreign Office, had been an administrator in Egypt from 1884 to 1897.

To John Kipling, 20 March 1913

ALS: University of Sussex

Avignon / Grand Hôtel d'Europe / le Mar. 20. 1913

Dear Old Man -

Your letter of the 15th was delivered to us as soon as we set foot ashore from the rolling *Cordillere*. I simply *can't* understand how it is that you could have gone 16 days without a letter: whenever I sent the diary-letter to Phipps I always (and so did Mother) sent another letter to you. Surely you got my letter written after the visit to the diggers as Bahr-el-Dahri[1] and the other when we were stuck on the sand bank.[2] We are both awfully upset about it because knowing what letters mean, we took special care to feed you up with 'em. I can sympathize because we went over a fortnight without a line from you. That was Cook! I think Phipps is a beast not to have written you for so long and I shall jolly well tell her so.

Your Easter-term troubles seem to have no end, and Pompey being away and the House in commission so to speak was the last straw.[3] We have got your half term report. All I can say is that the term seems to have been too vile for any one to be able to do justice to himself and I don't propose to count it. You were off your feed half the time; the masters were sick; the school disorganized and what else could you expect. I see W. W. V.[4] simply signed his initials. Didn't say anything about you but I *am* pleased that

Pompey said your conduct was "very satisfactory." You know how proud I am of you secretly – or if you don't you may have guessed it by now – and I was cheered to find that a Hellish turn hadn't lowered your house morale. You've got no end of character, my son. I don't care how much or how often or how fully you grouse or curse to me – I know and I understand and I sympathize, as you know; but it pleases me that you have carried on decently and quietly thro' the heavy burden of wet, discomfort and indifferent health. *Selah!* (as D. said when his harp-string bust).

I don't think I told you much about the voyage in the French boat – expect that she was dirty but comfy. They gave us no end of a cabin; the Captain made me free of the bridge and the chartroom and all his officers tried to teach me French seafaring words. *But* what they didn't tell us was that we had a whole mass of Syrian, Lebanon and Smyrna emigrants to America to disembark at a little quarantine station (an island close to Monte Cristo's island) *before* we got into Marseille. (*Note.* It is spelt without the S. Never knew this before). Well, we began decanting them and their baggage into steam launches (a bit of a roll on) both sides the boat at 4:p.m.: as each emigrant would perish sooner than be parted for an instant from his box, his bundle *and* his deck chair and as the passenger's ladder was the usual width of passenger's ladders, and as the men at the foot of it didn't like jumping into the tenders as they rolled, and as many emigrants who had gone into the tenders suddenly remembered that they had left a bundle behind and clawed their way up the ladder in the teeth of the downward traffic the result was Hades! [sketch of figure in fez with box, backpack, and deck chair]. Here is a lightly equipped emigrant. The French sailors simply lost their heads and added to the mess by shouting and hooting at 'em and driving 'em about like sheep. I don't think that our channel passage arrangements amount to much but this was like leaving the Boulogne boat in a nightmare. And it lasted till about 6.30!!!

So we landed at Marseille at dusk and the arrangements for our exit were about as crude as for the emigrants but we fell into the arms of Cook and he wafted us to the Hotel. But there was no sign of Landon or the car *or* Moore. Instinct told me that he might be at a certain hotel about 3 miles out of town – and even as I asked for him at that Hotel I heard *his* voice trying to get through to me! Soon he turned up with the undefeated Moore (by the way Mrs. M. he told me is in the family way. The event is expected in six or seven months: but don't you let on that you have heard). Landon was rotten with a running cold and ammoniated quinine but he said he'd had no end of a time running down from Boulogne with Moore and he ended by taking us all to *his* hotel which rises almost out of the sea, faces Marseille harbour, and is built like this [sketch of hotel] all among stone pines. The sea beats at the foot of it and they have a private salt pond where they keep their fish alive! It was the most beautiful view I'd ever seen. We had supper at 10.p.m.! It turned out that Landon had been busily trying to get at us with wireless all day. *We* (the Cordillere) had the apparatus but (having quarelled with Marconi) hadn't the operator. Needless to say the French Government calmly accepted the message, and trousered the money. As Landon says some happy P & O or B.I. boat probably took it in; or they had it at Malta. But we hadn't. This morning, we took [the] car (she runs a treat) and came here to Avignon where we stay for a day. Enclosed are two post cards of the "pont d'Avignon." I'll go on with my yarn later. This carries a heartful of love from us both.

the Pater.

Notes
1. 12 March 1913.
2. 3 March 1913 (ALS, University of Sussex).
3. There had been an outbreak of measles at the school.
4. William Wyamar Vaughan (1865–1938), Headmaster of Wellington, 1910–21, and of Rugby, 1921–31.

To Frank Henry Cook,[1] 1 April 1913
Text: Copy, Thomas Cook Group Ltd

Hotel Brighton, / 218, Rue de Rivoli, / Paris. / Ap.1. 1913.

Dear Cook,
    Here is a little tale, which may interest you, of what your people can do at a pinch.
    On Tuesday night we arrived, in the car, at Bourges from Marseilles[2] and I was met by the news that the King of Greece would be buried at Athens on *Sunday* and it behoved me to get a man down there in time for the affair.[3]
    Bourges is *not* what you might call a centre of civilization. It keeps one 10c: time table and the leading hotel lights itself with candles. So I threw myself heavily, by telephone, into the arms of Cook Paris and demanded how I was to get from Bourges to Brindisi, Brindisi to Patras, and Patras to Athens in anything like time. If you know that corner of the Mediterranean you'll remember that the Greek and Italian steamer lines are sketchy and chaotic.
    At the same time as I telephoned Cook I wired practically duplicate inquiries to Reuter because it seemed to me utterly impossible that the various European representatives could by any means get from their Capitals to Athens on the date given. Reuter (and this seems an additional feather in your cap) wired back: – "REFERRING COOKBUREAU". Meantime Cook – who in this case was a man called Manton whom I'd met once before – telephoned me exhaustively that *on the dates given* the thing was impossible by any known combination (he gave the combinations) of Greek or Italian boats. "You might

just pull if off" he said "by motoring to Milan". In that too, he was correct as I worked out afterwards. An hour or two later, when I had definitely abandoned the notion, Manton telephones again to tell me, *what Reuter should have done*, that the funeral was postponed till Wednesday; and presents me with two perfectly possible rail and boat combinations which would have landed me comfortably at Athens via Patras (all hotels given) in ample time for the ceremony on the postponed date. That information was timely and tremendously useful to the man who had to go down in the long run.

I don't suppose that this sort of thing is anything new to you but it pleased me as a client and an ex journalist more than I can say.

When I was at the Place de l'Opera[4] this morning I asked how the thing was done. As far as I make out he'd dug up both the Greek and British Embassies to get the second date *which Reuter didn't know* till Cook told him. In other words if I had depended on Reuter I should have been let down.

There was a crispness and an accuracy about the whole thing that I can't help boring you with.

Mrs Kipling joins me in kindest regards to you both and I am,

Very sincerely and gratefully yours,
Rudyard Kipling.

Notes
1. Cook (b. 1862), the grandson of the founder of the firm, ran Thomas Cook and Son with his brother Ernest until it was sold in 1928.
2. From Avignon they went to Albi on the 22nd and then to Limoges, 24 March. From Limoges they went to Bourges on the 25th, to Troyes on the 27th, to Rheims on the 28th, and arrived in Paris on the 30th of March (Motor Tours, 22–29 March 1913; Rees extracts).
3. King George of Greece (1845–1913) was assassinated at Salonika on 18 March. RK's party spent Wednesday, 26 March, in Bourges, "alternately in Bourges Cathedral and at the telephone making love to Cook. L[andon] was taken with spasms about going to the King of G's funeral" (Motor Tours, 26 March 1913). The "Sunday" RK refers to is 30 March.
4. One of Cook's Paris offices was at 1, Place de l'Opéra.

To Edward Lucas White, 8 April 1913

ALS: University of Texas

Bateman's / Burwash / Sussex / Ap. 8. 1913

Esteemed Younger Brother,

A line (as I am still heaving after the channel passage) on our return from Egypt and France to thank you for yours of Jan 25th.[1] By Allah, I thought I had included all that was to be included in my *Songs from Books*, and you are but one of many who now tell me that I have not! What can I do? The fault is mine. Nor can I extend all my "quotations" to full songs or there would be no end of it.[2]

I haven't your copy of the *Quest*[3] – but if it begins "The knight came home from the quest" – I wrote it. I forget when or why and I don't think it was published anywhere. Probably I wrote it for somebody. It ain't any allegory.

Now I will go and attend to an accumulated mail of three months – a most awful Job.

> Very sincerely
> Rudyard Kipling

Notes
1. They went from Paris to Folkestone on 6 April and arrived at Bateman's on the 7th (CK diary).
2. A number of verses of which a few lines or stanzas only are used in the books in which they first appeared are expanded in *Songs from Books*. Presumably in most cases RK wrote only what he needed in the first instance and was then tempted to expand his texts on collecting them for *Songs from Books*: cf., e.g., the texts in *Songs from Books* of "Gallio's Song" or "The Juggler" with their first appearance in, respectively, *Actions and Reactions* and *Kim*. See also 25 October 1913.
3. First published in *The Book of Beauty*, 1897. A typed copy of the poem at Sussex bears a rubber stamp reading "Edward L. White / 1223 Mt. Royal Avenue / Baltimore, Maryland" and at the head a note in RK's hand: "M.S. sold in 1912 or 1913 – unpublished verse." I do not know what he was thinking of.

To Sir Max Aitken, 9 April 1913
ALS: Harvard University

> *Bateman's / Burwash / Sussex /* Ap. 9. 1913.

Dear Aitken

A letter from Lady Aitken to the wife tells us that you are both laid up but since the letter was written on the 3rd we are hoping you are better. *Anyhow* send us a line to let us know how you are and when I can see you and, generally, what you have been doing.

I've been moving in exalted Financial Circles (French) of late and can tell you things about Kitchener and his policy in Egypt which will amuse you. Otto Kahn[1] (you were at the back of it) has sent me the duplicate of that glorious Field Marshall's baton which he gave you.

How the deuce are two uncommonly plain men, like you and me, to dress when they go abroad with 'em? The wife says our only possible chance is to turn out the Liberals and have you and me given offices at Court which shall as much surpass the billet of Gold Stick in Waiting, as our walking sticks surpass common ones.

As to the Liberals. My insular mind hasn't got further than saying: – "Thank God they ain't white." After all a Jew lawyer[2] and a Welsh solicitor[3] and Jack Johnston[4] and rabbits are much of a muchness. But if they have, under pressure, owned to this much, what in earth have they really done? D'you know.

I haven't much time but I've got some money which I want to invest in *my* way – not the Welsher's – to bring me from 5% and to keep. At any rate to pay for on delivery. Have you anything that you can recommend just now? I pause for a reply.

Dear love to Peter Rudyard, Janet and John.[5] It would be a good thing and a nice thing if you could come down any day but Monday of next week (or any day of this week) to see us.

Keep the 22nd open and go and see the first night of my little curtain raiser at the Royalty.[6] I shan't be there but there may be some fun.

All good wishes to you both from us two.

Ever

Rudyard Kipling

P.S.   I don't know what's the matter with you but, anyway, I told you it 'ud happen.

Notes

1. Kahn (1867–1934), German-born American banker, was a noted patron of music in New York. He was on the board of the Metropolitan Opera from 1907 until his death, and was a vice-president of the New York Philharmonic.
2. Sir Rufus Isaacs. The reference is to the Marconi scandal: see 22 December 1912.
3. Lloyd George.
4. I guess that RK means Jack Johnson (1878–1946), African-American heavyweight champion of the world from 1908 to 1915.
5. Janet (b. 1908), afterwards Mrs Edward Kidd, was Aitken's daughter. John is John William Maxwell (b. 1910), the elder son, who refused the barony but retained his father's baronetcy.
6. *The Harbour Watch*, first produced at the Royalty Theatre on 22 April 1913 as a curtain raiser to a three-act comedy called *Thompson*, by George Calderon and St John Hankin. Elsie Kipling claimed to have had a part in the writing of this (see Carrington, *Rudyard Kipling*, p. 514); RK speaks of it in writing to Elsie as "*our* play – the Pyecroft one" (21 March 1913: ALS, University of Sussex). The play is first referred to in CK's diary, July 1908, when Elsie was only twelve. It has never been collected. On 29 April CK took the children to London to see *The Harbour Watch* but RK did not accompany them. Instead, he came up in the evening "and we all go to a music hall" (Rees extracts, 29 April 1913).

To John Kipling, [4 May 1913]
ALS: University of Sussex

Bateman's / Burwash / Sussex / Sunday

Dear Old Man –

Just a line to say I'm back at Batemans after the Academy dinner[1] – d–d Dull: but I met Ward (Sir E. Ward Under-Sec. for War there) and talked to him about your getting into the Army.[2] He says he is going to write to the head of the examining (physical) board and suggests you might be examined privately just as a preliminary canter. This isn't a bad idea. In the mean time I suggest that you wear your *pince-nez* as much as you can and try to get used to 'em. They give a man a different expression as compared to spectacles. No news except its beastly cold and I'm rather lonesome for lack of a Friend and Ally to play with. Remember to dig out this term and let me know what a "presentation" to Sandhurst means. Is it a sort of letter of recommendation from your Head Master or what? You'll never get it if it is.

Ever your own
Pater.

Notes
1. The dinner, Sir Edward Poynter presiding, was on Saturday, 3 May.
2. When RK called at Wellington on 2 May he learned that "John now wants to go into the Army" (CK diary).

To Sara Norton, 6 May 1913
ALS: Harvard University

Bateman's / Burwash / Sussex / May. 6. 1913.

Dear Sally –

Telepathy again! I was thinking about you only a week ago and talking to Carrie and wondering what your news might be. Now comes your letter. Like you I'm up to my neck in work – sad result of three months holiday. But it's worth it. We spent six weeks in Egypt and there, by the way (literally in dahabiyah, on the Nile by Abu Simbel) met the Newmans – the artist – whom Ruskin discovered – and who I think knew your father. He paints the temples as most men would like to paint their loves and she is all that is left of the sweetest and best mid-Victorian.

As to the extract from the letter to Weir Mitchell I'd a vast sooner not have it printed for two reasons, First because it was a bit of talk between me and your Father and therefore, to me, a thing apart and rather sacred.[1] He always used to be down on me for calling him "Sir" but I always looked on him as a Father.

The second reason is quite a base one – born out of contemplation of a stack of mail not much smaller than a washing basket. The world, my dear Sally, is swarming with misbegotten people whom Eblis has cursed with unlimited leisure that they may be the more effectually damned. These people (may their days be shortened) write to me on any conceivable subject for no conceivable object except the gratification of their own uneasy curiosity. Were it to be put out that I had said what I had said about Longfellow, a multitude (*not* enclosing stamps) would instantly write and ask "But *why* did you say so? and don't you think that So and So is worthier than Longfellow. For my own part I am a student of such another in whose honour I have composed the enclosed verses which kindly get published for me in order that I may devote the proceeds towards a college for the education of neglected Pullman car porters."

And there would be excursuses and variations on the theme and theories would be built on it and the last state of your poor coz would be worse than the first.

So if it don't matter please let the thing be cut out and I'll bless you.

With all our loves ever affectionately.

Ruddy.

Note

1. Miss Norton was about to publish *Letters of Charles Eliot Norton with Biographical Comment by His Daughter Sara Norton and M. A. DeWolfe Howe*, 2 vols (Boston, 1913). The preface notes that the absence of letters to "Burne-Jones, Rudyard Kipling, and still other friends, is greatly to be regretted" (I, vi). The passage that RK objects to printing probably occurred in Norton's letter to Mitchell of 31 January 1907, in which Norton discusses some of RK's poems and then goes on to the topic of Longfellow's centennial (II, 166–8).

To John Kipling, 16 May 1913
ALS: University of Sussex

Bateman's / Burwash / Sussex / Sat[1] May. 16. 1913

Dear John,

There is to be a medical board to sit on you at Aldershot at 12:45 on Monday. I shall be at Coll. with the car at 12.30: and shall want you with your leave in order *and dressed in your best kit* which you had better put on that morning when you get up, the minute you come out of school. I have asked Pompey to see that your leave is ready signed before hand but I expect you to see that it is.

Then we'll nip over to Aldershot and see what the medical board says about things. It will be rather a rag.[2]

Ever
the Pater.

Notes
1. The 16th was a Friday in 1913.
2. The result was that John's eyesight was found to be "below standard" (CK diary, 19 May 1913).

To John Kipling, 24 May 1913
ALS: University of Sussex

Bateman's / Burwash / Sussex / May. 24. 1913

Dear Old Man,

Congratulations! It always looks well to bustle in at the end of a lesson with the air of one who has had the cup of learning rudely dashed from his lips. Well, that means *two* lessons that I got you out of – *plus* a decent lunch.[1]

I don't know when I've enjoyed a time more than our stolen afternoon among the æroplanes. Didn't that Lieutenant in the E. Lancashire tell you that a new carburettor would make your present byke a T.T.?[2] I fancied he told you it was only chucking money away to get a new one. Also, I don't see how you are going to test and tune a new byke before you go to camp. Suppose you give your order. This present byke will have to be sent up; the new one will come down – here? or to you? It can't very well come to you after W.W.V[aughan]'s attitude and I don't see how the deuce it can be fixed up here and sent over to you in trim for you to mount and ride away to camp.

I don't say that the thing can't be done. I only want you to consider the plan of campaign and think it all out before we meet so that we can discuss it seriously.

Also, I've a kind of suspicion of Friend Douglas.[3] Looks *to me* as though they lured one on from one game to another. However, that's your look out. Let's know precisely what sort of nickel-plated devil stink-puff they propose to give you in exchange for the present one *and* a fiver. (Thanks, by the way, for cheque. You couldn't have cashed it as it was made out to me).

I like the idea of the Thursday parade.[4] I fancy we'll all be there. It ought to be a very big show. I didn't tell you how delighted Mummy was over your jump-up in form. She fairly whooped. For goodness sake stick to it. I don't like the idea of your being even nominally able to be fagged by clever young shits – I mean squirts. Also I want you to be a *pre* before I die. I think with your knowledge of mixed human nature you'd make a good pre. I never was one.

My own idea at present is to slip up to Rugely[5] in the car and see the camp there on my own. If I pass you and King on the road you needn't expect me to take any notice of you or to reserve bedrooms en route.

I've got to go to the Guards camp in July or June[6] (I forget which) and I'd like to see an O[fficers'].T[raining].C[orps]. Show in full blast. Well. So long till the 5th. *Do* get your bicycle scheme clearly arranged in your head by the time we meet.

Dearest love from all.

Ever and ever
Your Pater

Notes
1. On the 19th, when RK took John to Aldershot for his physical: that must also have been the afternoon referred to in the next sentence of the letter.
2. Possibly "Tourist Trophy", after the motor race of that name.
3. The firm that made John's motor bike.
4. On 5 June, when they evidently went to Wellington to see John.
5. In Staffordshire.
6. At the end of June: see 9 July 1913.

To Colonel Lionel Charles Dunsterville, 6 July 1913

Text: Copy, University of Sussex

Bateman's. / July 6 1913.

Dear old man;

We've been a sort of Hotel of all Nations since I came back from Egypt so I haven't been able to get across to Cranbrook to collar young Lionel.[1] However I got him yesterday at 12.30 for the week-end i.e. he has to go back to-night at 6 p.m. He is a nice little chap as ever walked – with your rummy bulgy eyes and your precise (it is the only precise thing about you) way of reading sitting up bolt-upright in a chair. He doesn't talk much – looking on me, I doubt not, as one wrapped in the mists of antiquity. But he expands a bit with my girl Elsie who is used to boys. He has beautiful manners and poise – carries himself like a quiet self-contained sahib. They call him "Flea" at school, he tells me, which is a fair sign that he is about the smallest of the crowd. He says they feed him well and volunteered that the other day he had a strawberry tea at which he ate all the strawberries he could hold. Fancy the old Coll giving us strawberry teas! He is very fit: of a good colour, owns to no diseases and is a dam sight tidier than ever *you* were about folding away his kit at night. He has John's room and the run of John's books – settled himself down comfily under the electric with a book on mechanics "How it Works". I let the little beggar read at leisure. He tells me he wants to be a Sapper, and is certainly keen on machines. Our turbine interested him greatly and so did our oil engine for the electric light; also the accumulators.

But his main interest I should say was music. He steered straight for the piano in the schoolroom after he came and this (Sunday) afternoon having written his weekly letter to you he is strumming away most happily. Elsie and he had a long concert on the gramophone yesterday evening. Elsie reports his taste is good. We had a lot of rag-time records which Lionel didn't approve of in the least. There I am entirely with him.

Yesterday I drew the pond for him: found a wasp's nest and fagged him to help me carry rubbish to a bonfire. Lighting a fire is always a sound game for the young. (As I write I can hear that he has got into the Marseillaise on the gramophone and is trying to run an accompaniment on the piano). Now it has changed to God Save the King; both tunes are on the same record and as he knows that tune he is accompanying very well. I wish you could hear him. He has changed the tempo to suit his own ideas and – I write while he plays – he is handling the tune largo as you might say. We haven't worried him to do anything because I well remember that when a chap gets out of school in mid-term he only wants to slack and let the learning run out. So he goes from his book to his piano and back again at will. (Also it is raining hard).

We mixed a deadly mixture of honey and whiskey and dregs of liqueurs for our wasps this afternoon in a pickle bottle, but all our blandishments didn't avail to get 'em inside. Also I showed him my bees at a safe distance and he had a game of squash with Elsie. He told me, by the way, that bully-ing does not exist at schools any more – which is much what John says. He can nearly swim and intends to learn this term. They have fed him up a bit with cricket in the English fashion, and he ought to have tennis for a change.

He eats very well which is the main thing at this time of life. I had an idea from something I had heard that the little chap was delicate. He doesn't look it but he is certainly sensitive. Of course his first visit doesn't count. I'll get him over next term if I live when he is in the middle of one of our foul English autumns; Cranbrook isn't more than 30–40 minutes from us. The only drawback is that his Headmaster waylays me with intent to catch me to present prizes, so I have to walk carefully.

He is about a year younger than you were when we first met and I find it difficult (he doesn't) to remember the difference between our ages. He has not uttered anything noteworthy and I purposely am not taking too much notice of him. Remember our youthful opinions, when grown-ups insisted on importing themselves into our lives?

I had a note from Baugh t'other day saying you'd had your command extended a bit. Do you like it? When do you come home?[2]

Now I'll go down to tea. More later if the kid says anything a father or mother should hear.

Ever yours
Rudyard.

They sent him in his best Sunday jacket! I've told him next time to bring a dirty suit.

Notes
1. Lionel Walter Dunsterville (1902–70?), Dunsterville's eldest child, was now at Cranbrook Grammar School in Cranbrook, Kent.
2. "In January 1914 my tenure of command, with one year's extension, making six years in all, came to an end" (*Stalky's Reminiscences*, p. 239).

To Lawrence Cornford[1], 8 July 1913
ALS: Harvard University

Bateman's / Burwash / Sussex / July. 8. 1913.

Dear Lawrence

Congratulations in the first place on your passing so well into Wellington. I think you'll like the place, and all about it.

As to coming to Ascot, there isn't a ghost of a chance of my getting anywhere just now. I haven't a motor or what comes to the same thing I haven't a chauffeur[2] and there's no way of getting round England anywhere so as one can get back the same day if one uses the train.

You've got a big part in Feste – specially the piece where you rag Malvolio in the dungeon. Likewise a song or two. I wish I could see you at "and so the whirligig of time brings its revenges."[3] That's the best bit of the part.

But for me I must sit still and pray Heaven to send me a competent mechanic.

Ever affectionately,
Uncle Ruddy.

Notes
1. Lawrence Rudyard Cope Cornford (d. 1966), RK's godson, entered Wellington College in the Michaelmas term, 1913, and remained till 1917. He graduated from Cambridge in 1922 and was afterwards a solicitor and a schoolmaster (information from the archivist, Wellington College).
2. RK had fired his chauffeur George Moore on 16 June after six years' service: "His hot temper makes him do impossible things" (CK diary).
3. *Twelfth Night*, V.i 384–5: "And thus the whirligig of time brings in his revenges."

To John Kipling, 9 July 1913

ALS: University of Sussex

Bateman's / Burwash / Sussex / July. 9. 1913

Dear Old Man –

Just a line to beg you, as I am sure you will, buck up through the final term exams and come out with a good place. I am thinking a great deal of you these days.

There's nothing to tell in our events here except that we have no rain and the springs are low. I had an immense time out with the troops on Monday[1] – walked for miles with Gwynne and saw battle all round me at close hand. The drill of the men and their physique is magnificent. I am dining next Monday with the Kings Guard at St James's palace[2] – a new experience for me. It is supplied by the Coldstreams.

Moore leaves us on Saturday.[3] I'm rather sorry and very glad.

Ever your loving
Pater

Notes
1. RK means Monday, 30 June, when he and Gwynne observed the Army manoeuvres at Aldershot. The next day he came home and began a "story of his experiences at the camp" (CK diary, 1 July 1913). This, no doubt, was the story that RK describes at length in *Something of Myself*, pp. 214–15, about how the dead of the Boer War intruded upon the manoeuvres so that "there was a hurried calling-off of all arms by badly frightened Commandants – the men themselves sweating with terror though they knew not why". This story, he says, he finally threw away, in order to avoid questions about "psychical experiences". In a letter to Gwynne, 18 July 1913, RK writes of a suggestion for this story: "Yes. That's distinctly a good idea. You mean some old chap – not a special correspondent – who had served in the war – say an ex-major of Yeomanry – the local Squire. He sort of strolls out to see the show; and joins the procession (or rather meets it) of retiring and blue funked seniors" (ALS, Dalhousie University). On 22 July RK wrote to Lieutenant-Colonel R. J. Marker about the story: "I'm at my yarn now and when it's in type

should be very thankful if you'd just run an eye over it and check it for detail. I've made a pom-pom heard opening on a battery, 1200 yards *behind* the Coldstream's maxims which are hosing it down at 1100. I'm not quite sure of my ranges: tho' I believe the pom-pom could make a battery hop at 3500. Is that right?" (ALS, photocopy, Sussex).
2. On 14 July, on the invitation of Lieutenant-Colonel R. J. Marker (to Marker, 4 July 1913: ALS, Library of Congress).
3. See 8 July 1913.

To Frank N. Doubleday, 13 July 1913
TLS: Princeton University

Bateman's / Burwash / Sussex / 13th July, 1913.

Dear Frank,
    You are quite right. It was a great advantage of you to have sent your letter direct to us, as letters from the United States arrive on a Saturday and so it saves us several days. The particulars that you sent us don't bore us in the least, on the contrary, they are of the greatest possible interest and value to us.
    We have read through your ideas re the new Garden City Campaign and have given it our best and fullest consideration. Here are the conclusions we have arrived at: –
    The "Seven Seas" edition[1] Can only be twenty-three volumes unless you do not finish publication of the set till after October 1914, on which date I shall be publishing a volume of short stories.[2] This you could include. There isn't another volume ready. Note here that the "Seven Seas" edition includes the Letters to the Family – the Canadian letters which have never been published in book form before.[3] I take it Nye[4] took back a copy of the Bombay edition with him. You will see that, in it all the stories and verses are dated which, for the type of person who will buy such an edition, is a great advantage. I do not see that the people who would buy such an edition, is a great advantage. I do not see that the people who would buy such an edition would be any more inclined to purchase it on account of a facsimiled piece of M.S. From my point of view this is impossible, and from yours – isn't it a pity to make an edition which is quite different from anything you have done before and to include in it an old feature which you worked with the O. Henry?[5] It's a mistake, don't you think, to rub in a great success. An edition of this sort, as I see it, *must* be dignified and must be carried by its own weight; and Mr. Nye seemed to think, when he was here, that there was no chance of its not being sold. It isn't, after all, in view of the nation's population, a large number to get rid of. Here the Bombay Edition is already

at a premium. You make no mention in the "Seven Seas" edition that it is a signed one. I am ready to sign when you send the sheets over.[6]
The dummies reached us on Sunday. As you will know by now we have decided to have the paper of Dummy A. which feels and looks the richest, and the type, the "Scotch-face" type, Dummy B. If you find any difficulty in matching the blue of the Bombay Edition for initial letters you might have them in a good red. I should also like the binding to be a little darker in tone than in the Bombay Edition which strikes me as rather pale and delicate. I suggest that the imprint at the end should be the "Swastika" alone and not the elephant's head. Both are my trademarks in a way but we have used the elephant's head so much in the "Outward Bound."

The real interest of Mr. Nye's visit to me was not however the "Seven Seas" edition. It was the ideas that we talked about together in Paris – the Searle-Roebuck[7] Deal and the attack on the general market which is going to swamp the pirates. I think the Kipling book-case idea is excellent, as also is your larger distribution of the Kipling Index,[8] and I take it that you will be able to get the "Century" to go in with you on all your deals. I do hope that the S. R. proposition will go through. *I should like a copy of the Kipling Index.*

In regard to your suggested Note A. It is very good but it seems to me that you make too little play with the large and steady sales in France and Germany, of the translations. The sales in Italy, Russia, Scandinavia, Norway, Sweden and Denmark, and Finland are also very continuous, as well as the translations into the vernacular in India. I haven't the figures by me, but the aggregate is hundreds and thousands every year. Turkey is about the only country that does not translate my books *en bloc*. She confines herself to "If", which in Turkish looks very noble.[9]

Yours truly,
Rudyard Kipling

What you tell me about Nelson is delicious! My best congratulations on the $700 magnate. He'll never enjoy his millions as much as that sum![10]

Notes
1. The American counterpart of the Bombay Edition (see 22 December 1912). The Seven Seas Edition appeared in 27 volumes, from 1914 to 1926.
2. *A Diversity of Creatures*; its publication was postponed by the war until 1917.
3. Volume 5 of the Seven Seas Edition was the first American publication of *Letters to the Family* in book form, but it had appeared as a book in Canada in 1908.
4. Doubleday's representative, who had called at Bateman's on 12 May (Bateman's Visitors Book).
5. The Manuscript Edition of the *Complete Works* of O. Henry, 14 vols (Garden City: Doubleday, Page, 1912–17). A sheet of MS is inserted in one or more volumes of each set.
6. The edition was limited to 1,050 sets, the first volume of each set signed by RK.

7. Thus in MS, for Sears, Roebuck, the great American mail-order firm.
8. A *Kipling Index*, compiled by Eugene F. Saxton and first published in 1911, was being offered for free distribution in, e.g., Doubleday's *Country Life in America* magazine, November 1913. This was presumably the model for the *Kipling Index*, based on the English trade edition, that was published in London in 1914. The American version of the *Index* was reprinted in subsequent years in various forms: see, e.g., 18 March 1919.
9. RK received a Turkish version of "If" from his cousin Hugh Poynter: "Thanks very much for the Hakk with its translation of If, which made me feel very proud. I'd love a literal translation" (27 May [1912]: ALS, Sussex).
10. The postscript is added in RK's hand.

To Arthur Gibbs[1], 22 July 1913

ALS: Mrs Marjorie House

Bateman's / Burwash / Sussex / July. 22. 1913

Dear Gibbs,

If you can possibly get a man *please* pass him along. The R[olls]. R[oyce]. Co. don't seem to be able to find one. I want him married: I'll give him a cottage and garden and £2 (two pounds) a week. He has about 2 months to himself in winter on full pay and he don't have anything in the way of hard work. But he has to have entire charge of the car, *and to be civil.*

I'll sell the car for £1100: it cost £1400 – if I can't get a man and spend the money in a squadron of Fords.

Ever so many thanks for your kindness and for your invitation but don't you think it's rather rubbing it in to write a chap whom you know to be a notorious paralytic (as far as transport is concerned) to come up and see you. I'm borrowing a man now from the R.R. to get my boy back from Wellington.[2]

Thanks for the Stepney[3] tale. You see I couldn't take a "Stepney" now – I can't even take a lawful wife anywhere! We go and look at the darn thing and want to kick it! The wife is so lost as to point out that a Silent Knight[4] (last pitch of degradation) wouldn't fill up the garage as much and might be driven.

Ever yours
Rudyard Kipling

Notes
1. Gibbs (1868–1960), of Birtley House, Bramley, Surrey, was a member of the Stock Exchange, 1889–1948, and was associated with the flotation of companies promoted by Lord Beaverbrook and the founders of Rolls-Royce. It was Gibbs who provided Eaves (see [13 October? 1913]) as a temporary chauffeur for RK (RK to Gibbs, 29 August 1917: ALS, Mrs Marjorie House).

2. John was brought back from Wellington on 2 August (RK to J. St Loe Strachey, 3 August 1913: ALS, House of Lords Record Office).
3. According to Partridge, *Dictionary of Slang*, 8th edn, a "Stepney" is both "a spare wheel carried on a motor-car" and a "white-slave".
4. See [*c.* early March 1911].

To Colonel J. M. Fleming, 23 July 1913

ALS: University of Sussex

Bateman's / Burwash / Sussex / July 23 / 13

Dear Fleming,

We went to see Trix at Scarboro' last week[1] and I confess, so far as I was able to judge, I found her very much improved since I had seen her last. She seemed steadier in herself, more communicative and less self-absorbed. I went for a short motor drive with her one evening and for nearly an hour's walk on Scarboro beach after breakfast the next morning. All that time she was, of course, not normal but in no sense out of the ordinary in her talk and behaviour. She made one or two remarks about things that she had seen which proved that she was thinking and reasoning about what she saw. She has, too, much more initiative, it seems to me, than she had last year – gets up and does things on her own. Her nurse reads to her a good deal which Trix told me that she likes.

We are taking a house at Kessingland near Lowestoft Norfolk, for three weeks this autumn.[2] The children and their friends will fill it for the first fortnight, but one of the inducements to me to take it was that it was so near to Trix that it would be possible for her to come to us there if you approved – for our last week. We haven't quite settled our dates yet but it would be early in September and if you thought well of the idea I will give you the date later. I very much liked Trix's nurse, as well as Mrs. Kemp, and I fancy that the change might amuse and interest Trix.

Very sincerely yours
Rudyard Kipling

Notes

1. Trix had only recently returned to England from Jersey, where she had been since 1911, and was now staying in a village near Scarborough. RK and CK saw her in Scarborough on 15 and 16 July (Rees extracts).
2. The house belonged to Rider Haggard, and RK had rented it sight unseen (to R. W. K. Edwards, 23 July 1913: TLS, Syracuse University). It is described as a "two-storied building perched on a cliff, its many windows looking out over nine acres of land and miles of churning water. U-shaped, it had once been a

coastguard station and was filled with the sounds and the smells of the North Sea" (Cohen, *Rudyard Kipling to Rider Haggard*, p. 79). The family went there on 24 August and returned on 10 September (CK diary). Trix did not visit them there.

To Sir Max Aitken, 29 July 1913

ALS: Harvard University

Bateman's / Burwash / Sussex / July 29. 1913.

Dear Aitken:

We're both rejoiced to learn from your wife's last letter that you're on the mend again. Too much London – air, grub, hours etc. – taken in a gulp *is* apt to be disconcerting. One of the funniest things I know is to watch doctors giving names for the troubles which overtake one after one has overdone (I've been there: so I know). I merely mention this in order that you should not be surprised or annoyed if the medical men find out that you have nineteen separate and serious complaints, each demanding a special (*and* expensive) treatment.

Likewise do not forget my gentle hint of some months ago that the richer the patient the more obscure and interesting are his diseases. So cheer up and let us have a word from you now and again.

Things here stink pretty much. We are going to have Gehazi for Lord Chief Justice,[1] They tell me: also young Locker Lampson[2] tells me he's going to bring a law suit about the Marconi business, but Allah only knows if he will be let. I spent the week end with St Loe Strachey and, whatever we did, the talk turned on Marconi.[3]

Gwynne and I had a joyous 2 days in camp with the troops the other day – sleeping in a tent and trying to imagine it was the old life back again after 13 years. I met a lot of the old war-birds and saw the new troops who are not so bad. Otherwise I've been more or less at work with more or less good results. I've got a little less than two thousand pounds by me just now ready for investment but *not*, I think, in U.S. rails. There may be a big break if we have the Rand Strike[4] but I'd like to have a list of possible investments.

I wish you'd been out with me today before lunch. I was picking mushrooms in the fields. Got about 10 lb weight off one meadow in an hour which gave me exactly the feeling of getting something for nothing which Lloyd George is always appealing to.

Here's a Norwegian fisherman's prayer that a man sent me the other day.

> "Lord give me grace to catch a fish
> So big that even I

In talking of it afterward
May have no need to lie."

That strikes me as very sweet.

Now you write me a few lines telling me truthfully how you feel and I'll tell you what your symptoms mean. This is a great offer. But, seriously, *write*.

With all our love to you both

Ever yours
Rudyard Kipling

P. S.   I have some money in Canada too. Altogether I have about £3500 for investment. That's what I call solid wealth!

Notes
1. That is, Sir Rufus Isaacs: see 22 December 1912. Rufus Daniel Isaacs (1860–1935), 1st Marquess of Reading; after a successful career as a barrister held office as Solicitor-General and then Attorney-General, 1910–13; he was appointed Lord Chief Justice in October 1913, Ambassador to the US, 1918, and Viceroy of India in 1921; created Baron, 1914, Viscount, 1916, Marquess, 1926. The rumour of Isaacs's appointment to the Lord Chief Justiceship is what provoked RK to begin "Gehazi": see 31 July 1913.
2. Oliver Locker-Lampson (1880–1954), younger son of the Victorian writer of light verse, Frederick Locker-Lampson, was currently MP for North Huntingdonshire.
3. The company included "Lord and Lady Strachey, Lord O'Hagan, George Lloyd, Locker-Lampson" (CK diary, 26 July 1913).
4. White miners on the Rand struck in May and June 1913; in July police broke up a strikers' rally in Johannesburg and troops were called out. A settlement negotiated in early July did not satisfy the miners; a general strike was then threatened but did not materialise.

To Arthur Steel-Maitland[1], 31 July 1913
ALS: Mrs Lisa Lewis

Bateman's / Burwash / Sussex / July. 31. 1913

Confidential
Dear Mr Steel-Maitland

Many thanks for your formal conveyance of copyright in Gehazi – noble word! – to whom I am attending.[2]

In the meantime would you let me have as soon as possible from the office,

(α) exact figures, with dates, of money made by Shoofus in his deal in Marconis

(β) exact words of his declaration before the House in Oct (?) 1912.[3]

(γ) exact words of his admission before the committee that he had told Handel-Booth and Falconer that he had had Marconi dealings.[4]

(δ) exact terms of the original charge to which he objected so strongly.[5]

I have not yet got my Marconi papers in proper shape or would not have bothered you. Please let me have 'em as soon as may be.

Very sincerely yours
Rudyard Kipling

Notes

1. Steel-Maitland (see [July? 1908]) was now MP for East Birmingham and chairman of the Unionist Party.
2. In the poem called "Gehazi", RK's attack on Sir Rufus Isaacs for his part in the Marconi scandal (see 22 December 1912). RK began work on the poem on 25 July, "moved thereto by the rumour of Mr. Isaac being about to be made Lord Chief Justice" (CK diary). RK credits Steel-Maitland again with the idea for "Gehazi" in 14 November 1913.
3. In the debate on the Marconi contract in the Commons on 11 October 1912 Isaacs declared that he had had not "one single transaction" in the shares of the Marconi Company. This was true as regards the British Marconi Company, with which the government had entered into contract; but Isaacs made no reference to the fact that he had bought shares in the American Marconi Company, and it was on this point that he was widely held not to have acted honestly.
4. There was no such "admission". In testimony on 27 March 1913 before the parliamentary select committee appointed to inquire into the Marconi contract, Isaacs was asked whether "he had made any communication to the chairman or any member of the Committee of the fact that he had purchased and sold the shares in the American company". The question was objected to by Isaacs's political friends on the committee, and it was decided that Isaacs was not to answer it (*The Times*, 28, 29 March 1913). Frederick Handel Booth (1867–1947) and James Falconer (1856–1931), Liberal MPs, were both members of the select committee of inquiry and both had in fact been informed in confidence by Isaacs of his dealings in American shares "so that they might be able to head off any awkward questions on this score" (H. Montgomery Hyde, *Lord Reading*, 1967, p. 138). Hence the lines in "Gehazi":

    > Take order now, Gehazi,
    > That no man talk aside
    > In secret with his judges
    > The while his case is tried.

5. RK probably means the story printed by *Le Matin* of Paris on 14 February 1913 stating that Isaacs and Sir Herbert Samuel, the Postmaster-General, had used their insiders' knowledge to make a profitable speculation in Marconi shares. Isaacs and Samuel at once sued the paper for libel, and the story was shown to be groundless: see *Annual Register, 1913*, pp. 71–2.

To Frank N. Doubleday, 4–5 August 1913

TL and ALS: Princeton University

Bateman's, Burwash, Sussex, August 4. 1913.

Dear Mr. Doubleday,

Your letter of July 25th is just in. The circular of Macmillan in regard to the Bombay Edition was a very choice affair, and went into no details whatever – as I remember it – in regard to the subject matter of the Edition. It had two pages: one page dealt with the Author and his position in Letters, and the other with the proposed Edition from its printing, binding, and book-making point of view generally. And the only suggestions that you might gain from it would be that it was in size the size of the book to be, the print was from the Florence type, and the paper was the paper to be used in the Edition. I only saw the circular for a minute or two, but this is my recollection of it.

I am very much interested about Mr. Gillis[1] and his interest in the Seven Seas Edition, and I am quite sure that it will turn out admirably. Mr. Nye's interview with Sears-Roebuch, however, excites me far more, and I shall be glad if we are able to deal a proper blow to the pirates. I was quite clear in my talk with Charles Scribner on this subject,[2] and told him quite plainly that my great interest at present was pirates, and that pure spite more than anything else had influenced me in my desire for a free hand, so that I might strike at the pirate.

I have no wish or desire that a Kipling Index should be published and sold; in fact I object to it; but I should like to draw your attention to the "Kipling Dictionary"[3], published by George Routledge, whose American publisher is E. P. Dutton, and done by a man called Arthur Young. We had some correspondence with you on the subject at the time it was done. If you want details and facts, that would not be a bad place to get them from, – though I am far from wishing to say that the man is accurate. He did not trouble to consult with me because, as I remember, I wrote to him that I would not let him do it advertised "with my sanction." But I have given a promise to another man, and he is in progress of making a book which is going to be extremely valuable to us all, of answers to leading questions in all the volumes.[4] I think it would not be a bad idea for you to have this book in America: Hodder and Stoughton are doing it here, since they know that I do not object.

As to the Glossary, – I cannot see what earthly help it is to include it with the "Kipling Index". I cannot see a customer going to a book-seller and asking him for the meaning of words.

I have to apologise for the mistaken address: it comes because of a change of secretaries,[5] and the out-going secretary seems to have left her address book in the middle ages.[6]

I now take on in my own hand – trembling a little after an hour's fierce work in the brook with John at hauling out stumps and logs up the bank.

However we got out nearly half a cord of decent firewood and so I feel richer by $2.50 of my own earnings.

How on earth did you, with your own Page[78] as Ambassador, get into that mess with Uncle Sam about the Bombay Edition? Can't a copy be got into the U.S. even for the laudable purpose of increasing business?

Delighted to learn that Nelson is forging (I mean publishing) ahead.[8] Here are some "slogans" for him: "$\frac{\text{Knowledge}}{\text{Wisdom}}$ and gold are never second-hand." "Take care of your facts and your fiction will take care of itself." Also he *must* have a trademark. What do you think of a second hand itself [   ][9] helping mankind? I want to see more of his circulars and I should also like some figures of his sales. It's an exciting enterprise and one that looks as if it might be developed.

But to return to the 7 Seas Edition: Letters to the Family *are* Canadian letters – that is to say there is only one lot of 'em – I think the Fleet in Being is included in some other edition.[10] If not, of course you will include it.

We are both very excited to see how the venture will turn out and are already building joyous castles in the air.

Tuesday: 9 p.m.

I've just put in *all* day with two men, one pony and a long chain, hiking all the logs that John and I couldn't handle yesterday out of the brook. I am stiff, sore and dead tired but we've got up every dam log and only broke the chain twice. Also the pony is quite unbroken. Wish to goodness you and Nellie could have seen the fray. Tell her that her cypripediums[11] seem to have taken out their naturalization papers in England. With love to all.

Ever
Rud

Notes
1. Walter Gillis (1855–1925), printer, designer, and bibliophile. Doubleday says that Gillis "acted as our advisor on typographical matters and stimulated us to produce better and more attractive typesetting" (*The Memoirs of a Publisher*, New York, 1972, p. 184).
2. Scribner was at Bateman's for lunch on 1 August (Bateman's Visitors Book).
3. Young's *Dictionary* of RK: see 15 August 1912.
4. Ralph Durand, *A Handbook to the Poetry of Rudyard Kipling*, published in both London and New York, 1914. As this letter suggests, RK seems not merely to have permitted Durand's book but to have assisted with it. Durand (1876–1945) called and had tea at Bateman's on 13 October 1913 (CK diary). The book is still a notably useful commentary on RK's verse down through 1911.
5. Miss Hogg, who came in 1911, had been succeeded by Miss Bowman (CK diary, 3 July 1913). She proved unsatisfactory: "slow in her work and I greatly fear her wits" (Rees extracts, 4 July 1913). Miss Bowman left at the end of July and was succeeded by a Miss Veysey, who came on trial for a month (Rees extracts,

22 July 1913). Then came Miss Chamberlain, who arrived on 23 September (CK diary, 23 September 1913).

6. The letter from his point on is in RK's hand.
7. Walter Hines Page (1855–1918), partner in Doubleday, Page and Co. from 1899, and thus RK's publisher from that date; he had been appointed Ambassador to Great Britain by his old friend Woodrow Wilson in March 1913.
8. Beginning in 1910 Nelson had developed a business, first in selling out-of-date magazines at reduced prices, and then in reprinting books to be sold to the list of his magazine subscribers. He used such slogans as "Pay no money now" (John Tebbel, *A History of Book Publishing in the United States*, II [New York, 1975], 330).
9. Word illegible: nobly?
10. *A Fleet in Being* had just been collected for the first time, in the Bombay Edition; it is also included in the Seven Seas Edition.
11. Lady slippers.

To Cameron Forbes,[1] 21 August 1913

TLS: Harvard University

Bateman's / Burwash / Sussex / August 21. 1913.

Private.

Dear Mr. Forbes,

Yours of the 4th. And now you see that I am taking a leaf out of your book and answering you in type-writing. Unlike you, I cannot dictate for nuts. But my desire is *not* to learn to write; I often wish that pens and ink had never been invented.

I am very pleased to learn that you are better, though I cannot see how a man with any sort of kidney complaint can play Polo; but of course if that gentle exercise does not kill, it must cure.

Thank you also for the figures which you sent as to the moral and material progress of your little brown brother. The figures about the rise of trade in the Islands under Free Trade with the United States are especially significant, and I am having them used for my own base ends in newspaper quarters.

I am grieved to notice your enthusiasm for education in the abstract, and your pride in the increase of educational facilities. In due time, say in two generations, you will reap the reward of your beneficent policy – as we are already reaping the reward of ours in India – in the shape of prolonged and elaborate rebellion, sedition and treason: – this is almost axiomatic. The beauty of education is, that like drink, it awakes all the desires and at the same time inhibits (if this is the correct medical term?) most of the capacities. But these are things which I know I cannot persuade you of. The only things that matter in this fallen world are transportation and sanitation.

I have been watching the Mexican situation[2] with a great deal of interest, because it seems to me that with any luck Dr. Wilson will be landed in a war, compared to which our Boer War was a flea-bite.

We are just off now[3] to the East Coast for the sacred English August holiday, else I would inflict on you a longer letter; but I consider your health and forbear. Do write me again before the close of the year, and send me what papers you can.

Very sincerely,
Rudyard Kipling.

Notes
1. See 7 May 1912.
2. President Wilson had refused to recognise the government of General Huerta in Mexico following the murder of President Madero; Wilson wished to avoid involvement in the Mexican revolution, but there was much American pressure for intervention.
3. They did not in fact leave until 24 August.

To John Kipling, 27 September 1913
ALS: University of Sussex

Bateman's / Burwash / Sussex / Saturday 27th. Sep / 13.

Dear Old Man –

I don't know what *your* weather has been but ours, for the last three days, is simply tropical! Cloudless skies and steady damp heat.

Uncle Edward – the President of the Royal Academy – is here doing a water colour drawing of Bateman's for us.[1] He sits out in the garden under a white sketching umbrella, works without a break from 10 till 1. Then from 2. till 4-30. Never saw such an industrious old bird! He has also got a commission to make a drawing – not an oil painting praise the Lord! – of me.[2] I don't know how long that will take but he says only two (or three!) sittings. He is coming down in a week or two to do it and I confess I don't look forward to the prospect. This afternoon we are all going to Knole to see the place with Lady Sackville[3] for our guide. She was the woman that won the lawsuit the other day when a man called Scott left her a pot of money and his sisters tried to prove that he had no business to have done it. They say she is a most interesting woman and she certainly wiped the floor of the court with F. E. Smith[4] when he tried to cross-examine her! You will have seen, I fear, that I had to attend a National Service meeting at Burwash.[5] I'm awfully

3. Pencil portrait of Kipling by Sir Edward Poynter, made at Bateman's, 5–10 October 1913, for Sir Max Aitken.

sorry, for your sake, that I couldn't get out of it. Lord Roberts asked me and as I want to keep solid with him for *your* sake you ungrateful little devil, I agreed. 'Twasn't a bad meeting and I always like speaking to a crowd in the dark. But I thought of you and was brief. Thank you very much for what you tell me about Supering.[6] I do hope to goodness that you'll escape it. It may not be a disgrace but it's not nice and there will, in your case, probably be a heap of publicity about it. *Don't* say Damn! I'm only telling you the cold facts of our case.

I do most deeply sympathize with you old man about being cut out from running this term. But what *can* you do? I'd sooner have you well *not* running than sick even tho' you ran like three bloody hares. See how your literary style has corrupted mine.

Mother has been in bed for two days with a beastly cold. She is better now but Elsie is dribbling at the nose now. By the way Fipps is doing up the schoolroom *quite* regardless. It seems to me it will be a ladies boudoir by the time you come back. I note what you say about a motor-byke. We must wait till next year's models are out. *I* say that in a year no one will ride a motor byke except clerks and road-surveyors. There's rumours of a new road car that is going to knock spots out of all other cars. I am fairly bewildered with the choice of small ones. They *don't* kick at a boy under 17 driving cycle engines on two or *four* wheels. Dearest love from us all.

Ever
Your Pater

Notes

1. The painting of the house, with another by Poynter also dated 1913, now hangs at Bateman's.
2. The drawing had been commissioned by Sir Max Aitken; RK sat to Poynter on 5 and 10 October 1913 (CK diary). The drawing, in black and sanguine pencil, is now in the Beaverbrook Art Gallery, Fredericton, New Brunswick.
3. Victoria Sackville-West (d. 30 January 1936), wife of the 3rd Baron Sackville and mother of the writer Victoria Sackville-West; they lived at Knole, a great Tudor palace, near Sevenoaks, Kent. Lady Sackville was the principal beneficiary of the will of Sir John Murray Scott, her intimate friend, who died in January 1913. Scott's brothers and sisters brought suit against her, charging "undue influence". The case was the summer sensation of London and was decided in Lady Sackville's favour on 7 July. She received nearly half a million pounds from Scott's bequest. For Smith's cross-examination of Lady Sackville, see *The Times*, 4 July 1913.
4. Frederick Edwin Smith (1872–1930), 1st Earl of Birkenhead, barrister and Unionist MP, 1906–18; a cabinet minister during the war; Lord Chancellor, 1919–22; Secretary of State for India, 1924–8; created Earl, 1922. He had one of the largest legal practices in London in the years before the war.
5. RK addressed an open air meeting for the National Service League at Burwash on 25 September; the speech (uncollected), on the horrors of invasion, was widely reported in England and in France. It was the subject of a leader in *The Times* on 26 September, mildly endorsing the idea of compulsory service.
6. I.e., being "superannuated": that is, being compelled to leave school on grounds of age. John had turned sixteen on 17 August. After missing much of the autumn term at Wellington, he returned at the beginning of the new year but left for good in April 1914.

To Andrew Macphail, 5 October 1913
ALS: Photocopy, National Archives of Canada

Bateman's / Burwash / Sussex / Oct. 5. 1913.

Dear Macphail –

It arrived. Didn't it just! It came in a solid web – seven yards long – bearing an Old Bond Street address but a smell of honesty which one don't associate with that part of the world. And, as you say, it is of stuff that used to be handed down in wills – "my camlet riding-cloak" – "my frieze breeches with the steel buttons." The family fought over it but I think I've won and am going to have such a shooting-coat or maybe motor coat as was never yet built. Herein I have defeated Elsie who talked of tailor made sheets; and the wife who said something about a cloak. A most noble gift!

We have just finished the biggest job we've ever done yet: and feel like two Gibbonses at Lausanne[1] – if that was where he finished his "Decline and Fall." Three hundred and eighty-five yards of road – bottomed on split iron-stone rock and topped with iron-stone gravel out of the brook – where never yet road was but only a foul slimy track. And the four or five men who did it as keen as artists should be on their work. *That* is going to outlast all my printed stuff. It's drained with 4 and 6 in. drains on either side – 1000 carts at a low estimate have tramped and consolidated it in the making. Thus I – I alone who discovered in a suspicious dimple of a meadow an outcrop of sandstone which presently turned into iron shale – stuff that in the old days was melted at the Forge. T'was not I but a visitor who spent a pious Sabbath drilling holes into the great dull red sheet of rock and trying to blast it. But he didn't know enough to tamp his charge (which when you come to think of it is all life in allegory) whereby the dam' charge blew out like a gun and the air was thick as partridges with chunks of rock that whizzed past our heads. However no one was hit and we went to work on that quarry with crow and pick and … . but you shall see when you come. *Why* is it that one gets more pure joy and satisfaction out of a job of dirt and sweat and manual design than out of any brain-child? Here's my play (a one-acter it is true) turning out a success[2] and demanded by music halls (which must surely mean Popularity among the People) and here am I all full-chested and puffed up at the thought of a dirty little bit of road. You have the same feelings. They ooze out all through your letters. Of course if you use dynamite you are socially far above us. We only tried black powder. However, when I need more stone from our quarry I'll hire a blaster and dynamite it good and plenty.

I am pleased about your child and the Gaelic also the teacher who doesn't think much of English. A bad look out for Willie Shakspeare. I had a man the other day from the interior of Wales poisonous-full of his own "nationality" and its tongue and the teaching thereof.[3] But I entirely agreed with him and was prepared to help in giving funds for the teaching of Cymric and Ogham[4] and all the rest – compulsory if need be. Says he gratefully: – "But I shouldn't have expected this of *you* Mr Kipling." "Man" says I, "anything that cripples and diverts and renders more unintelligible the inferior and crippled breeds of the earth has my blessing and support."

Which reminds me a man from S. Africa[5] has been staying with me and telling wildly funny tales of the Dutch "administration" down there. You see, they never knew how to administer other than primitively: and the moment they are confronted with the most elementary sorts of organization have (swearing horribly) to employ Englishmen. But they take it out of us by renaming all the towns in what they fondly conceive is Dutch – their hideous taal-patois.[6] And here in England we are oppressed and lectured at by fancy races and fancy breeds. Herod died as we are dying.[7]

But the revolt in Ulster[8] is giving us all new hope – a thing that was bound to happen. It may very well be put down. There is a rumour that our menials intend to send Catholic troops against the North. This will be very interesting. But whether the trouble is suppressed for the time being or not, it will give us the habit of rebellion and when decent folk learn at last to rebel against oppression, much may be expected. Just now, the main question among "politicians" is how corrupt the present government is.[9] Estimates vary. Some say that several members of the Cabinet are untainted but this seems extravagant. The charge now is that they gambled on English railway stocks at the time of the big Railway strike[10] – they being at the time busy in composing the said strike.

Can you beat that?

But on the whole I am hopeful. Both parties are in the melting pot and our party is the more stupid of the two but people are getting weary of clever scallawags.

Incidentally, the women are burning houses.[11] I have now an empty farm house down the valley[12] which I should not be a bit surprised to find lit. It's a curious thing to hear people discussing the possibilities of arson when they go to the sea-side. But I confess I admire their outlook. The tacit assumption is (quite rightly) that what a woman does – outside certain lines – does not matter. And the women who do the jobs are *so* pleased and *so* violent and (by a law which you and I know well) vary outrage with printing and talking smut on a flamboyant scale. Meantime I have done another play[13] and meditate yet others. It's a bad thing to have a first play a success. One begins to think that the drama is easy. I shall probably come a "howler" in this belief.

Now I will go away from my desk. I am being pourtrayed (in pencil but except for certain licenses that is *just* as bad as oils) by my uncle Sir E. Poynter who has been incited thereto by a friend of mine.[14] I love my uncle and my friend *much* less than I used to: but I must go and sit to my uncle (who hates the smell of tobacco) in order to please my friend who is an inveterate smoker. "And thus the whirligig of time etc."[15] The wife – praise Allah – is very well and jubilant over the Road: Elsie too is well and happy. John is *not* so fit. I hear from school again that his glands are bothering him but I am assured on good advice that he will "grow out of them."[16]

Meantime I am as ever

Affectionately,
Rudyard Kipling

Our woods now are at their most admirable. Peacock blue in the shadow with orange splashes of bracken. Would you were here!

Notes

1. See Gibbon's account of how he wrote "the last lines of the last page" of his *History* "in a summer house in my garden" at Lausanne (*Autobiography*, ed. John Murray, 1897, p. 333).
2. *The Harbour Watch*: see 9 April 1913. RK wrote to Macphail on 21 August 1913 about "the accident of a small curtain-raiser which I perpetrated this Spring, and which to my unbounded surprise is seriously accepted as a play" (TLS, National Archives of Canada).
3. Not identified.
4. A twenty-character alphabet used by the ancient British and Irish in the oldest form of Gaelic known.
5. Perhaps Sir Charles Crewe, who, with his wife, was at Bateman's on 20–22 September 1913 (Bateman's Visitors Book).
6. Afrikaans.
7. Acts 12:23: "and he was eaten of worms, and gave up the ghost".
8. Over the question of Home Rule for Ireland: an armed volunteer force had been formed in Ulster, and was vowed to resist Catholic authority at all costs: see 2 December 1913.
9. See 22 December 1912 on the corruption charges against ministers.
10. In 1911: see 16 August 1911.
11. In the Suffragette campaign of arson, under way since late 1912 and intensified after the withdrawal of the Franchise Bill in February 1913. A house being built by Lloyd George was among the casualties.
12. Keylands.
13. Not identified, though it might be the undated one-act play entitled "Upstairs" published in the *Times Literary Supplement*, 7 April 1995, from the MS in the Berg Collection, New York Public Library.
14. See 27 September 1913.
15. Shakespeare, *Twelfth Night*, V, i, 384–5.
16. See [13 October? 1913].

To John Kipling, [13 October? 1913][1]
ALS: University of Sussex

Bateman's / Burwash / Sussex / Monday

Dear Old Man –

A Heavenly morning – I only hope it is as good with you!

We got home in three hours running time – in spite of fog. I'm rather obliged to you for what you told me about cutting off the engine so as to prevent backfiring and I am going out to tell Eaves[2] about it – as though I had thought it all out myself! I can't tell you what a delight it was to us all – and to me specially – to see you again. You know I'm rather found of you – though you *are* a dam young sweep. I recognize *quite* well how difficult it is for one to keep on with one's work[3] when one is hove into Sanny at uncertain intervals but I *do* believe in what your "small specialist" Bland Sutton[4] said – you'll grow out of it if you hang on.[5]

I'm going to call on B.S. the next time I'm in town to ask him when you ought to see him again. Not till after the 1st however. No need to [   ][6] again a day off. Tell me if you think *red* leather goes best with grey paint on a G.W.K.[7] My own idea is green but here I am willing to bow to your views.

Dear love from us all

Ever
Dad

Notes

1. Date conjectured from internal evidence.
2. The new chauffeur, who arrived on 16 August (Rees extracts). RK wrote to Arthur Gibbs on 29 August that "I owe you thanks also for Eaves who has a pleasing touch on the wheel a sympathetic manner and what looks remarkably like a professional conscience" (*Kipling Journal*, December 1985, p. 19).
3. The MS reads: "for one to keep one with one work".
4. Sir John Bland-Sutton (1855–1936), distinguished surgeon, President of the Royal College of Surgeons, 1923–6. When RK first met Bland-Sutton is not known, but they were friends by 1908, when RK gave his speech at the Middlesex Hospital at the request of Bland-Sutton (see 4 October 1908).
5. John had had mumps in August (RK to Lady Edward Cecil, 15 August 1913: ALS, Syracuse University) and seems to have been troubled by "glands" thereafter. RK took John to consult Sir John Bland-Sutton on 15 September; he diagnosed a "slight thickening" of the thyroid and said they must not go to Switzerland for the winter (Rees extracts: Bland-Sutton later withdrew his prohibition of Switzerland). John was twice in the Wellington sanatorium for "swollen glands" in October 1913 (Baker, *Kipling Journal*, June 1982, p. 12). On 1 November John was operated on by Bland-Sutton for "enucleation of the tonsils" (RK to Dr Curteis, 1 November 1913: ALS, University of Sussex).

6. World illegible.
7. A friction-drive, rear-engined English car built from 1911 to 1926; it was light and inexpensive (Georgano, *Complete Encyclopedia*, p. 260). RK evidently intended to buy one (see 5 December 1913) but in the event did not.

To Sir Herbert Stephen, 25 October 1913
ALS: Cornell University

Bateman's / Burwash / Sussex / Oct. 25. 1913

Dear Stephen,

You're a brick to take this amount of trouble and I'll be more than grateful if when you find more peas, not to say brickbats and tin cans, under the mattress you'd spare a line to let me know.

Now for the indictments. I begin with *mea culpa, mea culpa, mea maxima culpa* which is French for dam carelessness. All the same I wish *you'd* had the job.

(1.) I thought I'd dredged out pretty nearly everything but "Where would I be etc." as well as Jane Ardin' (which a man has written to me about *most* arbitrary) were oversights.[1] "Taught 'em to respec' etc." is *not* mine but a genuine Barracker.[2] "Ho my etc."[3] – I can't at this distance of time be sure of; but I do know that if by any slip I put in something that wasn't mine the Rowton lodging houses[4] would give up their dead to prove that I had deliberately stole it from some Regimental Bard of the neolithic 80's. That's what flummoxed me when I began the overhaul. Nota Bene – one man weighed in with a stanza from Longfellow: ditto Clough and wanted to know why the dooce I'd left 'em out![5]

(2) You're right about Philadelphia.[6] I omitted it because of unintelligibility – in spite of the last verse which I liked. Now I see I was wrong.

(3) The Song of Queen Bess was originally written as in Songs from Books because it bore directly on the locale of The Story of *Gloriana* in R[ewards]. and F[airies]. It ought to have been in that form in R. & F. and simpliciter in Songs from Books.[7]

(4) You may know the British criminal but you don't know the British public. I did *not* asterisk "Pharisee" in the original ballad:[8] whereby my mail and correspondence was increased. But there is a chap now laboriously preparing a full set of notes to my versified work which will make you giggle.[9] *Would* it surprise you to know, in the language of cross examination, that most people consider "Pharisee" to have something to do with Gospels? It did me.

(5) The line in "Frankie's trade" is wholly damnable – and the worse because it ruins "of a three day etc." in Rewards and Fairies. I've noted it:

I can't think it's my own error but more like that of a cultured proof reader.[10]

(6)   If you'd tell me the whole tangle of *"Gow's Watch,"* I'd be your debtor. It's an ungodly hash of (a) a play that I began (b) another play that I began under another name (c) two extracts from a third play that I didn't begin at all and (d) a lying ascription to Lyden his Irenius which has already brought me much woe. But to save myself I can't disentangle it.[11]

Per contra: Old Mother Laid in Wool is *all* new except the two first lines which come from an old Sussex song about hopping – and I wish to goodness I could recover the rest of it.[12] All the Prodigal Son[13] except verse 1 is new: the last verse of Gallio's Song[14] is new. Heriot's Ford[15] is new except one and a half verses and I do frankly admit that the extra verses in the Two Sided Man[16] strengthen naught. I don't suppose it would be fair to rake in the few that I have omitted of my chapter heads in a later impression but I think now, thanks mainly to correspondents, I've about got the run of 'em with accuracy. But, as I said, you go ahead and of your goodness, let me know about everything that you object to.

Gratefully yours ever
Rudyard Kipling.

Notes

1. Both verses from *Plain Tales from the Hills* are omitted from *Songs from Books*: "Oh! Where would I be when my froat was dry" is the heading to "The Madness of Private Ortheris" and is identified as *"Barrack Room Ballad"*. "Jain 'Ardin' was a Sarjint's wife" heads "The Daughter of the Regiment" and is identified as "Old Barrack-Room Ballad". Neither was ever collected by RK in any edition of his verse.
2. From the verses heading "The Three Musketeers" (*Plain Tales*).
3. Heading to "The Taking of Lungtungpen" (*Plain Tales*), identified as *"Barrack Room Ballad"*. These verses are collected in the *Definitive Verse* of 1940, presumably on RK's authority.
4. The inexpensive lodging houses established by the 1st Baron Rowton in 1892 in poor sections of London: six were built between 1892 and 1905. RK refers to "what they call a Rowton lodging-house" in "Uncovenanted Mercies" (*Limits and Renewals*, p. 388).
5. Longfellow supplies the epigraph to *The Light that Failed*, ch. 8, and is quoted in several of the stories, e.g., "The Finest Story in the World". The epigraph to the second part of "Baa Baa, Black Sheep" is from Clough, though in the early editions of the story (and some later) the lines are credited to James Thomson's "The City of Dreadful Night".
6. The introductory poem to "Brother Square Toes" (*Rewards and Fairies*).
7. By "The Song of Queen Bess" RK means "The Looking-Glass", the poem that follows "Gloriana" in *Rewards and Fairies*. In *Songs from Books* the poem has an introductory stanza and a refrain omitted in *Rewards and Fairies*.
8. In the last stanza of "The Ballad of Minepit Shaw", the poem introducing "The Tree of Justice" in *Rewards and Fairies*: "A Pharisee so bold". Durand explains that

the word is Sussex dialect for "fairy". "The colloquial plural for fairy – fairieses – was probably well rooted in the dialect long before the translation of the Bible, and its subsequent use in church made Sussex men familiar with the word Pharisee"(*A Handbook to the Poetry of Rudyard Kipling*, New York, 1914, p. 339).

9. Durand: see 4–5 August 1913.

10. The last line of the sixth stanza of "Frankie's Trade", the concluding poem to "Simple Simon", reads "By what he could see of a three-day snow-storm" in *Rewards and Fairies* but "By what he could see in a three-day snow-storm" in *Songs from Books*.

11. The fragments of the play called *Gow's Watch* that RK had published at this time are as follows: heading to ch. 10 of *Kim* (attributed to "Old Play"), expanded in *Songs from Books* as Act II, Scene 2; and an extract identified as "From Lyden's 'Irenius' Act III. Sc. II" prefacing "Mrs. Bathurst" in *Traffics and Discoveries* (not included in *Songs from Books*); later he published two extracts in *Debits and Credits*: "Gow's Watch, Act IV. Scene 4" following "The Prophet and the Country"; and "Gow's Watch, Act V. Scene 3" following "A Madonna of the Trenches". Three of these are brought together in RK's *Verse: Inclusive Edition 1885–1926* (1927): Act II, scene 2; Act IV, scene 4; and Act V, scene 3. These are described as having been "enlarged from various sources". The extract "From Lyden's 'Irenius'" is collected only in the Sussex and Burwash Editions.

12. Four (not two) lines from "Old Mother Laidinwool" appear in the early pages of "'Dymchurch Flit'" (*Puck of Pook's Hill*); RK has added thirty more in *Songs from Books*.

13. First published as the heading to ch. 5 of *Kim*: RK has added five stanzas in *Songs from Books*.

14. First published following "Little Foxes" (*Actions and Reactions*).

15. First published as "The Fight of Heriot's Ford", the heading to ch. 10 of *The Light That Failed*: RK has added six stanzas to the ballad.

16. First published as the heading to ch. 8 of *Kim*; RK has added three stanzas to the original two.

To Sir Max Aitken, 14 November 1913
TLS: Harvard University

Bateman's / Burwash / Sussex / 14th November 1913

Private
Dear Sir Max,

It's all right about Steele Maitland. He had the idea of "Gehazi" when I wrote the verses, and I believe has used it once before in a speech.[1]

I can't "garble" my "Gehazi". It's meant for that Jew boy on the Bench and one day – please the Lord – I may get it in.[2] As to the Globe:[3] one thing I feel is a great mistake is the way it skirts the Marconi business. The fence is very crowded already. Isn't there a place for someone on *this* side of it. If the Stock Exchange finds the financial methods, of which the Cabinet avail themselves, too stiff and too shady, can't some one paper try to speak the truth. I am feeling rather sick. I've just been visited by an American Administrator[4] – also a financier and millionaire. You should have heard the things that he felt able to say about England – not so much what the Government had done as the way the people took it.

Yours sincerely,
Rudyard Kipling

Notes
1. See 31 July 1913.
2. RK had offered "Gehazi" to Gwynne for the *Morning Post* (to Gwynne, 26 September 1913: ALS, Dalhousie University); evidently Aitken refused it too. The poem was not published until 1919, in *The Years Between*.
3. Aitken had purchased a share in *The Globe*, the oldest surviving London evening paper, in 1911.
4. Cameron Forbes, who had just been removed as Governor of the Philippines. He was at Bateman's on 11 and 12 November (Bateman's Visitors Book).

To J. D. Hamilton,[1] 27 November 1913
TLS: National Library of Scotland

Bateman's / Burwash / Sussex / 27th November 1913.

private.
Dear Sir,

You are the first who has noticed the extra "S" in "The Wrecker",[2] so I greet you as a good Stevensonian, properly jealous for the master's honour.

Now I can point out to you that "I" (the teller of the tale) did not use the word at all. It was Mr. L. O. Zigler's version of what he understood Mr. B. Walen to have said to him. As the statement was made only a very short time after the double murder and, as I recollect, in the presence of the corpses, it is possible (a) that Mr. B. Walen may have misquoted the original title or (b) that Mr. L. O. Zigler may have misquoted Mr. B. Walen.

You will note that in such minor matters as "braces" and "suspenders" Mr. Zigler was scrupulously careful to give both readings, but in referring to "Westminster" he inserted an extra "i".[3]

My own theory, therefore, is that Mr. Zigler not being a Stevensonian (as you and I are Stevensonians) misquoted through inaccuracy of ear. At least, I was at some pains to write "Wreckers" not "Wrecker", and I purpose to keep it so in the book-form.

But I am glad and pleased that you were so prompt to descend upon me for the mis-spelling.

Yours truly,
Rudyard Kipling.

J. D. Hamilton Esq.

Notes
1. Perhaps the John D. Hamilton of Glasgow who is mentioned as a Stevenson collector in George L. McKay, comp., *A Stevenson Library: Catalogue of Writings By and About Robert Louis Stevenson formed by Edwin J. Beinecke*, V (New Haven, 1961), 1893.
2. In "The Edge of the Evening", then just published in the *Pall Mall Magazine*, December 1913, the American Laughton O. Zigler reports a conversation in which "a book called *The Wreckers*" – meaning Robert Louis Stevenson's *The Wrecker* – is mentioned (*A Diversity of Creatures*, p. 292).
3. "The Edge of the Evening", pp. 288, 274.

To H. A. Gwynne, 2 December 1913
TLS: Dalhousie University

Bateman's / Burwash / Sussex / 2nd December 1913

Private.
Dear old Man,

I should feel more knocked out over your letter than I am, if it hadn't been for the fact that within the last week or two I've had the whole line of argument developed to me, much as you've developed it, by a Radical.[1] So I expect they are on the nibble at our out-posts all round – same as in 1910. They make very strong play to me with the idea that the situation is, *au fond*, in the hands of the Government who can make concessions at the eleventh hour and get us badly laughed at etc. etc. And that's where they err, and that is where time is against them and *not* on their side as they pretend.

They say that the movement is led by politicians. So it is. But the politicians did not *make* the movement. They only headed it, and as I see things, the movement can't be checked by politicians any more. You can't let 80,000 men arm themselves and spend time drilling and keeping their tempers while they are being insulted, and then expect the whole lot to file back quietly to quarters as soon as a "compromise" is announced.[2] It's like getting the Djinn back into the bottle. There's the Oath of the Covenant[3] for one thing, which pledges resistance to any form of Home Rule in Ireland. People who aren't politicians will not lightly slide out of an oath of that sort.

So I argue that if, and when, the politicians balk – they'll be pushed aside by the movement which will throw up its own leaders. At the best, all that the Government can offer is the betrayal of the whole of the South! All that will be saved will be 4 or perhaps 6 counties of the North. *Do* you think Ulster will buy herself off at that price? I don't. You forget that her own strength is growing every week – certainly every month. The terms she might have accepted last year are not the terms she will accept next year.

You talk of the German danger.[4] Does it occur to you that a betrayed Ulster will repeat 1688 in the shape of a direct appeal to Germany? And that in doing this, she will have the sullen sympathy of a great many people in England who are suffering under intolerable misgovernment? Ulster is nearer than S. Africa; and a betrayed Ulster is more dangerous than twenty South Irelands in open revolt. The South Irish have no passion for Home Rule as such. They realize it would be against their business interests; their leaders know that the money to finance a new revolt could not come from Ireland but must come for the U.S. Which is the more dangerous enemy? The South playing a game it has not got its heart in, or the North in a blind rage, *led by its own leaders <u>not</u> by politicians.*

The Radicals insist on telling you that there can be no fighting when all the fighting is on one side. Imagine a small Protestant–Catholic riot in the centre of Ireland – anything might provoke it. Then, imagine Ulster sending men down to help the Protestants. All the fat's in the fire at once; and until English troops are sent over, the North would probably be knocking hell out of the South!

As to politicians again. I don't know whether Carson will go back on his own people.[5] If he does, in all likelihood he will not live long, but someone else will take his place. You aren't watching a skirmish of politicians, old man. You are just seeing the head of an army move into position. Incidentally, you are watching the first move in the Revolt of the English. Think back to 1906–9.[6] People then said it was only a small political upheaval. I always said it was the beginning of a new '48. *And I was right.* This Ulster business is the beginning of the counter-revolution. I don't know which side will win, but I can quite understand why the Rads are so keen on knocking the heart out of us beforehand. But don't you be depressed, old man. *Don't follow the politicians.* The South Irish aren't going to get more money out of the U.S. I had a big American here the other day (Governor of the Philippines).[7] He says the Irish movement in the U.S. is as dead as Queen Anne. Pat Ford[8] was the only man who kept up a semblance of vitality in it. With his death, it's dead. Our game is organised resistance *to the end* – and the Government will crumple. What is more important the English revolt will begin.[9]

Ever
Rud

Notes
1. The subject was the question of Home Rule for Ireland. The bill had been first introduced in 1912; it passed its first reading in January 1913 and was then rejected by the Lords. The bill passed again in July and was again rejected. It had now been introduced a third time and would therefore inevitably pass, under the rules established by the Parliament Act of 1911. Meantime, an armed volunteer force had been organised in Ulster, civil war threatened, and no compromise appeared likely: "The year closed amid anxiety and gloom" (*Annual Register, 1913*, p. 262). RK had written to Gwynne on 26 November urging him to keep up the fight in the *Morning Post* against Home Rule: "if we fight we may win" (ALS, Dalhousie University).
2. In a speech of 25 October Asquith had said that he was prepared to consider any scheme "for the adjustment of the position of the minority in Ireland", but that "nothing must be done to erect a permanent or insuperable bar to Irish unity" (*Annual Register, 1913*, p. 220).
3. Introduced in September 1912, this obligated the signer to use "all means which may be found necessary to defeat the present conspiracy to set up a Home Rule Parliament in Ireland". Published figures gave the number of signers as 471,419 (*Annual Register, 1912*, p. 211).
4. Arms from Germany were being sent to the Ulster volunteers. RK's reference to 1688 evokes a parallel between the Jacobites of 1688, who invited a French army to Ireland, and the Ulstermen of 1913, who could be imagined as inviting a German army to their defence.
5. Sir Edward Carson (see 2 December 1900) led the militants in Ulster who vowed to resist Home Rule by violence.
6. The first phase of the Liberal government; after the elections of 1910 the government was dependent on the Irish vote and hence obliged to maintain a Home Rule policy.
7. Cameron Forbes: see 14 November 1913.
8. Patrick Ford (1835–1913), Irish-born journalist, editor of the New York *Irish World* and founder of the Irish Land League; devoted to the cause of Irish independence. He died on 23 September of this year.
9. This last sentence is in RK's hand.

To Brander Matthews, 4 December 1913

ALS: Columbia University

Bateman's / Burwash / Sussex / Dec. 4. 1913

Dear Brander,

My boy's had to have an operation[1] – not a big one but slow and annoying whereby, also, he has been out of school for most of the term and the demands etc. of an unwell youth of sixteen at war with his fate and yearning to return to his kind, keep one pretty busy. Also there is anxiety. So I've not been an even moderately decent correspondent.

But I'll tell you a quaint thing about your Shakespeare.[2] I read it first and then began reading bits aloud to my Elsie daughter who said: – "Let *me* have a look" – after the manner of children. She plunged into it and swallowed it whole – which again is rare in the young. She said at the end: – "That's *the* most interesting book about him I've ever read. It shows what he was really driving *at.*" You see? I think she hit the nail on the head. It's the only book *I* know that represents William as "a craftsman conditioned by his environment" (can't I use slang!) rather than as an irresponsible demi-god. And of course, touching his craftsmanship he was first and foremost a good workman with his eye on his actors. I've read it again and again. His soul-development doesn't matter (every man has his own notions how William grew internally) but to all you say and hint and deduce about this stage-work I do most heartily subscribe.[3] Likewise it has given me the idea of a story – which may pan out later.[4]

You're dead right about "wise *to*" and not "*on.*"[5] It was inexcusable carelessness on my part – the worse since I had that amazing New York "Horace" man[6] in the bookshelf. By the way you ought to review him. *Nota.* Zigler quotes the Detroit man as saying "a government of the alien etc."[7] Remember too he has married a southerner of extreme views and has become wealthy.

Oh! I had a rampant Stevensonian down on me for making Zigler misquote "The Wrecker" as "The Wreckers" and I had been *so* careful to make him make that error![8] But thus is the artist ever miscomprehended.

I'm up to my eyes in work of sorts: having more things in my head than I can get out with my fingers. This sounds like – other things but isn't. All good wishes for the coming year.

Ever sincerely
Rudyard

Notes

1. See [13 October? 1913].
2. Matthews's *Shakespeare as a Playwright* (New York, 1913), published in October.
3. In ch. 10, "Shakespeare's Actors", Matthews argues that Shakespeare wrote for a particular company and was "moved in his choice of subject by his intimate knowledge of the histrionic capability of his fellow-actors" (p. 191).
4. Nothing that RK published fits this context.
5. In the texts of "The Edge of the Evening" in both the *Pall Mall Magazine* and the *Metropolitan Magazine* Laughton Zigler says "Walen's talk put me wise on the location and size of some of the kegs" (Uniform Edition, p. 286). This is not altered in any later text of the story that I have seen.
6. Not identified.
7. "The Edge of the Evening", p. 283: "You heard what that Detroit man said at dinner. 'A Government of the alien, by the alien, for the alien.'"
8. See 27 November 1913.

To Lieutenant W. H. Lewis, 5 December [1913]

ALS: University of Sussex

Bateman's / Burwash / Sussex / Dec. 5: 9. p.m. (cold and windy)

Dear Lewis

Ever so many thanks for your jolly letter. By *all* means send along the Diary. I'd love to see it. You got better luck at Lahoul[1] than you deserved – specially in the matter of the 3 ibex. That reminds me of a wealthy chap I met thing spring on my way back from Egypt. (The wife and I spent six glorious weeks there). He'd hired a sporting dahabiyah with shikari, ice-box, palms and punkahs all complete (£1500 per mensem!!) from Khartoum to Gondokoro. Had put in several weeks and had not seen one single dam' thing. His language was not a bit refined.

Much interested in what you tell me about your idea of going into the Egyptian Army. Of course every one swears that it is not what it used to be – but then things never are. It's a fine service with heaps of administrative jobs going: but a foul climate or rather choice of climates and it's a *very* tight corporation to climb into. At least that's what I've heard. *Entre nous* if you get in your first job must be to conciliate Lady W.[2] *She* governs the Soudan as I am credibly assured by many officers. As far as I know I don't believe there is going to be any increase of pay for the Indian Army. We are going to use the English one to help shoot Ulster loyalists in Ireland. This is filling the Army with great joy, as you can imagine. Also, I'm told we've chucked the new rifle[3] on account of expense but you probably know more than I. It is said to emit a scarlet flame a fathom long and to turn white hot after 75 rounds. Subject to these limitations it is a first class *banduk*.[4]

You will of course have heard the sad news about Mrs. Leonard.[5] It seems that she was suffering from Bright's disease for years. We went to her funeral in a London cemetery. Ghastly! Thank God the girls[6] didn't come but stayed at home. Leonard came and was, as you can well believe, nearly heartbroken. They have all gone off now to the Cape as I expect Daisy will have written you by now. I am sorrier for Daisy than for any one else. Vi has at least her husband and Leonard has his memories but poor Daisy has nothing – so it seems – but sorrow. She is a good girl.

John has been knocked out of school for more than half a term owing to having to have an operation. It was only for removal of tonsils but he hasn't come round quite well and is now definitely to be kept at home till the end of the Xmas holidays. It has knocked him out of running which was the one thing he could do. Elsie is very fit and is now a young lady – when she remembers that she is close on eighteen.

The wife I'm glad to say has been fitter this year than for many a long day and as you know, I'm always pretty much the same. We're getting a new car and also a small G.W.K.[7] for the juniors. I'm told it's the best car on the market. I've taken John to divers music-halls which always make *me* inclined to weep but J. thinks them "top-hole."

Politically we are about as rotten as we make them and I'm on a league of sorts to help to wage civil war.[8] I never thought I should end as a rebel in my old age but all the best people are doing it. You never knew such a mad state of affairs!

This letter carries with it our best wishes for Xmas and the new year. All luck and promotion attend you.

Most sincerely
Rudyard Kipling

Notes
1. A valley in the high mountains of the Kangra district, Punjab.
2. Lady Wingate, wife of Sir Reginald Wingate (1861–1953), Sirdar of the Egyptian army and Governor-General of the Sudan since 1899.
3. According to *The Times*, 8 September 1913, the new 276 rifle was to be withdrawn for reasons not known, though it was reported that the rifle developed excessive heat during sustained fire. In December the War Office ordered a large number of "the old magazine Lee-Enfield Mark III pattern" (*The Times*, 22 December 1913).
4. Musket, rifle.
5. Mrs Charles Leonard.
6. The two Leonard daughters, Violet, now Lady Cobham (see 1 May 1912), and Daisy, unmarried.
7. RK had been negotiating for a new Rolls-Royce since July 1913. The car, for which he paid £1350, was his third Rolls-Royce; he kept it until 1921. There is no evidence that RK actually acquired a G.W.K. (see [13 October? 1913]); in June 1914, he bought a Ford: "A new car, a Ford arrives – the idea being it is to take the place of the Rolls Royce for station work" (Rees extracts, 30 April 1914).
8. RK probably means what became the League of British Covenanters (see [23 February 1914]), which must then have been in process of organisation.

To Colonel H. W. Feilden, 25 December 1913
ALS: Syracuse University

Château d'Annel[1] / Longueil-Annel (Oise) / Xmas. 1913

Dear Colonel Sahib

The crowded horrors of a "last day" at home prevented me from coming up the hill on Sunday to give you news of our Feast at Keylands.[2] It was immense! Some sixteen sat down to the hospitable board – Landon had Fred Brook (Tom couldn't come) Jenner: Jabez Petit, Willett and a few others at his end of the table. I had Pennels: Holmes: Isted: Weekes (a blackguard if ever there was one) and yet others including a Sprightly Youth called Hicks – whom I faintly recalled as a most inadequate bricklayer's assistant in real life but who now met me as man of the (lower) world.

There was a certain amount of gêne at the very beginning but the upset of an oil lamp by Landon rapidly put us all on a friendly footing. Our jokes were few and simple, but highly appreciated. The menu was roast beef, potatoes, pickles, and beer – beer – Beer! Plum pudding and mince pie to follow of course.

Landon's orders to Dale his man were not to let the pewters stand empty. I never saw orders more comprehensively and liberally fulfilled. Even in Weekes his tankard (and W. went out at least four times to ease his uneasy bladder) the beer stood level. (*Nota Bene*. Total consumption at end worked out to within a shade of a gallon each: and Landon, John and I drank about $1^1/_2$ pints between us). So conversation got animated. Everybody had two helps of beef – some had three – Holmes is reported to have had four! Then came pudding in brandy, with about a bottle of brandy somewhere in its original composition. Then a few – not many – mince pies and a delicate picking of bread and cheese. Holmes and Pennels on my right turned a delicate rosy pink (like good damp bricks) but their conversation might have been overheard by all the archangels. Then – ah then! – we got to songs. The Youth Hicks led off with a dolorous ditty (we know it well at the Rose and Crown) of an engaged youth in the service who went to the burning sands of Egypt treasuring "her dear lock of hair" and was promptly shot for so doing. And after the felon bullet had driven "the dear lock of 'air" through his heart he sang a chorus of eight lines in slow time. To him succeeded one Crouch with a fine voice and another amazing sentimental ditty – more deaths in the desert immediately after engagement. *Then* came the surprize of the evening; 'Twas Pennel's suggestion we should call on Jabiz to sing. You who know the hearts of Burwash probably know that Jabiz Petit is a Harry Lauder.[3] I had always regarded him as a blear-eyed, senile emptier of earth-closets, digger of weeds in paths and a forgetter of the plainest orders. He rose, with a neatly smoothed face that would have done credit to a Scots Kirk elder and in the remains of what must have been a true and fluty voice delivered a song on non-interference with the refrain:–

> "I never interfere – no matter what I may see
> Let everybody do as 'e likes. It's nothing to do with me."

Which by carefully graduated steps rose to heights of studious impropriety. And we all shouted like the men of Ephesus![4] All except me! I was lost in wonder. Then Holmes – Holmes ye Gods! – without prelude, without even rising from his place – Holmes being full of beef and beer and pudding and smoking acrid shag in a brand-new pipe, burst into song of excruciating sentiment. "Annie dear I'm called away." I thought earth had no more surprises for me but after more songs, Petitt went out and returned disguised in his working clothes to sing a song as a tramp!!! True he couldn't recall all the words but the effect was stupefying.

And at last they left, after an appropriate speech by Jenner, seconded by Holmes, topped off with hot punch! Then they leaned against each other outside and sang: – When shepherds watched. They couldn't go far wrong over *that* – 'Tis a carol that sings himself but when they tried to sing yet another and forgot both words *and* tune, we reluctantly decided that perhaps they had drink taken and so shut the door while they wound, deviously and hooting, up the hill.

But as we all said – *if* you had only been there!

We had a very good crossing on Monday and got here at 6.23: p.m. in hard frost with a hint of snow in the air. We were the first of the Xmas party in this huge Chateau and so were pressed into helping to decorate the huge Xmas tree which tonight will be exhibited to all the inhabitants of the village and the estate. It is over 15 feet high – one blaze of tinselries and coloured glass balls with solid stacks of presents, including coffee and tobacco, and bats and [   ][5] and toys, for about 200 people.

Last night (late having missed connections) came from the Hague, Henry Van Dyke,[6] U.S. Ambassador to Holland, his wife and two daughters – one a delicious flaxen haired thing of eleven. Also a young Uraguayan rather wrath to be taken for an Argentinian: and today motors have been piling in with alternate cargoes of American boys and French maidens. One boy – Wordner[7] by name – spent 15 months on the W. coast of Africa in the employ of the West African Consolidated Gold Fields. He nearly died several times but, as you can imagine, it was *the* time of his Youth life. He had to work underground – 1200 feet – superintending niggers. He told me that the sacramental phrase over the evening cocktail is "Damn all!" which is new to me! It shed rather a lurid light on the conditions of life yonder. Also he said that every man in the mines kept a little calendar and each evening scratched off one day as a thing safely survived. Seven out of the eleven of his batch perished in a year. And *so* the boy wants to go back again!

Snow fell last night and froze today. The young folk this morn went forth with tea-trays and boards and biscuit boxes and barrel-staves with intent to toboggan and to ski. They made themselves gloriously warm at any rate. This afternoon they extemporized a sleigh. Here is a faithful picture [sketch of sleigh made of wooden box and boards]. And hitched it behind a small pony which ran in circles round the courtyard of the Chateau. Several people were *not* thrown out but all the others were. And they are playing touch-last out in the snow and I am up in my room writing to you because I do not want Van Dyke to bore me stiff with the excellencies and virtues and futures of the United States of America.

On Saturday we go to Paris and on Sunday afternoon we have tea with Clemenceau and (D.V.) get to Engelberg on Monday morn.

Drop me a line at leisure and let me know about your honoured health.

Ever affectionately
Rudyard.

Notes

1. RK and family left on 22 December and arrived that day at Château d'Annel to visit the Depews. They left for Paris on 27 December and were in Engelberg on the 29th.
2. This must have been on the occasion of the completion of the remodelling for Landon's occupancy.
3. Lauder (1870–1950) was a celebrated singer and comedian.
4. Acts 19:34: "all with one voice about the space of two hours cried out".
5. Word illegible.
6. Van Dyke (1852–1933), Presbyterian minister, poet, essayist, and popular religious writer, had been Professor of English at Princeton since 1899. He was appointed Ambassador to the Netherlands in 1913.
7. Not identified.

To Sir Max Aitken, 15 January 1914

ALS: Harvard University

Grand Hotel and Kurhaus / *Engelberg* / Jan. 15. 1914.

Dear Aitken

Many thanks for your two letters and for the news you send. I admit my own idea is that just at the very last Asquith will chuck us the exclusion of Ulster as you'd chuck a bone to a dog and that we shall accept it! Here, I am devoutly hoping that I am wrong. I heard recently from someone who has seen the Londonderrys[1] and I have had a long talk with the Earl of Arran[2] who is staying here: and it will be very welcome news if you can send me any word that our side are *not* weakening.

I have been watching the development of the Winston Churchill game with a little amusement and a good deal of disgust – specially when F. E. Smith came into it.[3] I believe you can cure a woman of being a personal prostitute – sometimes – but it is impossible to cure a political prostitute from whoring. Meantime the ship is alight at both ends and in the middle – S. Africa, India, and Ulster – and for that reason the conservatives will probably accept Winston when it suits him to come over. We are a Great Party!

I see that the M[orning]. P[ost]. alone has the courage to hammer at Murray and the Marconis.[4] The *Globe*[5] ought to be more bitter – as comic as you please but savage. A man here, a casual stranger talking to me about papers said that he didn't think the Globe was hitting as hard as it used to. "It grinned more" he said "but it didn't get home." A hotel of this kind swarming with busy men, idle for the moment, is a very good place for collecting opinions from people one wouldn't get at at home.

We hope to be back the 7th February in England. We go to St. Moritz on the 22nd of this month[6] and it would be delightful if you'd come along if only for a few days.

Best love to Peter (no, I do *not* want a pony or poney, thanks) and the other babes and all our good wishes to you both.

Ever
Rudyard Kipling

Notes
1. Charles Stewart Vane-Tempest-Stewart (1852–1915), 6th Marquess of Londonderry, Conservative MP, 1878–84, when he succeeded to the title. Viceroy of Ireland, 1886–9; a signer of the Ulster covenant.
2. Arthur Jocelyn Charles Gore (1868–1958), 6th Earl of Arran, commanded the Officers' Training Corps in Ireland, 1909–12.
3. Churchill and Smith, who cooperated as friends across political boundaries, worked together for the exclusion of Ulster from Home Rule. But probably RK has in mind the speech that Smith made on 9 January 1914 to a Conservative club defending Churchill's naval policy against criticism from Churchill's own party (*The Times*, 9 January 1914). Churchill at this time was alienating many Liberals and compelling the applause of many Conservatives by his commitment to increased naval expenditure. Churchill did not return to the Conservative Party until 1924.
4. The *Morning Post* published a leader on 12 January, on the occasion of Lord Murray's return to England from the US, deploring Murray's absence at the time of the select committee's hearings in the Marconi scandal (see 22 December 1912). The leader also reports that Murray had refused to answer written questions put to him by the *Morning Post*, and demands that inquiry be made into the management of Liberal Party funds under Murray, who had been Liberal chief whip.
5. This was still one of Aitken's properties.
6. They went to Suvretta House, St Moritz, on the 21st, where they were joined by the Baldwins and other friends, but not by the Aitkens (CK diary, 21 January 1914; RK to Aitken, 23 January 1914: ALS, Harvard). On 3 February they left for Paris; on 7 February they returned to Bateman's (Rees extracts).

To Edward Lucas White, 20 January 1914
ALS: University of Texas

Grand Hotel and Kurhaus / Engelberg / Jan. 20. 1914: / (close on Zero)

Esteemed Younger Brother

Yours of the 20th comes here in 4 foot of snow and deep continuous frost – an old fashioned New England winter. Six hundred folk of all nationalities with a heavy sprinkling of Americans are disporting 'emselves in it in all the tongues of the pentecost – and I'm supposed to be trying to finish a bit of work! It's not easy with distractions outside at every turn and two nigh-grown children whirling in to ski-ing and skating and dancing. We go on to St Moritz tomorrow for a few days and then – Allah be praised! – home. Last year we went to Wady Halfa down the Nile – whereof you may, perhaps, see some record in some of the papers shortly.[1]

Glad you liked the Edge of the Evening. There's another coming out soon in the Metropolitan – a "tender rural fancy," that I much enjoyed doing.[2]

With numbed hands, between a turn on the rink and the last packing-up, in vile ink of the hotel brand (your well-thought-of blotters will be at home to meet me!) but with all good wishes

Most sincerely
Rudyard Kipling

Notes
1. *Egypt of the Magicians* began publication in *Nash's Magazine*, June 1914, and continued through seven instalments to December. American publication was in *Cosmopolitan*.
2. "Friendly Brook", *Metropolitan Magazine*, March 1914 (*A Diversity of Creatures*).

To Cameron Forbes, [21 February 1914][1]
ALS: Harvard University

Hôtel Brighton / 218. Rue de Rivoli / Paris[2]

Dear Cameron Forbes,

Behold me in Paris on our way to Vernet les bains on the Spanish border – with your Boston address carefully laid away at Bateman's and Sir Francis Younghusband[3] K.C.S.I. (Thibet, India frontier and such trifles) on the eve of sailing to the U.S. to lecture about British administration in India. He wants to get the U.S. interested in our work because the Anglicized oriental sets great store by U.S. public opinion. Also there are (as well as you know it) agitators of the coloured type who are always urging the "down trodden" to look towards the U.S. (*you* know the sort of stuff!)

I have given Younghusband a card to you as *the* best man I could think of to help him towards meeting the men who will help him in his game which is the Imperial game.[4]

I met him at the Royal Geographical the other night.[5] Hadn't seen him for ages, but he is a good man all through with a big record. I've told him to hunt Boston for you *via* the nearest Boston club.

Hope all goes well with the pretty gee-gees and that you don't find the weather too infernal. Did I tell you we met your Deputy (Gilbert)[6] in Switzerland. He and she both love the land.

With our united kindest regards

Every sincerely
Rudyard Kipling.

Notes
1. Dated from postmark.
2. RK and CK went to Paris on 19 February and left for Vernet-les-Bains on the 22nd (CK diary).
3. Younghusband (1863–1942), soldier, diplomat, and explorer, served in India and made notable travels in China and central Asia before transferring to the foreign (political) department in India. He headed the mission to Tibet of 1903–4, and was Resident of Kashmir, 1906–9. He published *The Heart of a Continent*, 1896, and, after his retirement in 1910, was active in the Royal Geographical Society. Younghusband had known RK in Simla, where, he recorded, RK was looked on as "bumptious and above his station" (George Seaver, *Francis Younghusband: Explorer and Mystic*, 1951, p. 37).
4. In his letter to Younghusband enclosing cards to Doubleday and to Forbes, RK says of Forbes that he is "ex-governor of the Philippines – millionaire, Harvard man, administrator and creator of the finest polo ground in the world... . He knows all the Asiatic problems and sympathizes with 'em" (21 February 1914: ALS, India Office Library).
5. 17 February 1914, when RK made a speech to the Society, collected as "Some Aspects of Travel" (*A Book of Words*).
6. Newton Whiting Gilbert (1862–1939), a lawyer and congressman from Indiana, was Vice-Governor of the Philippines, 1909–13, and acting Governor-General, 1912–13.

To Lord Milner, [23 February 1914]

ALS: Syracuse University

Hôtel du Parc / *Vernet-les-Bains* / P[ost]. O[ffice].

Dear Lord Milner

I found your letter of the 18th had been sent on from England and was waiting for me on my arrival here this afternoon. I wired you at once but am very sorry that an answer should not have gone sooner.

I have signed the declaration[1] (returned herewith). It is about time that some one began to try to look at some of the facts in the face. What people *can't* understand is, that we are on the edge of a change of dynasty – not of Ministry – if Home Rule in *any* shape goes through. It is inconceivable that the Celt should hold the Teuton people without those Teuton instinctively leaning towards the Teuton: and that means 1688 or 1066 over again. *That*, as I see it, is the peril – the deliquescence of a sulky people; even as they stood still on the *Hermione*[2] in the old days. And it is perfectly conceivable that Home Rule might be put through (by purchase of the sort we are familiar with) at the next election. In which case, another form of declaration would be necessary for some of us – yourself I hope among the number.

I am glad that you think this action may help to open purse-strings. When I see you in town that is a subject I should like to have some light on. Also I want to know whether a refusal of taxes can be worked on a large enough scale to give our Outlaws something else to play with.

I know some men who are talking a good deal but I don't know whether they intend to do much. Personally, after reading the week's *Spec*, I feel that St Loe Strachey ought to be bricked up for life in one of his hundred-guinea cottages.[3]

We are here for a "cure" for three weeks or so. I will let you know my change of address: but I expect we shall be returning to England early in April. Bateman's isn't habitable owing to some internal domestic changes which include plumbing *and* kitchen range. You know what things these are to cope with. If you are busy which you are, do not answer this letter. Sec. or typewriter is perfectly understood.

Ever most faithfully
Rudyard Kipling

Met Briand,[4] the day before yesterday in Paris at lunch, says he to me "Politics is all suggestion."

"Perfectly" says I, "but when the hypnotized one wakes up there is the devil to pay."

"And what is your Lloyd-George like?" says he upon this.

Now facially and in regard to a certain greasiness of hide and I take it, moral texture, Briand is most tremendous like Ll-George so, for delicacy's sake, I turned the talk to Caillaux[5] who, B. swears, is Ll-G's political child. How these socialists love one another!

————·————

Be thankful that you never got an eight-page letter from me all about the S.A. strikes; and "Uncle Louis"[6] and the late Mr. Kruger and my own unbounded joy and satisfaction. I posted it in the W.P.B. but it did me good to write it. I knew 'twould come but I didn't think 'twould come so soon and so perfectly.

Notes
1. A "British Covenant" on Ulster was published in a letter to *The Times* on 3 March, signed by RK, Milner, Lord Roberts, Edward Elgar, and other eminent names. It declared that, if the Home Rule Bill were passed without submitting it to a general election or to a referendum, the signers would hold themselves "justified in taking or supporting any action that may be effective to prevent it being put into operation, and more particularly to prevent the armed forces of the Crown being used to deprive the people of Ulster of their rights as citizens of the United Kingdom". The declaration was to be made available for signing to the country at large, and its supporters were to be organized as the League of British Covenanters, officially formed in April.
2. The crew of the *Hermione*, a British frigate on the Jamaica station, mutinied in 1797 and murdered all of their officers before handing over the ship to the Spaniards.
3. Strachey favoured the compromise measure of excluding Ulster from Home Rule, but in arguing for it cautioned that "till Exclusion is passed, and we are out of the wood of civil war, it is the duty of all good citizens not to say or do anything which may cause heat or aggravate the crisis" and that the Unionists should seek "not to embarrass the government, not to keep them in their tight place, but to help them out of it" (*Spectator*, 21 February 1914, p. 288). The same number of the *Spectator* offered plans for a model "Hundred-Guinea Cottage" (pp. 296–7).
4. Aristide Briand (1862–1932), Socialist politician, was eleven times Premier of France between 1909 and 1929 and a member of the Chamber of Deputies for thirty years. The lunch was given by Princess Marie of Greece, and the guests included the Vicomte D'Humières, Gustave Le Bon, and Jean Richepin (CK diary, 21 February 1914).
5. Joseph Caillaux (1863–1914), French Minister of Finance, who was then under unremitting political attack by Gaston Calmette, editor of *Le Figaro*. On 16 March 1914 Mme Caillaux called at the offices of *Le Figaro* and shot Calmette dead. The resulting trial was the sensation of Paris immediately before the war.
6. Botha, who was in political difficulties. General Hertzog, having broken with Botha on the question of Dutch supremacy (see 22 December 1912), had now broken with Botha's South African Party by walking out of the party's congress in November.

To Colonel H. W. Feilden, 6 March 1914
ALS: Syracuse University

Hôtel du Parc / Vernet-les-Bains / Mar 6. 1914

Dear Colonel Sahib,

Damn the Gaulois *and* the Standard![1]

The statement (about which I have already received a lot of wires and letters) is an absolute lie. I am not ill – I haven't been ill. Haven't even been afflicted with a cold or a tummy ache. As a matter of fact I haven't had the time to do anything so exciting. I have been taking baths – to keep the wife in countenance – a process which reduces life rather to the level of a convict prison. One day I am massaged under water which is (as I wrote you when I was here last)[2] a lengthy operation that ends in sending me to sleep for about an hour. It's practically a Turkish bath multiplied by 5. One feels washed within and without same as the ark was pitched.[3] On alternate days I swim (and that's a treat) in the big hot sulphur bath. Result I am getting elegantly narrow round the [   ].[4]

The wife's treatment is the same, barring she doesn't swim and she is standing it very well. She benefits by it afterwards: and gladly suffers the pains of dislocation and disarticulation.

It's a late spring here – raw cold for the most part with nothing doing in nature's line except the wild hellebore; snowdrops and violets. Birds few and shy *except* the hawks who I imagine have had their rations reduced by the late snows. Today is muggy and raining – an attempt at springlike weather. Words cannot paint the unbelievable but delightful dullness of life. We make our washing the excuse to live in utter peace – consequently we can keep abreast of our letters and do some work. I've been having a lively time over the declaration of Help to Ulster[5] which I hope may be of some use. But I can't see any *useful* end to it except civil war, or complete surrender of the Govt. This last is not to be feared so if we *only* sit tight we may have the show fought out to a finish.

Send us your news I pray and believe me with all our good wishes to you both.

Affectionately
Rudyard.

Notes
1. I have not found either of the items in question: they must have appeared around 22 February, when RK left Paris for Vernet (CK diary).
2. 18 February–25 March 1911: the letter to Feilden does not seem to have survived.
3. Genesis 6:14.
4. World illegible: "troste"?
5. See [23 February 1914].

To H. A. Gwynne, 10 March 1914
ALS: Dalhousie University

Hôtel du Parc / Vernet-les-Bains / Tuesday / Mar. 10. 1914

Dear Old Man,

You're a brick, and we're immensely grateful to you for the trouble you took in going down to see John and putting in an afternoon with him.[1] I'm sure it will buck him up and do him no end of good. He is not bad on games – specially his footer, tho' his best lay is ice-hockey. He *can* skate like a fiend.

You are quite right in what you say about his being old for his years but what *can* one do? When I was one month older than he is I was in receipt of a salary of £10 per month, with whiskers down my face.[2] Anyway he has only got a moustache. I am going to try to fill and interest his mind as much as possible and if he wants to know about vice I'm ready to tell him more than I have already. And that's a fair amount. But – oh Lord! – the care of a son is no light job. One sees oneself and yet *not* oneself looking at and talking at one and its difficult to know how much is heredity and how much is the independent new soul.

Your wire came in at breakfast today: for which I am grateful. I can't say how glad I was to read the M.P.'s leader in Monday's paper:[3] and I only hope and pray that the fools on our side won't be seduced by that muzzy lawyer's[4] traps. As you say, if we only sit tight we are all right. If we touch any of their plans with a barge-pole or admit the possibility of dealing with them we give away the whole case for the Union. It's the damned impudence of the thing that gets me. It's exactly like the family ne'er-do-well who by virtue of his very follies and crimes and the fuss he expects his people to make over them, establishes himself in a sort of privileged position wherein his original fatuity and no-accountness is overlaid by his demands and postulates and suggestions till at last the whole family and all the connections abandon their own job to sit in tearful enclaves over the sad case of "poor Willie" and how many of his preposterous and baseless claims can be admitted. But I feel happier – a little – now for even *my* pessimism don't carry me to the length of believing that Ulster can accept the absurd six-year suspense that is offered.[5] If *only* our people would stiffen up and get to work, I believe we should do better as mere fighters than we have done as politicians, "thinkers" (God help us!) and statesmen.

But make no mistake about it, old man, *an Ulster or an Ireland handed over to the Celt means an appeal for outside intervention* as in 1688. That is what I fear horribly. For the moment – we can[6] depend on much more than a few weeks – the Teuton has, or pretends to have – his eye glued on Russia. If by any conceivable means we can force an election now and come in, we're all right. Redmond's "revolt"[7] and making the government of Ireland "impossible" won't come to much for this good reason – Ulster has spent time and money in making an efficient army – perhaps the only efficient *manhood* army we have in England now and if I know human nature that army will never be wholly disbanded or left undrilled. Ulster herself doesn't realize yet what sort of weapon she has forged. Very good. With *that* sword hanging over him from the North the South Irish will walk delicately for fear lest, when he "revolts," men may come and call on him in motor cars and hurt him very badly.

If we lose the Election, as I see it, Ulster will really fight *and* will make her appeal for outside aid because that will be the deliberate smash-up of the Empire and the Union. Can you imagine an Ulster fighting for her life? I can: but it isn't a pretty picture.

For goodness sake try to get the Unionists to touch nothing and treat with nobody. It is not our business (we've been criminally weak already) to wipe up any mess that has been made. It is only cruelty to the empire and the Union if we do – as cruel as that last five pound note given to the family prodigal out of a sort of feeling that, after all, he is a connection of ours.

Well, here I'll stop. I see I'm slinging blots all over the place. Best love and renewed thanks.

Ever
RK

Notes
1. RK had asked Gwynne, when he called on John, to "buck him up *and* talk to him like an Uncle. He'll be grateful for it. He's reaching out in every direction for something to chew on mentally. I never take him off my mind for any length of time as he's reached the moment, which we both know so well, when he is dissatisfied without knowing his trouble – Do make him talk and let me hear what you think" (3 March 1914: ALS, Dalhousie University). John was just on the point of leaving school: see 19 March 1914.
2. That is, in September 1882, when RK left for India to take up his newspaper work.
3. Arguing that no offer Asquith might make on the Home Rule question short of maintaining the Union could be accepted: "Any form of Home Rule must involve a Nationalist ascendancy, must condemn the minority to a permanent position of inferiority and subjection, which they regard as degrading and unbearable" (*Morning Post*, 9 March 1910). For the terms that Asquith in fact offered that day, see note 6, below.
4. Asquith's.
5. Asquith's speech on 9 March, on moving the second reading of the Home Rule Bill, proposed that the Ulster counties might have the option to remain outside the Home Rule scheme for six years, after which they would come under the authority of Dublin unless, in the interval, Parliament determined otherwise. Sir Edward Carson, the Ulster leader, said of this scheme that it was "sentence of death with a stay of execution for six years".
6. Thus in MS: "can't"?
7. Redmond, as head of the Irish nationalists, could not officially accept any compromise of Home Rule.

To Lord Newton,[1] 14 March 1914

AL:[2] University of Sussex

[Vernet-les-Bains] Mar. 14. 1914

My Lord

A number of people have written to me commenting on the enclosed extract from a recent speech of yours in the Upper House.[3]

Your Lordship is in error in suggesting that I am "probably thoroughly ashamed" of having written the verses from which you did me the honour to quote a line in support of your own views.

The verses were carefully pitched in a certain key for a definite purpose and I am and always shall be extremely proud that, owing to this, they were the means of raising close upon a quarter of a million pounds to relieve some of the sufferings of our troops during the war in S. Africa.

Notes

1. Thomas Wodehouse Legh (1857–1942), 2nd Baron Newton, Conservative MP, 1886–98; succeeded to title, 1898, and was thereafter active in the House of Lords. He was a founder of the National Service League, 1902.
2. At the bottom of this letter, which is in RK's hand, CK has written: "copy of letter written Lord Newton re The Absent-Minded Beggar".
3. Lord Newton, in a speech in the Lords on 12 March, on the Territorial Bill, referred to RK thus: "Years ago when the Boer War was going on I remember a dreadful jingle, of which the author, Mr. Rudyard Kipling, is now probably ashamed, which ran –

     'Duke's son, cook's son, son of a belted earl,'

   or something to that effect. The poetry is, of course, deplorable, but the sentiment is an excellent one" (*Parliamentary Debates*, House of Lords, 5th Series, XV, 474–5: 12 March 1914).

   In his autobiography, *Retrospection*, 1941, Lord Newton says that he replied to RK regretting that he had "hurt the feelings of himself and 'his friends'... a second letter arrived, saying that his friends were still dissatisfied. To this I made no reply, as there is no law, written or unwritten, which compels one to admire poetry which is distasteful" (p. 204). The phrase about "friends", upon which Newton lays such stress, does not appear in RK's copy of this letter.

To Andrew Macphail, 19 March 1914
ALS: Photocopy, National Archives of Canada

Hôtel du Parc / Vernet-les-Bains / Mar. 19. 1914

Dear Macphail –

Your letter has just come in and I feel that you ought to know at once that "I am holier than thou."[1] Maybe you've bathed in your life: possibly washed a bit in hot water with soap but – *I* have been through a Course of Baths; and, within and without, and even to the marrow of my bones, I am of a purity and cleanliness and delicacy and suppleness which fills me with pride and amazement. Also I've drunk the beastly stuff and swum in it – same baths which Cæser took on his return from Great Britain – and all I want now is an ephod and a phylactery and a few of those things to be an Immaculate Archemandrite!

But I shall be beautifully dirty again by the time that you come over: and it will be a joy to show you England in Autumn. Assuming, that is, that we have an England fit to be shown: for we are really nearer big trouble – of the 1688's type – than we have ever been before. And like all shattering catastrophes it is wickedly and wantonly unnecessary.

We expect to leave here the day after tomorrow in our car to Paris – for the fourth time.[2] This year it will be Avignon, Arles, Les Baux and the Pont du Garde once more because I love Rome and specially her aqueducts: then up the Rhone valley to Grenoble: and then to Autun for certain cathedrals and things. The daughter we have left in Paris (which she loves and what is rarer *knows*) for the last six or seven weeks.[3] She attends lectures and conferences – but by no means to improve her mind thank God – and dress making and cookery classes which she *does* seriously incline to and generally is more of a Gaul than the Gauls – for which she has hereditary right. The boy is at school still: but I want to get him over and to take him along the forts and garrisons of the Eastern Frontier – Belfort, Nancy, Longwy etc., etc. – that he may realize the tension of the boiler plate on which he will have to live.[4] The more I know the French the more I respect and love 'em, and this indomitable *wisdom and sanity* – and laboriousness. Also, while I was in Paris – I've been several times this Spring[5] – I've been seeing a bit of certain orders of French society at closer quarters than usual and that has interested me too immensely.

You ought to see the peach and almond trees in bloom all down the valley here – like pink cream against the grey and yellow bones of the great hills. Not unlike the actual life of the land with the eternal menace across the border. Oh Lord! *What* a lot the Dominions have to learn and how slow they are to grasp it. When I read, as I sometimes do, of grave fat men who have done nothing but make money all their lives, talking about paying "tribute to England" if they help build a battleship I do not know whether to vomit or laugh.[6]

And that reminds me. We sent our car from London to Bordeaux in a 2,000 steamer and, incidentally, through what happened to be the worst gale of this wild winter. With it came my new chauffeur[7] – a young man just married, with a taste for beautiful things and a curiously mobile and sensitive face. *But* he had no knowledge of the sea: which saved him for he took to his bunk after a short while and remained there till nearly the end. And all that time wild telegrams were pouring into the papers of havock and wreckage, twenty steamers ashore between Bordeaux and Archachon and general devilment of flood and cyclone from Land's End to the Black Sea. But at 5:30 yesterday – while I was wondering how the little *Fauvette* would report herself, arrives my car from Bordeaux about 300 mile away and my chauffeur driving her. He ascends to my chamber – the unperturbed English servant all over. "Had a bad time?" says I. "Didn't notice anything unusual Sir" says he. "Only the Captain *he* was sick an' the officers *they* was sick." "And you?" says I. "Oh *I* was sick but then *I* wasn't on duty" was the reply. "Well" I says, "if it's any comfort to you, you've gone through the worst gale of the year." "Have I?" says he. Then reflectively, "Well I *am* pleased. It didn't do the car a bit of harm," turned on his heel and went to clean her off.

But I perceive that I babble. The main thing is you'll be over this year with the boy. Kindly report movements *and* dates. The wife I rejoice to say has found great good out of her course of baths and is really set up by it: which is a thing worth all the rest. She joins me in best love and I am, as ever

Affectionately
Rudyard Kipling

P.S.   If *I* were the Editor of the University Magazine I would have an article on the U.S. sense of humour – in the light of Page's latest utterances and their reception.[8] But Page *does* talk too much. But it's a funny thing to have to start in, at middle age, in the "treason" line. I believe I've done several things which are not strictly lawful already. Think of *that*, now!

When does your boy come over? You've got to bring him down to Bateman's. I can't take in the other five Orlandos but he must bring 'em down for a meal, and we'll set 'em wrestling on the edge of the pond. Don't make fun of our Via Sacra. It was only 340 yards but – it has stood this winter without flaw or gulling or wash-out and we've had the devil of a winter too, our side the water. The wife and I had to go back in mid-February for ten or twelve days.[9] 'Twas an interregnum of mild airs and sunshine and all the bulbs were very brave about it. And the primroses began. *Then* came winter in earnest. But the peculiar joy of our return was that Bateman's was in the hands of carpenters and plumbers and we (with joy inexpressible) lived in the Secretary's cottage – the one with the round rooms. D'you remember [sketch of cottage]. Five baby rooms *in all*. One little maid of all work. No changing for dinner. No dinner – just a two dish supper and if you wanted anything you reached out for it with your proper hand. We hadn't been so riotously happy for twenty year. It was the sort of thing Lear should have arranged for when he abdicated instead of being a snob about equerries and grooms in waiting. William didn't bring that point out properly.

Notes
1. Isaiah 65:5.
2. The three earlier trips were made in 1910, 1911, and 1913. Their itinerary for this one is as follows: 21 March, Vernet–Avignon; 22 March, Avignon, Arles, Les Baux, Avignon ("Thanked God we had seen Les Baux"); 23 March, Avignon, Vaucluse, Avignon; 24 March, Avignon–Grenoble; 25 March, Grenoble–Lyons; 26 March, Lyons–Autun; 27 March, Autun; 28 March, Autun–Orleans; 29 March, Orleans–Paris (Motor Tours).
3. Elsie must have remained in Paris on their return from Switzerland in the beginning of February. She stayed at a *pension*: see 27 May 1914.
4. I have no evidence that this trip was actually made. If it was, it must have been at some point between 4 April, when RK mentions his plan to make the trip in his letter to Mrs. Hill (q.v.), and 14 April, when they left Paris for England. John had joined them in Paris by 8 April (CK diary). This marked the moment of John's leaving Wellington College; in May he went to the establishment of a Mr Lee Evans, a "crammer" for the Army examination, at Bournemouth (CK diary, 13 February, 5 May 1914).
5. Twice, to be exact: briefly on his return from Switzerland in early February, and again, 19–22 February, on his way to Vernet. He was about to travel there for a third time.
6. Specifically, the Canadian programme to assist Britain in naval defence was stalled by Liberal opposition in the Canadian Parliament: see *The Times*, 16 March 1914.
7. Eaves.
8. In a speech to the Associated Chambers of Commerce in London on 11 March Page jokingly said that, though the US had not built the Panama Canal for the British, it was the British who would mostly profit from it. The next day the US Senate passed a resolution calling on Page to explain his remarks. The affair was only an opportunity for some skirmishing on American political questions at the time and soon dropped from notice: see *The Times*, 12, 13, 14 March 1914.
9. Between Switzerland and Vernet they were in England, 7–19 February: the main reason appears to have been to allow RK to make his speech to the Royal Geographical Society on 17 February (see [21 February 1914]).

To Edmonia Hill, 4 April 1914
ALS: Library of Congress

Hôtel Brighton / 218. Rue de Rivoli / Paris / Ap. 4. 1914.

My dear Mrs Hill,

Your last kind letter came to me in a sort of Mussoorie-under-snow – a huge hotel near St. Moritz, 5000 feet up and full of all the races of the earth, but mainly Germans, playing about in the snow. I should have answered it at once and did, indeed, make a beginning but I had to go to Paris and then down to the South of France. An intelligent French paper took the opportunity of announcing that something was wrong with my health – I suppose they couldn't understand anyone leaving Paris. It didn't happen to be true in any way: but I had quite a cheerful time explaining it to people who wanted to know.

We are back in Paris now: having come up in the car from Vernet – an eight day trip through at least sixteen varieties of bad weather ranging from snow to howling gales and flooded rivers. When the Rhone really floods it makes a very respectable little Ganges and Jumna.[1]

But the year has gone crazy as far as weather is concerned. We found Spring waiting for us here – very French and very pretty and have been out to Versailles and Fontainebleau. I *do* wish you had come over to Torquay last year. The climate wouldn't have pleased you but you would have found any number of delightful places close by where there is good air *and* sunshine.

We are in a shocking state, politically, in England and no one seems to know exactly what is going to happen. I wouldn't mind so much but for India where things are anything but satisfactory. Last year, we went as far as Cairo and down to Wady Halfa. I am writing a set of letters about it which are coming out in one of the magazines but nothing I could write would give any idea of the effect of the land which is so like all India in aspect and smell and association: and yet so unlike. I felt as though I was moving in a sort of terrible, homesick nightmare and as though at any moment the years would roll away and I should find myself back in India. But it is twenty five years and twenty six days since I left it.[2] Everything came back as vividly as ever with the bazar smells and the sight of the sand-banks in the river. I have kept as much of it as I could out of the letters – they will be called – "Egypt of the Magicians" – but you will see that a good deal has got in.

I am rather busy about odds and ends in Ulster; and hope to get back to England in a few days after a trip to the Eastern Frontier of France.[3] Then I don't expect to leave England for some time.

Meanwhile I have been meeting some rather interesting Frenchmen here. Briand: and Clemenceau – and your Ambassador to France[4] as well as Van Dyke, the U.S. Ambassador to Holland who is a very interesting man. Naturally one is a good deal interested in Mexico and I must confess I should like to see the U.S. take hold of Mexico and start in and administer it *more asiatico*.

Did you ever notice that Parke who used to be on the *Pioneer* and is now editor of the Cape Times (I was responsible for that little move) has got a Knighthood.[5] He and his wife are very pleased with it and I confess I'm glad too. He has worked very hard.

I haven't been doing much work of any account lately except a few stories and bits of verse. Life is so exciting from the political point of view that one has only time to watch it just now and wonder what new smash will turn up.

It was *very* kind of you to write and I am

Always sincerely yours
Rudyard Kipling

Notes
1. Allahabad, where RK had known the Hills, is at the confluence of the Ganges and the Jumna.
2. 9 March 1889, in company with Mr and Mrs Hill.
3. See 19 March 1914.
4. Myron T. Herrick (1854–1929), a lawyer, banker, and Republican politician from Cleveland; appointed Ambassador to France by Taft, he resigned on the election of Wilson but at Wilson's request remained on duty till the end of 1914. After the war he served again as Ambassador to France, 1921–9.
5. Park was knighted in this year's honours list. RK wrote to him on the occasion to send congratulations "in sincerity and admiration" (2 January [1914]: copy, Kipling Society).

To Sir James Dunlop Smith,[1] 14 April 1914
ALS: Tyler Collection, Yale University

Hôtel Brighton / 218. Rue de Rivoli / Paris / April. 14. 1914.

Dear Dunlop –

I want your help and unscrupulous interest on behalf of a Pottinger – grandnephew of Eldred and one of a line, as per enclosed pedigree, that have done the state some service.[2]

He comes out of Sandhurst at the end of this term but not, I fear, quite high enough to get his commission in the Indian Army – and I can't imagine a Pottinger outside the Indian Army or Civil.

His father[3] is Collector of Bhuj – a good man, left with a family. I met him last year en route from Marseilles and took to him a lot. The boy I know by report to be very good. He was educated at Cheltenham.

If by any means you can help to get him chosen for the Indian Army on his name's sake, I'll be very grateful and I don't think the army will suffer.[4]

We've been motoring all over France (and looking at the French army in between) and are now on our way home. I wish you'd been with me at an amateur inspection of a French Cavalry school at Autun a week or so ago.[5] They gave me three hours solid walk round – from the riding-school to the cellars – and I never saw instruction to match it. But as the wretched C.O.'s say: – "We've had practically 200,000 men added to our strength but no more officers! So we work eleven hours a day."

Every sincerely yours
Rudyard.

Notes

1. Smith (see 21 June 1900, to Lawrence) had returned to England in 1910 and was now political advisor to the Secretary of State for India.
2. The Pottingers, an Irish family, were a prolific source of supply to the Indian Army. In the nineteenth century at least twelve Pottingers – brothers, cousins, nephews – saw service in the Bombay or Bengal armies; others were in the Indian Civil Service or the British Army. The later generations were mostly educated at Cheltenham. The most famous of the family was Eldred (1811–43), the "hero of Heart". The Pottinger about whom RK is writing is Robert Ormonde Brabazon Pottinger (1895–1915); he did not receive an appointment in the Indian Army but instead served in the Royal Munster Fusiliers. He was killed in France in May 1915. He was, incidentally, not the grandnephew but the great-grandnephew of Eldred Pottinger.
3. Robert Southey Pottinger (1870–1943), commissioned in the Royal Artillery in 1889, had been in the Indian Political Department since 1893 and had been Collector of Bhuj, in the native state of Cutch, since 1912. His wife died in that year, leaving him with four children.
4. On 2 May RK wrote to Dunlop Smith: "It was more than kind of you to have taken so much trouble and to such effect: and Pottinger will be a happy man" (ALS, Tyler Collection, Yale). Since Pottinger failed his last term at Sandhurst and could not enter the Indian Army, it was perhaps the commission in the Royal Munster Fusiliers that was in question (information from the Curator, Royal Military Academy Sandhurst Collection).
5. This was on 27 March: "They all know him everywhere and are delighted to show him things" (CK diary). RK wrote of the visit thus: "In aft. asked French General if I could see cavalry school for children of his officers which I did on most extensive scale. 2–4.30 in company with Commandant of School and Colonel of 29th line and two or three other officers. Gym instructor turned double somersault backward from a high scaffold. Saw kitchens, dormitories, infirmary, etc. etc. and talked for an hour afterwards with Col. of 29th. An amazing insight into a new world" (Motor Tours).

To Sir William Osler, 10 May 1914

Text: Harvey Cushing, *The Life of Sir William Osler*, 1925, II, p. 408

[Bateman's] May 10, 1914

Dear Osler,

    I can't tell you how shocked I am to find the practice of medicine at Oxford (Roger's own university) so grossly behind the age. It was Galen who laid down that "anger at meat" (by which he meant all mental emotion save of the mildest) is the mother of evil; and here are *you* – Regius Professor – counselling me to recite my own verses "at" not before or after but *at* – a bountiful meal.[1] May I refer you to "Libellus R.B.A. etc., etc., de retardandis senectutis accidentibus et de sensibus conservandis" (Oxford 1590).[2] But seriously, much as I should love to be of use to you I fear I am no good in this matter. I don't know Bacon except from the popular legend; I have no Brewer[3] and I can't get up to Oxford on the 10th and I am up to my eyes in work and arrears of work of all sorts. Forgive me, and send me, as soon as you can, your paper on R.B.[4] to file with my old doctors. Nicholas, who could write even if he couldn't cure for nuts – says at the beginning of his Herbal, "I knew well enough the whole world and everything in it was formed of a composition of contrary elements, and in such a harmony as must needs show the wisdom and power of a great God."[5] That seems to me to cover Roger Bacon's outlook and I present it to you for a quotation. The wife joins me in kindest regards to you both and I am,

Yours ever sincerely,
Rudyard Kipling.

Notes

1. Osler had invited RK to attend the presentation of a statue of Roger Bacon to the Oxford University Museum on 10 June (Bacon's 700th birthday) and to write something to be recited at a Merton College lunch afterwards (Cushing, *The Life of Sir William Osler*, 1925, II, 408).
2. *Libellus Rogerii Baconi Angli, doctissimi mathematici et medici, de retardandis accidentibus et de sensibus conservandis*, Oxford, 1590: "The Cure of Old Age and Preservation of Youth".
3. J. S. Brewer, ed., *Fr. Rogeri Bacon Opera quaedam haeterus inedita*, 3 vols, 1859.
4. I find nothing on Bacon in M. W. Blogg's *Bibliography* of Osler, 1921.
5. Nicholas Culpeper, *The English Physitian*, 1652, p. [vi]: for Culpeper see 8 May [1893].

To Sir Max Aitken, 15 May 1914
TLS: Harvard University

Bateman's / Burwash / Sussex / 15th May 1914.

Dear Sir Max,

Thanks for your letter. I shall be glad to sell my Puget Sound Light and Tractions, and shall we say at 101, and I will put the money into the Chicago Milwaukee and St. Paul's. I am glad to hear what you have to say about the situation in America, and I am quite ready to invest money there if you will say what you think in the matter. I have some now ready for re-investment, and it seems to me a mistake to wait until the Calgary Mortgage falls in to settle affairs.

I am very sorry to hear that you are not well. I wish that the wife and I could come over to Cherkley to see you, but I have got the speech at Tunbridge Wells[1] to-morrow night, and I have been busy; putting all my other work aside to do that and some verses,[2] so I do not see any prospect of getting away just yet. Another difficulty is that at this time of the year the American publishers come to England, and I am constantly having business with them through my Agent. Can't you come down to stay the night with us next week. I should so like to see you and to hear your news. In the meantime write to me and say what you think of investments.

Yours sincerely,
Rudyard Kipling.

Notes
1. The speech attacking the government over its Ulster policy, made to an anti-Home Rule meeting on Tunbridge Wells common, on the afternoon of Saturday, 16 May; there were, according to CK's diary, some 10,000 people present. The speech was reprinted in pamphlet form at the time and was widely reprinted in the press, but it was never collected by RK. It was violent beyond anything else that RK had said in public, accusing the ministers of acting on nothing but venal motives on the question of Home Rule. Of the bill, RK said that "it officially recognised sedition, privy conspiracy and rebellion; it subsidized the secret forces of boycott, intimidation, outrage and murder". He went on to call the ministers "conspirators" and "outlaws", and concluded that civil war was "inevitable" under present conditions ("Rudyard Kipling's Indictment of the Government", pamphlet reprint published by the *Daily Express* [May 1914]).
2. "The Covenant", written for the first number of the *Covenanter*, 20 May 1914, the journal of the League of British Convenanters. The poem, a sonnet, was written on 9 May (CK diary). The League published a pamphlet reprint of the Tunbridge Wells speech under the title of "The Secret Bargain and the Ulster Plot".

To Frank T. Bullen,[1] 20 May 1914
ALS: Syracuse University

Bateman's / Burwash / Sussex / May 20 1914

Dear Bullen –

Ever so many thanks for that splendid collection of chanties. What I value is the application of the same; which no one that I can recall has ever set out before. I knew "Paddy Doyle's Boots"[2] was kept for getting up the bent of a sail but I never knew 'twas kept for *that* only.

I wonder what they sing on dhows and puttomars?[3] As soon as I can get a man with a voice I shall make him render them all: and with luck perhaps one may be able to get some words to fit the swing of one of the tunes.

Glad you liked what I said at Tunbridge Wells.

With every good wish

Sincerely
Rudyard Kipling

Notes

1. Bullen (1857–1915) in early life had been a sailor; his first book, *The Cruise of the "Cachalot"* (1898), had an introductory letter by RK. He published a number of books on sea life, including the one discussed in this letter, *Songs of Sea Labour (Chanties)*, compiled by Bullen and W. F. Arnold, 1914.
2. See "The Merchantmen", line 12: "And that's the way we'll pay Paddy Doyle for his boots!"
3. The dhow is the traditional boat of the Arabian seas; a pattamar is a lateen-rigged ship common on the west coast of India (*Hobson-Jobson*).

To Joseph B. Gilder,[1] 25 May 1914
Text: Copy, Library of Congress

Bateman's / Burwash / Sussex / 25th May, 1914.

Private.

Dear Gilder,

Many thanks for yours of the 16th May and for the enclosure. I did not know that the President had done me the honour to quote me in his memorial speech,[2] and am correspondingly pleased. Mr. Oler's[3] note was very gratifying, too, but, as you will see, quite unanswerable. Praise on that scale leaves one dumb. But please tell him how I appreciate it and how glad I am that he found the verses useful.

I am waiting with joy the encounter between Landor of Brazil and elsewhere and Roosevelt of the United States.[4] There will be a description of Landor which I venture to think will live.

With kindest regards and good wishes,

Rudyard Kipling.

Notes
1. Gilder (see 30 November–8 December 1902), the brother of Richard Watson Gilder, was for many years a journalist and editor in New York before becoming an insurance company officer.
2. In a memorial speech at the Brooklyn Navy Yard, 11 May, on the servicemen killed in the attack on Veracruz, Mexico, Wilson spoke of "men who can do what Rudyard Kipling in one of his poems wrote, 'Meet with triumph and disaster and treat those two impostors just the same'" (Arthur S. Link, ed., *The Papers of Woodrow Wilson*, XXX [1979], 15). The lines are from "If".
3. Wesley Oler (1856–?), a businessman in New York.
4. Roosevelt had just completed a dangerous expedition in the Brazilian jungle, and was reported as saying that the results would correct statements made by Landor (*The Times*, 9 May 1914). Arnold Henry Savage Landor (1865–1924), the poet's grandson, and a world traveller, had spent 1910–12 in South America, chiefly in Brazil, and had published *Across Unknown South America* (Boston, 1913). Roosevelt's *Through the Brazilian Wilderness* (New York, 1914) speaks of "those alleged explorers, among whom Mr. Savage Landor stands in unpleasant prominence" (p. 173) and prints a note affirming that Landor made no genuine explorations in Brazil at all, though paid by the Brazilian government to do so (pp. 347–8). The obituary of Landor in *The Times* praises his narrative ability but notes his "innocence of any adequate knowledge of natural history, physics, botany, physiology, ethnology, and tropical medicine" (29 December 1924).

To Andrew Macphail, 27 May 1914
ALS: Photocopy, National Archives of Canada

Bateman's / Burwash / Sussex / May. 27 / 14

Dear Macphail

To yours of the 8th a bit of a swift answer between the World, the Devil and Ulster: In the first place it wasn't a school to which my daughter went but a pension where they took and had taken for many years girls who had a governess with them. You see a girl needs so much chaperoning in Paris (this is vital) that she *must* have someone to take her out. This was a most quiet flat on the Sixth:

45 Rue Poncelet
Avenue Wagram

Kept by a Mme Sabatiere (Sabatière)[1] and her daughter – both charming. With my maiden were her two cousins and their German governess;[2] and also a female English girl with her more than English governess. Elsie had a woman who came and took her out to her cooking and dress-making classes and her lectures. Also the cousins' Fraulein conveyed all three of 'em to a sinful amount of theatres. But what's all right for 18, with experience of Paris and France for four or five years before, won't be good for 16 1/2. I fancy what *you* want for your Dorothy[3] is more in the nature of a finishing school where the girls go out to lectures etc. in coveys. Here speaks Mrs Kipling from the sofa in the drawing room. "But I know of mothers who have sent their daughters to those schools and I know the girls who have been. If you care to continue the matter I can get you addresses and details of some schools and could investigate when you come over."

And that's our contribution. But *given good care*, for Paris is a Hades, I can't imagine a better thing for a maiden than a dip into it. It is logical and it works and it knows how to enjoy life. Ours has been a wild and harassed one ever since we came back. Things are boiling politically and, lo, I boil with 'em and do now address crowds in the open air which I perceive is the straight cut to Tophet and so resolve to taste sparingly of that drink. But it taught me *quite* clearly a few things about Cleon *and* the sausage seller[4] that I had only believed academically before.

The main thing however has been the sudden and mysterious illness of a close friend of mine[5] who has rented a cottage of ours (we built it for him) about a mile across the fields. I met him first in the war. Since then he has travelled in Persia, been to Lhassa; up and down the Persian Gulf, even into Ur of the Chaldees and deuce knows where else. Suddenly six weeks ago, he being packed to accompany the King to Paris, he fell very literally sick. To him the doctor: – "Go you now to bed for six weeks and lie there. Also, since this is an uncertain world, put your affairs straight. If you go to Paris you die."

"Amen" quoth he "but I have no pain now the sickness is passed."

"Bed and a trained nurse" said the doctor. "You only get up for your bath. It's kidney sauté." Mercifully the little cottage had been built for weekends, and he had planted his garden and down he came five weeks ago, debonair as ever, and to bed he went in his big study (which might have been built for this end) with all the spring pageant starting round him. And God sent us 3 weeks of God's own weather and he lay and watched it and we tramped over to see him twice a day and behold – all his trouble passed from him altogether so that at the end of three weeks the doctor let him get up. And he has been up for two weeks now, and the doctor swears there is not a single organ in any way wrong: so we all rejoice. Only my friend is as one upon [whom] Allah has laid a Remembering Finger. He walks quietly and is not too keen (thank goodness) to get back to his work. But it was a strange experience talking with this sound man in his bed, in all that riot of spring heat and colour; and he not sure (nor we) whether he would see the magnolia he planted last year come into flower. But it's no bad thing for any man to go into retreat – willingly or perforce. I had mine at Vernet among the water taps and hills, and here for a while I end.

Ever
R.K.

Notes
1. RK has written the name somewhat unclearly in the first instance and so repeats it between parentheses.
2. Margot and Lorna Baldwin with their "French/German governess" (Lorna Howard, "'Uncle Ruddy', Remembered", *Kipling Journal*, March 1987, p. 34).
3. Macphail's daughter Dorothy (1897–1988), afterwards Mrs Lindsay.
4. That is, both sides in an extravagant political contest of accusation and counter-accusation: see Aristophanes, *The Knights*.
5. Evidently Perceval Landon: I have no other information about this episode.

To R. D. Blumenfeld, 12 June 1914

ALS: University of Sussex

Bateman's / Burwash / Sussex/ June 12. 1914

Dear Blumenfeld –

If you have any money to divvy out of the Penny Kipling[1] please send it to Mrs Kipling who wants it for Ulster refugees. She's on a clothing committee and I gather it won't be long before the first of the refugees are coming over.[2] I am busy with similar matters and want money where it can be got.[3] I do hope, by the way, that the speech did sell. Certainly it has caused much annoyance.

Any good in a cartoon representing one bobby holding back rush of crowd from suffragettes. Label "Their only friend" or

W.S.P.U.[4]

We seem *pretty undesirable.*[5]

RK

Notes
1. The *Daily Express* reprint of RK's Tunbridge Wells speech (see 15 May 1914) was offered for sale at a penny, with discounts for orders in quantity (*Daily Express*, e.g. 29 May 1914).
2. CK was a member of a committee formed to assist the women refugees expected from Ulster (CK diary, 10 June, 28 July 1914). In the Kipling Papers at Sussex is a typed copy of a document headed "Ulster Refugees meeting 15 Dec. 1913. Original draft resolution by Rudyard Kipling." It reads: "This meeting desires to express its deepest sympathy with the women of Ulster in the present crisis and pledges itself to do its utmost towards alleviating the necessary changes and discomforts that will overtake them in the event of civil war." The meeting was "at Mrs Hussey's to try and start the sub-committees for looking after women and children from Ireland when civil war comes" (CK diary, 15 December 1913).
3. According to Angus Wilson, *The Strange Ride of Rudyard Kipling* (New York, 1978), p. 258, RK contributed £30,000 to the League of British Covenanters. I do not know the evidence for this extraordinary statement.

4. The Women's Social and Political Union, founded by Emmeline Pankhurst in 1903, the principal militant society in the women's suffrage movement.
5. I find no such cartoon in the *Express*.

To Sir Charles P. Crewe, 14 July 1914

ALS: East London Museum, South Africa

Bateman's / Burwash / Sussex / July 14. 1914

Dear Crewe –

Allah knows how many of your good letters I have *not* acknowledged in the past few months but – I am far beyond apologies. When one is watching the sure smash-up of a ship in open day on a naked coast, to the noise of trumpets and shawms, one hasn't much time for aught else. *Nothing* I could say could give you any idea of the laborious insanity of the whole situation or the chaos into which, administrative matters of all kinds, have drifted. The one fixed point is Ulster – and Ulster is gradually coming to realize her strength. Of course it is the first adumbration of the military power that invariably evolves itself out of a tyrannical democracy but nobody ventures to hint that aloud – yet. Milner, as you can see, is doing wonders[1] but the people here don't care much, if at all. The war is not present to their eyes and what they cannot see they do not follow. I have been most desperately busy in all sorts of directions – legal and illegal chiefly the latter. It's hard to have to envisage civil war in one's declining years but – every one is doing it; and there is a ghastly likeness to the situation just before the Raid ever so many years ago. Mrs Kipling is busy on refugee committees – the women who are expected from Ulster with their children – and camps and underclothing and possible outbreaks of disease. Meantime the Law – in Ulster at least – is not and nobody pretends that the Government have any control of anything.

But a week here would convince you more than volumes of mine. I met Jameson at a week end party the other day[2] and found him *very* fit and well. He is openly agin the Government on Irish matters and takes, for him, a very gloomy view of things.

I expect that we, like your Labour men, have got to go through with it and learn our lesson. *If* England pulls through (it's a large if) I fancy there won't be a Liberal party for a generation or two.

This is a hurried scrawl between floods of letters. Please forgive me and with love from us all to you both.

Ever yours sincerely
Rudyard Kipling

Notes
1. Milner was speaking throughout the country against Home Rule.
2. This was at Cliveden, the home of Mr and Mrs (afterwards Lord and Lady) Waldorf Astor, on 4 July (CK diary). Among the guests was Mrs Asquith (RK to Lady Astor, 7 July 1914: ALS: University of Reading).

Part Two
The Dark Days of the War

August 1914–March 1917

INTRODUCTION

When the war broke out, Kipling was on holiday with his family at Kessingland Grange, a house on the Norfolk coast belonging to Rider Haggard, and his first response appears almost casual, even relieved: "I am not an optimist by nature" he wrote, but "I can't help feeling cheerful over this" (7 August 1914). He acted at once to put his son John into the fight, begging a commission in the Irish Guards for him from Lord Roberts. John, who was barely seventeen when he went off to barracks to begin his training, would not go out to the war for many months, and in that interval his parents hovered uneasily around him, knowing, as everyone had to know, what the probabilities were. They would send the Rolls to John's barracks so that he might make short visits to Bateman's. They often made a point of being in London on weekends so that John might join them there from Warley, not far distant in Essex, for dinners and theatres and music halls, a style of amusement quite unlike the family's usual routine. At the end of his year in training, John was sent to France in August 1915; on 27 September he was killed in an action associated with the battle of Loos. If any of the cheerfulness with which Kipling had greeted the outset of the war remained, it was gone now, never to return. Kipling allowed himself no direct expression of his grief, but something of its intensity may be guessed at from indirect expression – the growing violence of his language against the Germans, for example, or his intemperate notions about the treatment of conscientious objectors or of anyone who suggested negotiating a peace. The suffering caused by John's death was made even more poignant by the fact that his grave was unknown.

Before and after John's death Kipling busied himself completely with the war. "For All We Have and Are", his hymn of dedication to the war, appeared in *The Times* on 2 September. He wrote long letters to his American correspondents setting them straight on the questions at issue. He made speeches in support of the war effort. He visited the wounded in hospitals around southern England. He was active in organising a club for Canadian soldiers in London. While his wife and daughter knitted stockings for soldiers at the front, Kipling made scrapbooks to amuse wounded soldiers in England. Bateman's was developed as a working farm in order to help feed the country, and was several times offered for use as a hospital, though the offers were never accepted.

The quantity of writing that Kipling managed to do during the war, though no doubt the least-read part of his *oeuvre*, is quite considerable. It began with *The New Army in Training*, a series of articles for the *Daily Telegraph* published in December 1914. In August 1915, Kipling went as an official correspondent to the front in France, visiting the lines from Soissons to Belfort in company with his friend from the days of the Boer War, Perceval Landon. The result was *France at War on the Frontier of Civilization*, a series of five articles appearing originally in the *Daily Telegraph* in September 1915. "The Fringes of the Fleet", a series on submarines and the auxiliary ships of the Navy, was written at the request of the Ministry of Information. This was followed by "Tales of 'The Trade'", on submarine warfare ("The Trade"), written in 1916 at the request of the Admiralty from confidential reports. Then came "Destroyers at Jutland", also written up from reports. The three naval series – "The Fringes of the Fleet", "Tales of 'The Trade'", and "Destroyers at Jutland" – were collected in the volume called *Sea Warfare* in 1916. *The Eyes of Asia*, about Indian troops in Europe, was also written in 1916, though it did not appear until 1917. Kipling did not accept every official request for his pen; at least once he declined to help, on the grounds that the censorship involved would make it impossible to write anything useful (see 9 December 1915).

In these years he published nothing that did not have to do with the war, until, in 1917, he decided that the collection called *A Diversity of Creatures*, originally intended for publication in 1914 but held back on Kipling's instructions, could now be allowed to appear. Even then he was careful to date each of the stories to show that, with the exception of "Swept and Garnished" and "Mary Postgate", which needed no excuse, they all antedated the outbreak of the war.

Life at Bateman's was outwardly undisturbed, except for the new activity of farming and the stream of soldiers and sailors who came through at Kipling's invitation. Inwardly it was transformed. They could sometimes hear the sound of the guns in France and were aware of them always, whether audible or not. Caroline Kipling's health, already troubled before the war, continued to suffer during the war: in 1915 she began what was to be a series of visits to Bath for the sake of the waters. Kipling, too, began to feel the first pangs of the affliction – a duodenal ulcer – from which he suffered for the rest of his life. There had been a few ominous signs in earlier years, but the first real attack coincided almost exactly with the news of John's death. He was never thereafter to be quite free of pain, or of the threat of pain, though he did not burden others with complaints about his condition. That pain, however, must have had its part in darkening Kipling's outlook in these years. That outlook was, in some ways, no doubt dark enough already. He resigned from the Society of Authors in January 1917, in protest over its interference, as he thought, with the freedom of authors to publish where and with whom they chose. Thus he broke a connection that went back to his first days in London and his admiring friendship with the Society's founder, Sir Walter Besant. He cultivated a hatred of Germans, and he extended this to include pacifists, liberals, labour leaders, Irish nationalists, and anyone else who might be imagined as in any way interfering with a determined prosecution of the war.

To Colonel H. W. Feilden, 4 August 1914
ALS: Syracuse University

Kessingland Grange[1] / Kessingland. / Aug. 4. 1914.

Dear Colonel Sahib

Many thanks for your two letters. Yes, I feel like Jonah or whoever it was who went about saying: – "I told you so."[2] The whole thing seems to be working out with the usual serene logic of fact *but* – and it's a big but – it strikes me as tho' the Teuton had a little bit lost his head. Wind in the head is an awful disease, but I *do* think the Germans frankly and fully left us out of the show altogether.[3] I don't blame 'em – seeing what your[4] record has been but I think they err a shade in under-estimating as much as they do. I love your Suffolk–Norfolk folk. They don't howl or grouse, or get together and jaw but go about their job like large horses. It's a good harvest and ripe to cut.

As to sheep. The idea is a very good one but, you see, I'm not there. Rye Green[5] is in our hands and the ricks belong to us, but – who is to buy the sheep?

I don't know enough to know when I'm being swindled and my experiences with Jern's[6] haven't enlightened me. Would *you* send us a word of enlightenment as to what they're costing and whom you'd recommend us to buy from?

With our best greetings to you both

Ever affectionately
Rudyard K.

Notes

1. RK and CK had gone to Kessingland (see 23 July 1913) on 23 July 1914; they remained there until 10 August (CK diary).
2. England declared war on Germany on 4 August. The deadline for Germany's reply to England's demand for assurances regarding Belgium was not until 11 p.m., but it was already taken as certain that war would follow.
3. The Germans hoped for British neutrality in their war with Russia and France.
4. Thus in MS: for "our"?
5. See 2 August 1910.
6. Not identified. The name is not quite clear.

To R. D. Blumenfeld, [4 August 1914][1]
ALS: University of New Brunswick

Kessingland Grange / Lowestoft

Dear Blumenfeld,

Many thanks for your wire *re* ultimatum. I somehow fancy that these sons of Belial[2] will wriggle out of the mess after all – or it may be worth Germany's while to avoid Belgium *if* we stay neutral. *How* the Teutons must despise us – and how justly! Meantime we look as tho' we were losing time.

I'd be greatly your debtor if you could tell someone in the office to send me a wire of evenings when they have time, giving me the day's news. This place we have taken here is, for practical purposes, the side of a ship. The garden runs about 15 yards to a cliff – then the sea and all the drama of the skirts of war laid out before us. Destroyers going up and coming down in twos and fours – then a gun boat or so – then a N.Y.K. (Jap boat) all white and disinterested going to London; then a Nelson liner with a sort of "Mike you're wanted" look on her; then steam trawlers and the usual procession of tows and barges.

This afternoon entered from the South a racing cruiser (bow and tail wave in white wedges fore and aft). She signalled to two destroyers who were larking round here and they ran like whippets towards a certain quarter of the horizon. All inexplicable of course; but more than likely to be history if one knew.

The strain on you must be awful but there is the ancient text of the Rabbi (I think t'was Hillel or Ben Meir) to console one with. It says, substantially, that the worst that men and women meet in this world is just men and women and their actions.[3] The old boy was a bit of a free thinker like so many of the old Rabbis were at heart. My father used to quote it to me as: – "Nothing worse in the world than yourself and nothing better". I am tremendously interested in the Government's psychology and shall never cease to thank Allah that they are in charge with us loyalists to back 'em instead of 'other way round. Frankly I have high hopes – higher than I dare say out loud. It's the old Napoleonic idea over again, *not* evolved by direct action and one step after another, but *hatched* after 40 years of brooding. That cheers me to think of.

Well, Allah be good to you!

Ever
R.K.

Notes

1. The letter is not dated by RK; another hand has dated it "August 4 1914" and then substituted a "5" for the "4". The internal evidence makes 4 August much more likely.
2. That is, the English Liberal government.
3. I find nothing resembling this in Pirke Aboth, the sayings of the Fathers.

To H. A. Gwynne, 7 August 1914
ALS: Dalhousie University

Kessingland / Aug. 7th. 1914

Dear Old Man –

Ever so many thanks for your wire but I've been trying to do some verses about the English situation – not of course from the party point of view.[1] My notion is that the Dago knows dee well which side (or end) his macaroni is buttered and is not going to get into trouble if he can help it.[2] What I can't understand is the Austrian ambassador staying on with us, while Vienna moans about her friendship to England.[3] Surely that can't mean that Austria is getting scared at the shower bath she has pulled? I take it the Teuton, who is not tactful, has explained what sort of a Hell of a King-Empire Germany will be after she has won; and maybe the Austrian like the Italian begins to realize that his chance of a place in the sun is very slim after all the row is over. Anyhow it's an amazingly curious situation. I cherish a hope that by the time the wandering Americans have spread themselves through the U.S. on their return, they will tell tales that will not improve the temper of the U.S. towards Germany.

Meantime, here C. and I and the kids sit in the most easterly house in England not 100 yards from the sea with a light wire fence and a 50 foot earthen cliff between us and it. Last night it seemed to us that we heard guns – a queer sensation – at sea – 9 [ ][4] and big 'uns. It seems that the hand of Fate must have guided us here. Haggard lent it us a year ago. We then hired it for a twelve month and only came up on July 23rd – which is a long time ago. We are going to stick here a bit because I don't see the sense of lugging a family about England while all the lines are needed for troops. The simple Suffolker doesn't panic. He just carries on all serene.

I confess I feel rather proud of the way in which England has bucked up at the pinch and tho', as you know, I am not an optimist by nature I can't help feeling cheerful over this. I always said the Kaiser was our best friend. I see K[itchener] has asked for 500,000.[5] Here's a bit of a bet. When Liège falls the German army will make such a ghastly "example" of it (with a view to striking terror) as will send every other available male in England scuttling into the ranks in order to get a gun to have a pot at the Germans. That's where the policy of "striking terror" breaks down as applied to English folk.

John goes into the territorials as soon as we get back home. It's a bit of a wrench (he not being over strong) but I don't see what else can be done. I shall have my hands full of local relief business I expect.

We all send our love to you. You must be working like 7 devils.

Ever
Rud

P.S.   Are you cheered about K? Where is The Brat?

Notes
1. Perhaps "For All We Have and Are", published in *The Times* and other papers on 2 September 1914.
2. Italy declared neutrality despite its alliance with Austria. In May 1915, Italy entered the war against Austria.
3. Austria, after its eagerness to deal with the Serbs, tried to temporise as the conflict became general.
4. Letter not clear: "f"?
5. In his speech to the Commons on 6 August Asquith reported that Lord Kitchener had been made Secretary for War and had asked for an additional 500,000 men (*The Times*, 7 August).

To H. A. Gwynne, 18 August 1914
ALS: Dalhousie University

Bateman's / Burwash / Sussex / Aug. 18. 1914

Dear Old Man –

I took John over to Maidstone yesterday (for commission) and they turned him down for eyes.[1] Past as physically fit in every other way. But surely, in view of our butcher's bills, they are not going to stick to this. They seem to be turning men down here very freely. This has a double effect. It disheartens offering recruits and their neighbours and gives excuse for "sticky chaps" to fall out and hang back.

As to the *Hymn before Action*[2] – never mind the other papers. The old order of things has passed. Reprint it in some corner. No need to make a feature of it. Also reprint any thing else of mine that seems useful. There is the work of twenty years, ready to your hand and prepared for this moment. Use it.

Like you I have been speaking[3] – trying to get men to go into K's new army: but they are a bit slow and will be till we get our knock. Also our recruiting offices are not well placed or advertized. A marquee in the middle of the market square of all towns is what is wanted. As to Italy. This is no time for tickling. Italy will probably come in when she thinks it's safe and will stay out so long as the issue is doubtful.

I bear in mind all you say about verses. Believe me I am as hard at work as I can be. Send us a line from time to time if you have leisure. With love from us all.

Ever
Rud

Notes
1. John had gone to the War Office to apply for a commission on 10 August (CK diary, 17 August); evidently the visit to Maidstone was for the physical examination. Carrington explains John's situation thus: "forty years ago, when education beyond the primary stage was enjoyed only by a small minority, any reputable young man with a good education and a good character was eligible for appointment as 'Temporary Second Lieutenant', and might get a commission as soon as a regimental commander applied for his services" (*Rudyard Kipling*, p. 428). Following his rejection, John "talked of enlisting" (CK diary, 17 August): the date was that of his 17th birthday.
2. First published in 1896: see 3 March 1896.
3. I have found no record of any speech by RK at this time.

To Sir Max Aitken, 3 September 1914
TLS: Harvard University

Bateman's / Burwash / Sussex / 3rd September 1914

Dear Sir Max,

I was not able to attend to your letter of August 31st yesterday, as I was in town trying to arrange about John's commission,[1] and the wife was busy with a most tremendous lot of telegrams. Now I have wired that I should like to take up those securities of which you write in this letter, and I shall be very glad if you will ask your people to send me an account, giving details of recent transactions, and letting me realize how much balance I have with you.

The London "Times" has really excelled itself this time in their note to my verses.[2] Any other time one would have been simply distracted at their having done such a hopeless thing, but somehow nothing seems to matter much these days.

Yours very sincerely,
Rudyard Kipling.

Notes
1. RK asked Lord Roberts for an appointment for John; Roberts obliged, and John received a commission in the Irish Guards. He reported to his regiment on 14 September (CK diary, 2, 10, 14 September 1914). "We sent our John away yesterday to his new life with outward good spirits and inward misery" (CK to Mrs Balestier, 15 September [1914]: ALS, Dunham Papers).
2. At the end of "For All We Have and Are" *The Times* printed this note: "At the request of Mr. Kipling we are sending £50 to the Belgian Relief Fund in his name" (2 September 1914).

To R. D. Blumenfeld, 5 September 1914

TLS: University of Sussex

Bateman's / Burwash / Sussex / 5th September 1914.

Dear Blum,

I am going to make a short speech at the Dome in Brighton on Monday evening about urging enlistment.[1] I don't know [if] you think it would be useful to publish this speech in leaflet form, but if it is I shall be glad for you to do it. We shall use all the profits for either the Red Cross or the Belgium Relief Funds.

Yours
Rudyard Kipling

Notes
1. RK gave the speech twice that day, 7 September (CK diary): the speech was reported under the title "As They Tested Our Fathers" in *The Times* and other London papers, 8 September (uncollected). No separate publication is known.

To Frank N. Doubleday, 11 September 1914

ALS: Princeton University

Bateman's / Burwash / Sussex / Sep. 11. 1914

Dear Frank

Many thanks for your last note to Carrie. We are all settling down to the business of war now. John goes off in a day or two to join his battalion at Warley[1] in Essex and – the rest is as God shall dispose.

Now I want you to read carefully what I am going to say. Germany is running this war, of set purpose, without the faintest regard for any law human or divine. You've heard, of course, of Louvain, the burning of Dinant and all the other things. They are done in order, as the Germans say, "to strike terror into the world." And, by the way, the United States represents about all of the civilized world which is unaffected by the war. We have an American friend who has been living in France for years in a chateau which she converted into a 50 bed hospital and had to abandon as the Germans advanced.[2] She escaped to Havre in a motor which her daughter drove. Her accounts of the horrors committed is something ghastly. They cut the hands off a surgeon whom they took prisoner in order that he might never practise again. A Belgian officer, a friend of hers and a man whom I know also, told her that women and girls were *publicly* raped in Belgium by the command of their officers; and – but there is no need to go across the water for details. The Belgian refugees who are pouring into Folkestone all bring their tales of unbelievable horrors which they have suffered or witnessed. I know it must be difficult to give you any idea of it but – believe me – it is true: and the half of the truth has not yet been revealed – for obvious reasons.

And so this Hell-dance goes on: and the U.S. makes no sign. Nobody wants her to take part in the war but for her own conscience' sake; for the sake of her record in history, and her position as the one untouched civilized power, she ought to enter her protest against three atrocities. Be as neutral as you like; but do not pass these brutalities over in silence officially. If there is any means of making people see that this is a matter which touches the whole foundation and future of civilized life, *try* to bring it home to them. They cannot, if they will only think for a moment, sit dumb in the face of the negation of every idea and ideal that they have stood for since their beginnings. Remember, these atrocities at the present moment are being practised on a scale we have no record of in history – and they are increasing.

And the amazing thing is that the Germans assume that the U.S. don't count, in any way. Here is an incident that you can check. Two women that I know[3] one with a son and one with a nephew missing went to see Page[4] last Friday to ask him to get news from Berlin if they were prisoners. This is of course the most ordinary courtesy in war time for a neutral nation to undertake. Page told them that he was unable to get answers to his telegrams to Berlin! And he is the Ambassador of the United States!

You can see how incredible such a state of affairs seems to us. For all the purposes of neutrality the U.S. are wiped off the map by the Germans. And at the same time they are trying to conciliate your public opinion. Isn't the answer to their attempts, a suggestion that they should keep a few of the laws which they, in common with you, agreed to at the Hague convention?[5]

Ponder these things in your heart. The end of this war is a long way off and many awful things will happen. I don't know whether *you* realize but we do, very clearly, that all and more than all the horrors of Louvain, Aerschot, Dinant etc. etc. will be duplicated here, if we can't keep them out. Odd – isn't it? – in the 20th century?

With love from us all to you all

Ever
Rud

Notes
1. Warley Barracks, at Brentwood, Essex, where the reserve battalion of the Irish Guards was in training. John went there on 14 September. RK describes Warley as "old, crazy barracks", "condemned as unfit for use by the Honourable the East India Company a trifle of fifty odd years ago" (*The Irish Guards in the Great War*, Outward Bound Edition, II, 1).
2. Julia Catlin Depew, of the Château d'Annel, near Compiègne: she arrived at Bateman's on 9 September (CK diary).
3. One of them was Lady Edward Cecil, whose eldest son George had been killed on 1 September, though she did not yet know that: see 3 December 1914.
4. Walter Hines Page.
5. The International Peace Conference at the Hague, 1907.

To Theodore Roosevelt, 15 September 1914
ALS: Library of Congress

Bateman's / Burwash / Sussex / Sep. 15. 1914

Dear Roosevelt –

Your letters from England will have given you an insight into things as they are here. But I wish you could spend half a day with the Belgian refugees as they come into Folkestone. The look on their faces is enough without having to hear their stories which are like tales from Hell. When people congratulate each other that so and so's women folk were shot outright one realizes a bit about German culture. As far as one makes out the rapings etc. were (and are) put through as part of a set plan to "strike terror into the world."

Of course we in England may have these things happen to us: but frankly we are aghast at there being no protest from the U.S. against the Belgium dealings. It seems almost incredible that America which has always stood so emphatically against these horrors should be silent now. Neutrality is of course understood but surely neutrality cannot bar her from putting herself on record as officially opposed to Louvainism etc.

But the really important thing is, what is going to happen to the U.S. if Europe fails in this war? Germany's victory would mean Germany dominating the Eastern hemisphere by land and sea. In which case where does the U.S. with its present fleet and no army come in? For once I agree with the advanced Germans (they have left the Pan-German school behind) who say that, with England out of it, Germany holds the U.S. in the hollow of her hand. I needn't point out to you that the Monro doctrine would become a scrap of paper not worth tearing up.

I can only lament that you are not at the head of affairs to explain this to your people and to get them to arm steadily but at once by land and by sea. Otherwise, if Europe fails, there will be no place left for Freedom and the decency of things in any part of the earth.

Another reason that I wish you were in office is that I don't think you would sit and bite your nails at the White House while your accredited representative at St James's admits that he can't get any answer to his telegrams to the U.S. Ambassador in Berlin. You might regard that as discourteous – if not as an insult.

England is rather set and determined to see the thing through though it says nothing of its losses individually and collectively – and we are all hit in our degree. No one can get any news of wounded or missing. Berlin refuses to furnish it because the refusal increases the agony of the relatives.

Lord knows how long the show will last but we are planning it on a three years basis, which seems to me to allow a fair margin. But it is extraordinary to see the frank methods by which the Teuton sets out to destroy: and, to do him justice, his leaders and philosophers for the past generation never took the trouble to disguise what their methods would be. But we wouldn't heed.

Kermit and his bride paid us a most delightful visit on their way to South America.[1] And Happiness wasn't the word to describe 'em!

Please give them our best remembrances and with our heartiest good wishes

believe me

Ever yours sincerely
Rudyard Kipling

Notes

1. Kermit Roosevelt (see 2 August 1910) had married Belle Wyatt Willard on 11 June 1914. They were at Bateman's on 7 and 8 July (Bateman's Visitors Book), en route to Buenos Aires, where Roosevelt worked for the National City Bank.

To Elsie Kipling, 28 September 1914
ALS: University of Sussex

Bateman's / Burwash / Sussex / Sep. 28. 1914.

To the Hon
  Miss Lofter-Brassey
    Castle Driver
      Niblinks
        N. Bunker![1]

But the idea of *you* as a hard bitten golfer, oh my best beloved, fills me with amazement. I don't somehow seem to see you swinging your fat self round after the stroke – following through, keeping your eye on the ball and all the rest of it. But if it's going to really take hold of you it will be great fun. You'll have to join the Burwash golf-club and play with the Chamberlains.

Words can't say how pleased I am that you are having a good time. 'Just like you. First: – "*Must* I go?" next: "I don't want to go. Tell me to come home as soon as possible." Then "Please may I stay longer." Yah!

We too (or two) greatly wish we could come up but it's an over long journey for a very short time and frankly I'm not up to it. You know I am not much given to lying abed (except o' mornings) but I was abed for four full days with a variorum mixture of neuralgia, toothache and temperature – at which I was in great indignation.[2] Mummy was more different sorts of an angel to me than even *she* had ever been before – and you can guess how much *that* meant! Now I am dressed indeed but rocky and Saturday[3] came John in full canonicals by the 5.44. He *very* much becomes the uniform, as you Scotch would say. It was a changed John in many respects but all delightful. A grave and serious John with an adorable smile and many stories of "his" men – notably Beggie his mad Irish servant whose idea of cleaning J's room is "to keep a broom about" – as an earnest, I suppose, of what he might do. The Irish Guards I gather are racially and incurably mad – which of course suits J. down to the ground. For goodness sake try to get some of his stories out of him – notably of drunken men trying to kiss sentries, while the sentries presented arms. He meant to write to you yesterday (he left at 6.30) but he didn't. I am immensely pleased with our boy. The old spirit of carping and criticism has changed into a sort of calm judicial attitude. Evidently he gets on well with his men – he talks to 'em when he can which is one of the great secrets of command. He speaks well of the food at mess "almost as good as Brown's" says he; and I think he is growing. We had a perfectly lovely day together; broken by occasional grunts of "wish to the devil Phipps was here," which indeed we all did.

Tho' I am sorry for your disappointment Mummy and I both feel that he will appreciate you more when you meet. (Please forgive this abominable handwriting but the pen feels as strange to me as an oar, after all these days). We talked, and we talked, *and* we talked – this grown up man of the world and I. Mother is trying to arrange a meeting between you and John at Brown's on Saturday but we mustn't be disappointed if it doesn't come off because he doesn't know five minutes beforehand what he can do or when he can be spared. When he came down to us on Saturday, for example, he had to change all his train because, though he knew he was free, he had to go to the adjutant to report that he was leaving; and the adjutant was engaged with prisoners. The Irish Guards are rather given to prisoners – "not an ounce of vice in 'em even when they are drunk" says John "but *quite* mad." He mimicks their dialects perfectly.

And now I will stop. No one will be more pleased that you have had this lovely time than we shall be. But there is worrk, madam – shirts and socks madam to be undertaken. The fame of your socks has spread. Mummy's order for nine pairs (with shirts) has brought her a fresh order from the same troop – a modest man who says he is rather thin and five foot ten and 22 inches from elbow to wrist, or else it's shoulder. I enclose copy of his letter which Mother asks me to send you.

A whole heartful of love from us both and best remembrances and heartiest thanks to Mrs. Lowe.

Ever your own
Daddy

Notes
1. Elsie had left on 18 September to stay with Juliette Gordon Low (see 2 December 1900) at Castle Menzies, near Aberfeldy, Perthshire. As her mother wrote, Elsie "has been working so hard and been so upset by the war and went away sad for a loss of another friend news of whose death was in the morning paper. Killed in action. She says very soon she won't know any man *who is alive*" (CK to Mrs Balestier, 18 September [1914]: ALS, Dunham Papers).
2. This attack followed a visit to Sir Max Aitken at Cherkley on 21 September (Rees extracts and CK diary, 21–6 September). CK wrote that she was "sure his illness is the form the strain anxiety and sadness of these last dreadful weeks have taken" (to Mrs Balestier, 26–9 September [1914]: ALS, Dunham Papers).
3. 26 September.

To Andrew Macphail, 5 October 1914
ALS: Photocopy, National Archives of Canada

Bateman's / Burwash / Sussex / Oct: 5. 1914:

Dear Macphail

Many many thanks for your good letter just in with its cheery description of your "contemptible" (the word is now consecrated by Teutonic culture) Engineers.[1] You see one doesn't know – isn't told – where the various contingents are or when they landed – for obvious reasons: but if by any chance I find out about your brother[2] you may be well sure that I will go and see him. I like the idea of writing sonnets and building bridges for cannon, with either hand so to say. Well, they are all needed and welcome they will be. Evidently Allah intended that the Kaiser should die in the high act of welding the British Empire. There used to be a lot of questions about the Federation of the future. He has kindly settled them all for us. But do not let the good work of getting more men slack off even for a day. Trouble comes not before but on the heels of victory as some eminent Greek remarked a few thousand years ago. It will be a long long job to put through to a satisfactory finish. We have half a million men under training now, with the eagerness of men who want desperately to be taught and we shall have twice that number in a few months. This, over and above the army in the field, the 500,000 territorials and the contingents as they come in. It's curious how quietly – for our note is ever quietude – the English have taken to the grim business of arms and how well the afflicted bear their sorrow. Conceive for a moment – as it will appeal to Dorothy – that *every* young man, with *one* exception (and *he* isn't in favour) with whom Elsie danced at the beginning of the season is at the War; the vast majority wounded dead or missing. Almost all the men I used to know are gone – some past recall: and the staple of conversation when one meets is as to the whereabouts of such and such an one, son or husband or father of so and so. It is the uncertainty that kills. *Exemplia Gratia.* An old friend and neighbour of ours had her son reported wounded and missing more than a month ago.[3] She went over to Paris the other day and covered all the country near where he fell, in vain search for news. A sympathetic French peasantry assuring her he was all right; the guns growling far off, and she wandering from one piled mound of graves to the next. She hears nothing save a report that he was seen dying in a ditch (the boy is eighteen). She comes back to England and receives a report that he is a wounded prisoner in Germany. Writes for confirmation of the report and has it strongly confirmed. On that very day comes word from the boy's battalion that a returned prisoner saw the lad blown to pieces by a shell. And so the horrible see-saw goes on; she dying daily and letters of condolence *and* congratulation crossing each other and harrowing her soul. Meantime the boy's father thousands of miles away and cut off from all save letters and wires. And that is but one case of many, many hundreds. *Per Contra* one comes across cases of the reported missing miraculously restored and then one sees the envy in the eyes of the other women.

My boy turned up here last Sunday in uniform – a grave and serious person much attracted by his Irish soldiery with whom he had been playing football as well as accompanying on night marches. As he says "a second-lieutenant is less valuable than a private." When one is my age and has toiled *very* hard to make life pleasant for one's children, one resents bitterly that their youth should be blasted by this shadow: But *they* don't and that's what it is so hard to realize. They have the world to carry on; with the spring and passion of their own youth and, not having played the game of life, do not in the least care what sort of game it may be. This is very curious to meditate upon. And I remember in my youth I lived through what I was told were grave crises but they did not touch me, because I was young.

We rejoice, both of us, at your hint that you may be coming over. *Do!* If we have any luck you come down to Bateman's and see how this world goes on. By the way the enclosed anonymous letter came to me in the mail that brought yours. A woman evidently but she crossed out the address clumsily. So I return it to you if you think it worth while to hand over to your police. One doesn't like letters of that kind to be written from a known address – at least we don't in English. Have constables go and take note of the age and profession of the writer and then invite them to explain themselves to magistrates. All the same, we are crazily lenient about Germans in our midst.

Now I will stop. It was a joy to get your letter and I do hope and pray I may come across the Canadians on their way through England. What you say about the "farming machinery" is most helpful. Yes I know the name of that Reaper and (Empire) Binder very well. With all our best wishes to you and yours.

Affectionately,
Rudyard Kipling

Notes

1. A Canadian Expeditionary Force was now on its way to England; the first contingent landed at Plymouth on 15 October and went into camp on Salisbury Plain. RK visited the camp on 24 November (CK diary) and described it in "Canadians in Camp", originally published in the *Daily Telegraph*, 19 December 1914 (*The New Army in Training*). "Contemptible" had been in popular use since the Kaiser, in an Order of the Day on 4 August, had urged his soldiers to "walk over General French's contemptible little army".

2. James Alexander Macphail (1870–1949), Major (later Colonel) in the Canadian Engineers; in civil life he was professor of engineering at Queen's University, Kingston, Ontario.

3. This was Lady Edward Cecil, who evidently did not yet know for sure the fate of her son George, killed on 1 September (see 3 December 1914). She called at Bateman's on 1 October to tell of "her adventures in Paris" (CK diary).

To Theodore Roosevelt, 20 October 1914
ALS: Library of Congress

Bateman's / Burwash / Sussex / Oct. 20 1914

private

Dear Roosevelt

Many thanks for your letter of the 3rd and for the *Outlook* etc. that accompanied it.[1]

My only criticism of your articles would be that they are a little too remote in tone for the actual facts of the case: but of course much water – or shall we say blood? – has flowed under the bridges since they were written.

The necessity for immediate military preparation is not insisted upon strongly enough. As I see it, the U.S. for existing Teutonic purposes *is*, practically, Belgium. That is to say she has much the same assets as Belgium had – a vociferous public opinion and large financial means. Neither of these assets much concern the Teuton since he disregards the one and annexes the other.

It all seems to me to boil down to one point. The allies are shedding their blood (and the butcher's bill is a long one) for every ideal that the United States stands for by the mere fact of her Constitution, not to mention her literature, press and daily life.

If the Allies fail all those things (which one has been taught to believe are Eternal Verities) will be challenged, and challenged very soon, by the conqueror. If the U.S. cannot bring sufficient force to repel the challenge, she will have to conform to the conqueror's ideals.

Meantime–and this is my point – the U.S. is *not* arming in order that she may possess that sufficient force. For that reason very little that she says now matters much and whatever she may say later will matter less. The facts set forth in the *Outlook* – that her prestige never stood higher and that she has made £100,000,000 by profits on war-wheat alone – have no bearing on the situation.[2] If she has not armies and fleets she will go under.

I am sorry that there is a schoolmaster instead of a man at the head of the U.S. today because I know something of the limitations of the schoolmaster's mind. As to what you say about atrocities,[3] we are in rather close touch with that arena. Our hospitals are full of our own wounded as well as Belgian wounded (I am off to see some of these latter this afternoon).[4] Also the county is full of Belgian refugees. Women who have been raped to any large extent don't talk about it, but those who have lost children and relatives are very eloquent. Belgium was scientifically vivisected on Holland's doorstep in order that Holland might draw instruction from the lesson.

Lee[5] is out at the front I believe so I will not risk your letter in an envelope on his trail.

With every good wish

Most sincerely
Rudyard Kipling.

Get your people at any rate to begin to arm.

Notes

1. Roosevelt published "The World War: Its Tragedies and Lessons" in *The Outlook*, CVIII (23 September 1914), 169–78. In it he is at pains to make clear that he is "not passing judgment one way or the other upon Germany's actions" (p. 172); but he affirms that "every circumstance of national honor and interest forced England to act precisely as she did act" (p. 170). As for the US, the lesson to be learned from Belgium is to "speak softly and carry a big stick" (p. 175). The other articles referred to in this letter were "certain newspaper articles I have written" (Roosevelt to RK, 3 October 1914: TLS, Library of Congress). These would have included something from the series that Roosevelt wrote on the war for the *New York Times* beginning 27 September 1914, reprinted in *America and the World War* (New York, 1915).

2. An article on commerce and finance in the September *Outlook* reports an increase, owing to the war, in "the value of an unexampled grain crop by about $500,000,000. … Meantime, directly as a result of the war, we have an immensely increased prestige as a Nation" (p. 222).

3. In his letter of 3 October to RK Roosevelt says "I have not touched on the outrages against individuals because there is much conflict of testimony and because in huge armies of many millions of men it is perfectly certain that some thousands of unspeakable creatures will commit unspeakable acts of infamy and moreover my own experience in the Spanish war has taught me that there is a tendency to exaggerate such outrages. At the time I firmly believed things of the Spaniards which, with the knowledge I have since acquired, I am positive never occurred at all."

4. The Belgian soldiers were at Hawkhurst; RK visited them on 21 October "to take them some books in French" (to John Kipling, 21 October 1914: ALS, Sussex).

5. At the end of his letter of 3 October Roosevelt writes: "I have written you very freely. I shall ask you not to show this letter to anyone except Arthur Lee, to whom you are entirely at liberty to show it." Arthur Hamilton Lee (1868–1947), 1st Viscount Lee of Fareham, had served as military attaché with the US Army in Cuba during the Spanish-American War, when he was made an honorary member of Roosevelt's Rough Riders and became one of Roosevelt's intimate friends. He was in Parliament as a Conservative, 1900–14; on the outbreak of the War he rejoined the Army and was now at the front. Lee afterwards had a career of high public distinction, in office and out of it.

To Edward Bok, 28 October 1914

TLS: Syracuse University

Bateman's / Burwash / Sussex / 28th October 1914.

private and confidential

Dear Bok,

Many thanks for your letter of the 19th. In view of the magnificently organized campaign for your education that Germany has been working, it would be strange if there was not some change of public opinion in the United States. I only wonder that the big financial interests, plus the large German and German-Semitic elements of the population, have not made more of a change. And I freely admit that German efficiency is very impressive, and loses nothing as it is described by the correspondents of the United States papers. These men have been suffering, until lately at any rate, from the restriction imposed by our censorship, and, as our "Times" points out, it is a serious thing – even for a nation fighting for its existence – to antagonize the press.

Then again, the position of your country is very difficult. The United States declared herself neutral at the outset, and her neutrality has not been shaken by anything that has happened in Belgium or in France. At the same time, a large proportion of her public opinion has up to date expressed itself as in favour of the Allies. This from the German point of view is a culpable exhibition of partizanship for which, as the German papers announce, the United States will in due time be called to account. And I have heard that the same threats are employed in the United States by German-born interests and associations. Now, those who are responsible for the control of the United States by now realize – what their Naval and Military men have been telling them for some time – that as a fighting power the United States does not exist. Consequently I should not be at all surprised if there was a general feeling in those quarters that the press might – in view of "the efficiency of the Kaiser's fighting machine" – mitigate its transports a little. I do not say that the feeling has been crudely put into words but – there it is. After all a nation can only do what it can, as one sees daily in the case of poor Italy who, so to speak, lies under the guns.

And in regard to outrages, I can quite understand the position of the United States. Any people that passed over in official silence the horrors in Belgium – I do not speak of those in France – *must*, if it is to continue to live with itself – believe that those horrors are exaggerated or, better still, have never taken place. I fancy, therefore, that, in exact proportion as those horrors are revealed, there will be a rising outcry in the United States that they were invented. My work brings me into contact with, among others, Belgian wounded and refugees who are all around us here in private houses etc. which have been converted into hospitals. At Hawkhurst, at Cranbrook

(I think I once took you and Mrs. Bok there to see a window in the church that had been put up by some relatives of Mrs. Eddie[1]), at Lamberhurst and so on. Yesterday I saw a lad of eighteen who, I was told, was in danger of "melancholia following shock." The Germans, it is true, had done him no hurt, but he had to see his father, mother and sister killed in his presence. They say their throats were cut but it was probably done by the bayonet. He sits and stares into the fire without saying anything. When he shuts his eyes the scene repeats itself behind the closed eyelids.[2] At Folkestone refugees have been arriving by the thousand daily. They are sent up to Charing Cross with what they stand up in, and are distributed to hospitals and shelters. There is one hospital in London where they try to treat the women and little girls who have been raped, and where arrangements are being made for the care of those who will become mothers. I have not yet seen any mutilated children, but they can be verified. These matters which must, of course, seem strange to you form part of the fabric of our daily lives nowadays.

You can easily ascertain how far the atrocities have been invented. If you care to send a representative to Folkestone, or to Oxford or Cambridge where they are taking in Belgian professors, or to any hospitals or refuge shelters, you would get very precise information as to the "efficiency" of the Germans. France also is open. Our people come and go there regularly, and the record of bestiality, deliberate wreckage and systematic defilement is the same as in Belgium. Here is an extract from a letter I got this morning from a Frenchman who has returned to his village after the Germans had retired. He writes: – "The soldiers and officers have pillaged and stolen, and violated women and little girls (the Teuton taste seems to run in that direction). They have mur-dered and shot non-combatants without cause – through mere Sadism and drunkenness. ... The people are without food, clothes or shelter." And so the record runs wherever the Germans are in possession. As I have said it is open to you or any other journal to get details of it from direct evidence.

Your people do well to try to believe that the atrocities "have not been and cannot be verified" for if you believed otherwise you would be disturbed in your souls.

Now as to my writing verses about "America next". That it seems to me is a matter which might be misunderstood and construed as an appeal for the help of the United States. I think, if you look back, you will see that this is a thing we have never for an instant contemplated since your President announced the neutrality of the United States. Nor do I feel myself justified in writing one line which could lend itself to this impression. I have written privately to men I know in the United States urging them to use their influence with their people to make the country realize the peril in which it stands. But this I did solely because I loved the land which gave me my great happiness in my youth. For the rest, my duty it seems to me, is to the Empire and the Allies. I have given my only son to the Army: I am giving my time and substance to the work that lies before us. It will be a long task but I think we shall win. If we win the position of the United States is perfectly sound. It will merely have made a wrong estimate of German efficiency for which the Allies will not call it to account. If we fail, it will have the opportunity of experiencing, as you say, "a perfect wave" of that efficiency at close quarters and at once.

In these days one reaches out to one's friends abroad and is glad and grateful for their sympathy, and I thank you for giving me the opportunity of saying these things to you.

Yours sincerely,
Rudyard Kipling.

Notes
1. RK means Mary Baker Eddy, the founder of Christian Science, whose third husband was descended from William Eddye, Vicar of Cranbrook. A memorial and three memorial windows to Eddye are in St Dunstan's, Cranbrook (information from the Reverend Canon M. L. Cooper).
2. CK amplifies this story: "Rud tries to see as often as he can a poor young Belgium refugee who was a teacher at Liege. ... Such a charming young fellow who they fear will go crazy. He saw the Germans cut the throat of his father and mother and sister of 12 after they had raped the latter and can not be got to close his eyes because he says then he can see it all again" (to Mrs Balestier, 28 October [1914]: ALS, Dunham Papers).

To Oliver Baldwin, 31 October 1914

ALS: Photocopy, University of Sussex

Bateman's / Burwash / Sussex / Oct: 31. 1914 /
Bateman's drawing room: / 8.45. p.m.

Dear Ollie

Many thanks for your letter which I observe is occupied mainly with John. He is on 24 hours leave here – came down from Warley in the car this afternoon – and at the present moment sprawls on the old green sofa in *mufti* – first time I've seen him in mufti for six weeks. He is snorting audibly over Edgar Wallace's article on "turning out a Tommy" in the Royal.[1] What moves his wrath is the description of "delightful route marches" on frosty mornings in October! As J. has been doing 17 miles route marches in poisonous wet, as well as night attacks under the same inspiring conditions John is a bit of a Sadducee about delightful route marches. When I picked him up this morning he had just come off an inspiriting sprint of 4 miles with his company in 38 minutes. But he shall now dictate to you himself:[2] –

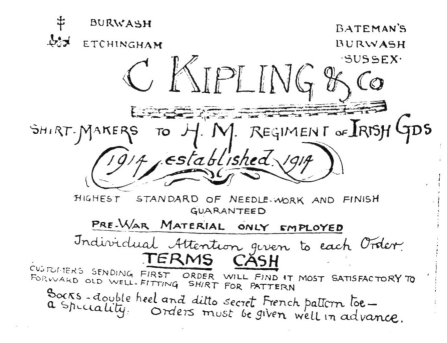

✝ BURWASH   BATEMAN'S
    ETCHINGHAM   BURWASH
                                                 ·SUSSEX·

C KIPLING & Co

SHIRT-MAKERS TO H. M. REGIMENT of IRISH GDS

(1914, established 1914)

HIGHEST STANDARD OF NEEDLE-WORK AND FINISH
GUARANTEED

PRE-WAR MATERIAL ONLY EMPLOYED

Individual Attention given to each Order.

TERMS CASH

CUSTOMERS SENDING FIRST ORDER WILL FIND IT MOST SATISFACTORY TO
FORWARD OLD WELL-FITTING SHIRT FOR PATTERN

Socks - double heel and ditto secret French pattern toe —
a Speciality.   Orders must be given well in advance.

4. Tailor's label by Kipling, with letter to Oliver Baldwin, 31 October 1914.

He doesn't look half a bad officer. The cup ought to be along shortly: but all the shops are slower than time nowadays. Let us know as soon as ever you can come down here.

May the Lord shine on you and your *future* Sam Browne.

Ever
RK.

Notes

1. The name is not quite clear. I have not found the article in question. Wallace was then writing regularly for *Town Topics*.
2. This letter is a round-robin from RK, Elsie, and John: John's message reads thus:

   "Just a line to say what rotten luck it is on you that you can't join, but you are bound to get a biff at the Teuton soon.

   We have a pretty stiff training in the Brigade but it is great fun. With luck I ought to be out at the front in eight weeks, but it is mostly a question of luck.

   If I am stationed at Windsor I will come over and have tea some day and we will 'gas' about the dirty German."

To Captain W. H. Lewis, 1 November 1914
ALS: University of Sussex

Bateman's / Burwash / Sussex / Nov 1. 1914

Dear Lewis,

And I ain't surprised either.[1] Every one is back or gone across that ever I knew and I don't think anything of meeting three old schoolmates from three different ends of the earth in one day at the Stores.

I'll surely come over if I can. I've been visiting camps like any thing and I expect to be in Salisbury before long.[2] Then I'll stretch over to Lyndhurst (Golly! how filthy wet you must be under all those falling leaves and on top of that soaking heather). John – he's here for today on 24 hrs leave – is at Warley. He's in the Irish Guards, very much interested in his job and very fond of the Irish. I don't expect he'll be able to get away, tho' he'd like to see you awfully. I'll bring Mrs Kipling and Elsie if by any means I can.

With much love from us all

Ever
Rudyard Kipling.

But where the dooce are you going to get your mountains? In the Ardennes?

RK

Notes
1. Lewis's note on this letter says "On my arrival with 5. M[ountain]. B[attery]. from India for the War."
2. RK was at work on the six sketches published as "The New Army in Training" in the *Daily Telegraph*, 7–24 December 1914 and, revised, in volume form in 1915. In preparation for this RK, between 13 October and 24 November, visited camps at Crowborough, Aldershot, Maresfield, Uckfield, Sevenoaks, and Salisbury Plain, as well as Indian troops in the New Forest, where, presumably, he was able to see Lewis. The work was finished on 2 December (CK diary, 13 October; 9, 13, 16, 21, 22, 23, 24 November; 2 December).

To Lady Edward Cecil, 3 December 1914
ALS: Photocopy, University of Sussex

Bateman's / Burwash / Sussex / Dec. 3. 1914. / 5. p.m.

Dear Lady Edward

We are just back from Gatcombe House.[1] I think it better that I should give my account in writing and if you have any questions to put to me that you should write them and not see me till I have seen Snowden[2] as I want to keep my impression of the talk with the three grenadiers at Gatcombe House undisturbed and distinct.

As you know there were three men – James, Barker and Titcombe.[3] James was a fine handsome man with a certain amount of self consciousness and a moderate gift of words. Barker was fair, thin-skinned, fine-handed and an obvious "sensitive" all over. I was glad that he confessed throughout that he knew and remembered but little of the affair as he was of the type that is given to imaginations.

Titcombe was slow, unlovely, thick skinned and phlegmatic – not at all a man of many words. He did not strike me as the sort that embroiders or varies its statements.

The map was of the greatest service as it helped the men to compare notes while they handed it about. For some unknown reason, James knew more about the actual hours when events took place. He didn't tell me why but he was most definite about times.

At about one o'clock or five minutes after, on the day of the fight, the Irish Guards retired through the grenadiers who were then in the wood and, as far as the three men could be sure, that I. G. came across the flat-plateau marked in the map.[4]

Platoons Nos. 13: 14: and 16 of the Grenadiers were then thrown forward to protect the retreat. The three men all had an idea that the platoons were sacrificed to save the rest of the regiment. They do not know by whose orders the platoons were thrown forward but James said he heard one officer say or shout to a companion: – "We must hang on here till two o'clock."

Titcombe remembers that No. 13. platoon in charge of Needham[5] advanced, as I have indicated in pencil, through the wood on the flat plateau. He is not precise as to the location of platoons 14 and 16, because the Germans were already advancing in great numbers through the wood and were surrounding them on the North; East and South. Titcombe asserts, on hearsay, that possibly a few men of Platoon 16 were not surrounded but he is quite certain that 13 and 14 were absolutely surrounded.

The shrapnel fire had ceased as the Germans came to close quarters; each man and officer had to do the best that he could for himself. The platoons were all mixed up in this blind hilly wooded country.

A certain number of men, – he does not know of which platoon – lay down behind a bank on the ride where I have written "men lying down." This detachment fired towards the north at the advancing Germans. At the same time the Germans were streaming across the same ride further towards the Eastward to join the Germans who had already got south of our men.

It was as you can understand a case of our men being rounded up and fired at from all sides. Our men tried to break through where they could – north south or east or west.

At the time when the surround was complete Titcombe saw George, with his sword drawn, running behind the line of men who had taken cover lying down to the south of the bank of the ride. Titcombe does not know whether those men had been posted by George's order and so far as his memory serves him George had not then been hit. George was running down the ride to the East in order to stop the Germans who were streaming across it. George had got about a hundred yards down the ride – or was one hundred yards from where the ride joins the main road – when he was shot at least twice. The fire was coming from all quarters and he may have been shot more than twice. Titcombe's impression is that George was shot in the chest and the shoulder.

He fell and died at once in the ride. Titcombe was wounded shortly after – he has no very clear sense of time – and dropped beside George. He thinks that George was shot about half way through the action.

The Germans themselves sounded the Cease Fire at 2:30 – the three platoons being wiped out. They then removed the dead and wounded from the road to the side in order to let their transport pass and Titcombe saw them do it. Titcombe lay beside or near to George's body till the next day when he was picked up by our men who were prisoners and they buried George the body having lain by the side of the road for close on twenty four hours. The same party that picked up Titcombe buried George.

This then is all my story. It was difficult to unravel because all three men, naturally, interrupted or checked each other – and that brought in the names of other men. They were – all except James – doubtful about their times: and it is possible with the best will in the world that I may not have fully comprehended all that they said. However I summarized Titcombe's statement to him before I left and he told me that it was correct.

I carefully left out any personal note; reserving that for Snowden: and the picture that Titcombe gave me was a clear one or as clear as the confusion of that fight permitted. What stuck in Titcombe's mind was the little party of Grenadiers behind the bank of the ride and George running towards the East at the Germans crossing on his right flank, and the bullets at the same time coming from the rear.

Knowing the boy, I allow myself one piece of supposition, which, I intend to work up to with Snowden. I imagine George posted the party under the bank and was hurrying off to secure his flank if he could. Snowden in his platoon may have been one of that party. I shall ask him if he recalls George's last order.

Titcombe was in Manners'[6] platoon. He told me he saw Manners shot through the head and die at once.

James saw Needham wounded and asked him if he was badly hit. Needham said he believed he was wounded in two places. He was then conscious but very faint.

The wounded after the action were not all kept in the Church till the retreat. For example James says that he was transferred to a "shooting-box" – a sort of chateau near by.

James also added the significant fact that no English prisoners were allowed to see the Germans bury their dead: and that the German doctors were three days working at full stretch before they could put a first-dressing on all their wounded. When they had done this once they asked the English doctors if they, (the English) had any serious cases which needed elaborate operations as the German doctors would take those cases before they began putting second dressings on their own wounded.

"So" said James "we did them some damage."

I have told you all and everything that I have gathered from these men and you will sift it and fit it in for what it is worth.

Most sincerely
Rudyard Kipling.

Notes

1. Near Newport, Isle of Wight; there is no record of its having served as a military convalescent home during the war, but RK's letter seems to make clear that it did, at least for a time. RK had gone there to investigate the death of George Cecil (1895–1914), Lady Edward's eldest son. George, a Lieutenant in the Grenadier Guards, had been killed on 1 September during the retreat from Mons in the episode described here.
2. Probably Frederick Snowden, an enlisted man in the Grenadier Guards since 1906; he was perhaps George Cecil's soldier-servant.
3. Two of these men are identifiable from the records of the Grenadier Guards as Private Stephen James, later killed in action; and Private Walter Titcomb, who did not return to action. Barker is perhaps Lance-Corporal S. L. Barker (Lt-Col. Sir Frederick Ponsonby, *The Grenadier Guards in the Great War of 1914–1918*, 1920, III, 301).
4. RK's sketch map of the battlefield accompanies the letter.
5. Lieutenant (afterwards Major) Francis Needham (1886–1955), Grenadier Guards, son of the 3rd Earl of Kilmorey. He was "slightly wounded" in this engagement (*The Times*, 15 September 1914).
6. John Nevile Manners (1892–1914), elder son of the 3rd Baron Manners; like George Cecil, he was a Lieutenant in the Grenadier Guards.

To Theodore Roosevelt, 4 December 1914
TLS: Library of Congress

Bateman's / Burwash / Sussex / 4th December 1914

Private and Confidential
Dear Roosevelt,

I'm afraid I've been a long time answering yours of the 4th November, but I have had to be away from home a good deal, among the camps of the new armies.

Your articles, to my mind, cannot be bettered.[1]

With your usual courage, you have stated aloud, in regard to the position of the United States, what everyone in Europe has been thinking since the war began. Obviously, it is not a thing that any foreigner could utter. I see from the cabled summary of your later articles that you outline the possibilities of the situation after the was is ended. So far as the United States are concerned, I think your forecast will come true.[2] The more life and treasure spent in winning this war, the less will the victors be disposed to listen to any neutral's suggestions when the time comes to deal with the loser. That is only natural, but, in addition to this, the United States is on record as having made no protest against any action that Germany took – from the invasion of Belgium to the violations of the Hague Convention. By what logic, then, will the United States protest against any action taken by the Allies? That – to put it shortly – is the impasse into which Mr. Wilson (bless you, for your illuminating flash-light on his family history!)[3] has prayerfully led his people. I imagine that later they may demand explanations of the "great and good." At present they do not quite understand where they are at. You, who know world-politics, do. As Lowell says: – *"Once* to every man and nation comes the moment to decide."[4]

But you yourself have said it all. There's no gratitude in a democracy, or they might realize you have put them under the greatest debt of your career. Instead of which you will get simply cursed.

Things are not going so badly here. I am, as you know, a black and unbending pessimist, but even I am beginning to feel, after much consultation with the men at the front, that we are turning the corner. Equipment is drawing abreast of men. (As you know we have had to equip our Allies rather as it was in the old Napoleonic days). The Artillery question is being settled and much transport and troops have been shifted. Our garrisons are rearranged – from Hongkong to Gib, and the Colonial contingents are in place. At present we haven't more than a million men under training. (I've been going round looking at them for the last six weeks in their camps and huts. They are rather interesting, both in physique and intellect and zeal to learn.) I don't say all England is yet an armed camp because there are gaps where you can go for ten miles without seeing troops, but so far as my wanderings have led me there is no road where you can go twenty miles without running into them in blocks. The second million will be coming on as soon as we can get the accomodation for them, and they ought to be able to fill the wastage in the first million. But we prefer to have our men thoroughly equipped and trained before using them.

The game is not going badly at the front either. (The said "front", by the way, is five hours from London.) Joffre[5] seems happy and our people are not kicking. The French and we are carrying the weight of about two million Germans. They have been sending up their younger men and boys lately on our front. This is valuable because those are prospective fathers, and they come up to the trenches with superb bravery. Then they are removed, and new corps are sent in who have not seen too many of their dead. There are not many tactics or finesses on either side – the aviators block that – and so the game reduces itself to plain killing. Our losses are not light but by the circumstances and training of the German armies the German losses are not less than three times ours – which is a reasonable proportion. But don't believe that the Germans will slack off. They are good for at least a million more losses on our front alone – besides what they can stand from the Russians. They ought not to begin to weaken till they have lost a flat million of dead – not counting sick and wounded. We have got our bigger artillery into shape on the western front, and I believe are reaching them farther back than before.

I don't know for sure what the Russians are costing them but, my information is, that in the cold on that eastern frontier, a wounded man who has to lie out even one night before being picked up, is quite dead.

I fancy it is going to be a much longer game than people in the United States think, and, of course, Germany will do everything in her power to make friction between us. I can trace the effects of her agents, just like the smooth smear of water above a torpedo, in the letters that I get from the other side. The latest dodge is the "unparallelled efficiency" boom and the stupidity of backing the wrong horse in a war that "can have only one end." I expect later that trade questions and "conditional contraband"[6] will be played for all they are worth. And we must put up with that too. We are expected to do the world's fighting and to keep the world comfortable while we are doing it.

But has it ever struck you that if the game goes our way, the largest block of existing Germany may perhaps be the eight million within your Borders? And precisely because, to please this contingent and to justify his hereditary temperament, Wilson did not protest against the invasion and absorption of Belgium. Wilson will not be able to save for them the sentimental satisfaction of having a Fatherland to look back upon from behind the safety of the United States frontier. It seems a high price to pay for "domestic politics"!

Thank you for what you say about my boy.[7] He was not seventeen till the 17th August, but he managed to get in by September 6th. He is in the Irish

Guards. Suppose my only son dies, I for one, should not "view with equanimity" Mr. Wilson (however unswayed by martial prejudice) advising or recommending my country how to behave at the end of this war; and I am but one of an increasing number of fathers. As I have quoted: – "*once* to every man and nation", and Lowell was no small prophet.

Give my love to Kermit and his bride. I haven't heard from the boy in ages. With every good wish,

Believe me as always,

> Most sincerely,
> Rudyard Kipling.

Notes
1. The articles reprinted by Roosevelt as *America and the World War*, 1915: see 20 October 1914.
2. Roosevelt wrote that the US could have no influence at a peace congress owing to its failure to take any action or to make any protest: "we shall be treated as we deserve to be treated, as a nation of people who mean well feebly, whose words are not backed by deeds, who like to prattle about both their own strength and their own righteousness, but who are unwilling to run the risks without which righteousness cannot be effectively served" (*America and the World War*, p. 259).
3. Roosevelt wrote in his letter of 4 November 1914 that none of Wilson's family fought in the Civil War: see 10 April 1915.
4. "The Present Crisis", stanza 5.
5. Joseph Jacques Césaire Joffre (1852–1931), Marshal of France, Commander-in-Chief and in command of operations on the front until he was recalled in 1916.
6. The US protested at the English declaration that such things as foodstuffs, clothing, and fuel were "conditional" (i.e., not absolute) contraband.
7. "I hear your son has gone to the war. I heartily congratulate you" (Roosevelt to RK, 4 November 1914).

To Edward Bok, 5 December 1914
TLS: Syracuse University

Bateman's / Burwash / Sussex / 5th December 1914

Private and Confidential

Dear Bok,

I ought to have answered yours of the 9th before this, but I have been rather busy, and away from home going round the camps where the New Army is in training. I am doing a set of newspaper articles about it, though, for obvious reasons, I am not telling more than I can avoid. The Germans have a theory that the New Army is small and contemptible and that the hearts of the English are not in the war. Personally, I do not want to destroy that theory, so I have kept the note of my articles as low and as grey as possible.

I visited the Canadian Army a few days before your letter came. They are rather well equipped, and I think I may go so far as to assure you that their ammunition *does* fit their guns. But, knowing the facts, I quite see why the Germans put that idea into circulation. They have, as I have already said, a wonderful press bureau, and nothing has interested me more than its adaptability. When the atrocities could no longer be denied, it switched off on to the "unparalleled efficiency" note and is, or was till lately, engaged on pointing out that the war could only end one way. I don't know what it will do next, but I am sure it will be something perfectly calculated for neutral consumption – and to make friction between the Allies and the United States.

As to the progress of things I cannot, of course, tell you what has been and is being done, but I can say that as far as England is concerned we have resorted and rearranged our garrisons, shifted troops as necessary, and put certain contingents into their places throughout the Empire from Hongkong to Gibraltar; an amount of necessary stores and equipment has been delivered to our Allies; the artillery is well forward, and the new factories necessary for keeping up with material wastage are at work. We have, as you know, a certain number of troops at the front which are being kept up to strength, though we have already lost 50 per cent more than the full strength of the entire United States army.[1] We have in England a certain additional number of troops which are being added to as we have the accomodation for them. You may have seen estimates of these numbers. These certainly are *not* exaggerated. I have seen their training, physique, and intelligence. They appear to me not unsatisfactory.

One point I can touch on is the large number of the recruits who, thanks to Lord Roberts's miniature Rifle Clubs, come to the ranks with a sound knowledge of shooting and the habit of handling a gun.[2] I don't know whether you ever saw our shooting range in this village. It is one of five within a radius of seven miles. I gave the ground for it and used to give prizes to be shot for. I think Frank saw it, and didn't quite understand what it was all about! The men from the towns where miniature ranges are more accessible than in the country are even better prepared in this direction than the agriculturists. You will not find any reference to this and other matters in our papers. But you will find a tremendous outcry against professional footballers and the crowds who watch football matches, on Saturday afternoons. The *professional* football players number less than 5,000; the crowds who watch them run from 150,000 to 300,000 per week, a large proportion of that number are operatives in various industries which are now running night and day for the service of the army, and a certain percentage consists of troops in training for whom football is their national game and Saturday afternoon their only holiday. I notice that the German press bureau is making great play with this feature, as proof that the English are weakening. We have, too, a brisk and spirited correspondence from old maids, country parsons, and earnest well-wishers in arm-chairs deploring the disgraceful laxity of the young men in coming forward. You will also find in my articles much declamation to the same effect.[3] But you will never get at the actual figures of the recruiting or the strength of the new army.

Which things, my dear Bok, are an allegory!

I can quite understand the impatience with which the United States looks on this long and deadly slow game. But it is worth while remembering that the prepared desperado strikes when he is ready; the decent citizen naturally needs time to get his resources together. Time, and the Navy, have been good to us Allies so far; and we are beginning to have reasonable hopes that in the fulness of time we may be able to save both ourselves and incidentally – you. At the present moment we are fighting for civilization all over the entire planet; human nature being what it is – we are expected to save the world and to keep it comfortable, as well as to supply it with heart-warming emotions and good chances for making money, while we are at the task.

And so we go on with the monotonous job of destroying Germans where possible. Up to the present their casualty lists are over one million on our side only, exclusive of what the Russians are costing them. But they are a long-enduring breed, trained for a generation to just this issue, and nobody who has been at the front sees any hope of their weakening till they have worn down by at least a couple more million of casualties.

I am glad to hear the United States is sending food to the Belgians, but I trust you will make quite sure that it will not be taken by the Germans for their own use. They are, quite reasonably in view of what they have done, anxious to reduce the native population of Belgium as much as possible.

With my good wishes and the hope that these details will not bore you,

Yours sincerely,
Rudyard Kipling.

Notes

1. The US Army in 1914 had a strength of 98,000 men. In December *The Times* military correspondent estimated that the British Expeditionary Force had then suffered about 84,000 casualties (*The Times*, 2 December 1914). This is very close to the number published by the War Office (80,796) in *Statistics of the Military Effort of the British Empire during the Great War*, 1922. RK doubtless heard many different voices on the matter of casualties.
2. A note to part 6 of RK's *The New Army in Training* reads: "Thanks to the miniature rifle clubs fostered by Lord Roberts a certain number of recruits in all the armies come to their regiments with a certain knowledge of sighting, rifle-handling, and the general details of good shooting, especially at snap and disappearing work" (Outward Bound Edition, XXXIV, 282).

3. In part 2 of *The New Army in Training*, for example: the volunteers, RK writes, "think it vile that so many unmarried young men who are not likely to be affected by Government allowances should be shy about sharing their life. They discuss these young men and their womenfolk by name, and imagine rude punishments for them, suited to their known characters" (Outward Bound Edition, XXXIV, 237–8).

To Andrew Macphail, 3 January 1915
ALS: Photocopy, National Archives of Canada

Bateman's / Burwash / Sussex / Jan. 3. 1915

Dear Macphail

This goes west in immediate reply to your letter: for the Lord knows where the second contingent[1] may be ordered to. Malta – Hong Kong – Egypt – anywhere. Oh but we are giving the Empire a personally-conducted tour of education! Several battalions of my acquaintance – cheery agriculturists from Sussex – have been sent off to India! Their letters home are amazing. They were Territorials you see and in their wildest dreams never expected temples and elephants. Egypt I learn is filled with profane Australians and equally profane New Zealanders. Princess Pat's batt'n[2] is out in Flanders. The rest, I believe, still churns the mud of Burford and West Down South.

I saw the boy[3] – and a superb young 'un he was. Also I saw his uncle[4] and schemed to get 'em both down to Bateman's – for Xmas for choice.[5] Since that date, I have lived the life of a houseless dog; not being at home two consecutive nights.[6] When I wasn't busy about troops – I wrote some things about 'em and had to do some things about 'em also – I was hanging on after my boy who being an ensign in the guards naturally leads the life of a general maid of all work in quarters which – but we won't describe 'em. Others have worse. When he gets a bit of spare time we chase after him: and there are happy periods when he hangs as it were in the loop of a telephone wire liable to instant summons. I don't think your boy will be allowed the decent obscurity of N.C.O. rank for very long. They are looking hard for officers and in the past few months men have had opportunity to show their fitness and the reverse. Of course all contingents and improvisations begin with a certain deckload of incompetents which are jettisoned as the weather gets worse. One advantage is that these men have *not* passed any sacred Examination which gives 'em the right to be where they are. I had a glorious time in the Canadian camp. They were *so* good and *so* damned young and conscientious and *so* full of their own small sins. Reminded me somehow of a revival meeting and the anxious seat. O Lord if I only had you here for half an hour what tales I could tell you about 'em. The boy's salute was an impressive thing – so was his size and his poise and his gravity.

We in England are getting on for $1^1/_2$ millions in the New Army alone. You see our rate of recruiting is conditioned by our equipment: and so we can't for the present at least take over 30,000 a week. But in mind and body it's not bad stuff: and it is deadly keen to get wisdom.

I get amazing letters from all parts of the U.S. where the persons inhabiting that section of the world seem to have 'verted to origin in a shameless way. All this precious talk about "assimilation" seems to have gone by the board. We have to deal with fugitive European "citizens" mourning for the lands they left in order to get rich. "What" writes a most eminent U. Esser to me "is going to be done with my own little country which I love."[7] He means Holland, so please you! His parents came from there. And all the others are like him – standing well back from the fuss, tremulous, querulous, exhorting and cackling. But devil a one of 'em shows any trace – save Roosevelt – of the "Americanism" that they have been fed on.

And really the attitude of the U.S. now makes one blush all up the back. Louvain touched them not nor Aerschot[8] either but when it came to copper and cotton the Flag bellied![9] This war has come like the Judgement Day to show out character.

I know that feeling about lying under conviction of sin. I had my dip into it ere I found my job and I've hove all my small assets into the same. We need doctors the worst possible way though the percentage of recoveries from wounds is very high – when you can get at the wounded in time. You won't have much to do with a horse at the front I expect. More and more the motor-car is coming up to the lines and the conspicuous and slow moving Beast is being cast aside. I don't expect – but one never knows – any big developments before the spring. It is hard to deal any telling blow at a section in trenches but I believe that our contemptible little army at the front is growing quietly and I know that the French are hard at work, fighting with a cold white fury that is very awestriking. The Boche won't begin to see reason till he is decimated – i.e. has lost about 5,000,000. Up to date we haven't accounted for more than 2,000,000 exclusive of sickness (of which we have no details) and of slightly wounded who come back to the firing line in a few weeks. My reason and my instinct jump with yours. It may be three years or it may be sooner. If sooner, the greater and more spectacular smash.

I am sorry to say that the wife is very ill with neuritis[10] – the result, I doubt not, of strain on the boy's account *plus* years of hard work and as soon as she's better I must get her to a doctor. This goes to catch the mail with all my best greetings and wishes.

Affectionately
Rudyard Kipling

Notes

1. Of Canadian soldiers: Macphail went out with them to England on 15 April 1915. Macphail, though now fifty years old and nearly blind in one eye, pulled strings to get an appointment as a medical officer (Ian Ross Robertson, "Sir Andrew Macphail as Social Critic", PhD thesis, University of Toronto, 1974, p. 274).

2. The Princess Patricia's regiment of Canadian Light Infantry, raised under the Governor-Generalship of the Duke of Connaught and so called after their Colonel, Princess Patricia, the younger daughter of the Duke, who travelled to South Africa with the Kiplings in 1905–6 and who drew CK's portrait on shipboard (Rees extracts, 6 January 1906).

3. Macphail's son Jeffrey, who had enlisted on the outbreak of the war. RK presumably saw him on his visit to the Canadian camp at Salisbury, 24 November 1914 (see 5 October 1914).

4. James Alexander Macphail: see 5 October 1914.

5. Both Jeffrey and James Macphail were at Bateman's, 14–16 January 1915 (Bateman's Visitors Book). "Nice people and so happy for the rest and quiet of a home. They had not been inside a house for 5 months" (CK to Mrs Balestier, 17–18 January [1915]: ALS, Dunham Papers).

6. No doubt an exaggeration, but he had been sufficiently busy since his visit to the Canadian camp on 24 November. He travelled to the Isle of Wight on 3 December to make enquiries about the fate of George Cecil; he was in London on 8 December to dine, for the first time, at The Club; he was at Cherkley, Sir Max Aitken's house, on 20 December, entertained Cameron Forbes at Bateman's on 21–2 December, attended the production of E. W. Hornung's *Raffles* in London, 23 December, on the invitation of the author, and spent Christmas at Cherkley with CK, John Kipling, and the Bonar Laws. Early in December he finished his series of articles on *The New Army in Training*, published in the *Daily Telegraph*, 7, 10, 14, 19, 21, and 24 December 1914.

7. This was Edward Bok. RK wrote to him on 4 January 1915: "As to Holland, she missed the great moment that Belgium took" (ALS, Syracuse). Holland remained neutral throughout the war.

8. Belgian towns, both in the path of the German sweep through Belgium. The destruction of the University library in Louvain was one of the most-publicised German atrocities in the early months of the war. At Aerschot 150 civilians had been killed on 19 August 1914.

9. The US and Britain were quarrelling over the freedom of neutral trade, including the trade in America cotton and copper with Europe. The British, eager to deny resources to Germany, identified such trade as contraband and had detained and searched American ships. On 29 December the US presented a note of protest to the British government over "unwarranted interference with the legitimate trade of the United States" (*The Times*, 30 December 1914). The British reply on 17 February conceded nothing, especially since the Germans had declared their blockade of British ports in the interval. The issue remained unresolved until the American entry into the war, though American trade with Europe steadily increased during that time.

10. CK was ill on 26–7 December 1914 (CK diary); on 11 January she was examined by Bland-Sutton who said that she must go to Bath for a cure (Rees extracts, 11 January 1915). The visit to Bath was duly made from 29 March to 24 April (Rees extracts).

To H. A. Gwynne, 7 January 191[5]
ALS: Dalhousie University

Bateman's / Burwash / Sussex / Jan. 7. 1914

Dear Old Man –

With regard to notions about clearing out trenches at close quarters, I have, as I think I've told you, been deluged with letters on this subject from all sorts of cranks.[1] Here are some.

One man wrote me:–"If you can compel any body of men to perform any natural act when they should be loading and firing you have them help-less." *His* notion was a powder that induced sneezing. Obviously a man sneezing is even more helpless than a man with his breeches down. The latter at any rate can fire a rifle: the former is helpless down to the waist. My correspondent's ideas, however, did not extend further than chucking packets of sneezing powder, though he thought well of chlorine. Another man put before me the idea of a petrol engine not bigger than a vacuum cleaner to generate carbonic and pipe it into adjacent trenches. His idea was painless extinction through a hose applied at night – specially if the Boches' trench was on a lower level. I don't see what he wanted with a petrol engine which would make an infernal row. Surely carbonic can be generated in silence.

Yet another suggests a skimming æroplane – small with shortened wings so that it would just not leave the ground – "roll" I think he called it – which could be used at night with a small *pistol*-maxim (the kind they used to make for suppressing riots in S. American republics) to skim down a line of trench. He seems to think that a twelve-foot spread of wing and a very broad wheel base to guard against upsetting would do the trick. It might for once or twice but the row of the motor getting ready is against it. Practically his notion amounts to a skimming dish armoured car – the pistol maxim being pointed through the floor.

Yet another man wants small model æroplanes or skimmers simply to carry bursting charges of forty or fifty pounds across the dead ground into or towards the next trench. Another suggests a $\frac{1}{8}$ scale modification of the Brennan torpedo[2] for land purposes. This as you know is controlled from the launching station by wires on reels. Any dam form of mechanism from clock-work up which would carry a 50 lb charge a hundred yards would do the trick, he says.

Another chap, who interests me, goes bald headed for kites sent up with the proper wind and the bomb sent up along the string as one used to send a "runner" up a kite string when one was little. Thus: – [sketch of a kite string carrying bomb over trench; parts captioned: "kite line"; "50–100 yds"; "Germ. trench"]. He says kites are d. difficult to hit. He also adds that a runner-bomb sent up the string might be allowed if it missed the trench to travel up to the kite. The string could then be cut and the whole shoot would plunge to earth down-wind somewhere at the back of the German lines, thus adding injury to anticipation. A kite has no nerves, he says, to be shot at.

My own views incline me more to some shape of mechanical runner or land Brennan which might be at least worth experimenting with. I object to explosives that explode on impact as they can be set off by rifle fire: but a silent *timed* bomb, once got up quietly to the enemy-trench, is a much more difficult thing to deal with, and more nerve shattering. Of course such a thing couldn't be dropped into a trench because it gives itself away but a selection of variously timed bombs shot in the dark near a trench might do much. Civilization has not yet reverted to the stink bomb of ancient gunnery whose component parts were human-ordure, verdigris, sulphur and such trifles but a fizzing carcase-shell on these lines – a shell that couldn't be picked up or handled, would clean a trench out better than any threat of violent death. Men don't mind dying but they fear being made uncomfortable. Here's a 200-year old receipt for a stink-bomb entirely at your service: – Brimstone 2 lb: Rosin 1 b: fat of the worst sort 1 b. Mix with a little horse dung and as much man's dung and chips of horse-hooves as the stuff will take up melted, smear on old woollen or flannel or carpet for choice well soaked in salpetre to make it burn bright and drop to windward of trench required and see what happens. A bow (6 ft of 80 lb pull) or cross-bow can throw a surprisingly heavy weight for fifty yards *and it makes no noise*.

So there, you've got the following separate forms of annoyance: –

(1)   manufacture and pipage of deleterious gasses into trenches: which is out of the question.

(2)   skimming or ground-shaving æroplane with pistol-maxim in floor or bow to skim along trench: which seems to me too cumbrous.

(3)   controlled land-torpedo (a la Brennan) or mechanical runner to carry explosives 50–100 yards and then bust. Possible but too elaborate and liable to be blown up.

(4)   Kite which would amuse men and make 'em expose 'emselves too much. Not bad though:

(5)   The simple good old bow and arrow, which in itself is exercise for the bored men, carrying either the stink-ball or the light $3/4$ lb bomb or grenade. As a night weapon the bow and arrow leave nothing to be desired: though the more particular may prefer the cross-bow. The simpler the weapon the better. So turn your Royal Society minds on this aspect of the second most wonderful game in the world.

Ever
R.K.

Notes
1. "I get letters from every sort of patent-invention man on the subject of offensive weapons. One chap urges – with some truth – that the only thing which will *infallibly* clean out a trench is a hive of bees" (to Gwynne, 2 January 191[5]: ALS, Dalhousie).
2. A torpedo controlled mechanically from the shore, used in coastal defence by the Royal Navy from 1890.

To Edith Plowden,[1] 15 January 1915
ALS: University of Sussex

Bateman's / Burwash / Sussex / Jan. 15. 1915

Dear Edith

Thank you very much for your kind and generous letter.

Long may you live to the despair and confusion of your executors! They are an objectionable caste, all executors. I have several of 'em and they talk about one's "estate."

I gladly accept your offer of my copybook of early verses with the Father's drawing[2] and I shall be more grateful than I can say if you would extend your kindness so far as to give me the copies of the schoolboy poems on note paper.[3] After all, they were sent from me to *you* and if they are going to be given or willed away why shouldn't they come back to me for myself and my children. They are of more interest to me than any one else and though I am quite certain that Stan[4] would deal honestly by them, I know by bitter experience, how difficult it is to prevent other people from gaining access to such things and giving them a baleful publicity.

Whence got you the idea that I am "reckless" about my letters and poems? For more than twenty years I have done my best to try and get all such letters and papers into my possession. That I have not always been successful is proved by the fact that I have seen the most sacred and intimate matters concerning myself and my people printed in newspapers and periodicals; and it has been the same with a good deal of my early work.[5]

It is for this reason that I hope you will, of your kindness, give me all the old work that you may have of mine and above all that you won't have Father's drawing photographed. *Nothing* is safe from the press these days! How like your kindness to have gone to see my uncle Joseph.[6] They wrote me of his wife's death and he is now going to stay with my Father's sisters. I have heard from him at intervals since my Father's death and have sent him assistance from time to time. I have done a good deal, as regards the war, in the U.S. but I think the time has arrived when further explanations may be misunderstood by them. With every good wish for the coming year

Always yours affectionately
Rudyard

Notes
1. Edith Plowden (see [August 1881]) was now living at the Briar-Patch, Knebworth, Herts.
2. Miss Plowden describes the "copybook of early verses" thus: "Before he went back to India in Nov 1882, he gave me a thick school copy-book filled with his poems, written straight off. His father, as an opening illustration, drew in sepia a procession of poets led by Love (a little cupid) followed by Homer with his hand on Love's head, then came Dante, Chaucer, Shakespeare, Rossetti, Browning, Russell Lowel, closed by a spectacled little Rudyard following with adoring spectacled eyes, pen in hand and copybook under [his arm]" (typescript, Baldwin Papers, Sussex, quoted by Rutherford, *Early Verse*, p. 23). RK himself wrote of these early poems that they "had been first written in a stiff, marble-backed MS. book, the front page of which the Father had inset with a scandalous sepia-sketch of Tennyson and Browning in procession, and a spectacled schoolboy bringing up the rear. I gave it, when I left school, to a woman who returned it to me many years later – for which she will take an even higher place in Heaven than her natural goodness ensures – and I burnt it, lest it should fall into the hands of 'lesser breeds without the (Copyright) law'" (*Something of Myself*, pp. 206–7). The "scandalous sepia-sketch" survives, however; it is now at Sussex, and has been reproduced in Rutherford, *Early Verse*, p. 25.
3. Perhaps the notebook of early verse described as "Notebook 1" in Rutherford, *Early Verse*, p. 24.
4. Baldwin: Miss Plowden was particularly close to the Baldwin family, and some of her papers are now among the Baldwin papers in the University of Sussex library.
5. Much of RK's early work had been reprinted without his permission or knowledge – e.g., the volume called *Abaft the Funnel* (New York, 1909). I do not know what RK can mean by the publication of "sacred and intimate" matters; his application of the phrase would probably not be generally allowed.
6. Joseph Kipling, JLK's only brother.

To Sir Max Aitken, 19 January 1915
ALS: Harvard University

Bateman's / Burwash / Sussex / Jan. 19. 1915

Dear Colonel
In the first place congratulations![1] The Chief of a staff is one Hell of a chief as you will discover, but he also has one Hell of a time owing to fool subordinates. You'll find finance is simple beside this job. Your head A.D.C. has got

to be a *first-class* man, of good social standing but *not* a snob, with enormous tact, with full knowledge of military matters and a graceful way of imparting it to his chief. (When you have sucked him dry sack him and get a new one). He must also have a knowledge of Canada and the Canadians and their sensitiveness. But, of course, your chief difficulty will be to club off the people who can't do these things. God help you! I wish *we* could but I might throw some light on some of the candidates who are probably now offering themselves to you.

R.K.

Notes
1. Aitken had sought, and had now been officially appointed to, the position of "the voice of Canada in Great Britain" charged with reporting to the Canadian nation. He had been left to invent the duties of the position. "Aitken's first invention, as befitted a believer in publicity, was to make himself Canadian Eye Witness [attached to the Canadian Expeditionary Force]. He acquired the rank of lieutenant-colonel in the Canadian militia and was authorized to attend GHQ in France" (Taylor, *Beaverbrook*, p. 87). In this capacity Aitken wrote a weekly communiqué and published the first volume of a narrative called *Canada in Flanders*, 2 vols, 1916–17. A. J. P. Taylor calls this "a fine piece of war reporting, the more striking because it had then few examples to follow. Kipling, calling himself a 'wordsmith,' helped Aitken with the style, but this help was hardly necessary. The inspiration came partly from the Old Testament and partly from Stevenson" (*Beaverbrook*, p. 88). There is no reference to RK's help in Beaverbrook's book, which has as its prefatory motto a stanza from RK's "Our Lady of the Snows". Other references suggest the sort of help that RK may have given: "Rud re-writes Canadian eye-witness letter to fit in with more sombre state of affairs (Rees extracts, 12 May 1915). See also 6 December 1915.

To H. A. Gwynne, 22 January 1915
ALS: Dalhousie University

Bateman's / Burwash / Sussex / Jan. 22. 1915

Dear Old Man
    Many thanks for your kind note. Yes. You're quite right about Haggard.[1]
    As to John. Surely you don't think we leave him on his own in town! I'm enormously glad for any help I can get for him and you of course would be most invaluable.
    He's coming up to town on Monday for a signalling class. I'm coming up on Wed. to see him because, I've got a speech at the Mansion house.[2] I shall see him then. As soon as I heard of the course we arranged to come to town

and stay at Brown's and I fancy that he'll stay there too. Specially as I've asked him to be my guest there. He's a domestic lad in most respects and Brown's are his head-quarters where he has been known since his babyhood and the old butler there keeps a faithful eye on him.

Of course I've realized the danger of J. being in town alone and I've put out life-lines in every direction among my friends and we've been up to town often twice a week ourselves for theatre and dinner with him. While the signalling course is on we have no intention of *not* being in town. Elsie, as you know, is having a splendid time with the Bland-Suttons and I understand he has engagements with them. I'm a heap more afraid of town than I am of the trenches – as I think I wrote you. He's moderately safe at Warley but if the Batt'n comes to town then we realize we must come up too.

Ever yours
Rud

I heard from Cuthbert[3] that the signalling course was only a fortnight.

Notes
1. Rider Haggard's brother Arthur, to whom RK had given a note to Gwynne on 20 January: Haggard wanted Gwynne's help in founding a veteran's club (to Gwynne, 20 and 21 January 1915: ALS, Dalhousie).
2. In support of military bands to be used to stimulate recruiting, 27 January 1915: printed as "National Bands: a Speech delivered at the Mansion House on Jan. 27, 1915", 1915 (uncollected). RK had lunch with the Lord Mayor at the Mansion House before the speech (Rees extracts, 27 January 1915).
3. Captain James Harold Cuthbert (1876–1915), then adjutant of the reserve battalion. As an officer of the Scots Guards he was lost in the action in which John Kipling was killed: see *The Irish Guards in the Great War*, Outward Bound Edition, II, 16.

To Mrs Humphrey Ward, 18 February 1915
ALS: Pusey House, Oxford

Bateman's / Burwash / Sussex / Feb. 18. 1915

Dear Mrs. Humphrey Ward,

Forgive my not having answered your kind note before but I've been moving about a good deal lately. I got *Delia Blanchflower*,[1] of course, as soon as it came out and we read it at once. It is a wonderful study of the suffragest temperament and I am sure that, 'spite of the fact that war seems to hold everyone's attention, it will arouse enormous interest. It may – but this is a rash prophecy – even make people think. Meantime I am wondering in my mind, what "Delia" and the rest are making of this changed world. With many thanks for my own special copy

Most sincerely yours
Rudyard Kipling

Notes
1. *Delia Blanchflower*, 1915, the story of a militant Suffragette who repudiates her ways. Mrs Ward was the founder of the Women's National Anti-Suffrage League.

To John Kipling, 23 February [1915]
ALS: University of Sussex

Brown's Hotel, / London. W. / 23 Feb. Tues: 9.40. a.m.

Dear Old Man –
    The enclosed came this morning and we are duly sending it on. We think it is an ode of thanksgiving from Girlie[1] for the photo.
    Lunched at the B-Suttons yesterday where we met Sir Charles Wyndham[2] the actor who, it seems, is Lady Bland Sutton's cousin. I never knew *that* before. He used to be a great man in his day but is now quite ga-ga and seems to have difficulty in remembering the end of a sentence after he has begun it. Then I went on to the Empire Hospital to carry Long-Innes[3] a sort of arrangement for the blind (with metal lines across the paper) which might make it easier for him to write with the left hand. It amused him for a minute or two which was all that I cared about. He can really write not half badly. His sister came in after I had been there about ten minutes and then I got out.
    In the evening dined at the Marlborough[4] (now *that's* an exclusive Club if you like) with Aitken, Bonar Law, Rothermere,[5] young Neil Primrose[6] *and* Sir Reginald Braird[7] Permanent Under-Sec. for War. He (Braird) told me with his own lips that K is "as pleased as Punch at being made Colonel of the Irish Guards."[8]
    Well now I'll go to brekker and get shaved. With all love

Ever your most attentive
Dad

Notes
1. As the former governess Miss Mary Blaikie was known (see 22 August 1907). She had left the Kiplings in 1910 after six years of service.
2. Wyndham (1837–1919), actor-manager particularly distinguished in comedy; opened Wyndham's Theatre, London, in 1899. A failing memory led to his retirement.
3. Captain (later Major) P. S. Long-Innes, MC, of the Irish Guards, had been wounded on 1 February (*The Irish Guards*, Outward Bound Edition, I, 88–9). He was wounded again in 1916, in the action in which he won the MC.
4. The Marlborough Club, 52 Pall Mall.
5. Harold Sidney Harmsworth (1868–1940), 1st Viscount Rothermere, younger brother of Lord Northcliffe, prospered in partnership with his brother, and was himself proprietor of several papers. After Northcliffe's death Rothermere succeeded to the control of their newspaper empire.
6. Primrose (1882–1917), younger son of the former Prime Minister, Lord Rosebery; he was currently Parliamentary Under-Secretary to the Foreign Office. He was killed in action, 18 November 1917.
7. Thus in MS, for Sir Reginald Brade (1864–1933). There was no such office as that of Permanent Under-Secretary for War. Brade had been Secretary of the War Office since 1914 and was also Secretary of the Army Council.
8. Kitchener had been appointed Colonel of the Irish Guards in December 1914, in succession to Lord Roberts.

To Colonel Lionel Charles Dunsterville, 24 February 1915

ALS: University of Sussex

Bateman's / Burwash / Sussex / Feb. 24. 1915

Dear Lionel

Thank you ever so much for your letter with cheque enclosed which is duly noted etc. etc.[1] I've been away in the North[2] looking at things or I should have answered it before.

Of course I'm only a dam civilian so I can't see *why* an ex-C.O. of a Native Infantry regiment has to fester on trains in the disguise of a Cook's tourist agent.[3] But the ways of the W[ar]. O[ffice]. are wonderful! If there's anything I can do to be of any use to you please let me know.

I've been down at Brighton looking at the Indian wounded and having a lovely time with the Punjabis.[4] The little *Larrai*[5] has filled them with great respect for the manners of sahibs when they fight. As a young Peshawuri *naik*[6] said to me: – "It was a war of a kind which has not hitherto been shown to us."

What you say about the Anglo-French relations is most cheering. I wish to goodness I could get at you for a bit to swap yarns. I've got some beauties. I gather that the French rather go in for interesting but sterile whores whereas our practical men cohabit (precisely as you say) in a respectable manner with the married women and raise up seed to the Entente. This is as it should be.

I'm awfully busy with a whole lot of odds and ends including the bands.[7] We've got a few going now and they don't 'alf make a row neither! But it *does* help recruiting and marching. Just got orders to billet six officers of the North Lancashires.[8] How I wish you were one of 'em. There's no O.U.S.C. news. My boy has done his signalling course in London where I've been on and off for the last few weeks and now he tells me that he's due to go out in a few weeks. He's rather like what I was, to look at, at his age – anyhow like enough for you to recognize if you came across him.

With every good wish

Yours,
RK

Notes
1. Dunsterville, who had left his command in India and returned to England in 1914, wrote that his finances were then in a "tragic state" (*Stalky's Reminiscences*, p. 242). RK loaned him £500 at 4% without security (to Dunsterville, 17 February 1914: ALS, Sussex).
2. RK went to Newcastle sometime in February (CK diary, dated only "February"), and probably visited other places as well. I have found no report of the trip.
3. Dunsterville volunteered his services on the outbreak of the war but was only able to get an undistinguished assignment as a "train-conducting officer" in France: "it was our business to see that the train reached its proper destination ... and to bring back the empty trains to the Base to be refilled. It was extremely interesting work, though not of a heroic nature" (*Stalky's Reminiscences*, p. 243).
4. On 23 January (CK diary).
5. Fighting.
6. Captain or headman; here, non-commissioned officer.
7. There were now eleven such bands, known as the Lord Mayor's Recruiting Bands (see 22 January 1915).
8. Their visit to Bateman's is described in RK's letter to John Kipling, [27 February 1915] in Gilbert, *O Beloved Kids*, pp. 175–7.

[To Sir Max Aitken, February 1915][1]
Text: Copy, House of Lords Record Office

Morale of Civilians and the Censorships.

———

Suggest study of the soldier – especially the officer.

It is to be remembered that, in spite of all the alleged advance of science the practice of War is not an exact art; every detail hinges at the last on the strength and intelligence of the individual man. Therefore the Army – the armies of all nations are arranged on the basis that every man is a fool, which in a War he mostly is. Therefore the officer is a man who deals with fools. That is why all Army explanations and orders are repeated and multiplied and every detail which has to be done is set out with an enormous amount of elaboration. The civilian running a small business does not understand this. Nor, can he understand how a thousand men acting together are, where their food, transport, etc. is concerned, as helpless as so many slates. Also, most of the things which are done by the Army as regards camp and barrack life are the outcome of ages of special experience in the handling of men. These means may appear slow and cumbrous but there is generally very good and sufficient reason for them.

This is the first thing that the Civilian mind must try to understand, and to interpret to fellow-civilians.

Again, in a War of this enormous size the Civilian must remember that very little effect is produced by the movements and actions of any body of men. That is, very little effect which the Civilian is competent to see and pass judgement upon. The net result of weeks of slow preparation may be nothing more than the advance of a few troops to the crest of some slightly rising ground which gives them command over a few miles of country. The preparations and the sacrifices of human life may seem absurd and disproportionate to the Civilian, but it is to be always remembered, that till he has been at least a couple of months in the field he is not in any way competent to judge.

If he listens to the talk of military men among themselves he will learn more than by asking questions direct.

Also, behind the firing line the Civilian comes into contact with all the stories of desertion, self-mutilation, and the other phenomena connected with weariness and loss of nerve. He must remember that this is no more than a part of the normal and inevitable wastage of men in every army, and he must not attach undue importance to it or allow the knowledge of it to colour his reports.

The most fatal attitude of mind he can take up is that of always thinking: – "Oh, if only a little civilian common sense were applied to the problem". The problems of War and the handling of men in camp are *not* Civilian problems and in nine cases out of ten civilian methods (excellent where only a few men are concerned) would lead to more delay and perhaps disaster.

It is almost impossible for a civilian who has had a civil education all his life to approach military life with a clear mind but this is the first lesson that he must learn.

The mental habit of the Canadian and his instinctive revolt against the outer signs and evidences of discipline – such as saluting – is his very great handicap. The Australian and the New Zealander have had the advantage of having adopted for some years past a form of compulsory training which has made them used to the forms of discipline and at least a large percentage of them realize the necessity of discipline. The Canadian has not had that experience. For that reason he is still, consciously or sub-consciously, wasting his own energy in kicking against it. The worst of it is that his own country and its journalism more or less upholds him in this attitude: so his situation is doubly dangerous.

The experience of the South African War has shown us that undisciplined troops from the Dominions, when they get into trouble through lack of discipline, instinctively try to throw the blame of their own failure on "The rigidity of the British system", "the hide bound regulations of the British Army" or some such silly form of words. At the same time the journals of the Dominions in order to uphold, as they think, the honour of their countrymen are inclined to back up the wild statements of officers and men.

This is a very grave danger: The important thing is to exercise a very strict censorship of the men's letters home. The English system of censorship prevents foolish or depressing letters from being made public in English or Indian papers. It is *ten-fold more important* that no Canadian letters of a stupid sort should go to Canada because they will not only be immediately published in Canadian papers but will also be exploited in the pro-German interests by the U.S. papers across the line. *The censorship of Canadian Army correspondence is therefore a vital link in the chain.*

Notes
1. A MS note on this memo reads: "Original in Bank Box. Feby. 1915." RK evidently wrote the memo for Aitken's guidance in his role as "Canadian Eye Witness": see 19 January 1915. At the time there was much protest over British censorship of war reporting: see Chisholm and Davie, *Beaverbrook*, p. 126.

To Sir Charles P. Crewe, 13 March 1915
ALS: East London Museum, South Africa

Bateman's / Burwash / Sussex / Mar. 13. 1915

Dear Crewe

Yours of St Valentine's day! Golly what Valentines for the world, this year. I've followed the S. African situation[1] with homesick interest and it seemed to me from here that things would go pretty much on the lines you indicate: i.e. Botha to be played up to and the whole tone of things let down several pegs in consequence. And so it would be did the S.A. show stand by itself. If, let us assume, De Wet had rebelled etc. in time of peace, Botha would, presumably have acted much as he does now; all the Empire would have slavered him with gratitude and the Loyalist would have had to treat the non-actively disloyal dutchman, the passive sympathizer and all the other shades of disaffection sedition etc. as saviours of the land. BUT, and this is a big but, we are not at peace. On the contrary we are at war and people's tempers and tones are hardening with their losses and their discomforts. Nor is the civil control in England at all the thing it was only a few months ago for the reason that we have got 1,000,000 + x men under arms and, with the best will in the world to keep a supremely-civil administration, military interests, by the necessity of the case, predominate and will predominate still more

Very good. At the end of the war neither the army which has been created, nor, more vital still the temper that has been created, can be shut up like a book that is read. There will be a rearrangement of ideals and methods that will be very striking indeed. So cheer up! A South Africa deprived of any German backing or sympathy – a South Africa which has nothing to appeal to except the Empire's idea of what is expedient for the Empire; and with no card to play in politics except that it has had German affinities is *quite* a different thing from the same country with undefeated Teuton hosts in Europe and at Windhoek.[2] Moreover there will be armies to be disbanded – lots and lots of men who have tasted freedom and adventure and who aren't going back to the shop and the mill. They are persons who already think a heap of themselves and have a certain contempt for men who haven't gone with the game. I do not think they will be any less – insistent shall we say – after the war when they knock about over the face of the earth. Already I have heard territorials – *territorials* mark you – discussing the advantages of a punitive campaign in South Africa as a treat and a training! You see, after the war, there will begin a war to root out German influence because we all know it is bad and costs lives and money. Consequently people who make trouble or initiate fancy particularist legislation (except in the direction of making Germans pay extra taxes and report themselves to the police, as Australia will probably do and as Canada may do) will not be very well looked upon. You, remembering the old war will laugh and say: – "We shall forget." We shall not because *now* the common people and all classes are paying with blood and money. They object most to losing their kith and kin.

Summa. What the Dutch do now doesn't matter a damn. You can play up all you care to. With Germany defeated the Loyalist is set free with the public opinion of an Empire behind him and men to back that opinion. Nor does it greatly matter whether you are in Windhoek or Wynberg by July, if the German crocks in Europe. We are at last realizing that this war is to the dead finish and under all the silence and apparent sloth which impresses the foreigner as apathy, a good deal is being done, and more will be. Of course *if* we get through the Dardanelles[3] there will be a quick shift of scenery and almost anything may happen. At the present moment the Teuton is being bled in men, which matters more than anything else to him;

and in stores which he can manage to get on with. Our people – confound 'em – aren't touched yet in their pockets and the Government money is making the lower classes horrid rich. We have soldiers billetted in our village at 3/4^d per head per night. It's a silver mine to the poor widow and the small she-shopkeeper.

We are shoving out troops as fast as we can and, better still, we are getting more level on equipment. I've been up among the big factories (ships guns and plate) in the North and have seen the new buildings literally quadrupling the old ones.

And we are only at the beginning. The submarine blockade has in many ways been rather a gain to us inasmuch as the submarines have had to show 'emselves and we have got a few above water. We have got more of 'em *under water* but on that of course, the admiralty keeps quiet. We have also sent across some new and rather interesting types of big gun and – best of all – the honeymoon with our Allies continues and gets better as *our* losses increase. This is only human nature. The Muscovite will do anything to get Constantinople and one can hear him smiling from this distance at the prospect of it.

One curious phase of the national psychology now is the desire that the agitated neutrals should *not* mix themselves up in the quarrel. (You have seen aas vogels[4] round a dying trek ox? Among the neutrals you can see now just the same nervous lifting of the shoulders and little half-flutters and hops forward.) That I take it is a good sign.

The Teuton as a people is still assured that he will win and win heavily and he comes up to the attack, specially against the Russian, regardless of losses. Our very free talk of our own strikes (Lord! what a lot of voters will sell their country for 2^d an hour extra) and our disconcerting habit of playing with all the cards on the table, cheer the enemy in his beliefs, which again is an advantage. The papers and the Government (but chiefly the papers) are very insistent on the seriousness of the situation and the sacrifices we must be prepared for: and I welcome that sign.

One can get no labour; wages have risen; we find little or no want, certainly none traceable to lack of employment among the lower classes and the recruiting goes on secretly and satisfactorily.

But oh how I wish you were here to study our politics. There is *nothing* lower than an English politician in peace – except the same animal in war, and his struggles to stay in the limelight and to coax himself to believe that nothing has changed in the world of irreverent, and openly contemptuous, *khaki*, are beautiful to see. They suggest the emotions of an ancient and undisturbed tapeworm in the bowels of one who has taken a dose of – antithelmintic[5] (I think that is the word) medicine.

My boy has not yet gone out: for which I praise Allah since every day that dries the trenches is a gain. After that, we shall have losses on a scale that will make the pomp of abatoirs ridiculous; and then we shall really be at war.

Forgive this long yarn and don't trouble too much about the Dutch for the present. They are only a leaf at the end of a branch which is being lopped off. With all our best love to you all

Ever sincerely
Rudyard Kipling

Notes
1. General De Wet (see 23–24 August 1901) had sided with General Hertzog against the government of General Botha in Hertzog's campaign to take South Africa out of the Empire and to re-establish the Boer republics. At the end of October 1914, De Wet attempted an armed revolt. He was put to flight by Botha in November 1914, and captured early in December. In June 1915, De Wet was tried and found guilty of high treason but was pardoned in December 1915.
2. Capital of German South West Africa. The South Africans sent a military expedition against the Germans in South West Africa in August 1914, and successfully concluded the campaign in July 1915.
3. The attempt to force the strait by Anglo-French forces beginning 16 February 1915 was confined to naval action; landings began on 25 April but were unsuccessful. After heavy losses the Allied forces withdrew, an action completed in January 1916.
4. South African vultures.
5. If there is such a word it would be "anti-helminthic".

To John Kipling, 30 March 1915
ALS: University of Sussex

Bath Spa Hotel,[1] */ Bath. /* Mar. 30. 1915 / 6: p.m. (the sun shining hard)

Dear Old Man,

This is a rummy place – a sort of mixture of Madeira, the South of France, bits of Italy and Bournemouth all tumbled into a hollow between hills and populated with invalids and soldiers. The town is full of soldiers – the 10th Devons have their headquarters in one of the most fashionable streets and what used to be elegant private houses now bustle with privates and great coats and rifles. They are going to have inter-Regimental sports in a few days. This explained the spectacle I saw this morning of six perspiring privates in obviously civilian knickers chasing round one of the squares hounded on by a long corporal while the cooks of a battalion camped in one of the parks hung over the railings and criticized their action. I believe there is some artillery here too; though I haven't come across it yet.

Mother has started in on her treatment which means a hot bath one day and a hot bath and massage the next and a sort of dry massage every evening at 9:p.m. It is a devilish strenuous undertaking for so small a woman.

Elsie and I went out this morning to the Pump Room where the hot waters of Bath are dispensed by two virgins at 2d. a glass. It isn't an exciting spectacle except for the invalids. Some of 'em are fat – as fat as swine: others cough: others limp and the rest look like lepers. The hotel boasts one old gentleman who knits comforters for troops. We overheard him say proudly "This is my third." I believe he finds it soothing for the nerves.

And talking of nerves, I owe you two Bob – for I see in the papers that Wells[2] was knocked out – a half-hook on the point. I don't know whether he has guts or not but surely this finishes him on the stage of pugilism.

Did you see, by the way, that the much advertised Football battalion[3] only roped in a few score men out of the 1800 pros. who play. *What* a stinking game is soccer. We expect to have the car over by Friday morning, with the new man[4] to drive; so if by any chance you can get to us for Saturday we might be able to go for a little run about the country. It's a pretty part of the world.

You had better look up the A.B.C.[5] and see how the trains go. There is one which gives you your lunch aboard – a most useful train and there is a splendid one (we took it) at 4:15 from Paddington which comes on without a stop, getting here at 6.6. There are also good trains in between – one at about 3. o'clock I believe but if you miss the lunch train you will find the 4:15 will give you tea. Uncle Stan always loved his food and he feeds his Great Western passengers well.[6] But you may be going to Bournemouth or somewhere.

We haven't met any one we know yet but I expect that experience will not be long delayed. The town clerk is coming to call.[7] God knows why. It makes me feel as though I were a deserter or a defaulting debtor. The grub here is good and the rooms are beautifully clean and comfy and as the hotel really *does* stand in its own ground (see advts) one feels decently secluded.

There's a prep-school at the back of us – up the hill side, which moved us nearly to tears. Two kids began playing golf with cleeks. It ended in a hockey match and a scuffle – precisely as it would have done with you and me not so long ago.

Best love from us all.

Ever your
Dad

Notes
1. They went to Bath by train on 29 March (Rees extracts). This was the first of the visits to Bath that they regularly paid over the next six years for the sake of CK's rheumatism. In a letter of 1916 she describes her routine at Bath thus: "I have my bath at 10 a.m. and am not back until 12; then my woman rubs me for an hour. I rest an hour the last fifteen minutes of which I start my lunch in bed; start to dress at 2.15 out at three for a walk drink my water in the Pump room at 4.15 and home" (CK to Mrs Balestier, 2 February [1916]: ALS, Dunham Papers).
2. Bombardier Wells, British heavyweight champion, was knocked out in the tenth round by the American Frank Moran in a fight in London, 29 March.

3. The 17th (Service) Battalion of the Middlesex Regiment was formed in January as the "Football Battalion". Its commander reported at the end of March that only 122 men had joined (*The Times*, 30 March 1915).
4. This was a man named Stern, who came at the beginning of April and quit after ten days; RK was always anxious that his chauffeurs "understand" the Rolls-Royce and wished them to take special training in order to qualify. Stern took the position that "A Daimler and a Rolls-Royce are practically one and the same machine, and a Daimler is good enough for me." And so saying he left (to Arthur Gibbs, 13 April 1915: ALS, Mrs Marjorie House).
5. *The A.B.C. Railway Timetable*, published monthly.
6. Baldwin inherited his father's financial interest in the Great Western Railway.
7. This was a Mr F. D. Wardle (RK to Wardle, 30 March 1915: ALS, Duke University).

To Captain F. H. Huth,[1] 3 April 1915
ALS: Syracuse University

Bath Spa Hotel, / Bath. / April 3. 1915

My dear Captain Huth –

It is a most priceless gift that you have sent me – the finest Koran I have ever laid eyes – much less hands – upon.[2] I have never seen anything to come near it. There was one that I remember in the Jaipur museum[3] but that was of a later date and not as well written. It shall take rank with the greatest of my treasures and I thank you most heartily for your Hatim-Tai-like[4] spirit in giving it to me.

I hope, if you will let me, to come over to Beckford House and thank you by word of mouth.

Very sincerely yours
Rudyard Kipling.

P.S.   I am more than a bit of a fool about horses: and I didn't know, till I had read your *memoria technica*,[5] the relation of the groove in the corner tush to the animal's age. Now I shan't forget it.

Notes
1. Frederick Henry Huth (1844–1918), Captain in the 1st Dragoon Guards, who lived near Bath. His father and two uncles were all notable collectors, as was Huth himself; he made gifts of pictures, books, and other items to the City of Bath and was a trustee of the Bath Art Gallery.
2. The inventory of books at Bateman's made in May 1940 lists two copies of the Koran, both in George Sale's translation: London, 2 vols, 1764; and "new ed.",

Philadelphia, 1853. Neither is now at Bateman's, but neither seems likely to be the one referred to in this letter. Beatrice Dunham refers to a "beautiful illuminated Koran" that she was shown as Bateman's in 1931 (*Kipling Journal*, December 1996, p. 44).
3. RK began the tour recorded in *Letters of Marque* at Jeypore at the end of 1887; the museum is described in Letters IV and V (*From Sea to Sea*, I, 31–6).
4. Not the elephant of RK's story "The Killing of Hatim Tai" (*The Smith Administration* in *From Sea to Sea*), but the model of generosity in Arab folklore.
5. I have not identified this. Huth published two bibliographies on horsemanship: *Works on Horses and Equitation*, 1887; and *Works on Horsemanship and Swordsmanship in the Library of F. H. Huth*, Bath, 1890.

To C. R. L. Fletcher, 10 April 1915

ALS: University of Sussex

Brown's Hotel, / London, W. / April 10. 1915.

Dear Fletcher

As to handwriting, I sprawl in dust and ashes, because I've had my own punishment. It's one of my correspondents who writes absolutely the foulest fists that ever was and I've had to puzzle and swear my way through his infernal communications for weeks past. The wife stands by and reads me Moral Lectures saying: – "Oh! *Now* You see what it means!" I do! I'm sorry. Bad writing is a Crime besides being an Insolence and an Outrage and a Waste Of Time. I am full of the zeal of the convert.

We're up for the weekend to meet my boy who has a night off. I thought I told you John got a commission in The Irish Guards last September, about three weeks after his seventeenth birthday. Since then he has learned what work means and has liked both it and his Irish. He's at Warley in Brentwood which isn't a gay place and he is, or was, Senior Ensign. It's an amazing world!

Of course I skated off the Eton question – after you had clubbed me over the head with a loaded stick. (By the way I've turned in the facts you gave me about the College to a man who needed enlightenment and they have eased his mind.) But you *did* defend Lyttleton.[1] You said in effect "the prisoner is guilty but violently insane" – or words to that effect. And, as I said, I call that a very efficient defence. 'Glad you told me about L's "scholastic attainments".[2] I'd hate to think that he was accurate about anything.

Your deep and welling affection for Cambridge reminds me of what Roosevelt wrote me about Wilson a few months ago. "*He comes of a Virginian family no member of which took any part in the fighting on either side, during our*

Civil War."[3] I have a notion that I may have written you this before but it is a beautiful sentence.

In my spare times at Bath I've been reading Jane Austen and the more I read the more I admire and respect and do reverence. What are *your* views? When she looks straight at a man or a woman she is greater than those who were alive with her – by a whole head. Greater than Charles;[4] greater than Walter[5] – with a more delicate hand and a keener scalpel. I have suspected it for a long time but, like my friend the South African millionaire who discovered the Bible, in my presence, in his thirtieth year,[6] now I am sure.

A man told me what he insists is the only authentic ghost-tale of the War. He asserts it is known throughout our Army at the front. This is it. Thrice in the great attack at Ypres[7] our line was worn down to a thread – as you know – which the Huns might have smashed at pleasure. Thrice when the game was all their own they turned back and we were saved. Our people were naturally curious to understand what had so worked on the Barbarians. They asked their prisoners – many prisoners at many times and in many places: "*Why* did you break back?" And in each case, the story goes, those prisoners replied: – "Because we *saw* the enormous reserves that you had waiting to attack us." And there were none – none at all: for the last cooks and orderlies had taken up their rifles in the final scrum!

Now *whose* were those Reserves? "Our Army in Flanders": Marlboro's men: old militia regiments of Wellington's time, stiffened with the bulk of the August expeditionary force? It's a strange notion – that waiting reserve that was never there! If one had the turn for it – as, these days, I have not – one might do verses on it.

My suggestion was not about the history of the War (*that* is being linotyped in Hell, and it is using all the machines) but a study of one small battle. The present work is being done baldly and butcherly, by men who can't weigh evidence.

Good luck to your Tobacconisterie[*8] – but 'tis a venal method of winning affection. In the Boer War I controlled many many pounds of cake tobacco and millions of cigarettes to distribute; and the Entire British Army ran after me wagging its tail.

But the talks must be wonderful. By the way I met Andrew Fairservice and Alan Breck[9] side by side on the same settle in a Bath hospital last week – and they described each from his own angle the details of one affair they had been through together. Finally Andrew: – "If I had ma leg off I'd be kidding I wanted to go back to the trenches. But I'm a sound man and I'm no enthusiaastic". Alan, explosively: – "But it's God's truth *I* am and *I*'m a sound man." Andrew, very tenderly: – "Then you're a damned loo-natic."

Sometime when you have the liking tell me about your parson. I'm sick at heart over the way the Church has not, to my mind, taken her right and righteous part in this, and I'd like to be cheered by one good priest. The others are too good.

Ever
R.K.

*also cheque

Notes
1. Edward Lyttelton (1855–1942), brother of Alfred Lyttelton (see 11 July 1902), was a master at Eton, 1882–90, headmaster of Haileybury, 1890–1905, and headmaster of Eton, 1905–16, where Fletcher was now helping out as a teacher of history during 1914–15. Like his brother, Edward Lyttelton was a notable athlete; as a teetotaller, a vegetarian, and a man of strenuous spirituality, he was regarded as an eccentric. RK had had lunch with Lyttelton on 4 June 1913 at Eton (CK diary) and was no doubt fully aware of his reputation. Lyttelton had preached a sermon at St Margaret's, Westminster, on 25 March in which he argued that, when it was possible to treat with the Germans again, they should be treated with Christian charity rather than in a spirit of competition and vindictiveness. He said, for example, that the English could not demand the internationalising of the Kiel canal without allowing the internationalisation of Gibraltar. For this he was called "pro-German" and worse. Lyttelton's resignation from Eton in April 1916 was in some part a consequence of his unlucky sermon.
2. Lyttelton was without scholarly ambition.
3. "Wilson is a scholarly, acrid pacifist of much ability and few scruples. He was born in Virginia, and comes of a family none of whose members fought on either side in the Civil War" (Roosevelt to RK, 4 November 1914: TLS, Library of Congress).
4. Dickens (though only just a contemporary of Jane Austen's: he was born in 1812 and she died in 1817).
5. Scott.
6. As a guess, Sir Abe Bailey.
7. The first battle of Ypres, 19 October–22 November 1914.
8. Fletcher was supplying tobacco to wounded soldiers at Oxford: see [May 1915].
9. Characters from Scott's *Rob Roy* and Stevenson's *Kidnapped* and *Catriona*, the one cowardly, the other bold.

To Laurence Alma-Tadema,[1] 21 April 1915
ALS: Cornell University

Bath Spa Hotel, / Bath. / April 21. 1915

private
Dear Miss Alma Tadema –

I must protest most emphatically against your appeal for the Polish Victims Relief Fund[2] which I have just read, and for which the various patrons and patronesses of the Fund are made to appear responsible.

I should never have acceded to Mr. Paderewski's request for my name if I had thought that the appeal would be worded so as to include an affront to one of our Allies: and I am exceedingly annoyed that my name should have been coupled with anything of the kind.[3]

Though the harm has been done, I must ask you to remove my name from the list of patrons. I am of course in deep sympathy with the needs of Poland at the present time and enclose a cheque for the Fund.

I am forwarding a copy of this letter to the Russian Ambassador.

Sincerely yours
Rudyard Kipling.

Notes

1. Laurence Alma-Tadema (d. 1940) was the daughter of the painter Sir Lawrence Alma-Tadema (see 4 January 1911). She was co-founder with Paderewski of the fund for Polish relief: see note 2, below.
2. On 29 March Ignace Jan Paderewski, the great Polish pianist and patriot, published an "Appeal for Poland" in *The Times*. This was followed by the establishment of a "Polish Victims' Relief Fund", having among its patrons such artists as Thomas Hardy, Sir Edward Elgar, John Singer Sargent, and RK. Miss Alma-Tadema was its honorary secretary (*The Times*, 15 April 1915). Paderewski contributed the proceeds of his wartime concerts to the Fund.
3. I have not found the text of the appeal in question. On 21 April *The Times* reported that in a recently published appeal by the Fund the "Russian policy in Poland and the action of the Russian Army were represented in a light unacceptable to his Excellency the Russian Ambassador." In consequence, the Ambassador had withdrawn as a patron of the Fund.

To C. R. L. Fletcher, 5 May 1915

ALS: University of Sussex

[Brown's Hotel, London] May. 5. 1915

Dear Fletcher

No! No primroses or cowslips yet awhile for me. We're in town waiting on events as those affect our son and also Mrs Kipling is trying to recover from the effects of the Bath treatment.[1] It's drastic but it appears that if the patient does not at once perish, there is a reasonable hope that a cure may set in later. Meantime I've been hospitalizing and doing bits of things without value or use. I like the hospitalizing best though a big bout of it rather pulls one. Isn't their dignity and their patience splendid. I've met but one exception among the officers and he was a promoted ranker – doubtless an excellent man and full of attainments but unduly eloquent on his own sensations. 'Twas a hand wound: the rest of his physique unimpaired – indeed built up and strengthened by the long rest but – God forgive me, since he had been helping to save mine own unworthy carcass! – I couldn't but detect his blood-sister the voluble impatient house-maid with the toothache, as his voice lost its superimposed "gentility" and broke into the chords of his own civilization. And I've been seeing men from the Canadian army in this last Ypres affair[2] and hearing *their* talk. It's the first time that Canada has had a bill sent in to her in earnest and she feels it, as a young man or maid resents sorrow in this life. Of course, in the Dominion they do not yet realize how small an item is their contingent in all that mass and their natural instinct will be to ask: "But *why* were our men sacrificed?"

And "Sacrifice" is a word that young things use very ignorantly, ain't it?

The actual men concerned seemed to me sombrely proud and with a new and most active hate towards the German, proportioned to their own tolerance in the past in Canada. *And* their views on the United States. ... Oh Lord! They spoke, drawled rather, with a cold contempt that was worth hearing and mixed with their contempt there was disgust that this Thing and its influence should have corrupted their own politics and commercial life. You've probably come across the same.

And now the Australians have begun to lay their sacrifice on the altar[3] and I'd give a good deal to know how their national psychology will be affected. I have always stuck to it that they are the most vindictive haters within the Empire on account of their heavy meat diet and the advantages that they were given for nothing. I shall be curious to see how it works out.

Apropos {to/of} taking wounded out for motor trips – here's a yarn that I got fresh from the lips of an Irishman whom a kind lady had taken to the Zoo in her car: – "I've been through the b. Marne an' the b. Aisne, but to set behind a b. lady in a wounded car that can't drive, tears the hearrt out o' me!" After all how should he know whether a woman can or can't drive. He's never trusted himself to that make of chauffeur before and I have a vision of him holding on with desperate white-knuckled fingers to the side of the car, with a rowling eye of apprehension, and a nervously polite tongue.

I'd like to come and see you shepherding your flock through Oxford, and I bet the beauty of the place and your explications are balm to 'em. And have you noticed how wide a range of interest they possess and what queer funds of knowledge. We had an aged housemaid once who took all English history (in primers to be sure) for her province. And the tale was alive to her and she held it in very decent proportion.

Yesterday I met and had talk with a man in from the Philippines[4] where he'd captained U.S. police and Filipino police through six years jungle hunting against Moros and semi-cannibals. I'd corresponded with him for years but never seen his face. The War came: he was an Englishman; married with 2 kids. He chucked and fled and is just gazetted Captain to a

K3 battalion – deeply grateful for that post. 'Funny how all the U.S. had peeled off him en route and he was every minute more the Ex-Army Officer of the Boer War. But as he said his drill will be more painful to him than to the Youngest Second-Lieutenant for he is naturally soaked in U.S. drill where a platoon is 30 men.[5] He goes humbly on to the square in a day or two.

And now I'll to bed. I had very little sleep last night and whorson aches all over me.

But write – write to me and tell me more about your peoples in the hospitals. I've never connected you much with Saint Martin, but I do now.

Ever
R.K.

P.S.   And will you kindly let me have your views on the Beatification of Charles the Martyr as the "Church's one creation" at this crisis.[6]

OXFORD of the FUTURE[7]
(circa 1917)

Tutor to undergrad (aged 23: D.S.O., Legion d'Honneur and medals with 7 clasps)

Then I presume Mr. Golightly we may take this as your considered translation of the passage? etc. etc.

Undergrad (*mechanically*)

Fall out that man! What the hell d'you mean by presumin' an' considerin' to your super. ...   Oh I *beg* your pardon Sir. I – I – I'm afraid I didn't quite look it up before coming here.

Notes
1. They left Bath for Brown's Hotel, London, on 24 April and remained until 12 May (CK diary and Rees extracts).
2. The Canadians had been heavily engaged in the second battle of Ypres, beginning on 22 April 1915; this was the first occasion on which the Germans used gas on the western front.
3. Two of the five divisions employed in the landings on Gallipoli, beginning on 25 April, were Australian and New Zealand troops.
4. Duckworth Ford: see 16 September 1907.
5. The English platoon (a term not restored to use in the English army until 1913) was slightly smaller, though the number in question seems to vary.
6. Charles I was restored to the calendar of saints of the Church of England by Convocation on 28 April (*The Times*, 29 April 1915).
7. RK has written this addition in a corner of one sheet, at right angles to the rest of the letter, and drawn a border around it.

To Colonel Lionel Charles Dunsterville, 5 May 1915

ALS: University of Sussex

Brown's Hotel, / *London, W.* / May 5. 1915

Dear Lionel

Yours of the 13th of last month en route for the Shiny[1] once more. Take my heartiest congratulations though I should have preferred you in a K[itchener]. Brigade here. Dam-well did Maxse[2] remember you I hope, for it wasn't me that shut my mouth about you when I was at manœuvres the year before with him. But perhaps, in view of your Asiatic past, a Jhelum brigade is best. Anyway the new K armies are a breed apart[3] – extraordinarily interesting and, as far as I can see, extraordinarily good. They are all a bit stale now, over-marched and over-drilled with not enough leave for either officers or men to reconcile 'em to coming back to their work. Hence leave breaking among the men (which appears to be their only crime) and grousing at the messes.

I am horrid busy as usual over a lot of things that don't count – also as usual.[4] I believe my boy's battalion goes out before long. We are sending troops across pretty thick. The Holy British Public have at last realized that this is Bloody War and it's impressing 'em. Send us a line from time to time as you can and never forget how keen an interest I have in you and your doings. I've always stuck to it you'd go far.

Ever
Rudyard

Did you see H. E. Napier[5] was killed at the Dardanelles? Ours, I think.

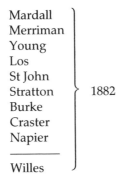

Mardall
Merriman
Young
Los
St John
Stratton
Burke
Craster
Napier
———
Willes

} 1882

RK.

Notes

1. Army slang for India. Dunsterville had been appointed, at his own request, commander of the Jhelum Brigade in India and had sailed for his new post in April

1915. He was soon transferred to the 1st Infantry Brigade at Peshawar, where he remained for the next two years (*Stalky's Reminiscences*, pp. 251–2).

2. General Sir Ivor Maxse (1862–1958), older brother of RK's friend Leo Maxse; a veteran of the Sudan and South Africa, at the outbreak of the war he was commander of the 1st Guards brigade. He commanded the 18th Division, one of the New Army formations, in France, 1915–17, and the XVIII Corps, 1917–18. RK saw him at Farnborough on 28 June 1913 (CK diary) before going on to the manoeuvres at Aldershot (see 9 July 1913).

3. RK had gone to Aldershot on 26 April to "see some of K's army finished" (Rees extracts).

4. RK had been busy at stories: "Sea Constables" and "Mary Postgate" in March and "The Tie" in April (CK diary, 8 March, 22 April 1915). He had also been visiting hospitals (CK diary, 22 April 1915) and had been to Aldershot to see the army in training (note 3, above).

5. Colonel Henry Edward Napier (1861–1915), at USC 1875–80, commanded a brigade at Gallipoli, where he was killed in the first landing, 25 April 1915. The other names may be identified thus from the *OUSC Register* [Canterbury, 1936]: Colonel William Mardall (1862–1912), at USC 1874–8, commanded the 31st Lancers, Indian Army, and died of peritonitis at Kohat, North West Frontier, 1912 (see 29 July [1911]). There were three Merriman brothers at USC; the likeliest is Colonel Reginald Gordon Merriman (1866–?), at USC 1879–82, who served in the Royal Artillery until retirement in 1919. Of the several eligible Youngs, my guess is that RK means Lieutenant Arthur Frederick Young (1866–88), at USC 1879–84, who died of enteric fever at Ferozepore, India, while serving with the East Lancashire Regiment (see 30 January 1886). There were two brothers named Los; one, a ship-owner, died in 1930; the other, Lieutenant Ernest Daniel (1859–80), at USC 1876–8, died of enteric fever in Afghanistan in 1880 while serving with the 25th Foot. Captain Arthur St John (1862–?), at USC 1876–9, served with the Royal Inniskillin Fusiliers and retired in 1894 (see 9 May 1896). Colonel Wallace Christopher Ramsay Stratton (1862–?), at USC 1875–9, served in the Political Department of the Indian Army, 1885–1917, and was Chief Commissioner, Ajmir (see 24 April 1883). Henry Morton Burke (1863–?), was at USC 1875–80; no further information about him is given. Craster may be Colonel Shafto Longfield Craster (see 24 April 1883), at USC 1874–9. There were three Willes brothers at USC; the likeliest is Arthur Herbert (1864–96), at USC 1876, reported dead at Darjeeling, 1896. Apart from the facts that all were at USC at some time during RK's years there and that most were in the military, I can find no common denominator among these men. Nor can I explain the rubric "1882".

To Lady Edith Bland-Sutton,[1] [9 May 1915]

ALS: Royal College of Surgeons

Brown's Hotel, / London, W. / Sunday night

Dear Lady Bland-Sutton

The memorial service to the Canadian dead will be held at St Paul's tomorrow evening and it is imperative that I should be present.[2] I find that it will be held at 7.30. p.m. I would not have missed the dinner tomorrow night for anything less than this but I am sorry to say that I shan't be able to come. The wife and John and Elsie will be coming to you but they can't tell you how very sorry I am that anything should have interfered with an engagement that I have looked forward to for so long.

Ever sincerely
Rudyard Kipling

Notes
1. Edith Heather-Bigg married Bland-Sutton as his second wife in 1899. She presided over his Brook Street house, where they entertained frequently.
2. RK attended the service in order to write an account of it for the Canadian press. The article duly appeared in the *Montreal Gazette*, 14 May 1915 (and doubtless in many other Canadian papers) as "Mourning and Rejoicing at Old St. Paul's". For some inexplicable reason this item seems to have escaped all of RK's bibliographers, despite the fact that it appeared in a major newspaper, is signed by RK and is explicitly identified as his in the text. A MS of the article is at Dalhousie, and a printed text is pasted in one of the scrapbooks of RK's work among the Kipling papers at Sussex (Sussex 28/7, p. 124).

To Lord Desborough,[1] 29 May 1915
ALS: Hertfordshire County Council

Bateman's / Burwash / Sussex / May 29. 1915

My dear Desborough
    We saw the news yesterday – side by side with the poem that rounded out that splendid young life.[2] No words can mean anything to you now, nor even the knowledge that we all lie under the shadow of a similar loss sooner or later: but we both send our love and our sorrow and our sympathy to you two.

Ever most sincerely
Rudyard Kipling.

Notes
1. William Henry Grenfell (1855–1945), 1st Baron Desborough, had a parliamentary career first as a Liberal and then as a Conservative; after being raised to the peerage in 1905 he continued an active career in local government, was chairman of the Thames Conservancy Board for thirty-two years, and held many other administrative offices. He was one of the outstanding athletes and sportsmen of

his day, twice swimming the rapids below Niagara and twice climbing the Matterhorn, among a host of other such feats.

2. Captain Julian Grenfell (1888–1915), eldest son of Lord Desborough, had been wounded at Ypres in May and died on 26 May. After Eton and Balliol Julian Grenfell joined the 1st Dragoons in 1910 and served in India and South Africa before his regiment went to France in October 1914. *The Times* of 28 May, which carried the announcement of his death, also published his poem "Into Battle", dated "Flanders, April 1915".

To C. R. L. Fletcher, [May 1915]
ALS: University of Sussex

Bateman's / Burwash / Sussex

Then I saw in my dream how Great-heart was carried into Oxford to mend him of his wounds which he had gotten against Apollyon; for he had met with some notable rubs. And that town is more full of Learning and Loveliness that can well be reckoned. Neither is it all vanity as in most but, generally, a fair record and register of great good things done in the past and very wonderful towers and palaces set among pleasant meadows by delicate waters and under a variety of trees.

Then said Greatheart, when the sisters had shifted him out of his grisly clothes and he lay abed: "I think I am as well in this place as anywhere. The "place suits with my present temper. Methinks, here, one may without much "molestation be thinking of what a man is and what he has done and to what "his King hath called him."

So then, he lay abed until his wounds had taken to an healing and when he could make shift to hobble, he went abroad in the streets between the palaces. He found that he could make nothing out of them out of his own knowledge, neither what they represented nor when they were builded nor for what ends.

"Here am I" said Mr. Greatheart "set down, and like to stay awhile, in this Oxford with no more knowledge of the stones about me than a mere ox at market." Next he asked questions of the passers by and they answered him either according to their ignorance which was great for it is always darkest under the lamp, or according to their knowledge which, when they had it, was too much to be digested all of a heat by a sick man. So it fell out that between the two sorts, Greatheart got no good and an ache in his sore head to boot.

He had a month's mind to go back again to his fight against Apollyon where at the least an honest soldier did not doubt of the words that he heard: but that, by force of his wounds, could not be yet awhile. So then he lay abed and smoaked a pipe on it and put the matter fairly before a scholar of Oxford[1] that had helped him to the tobacco.

Great-heart. How do you go about to get knowledge?

Scholar. As I used to hold, by the reading of books: but, as I now perceive, by dealings with men.

Great. Alas! And I have met with no more or less than men all my life: but my knowledge is naught.

Schol. Would to God that I had an hundredth path of it, Mr. Greatheart!

Great. If either myself or my crutches can do thee any service they are both at thy command Mr. Scholar.

Schol. Nay! Nay! What I would have thee understand is that thou hast already saved me and, what is as dear to me as mine, this city of Oxford against Apollyon.

Great. It is a fair city as I have seen but, as I should think, not a new or even moderate old city. (He said this doubtingly to probe the other.)

Schol. You may hold to that Mr. Great-heart. 'Tis a very ancient city which, like diamonds or other jewels, her worth augmenteth with the ages. (And he gave him fresh fire for his pipe.)

Then said Great-heart puffing merrily: – Scholar, how wouldst thou go about to clean and strip an harquebuss or a musket?

Schol. By instruction. How else? For there are as I am told three-score separate named pieces screws and bands in her and to each its appointed place upon assemblage.

Great. How many pieces or, I should say, notable and antique places in this city, Mr. Scholar? I cannot keep fair tally of 'em.

The scholar then gave him the right number of these places with which I will not stretch your belief.

Great. In how many books is the history of them written?

Schol. Indeed I cannot guess to a near hundred or so; but I do not judge it to be any more than forty thousand books in the English tongue or maybe some few more.

Then Greatheart fetcht a heavy sigh and fell to his pipe more than ever. "I see clearly," said Greatheart, "I am like to die in ignorance."

"Not if any art of mine can save thee" said the Scholar, "for that a man who hath saved so much should be denied any knowledge of what he hath saved is unjust in the highest. What is it in chief that thou wouldst know Mr Greatheart?"

Great. Even as much as a simple man may of this great fair city where my hurts have been mended and which I would not forget in my after-travels. But I will read no forty thousand books nor yet forty, and you may hold to that Mr. Scholar.

Schol. I doubt I had been a better man if I had followed thy rule. Will one book content ye?

"So as it be a small one" said Greatheart "and inset with pictures which I may compare against the very buildings. And, I think, too, a map for we used maps in Flanders."

Scholar.   You have said right, Mr. Greatheart, and I will go about now and get it done. And I count it a singular honour as well as delight, for that love that I bear to the city and to you its saviour, that I am enjoined to this work.

So then, after a while, this book was made even as you see it now, to the end that Mr. Greatheart, while his wounds are on healing, might no more be vexed and bemused by the chance informations of chance met people upon bridges or under arches or in streets or the aisles of chapels when he would discover the history and the meaning of such places, in Oxford.

Let him take this book in his hand when he is minded to walk abroad and let him direct himself by the letters and numbers upon the map and if he read in the book he will find that each place is spoken of in order and its use and meaning and age is written down, in truth and for the love that the City bears to him.[2]

Your proofs haven't come yet.[3] Is it worth while for you to tinker this up a bit on the old O[xford] P[ress] lines?[4]

RK.

Notes
1. Fletcher.
2. The closing and signature have been cut away. The final two sentences are a PS written at the head of the letter.
3. Of Fletcher's *A Handy Guide to Oxford Specially Written for the Wounded*, Printed for the Author, Oxford, June 1915. The title page states that the "Price for the duration of the war to the public" is "One Shilling net" and that "Until the Peace the Profits of sale will be given to the Fund for supplying Tobacco to the Wounded in the 3rd Southern General Hospital."
4. RK's little sketch, playing on Part Two of *Pilgrim's Progress*, was altered and reduced (presumably by Fletcher) to appear as the preface to Fletcher's *Handy Guide*, where it reads thus:

> And I saw in my dream how Mr. Greatheart came to Oxford city, to be healed of the wounds that he had gotten in the fight against Apollyon. When he had lain a month there, tended by Christiana and Mercy and Faith and the other sisters whose names are writ in the Book of Life, when, I say, his hurts began to be on an healing, he made shift to go abroad betwixt his crutches to view that city. Now the city, as all pilgrims know, lyeth amid pleasant meadows beside delicate waters, and is all full of fair palaces, towers, and temples. Yet all these, as it seemed to Mr. Greatheart, were without plan, or name writ large upon them, whereby a stranger might know them one from other. And when he asked of those who stood in the public wayes, agape at his sad estate, how he should go about to learn of these same buildings, by whom, and when, and wherefore they were made, for a great while he gat no help. For some of the people in

their ignorance knew naught (since it is always darkest under the lamp); and other some there were, of too great knowledge, that told him how the town's history was writ fair in many score of learned books. "Alas," said Mr. Greatheart, "these I have no leasure nor liking to read, for my trade is not of books, nor have I skill of hard words." But there met him presently a man with white hair who spake very civil-ly to him thus, "Mr. Greatheart, you have saved me and this my city from Apollyon, and I should reckon it an honour if you would take this one small book that I have made for your sake. You shall find it tells a little, and, as I hope, in plaine words, of the notable things which you may view while you sojourn in our city." And herewith he proffered the small book, which the other thankfully took and thrust in his bosom; for what with the manage of his crutch he lacked an hand to hold it as he hobbled along. And the white-haired man went upon his way and Mr. Greatheart saw him no more.

To John Kipling, [6 June 1915]
ALS: University of Sussex

Bateman's / Burwash / Sussex / Sunday afternoon / 2:15. p.m.

Dear Old Man –

It seems the deuce and all of a time since you left but we are still smacking our lips over the good time that we had.[1] It *was* good! And you got the best of the weather too, for it has come off cold and raw. We are thinking of coming up to town on *Wednesday.* Do let us have a wire Wednesday morning to say if you can come up on Wednesday evening. If you can't come up we can put it off till Thursday if that is a better day for catching you.

Yesterday Mums and I took Vincent[2] to Mr. Allen's at Free Chase. He is still an arrant fool about his gears but his driving has much improved and on the whole he makes better time than Eaves did. Also, thanks to his hair being cut, he keeps his hat on his melancholy head. But it is awfully exasperating to have to watch the road every minute for fear he should take a wrong turning. Coming down, after I left you at Brown's, he made *four* mistakes – one at each main turning beginning at Elmer's End. I note that when agitated the tip of his nose gets red and his eyes begin to stick out. But, I don't despair of making him a decent chauffeur yet. I think he is an hen-pecked animal in his domestic life. At least, I should imagine this from the way in which his two daughters treat him.

Did you see in yesterday's casualty list that Allen Aitken,[3] Sir Max Aitken's brother, has been wounded at the Dardanelles?

We should most deeply appreciate a line from you to let us know how matters stand in the Irish Guards and what the prospects are of additional drafts being sent out. You see one doesn't get really important news in the papers. We expect Sir Maitland and Lady Park down here for tomorrow night from London.[4] They will be the first outside visitors that we have had for ever so long; and I expect that she may be a bit of a trial with her uncontrolled motherly emotions.

There is no domestic news to tell except that Mother's throat has developed into a bit of a cold, due to this infernal east wind, but she is getting over it. Elsie is well and making pajamas at an immense rate. There is a report that Benjie Noakes – the little chap with the spectacles – has got scarlet fever. The village has been put out of bounds for Elsie.

Yesterday we three went up to investigate that new built empty house on the top of the hill behind Keylands, with a view to seeing if it couldn't be turned into a convalescent officers hospital.[5] But it seemed to us too small for anything. It is big and showy enough outside but half of it appears to be coal-houses, W.C.'s and larders – excellent all of them but hardly giving sufficient cover for invalids.

We have no other news but we have a heart full of love each which we send to you and I am

Ever your loving
Daddo

P.S.   Did you get a new stick at Briggs'?

Notes
1.   John fell ill on 16 May, and on the 19th RK went to Warley to take John back to Bateman's, where he remained until 27 May (Rees extracts).
2.   Vincent, the new chauffeur, arrived with his family on 14 May (Rees extracts). RK called him the "pale Baptist" (to John Kipling, 10 June 1915: ALS, Sussex).
3.   Allen Aitken (1889–1959) was with the 4th Battalion of the Canadian Division. He survived the war and prospered as the manager of his brother's affairs in Canada.
4.   They were at Bateman's on June 7 and 8 (Bateman's Visitors Book). Her only child was now serving in the Black Watch.
5.   They were evidently thinking much on this possibility at the time. On 7 June they went to the War Office to offer Bateman's as a hospital; the offer was declined (CK diary, 7 June 1915).

To Henry James, 22 July 1915
ALS: Yale University

Bateman's / Burwash / Sussex / July. 22. 1915.

I saw you the other day at the Athenæum deep in talk with, I think, Curzon, so I went on: for which I'm sorry. And I'd do my best for this venture[1] but that I have got hold – or rather it's got hold of me – of some work which I can't put aside.[2] It isn't of a literary nature and will be taking all my time for some weeks to come. Otherwise, need I say it, I should have been at your command. Dear love from us both.

Ever affectionately
Rudyard Kipling.

Notes
1. James was soliciting contributions to a book edited by Edith Wharton entitled *The Book of the Homeless* (New York, 1916), published to benefit the American Hostels for Refugees and the Children of Flanders Rescue Committee. The book contained contributions from writers, painters, and composers, including James himself, Cocteau, Conrad, Hardy, Yeats, Sargent, and Stravinsky. RK's refusal was apparently misunderstood, and was resented by Mrs Wharton: see R. W. B. Lewis, *Edith Wharton: A Biography* (New York, 1975), p. 380.
2. He was about to go to France to visit the front as a correspondent: see [12 August 1915].

To Henry James, 28 July 1915
ALS: Harvard University

Brown's Hotel, / London, W. / July. 28. 1915.

We couldn't love or admire you more than we've done all these years but today's news in the *Times* makes us all very proud.[1]

You don't know what it means or what it will go on to mean not to the Empire alone but to all the world of civilization that you've thrown in your lot with them.

Ever affectionately
Rudyard

Note,
1. James's naturalization as a British subject on 26 July was announced in *The Times* of 28 July. James's stated reasons for the action are quoted thus: because of his "attachment to the country and his sympathy with it and its people" he wished "to throw his moral weight and personal allegiance, for whatever they may be worth, into the scale of the contending nation's present and future fortune". Leon Edel explains that another reason for James's taking this step was that, as an "alien", he could not inhabit his house at Rye without police permission (*Henry James: The Master, 1901–1916*, Philadelphia, 1972, p. 529).

To Edmonia Hill, 4 August 1915
ALS: Library of Congress

Brown's Hotel, / London. W. / Declaration Day. / Aug. 4. 1915

My dear Mrs. Hill

I was very grieved indeed to hear that you had been ill, and for so long as my last letter was before the war. You don't say what manner of illness it was so I am left wondering between operations (in our world today every one is operated upon) and diseases. I know however that there must be compensations when one recovers in Maryland in summer time. (I think I miss the birds and the smell of the mornings as much as anything). I haven't heard of Roland Park[1] as a specially good place for anything – as it might be Bath or Harrogate – and all my enquiries about it didn't help me. I imagined it was merely a summer resort, but I most fervently hope it will behave handsomely to you while you are getting better. The cool nights are a long way off but I don't believe your southern heat is as bad as our clammy sticky warmth.

Our world over here is a queer one – intensely interesting and quite natural. Now and again one recalls that one used to lead a different sort of life once, but those days are further away than the Pyramids; we live among troops, hospitals, refugees, French officers, Italian attachés and Russian agents, as smoothly and as unquestioningly as though we had always been what we are now, the most cosmopolitan people on earth.

My son, who has had nearly a year's service in the Irish Guards, goes out to Flanders this week.[2] So we are up in town waiting till he leaves. After that I go over to France where I expect to have a look at things before the troops settle down for the long autumn and winter campaign. Every one is busy at his or her different job – munitions, hospitals service, intelligence or whatever it may be and, being English, of course every one growls and grumbles at the top of his or her voice. As you know, the English can no more get on without grumbling than a nigger can wash dishes without singing hymns. But the Hun is not yet abreast of this fact and I fear the poor dear will be misled by his own deductions. So long as the grumbling and ostentatious pessimism goes on, one knows that things are running all right. The English are useless when they are winning for they then conceive it their duty to be conciliatory and polite. We ought to be unspeakably grateful that the issues are so clear and that the Hun has left us no loop hole to wriggle out of or back door to retreat by. His year of success (at a price) has made him very *zubberdasti*[3] so that he is now speaking out of the fullness of his heart.

Today is Declaration Day (one feels that it has existed since the birth of time) when we all go to church and renew our vow to carry on the good work. As a matter of fact our dead are enough to keep us mindful. Our losses up to date are about 350,000 (say 70,000 dead) and they have been

1. Perpignan, March 1911: standing, Lord Roberts and Kipling; seated, the Bishop of Perpignan and Lady Edwina Roberts. The Bishop was "a charming talker, a mountaineer, no mean archaeologist and an authority on Catalan poems and traditions".

2. Kipling and Sir Max Aitken at an election meeting, Ashton-under Lyne, 18 October 1912, during Aitken's campaign for re-election as a Conservative MP.

3. Kipling in 1913: the assured artist.

4. Kipling delivering a speech at the Mansion House on "national bands" to support recruiting, 27 January 1915.

5. John Kipling in the uniform of the Irish Guards, probably 1915.

6. F. Monroe, Kipling and Perceval Landon, taken near Thann, 19 August 1915, during Kipling's tour of the French front. Monroe, an officer of Scottish ancestry in the French artillery, acted as their guide in Alsace.

7. Sir Andrew Macphail in the uniform of the Canadian Army Medical Corps, *c.* 1917.

8. Kipling with Italian officers, May 1917, near Cortina d'Ampezzo.

9. Oliver Baldwin, Kipling's nephew, *c.* 1929.

spread evenly over the community so that all classes are in debt to the enemy. There is, as you say, no "glory" in the old world sense in this war. It is simply a job that has to be put through if the world is to be possible for civilized human beings hereafter. It may take another two or three years but the civilized world will do it, and do it with a thoroughness that even the Hun will admire. It isn't in the English nature to hate after the Prussian manner but we are as you might put it, a little annoyed at and wearied of, the Central Powers – and the men who make the New Armies are the people of England – a class which never before has had to go to war. Our common losses are drawing us together, nation by nation, as well as class by class and, for those who survive, the dawn of the new world will be worth seeing.

I wish I could make you realize how mutually and as a matter of course, the French and the Belgians use and occupy London and indeed all England and how the English do the same by France. It's almost that obliteration of boundaries that socialists used to dream about. *Their* slang is mixed up with our slang and ours with theirs and the music hall jokes (all the army of course goes to the music halls when it is on leave) are bilingual.

I've been too busy to write much but I've got a couple of stories coming out next month – one in the *Century* and one in the *Metropolitan* which may interest you.[4]

Yesterday I was at the opening of a club for Canadians on furlough, where we met the Premier of the Dominion and a lot of leading Canadians.[5] There is a large colony of them in London. The Dominion has done splendidly and is now keeping a permanent reserve of 50,000 men in England to fill up gaps in their own fighting line at the front. The Australians are in the Dardanelles with the New Zealanders so one only sees odd detachments of them here. The Cape lot are coming up shortly and the clubs where I lunch bristle with Indian Princes who have come over with contingents. The spectacle of a French (1) flying-corps captain tackling a Sikh Prince (2) in the *lingua-franca* of the trenches, while a French (3) Canadian officer interprets the French to an Indian (4) Army Doctor who translates it into more or less comprehensible Urdu is beautiful to behold. In spite of all that has been and of all that will come, these are good days to have lived in and I am thankful I have been permitted to see them. Forgive me for having filled this sheet with nothing but war but, you see, there is nothing else on any horizon. I wish you would write me a letter and let me really know how you are and what you do, for I am always

Yours
Rudyard Kipling.

P.S.   And yesterday I was told that George Chesney has, at last, retired from the editorship of the *Pioneer*.[6] It sounded like the upheaval of centuries of a dynasty.

Notes

1. There is a Roland Lake, a reservoir, just north of Baltimore in what is now Robert E. Lee Park; perhaps this was where Mrs Hill then was.

2. John's battalion did not leave barracks for France until 16 August. He left Bateman's for the barracks on 15 August: "He looks very straight and smart and brave and young as he turned at the top of the stairs to say 'Send my love to Dado'. In the evening the car returned bringing his kit" (Rees extracts, 15 August 1915). RK had left for France on 12 August.

3. "Zabardasti" means "Violence, force, oppression, tyranny" (Ivor Lewis, *Sahibs, Nabobs and Boxwallahs: A Dictionary of the Words of Anglo-India*, Bombay, 1991).

4. "Mary Postgate", *Century Magazine*, September 1915 (*A Diversity of Creatures*); "Sea Constables: a Tale of '15", *Metropolitan Magazine*, September 1915 (*Debits and Credits*). RK is reported as at work "on a new story, Mary Postgate", on 8 March 1915 (CK diary).

5. The Club of the Maple Leaf, Charles Street, Berkeley Square, for non-commissioned officers and men of the Canadian Expeditionary Force on furlough. CK was president of the committee of the Club; the official patrons were Earl Grey, Lord Milner, and RK (Sir Andrew Macphail, *The Medical Services* [Official History of the Canadian Forces in the Great War 1914–19], Ottawa, 1925, p. 345). On the occasion of its opening RK replied to the speech of Sir Robert Borden, the Prime Minister, thus: "Mr. Rudyard Kipling said it was extremely pleasant to know that Sir Robert Borden, with his knowledge of Canadian needs, was of opinion that the Club of the Maple Leaf promised to be useful. Like everything else in this war, it was created to fill a gap. When a man was wounded he went to a hospital and the hospital looked after him. When he was convalescent he went to a convalescent home; but in the interval between the convalescent home and his return to the front it was difficult, cruelly difficult sometimes, for a man who could not go back to his own people to find a home where he could be at ease and meet his friends. That was what, as far as possible, the club aimed to supply" (*The Times*, 4 August 1915: uncollected).

6. Chesney retired this year and returned to London as the *Pioneer's* representative: see 30 April 1886.

To Caroline and Elsie Kipling, [12 August 1915]

ALS: University of Sussex

Thursday 5 p.m. / On train between Abbeville and Amiens.[1]

Never was so curious a journey, oh my dears. In peace time, as you know, one may write days ahead for a cabin and not get it after all. But now – Landon went to the steamer while I was "baggage exempting" at the customs place at Folkestone, a formality which took me less than $1\frac{1}{2}$ minutes, and not only did he get a cabin but, as I lounged statelily outside it up comes the purser and says – "Wouldn't you like a cabin, Mr Kipling?" "They're plentiful today" says I. "Well, you see, people don't travel for pleasure these days" (are you aware that I'm writing this beautiful hand with one of L's blocks on my knee and the train swinging along at 30 miles?) Yet the appearance of the boat was tripperish in the extreme barring the uniforms of the nurses and a lot of French folk of severely businesslike (not to say Hebrew) aspect. (Here we are coming into Amiens through the tunnels, a couple of hours or so, late). Well, I was buttonholed by the Duchess of Rutland[2] outside my cabin and she told me all about a hospital that she wants to start at Hardelot[3] but the authorities, somehow I don't blame 'em, put obstacles in her light. She couldn't get nurses; she couldn't get Lord knows what all and people didn't love her. Right in the midst of this clack a man with tinted spectacles passes. She says to me "Ain't that Munter – doctor to the Queen of Sweden?"[4] As he passes she hails him and – Munter it was! Now why? Why? I fell into talk with him at once and he tells me of all his grief and sorrow to find that Sweden is so – not Pro-German but afraid of Russia – and how he has got into trouble in Sweden for his English and French leanings: and how he has dismissed himself from his Queen's service and how, but for the sad fact that our naturalization laws now insist that a man must put in twelve months continuous residence in England, he would have "already, my dear Mr Kipling, have been a British subject."

Of all which you may believe as much as I did. He was immensely curious to know where I was going and what for: but as I did not know myself of course I couldn't tell him. And I don't know that that made him any less curious. So have stirred him up I left him.[5]

Then we left the pier with a quick stealthy turn and two destroyers came out of the warm grey sea (or that was the effect of it) and fell in alongside us on either side, sort of lounging along to keep pace with our modest 22 knots. We weren't in any hurry. The Channel was full – packed with traffic – and there were certain arrangements for the discomfort of roving submarines which were very nice to watch. The only tough of abnormality were our boats slung out from the davits and a boat's crew standing by each.

Then L., who has a farseeing mind, bethought him how we should most easily land at Boulogne and spoke to Sir John Cowans[6] the Q.M.G. who was naturally looking after Princess Victoria.[7] "Come ashore with us" said Sir John, and while the rest of the passengers gathered in the smoking room for French officials to visé their passports, I talked to Princess Victoria Schleswig Holstein (you remember the passport that I misread as Lemberg Holstein). It was a funny conversation. She did the talking and except that she is all right it was curiously like Dr. Munter's. First she explained her own sentiments and the sentiments of her Mamma, and the excellencies of Louis of Battenberg[8] who "saved the nation." And she thought it cruel unfair that people should write insulting letters to her Mother. Then she enlarged on the peculiarly unfortunate position of Royalty these days. "You see, we are all cousins and relatives, and owing to our peculiar position we are more intimate with our relatives than you are with yours. We have to be because we are so limited." Come to think of it, that was true enough. But what worried her was what was to happen to them – this interconnected family – after the war. "We have talked it over and we think we can meet some of the women afterwards but the men – no – never." To which I pointed out that if we won she needn't worry about meeting the men as they would be tried for their offences. This struck her as rather a novelty. Then she wailed over the German Emperor whom she had known since a boy and "Who would ever have expected he would have done *this*." All exactly like a woman in any other walk of life explaining how her family had members who were no credit to it: and, underrunning it all, the anxious, quite natural, desire to set herself and *her* own people right with – shall we say public opinion. A conversation wholly inconceivable a year ago, and showing the keen enlightened apprehensions or rather, perceptions of modern Royalty. She was lyric about her father, and her brother's uprightness and the kindness of the Kaiser in "calling a cabinet council" to decide that the brother was not to serve on the western front.[9] Then she told me that "Daisy" the Crown Princess of Sweden[10] acted as a check on the older generation. Thus said Daisy: – "The Queen is one thing. *I* am very much the other. The Court you can believe is strictly neutral." Poor little anxious time serving court of Sweden skirmishing up and down these long passages. And so she ran on, always about her family – her family and all the great European family it was married and mixed up with, and every now and again she'd jerk in: – "But one's country must come first, mustn't it?" It opened whole new horizons to me – Royalty on the family side, desperate anxious for its pay, position and allowances.

As we came into shallow water our escort spread out and drew aside right and left of Boulogne Harbour just like two black retrievers forbidden to come into the house and we hove alongside the quay. No common gangway for *us* but a special one down which Sir J. Cowans herded the Princess, her lady in waiting etc. between rows of uniforms. And L. and I marched in the rear of that party and were free of France. True, I followed our baggage for a fleeting moment into the douane where a the sight of the exemption pass they dropped me like a hot potato. Yes, there was a *compartment* for me. Yes there were two seats at dejeuner. Yes, there was everything. And there was! I don't say it was a Royal progress because I don't know how Royalty travels and Mummy won't let me have an (extra) lady in waiting. But 'twas good enough for *my* simple needs. A good dejeuner: an hour's nap at full length after, a cup of tea and – *me voici*! I also had a careful wash *with* nailbrush on the boat.

I can't describe Boulogne, nor the country thence to Amiens because it was England. I never saw men looking so fit and well as our troops. Now and then one came across a sprinkling of French but the whole setting and background was *khaki* – jovial, tanned khaki, picked out with occasional nurses. Yes, I quite savvy why nursing is always popular. The nurse isn't always in hospital by a dam' sight.

We have passed Amiens and I think we shan't be *very* late at Paris after all. I will defer further considerations till I reach the Ritz where if there is not a brass band, milk white horses and red cloth I shall be bitterly annoyed. I sent you a wire from Boulogne, and *oh* how I wish you two were along to see the new France. While I think on it, dear love to John. I saw a sub like him, standing beside the line at Abbeville.

7:50. *Hotel Ritz.* Only an hour late after all. Got into Paris towards twilight, a flaming sky and a silhouette of black buildings. Then a taxi and a drive through Paris – always adorable, hot and still with great empty spaces – a Paris more beautiful now that you can *see* it than ever before. The station dimly lighted but full of folk and as proof that I really am here I continue on Ritz paper. But it's all so mad! The place Vendome empty, one military car outside the Ritz and about 30 names on the list of guests. Where *we* used to have tea an echoing corridor of emptiness. But the spirit of the dam place persists: and here is Landon making me change for dinner!

We have noble rooms, with a bathroom that would have delighted Delysea[11] – a profligate allowance of nickel plumbing. The price is *12 fr* per diem each. Talk of economy! Now I'll just run this into the post and go on later.

L. sends his best salaams. Dearest love to you all; and to my boy

Ever
Me!

Notes

1. RK left for the front in France with Perceval Landon on the morning of this day and returned on 26 August. The idea for the trip went back at least as far as March 1915, when CK wrote that "General French is anxious to have Rud come out to head quarters and have a look round" (To Mrs Balestier, 28 March [1915]: ALS, Dunham Papers). The trip took RK and Landon from Paris on a circular tour of the French lines from Soissons through Rheims, Verdun, Nancy, Belfort and Troyes before returning to Paris. The result was the series of articles collected as *France at War on the Frontier of Civilization*; they were first published in the *Daily Telegraph* and the *New York Sun* between 6 and 17 September 1915.
2. Violet Lindsay (d. 1937) married Henry John Brinsley Manners, 8th Duke of Rutland, in 1882. The Duchess had some reputation as a painter.
3. A small resort south of Boulogne.
4. Axel Munthe. RK had met him in Stockholm in 1907: see 16 December 1907.
5. The sentence stands thus in the MS.
6. General Sir John Cowans (1862–1921), Quartermaster-General, 1912–19.
7. Helena Victoria (1870–1948), whose mother was Helena Victoria, 3rd daughter of Queen Victoria, and whose father was Prince Christian of Schleswig-Holstein.
8. Louis of Battenberg (1854–1921), 1st Marquess of Milford Haven and Admiral of the Fleet; in 1917 he took the surname of Mountbattern. He was the son of Prince Alexander of Hesse, but came to England as a boy, was naturalised, and entered the navy as a cadet, with the patronage of Queen Victoria. At the outbreak of the war Battenberg was First Sea Lord, and it was by his decision that, on the eve of the war, the fleet was mobilized rather than being dispersed. At the end of October 1914, he yielded to the pressure of suspicion of his German origins and resigned as First Sea Lord.

9. The Princess's brother, Albert (1869–1931), had been brought up by his uncle in Germany and succeeded as Duke of Schleswig-Holstein in 1921. In the war he held a commission in the German army and served as a non-combatant.

10. Princess Margaret (1882–1920), elder daughter of the Duke of Connaught, 1st wife of the Crown Prince, afterwards Gustavus VI of Sweden. RK had met her in 1909: see 16 July 1909.

11. Alice Delysia (1889–1979), French-born actress and singer, made a hit in her first London appearance in a revue called *Odds and Ends* that opened in October 1914. One of the numbers, apparently, was "My Lady's Undress", which may account for her supposed pleasure in bathrooms.

To Caroline and Elsie Kipling, 13 August 1915
ALS: University of Sussex

> *Hôtel Ritz / Place Vendôme / Paris /* Aug. 13. 1915. 10. a.m.
> (in the rose pink bridal chamber)

A hot still day with plumps of warm rain that don't make anything cooler – just like Brown's in fact.

When we went down to dinner last night there were at least 15 persons sitting down in the vast echoing halls and we found that evening dress was *not de rigueur*. If you wear it at all, which is rare, you wear a black tie. So I jeered at Landon.

You can imagine the state to which the Ritz is fallen when I tell you that I saw one waiter playfully kick another man's behind right in the middle of the dining room – close to the serving table. They are only boys dragged in from the streets – poor and **anæmic** – and they treat the show as a sort of picnic and the seniors can't say anything. Imagine Holmes being obliged to put up with skylarking among the waiters at Bruins[1] while meals are being served! A Colonel Leroy Lewis[2] (military attaché I believe) told me that Meurice's is worse and the Continental worst of all. I see the Hotel Brighton is still in existence and has quite half a dozen guests. Maurice Baring[3] sat at the next inhabited table to us. He is in the Flying Corps and will fly back today to his job – whatever it is. He has just come up from Italy.

At the end of dinner there came up, the clean well groomed black moustached Ridgeley Carter,[4] once councillor of the American Embassy in London, and now a prominent member of Morgan's bank. He was very full of talk about the situation in general and, of course, about the attitude of the U.S. and our good Monsieur Wilson whose position (Lord! how wearied I am of hearing it) is "very difficult." I preserved, as L. can testify, a disinterested silence, even when Carter spoke of the Lusitania business[5] as "the

Lusitania accident – or tragedy – or – or whatever you like to call it." *You* wouldn't have been quiet. Here Landon interposes. He says that Carter did *not* use the word "tragedy" but pulled up for an instant after the word "accident" and then went on with a rush – "or – or whatever you like to call it." Carter also added that *if* Congress had been in session at the time of the *Lusitania* the U.S. "would have gone to war." He further added that *if* another American life were lost, the U.S. *would* go to war. 'Twasn't any of my business to affirm or to deny so I said nowt. Then to bed, after Colonel Leroy Lewis had given us a long aperçu of the present political situation in France which he says is full of intrigues among generals and politicians, – very much like our own situations, plus a certain French savageness.

I took great care with my unpackings and repackings and locking ups: and I nearly wept over the loving care and forethought that showed in every fold and package of my baggage. Everything that the mind and body of man could think of had been arranged for. Even I, can't go wrong. And this morning at 9: a.m. came the inevitable and polite French postman with a registered letter to sign for, from Fabulet with cheques for Frs. 2250* now safely locked up. This represents solid wealth, me love. I thought you'd like to know that I have it.[6]

When we are dressed (we've finished our dejeuner of horse shoe rolls and coffee in our connecting suite) we go out to the Embassy to see Lord Granville:[7] then Pindot lunches with us; and in the afternoon I shall see C[lemenceau]. I hope. He is as busy as the devil in a gale of wind by all that I hear. I gather that Julia[8] is still running her hospital at Compiègne: but I live in hope that she will be too busy to come into Paris.

As soon as Ponsot lets us know what we are going to do and for how long we shall be out I will communicate with you. Have just told the manager to cash Fabulet's cheque and deposit the money in the safe. Am clean, and washed and well dressed and always your lover. 11:10 a.m.

2.30. p.m. Well, at 11:30 we went to the Ambassador's whereby hangs a long and most interesting tale which I will tell you when we return. It would take pages to record.

At 12:30 came Monsieur Ponsot whom we lunched and who stayed two smitten hours. He tells that on Sunday morning Captain Puaux[9] (in plainer type PUAUX – pronounced Pew-oh!) will take us under his wing and we shall embark on the following itinerary – just Landon, Puaux and me: –

(Sun) 1st day: to Soissons via Compiègne: dine and sleep at Gonchery
(Mon) 2nd Day – to Rheims and go on to Verdun via Clermont en Argonne
(Tues) 3rd Day Toul, Nancy, Gerbevilliers and Remiremont
Wed.
Thurs 4th and 5th day. Alsace with General Sérree[10] – *not* Sarrail.[11]

From Alsace we can return to Paris in one day, though it is more likely that we shall stop a night on our road back.[12] So you see the whole thing is inside of one week and I gather that we are to be most tenderly shepherded. With only three men in the motor there ought to be ample room for baggage etc.:[13] – I shall write you the diary of my adventures and I think it will be possible to send the letters off each day in the military post bags. If it isn't then I'll post 'em all from Paris. I shall try, all being well, to get back by or on Monday next. If I get back to Paris on Saturday, I shall come on by the Sunday train but, of course, that all depends on circumstances.

It's gone a good deal cooler just now and I am now off to see if I can catch Clemenceau.

The Bird will be pleased to know that the little dog-shop in the Rue Castiglione is in full blast – Pekinese on cushions as usual. Many shops are shut but never – oh never – have I seen such attractive bargains in marqueterie and general fribbles. I feel it my duty to the Lighter side of France to bring back a ring or some small jewel.

And here am I, at the end of my paper. Dearest love to you all.

Ever
Me.

P.S.   Just met young Brassey[14] whom I last saw at Taplow[15] – spending a few days in Paris.

Friday
7: p.m:
And so back from that amazing human explosive Clemenceau who on the instant of my coming held forth without break and so continued for forty coruscating minutes. All truth too – backed up with very real power and the widest knowledge. I should say from what he said that *their* government is the twin of ours, mentally and spiritually – same incompetence, same lawyers explanations; same complete inability for any one to admit that they were wrong in any particular, and the same furious intrigues of, apparently, every one against every one else. I can't write it to you, for reasons, but the political intrigue is balanced by the military. On one point – the vital one – however there is complete agreement – that the war is to be won. I heard nothing, in all the torrent of denunciation, that even hinted at the existence of a peace party anywhere in the length and breadth of the land. They are free from that at any rate.

Otherwise it seems that the ministry made absolutely and surely every mistake that ours did – thought that the war would be short; thought that, if anything, France had more cannon than she needed and, in that belief, countermanded orders for guns: Then … but you can read the whole tale in the English tongue *except* that this French ministry never had any illusions about the supreme importance of making cotton contraband[16] (we all see our neighbours' faults with immense clarity).

Then he branched off into our (the Allies) diplomacy and the immense hash we had made, specially on the part of Russia, in our dealings with the Balkan states. He still sticks to the notion that it would be the best of good things to get Japan to send an Army through Russia and he tells me (told me repeatedly) that the German people, *qua* people, were fed up with the war of continuous victories "always in the same place." Somehow when one is on the same piece of land as one's enemy one seems to get more information about his *morale* than one does in an island. He was full of little touches describing the Germans and what they think. He assured me that they (the people of the Empire) have a growing horror at the thought of another winter campaign – a horror that it would need a lot of victories to counteract. He has no earthly doubt of the issue but – munitions, munitions was his cry throughout. I talked French.

And talking of talking French, Mons. Ponsot at lunch said to me: "If I had known you talked French so well Mr Kipling, I would have given you a most interesting French captain, the son of Berthillon[17] of the fingerprints, (measurement of criminals etc.) to take care of you." There. I hope you are pleased with my humble endeavours.

And now I have come in to find that Landon has gone out and since I have only an old Scribner and a St Nicholas, and since, also, I love you, I am filling in the hour between lights by filling in this little sheet to go out at eight o'clock.

I wish I could give you any idea of this changed Paris with the framework of the streets visible, so to speak, and the girls walking (beautifully dressed with the cheapest means) with the wounded soldiers, and the widows with their long black streamers and all the cheery, bright eyed resolution and smiling patience of it all! Be *very* proud of your France, my wife and my daughter. It makes me humble.

Dearest love.

Me.

What do you think of a general who, in order to find out if any one is intriguing against him orders *all* the officers letters to be opened by the censor? *All* includes his brother generals. Hence a flurry in the camp.

---

*two thousand, two hundred and fifty francs, which I acknowledged to Fabulet 176 Rue de Charelles Rouen.

Notes
1. Thus in MS, presumably for Brown's Hotel.
2. Colonel Herman Le Roy-Lewis (1860–1931); he served in the Boer War and commanded the Hampshire Imperial Yeomanry, 1902–7; 1st South-Western Mounted Brigade, 1908–13. He was now military attaché in Paris.

3. Maurice Baring (1874–1945), poet, playwright, novelist and journalist, served throughout the war with the Royal Flying Corps; he had just been assigned to the staff of Colonel Hugh Trenchard, commander of the Corps.
4. Ridgeley Carter (1864–1944) served in the American Embassy in London from 1894 to 1909; he joined J. P. Morgan and Co. in 1912 and was a partner in the French branch of the firm from 1914.
5. The Cunard liner *Lusitania* was sunk off the coast of Ireland by a German submarine on 7 May 1915 with large loss of life, including 128 Americans.
6. Perhaps this was money to RK's credit from Fabulet's translations into the French.
7. Granville George Leveson Gower (1872–1939), 3rd Earl Granville, was Councillor of Embassy at Paris, 1913–17.
8. Mrs Depew.
9. Their guide on the tour, "a charming boy of 30 with medaille militaire" (RK to CK and Elsie, [14 August 1915]: ALS, Sussex]). He was probably René Puaux, who had written a series of articles on the British army in France, collected as *L'Armée anglaise sur le continent (août 1914–août 1915)* (Paris, 1916). Puaux translated RK's "Some Aspects of Travel" as "Des voyages et des parfums" (Paris, 1917), and RK's "France" as "Poème à la France" (Paris, 1917). He also translated *Le pèlerinage du roi d'Angleterre aux cimitières du front et le poème de Rudyard Kipling* (Paris, 1922).
10. General Serret, governor of Alsace: this was the general of whom RK wrote: "But for his medals, there was nothing in the Governor to show that he was not English. He might have come straight from an Indian frontier command" (*France at War*, New York, 1916, pp. 79–80).
11. General Maurice Sarrail (1856–1929), commanded the 3rd Army at the first battle of the Marne and was commander at Salonika, 1916–17.
12. This was approximately the itinerary followed, though after the second day it was considerably altered in details.
13. In fact they travelled in two cars: a Renault limousine for RK and Landon, and a Mercedes to follow with the baggage.
14. Probably Captain Cecil Henry Brassey (1896–1949), son of Sir H. L. C. Brassey, 1st Baronet; young Brassey was at Eton, 1910–14, and was now in the Life Guards.
15. Taplow Court, Bucks., the home of Lord Desborough.
16. As late as January 1915 the British had not yet declared cotton to be contraband.
17. Alphonse Berthillon (1853–1914), inventor of a system of anthropometry applied to the identification of criminals; it included the "mug shots" that are still a standard item in police records.

To Caroline and Elsie Kipling, 15 August [1915]

ALS: University of Sussex

Aug. 15. 8.40 p.m. a villa (!) in Jonchéry

Very most dears –

I suppose this, as the first, will be the most wonderful day of all.[1] Anyhow I haven't words to describe it. We left Paris at 8.30 this morn in the grey blue Army Limousine closely followed by the baggage car, the Mercedes that I spoke of in my last letter. There was Landon, Captain Puaux and I and a military chauffeur and an attendant of a military nature. We took the north Road to Senlis (see Cartes Taride) and there, not more than 40 kils from Paris we saw the first evidence of houses that had been burned by the Germans a year ago. It was a pale white street of pale white stone and the houses were smashed about and burned, several scores of 'em – and on some the grass of a twelvemonth was sprouting between the stones. Behind one heap of wreckage lived the Veuve Simon who sold drinks and tobacco. L. invested in 5fr worth of Caporal cigarettes for the Army of France – blue and yellow Caporal. The Veuve served us with graciousness and we sped on and on, over pave and lack of pave with nothing on earth to bar our progress – no troops, no horses, no nothing except a few peasants working in the fields – we passed Compiegne and a little while after plunged into an adorable wooded valley with the chateau of a Banker called Pilly-Wille (!) gleaming through the trees. Here was our lunch place. Then, after a few turnings and twistings of the road I became aware that troops were hutted in huts of branches all alongside the road and in the park and as we got under the shadow of beautiful trees the huts sank into the ground and became more of the nature of dug outs. We were received on the chateau steps – it overlooked a heavenly valley and was surrounded on two sides by a platform of stone rather reminding me of Ewhurst[2] – in front of it stretched a heavily wooded park with [sketch of château] drives like Maresfield[3] – The General who was called Nivelle[4] told me that *his* mother was English but he didn't talk good English for all that. He was a charming man of gentle manners. We arrived at 12:15. Lunch wouldn't be till 1: would I come out and "see something." So we came. Got into the auto and went perhaps half a mile down a stately avenue with trees on either hand so close that no grass grew there and in the shadow of the trees roofed in with leafy roofs were a battery of guns. On the other side of the avenue more dug outs and bomb-proofs (I hope Pilly Wille the Banker will like what they've done with his park) all steeped in a sort of gloomy brown light for the day was a little wet.

Then we came to a tree – to a huge tree – an acacia, L. says, about 60 feet high with a ladder going up to a platform in the top branches. Up climbed the general, up went me and the rest of us – up and up and when we got to the top platform lo there was another! At last we came to a crow's nest in the tree, with a map under a little roofed table, a telephone and a man or two. The tree grew overhanging the outer wall of the chateau park, as it might have been the park of Anel. *Then* looking through the leaves and the branches – I saw the whole countryside falling away for miles in a long yellow slope (the Boshes had used gas weeks ago and the grass had perished for three or four miles. 'Twas like a stretch of lonely African veldt thus [sketch of desiccated landscape]. The things like chewed toothpicks were all that was left of some trees round a ruined farm of which not one brick was left on another. There was another set of buildings nearer apparently sound but when one looked twice one saw they were mere shells. And regularly all along the line of horizon, three miles away, the shells from our guns in the discreet park raised clouds of white smoke precisely like the spouts of waves up a breakwater in a storm. These were varied by bigger pillars of white smoke where a trench-torpedo was bursting. All slow deliberate and methodical in this vast emptiness: and from time to time the whirr of German shells spinning over us and ours spinning out past them. It was immensely, unspeakably wonderful – but, as I said, all so like the breaking of waves against rocks. I thought I heard one or two different noted explosions behind us but 'twasn't my job to ask. I learned later from a fascinating officer in charge of the guns that 3 had fallen in the park. So there we all stood on the platform watching this solemn affair where no men were visible, and across the yellowed grass. Then we climbed down the ladder (which I loathed but I didn't bungle) and were taken to a set of enormous limestone caves or quarries where troops were resting. The light and shade effects of the blue clad troops in the queer irregular caverns and the shafts of light were indescribable. And there too, in little rock cut kennels lined with straw lived the various sentinel dogs who are trained to go out with the pickets and the General said to me with a wave of the hand: – "*all* these men know your books". I smiled politely. He turned on the nearest group and asked 'em! "*Yes* oh yes" said they. "Specially the Jungle books!" He took me elsewhere and sentries with their rifles told me the same thing. Weird noncoms in dugouts echoed it till I nearly thought it was a put up job of the General. But 'twasn't. 'Twas true!

(The fuss about this tour is there's too much dam R.K. in it. I have to lead all the processions).

Well, after more wandering in dug outs back to lunch – a devil and all of a lunch of 15 covers: crayfish: filletted beef etc. – we got away and a new officer who seemed to know everything I'd written tucked me into a car of his own and led a procession (of 3 cars) towards Soissons (Soissons).[5] The Germans were commanding the main road so we had to dodge and duck through side lanes to reach it and in some places there were screens of boughs to hide the road. We were about 3 mile or kilometers from 'em. Presently we entered a *dead* town – with grass growing in the streets; and the gaunt ribs of the wrecked cathedral high in air. The silence was *very* curious. One heard a footfall a long way off and perhaps one saw a – woman or a girl, or the face of a woman out of a window. *I* thought that somewhere in the silence I heard voices singing, but said naught. And so like people in a church, we four and another officer, moved deeper into the city of wrecked houses, and fallen rubbish, and ever growing weeds, towards the dead and ghostly cathedral. It dawned on me after a bit by reason of sounds in the air that Soissons was being shelled. "Oh yes she gets it every day" said an officer. Like the other place, it was slow and methodical – rather like Devils ringing gongs. And the officers told me where the shells were going, or were intended to go. We came nearer to the Cathedral and again I thought I heard song. "Nonsense!" said the officer with me. But he forgot Sunday and he forgot France. In a little only partially wrecked side chapel some 100 people, mainly women, were gathered at service – kneeling before the altar and singing not knowing whether or when the next shell might lift 'em all out of the world. "*C'est stupefiant*" said one officer but I saw his eyes and Puaux's fill with tears. I have no words to describe those lines of pale faces in that unreal light through the window or the effect of that valiant little trickle of voices (and the priest's deep bass) against the silence. There used to be 20,000 people in Soissons. There are now perhaps 600 and of these a quarter were in the Chapel. We went into the main Cathedral – one side was half torn out, the high altar was protected with sandbags and the statues buried in 'em. And then we came away through the silence; dodged past the end of a street that the Germans can see down and ducked and dodged our way back. After an hour and a half we reached this place stopping en route to drink orangeade at a peaceful dreaming chateau whose proprietor is now chauffeur to some general. There were a lot of military men here and they were all polite and wanted us to do a heap more but we politely declined and fled after dinner to our quarters – three rooms in an echoing tiny villa where an old woman and her daughter look after us. The French are a great people but they want one to do too much. Landon and I are eloquent on this head. He sits opposite me with a map and a compass laboriously writing out his day's work. He says he has so many things to report that he'll write himself but that my aimi-ability (you told me to be nice) makes it impossible almost for us to get any time to ourselves at all. He sends his salaams and hopes all is well with John, any and all of whose stories he likes much. (It isn't yet 10 o'clock and I'm going to bed. Brekker at 9 tomorrow.) A glorious day but I don't like this incessant talking of French and this everlasting R.K. jaw who is ever and ever and ever

Your own Boy

Notes

1. The events of this day are written up in "On the Frontier of Civilization", the first chapter of *France at War*.
2. Village in West Sussex, about eight miles east of Burwash.
3. Village in East Sussex, two miles north of Uckfield.
4. Robert-Georges Nivelle (1856–1924) after early successes as an artillery comman-der was promoted commander of the Armies of the North and North East. On the disastrous failure of his offensive in the 2nd Battle of the Aisne, 1917, he was relieved of his command. A. J. P. Taylor says, in contradiction of RK's judgement, that Nivelle "spoke good English" (*English History 1914–1945*, Oxford, 1965, p. 80).
5. RK's first attempt at the word is not quite clear.

To Caroline and Elsie Kipling, [16]–17 August 1915

ALS: University of Sussex

C[ercle] M[ilitaire] V[erdun] Verdun, le 15th August / 6.15. p.m.

I have just despatched a couple of p.c.'s[1] to you on the off chance that they will get away tonight. This is a military club and the attendance is far from military.

I had a splendid night last night at Jonchery in a soft and flealess bed in deep peace from 11 till 7 when I was waked by the tramp of troops, turned round and went to sleep again till 8:30. An old woman and a fat young 'un ran the villa. The W.C. was reached through a bedroom – uninhabited I hope. There was a little prim French garden outside. When we asked for hot water they brought us a wee little potful just off the fire. The lamps were rather unwell and unhappy. Your electric torch saved me.

We had a little breakfast at nine and set off with Puaux and the indefatigable other officer whose name is Heilbrunner to have a look at a battery on a hill not far from Rheims.[2] It was more like the flat bit at the back of the hill at Vernet (where we used to go round the corner towards the cascade des Anglais) than anything else. Just scrubby pines and a steep hill and the wreck of an old stone wind mill. Finally, we came to a tunnel under an embankment and then (tho' we didn't realize it) we were all among the craftily hidden guns. They lived under bombproofs and by the sides of caverns and, apparently, *in* caverns half natural, half artificial and their ammunition which seemed inexhaustible was stacked in cellars beside them, and all their officers were enthusiasts. Gunners always are. But it was a dull grey day, very bad for shooting and, as they explained almost apologetically, the trenches in front of 'em were held by Saxons who "did very little." But – happy thought! – wouldn't I like to see a round fired. So they fired it at the silent Saxon at 4000 yards and I was amazed at the speed and simplicity of the 75. No apparent mechanism. One sharp turn of the breech to load – another turn ejects the spent case like a rifle cartridge. The discharge is a ringing bark. They were all very keen artillerests and apparently *all* (down to the corporal of the gun) had read the Jungle Book. You've no idea how ridiculous it is. I'll tell you tales afterwards that even *you*, darling, won't believe.

Then we went to look at the trenches from an operation tower – all most wonderfully hid and neat. The picture that one saw through the long oblong slit differed very little from the one I saw from the top of the tree at Offremont yesterday except that there were a few hills in it – and there was nothing doing. The Saxons were dumb; except for my single shot the French were silent – the line of the German trenches ran in an irregular curved line of whitish dirt about 2000 yards away and evidently they were not at all on the job. Somewhere, a long long way off, a single big gun lifted up its voice and grunted like a buffalo but nothing came our way. All about, there were neat pits in the earth about 3 foot deep and six across–some were quite new: others had poppies growing in them – the scars of old shells. The Germans seem to delight in placing them with almost mathematical accuracy – four at a time.

Then we left that Gallery, the keen clean handsome brown commandant and the bearded and scientific captain and ran on to Rheims which was only eight or ten miles away. Rheims held 100,000 people before the war; now there are less than 2000. At first one notices nothing in particular except the singular loudness of the few wheels that are moving in the echoing street. But when one comes out into the Cathedral Square and sees the shame of all the world fronting you – it's different. My dears they not only shelled the cathedral but they dropped incendiary shell on it and half the front is literally roasted to a horrible flesh colour. The towers are smashed, the windows most of 'em in little bits of tinkling lacery, the gargoyles maimed and defaced – the whole thing looks like some wretched mutilated human being. Inside, there is nothing. The stalls of the choir have been burned out; huge gaps ripped in the side of the chancel, the floor is covered with fine debris of splintered glass and pounded stone, mixed with fragments of shell, two immense old oak doors opening from the sacristy into the cathedral have been *bent* like two pieces of paper and jammed in that position by the mere wind of a shell that fell in the archbishop's garden – the archbishop's palace is a mound of ruins; and (to crown the infamy) for hundreds of yards all round the cathedral the houses are mere roofless facades – *whole* streets of 'em! That was done when the Boshes were getting their range.

Birds flew in and out of the windows making a noise like the whirring of a shell – the floor tiles were all bruised and broken with rubbish that had fallen from the roof; the great buttresses outside were brushed, as it were, with scrapes of shrapnel; there were floor mats on the wrecked high altar and the first thing that the guardian said to us was: – "Put on your hats Messieurs, this is not consecrated. The Archbishop has declared it desecrated." But – you remember Joan's niche where we burned our candles.[3] The status is gone indeed but there is a tricolour in its place and below it are the spiked candlesticks on which we fixed our candles. I can't tell you how I felt at the savagery and the brutality of it all. None the less, if the French Govt would only take steps and fetch them down and pack them up much of the window glass could be saved. L. and I were both sure of this. We went away, sick and heavy at heart and left that poor blinded burned horror slow in the great stillness. Rheims was not being bombarded that day on account I suppose of the fog. (*Nota*. Joan's statue on horseback in the square is *untouched* save for one splinter of shell which has bent the tip of the sword scabbard).

At Rheims the indefatigable Heilbrunner left us. We liked him but we were not sad for he was so dam' energetic, and Puaux and L. and I, sped in grateful silence in the Limousine to Epernay – G'd Hotel de l'Europe – where we made an adorable lunch quite at our ease and undisturbed by Generals.

(At this point L. interposes with a mass of misrepresentations which he calls a letter to you. Believe none of 'em. I am the model and pink of tact. *I* talk French to Generals. *He* can't. He lurks in the background and begs me ask for quiet dinners and time to do some work in. There isn't much. But we are having the time of our lives. Landon has lost his London belly. I walk miles and don't feel 'em. And *how* we laugh! To resume!)

After Epernay we went through alternate rain and fair toward Chalons; and that was perhaps the first time that we came among any large mass of French transport. There were a number of motor ambulances going in the same direction as ourselves. We proudly overtook and passed 'em at French rates of speed and in the midst of our pride the Mercedes punctured and we in the Limousine had to stop for her. 'Twas on the edge of a village which Bosches had burned and pounded to pieces months ago and the few little bits of white walls that remained were covered with the scrawled names and initials of soldiers who had billetted there. One house was merely a blur on the ground but its garden had gone on blooming quite civilizedly and made a brilliant patch of colour in the desolation. All along these parts we met troops of all kinds and occasionally weird motors hitched to big guns and ammunition lorries. The country side was cultivated to the last inch and over all there was a settled peace and calm wildly unlike any idea of war. The faces of the soldiers were throughout hale and bronzed and undisturbed, and the traffic managed itself without any trace of confusion. *That* impressed me throughout. It is a people settled down to war and all that war may bring.

Then on and on eastward till the country rose into little hills and villages atop – what one would call an eminently "touristical" land in peace time. We were nearing the Argonne where there is fighting. Occasionally a village showed, at one end or in the middle of the street, what the Bosches had done to it in their movement northward last year: and often one saw cemeteries of little crosses beside railway lines. Then one saw hospitals d'evacuation (clearing hospitals) in the villages – right *on* the main street of canvas and iron added to existing houses.

The rain cleared off and it became a lovely evening – or rather late afternoon and we entered the village of which I have sent you postcards. It was a hill village, built against a tree covered little mountain which in turn was crowned by a church – it reminded me something of Vernet, and it commanded a gigantic view across a fat plain towards a world of low wooded hills – say, an horizon of 70 miles from edge to edge. The winding road seemed to end in pale pinkish ruins blocks of shivered masonry and brickwork against the Italian evening sky; a flight of stone steps climbed up and up the hillside on the right through a desolation as complete as Les Baux (for one end of the village had been Bosched) and ended in a church bowered in tall trees. All the landscape across the plain shook with noise – not combined thunders of battle but single uproars of gigantic guns that raised plumes of smoke visible for ten miles. That showed where the Crown Prince[4] is fighting and has been fighting for weeks to get through and save his wretched life and his hope for the Throne. He has already lost 60,000 men there and God knows how many more in the same vicinity months before! And we looked at a landscape as lovely as anything in an illuminated mediæval book; and we saw it all torn and harried by the shells and the mines under this heavenly evening light. An observation balloon rose up a mile or so away; then an æroplane began to skirmish about like an uneasy dragon-fly. The balloon was at work taking ranges etc.; the æroplane was merely training some beginner! And while I looked and marvelled an unseen military band began to play a waltz up the hill side!!! (la suite a prochaine numero).

Aug 17. / 9. a.m. / (letter continues)

The music seemed to put the final touch of unreality on it all. We climbed the stone steps and found a military band playing to men in billets. They stood in a ring just outside a wrecked church. Then we climbed through woods by paths exactly like Vernet to a little group of soldiers, officers and a priest or two who were watching the monstrous battle across the plain and they identified the isolated roars of the guns saying: – "That's us! That's the Bosches" and so on; and all the while the peace and glory of the evening would have made you weep. Clermont in Argonne used to be a famous tourist spot. I don't wonder.

We came across a Lieutenant of the local Garde there who spoke a fierce and amazing English with only one gender – feminine. He helped me to buy some postcards at a booth in the bottom of the ruins and just as we were moving on he put his head in at the auto window and said: – "She play – for *you* – Tipperary!" And the Band played Tipperary. I make haste to tell this tale ere Landon puts in his version. Think you that France insists *I* am the author of Tipperary? Then to Verdun – which is like a tiny Florence inside a fort and after to dinner with a great and a most fascinating old General – a splendid dinner where we met a French staff officer who, I thought, was an Irishman. His mother was Canadian. At 9 o'clock (for we insist on keeping good hours) we returned to Verdun under the wheeling beams of French and Bosch searchlights. It looked as tho' the Bosch were all round us. My room at the Military Club overlooked a river that roared over a weir more loudly than the Cady of Vernet (a heavenly little peaceful view) and as long as I was awake (which was several minutes) I heard the clamour of big guns among the hills mixed with the roar of the river. But the Bosch leave Verdun alone because Verdun spanks Metz with big fat cannon if they drop shells here. The view from the front of the club was of fat barges in a canal and adorable houses all alongside.

We left the hotel at 9.30 for a review – for an unprecedented Review – Kitchener himself reviewing (with Joffre!) a French Army Corps – in a vast rolling landscape of reaped fields and bare downs. We reached the Army Corps in about an hour from Verdun. It lay by the side of the road in a sort of pale blue drift like myosotis – 50,000 veterans of this part of the world – men who had been at it for months, with a trifle of 150 cannon or so at their heels and a mass of cavalry. But *why* K should be reviewing armies in this part of the world and by what strange coincidence I should be at the place is wrapt in mystery. I don't fathom it at all.[5] It was decided upon only 4 days ago, they tell me, and it may portend that we shall send troops (English) to various places along the French line to show 'em. K turned up in an auto, with Wilson[6] and Fitzgerald[7] – walked all along the dull blue line while the band played God Save the King and The Marseillaise – and all the while 3 or 4 æroplanes swished over head and did stunts. Then he moved off about a mile in the auto and the whole line defiled before him in columns – an awfully impressive sight. They began one side of the plain and melted away on the other – this brooding dull blue cloud of men that at half a mile looked like the dull horizon itself. There were about a dozen peasant women staring at it and L. and I. The rest was *all* military and by what I can make out not a soul knew of the affair. It took about an hour and a quarter and moved me almost to tears. Puaux, my nice captain, frankly wiped his eyes. He hadn't seen an army before except in trenches. Then we came away; had lunch at Bar le duc; had a punctured tyre by the roadside during which I wrote you half this letter and at 3.30 p.m. behold us in Nancy whence we do not stir till tomorrow. We want to collect our impressions.

I wrote a line to John at Le Havre before I left Verdun this morn;[8] and had it expressed and passed by the military so he ought to get it without delay –

(5: p.m.)

Nancy is the deuce and all of a fine town; with more life in it that Paris. L. and I have just come in from a walk during which he found a glorified and quite logical and refined Harrods where they sell everything from cutlery to pots of honey – an enormous place. He bought a book; I a pirated translation of Naulakha:[9] also a clothes brush. Then we took a fiacre to the Cathedral which was the vilest shock we have yet sustained. I stayed outside but L. went in which he said was AWFUL. We are now discussing a glass of most mild cold beer and shall go up to our rooms in a little while and "collect our impressions." I fancy that means a nap.

The Grand Hotel sits in an immense square which is everywhere reached through bronze and gilt gates.[10] It was the first town which William proposed to enter as a conqueror: the women are very pretty; the shops are *very* good and the display of vittles makes one look forward to a good dinner.

One enjoys one's meals on the road in spite of the luxury in which one travels. And now, my love, I'll end for a little. Up to date this is what I have done.

Sunday – Battery at Offremont, lunched with general and bombardment of Soissons and inspection of a regiment of Moroccan troops (I forgot to put that in). Slept at Jonchery dined with General.

Monday – Another Battery at Martin Vevers; and Rheims. No bombardment. Slept at Verdun. Dined with General Herr![11] (He's an Alsatian).

Tuesday. Kitchener's Review. Verdun to Nancy at about 70 m.p.h. and shall dine and sleep at Nancy *without* generals.

Dearest love
Your Boy

Notes
1. They are views of the ruined village of Clermont-en-Argonne (Sussex).
2. The events of this day of the tour appear in "The Nation's Spirit and a New Inheritance", and "Battle Spectacle and a Review", chapters 2 and 3 of *France at War.*
3. They were in Rheims on 28 and 29 March 1913 (Motor Tours).
4. William (1882–1951), eldest child of the Emperor William II, was at this time nominally in charge of the German operations against Verdun.
5. Kitchener was there to hear Joffre's arguments to the reluctant English for a major assault on the German lines in the West in view of the failure of the Dardanelles campaign and the weakness of the Russians. Kitchener finally assented, and one of the results was the battle of Loos, in which John Kipling was killed.
6. General Sir Henry Wilson (1864–1922), the leading sponsor of Franco-British military cooperation and now the chief liaison officer with French headquarters. He was later made Chief of the Imperial General Staff and promoted to Field Marshal.
7. Kitchener's ADC: see [17 February 1913].
8. The letter (ALS, Sussex) appears in Gilbert, *O Beloved Kids*, pp. 195–6.
9. Perhaps the translation by Mme Charles Laurent, Paris, 1900. There are two copies of this in RK's collection of his own works, now in the British Library.
10. The Place Stanislaus.
11. Frédéric-Georges Herr (1855–1932): he had just taken over as commander of the fortified region of Verdun.

To Caroline Kipling, [20] August 1915[1]
ALS: University of Sussex

Grand Hotel St.-Laurent / Troyes / (by motor from Belfort) / Friday. Aug. 21.

Yesterday, O my love, was the only day on which I did not send a letter. But yesterday was a somewhat full day.[2] It began at 6.a.m. (coffee and rolls in the adorably quaint villa among the wooded hills of Alsace). I don't say where. Then at 7: a.m. we started in motors. The Limousine and the Mercedes trecked into the hills up a hill road *precisely* like the Himalayas till the Limousine (I don't blame her) stuck in the mud and the Mercedes driven by a devildriver who had had charge of six cars in Connecticut (!) and who I imagine was a road racer, came up and took us aboard with Captain Puaux and young Monroe (the officer detailed to look after us through this section. He (Monroe) came of an ancient Scots family about the time of Louis XIV. Sir Hector Monroe[3] is his clan head. He is a joyous youth of a gunner and his

English is as vile as his heart and soul are good. He *looks* as Scotch as Scotch and wears the *biretta* of the Alpinists). Well, what happened after that don't much matter except that we, after a while, stopped to look at a battery of mountain guns; got out and walked under the gloom of many trees till we came to a place like a tea garden full of little chalets with fantastic names on the steep hill side. Thence we got into the communication trenches and walked and walked *and* walked, till we met a fatherly and motherly Colonel who took us into the first line trenches which are 7. or to be exact $7\frac{1}{2}$ metres (say the length of a cricket pitch from the Germans). They were Bavarians and had been carefully attended to the night before with the result that they were *quite* tame and I had peeps at 'em through loopholes blocked with plugs. The Colonel pulled the plugs and bade me look. I saw green sandbags in a wilderness of tree trunks and stones and no Bavarians saw me. Our men were at dinner. The trenches were beautifully clean and kept like a museum. There was no smell save the smell of cooking. There was no noise because we were so close and – nothing whatever happened! It might have been luck or it might have been good management but I assure you that you and Elsie might have taken that walk with me (I'm glad you didn't). When we came away Puouaux drew his well trained diplomatic breath and murmured – "I am happier than I were when you was coming up." We got back to our village at 12. and had a divine lunch. At 4:30 we went to the town of Thann about 5 miles away. "Now this" said Landon "is *really* dangerous." The Germans are in the habit of shelling Thann in their leisure moments. It's a beautiful Alsatian town and well worth the defiling but the German was *not* shelling that day and it was deep peace and silence. We had an amazing tea with an old gentleman in a 200 year old house; the cellars of which were fitted as hospitals and refuges. Upstairs, grace, gaiety, macaroon cake, a pretty hostess and handmaid in Alsatian dress – downstairs, iodoform, beds, operating tables etc. etc. The cellars were about the size of a church crypt. A more marvellous contrast you couldn't conceive.

Then to dinner with no – not the General but a Colonel almost next door to our villa en [   ].[4] This morn at seven we went to Belfort along a road that the Germans usually shelled (but they did not!) We lunched at Vezoul (as good a lunch as Vezelay!)[5] and Captain Puaux who naturally wanted to get back to his wife, urged us along the road to Troyes. We have motored for 9 hours. Hence the vileness of my fist. We are now in the peace and luxury of Troyes. I am sending you a wire tomorrow (it can't be sent tonight as the officials are away) to ask you to send your news to the Hotel Brighton on Sunday. I have got to see Joffre (he wants to see me!) at Head Quarters before I can get away, which I hope to do on Tuesday and if luck holds to get to Bateman's on Tuesday afternoon. I have lived *very* many years and have oceans to tell. I am writing another line to John.[6] Tomorrow I will try to spend in peace (if Generals will let me alone) and get abreast of my work. I hope to get to Paris Sunday morn.

All my heart's love to my two dearest ones. I am wearied with motoring but otherwise in splendid fettle.

Ever your
Boy.

Please excuse fist: but nine hours in a car make one's hand jerky.

Notes
1. RK has misdated the letter: Friday was 20, not 21, August. The letter is endorsed in CK's hand as "Aug 20th".
2. The events of 19 August appear in "Life in Trenches on the Mountain Side", ch. 5 of *France at War*.
3. Sir Hector Munro of Foulis (1849–1935), 11th Baronet, was honorary colonel, 3rd Seaforth Highlanders, Lord-Lieutenant of Ross and Cromarty, and an ADC to King George V.
4. Word illegible.
5. 27 March 1913, on their motor tour across France with Landon following their trip to Egypt: "Hotel de la Poste and Lion d'Or where a most excellent dejeuner" (Motor Tours).
6. This letter does not appear to have survived.

To Caroline Kipling, 22 August 1915
ALS: University of Sussex

Hôtel Brighton / 218, Rue de Rivoli / Paris / Sunday: / Aug. 22. 1915: 8.20 p.m. Room 315. Landon 316: and the whole hotel crawling on its belly all around us. A beauteous damosel unpacks my clothes.

Most Dear and True

I got in at 7:30. here from Troyes – after a rather ludicrous time about the passport when we tried to buy our tickets to Paris. You are conducted *before* you are allowed to buy to an officer of sorts. He was a fat fleshly beast who merely grunted and said we must go to the Commissary of Police. He knew nothing about us – only that we hadn't leave to leave Troyes. Then uprose a very dirty little corporal with a thin restless face and haled us out. Once away from the presence of the officer his visage changed. "*I* know" said he, "you are that Rutyar Kiplen of whom we read. Our officers are all asses (*ânes*). I have a shop at Paris – close to the Boulevard St. Martin. Troyes is an awful place. Come along with me. I'll take you to the Commissary of Police. Our officers are *all* bêtes." So we went amicably along: he telling us how the place was still infested with spies whose papers "are more regular than the most regular." (Oh, I forgot to say that when I owned to being "Rutyar," he launched a long, friendly and enthusiastic: – "Ah God-dam!" which was the first I'd ever heard of that much described word.) Well, then to the Palais de Justice where we met the Commissary of Police who – God knows for what reason – made us describe what Monsieur Ponsot, who had signed one of my *sauf conduits* looked like. Landon for some reason (it was all quite mad out there in the sunny square, with the fat straw hatted little toad of a police commissary blinking at us) described him. "Ah" said he "then he isn't the deputy for the Eure. I thought he was. It's all right. Why did you bring these gentlemen here." "Well, you know what our officers are" said the corporal. "*I* knew all about 'em."

"Very good. But I'd like the gentleman's card as a souvenir of a great writer."

He got it (there's some good in this R.K. business after all) and back we went with our little shopkeeper soldier to the station and most comfortably got our train. (Please forgive this scrawl, my love, but it's hotel Brighton ink and pen).

And when we reached here I had your blessed wire and ran round to the Ritz and got your precious letters of Aug. 13: 15 16. 17: 19, and 20th, with the D.N.'s[1] dam cheeky wire and our boy's good letter (I'm writing him steadily. When I leave this room I see No. 301 across the landing, which was his little suite when he was with us here) and Henry James's Jamesish letter: and Mrs Hussey's[2] and Mrs. Gaskell's.[3] In return I send you a little trifling note from the *Times* which may amuse you. I wired you, for the mere joy of wiring, to tell you I'd got 'em all and, seriously, to ask your views about what we ought to do with the letters for France. The pressure for my views etc. is simply awful. Hurry up and let me know your Royal Mind, my Queen.

Yes dear. It is worth all and more that we have kept the Unit intact till now and that *you* have made the Unit what it is. D'you suppose I didn't think of that all his birthday while I watched the IVth Army Corps flow over those downs near V – past Kitchener. Haven't you got my letter describing it yet? Remember, I only missed one day and that was the day in the Alsace trenches, as I told you. I wrote John an account of it.[4]

I think your idea about Boulogne is good if it can be managed: but I *do* so want to get this set of impressions off my chest before they become mixed. Moreover I don't think that a Surgeon General's leave is sufficient to allow me to circulate in Boulogne. One has to appeal to French. But I don't think I shall come over on Tuesday since you are so generous. Assuredly I *do* expect (if it fits) to be met at Folkestone. Equally of course I will send you a wire when I come. But don't panic if the boats are suddenly discontinued. They have to be occasionally.

Julia was here as you will see from enclosed. Julia *is* here (at the Crillon) as I found out per the Brighton concierge just now. I am saying *nothing whatever*.

'Tis the safest way. And now my dearest dear I'll write a line to John.[5] Oh those last tearing days. What they must have meant to you! I don't suppose ever was a girl more loved than you by your family and a million fold more by

Your Boy.

P.S.   When I return be prepared for a new Domestic Tyrant. I'm somebody and I've – pulled the whiskers of death and don't you forget it.

Notes

1. *Daily News*?
2. The wife of Edward Windsor Hussey (1855–1952), of Scotney Castle, Lamberhurst, Kent; the Husseys were an old Burwash family. Mrs Hussey (d. 1958) was born Mary Rosamund Anstruther and had married Hussey in 1900. RK called her "the beautiful lady with the beautiful garden" (to Mrs Doubleday, 10 May 1913: ALS, Princeton).
3. Helen Mary Gaskell (d. 1940), founder of the War Library for sick and wounded soldiers in September 1914. She was a friend of Burne-Jones. The "scrap-book department" of the War Library was, according to the obituary of Mrs Gaskell in *The Times*, inaugurated "at the suggestion of Rudyard Kipling" (8 November 1940). See also [October? 1915].
4. This letter does not seem to have survived.
5. In Gilbert, *O Beloved Kids*, pp. 199–200.

To Caroline and Elsie Kipling, 23 August 1915
ALS: University of Sussex

Hotel Brighton (this is their ink) / Aug. 23. 1915 6.p.m.

My dears,

We are waiting till Joffre, who asks for us, shall see us. *But*, since you cannot telephone to his headquarters where Captain Puaux lives; and since you are equally forbidden to wire, and since the postal arrangements of France are of an unpunctuality the most profound – we are still waiting.[1] I sent my letter to Puaux, who conveyed me Joffre's invitation, through the French foreign office. Anyway I can't get over tomorrow to England – that's certain. And, if you don't mind, I'm glad of this margin in which to, as you say, digest. The time has been so filled with the most direct and poignant experiences that I hardly knew where to begin: But now, I think I see my way clear to at least three *first* class articles which, if translated into French, will do all you and I desire.

No letter from you today – I suppose because the boat has been held up and I have missed it sorely. The Hotel Brighton where they never admit that I am, is a very present refuge in time of trouble and, I believe that I am rather badly wanted by all sorts of persons "to express my sentiments." The pressure on the French side is *very* strong, and naturally; and the sooner I get the letters done the better. But meantime (and I hope you won't say it's wrong) I've done this: – L. and I have made up about 400 words of extracts from a private letter supposed to have been written by me to a friend which he has sent off to the D[aily]. T[elegraph]. this evening.[2] It says nothing about my experiences; it doesn't take the edge off anything I'm writing afterwards but it *does* give full and ample praise to the temper of France and hint that we might do more to help her. There isn't a word that, even the Bosch can twist into a misunderstanding and – it will be translated at once this side where it will do good. The French complain that the English misunderstand 'em and *vice versa*. I think, by the time I have done, I may be able to put a little of that trouble right. Here my d–d popularity will come in useful. My dears, it is absolutely terrifying to me to find what I am in France. I haven't told you a tenth of the unbelievable things that have happened. For instance the ex-avocat soldier in Alsace, who looked precisely like Grayson,[3] asked me, *under fire*, to explain *how* the idea of the Jungle Book had come to me. And a man, unseen in the darkness of a dugout, reached out his hands and shook mine murmuring, "*Le Grand Rutyar!*" And a Lieut. of Artillery begged me, headlong as a boy will, to write something about his beloved gun-mules. "But I *have*" said I. "You've *not*" he cried. "I know 'em all – *all!*" Then I told him about "Servants of the Queen"[4] and he exploded with satisfaction. And so it goes on – up and down, high and low, throughout *all the Army of France.* Certainly I ought to be able to be useful. Chevrillon writes me they will believe me before any one else.

I have written John another letter,[5] recapitulating my others in case they should have missed him and telling him about certain dodges and ideas in the French trenches. L. says *all* their trenches are better than ours. I only know that, as I told you, they are speckless clean, odourless and (as you see) *quite* safe.

I don't mind trenches. I *do* object to winding hill roads where the Bosches can shell you. One feels so impotent. Now I will stop. They tell me there is great delay in the post because of the censorship. So I fear my letters may have suffered. They were posted from queer places. I was at Tiffany's today to get a little silver knife for Landon and the assistants nearly tore me to pieces because I spent f.12.50!

Send me word of my Elsie and what she does. How I wish you were with me. Paris, quiet and calm, under the shadow of war, is lovelier than Paris at peace. I think I'll just pitch in a small *clearly written* letter to John[6] (I remember what you said about his preference for short letters) and then I'll turn in.

9.p.m. No reply yet from Puaux about Joffre seeing me. I told P. to tele-graph but as its only $1^1/_4$ hours en auto to Head Quarters I can do it early tomorrow.

Ever your own most loving
Boy

Notes

1. In the event, RK never did see Joffre. On 25 August he writes: "After keeping me hung up here for two days I find that Joffre can't see me. He's busy somewhere else. D–d impertinence isn't it? But he sent a message to 'excuse himself.' Can you see K. doing that?" (to John Kipling: ALS, Sussex).
2. This duly appeared in the *Daily Telegraph*, 27 August 1915, as "Rudyard Kipling on France", ostensibly the text of "a private letter of Mr. Rudyard Kipling".
3. (Sir) Rupert Grayson (1897–1991), 4th Baronet, was a fellow-officer with John Kipling in the Irish Guards and was twice wounded in the War. He visited Bateman's with John (CK diary, 17 July 1915) and after the War was often at Bateman's. For a time he was an ordinary seaman in the British merchant marine; for a time he was a publisher in London; for a time he wrote music in Hollywood. During the Second World War Grayson was an admiralty courier and foreign service messenger. He also wrote a number of adventure novels.
4. Published in the *Pall Mall Magazine*, March 1894, and *Harper's Weekly*, 3 March 1894 (*The Jungle Book*).
5. This letter appears not to have survived.
6. 23 August: in Gilbert, *O Beloved Kids*, pp. 202–3.

To John Kipling, [27 August 1915]
ALS: University of Sussex

Bateman's / Burwash / Sussex / Friday 7.p.m.

Dear Old Man,

Reached Folkestone last night at 6.15 and found Mums and the car. Got away at 7: old Vincent jogged us back steadily via Romney marsh and Appledore in 2 hr. 40 min. It was a bad mixture of mist and moonlight with no edge to the road – the sort of job Vincent must know by now. But why *does* he keep his engine going full tilt when we have to halt at a railway cross-ing? Got in to Bateman's about 10.40; supper and bed but not before I had read your last letter describing your Court Martial order. 20 miles on any old A[rmy]. S[ervice]. C[orps]. lorry is a fair treat![1]

I was busy all this morning getting my letter done about France and what I thought and saw. Certainly, I had wonderful luck.

The Bird is roaming about Scotland with John Bailey[2] who, she writes, looks on her with awe as one who has been to so many music-halls.[3] "Fame at last" says the Bird.

Well, forgive a fool's scrawl but I've nowt to tell save that I love you and that I shall probably continue to do so. Mums sleeps well, I'm glad to say and has a good appetite.

Ever your Dad

P.S.   They have a dam' awkward trick at the customs of asking you if you are carrying letters. I didn't know they were as mean as that. Landon came back with me and don't go out again for some few days. I've got a tale to tell you (can't and daren't write it) which contains absolutely the filthiest and most expressive phrase I've ever heard in my life. And that's saying something.

Your sword is on top of the credence in my study. I think of all the awful drudgery it has seen you through in the past twelve months and again I lift my civilian hat off to my son.

Notes
1. John had written to them on 22 August that "I have to sit on my first Court Martial tomorrow"; since it would be held some 20 miles away, he added, "I don't know how I am going to get there; it will most likely be on the back of some old A.S.C. lorry" (Gilbert, *O Beloved Kids*, p.201); on 30 August he reported that there had been four cases and that one man "came very near the extreme penalty" (*ibid.*, p. 215).
2. Abe Bailey's son: see 27 April 1910.
3. The music halls were the standard family amusement on their meetings in London with John in this year.

To Walter Hines Page,[1] 5 October 1915
ALS: Princeton University

Bateman's / Burwash / Sussex / Oct. 5. 1915.

Dear Dr. Page:
May I ask you to communicate with the American ambassador in Berlin to ask if he can discover any trace of my son:
John Kipling
2nd Lieutenant
2nd Battalion Irish Guards.

He is reported to have been wounded late in the afternoon of Sep. 27th, on the outskirts of a wood near Loos (LOOS) and to have crawled into a shed or building which was almost immediately afterwards occupied by the Germans.[2]

When I last heard from him he had lost his identification-disk[3] so I send a description of him over leaf.

He is dark with strongly marked eyebrows, small moustache, thick brown hair (straight) dark brown eyes with long lashes.

Height about 5.7 $^1/_2$. Small white scar on forehead and one front tooth slightly discoloured.

He is short-sighted and is most probably wearing gold spectacles.

He wears a small gold signet-ring with monogram J.K. All his clothes are marked.

His name has been sent in to you from the Regimental Headquarters of the Irish Guards but it was not then known that he was wounded. This information might facilitate the search. [4]

Very sincerely yours
Rudyard Kipling

Notes
1. The American Ambassador to Great Britain: see 4–5 August 1913.
2. RK and CK received a telegram from the War Office on 2 October stating that John had been "missing" since 27 September. For the next two months they attempted unceasingly to discover whether John were still alive, or, if not, what had happened on the fatal day. It was long before they were compelled to give up any hope that he might still be alive. They were never to learn where his body might lie, but through their persistent inquiry they were able to learn almost every circumstance apart from the location of the grave. The distilled account of what they learned and believed is given in RK's account of the minor action in the Battle of Loos in which John met his death. After describing how a party of the 1st Scots Guards had attacked Puits 14 bis and momentarily captured it, RK goes on:

> Their rush took with them "some few Irish Guardsmen," with 2nd Lieutenants, W. F. J. Clifford and J. Kipling of No. 2 Company who went forward not less willingly because Captain Cuthbert commanding the Scots Guards party had been Adjutant to the Reserve Battalion at Warley ere the 2nd Battalion was formed and they all knew him. Together, this rush reached a line beyond the Puits, well under machine-gun fire (out of the Bois Hugo across the Lens–La Bassée road). Here 2nd Lieutenant Clifford was shot and wounded or killed – the body was found later – and 2nd Lieutenant Kipling was wounded and missing. The Scots Guards also lost Captain Cuthbert, wounded or killed and the combined Irish and Scots Guards party fell back from the Puits and retired "into and through Chalk-Pit Wood in some confusion" (*The Irish Guards in the Great War: Part II: The Second Battalion*, Outward Bound Edition, p. 16).

John's name was ultimately inscribed on the memorial at Dud Corner, together with those of thousands of other soldiers whose bodies had never been found or identified. Not until 1992 was it discovered by the Commonwealth War Graves Commission that the body of an unidentified Lieutenant of the Irish Guards buried in St Mary's cemetery at Haisnes, north of Loos, must be that of John Kipling; because of a mistaken map reference the body had been recorded as coming from a region in which the Irish Guards had not been engaged. When the correct reference was established, all the circumstantial evidence pointed to the identification of John Kipling. See *Kipling Journal*, September 1992, pp. 9–10.

3.   John wrote on 19 September 1915 that he had lost his identification disk and asked them to get a new one for him (Gilbert, *O Beloved Kids*, p. 220).

4.   The letter is endorsed: "H[is] E[xcellency] ans'd by telegraph 6-10-15. Sent to Berlin Embassy 6-10-15."

To R. D. Blumenfeld, 6 October 1915

ALS: University of Sussex

Bateman's / Burwash / Sussex / Oct. 6. 1915

private

Dear Blumenfeld

Ever so many thanks for holding your hand about John. I don't suppose one straw more or less much matters at such a time but – Taffy has really excelled himself.[1]

As far as I can make out his wife picked up some rumour at a dinner-party; told Gwynne; who forthwith telephoned to the biggest ass in the Battn who seems to have given him another casualty ("*wounded believed killed*") instead of ("wounded: missing": which John was.)

The rest, including the remarks about his "youth" and his "delicacy" (John was a Gym Instructor among other things and as hard as nails) was fabricated in the M. P.! Result is, a congested mail and unlimited weeping willow and dithyrambic correspondence for us. We were hoping for a few days' peace before the news got out but – there's nothing like journalistic enterprize.

The worst is that it was all so damn kindly intended (specially the obituary notice) and the best is that one is only one atom in this ten-million man power welter, and so one sticks it accordingly. Good luck to you and yours.

Ever sincerely
Rudyard Kipling.

Notes

1.   Gwynne published the following notice in the *Morning Post*, 6 October 1915:

THE DEATH OF MR. JOHN KIPLING.

We have the heavy burden of announcing that Mr. John Kipling, of the Irish Guards, is reported "missing, believed killed." John Kipling was the child for whom his father wrote the *Just So Stories*, the boy for whom Puck told immortal tales of the beloved land, for which this supreme sacrifice has now been made. Mr. John Kipling was barely eighteen, a boy of delicate health but indomitable zeal and resolution. He had been nominated for the Irish Guards by Lord Roberts, and was determined to take his share in the war. In assenting to his urgent pleas the father – and the mother also – offered the dearest of all possible sacrifices on the altar of their country – an only son, whose youth and health might have given them a good reason for evading the ordeal. The sympathy of the whole Empire will go out to Mr. and Mrs. Rudyard Kipling in their sorrow.

Gwynne, among RK's friends, had been perhaps closest of all to John. The statement about "delicate health" was no doubt an exaggeration, but Gwynne would have known of John's ill-health at the end of his school days and of such episodes as John's being brought from Warley to Batemen's when he was ill in May 1915. When Gwynne learned of John's death he at once went to Bateman's "to poor old Kipling and spent the day with him. Such splendid pluck. When I arrived, he said 'What did you come down for?' I said 'to see what I can do'. 'You can do nothing' he said but I saw a quiver in his lips which showed how the thing had gone home" (Gwynne to Lady Bathurst, 7 October 1915: Keith Wilson, ed., *The Rasp of War*, p. 132).

To Major General J. B. Sterling, 9 October 1915
ALS: Cornell University

Bateman's / Burwash / Sussex / Oct. 9, 1915

Dear General Sahib

Many thanks for your note which tells me something I had guessed but hadn't known before. I send you a copy of a letter the boy's Colonel (Butler)[1] wrote to me as well as one from a brother-Lieutenant. I have been down for some time with a go of gastritis[2] (picked up on the beach)[3] so I haven't been able to get up to town. I'd be very grateful if you would tell me what happened around Puit 14 where the Scots and the Irish fought together. Who broke? Was it a K[itchener] division? And who saved who? There was a piece of damned silly nonsense in the Morning Post about the boy. The *M. P.* had picked up the news somewhere in town I suppose and went out of its fool way to represent the lad as young and "delicate." He was physically three years ahead of his age and was as fit as a fiddle. I'm rather sick about it for it's specially rank when you remember he was in the

Brigade which doesn't encourage unfitness. Also, he was shaping excellently as an officer.

I don't regret anything except the uncertainty.

Ever most sincerely
Rudyard Kipling

Notes
1. Colonel (afterwards Brigadier-General) L. J. P. Butler (1876–1955) took command of the 2nd Battalion, Irish Guards, in July 1915.
2. RK returned to Bateman's from a trip to London on 27 September "feeling very ill"; on the 29th the doctor diagnosed "gastritis" and put him on a strict diet. By 6 October RK was "much better and begins to eat proper food" (Rees extracts). As RK described this "attack of indigestion" some months later, it "came on last autumn after a tour in France, a visit to certain sections of our fleet where I got a chill, a good deal of hard work and a good deal of strain and anxiety caused by the disappearance of our son after the battle of Loos" (to Dr A. W. S. Curteis, 3 June 1916: ALS, Sussex).
3. That is, from his visits to the headquarters of the east coast naval patrols at Dover and at Harwich for the articles that became *The Fringes of the Fleet*. RK went to Dover on 18–19 September and to Harwich between 22 and 25 September (Rees extracts). It was perhaps on this tour that he was the guest of Admiral G. A. Ballard, commanding the east coast naval patrol, who writes that RK occupied the spare cabin on the Admiral's flagship "and sat at my table with my personal staff and self" (*Kipling Journal*, October 1946, p. 3). But CK wrote at the time that RK "had slept in a different ship every night during the week and had travelled every day" (to Mrs Balestier, 27 September [1915]: ALS, Dunham Papers). The six articles that resulted were sent off on 3 November and the verses accompanying them on 11 November (Rees extracts, 3, 11 November 1915). The series was published in the *Daily Telegraph* in England, 20 November–2 December 1915; it appeared simultaneously or slightly later in papers in "the U.S., France, Australia, Greece, Italy, Russia, and French Switzerland" (Rees extracts, 11 November 1915).

To Henry Van Dyke,[1] 14 October 1915
ALS: Princeton University

Bateman's / Burwash / Sussex / Oct. 14. 1915.

My dear Van Dyke

Thank you very much for your kind letter from the Hague of Oct. 10. We are still hoping that our boy, who was wounded and missing on the evening of Sep. 27th in the fighting between Loos and Hulluck, may be a wounded prisoner in some hospital or, if he were slightly wounded may, by now, be better and in some prisoner camp.

Might I ask you of your kindness to see if you can find any trace of him. He was a 2nd Lieutenant in the Second Battalion, Irish Guards: and I have reason to fear that he had lost his indentification disk before he went into action and so could only be identified by his clothes, all of which were marked. He wore a small gold signet-ring with monogram J.K. and though he would have been wearing spectacles in action the mark of pince-nez which he usually wears is very distinct on both sides of his nose. He has a small scar on his forehead. For the rest he was 5 foot 7 or thereabouts, with slight dark moustache, dark brown hair and very strongly marked black eye-brows over brown eyes.

I do not suppose you will recall him but he was one of the little company at Mrs. Depew's chateau at Anel in Xmas 1913[2]

Very sincerely yours
Rudyard Kipling

Notes
1. The American Ambassador to the Netherlands: see 25 December 1913.
2. See 25 December 1913.

To Stanley Baldwin, 23 October 1915
ALS: Dalhousie University

Bateman's / Burwash / Sussex / Oct. 23. 1915.

Dear Stan

We had a very jolly time with Oliver[1] who looks to me as though he were going to shape splendidly. His height deceived me. I had no idea till I ran the tape over him that he had such a chest expansion or such depth of chest. It's an ideal frame to hang muscle on and his feet are hard for road work.

Talking of the service and O's heart being opened on account of John, I saw that the boy was *very* keen to join the Irish Guards "as John did." I said nothing to persuade him that way but I think you'll understand my repre-senting to you what I gathered from our talks. I was always very glad of any side-lights from John on his own career.

If Oliver joins the Irish Guards he'd have a right and a claim to the Regiment as much as though he were a younger brother of John's: and the Brigade is very keen on the idea of family continuity. This would mean that O. would have his road made easier for him with the C.O.: the senior officers, the adjutant and, most important of all, the permanent sergeants who train them and who are quite as keen as the officers on Brigade custom. Morover it's no bad regiment and I should think that the Celts (they are pure Irish rank and file) would suit O's temperament as they suited John's. They have to be handled on imaginative lines.

If you think well of the notion, there'd be no bother. You know Kerry[2] and he'd jump at O. of course and I'm sure you'd like Lord de Vesci[3] the regimental adjutant at Buckingham Gate. There would be no likelihood of O. being sent out before he was eighteen and that *ought* to mean, the army of occupation. He'd put in a hard year first of being trained and training men and that's as useful as anything else.[4]

Ever
Rud

Notes
1. Oliver Baldwin had left Eton at 16 at the end of this summer; he had been at Bateman's, 16–19 October (Bateman's Visitors Book). CK wrote of this visit: "We have Oliver Baldwin for the week end … a nice boy and a great delight to see a boy about" (to Mrs Balestier, [16–19? October 1915]: ALS, Dunham Papers).
2. Henry William Edmund Petty-Fitzmaurice (1872–1936), styled Lord Kerry, son of the 5th Marquess of Lansdowne, whom he succeeded in 1927. Kerry was MP for West Derbyshire, 1908–18, and a Senator of the Irish Free State, 1922–9. He served as Lt.-Colonel commanding the reserve of the Irish Guards, 1914–16.
3. Ivo Richard Vesey (1881–1958), 5th Viscount de Vesci in the Irish peerage; Major, Irish Guards, special reserve, since August 1914.
4. Oliver Baldwin went to an Officers' Training Corps at Cambridge in May 1916, was commissioned in June 1917, and joined the Irish Guards. He did not go to France until the end of June 1918. The news of his orders came while he was at Bateman's: "One afternoon whilst I was paddling in the pond and the sun was shining its happiest, the telegram arrived. I capered round the lawn with joy, for at last the great adventure had begun. One of the family had fallen. I was the avenger. I never thought for a minute of being killed" (*The Questing Beast: An Autobiography*, 1932, p. 62).

To Rupert Grayson, [October? 1915]

Text: Rupert Grayson, *Voyage Not Completed*, 1969, pp. 85–7

Bateman's, Burwash, Sussex.

I am sorry to learn – though it isn't in the least surprising seeing what you have gone through,[1] that you are still a bit shaken up. However, I can assure you for your consolation that with your youth and temperament you will come through without damage. It is often the very strength of a young man kicking against the accident or shock to his body that makes him feel so infernally wretched. Older men don't, as they imagine, feel shock so much, that only means they haven't the elasticity.

So when you are feeling like "three penn'orth of tripe" as John used to say, remember that it isn't your weakness declaring itself but your strength coming back. I was never hoisted by a shell but I've been rather ill once in my life when I was young, and I know.

The serious matter seems to me the loss of your dog. A man has a feeling about a dog which is quite apart from other feelings. I only wish I had one that I could venture to recommend to fill the old one's place: but our animal Jack is rather a mongrel hound of reserved character and absolutely no morals. He began life as a poacher, under the able tuition of his sister, a brown and white rough-haired terrier bitch. And if ever that expressive word exactly expressed a lady, it did in her case. I have fished Jack out of rabbit wires in the woods at eleven o'clock at night and seen him sneak off for fresh trouble next morning. Obviously *he's* no good.

My own idea would be a sealyham. There isn't a wiser or more gentlemanly breed alive, and they are good for most things up to badgers.

Your mother says that when you feel fitter you will come down here, and that prospect is making us happy.[2]

There is a literary career open for you when you feel like it. I do a bit at it myself. It is the manufacture of scrapbooks for the wounded in hospital. Observe the process. You take a mass of magazines, weekly papers, *John Bulls' Life, Punch*, etc., – anything with fairly vulgar pictures and fairly vulgar jokes. You cut out the pictures, from ads of motor bikes to beautiful females without clothes (the hospitals like this) and you mix in the vulgar jokes in the proportion of about 3 to 5. Then you take 12 sheets, not more, of brown paper and gum the resulting mixture on to 'em. Sometimes one makes a refined scrapbook – pretty girls and squashy verses – for a delicate soul. Otherwise one goes in for purely comic effects. The curious thing is that a man who isn't equal to reading gets a sort of languid pleasure from turning over the collection. The pictures remind him of civil life and most men are keen on ads of cars, motor boats, etc.

Elsie invented this idea but they are called R.K. scrapbooks. There is a great deal more art in making them than you would imagine. You'll probably have to make or help make some at Bateman's.[3]

If this disgusts you let me know.

I've been among some of our ships lately – down in a submarine and so on and am now trying to write out any[4] impressions.[5] It was a most interesting time.

With all our best and warmest greetings to you,
believe me,

Yours sincerely,
Rudyard Kipling

Remember what I told you, the next time you feel more than usually wretched. "There are many liars but there are no liars like our own sensations."[6] I forget where that comes from but it is true.

Notes

1. Grayson had been wounded – "blown up by a shell" – in the same action in which John Kipling had been killed (*The Irish Guards in the Great War*, Outward Bound Edition, II, 21; *Voyage Not Completed*, 1969, p. 80).
2. Grayson was at Bateman's from 7 to 13 January 1916 (Bateman's Visitors Book).
3. Grayson recalled "one winter evening" spent at Bateman's when "we were compiling R.K. scrapbooks, sitting in front of the great log-fire in the hall" (*Voyage Not Completed*, p. 87). They were evidently popular: in 1917 the War Library appealed for volunteers to make "Kipling Scrapbooks" for the Library so that it could extend its circulation of them; instructions on how to make such scrapbooks were provided by the Library (*The Times*, 6 September 1917).
4. Thus in printed text: "my"?
5. *The Fringes of the Fleet.*
6. RK is quoting himself: "there are many liars in the world, but there are no liars like our own sensations" (speech at McGill University, 17 October 1907: collected as "Values in Life", *A Book of Words*, p. 20). See also *Kim*, ch. 15: "there are no liars like our bodies, except it be the sensations of our bodies".

To Colonel Lionel Charles Dunsterville, 12 November 1915

ALS: University of Sussex

Bateman's / Burwash / Sussex / Nov. 12. 1915.

Dear Lionel

I saw: and rejoiced, that you had been dealing faithfully with the Mohmands.[1] Now is the time to do as much killing as possible – in view of possible excitements that may follow on this German move towards Constantinople[2] – and to talk sternly to Jirgahs.[3] But I'm sorry about the diarrhæa, and the fever. You've *got* to look after yourself and you were always as careless as a goat about these things.

Our boy was reported "wounded and missing" since Sep. 27 – the battle of Loos and we've heard nothing official since that date. But all we can pick up from the men points to the fact that he is dead and probably wiped out by shell fire.

However, he had his heart's desire and he didn't have a long time in trenches. The Guards advanced on a front of two platoons for each battalion. He led the right platoon over a mile of open ground in face of shell and machine gun fire and was dropped at the further limit of the advance after having emptied his pistol into a house full of German m[achine]. g[un].'s. His C.O. and his company commander told me how he led 'em: and the wounded have confirmed it. He was senior ensign tho' only 18 years and 6 weeks, had worked like the devil for a year at Warley and knew his Irish to the ground. He was reported on as one of the best of the subalterns and was gym instructor and signaller. It was a short life. I'm sorry that all the years work ended in that one afternoon but – lots of people are in our position and it's something to have bred a man. The wife is standing it wonderfully tho' she of course clings to the bare hope of his being a prisoner. I've seen what shells can do and I don't.

We're pounding on in our perfectly insane English fashion. The boys at the front are cheery enough, (we've got rather a lot of artillery) and the Hun is being killed daily. It's the old story. *All* the victories were on Napoleon's side all through and yet he didn't somehow get further than St. Helena.

I've been, as I think I told you, among the ships and my lucubrations are coming out in the D. T. It was a gay time. I went down in a submarine.[4]

Poor old Buck![5] I can remember him at Coll. He tried, do you remember, to raise and train hawks! Much to Crofts' disgust. I'll send him a letter of sympathy.

Now, my dear old man, try and look after yourself a bit and keep fit. We've a hell of a year ahead of us but after that I think we'll be through.

Ever

Rudyard

Notes
1. In the autumn of 1915 Dunsterville, commanding the 1st Infantry Brigade at Peshawar, "marched out again against the Mohmands. ... Operations against these tribes continued on and off till the end of 1917" (*Stalky's Reminiscences*, p. 252).
2. A combined German, Austrian and Bulgarian force attacked Serbia on 6 October and gave the Germans control of communications throughout eastern Europe.
3. A *jirgah* is a council or assembly of the headmen of a Pathan or a Baluchi tribe; cf. RK's early sketch called "The Cow-house Jirga", published in the *CMG*, 4 November 1887 (*The Smith Administration*).
4. This was on his tour of 22–5 September (see 9 October 1915), in a submarine commanded by Captain Charles Stuart Benning, "one of the most charming men I had ever met – even on the salt water" (RK to Cope Cornford, 26 November 1915: ALS, National Maritime Museum).
5. Brigadier-General K. J. Buchanan (1863–1933), Indian Army (see 29 July [1911]), school-fellow of RK and Dunsterville. I do not know what is referred to.

To The Reverend James O. Hannay,[1] 12 November 1915
ALS: Dalhousie University

Bateman's / Burwash / Sussex / Nov. 12. 1915

Dear Hannay,

Your boy writes excellent matters and every word of it interests us. I like the idea of him and his tactful N.C.O. officiating at the mysteries of the Lewis gun – no man being able to withstand them.[2]

But why are you impressed with the behaviour of the Guards. They *are* the Guards. Thus do they behave and in no other manner nor ever have.

Ages ago they entered Bloemfontein after a march,[3] atop of many other marches, of 27 miles during which they had walked through exhausted regiments who sat by the roadside and cherished their poor feet. They had about three pairs of trousers per five men and their rations had been sketchy. But they entered the town as though it had been Hyde Park and when I dined with Pole-Carew[4] he hoped, very seriously, that I had made allowance for any irregularities and shortcomings in their demeanour and bearing. He himself, and his officers, made none.

It will be a joy and a comfort to your boy all his days to have been in and with the absolute Best.

If it isn't imposing too much, please keep on sending us his diary. It holds us in touch with the battalion.

Very sincerely yours
Rudyard Kipling

Notes
1. Hannay (1865–1950), Irish clergyman of the Church of Ireland, made a name as a novelist and humorist under the pseudonym of George A. Birmingham. He was Rector of Westport, County Mayo, for 22 years, until 1913. He served as a chaplain in France, 1916–17. From 1924 he held livings in England. His son, 2nd Lieutenant R. Hannay of the 2nd Battalion of the Irish Guards, commanded No. 6 platoon, as John Kipling commanded No. 5. The younger Hannay kept a diary which he sent to his parents in instalments, and the elder Hannay had been sending parts of them to RK since early in 1915. On 6 October he had sent some pages from his son's diary in which John is mentioned in a "casual and lighthearted way" (Hannay to RK: ALS, Sussex).
2. At this time, according to *The Irish Guards in the Great War*, "two Lewis-guns, which were then new things, had been supplied to the Battalion, and teams were made up and instructed in the working by 2nd Lieutenant Hannay" (II, 44).
3. At the end of March 1900.
4. Pole-Carew (see 14 April 1901) was then commanding the Guards Brigade in South Africa.

To Oliver Baldwin, 20 November 1915
ALS: Dalhousie University

Bateman's / Burwash / Sussex / Nov. 20. 1915

Dear Oliver

Your letter has come in, and I make haste to send you my view of things.

In the first second and third place keep your head and don't fly off the handle. A great many things are bound to happen before you are seventeen; and next March is more than four months away.

The check that you say has been laid upon you is the first part of your burden as a man and it must be met with patience and dignity – both which qualities you have.

I will do all I can to help you by developing the military point of view to your father which is the point I am most competent to speak about. You on your part must promise me not to sulk or storm.

I ask this because the relations between a man and his father are the most precious in the world and depend quite as much upon the son as on the father. Once injured they are awfully hard to reestablish. Your father is trying to do what he thinks best for you in view of your present age and if you show any uncontrolled signs of disappointment at his action you will only be justifying his idea that you are too young to go forward into training.

So remember that you are a man and must meet this situation as a man.

I can't tell you how thoroughly we sympathize in and understand your feelings and I believe your father will later on realize them too and will then release you from the indignities to which your size, rather than your age, exposes you daily.

I know that my advice is hard but I depend upon you to follow it – *as a test.* Though John often blustered and swore about at large when I gave him advice as a man to a man I can't recall any time when he did not in the long run follow it. And that I think gave him the start of the discipline that made him so good a young officer. I'll tell you about it some day. Believe me, managing a son isn't all beer and skittles.

Now go on and sit tight and shut your mouth and above all things keep yourself fit.

Ever your affectionate Uncle
Ruddy.

To Stanley Baldwin, 20 November 1915
ALS: Dalhousie University

Bateman's / Burwash / Sussex / Nov. 20. 1915.

Dear Stan,

I've never written this kind of letter before – indeed, I never cared enough about any one to write it: but my affection for Ollie and you must be my excuse.

Ollie writes now that you tell him he mustn't go up for the service till he is $17\frac{1}{2}$: I am sending you [a] copy of my letter to him wherein I naturally advise him to sit still. But from the boy's point of view it is pretty serious. It mightn't matter so much if he wasn't so large and didn't bear himself so like a man. As it is, his size lays him open to a fair amount of insult already – even in Brighton the Slacker's Home.[1] He can put up with that of course as long as he is under age but afterwards it will be hard on him and he is a sensitive lad.

Setting that aside, here is the other aspect. If he joins when he is seventeen he won't be sent out till he is eighteen and he will get a year's training in the Brigade which is equivalent to three in the Line. If he joins when he is $17\frac{1}{2}$ he is liable to be sent out at eighteen and then he'll only have six months' training behind him – which isn't enough. Moreover, the half year that he spends waiting till he is $17\frac{1}{2}$ will be extremely unpleasant for him. He won't be able to go out in public, or to attend public meetings or gatherings; he won't be able to open his head on recruiting matters and the fact of his being a civilian will be unscrupulously exploited in the constituency.

Add to this that, if, as is likely, we get group-conscription for the rank and file[2] his position will be almost untenable. Indeed, as I see it, he will be brought up with the flat choice between applying for a commission or going into the ranks.

Wouldn't it be better by all odds – on account of the training he'll get, and for the sake of his own peace of mind – if you let him know you'd have no insuperable objection to his joining after seventeen. Even so this doesn't bring him into the trenches much before sixteen or eighteen months from this date. We may then reasonably expect that the worst will be over.

I am afraid the young 'un feels rather sore about the delay which, as you can see, is my reason for writing to you. Having lost my own son in the flesh I'm the more keen that none whom I love should come within even the possibility of losing their boy in the spirit. Forgive me if I have blundered: but I am not very good at this sort of thing. I don't think my advice to Ollie is unsettling however.

Your affectionate
Cousin Rud.

Notes
1. Just after leaving Eton, Oliver Baldwin wrote, "I was given a white feather by a woman on the West Pier one day, of which I was very proud, since I had no idea I looked old enough to be a soldier" (*The Questing Beast*, p. 46).
2. The Military Service Act of January 196 imposed military service on unmarried men between the ages of 18 and 41.

To Sir Max Aitken, 6 December 1915
ALS: Harvard University

Bateman's / Burwash / Sussex / Dec. 6. 1915

Dear Aitken

I am sending you back all your proofs.[1] I have been through them but really there is very little for me to do. It is all, as I said, extraordinarily good and extraordinarily interesting and the very simplicity and directness with which it is told make it excellent. *Don't* try to fiddle about with it too much. I have purposely touched as little as I could. It's rather a new thing – from the literary point of view.

I can't think of any chapter headings for the chapters you refer to, but I suggest that since it is a book of national and Imperial interest you quote from the older poets as much as may be. Shakespeare and Milton for choice. That's why, I think, you'd better cut out the quotation from me.[2] It's all right in a newspaper article but it's too crude for such a book as this. Stick to William and the older dramatists. There's enough in Milton, in the fighting line, to give you all you want.

Ever
RK.

Notes
1. Of Aitken's Canadian Eye-Witness reports, collected in book form as *Canada in Flanders*, 1916.
2. Six lines from "The Return" (*The Five Nations*) are used as the epigraph to chapter 2 of *Canada in Flanders*.

To Admiral Sir Edmond John Slade,[1] 9 December 1915

Text: Copy, University of Sussex

[Bateman's] 9th December 1915

Dear Admiral Slade,

Thank you very much for your letter of the 8th. After consideration I do not think that anything would be gained at present by my attempting to describe the Grand Fleet or the Cruiser Patrol. The descriptions that have appeared so far of the Grand Fleet or the Cruiser Patrol. The description that have appeared so far of the Grand Fleet show quite plainly that nothing is allowed to be said about it. Otherwise I cannot see how so many and such various observers, Allied and Alien, could have succeeded in producing so uniformly unconvincing an account.

The matter of the Cruiser Patrol is different. Every civilian who knows anything knows that our alleged "blockade" is not a blockade, since the earliest days of the war it has been riddled by arrangements and understandings and Orders in Council which entirely nullify its intention.

When I wrote the Fringes of the Fleet I did no disservice by not telling things that the Censor would not have passed. With the Cruiser Patrol it is otherwise. The public has been so fogged and fooled over the conduct of the War, that I cannot use my pen to add to their confusion, by telling them those partial truths which are all that the Government intends them to know.

I trust you will see my difficulty and I hope you will understand my disappointment.

Yours sincerely,
Rudyard Kipling

Notes

1. Admiral Slade (1859–1928) was Director of Naval Intelligence, 1907–9); Commander-in-Chief in the East Indies, 1909–12. On the outbreak of the war he was employed in "various ways at the Admiralty" (*The Times*, 23 January 1928). He retired in 1917.

To André Chevrillon, 31 December 1915

Text:[1] Translated from *La Revue de Paris*, 1 February 1916, pp. 478–83

[Bateman's] 31 December 1915

Thank you for your good letter, which I have read and re-read. I am like you – not having been born in England and having had only a small part of my education there. There are days when I look at, or rather listen to, these people and say to myself: "If you people aren't mad, then I've gone crazy." But on looking closer at what they are accomplishing I find that they are saner than I had imagined.

Yesterday, for example, I met in one of my fields, where I have just had some dead trees cut down, the wife of one of my tenants who was gathering up rather heavy bundles of firewood: I helped her load them in her cart. I knew that she had lost a son, a soldier, this summer. Her indifference about the war was monumental. It was because she loved fish. She had written to her two other sons to send her some fish: they answered that it would not be worth the cost of shipping (all this, as you will imagine, slowly developed with infinite repetitions, while she collected her dead wood). "So, you have sons who are fishermen?" I said to her. "Yes, fisherman, all their lives." Finally, at the end of ten minutes, I find that she has two sons who serve on minesweepers, somewhere, between Ramsgate and Torquay – she doesn't know exactly. One of her sons was on two boats that sank: one time the boat was able to be beached; the other time – I repeat her own words – "it was stopped in its course by something that I don't understand." The other son, with his captain and three other members of the crew, "was called to see the king and to receive a medal for something. I don't know what, but it is supposed to be a medal for having saved lives from a boat that hit a mine some weeks ago." But her main worry is about the fish that she wants in order to "change her diet" and the high price of shipment. She also has two sons in the army (she had three but I have said that one was killed last summer). She does not seem to be much upset: but she wondered about her fishermen: "They have all the time they need for fishing." Is this a parable, or an allegory? I don't know at all: I tell you this so that you can understand from what a strange angle we approach things.

There are at the moment in our village about six young men who haven't enlisted. Our village does not talk about the 150 who have gone off, and whose names have been duly posted at the churchdoor – those of the dead enclosed in a neat little black border. All the talk turns on the shame and the sin of the six black sheep and on the punishments they'll get when their comrades come back. Our ministry is undecided and unhappy over the question of compulsory service: it is still very political. Besides, it won't accept the principle until every Englishman has been convinced that the government has said and done everything one could ask against the principle. Meantime, volunteers continue at the rate of 30,000 a week: people fear the dishonour of compulsion. People don't make any noise on that little matter. For my part, I think they are wrong, but that's not at all my affair. I share actively in the disapproval that falls on the six black sheep in our village. When they have gone off, I will transfer my attention to the next group on Lord Derby's list.[2] And everyone will do the same. It is thus that we get all the men that we need. We must expect some protests from the socialists and the pacifists: they won't protest except to save face. For many of our people, death is nothing compared to a change in "their principles". In a country where three million men have volunteered for the war, because it was "a matter of principle," it follows logically that one must find, here and there, those who, because it is also a matter of principle, will refuse to go until it is demonstrated to them that they aren't sacrificing their "principles."

Some of our workers feel the same way: hence the language that Lloyd George uses towards them.[3] When he has told them all, and he is thinking of the future when he talks to them, one will be able to say of the very small number of men who continue their resistance: "You are in the pay of Germany!" And it is very possible that one will be able to prove it. That will be a little occasion to make a big noise, whose effect will be to make the workers work harder and to call to account those who don't. You will hear more of all this one of these days.

And now, as for the progress of the war. These sombre, wet days aren't good for the soul. I have gone through several very dark moments, and no doubt I will go through worse. The German exploits all the psychological factors that he is capable of understanding, and his press is much taken up in confirming the world in the idea of an immovable and invulnerable Michael,[4] in control of Europe and scornful of his little adversaries. But the democracies have a sense of humour that is fatal to a war conducted on the heroic or Wagnerian scale. They will be busier in the spring. I don't blame them, for the idea begins to dawn upon the German mind that this is not a war of victories but a war of extermination for their race. We others, in England, are better educated about that today than we were a year ago, – that is to say, the general public begins to grasp the idea. When an entire nation has gone down into the trenches, there can be no victory. There can only be killing, butchery, and three nations, at least, desire ardently that the Boche be killed, – at retail, since one can't kill him wholesale. As I have said and repeat, the Boche can't go back from his present position: he doesn't dare, because it would be necessary to explain the thing to his own people. He must wear himself out – always in detail – whether it be in advancing and carrying off victories, or staying where he is. And when he is worn out, very little of the German problem will remain to consider. There is the end that the Fates are bringing us to despite all the efforts that we have made to evade it, to put aside, among us, even the idea; and nation after nation is beginning to understand it. The question of an "indemnity" for Germany has disappeared through the force of fact. If she continues to claim one, it is cheaper to go on killing. If she asks for peace without an indemnity, with a return to the *status quo ante*, what guarantees are there that, as soon as civilisation is disarmed, she won't throw herself upon it once again. Her own gospel, the moral law that directs her life, commands her to do it. That's why one can't permit her ships to go back to sea. She can't carry on more war than she is now doing, because she is engaged on all possible fronts. She can defend and "consolidate" her conquests (that's an always consoling word) but what will consolidation do for her when she must perpetually push more men into the rim of fire that burns all around her? Allah has decreed that she will perish through her own acts, as a consequence of the law she professes, and through her own temperament. If the Allies had won some five or six months ago, they would have left a Germany still capable of reviving. Now there will remain – this may seem extravagant to you – no Germany: only some people who will live on an eternal defensive, in moral, social, and political trenches. The mental attitude of the Boche is changing already to face up to this situation (he has always known what his clients require). One sees this very clearly in his newspapers.

And I write you all this on the assumption that the war has only meant the loss of men, as if they have not had to deal with sickness, with developing scarcity, with internal needs and troubles – as if their master, who *is perhaps at this moment entering upon his Hundred-Days,*[5] were immortal. Grant them everything: a defence impossible to break, a supply of food that one can't stop, a people unendingly zealous and ardent for the war; even then, – and I know that you all agree – one must hang on: your France, which has paid with the flesh of its flesh, and we, the English, with our half-million, to which we will add more and more – and Russia, with her dead beyond counting. All the rats are before us in a single pit and, so far as the English and the Empire are concerned, we can put enough men in the lines in France to hold the Boche as you are holding him. For the rest, it is for the Boche to consider this among his other things to worry about.

As for the financial situation, remember that you and I (I am fifty years old today) are men of mature age, who judge the future according to the past that we have known, a past that we imagine will return, one day, from this amazing present, – but it is not for us to think about such things. If I were younger, I would show how a wave of immense prosperity succeeds every war, a prosperity whose causes are as much psychological as material. But I leave these considerations to those who are twenty years younger, and I accept the fashionable thesis, the one that holds that universal ruin awaits us. Agreed. But when the whole world at once has been ruined (materially), everyone will be as rich as his neighbour. I imagine that among us, in England, where the little debt-holders are not numerous, a certain proportion of the debt will be simply wiped out or repudiated for the very just reason that men who were rich enough to lend great sums of money to the State are rich enough to lose it. It is immoral, but we will only smile about it – even the rich men who have been made losers. Perhaps we will give titles of nobility in compensation: that would be an admirable – but how practical – apotheosis of our national "snobbism." I see that an English paper has already put forth such an idea. Seriously, we will see some queer finances, and the spectacle of a central Europe administered as an estate for the profit of:

France	Serbia	New Zealand
Russia	Montenegro	Canada

England	Japan	South Africa
Italy	Australia	India
	Belgium	

will be not without charm. Then, the Boche will write a book to prove that the number 13 is an unlucky number!

What a long letter I have written you! Pardon me, but yours have a stimulating effect on me. It is raining, with a diabolical wind. I am filled with an entirely personal sadness, not at all public. Try to interpret us to your people as something less than or more than maniacs. We are strangely unconscious of the effect that we create; yes, there is in us something our friends might take for brutality, but which isn't. It is rather a curious variation of snobbery that I don't have time to analyse. Meantime, we are nearing four million men. When the war of endurance is ended, we will start, you and I, an international society for the assassination of our politicians, our pacifists, and our demagogues, or at least of those who remain. I will hang or burn yours, and you will burn or hang mine. I suppose that the Russians will prefer to hang theirs themselves.

Notes

1. An incomplete English version in typescript of this letter is at Sussex, but it is clearly a translation from the French of the *Revue de Paris* and has no special authority. I have therefore used my own translation. The letter was evidently intended for publication.
2. In October Lord Derby, an advocate of conscription, had been appointed Director of Recruiting in hopes that the voluntary system could be made more productive and the necessity for conscription avoided. Derby's scheme, inviting men to "attest" their willingness to serve, failed to satisfy the critics, and conscription soon followed.
3. Lloyd George succeeded in bringing the unions to agree to set aside restrictions on production in return for limitations on profits. When suspicions over this agreement grew serious, Lloyd George, in his capacity as Minister of Munitions, undertook to "rouse the workers to a sense of the gravity of the struggle" (*DNB*).
4. I suppose that RK means the archangel Michael in his aspect as a warrior.
5. *Les cent-jours*, i.e., the brief period between Napoleon's return from Elba and his final defeat at Waterloo.

To Herbert Baillie,[1] 12 January 1916

TLS: Alexander Turnbull Library

Bateman's / Burwash / Sussex / 12th January 1916

Dear Brother Baillie,

Many thanks for yours of last year with your news of the reinforcements. I was at a hospital the other day which held 900 samples of all the stock that

We raise, and I met a youngster from Auckland, a farmer, half full of shrapnel, but going strong. Also a Maori who interested me immensely.

You're quite right in what you say about the new relations between the Dominions. All that was small and petty in their rivalries has been washed out in blood. All that was best is better even than before. There is a sort of grave courtesy and affection now at the back of all the chaffing and joking that is very fine and touching to see. And they *do* chaff each other, too!

Don't you be too concerned over our bickerings and back talk at this end of the show. It is the ancient habit of the English to grouse and argue and growl over every job they ever engage in. I had to listen to a long lecture the other day from a wounded bank-clerk[2] on the sin of calling the Germans names. He said it was not right to abuse them for following their "national ideals". He was of opinion that no German was fit to live because his "national ideals didn't square with the ideals of civilization", and he looked forward to the complete wiping out of Germany as a power. *But* (and he talked about it for ten minutes) that didn't justify "coarse and vulgar abuse".

Well, that is a point of view that would not strike most people.

This sort of thing puzzles the German badly. He cannot understand why men who grouse and criticise their own side keep on hammering *him*. There was a man called Napoleon who, if you remember, was puzzled in very much the same way and the worry eventually killed him. The Germans do not yet understand why the "Colonies" as they call them have not "revolted" from England. I cannot help feeling for them. Here they are winning at least one victory per week and an extra big one once a month. And here are the Allies with their infernal stupidity not yet recognizing that Germany if properly approached would be ready to impose "a victorious peace". (They are rather keen just now on "victorious peace" in Germany – but nowhere else!). Instead of which the silly Russians and the foolish French and the fat-headed English and the deluded "Colonies" who cannot be making money out of the game, are sending up more men and guns against them. If I were a German I would really be grieved at the blindness of all the rest of the world, and judging from their papers they are grieving in multitudes. But I fancy, it is a long way yet for them and for us. They have *got* to go on winning victories for about another year, if their men and their money run to it. They will probably finish up with a splendid victory and then those damn fool allies will "reform their line" and pick up the pieces, and get ready to be beaten again – very likely not far from where the lines are now. Then the show will shut up with Germany victorious to the last, and the Allies methodically carving her up into nice harmless pieces. Maybe I am wrong – I hope I am – but that is the way I see it – Germany winning all the victories and the Allies winning the war.

As to what you say about spies, the one thing we *must* get into our thick heads is that wherever the German – man or woman – gets a suitable culture to thrive in, he or she means death and loss to civilized people, precisely as germs of any disease suffered to multiply mean death or loss to mankind. There is no question of hate or anger or excitement in the matter, any more than there is in flushing out sinks or putting oil on water to prevent mosquitoes hatching eggs. As far as we are concerned, the German is typhoid or plague – Pestis teutonicus, if you like. But until we realize this elementary fact in peace, we shall always be liable to outbreaks of anti-civilization. Make this clear by all means in your power. I see that Australia has begun to restrict German trade. That is right. Where a bale or a box of German goods comes into a civilized country, there is always the chance of exposing mankind to danger sooner or later. This has been proven before all mankind in every quarter of the world.

And now I shall end my much too long letter with every good wish for the new year and for all friends in New Zealand. Maybe, we shall pass another red Christmas but that, in one sense, is not our business. We must put the work through for the sake of all mankind and for the saving of our own souls.

Yours ever sincerely,
Rudyard Kipling

Notes
1. Baillie (1863–1941) was a bookseller in Wellington, New Zealand, when he served as RK's guide to Wellington in October 1891: see Tom L. Mills, "When Rudyard Kipling was in New Zealand", in Orel, *Kipling: Interviews and Recollections*, pp. 268–71. In 1901 Baillie joined the staff of the Wellington Public Library and served as chief librarian, 1904–28. He was also a long-time Mason.
2. In a letter to André Chevrillon, 7 January 1916, RK says the soldier was "un home-ruler protestant" and "un homme gravement blessé, éclopé, j'en ai peur, pour la vie" (*La Revue de Paris*, 1 February 1916, p. 484).

To Israel Gollancz,[1] 14 January 1916
ALS: Rosenbach Museum and Library

Bateman's / Burwash / Sussex / Jan. 14. 1916.

private
Dear Sir,

Thank you very much for your letter.

As I see it we are just now at the beginning of the most serious phase of the war and no man can say what the next few months will bring forth. It does not seem to me fitting therefore that we should turn aside by a hairsbreadth or divert any available energy from the issues that face us. In other words the best celebration of the tercentenary of Shakespeare is to help to save his country from the Germans.[2]

So, you see, feeling as I do, I should be of no use to you in the matter of the tercentenary. That is a most beautiful book which I have received from you and as a lover of books I thank you a thousand times.

Very sincerely
Rudyard Kipling

To I. Gollancz Esq

Notes
1. (Sir) Israel Gollancz (1864–1930), professor of English language and literature at King's College, London, 1905–30; a noted medievalist and Shakespearean scholar; founder and first secretary of the British Academy.
2. Gollancz edited *A Book of Homage to Shakespeare* (Oxford, 1916), to commemorate the tercentenary, with contributions from Thomas Hardy, Edmund Gosse, George Saintsbury, George Santayana, Henri Bergson, and many other notabilities and scholars from around the world (but no Germans among them). RK gave Gollancz permission to use the letter on *The Tempest* that he published in *The Spectator*, 2 July 1898, stipulating only that Gollancz should include the date of original publication (RK to Gollancz, 16 January 1916: ALS, Rosenbach Museum and Library). The letter appears in *A Book of Homage to Shakespeare* as "The Vision of the Enchanted Island".

To H. A. Gwynne, 8 February 1916
ALS: Dalhousie University

Empire Hotel, / Bath. / Feb. 8. 1916

Dear Old Man –

Your letter has come on to me here.[1]

There isn't the least use in my presiding over meetings at the Constitutional Club to discuss how to prevent air raids.[2] That ought to have been taken in hand years ago – but years ago there wasn't any one who believed in facts. What's the use of spluttering now. Surely we can at least try to take the gruel that we cooked for ourselves. Nothing will convince the country that most of the Cabinet isn't on the German side: and I can't say I blame 'em.

Is it true, what I hear in smoking carriages and smoking rooms, that F.E.[3] (in uniform) was locked up the other day in a guardroom in France – very tight – on his way to or from his beloved Winston?[4] If so, I am pleased.

Ever yours
RK.

Tell Paddy that I can't come to the Constitutional show. P. by the way was a rampant free trader not so long back.

Notes
1. RK and CK left for Bath on 1 February and remained there until 2 March (Rees extracts).
2. Lord Montagu was to preside at a discussion at the Club on 15 March on "The Need for a Strong Air Service" (*The Times*, 10 March 1916).
3. F. E. Smith (see 27 September 1913), now Attorney-General in the first coalition government.
4. Churchill, out of office since the formation of the coalition in May 1915, had in November joined the army in France. He was now commanding the 6th Battalion of the Royal Scots Fusiliers. The story about Smith is essentially true. Smith had dined with Churchill at his headquarters in Ploegsteert, Belgium, on the night of 30 January 1916 and had retired to bed in "pretty shot" condition. Smith had no pass to enter the war zone and was in consequence arrested at 4 a.m., taken to St Omer, and confined in a hotel room. Smith walked away from the room in the morning, despite the armed guards posted there, and, after some anger and confusion, the affair was quickly closed (Martin Gilbert, *Winston S. Churchill*, III [1971], 694–7).

To C. R. L. Fletcher, 9 February 1916
ALS: University of Sussex

Empire Hotel, / Bath. / Feb. 9. 1916

private and confidential
No! I won't! The man who stumbles on such a mine must work it his exclusive self. What a ripping idea! *And* what backgrounds![1]

The whole I submit culminating when Aristide Lemieux's great grandpapa of the Imperial Guard, immeasurably shocked and scandalized, takes him up before The Little Corporal himself!

(Dewy Waterloo corn – or some ghastly frozen angle of the Beresina with bluish-white ice-blocks on end? One moves so well in dreams).

"My degenerate descendant" says the choking ancestor; and coldly and dispassionately the Little Corporal argues it all out – at first to his hearers; then aloud to himself – recrystallizes as it were the possible course of *his* career if he had won such an Alliance. His pros and cons; his estimates of the English character as it then was. There's everything in it that you care to put in out of history and your own alive knowledge of yesterday to make it thrill and colour.

Hurry up with the scenario: You *can't* do it in less than 6,000 words (as I see it) and they'll all have to be ground and sweated fine.

Ever and anticipating Larks
R.K.

P.S.   Aristide Lemieux was a small (darkish) shopkeeper in Tours: He married (1903) Clotilde Dessaux or Dessaix from Perigord way near Rocamadour. Has issue one boy and one girl, 11 and 9: –

His father Bertran L. was a small bookseller in Tours 1837–1900; His Uncle Onesime a farmer. Aristide's mother was a Normand. She kept the family going, 1847 –. Jean L. (grand pa) was out on the barricades in '48. Rather a rolling stone. Travelled in Burgundies. Knew too much about wine and women. Grand Uncle was a priest. Knew a man of the name of Balzac – an author of immoralities mostly.

1.   If you get crowded keep it to the Napoleonic interview?

2.   What did the retainers of Duke William[2] think of the word "alliance": and how the deuce did the transient and embarrassed spirit of Aristide Le Mieux save itself out of all the riot and confusion and drinking of that first evening after Hastings? It wasn't the time or the place to propound his theories but it was his fate.

+. *Don't* tell all and sundry or some one will crib it. Anatole France would.

Notes

1. The subject is Fletcher's idea for what became a story he published as "The Treason of Corporal Aristide Lemieux", *Cornhill Magazine*, N.S., XL (1916), 623–40. The story is Lemieux's account of a dream in which he, a corporal on punishment duty, meets Napoleon during the retreat from Moscow. In the course of the interview the scene gradually becomes the western front and Napoleon gradually takes in the changes operating – from the presence of aircraft and machine guns to the astounding fact that France is now allied with the English and Russians. To the question, what to do with the Germans? Napoleon answers, Leave them to their own devices but hang a king for every European capital that has been "insulted".

    Among the points suggested by RK, these occur in the story as published: a grandfather in the Imperial Guards, who speaks of "my degenerate descendant" (p. 626); blocks of ice in the Beresina (pp. 623, 626); Lemieux comes from Tours (p. 633); his wife is from Rocamadour, and they have two children (p. 637).

    Fletcher, in a headnote in the *Cornhill*, writes that the figures of the story "were poor, wooden, sawdust-stuffed puppets until they had paid a brief visit to the greatest living artist in historical romance. They returned from that visit much more lively; yet they still remain but faint and feeble imitations of the immortal figures which fill the canvases of that great artist" (p. 623). RK evidently saw a draft of the headnote, for he wrote to Fletcher on 26 February that it was "all right about the introduction. 'Greatest of living artists in historical romance' disguises me quite effectually" (ALS, Sussex).

    On 16 February RK refused Fletcher's suggestion that RK write the story himself; he suggested instead that it be cast either as a letter home or as a one-act play (to Fletcher, 16 February 1916: ALS, Sussex).

2. Fletcher evidently intended a dream sequence following William the Conqueror's defeat of the Saxons as another episode in the contradictory relations of the French and the English over the centuries.

To H. A. Gwynne, 19 February 1916

ALS: Dalhousie University

Empire Hotel, / Bath. / Feb. 19. 1916

urgent
confidential
Dear Old Man –

You have been neglecting Haldane[1] again – with the inevitable result. As far as I make out there is a move going on to appoint "sympathetic" pro-german clerics to high places in the Church – men who believe in "reconciliation" after the war. *Exempli gratia.* A man called Barnes[2] has been appointed to the Temple. I understand (but you must make sure) that he is a member of the U.D.C.[3] and recently presided over its meetings at Cambridge. Also, find out who was put up for the Bishopric of Newcastle.[4] A decent candidate was, I am told, turned down on the grounds that what the Govt wanted was a "reconciler." The man at the back of this game is *Haldane* and for goodness sake go into it and work it up. If you can prove Barnes' complicity with the U.D.C. it will be a great step. But Haldane is the prime mover. Unless you keep him in a funk he will begin to do evil.

I have come across the diary of a prisoner in France – written by a soldier here.[5] It's the most amazing thing you ever read outside of Defoe. It ought to be published broadcast. The man for a wonder has written absolutely as he speaks. I am trying to get him to let me have it copied. What do you think could be done with it. Would the Censorship allow the horrors to be made public?

Ever
Rudyard

Notes

1. RK was among the many who, given Haldane's army reforms before the war (see 18 March 1911), his sympathy with German intellectual life (he had studied philosophy in Germany), and his fluency in German, concluded that he was "pro-German". Haldane had been excluded from the coalition government in consequence of this hostility, and could not now have anything officially to do with ecclesiastical appointments.
2. Ernest William Barnes (1874–1953), fellow and tutor of Trinity College, Cambridge, was appointed Master of the Temple in 1915 and became Bishop of Birmingham in 1924 on the nomination of Ramsay Macdonald. Barnes was a pacifist.
3. The Union of Democratic Controls, founded immediately upon the British declaration of war, aimed to achieve a lasting post-war settlement. Its programme was for "ending the war by negotiation and for open or democratic diplomacy afterwards" (A. J. P. Taylor, *English History 1914–1945*, p. 51). Inevitably, this position meant that it was seen as "pro-German" or "pacifist".
4. The Right Reverend H. L. Wild (1865–1940) had been appointed Bishop of Newcastle in September 1915.
5. See [*c.* 22 February 1916].

To H. A. Gwynne, [*c.* 22 February 1916]

ALS: Dalhousie University

Empire Hotel, / Bath.

confidential

Dear Old Man,

Here you are.[1] If the Censor passes it, you've got as big a scoop as you need. I suggest three or four articles (1 1/2–2 cols) in M. P. The whole thing is about 15,000 but you ought to get the guts in about 6,000. *It's an immense document.*

I have just been through it to cut out derogatory remarks about the Russians and also a reference to Captain Vidal.[2] Otherwise, I think it is all right. It gives the plain horrors of Wittenberg in the most awful form.

The "author" – Pte. A. Green 1st Somerset L. I. – is a hopeless cripple in the Mineral Waters Hosp. here. He wrote his record in an exercise book "to save himself the trouble of telling it all so often to his friends."

He is a long-service soldier – a resident of Bath. But don't mention his name, or give the name of any man mentioned in the record.

He showed me his "book" and I got him to let me have it typed. I told him I would send it to a paper and give him what I got for it. So cough up as much as you can – (it's worth anything over a tenner if the censor lets you print it) and send the cheque to Mr. A. Green care of me. That will convince Green of my bona fides. Be quick with the cheque please. Later on I want to have the record published in the U.S. specially with reference to Gerard's visit to Wittenberg.[3] It comes at the very best time in view of Vidal's return.

Go through it carefully and see that no comments on Russian prisoners are left in. It's an absolute mine of staff and revelations – notably the acct. of the munitions factory explosion near W.[4]

Ever yours
RK

Send the typed copy back to me when you have done. On no acct. mention my name or people will think I may have helped in it. It beats Defoe to *my* mind for sheer simplicity of horror.

RK

Notes

1. A narrative called *The Story of a Prisoner of War*, written by Arthur Green, a private in the 1st Somerset Light Infantry, whom RK met in a Bath hospital. The story is an account of the German prisoner of war camp for Russian, French, and English soldiers at Wittenberg, where an epidemic of typhus broke out in the winter of

1914–15. The mis-spellings and illiteracies of the author are left unchanged. It was published at RK's instance in the *Morning Post*, 13–22 March 1916, and then in book form by Chatto and Windus in April 1916. RK conducted the negotiations for book publication as well.

2. Captain Vidal, one of the British medical officers among the Wittenberg prisoners, had been detained by the German after the release of other British prisoners but was en route to England by 22 February (*The Times*, 23 February 1916).

3. James Watson Gerard (1867–1951), American Ambassador to Germany, 1914–17. Green records his visit to the Wittenberg camp: "Mr. Gerald, the American Ambassodor, came round about the 7th [September 1915]" (p. 79). Gerard himself wrote that "undoubtedly the worst camp which I visited in Germany was that of Wittenberg" (*My Four Years in Germany*, New York, 1917, p. 172). I can find no record of an American publication of the book.

4. *The Story of a Prisoner of War*, pp. 72–3: "there was a big explosion. ... I really thought it was the end of the world. ... It proved to be a big ammunition works had blown up, killing, they say, 300 women and girls."

To Dr W. S. Melsome,[1] 9 March 1916

Text: Copy, University of Sussex

Brown's Hotel,[2] / London, W.1. / Mar. 9. 1916.

Dear Melsome,

I enclose herewith cheque for your memo for two years' advice and good counsel. It's a ridiculously small part of the debt that I owe you.

Mrs Kipling, very wisely, has not been out of the hotel since she came. The weather has been more than infernal. My daughter on the other hand has attended several theatres as well as cinemas: so I suppose that averages things up.

I lunched with Bland-Sutton the day before yesterday and he started, of his own motion, to refer to you in terms that ought to have made your ears tingle – if you've given up blushing. I cheered him on.

My stomach is behaving with a certain decency which both pleases and surprises me. Those cachets of yours must have compelling virtues in 'em.

With all kindest wishes from us three

Most sincerely yours,
Rudyard Kipling.

Notes

1. Dr William Stanley Melsome (1865–1944), BA, MA, and MD, Cambridge, had been a fellow of Queens' College, Cambridge, 1888–95, before establishing himself at Bath, where he was in practice for over 40 years. He attended both CK and RK.

The "gastritis" that was diagnosed in 1915 (see 9 October 1915) was evidently becoming troublesome though not yet severe. It was in fact an undiagnosed duodenal ulcer, which would torment RK for the rest of his life. Dr Melsome appears in RK's "Clinical History" through 1919 but not thereafter.

2. They went to London on 2 March and on the 3rd attended the funeral of Henry James at Chelsea Old Church. They remained at Brown's Hotel until 18 March, when they returned to Bateman's (Rees extracts).

To Sir Douglas Brownrigg,[1] 24 April 1916
Text: Copy, A. P. Watt Ltd

[Bateman's] 24th April 1916.

Dear Sir Douglas,

I am sending you with this the draft of the first of three articles which I would propose to do from the notes sent me by the Admiralty.[2] If it is satisfactory, let me hear and I will go on with the work.

I must make one condition about these articles, and that is that your people shall be responsible for securing the American copyright in them, and that the copyright both in England and the United States of America shall become my property at the end of a year or at the termination of the war, whichever suits your arrangements best. In the meantime, of course, your people have the exclusive right to them to use as articles in newspapers or as pamphlets in propaganda work in all countries.

It is most essential that the articles should be properly copyrighted in America. This matter could be arranged for you by my agent, A. S. Watt Esq., (of the firm of A. P. Watt and Son, Hastings House, Norfolk Street, Strand, W.C.) who is also a member of Mr. Masterman's Committee[3] and works under him doing propaganda work.

Yours sincerely,
Rudyard Kipling.

Notes
1. Admiral Sir Douglas Brownrigg (1867–1939), 4th Baronet, retired from the Navy in 1913 but served as Chief Censor at the Admiralty throughout the war.
2. "Tales of 'The Trade'", a series of three articles about the Submarine Service ("The Trade") written from confidential reports to the Admiralty and collected in *Sea Warfare*. They were published in *The Times* and other papers, English and American, as follows: "Tales of 'The Trade' I: Some Work in the Baltic", 21 June 1916; "Tales of 'The Trade' II: Business in the Sea of Marmara", 23 June 1916; "Tales of 'The Trade' III: Ravages and Repairs", 28 June 1916. These articles were

distributed in mimeographed form to newspapers by the Official Press Bureau, care being taken to emphasise RK's copyright.
3. Charles Frederick Gurney Masterman (1874–1927), politician and author, was the director of Wellington House, the propaganda department, throughout the war. Before the war Masterman had been a high-church Liberal MP notable for his work towards social reform, including the National Insurance Act, and for his books on social questions, e.g., *The Condition of England*, 1909.

To George Saintsbury, 18 May 1916
ALS: University of Sussex

Bateman's / Burwash / Sussex / May. 18. 1916

Dear Saintsbury

I've been away from home for the past week:[1] and I wish to goodness "The English Novel"[2] hadn't been put on my table atop of letters to be answered. Don't think for a moment that I neglected my Duty. I merely had a look at the Four Wheels[3] (or Four Great Beasts) to assure myself of your orthodoxy. I don't see how I could have done less. But, anyway, none of my letters have been answered and I've raced through the whole of the book – as a preliminary to getting at it this afternoon with a pipe instead of working in the fields. It is infamously bound and of a cheap and ignoble aspect ("not given – only Dent")[4] which shall be remedied by clean leather.

I am specially beholden to you for the Marryatt and Bunyan estimates[5] – the dialogues of Pilgrim's Progress included and. …

But this is a matter one could go on with for the rest of the morning.

Has it occurred to you what a weltering geographical Hell the smaller literature of the Future is going to be immediately after the war? Only one background, mark you, and only one language – a sort of lingua-franca of the camps. Also, England (as part of that background) described from without by a whole generation of Australian, Canadian etc. novelists whose hero passes through the training-camps. London described by the *emigrés* of the French Revolution won't be in it for queerness.

Ever sincerely
Rudyard Kipling.

Notes
1. They were in London on 17 May (CK diary), perhaps the last day of a longer stay.
2. Saintsbury's *The English Novel*, 1913.
3. "The Four Wheels of the Novel Wain", Saintsbury's chapter on Richardson, Fielding, Smollett, and Sterne.

4. Possibly a play on the phrase "not given – only lent", though the application is hard to see. J. M. Dent was the publisher of *The English Novel.*
5. Marryat "has many of the qualities of the novelist in high degree" (p. 219). Bunyan is praised for dialogue written "as few have done it even since his time" (p. 56).

To Andrew Macphail, 21 May 1916

ALS: Photocopy, National Archives of Canada

Bateman's / Burwash / Sussex / May. 21. 1916.

Dear Macphail

I traced you by way of an officer at Bath, in charge of a clearing depot there so as to know at least you were alive and I had written you a long letter when yours of the 13th came in to our relief and joy. How I envy you your day with Geoff. By the way, as life runs now, he is about right for his triple stars – not that, I expect, he hasn't been doing major's work and more, for some time back. We expect a boy – (C[anadian]. R[oyal]. A[rtillery].) to lunch who at the advanced age of twenty two looks for a battery.[1] He has had a year, as well as some gas, but is now taking life with the abandon of his amazing breed. There's a regular Canadian colony at Shorncliffe[2] – well established by now where babies are born and folk come and go – mothers and sisters and such. In some ways it makes one think of the French emigrés of the Revolution. Curious to see how they modify the English around them and are in turn affected. I have studied the demoralization so to speak by English comfort of a young Canadian woman who by virtue of her husband's position, came into a two hundred year old house crowded with all the fat comforts of generations, and a red garden wall all round. The Australians being at this distance a kinless folk have not yet as far as I know established any colony but there is a scattering of South Africans. I spent a few months of last year and the beginning of this in the strange enjoyment of ill-health – and a civilian makes the devil of a fuss if he doesn't feel well. It was some internal kick up which gave me all the sensations of maternity with no benefit to the nation but, instead of growing gross I withered and shrank – a foretaste, just sketched in, of the lean pantaloon days to come. Very interesting to note in the looking glass. Then, after some time, the thing passed off – some said too much bolting of one's food; others gastric catarrh, and others other complaints. Anyhow I am not ill now but – there's no burking it – I feel as though I were older. Never having had the emotion before I was much annoyed: but one can't quarrel long with an Incontestable Fact. It's possible that I may be off to the Continent again ere long[3] – farther than France this time – a prospect that does not allure me. I've been among the ships a little, and liked them. Summer came on us in three great strides – and all the valley is one pale green fire, with warm nights and broom and gorze and lilac and the whole generation of wall-flowers up in insurrection together.[4] Unbelievably beautiful but, as you can imagine, a little too full of ghosts. We have no labour: we have 300 acres of land and small chance of getting in our hay but we have cattle and calves and Mrs. Kipling has found a Tasmanienne (which I take it is the feminine of Tasmanian) who, with the aid of a Dane is going to start in a cottage and make butter and look after poultry – with such developments as may develop. We have three or four women on the land already[5] – fat old things who somehow manage to do almost a man's work.

I have sent you – the only important part of this letter – a separate slip of memoes about Geoff's address and yours. Geoff and Dorothy must of course come down here[6] (*you* ought to have told her where we were as we can't get at her without address). You of course will come down here and I only pray I may be in England.

Forgive a scrawl but I have a hayrick and a half of a futile mail to worry through (what truck and tosh writing is) and I am ever

Yours
Rudyard Kipling

P.S.   Be of good heart as to the end. The Hun is not happy, nor certain of his future.

Memoes

No. 1.

Tell Geoffrey to let us know his address when he comes to England that he and Dorothy may come down here.

No. 2.

Let us have your address and your time of leave the instant that you know it.

R.K.

Notes

1. This was Lieutenant Harry Parker, identified as "C.R.A.", who had lunch at Bateman's on 16 April, 22 and 28 May, and 4 June 1916 (Bateman's Visitor Book).
2. Shorncliffe Camp, near Folkestone.
3. Whatever this possibility may have been, it did not materialise; RK's next trip to the Continent was to Italy in May 1917.
4. Cf. "Leaves from a Winter Note-Book": "No pen can describe the turning of the leaves – the insurrection of the tree-people against the waning year" (*Letters of Travel*, p. 103).
5. On 23 February CK recorded that "a lady comes down from London to discuss our offer of Rye Green farmhouse for a hostel for women's labour" (Rees extracts).

6.   Jeffrey, now Captain Macphail, MC, and Dorothy Macphail were at Bateman's on 22–3 June 1916 (Bateman's Visitors Book).

To H. A. Gwynne, 21 May 1916
ALS: Dalhousie University

Bateman's / Burwash / Sussex / May 21. 1916.

private

Dear Old Man,

I have been bothered all round the hat for a "message" to the Colonies etc. for Empire Day. So I have done the enclosed which goes to Canada Australia etc. and also to the London papers.[1] Here is your copy if you want to use it.

I hear Carson is suffering from a touch of weakness of the heart.

Ever yours
Rudyard Kipling

Notes

1.   "Empire Day Message", published in *The Times, Daily Express, Daily Telegraph* and other papers, 24 May 1916 (uncollected). This was the first officially-recognised celebration of Empire Day. The one-paragraph text begins "When Germany challenged us nearly two years ago to uphold with our lives the ideals by which we professed to live, we accepted the challenge not out of madness, nor for glory or for gain, but to make good those professions."

To Mrs R. A. Duckworth Ford, 26 May 1916
Text: Copy, University of Sussex

Bateman's / Burwash / Sussex / May 26, 1916

Dear Mrs Duckworth Ford –

This is just a line to tell you that your husband came down for a night on May 24th from town.[1] To my mind in spite of his Cameroons experiences, he looked distinctly better than when I first saw him in London nearly a year ago. At that time he was I fancy feeling the effects of our beautiful British climate in summer. This time though he was a little thinner he looked and moved much more fit in every way. He has no external trace of malaria in the shape of yellowish eyes or fever pallor. He is a uniform biscuit-brown colour. He eats well and I can testify that he sleeps well: and takes care of himself to the extent of travelling with a British warm coat. This is a trifle that men are apt to forget when they are in England. We didn't take any exercise but just loafed, though he insisted upon helping me sickle and clip a bit of a lawn (I let him do most of the work) in the sunshine. Evidently he has gardened before. We heard about your housekeeping in the tropics, which made us all rather envious: and we saw photoes of Dabs and Mick. Unluckily he had not brought down one of the new girl baby whom he profanely calls the Mushroom and, being a mere man, he couldn't tell my daughter accurately what "The Mushroom" was like.

Now he is up in town chasing round for a fresh appointment which I am very anxious that he should get: because there is no sense in England's losing the knowledge and experience of a man who has done Eastern and Tropical service. I only wish I were better able to advise him. But the main point is that he is very well and since (as I know) it is always comforting to hear from people who have seen one's man, I venture to write and tell you.

With our united best wishes to you and the family whom we feel that we know, very sincerely

Yours
Rudyard Kipling

Notes

1. This letter is enclosed in a letter of the same date from RK to Ford saying that "here's a small enclosure that I should like you to send on to your wife if you think fit" (ALS, Sussex). Ford had returned to England from the Cameroons early in 1916 and had been hospitalised with malaria and dysentery (RK to Ford, 28 February 1916: ALS, Sussex). RK had then arranged for the publication in the *Morning Post* of Ford's account of the Cameroons campaign (RK to H. A. Gwynne, 11 March 1916: ALS, Dalhousie). After his recovery, Ford visited Bateman's; this letter is RK's report of that visit to Mrs Ford, whom RK had never met.

To Lady Edward Cecil, 28 May 1916

ALs: Syracuse University

Bateman's / Burwash / Sussex / May. 28. 1916

Dear Lady Edward,

I am afraid there has been a little trouble over your last letter to Mrs Kipling.[1]

I did not know there was any *inland* censorship on letters but it seems that there is and that a Major E. M. Whistler-Titherington R.E. is Deputy Censor for East Sussex. He takes exception (the Defence of the Realm Act apparently permits this) to some of your remarks and he writes me that your references to the treatment of German prisoners would prejudice the Allies and Germany's relations on the conclusion of peace, and would give neutrals a wrong idea of our methods in dealing with prisoners. Apparently by a new ruling, if one has in one's house any printed or written matter that cannot be published, it is an offence under the Act. He has made *me* responsible for the letter though, as you will see, I have explained I have no control over my wife's correspondence and that you and she have long written to each other quite freely. I quite agree, privately, with your use of the term "Bloody Hun" as a justifiable epithet but – you know how *very* sensitive our Government are. Perhaps it would have been as well not to have actually written it down.

But, as I gather from Major T., the *real* trouble is your reference to their being made to travel in "dark bags" and, if you will allow me to say so, your even more unfortunate remark which Major T. seems to think is a direct incitement to murder, that they should be "very speedy in their journeys." There is no getting over the fact that the phrase *is* a trifle suggestive, though I don't in the least follow Major Titherington when he calls it "almost Turkish in its savagery," but I am sure that in your tactful hands it may be made to bear an explanation somewhat less sinister than that which he insists on attaching to it. I have done the best I could in the matter: but it appears that he referred the whole letter direct to the cabinet without giving you an opportunity to be heard in your own defence. I have of course disclaimed any responsibility, which I find I can do under the married women's property act: and it is, as I have told the Major, utterly impossible for me to produce previous correspondence between yourself and Mrs Kipling, which is what he wants me to do.

I enclose you copies of Major Titherington's letters etc. to me as well as the Cabinet's comments on the passage in your letter which seems to have landed us all in this rather unfortunate imbroglio.

As far as I read the situation they evidently don't wish to drag you *directly* into the matter; and Curzon's action in proposing a commission (which cannot be expected to arrive at a finding much before 1918) strikes me as singularly subtle and farsighted.

Very sincerely
Rudyard Kipling

Notes
1. What follows, it perhaps need not be said, is a joke. No doubt RK had prepared elaborate documentation to accompany the letter, but this has not been found.

To Frank N. Doubleday, 30 May 1916

ALS: Princeton University

Bateman's / Burwash / Sussex / May. 30. 1916

Private.

Dear Frank,

Many thanks for yours of the 15th. I did the verses[1] with some idea that they might be useful, but I had forgotten the Presidential Election.[2] As soon as I realized that the situation was going to be used for political purposes I cancelled them – and that was all there was to it. We'll let them repose in that safe of yours.

There is certainly no feeling whatever among the Allies against the U.S.A. for making money out of munitions. All the countries are full of contractors of sorts who are doing the very same thing. It happens in every war and is one of the penalties of being unprepared. As a matter of fact we have not heard much about the U.S.A. for some time past. The papers give us summaries, now and again, of your President's speeches and there may be an occasional leading article: but our main pre-occupation is, of course, the war and, for those who are not actually engaged in the war, the daily casualty list.

I haven't heard any one talk about the U.S.A. for months now and as far as I can remember I have only met a couple of U.S.A. citizens during the past half year. One of them was a person from the N.Y. *Tribune*[3] who was very careful to point out to all and sundry that he was pro-ally but not pro-British.

He complained to me, rather bitterly, that he could not get "good stories" and that we "lacked the personal note." I tried more or less to explain that we were not very keen on exploiting the blood of our own people for journalistic purposes and that our advertizing department was always behind the times. He went off to France and then wept loudly in his paper over English decadence. It was rather comic in one way because one could not tell him that the Allies are not as he seemed to think detached Powers each playing for its own hand, but a somewhat intimate union.

But to return to the U.S.A. This is, roughly, the position from the Allies' point of view. None of us expected the U.S.A. to take actual part in the war at its outbreak. She had not, nor has she now, men or material for one week's work under modern conditions. Nor was it conceivable if the Germans had done their preliminary political arrangements properly, that the various races etc. in her borders would have permitted the U.S.A. to embark on any such venture.

None the less, there was an expectation – I, for one, confess that I shared it for a short while – that the U.S.A. would have entered some sort of protest (formal) against the violation of Belgium since this was a matter which did not concern her relations to any of the allies but *did* vitally concern the principles and ideals which the U.S.A. professed to hold and under which she asserts she was founded. However, the U.S.A. did not put herself on record in any way except in so far as her President officially urged her people to be *"neutral even in thought."*[4] This somewhat astonished some sections of the public among the Allies.

Then followed certain difficulties between the U.S.A. and Germany.[5] We need not go into them but the attitude of the U.S.A. under them impressed most people as the second outstanding wonder of this war – the first, of course, being the revelation of Germany's scientific and well-matured savagery.

But all this happened many months ago, and since then the Allies have been fighting to save themselves and the rest of the world from a general return to the methods and ethics of Assyria. We have had no time to think of anything except the war which has changed every detail of our lives, all our thoughts and our whole outlook upon life.

Naturally, this is not a thing one talks about but when peace comes we shall all realize it and we Allies will have to get together and make the new world. The U.S.A. is still in the old.

If we Allies win, the U.S.A. will be all comfortable and will never know what she has been saved from. She will be able to present her claims for interference with mails, diversions of cargoes etc. in proper courts of Law and will probably make an extremely good thing out of it.

If we lose, she will, after an interval dependent not on her pleasure or her preparations but on the German convenience, perish utterly, for there will then be no effective power in all the world to enforce any moral principle or any old fashioned conception of right and wrong. And when the U.S.A. goes, that will be the formal finish of "Democracy." It will have been tried for a hundred years and proved incapable of protecting the life of man, the honour of woman or the property of either.

I know that you cannot realize this but *we* can. Look into Belgium and see the thing in full operation, and into the occupied portions of France which are now such a Hell as you cannot conceive. You write that it would be a good thing if England were to pay the U.S.A. "all the easy civilities possible" to "keep things going well" between the two countries. England, at present, has five million men under arms simply in order that things may go well with the world which includes the U.S.A. No people can do more than send out its best to die for absolute elementary right as against calculated and prepared wrong. You suggest also that at least one important man "should come to the U.S.A. on a mission – just a mission of friendship and good will." That is the talk of the old world which died on Aug. 4 1914. Men do not prove their friendship and good will now by their mouth but by their lives. We have stated our case – it is written in blood and fire where all the world can see it. The Germans have again and again most explicitly declared that they are out for "world-empire or go under." You yourselves best know what methods they have used against you, a neutral, in pursuit of their aims. It is not for us to send a man to compete with Bernstorff[6] or his agents in your country, or to threaten the awful things that will happen to private citizens of the U.S.A. unless the U.S.A. does what we demand. We can't give you "good stories" or interest you in the "personal note" of this war. Those of your citizens who are of English descent do not conspire against your Government or your institutions. Our Ambassador has in no way, on any occasion, overstepped the strictest lines of international correctness. At no time have we asked anything of you in the nature of a gift except, long ago, we expected from you one or two words of moral support which would have shown us that your people dared to disapprove of the unprovoked murder of a nation and a country.

And that you did not give. Not God Himself can now return to you the hour when you might have spoken – merely spoken – as a Power in the face of Civilization and when, in all likelihood you would have saved millions of lives and, certainly, would have saved that which is more precious than any life on earth. You chose, after full thought and mature deliberation, to commit moral suicide. There may be many reasons, and some justifiable, for a man to commit suicide; but the old rough rule of our world runs that suicide is confession and avoidance. As it is with a man when things have to be faced in their reality, so it is with a nation.

As I have said, people – except word-spinners like myself – are too busy now to think about these things. Indeed, I would go so far as to say that no one wants to think about them unless and until the U.S.A. seriously puts forward her belief that she may take part in bringing peace to the world. I see that the cables just now have many references to this idea – mainly, I gather, because it would be a feather in Mr. Wilson's cap if he succeeded.[7] I hardly think that is a safe line to take up since any serious attempt, if persisted in, would bring the U.S.A. up against the whole of that civilization which has paid with its blood to save Civilization. The terms in this war will be imposed by the winning side. A victorious Germany would not listen for an instant to any representations from the U.S.A. The Allies, if victorious, would not be disposed to attach much weight to the actions of a Power which is "neutral even in thought."

And herein, as I see it, lies a peril for the U.S.A. – that she may be led either by some idea of election advantage, or the quite human desire to "do something", to commit herself to serious peace diplomacy. In that event, you may be sure that, though the language of the Allied diplomats would be studiously correct and, since the Censorship is strong, the tone of the Allied press would be equally correct, the public opinion of the Allies could hardly be prevented from crystallizing against the U.S.A. A glance at the map will show you how wide-spread that public opinion would be.

From Quebec to Vancouver there is hardly one Canadian household which has not contributed to the Dominion's 400,000 men. From Vladivostok to the Russian European border the same holds good as regards Russia where the war is educating the Russian peasant enormously. Australian with her 260,000 – most of whom have seen the heaviest fighting along our line, and New Zealand with her 100,000 have each made their sacrifices on the same scale. India, with a number of troops which need not be specified, as well as every one of the Empire's eastern possessions, is equally concerned. South Africa which has run two, if not three successful campaigns against the German,[8] has her own interests to consider. We come, then, to Italy with her immense immigration to the U.S.A., France, which has borne the heaviest burden of all, and, lastly, England.

It does not seem to me a light matter for the U.S.A. to have herself and her actions misunderstood not merely by the politicians and the press but by every man, woman and child in all these countries, concerned in the war. And, remember that a woman who has lost her dearest in this war has a longer memory and a more enduring hate than a man. Also, women will have more political power in the future, with all the Allies.

Therefore, I am inclined to think it would be wisest for the U.S.A. at this juncture not to commit herself to peace proposals or even to indulge too much in pious aspirations after peace, because all those things help the German against whom civilization is at war.

You bring yourself up against the Question which, so far, has not been asked aloud: – "By what right, by what effort, by what sacrifice are you entitled to speak on *any* matter outside your own borders?"

I would not have volunteered this if you had not explicitly asked: and if it had been any one except you whom I love (and to whom in great measure I owe the fact that I am alive and able to bear my burden in these great days) I shall not have written a word in reply.

You may remember in the early days of the war that I wrote you, as I wrote some other people, urging that the U.S.A. should prepare against the reality of things.[9] I see now that it is too late for you to prepare. As far as our generation and the next is concerned, the U.S.A. except in material things, must be guided by the world and not as she would guide herself.

Ever affectionately yours
Rud

P.S.   And, after all, what have I said here that is not in "The Question."[10]

Notes
1. Not identified.
2. Wilson campaigned successfully for re-election in 1916 on the slogan "He kept us out of war."
3. Frank Simonds (1878–1936), American journalist, was associate editor of the *New York Tribune*, 1915–18. He was regarded by American audiences as particularly expert on the events of the war and published a five-volume *History of the World War*, 1917–20. Simonds was probably the unnamed journalist of whom RK wrote

to Lady Edward Cecil on 16 March 1916: "I saw him again Monday afternoon – after he had seen Law and just before he saw Milner. He spoke much as he has written you and I tried to explain that our mouths were shut. … I told him that by the time he had seen something of France he himself might be able to realize a little of the situation. But, I think, his main desire is to make the English 'tell their story' which he won't do" (ALS, Syracuse University).

4. Wilson's statement, published on 19 August 1914, declared that "the United States must be neutral in fact as well as in name. … We must be impartial in thought as well as in action" (Ray Stannard Baker and William E. Dodd, eds, *The Public Papers of Woodrow Wilson*, III [1926], 158).

5. Over the German policy, announced early in 1915, of unrestricted submarine warfare in response to the Allied blockade. Wilson steadily protested to the Germans and received some concessions, but his policy would certainly have seemed weak and discreditable to RK.

6. Johann-Heinrich, Graf von Bernstorff (1862–1939), German diplomat, Ambassador to the US, 1908–17. He hoped for American mediation in the war.

7. Wilson spoke on 27 May 1916 to the League to Enforce Peace, suggesting a league of nations and offering the US as a mediator in the war: "Our interest is only in peace and its future guarantees" (Arthur S. Link, *Wilson: Campaigns for Progressivism and Peace 1916–1917*, Princeton, 1965, p. 26). The speech was unenthusiastically received in France and Britain. *The Times* concluded that "the Allies are not and will not be disposed to allow American internal politics to be introduced into their righteous quarrel … they will listen to proposals for peace in such a quarrel only when they come from the beaten foe" (29 May 1916).

8. The South African forces had defeated the Germans in South West Africa in a campaign concluded by July 1915. The Germans had taken the offensive in east Africa, moving from their Tanganyika Colony into Kenya. A South African force had been operating against the Germans there since 1915 and had succeeded in driving them south, but the Germans maintained resistance until after the Armistice in 1918.

9. 11 September 1914.

10. "The Question" (or "The Neutral", under which title it also appeared) was first published at the end of *Sea Warfare*, 1916, and was collected in *The Years Between*: the poem parallels Peter's denial of Christ with the American failure to support the Allies.

To Sir J. R. Dunlop Smith, 9 June 1916

ALS: Tyler Collection, Yale University

Bateman's / Burwash / Sussex / June 9. 1916.

Dear Dunlop –

I'm extremely glad that a book *is* being done about our Indian troops' work in the war; but a foreword, I'm afraid, is out of the question. I'm *very* busy with a long job now,[1] and I have declined so many times to make forewords for books on various aspects (and troops) engaged in the war, that I couldn't do one now without putting myself wrong with the men I have had to refuse. Such a book ought to be done in the very best way possible.

As to the Censor's reports (Indian letters) I'd be immensely grateful for more of them. They are a complete revelation. If in my floods of work I can manage ever to do what I want and compile some sort of article out of them – not, of course, giving the source of my informations – may I send it to you to be checked?[2]

In great haste

Ever yours
Rudyard

Notes

1. The only long job RK had in hand now was "Tales of 'The Trade'", and that had been essentially completed by this time.
2. The first reference to what became the series of "Indian letters" published serially in 1917 and collected as *The Eyes of Asia*, 1918.

To Captain R. A. Duckworth Ford, 19 June 1916

ALS: University of Sussex

Bateman's / Burwash / Sussex / June 10. 1916

Dear Duckworth Ford,

Yes – I know Lugard,[1] not intimately but well enough to write him a letter which I shall be glad to do when you go out.[2] I agree with you that an administrative job out there would be best and – which is your luck – men with tropical experience are rare. I'm rather glad – from the point of view of the Imperial game – that you have elected for Africa again.

We've just had a man down here fresh from the Jutland action – a destroyer commander.[3] He was very well satisfied with what had been dealt out to the Hun and had a gay time *between* a couple of Dachshund cruisers at 200 yds both of whom tried to ram him!

Yes – I think the war goes steadily enough and the Hun is not happy. The fun will begin when he realizes that the world don't want him to be happy. Then he will curse his God (which is the Kaisar) and throw fits.

Thanks to various forms of skilled and unskilled white labour that came, as guests, to Bateman's; we have scythed, sickled *and* mown with the hand-mower, the strip of grass all round the pond – also the other semicircle of turf where there isn't a sundial! The effect is superb! Tomorrow, we hope for even greater things. MacIntosh is no friend of mine, being an immoral gander but Bowser, one of his wives (the brown one) now eats bread from my hand and makes snuffling noises like an affectionate puppy! I never knew geese had such a vocabulary.

What I mean to do about L. is to write him a full private letter about you and send you the formal "this is to introduce" chit. Will that be all right?

With every good wish

Ever
Rudyard Kipling

Notes

1. Lugard (see 12 November 1905), Governor-General of Nigeria, 1914–19.
2. I have found no record of Ford's service in Nigeria.
3. This was Lt.-Commander Lyon (Bateman's Visitors Book, 9 June 1916), who is probably Admiral (as he later became) Sir George Hamilton D'Oyly Lyon (1883–1947), who was at the Battle of Jutland. He held various commands afterwards, including the African Station, 1938–40, and the Nore, 1941–3. The Battle of Jutland had been fought on 31 May 1916. This was the only major engagement of the war between the British Grand Fleet and the German High Seas Fleet, or, as A. J. P. Taylor puts it, "the only battle between two great modern fleets ever fought in European waters" (*English History 1914–1945*) p. 63). The battle involved 250 ships and 25 admirals; the inconclusive results allowed both sides to treat it as a victory.

To Andrew Macphail, 15 June [1916]

ALS: Photocopy, National Archives of Canada

Bateman's / Burwash / Sussex / June. 15.

Dear Macphail

Yours of the 12th.

We are writing at once to have Dorothy down here, where her advice in agricultural matters (and it is needed) will be worth gold.[1] We have a houseful of women workers on the land – plus two kine and chickens etc. etc. They are all new and largely unrelated.

We are all hoping and praying that you will get your leave and will head here and be washed and put to bed.[2] We are expert in putting the wearied to bed. As to the Naval business, I take it that, by now, you are aware of the indescribably brutal carelessness that pitched that first summary all raw into our astonished faces.[3] It cost all our Empire a terrible night but I don't suppose it troubled Balfour's sleep for an instant. I can't tell you how savage we all were, and are, about it.

I had a destroyer commander down here last week, fresh from the Horn Reef.[4] He told me that when they returned to port (he towing a disabled destroyer) they were received by the shore-people as a beaten fleet. "And" he said wrathfully, "we were rather thinking we had done our bit, too." By all accounts the Fleet has more than done that. My friend being destroyer was naturally only acquainted with what his class had done. The round-up afterwards was just like men comparing notes after a battue. "How many shots did you loose? What did you get?" They compared notes all round, and – it wasn't a bad total – for destroyers only. My friend missed his bird – a light cruiser leaping on him out of the dark at 200. As he swung to get her, another cruiser came down on the other side and he had just an instant to straighten himself up between the two of 'em and they passed a few yards clear of him. One gave him her broadside by searchlight-point blank but she had allowed for 1000 yards and the salvo tore over them. A gay night, as light as day, he said, when the guns fired and one saw the destroyers running like black cockroaches over the lit up waters. I haven't met any of the big-ship men but they dealt faithfully with the Hun and Wilhelmhaven[5] is one scrap-heap, let alone those ships who did not return. We shan't get news out of the Hun in a hurry[6] but the North Sea is shallow and will give up its secrets in due time. One thing seems well established – that when fired at afloat the Hun's return fire is erratic and he does not love torpedoes one little bit.

So be cheered. I could give you details of the enemy losses but not officially. I think we may take it however that they were effactually sickened and more than our own losses were put down on their side *plus* the general hammering up of as much of their ironmongery as floated at the end.

And now we'll arrange for Dorothea her birthday.

God bless you and keep you.

Ever Affectionately,
R.K.

Notes
1. Dorothy Macphail visited Bateman's with her brother, 22–3 June (see 21 May 1916).
2. Macphail was at Bateman's with his daughter on 15–16 January 1917 (Bateman's Visitors Book).
3. Balfour, now First Lord of the Admiralty, issued a communiqué on 2 June 1916, the first public news of the Battle of Jutland, confined to the facts as they were then known. This was treated by the press as the news of a disaster. When a fuller assessment of the battle had been made, Balfour suffered much abuse for having seemed to exaggerate the losses. He defended himself on the grounds that truth-telling could not be grounds for regret.
4. Usually Horns Reef, a shoal off the coast of Jutland. The Battle of Jutland (the Battle of Skagerrak to the Germans) was originally called the Battle of Horn Reef in the British press.
5. Wilhelmshaven, home port of the German High Seas Fleet.
6. The Germans did, for a brief time, conceal their losses.

To André Chevrillon, 22 June 1916
Text: Copy, University of Sussex

Bateman's / Burwash / Sussex / June 22nd 1916

Dear Chevrillon,

I've just got your letter and am very glad you've held up the arrangement with Hodder Stoughton till you've communicated with Watt.[1] He is on the publicity committee and I am pretty sure it is for the U.S.A. that he wants the book.

As to my writing a preface. Assuredly I will do it and (it is pleasant to use a common form phrase in all sincerity) I shall feel myself honoured in the association. But, between ourselves, 'twill be the first time I've ever done a preface and I shall probably make a howling mess of it.[2]

Be a good man and give me a phrase or two as to the points one ought to bring out. I know more or less what I want to say but I don't know if I can get the balance and the poise as I'd like it. Behold the extraordinary delicacy of the situation!

We – all of us Allies engaged in the war, have, after generations of strictly materialistic training, after corruptions and imbecilities innumerable, after loss of faiths, morale, and convictions – we, I say, have been surprised or forced, or (as I prefer to believe) inspired into the most tremendous affirmation of the immanent goodness of man's soul that Earth has ever known. The choice was given us: – "Offer yourselves as a sacrifice for mankind or perish in the spirit". Through the great goodness of God we chose the sacrifice. We scarcely admit this even among ourselves: indeed I doubt if we yet realize it but – there it is. Aren't I right?

Now, for one horrible moment, imagine yourself a Neutral to whom also a choice had been given – not, necessarily, to add his proper body to the oblation but merely to give or withold his word of approval on the sacrifice. Conceive that, for a reason, for a multiplicity of excellent reasons, you, that Neutral had chosen at the beginning, *not* to give that word of approval. Imagine further that as time went on and blood ran, you perceived – were compelled to perceive in spite of your own neutral preoccupations – the splendour and the significance of the sacrifice that was accomplishing itself before your eyes? Surely, my dear Chevrillon, in order to exist upon any terms with yourself, in order to keep your sanity and belief in some sort of moral order, you would be constrained to discover, or invent and, having done so, to reiterate to yourself *any* statement, any excuse, *any* form of words which would allow you to feign to yourself that your abstention had been justified. And that, as I see it, is precisely the position of the neutral to-day. Here is his argument: – initially, the sacrifice of the Allies was inconceivable unless they were mad – "all mad together" as I believe one Neutral Statesman said. But people do not go mad on such a scale or (the Neutral argues) at least they have never done so in the world's history up to date. Therefore there must be another reason. Outside of insanity there is only one thing which, the experience of ages proves, will move mankind. That is commercial gain. *Ergo* the Allies were moved to war by the hope of commercial gain. For if this were not so – (it is the neutral who is still arguing) then am I a castaway who have betrayed civilization. *But* I cannot have betrayed civilization because I am visibly surrounded with the appliances of civilization such as water closets, elevators, beautiful furniture and automobiles, and a most eloquent press. Moreover, the evidence of my bank account shows me that I have gained the whole world. Therefore I must have saved my soul. Therefore it is incumbent upon me to save the souls of my misguided brethren who are surrounded with shell-holes, disease, dirt, blood and wounds – all of which are evidences of barbarism. Therefore I will continue in my good work of gaining all the world and of trying to save with my eloquent press and my excellent aphorisms the souls of my brethren who are mad. Then the argument repeats itself on the line that I have just drawn. It is a circle of torture in which the Neutral must continue to revolve for the simple reason that if he escapes from it – he knows himself as he is: and that is knowledge which no self-respecting neutral permits himself to acquire. I also have met a neutral lately who explained to me how England "embarked" (Mon Dieu! *what* an embarkation) on this war for "commercial gain". I suggested that it seemed to me rather a clumsy way to arrive at our ends but that did not trouble him. To his mind there could have been no other reason. He knew all about our motives. *You*, you will be interested to learn, "embarked" on the same dark vessel, for "revenge". In which case your preparations!! . . Russia was actuated by "motives of conquest" and "a desire to escape from the despotism of the ruling classes". It is all so damned simple when one is outside the fight, isn't it?

I am sketching (our National Respectability will never allow me to publish it) an interview between Judas and one of the Sanhedrin just before the thirty pieces of silver were paid.[3] Nobody admitted more freely than Judas and the priest the personal and social merits of the Person whom they were bargaining over. He was perhaps a little austere and self-centred but, left to himself, he would have been quite a decent member of society. It was his foolish principles that made the danger: they were subversive of all progress – reactionary to the last degree and in the interests of local and provincial peace, they ought to be gently but firmly checked. And the more I go into the tale the more I sympathize with Judas's point of view. Why be dragged around Palestine at the heels of a lot of rowdy peasants, when one could get money *and* consideration from the established and generous gentlemen of the Sanhedrin?

Meantime my personal heart is heavy for as the year turns round and dates and days repeat themselves one is dragged back to the past of last year and that is not pleasant. We are a very large band now – we parents who do not know where our dead are laid: and I think, it is that indignity which moves us as deeply as anything. Never believe again, that the English do not know how to hate: It was a long lesson and we were slow learners but we have our teaching by heart at last.

Still there remains some amusement in the world. It is all of one sort of course. I had a boy down to lunch with me the other day, about four days after the little affair at Horn Reef.[4] He was a captain of a destroyer and, not till we had half finished our meal, did he tell us, incidentally, that he had been through the business and had towed a disabled destroyer home. The destroyer is a class apart. After the fight they talked one to another, exactly like men after a battue: "How many shots did you fire?" "How many birds did you get?" They got a good many. In one case, one boy had to let a flying cruiser go. (The light cruisers were bolting all across one flotilla like flushed partridges). He daren't fire for fear his own torpedo would explode *in* its tube. Judge how close the two ships were. And they missed – the Huns missed – *at two hundred yards* with salvoes of 4 and 6 inch stuff! It was a holy mess. What annoyed my friend when he came back to port, thinking, as he said: "We'd rather done our little bit" was to be received in dead silence by the natives of a "beaten fleet"![5] It was that immortal First Despatch. Some day I will tell you about it and you shall decide whether National Temperament isn't tenfold more bewildering to the enemy than acquired machiavellianism. I haven't met any of the big ship men but I am told that they didn't do so badly. Williamshaven is full of unusable ironmongery and there is stuff at the bottom of the North Sea which will have to be fished up one of these days.

I have a theory – I haven't developed it to anyone but you – that knowing the Hun would make a tremendous victory of it whatever happened; knowing also that he was fighting off his own shore where he could cover up his losses and get away with his lame ducks – our authorities decided to let him have all the victory he wanted to advertise, and to take the chances (which of course were a certainty) of his people being more knocked out by the gradual leakage of facts afterwards than our people would be by the "inspissated gloom"[6] of Despatch No. 1. As I have frequently remarked – we are a brutal people where our own feelings are involved.

One charming child, demonstrating on the table-cloth with knives and bits of bread, a position of variegated peril through which he had lately passed, wound up his tale with: "Of course if I'd got her ('she' was a Hun ship) it would have meant promotion for me and I rather wanted to get her because I want a bigger destroyer to command. My present one is too wet for my taste." As it was someone else "got her" and the consequent promotion. My friend merely drove her towards his friend. He said it was like chasing a hare.

And now we in England have cleaned up all the crumbs. Every one is up or under notice to be called up who has not already gone. Me voici, with one man over age, to look after 160 acres of land and 27 cattle. My sole gardener under orders and my sole help a youth and a boy and a scattering of female labour. It's absurd and trivial enough in the face of what you have to endure but I grow very eloquent on the "hardships of war". You who know all English literature know the Ingoldsby Legends and the Lady of whom it was written: –

> The hard iron gauntlet her flesh went an inch in.
> She didn't mind Death but she couldn't stand pinching.[7]

My sentiments exactly when I act as electrician in charge of our electric lighting plant and cover myself with oil from my eyebrows to my boots. The literary temperament is *not* mechanical.

Have I told you we have fitted up one of our farm-houses as a place where a convalescent officer can come with his wife and rest a bit. We did it all ourselves and it has been full since the 1st of May.[8] Our present case is gas and shell-shock – a young civilian with no thought of war, predestined to be a bank-clerk and now, with a military cross and a year's war behind him, a man of new thoughts and ideas – one of many thousands who have little patience with politicians. I think the politicians will be surprised but they live in a world of their own where all the old dead things and words are still alive and worshipped.

And now I will go out and attend to various matters about the farm. We have much hay and no labour to get it in with. My heart is too full about Verdun[9] to say what I would say. It is beyond admiration as it has been almost beyond belief. Yes, I suppose I must strike you sometimes as Doctor Pangloss[10] (and you should see me cultivate my garden) but I deny vehemently that I am optimistic. It is only that I do not admit the Legend of the Hun: I was saved from that by not knowing the German language whereby (Allah be praised!) I have walked all my days quite immune to the German. So I repeat that we *are* compassing his destruction, utter and irremediable. We are appalled now at what he has done to us. The time is at hand when we shall be appallel at what he has done to himself. The Neutral will then say: "See what you have done to him." *That* is the time we must be on our guard for our dead will have been buried but his will lie out in the open to solicit the weak pity of mankind. . .

> Ever with all sincerity
> Rudyard Kipling

Notes

1. Regarding the arrangements for the English translation and publication of Chevrillon's *L'Angleterre et la guerre* (Paris, 1916). RK had written to Chevrillon on 15 June 1916 recommending that he put the book in Watt's hands (copy, Sussex). It appeared in England as *Britain and the War* and in the US as *England and the War* (London: Hodder and Stoughton; New York: Doubleday, Page and Co., 1917), with a preface by RK (uncollected).

2. He had done no formal preface before, but letters from RK had been used, no doubt with permission, as prefaces to Frank Bullen, *The Cruise of the "Cachalot"*, 1898, and Robert D'Humières, *Through Isle and Empire*, 1905; RK also wrote introductory verses ("The Sea-Wife") for John Arthur Barry, *Steve Brown's Bunyip and Other Stories*, 1893.
3. This is the only record of the work that I know of.
4. That is, the Battle of Jutland: see 10 June.
5. Thus in copy. In the French translation of this letter published in the *Revue des Deux Mondes*, 15 September 1959, the passage reads: "ce fut d'être reçu par les gens du pays comme une "flotte vaincue", au milieu d'un silence de mort!" (p. 199).
6. Boswell, *Life of Johnson*, 16 October 1769.
7. Richard Harris Barham, "The Tragedy", *Ingoldsby Legends*.
8. They received a wounded officer named Savill and his wife at Dudwell farmhouse on 3 May; when the Savills left, a Lt. Hall, his wife, and his sister-in-law moved in (Rees extracts, 25 April; 3, 31 May; 1 June 1916). There were at least two further soldier occupants until 20 September 1917, when RK's sister Trix and a companion arrived to take up residence at Dudwell Farm (Rees extracts).
9. The German offensive against Verdun, beginning on 21 February 1916, was the longest single battle of the war, lasting until December. The casualties were more than 650,000.
10. The optimistic philosopher of Voltaire's *Candide*.

To Lord Selborne, 29 June 1916

ALS: Bodleian Library

Bateman's / Burwash / Sussex / June. 29. 1916

Dear Lord Selborne

I can't tell you how your resignation[1] gives one belief and hope, in these fantastic days, of confused issues. Of course the position as you put it is quite a straightforward one.

It is difficult to understand why a man should be expected to go back on all his conviction and all his experience, merely because Ireland has proved the truth of them up to the hilt.

Believe me you have heartened us all and I, for one, am very grateful.

Sincerely yours
Rudyard Kipling.

Notes
1. Selborne (see 27 March 1906) resigned his office as President of the Board of Agriculture and Fisheries on 25 June on the government's Irish policy. Following the Easter uprising in Ireland (see letter to Almroth Wright, [1916]), Asquith had moved to grant Home Rule at once, but the opposition of Selborne and others so long as the Ulster question was unresolved defeated this move.

To Louisa Baldwin, 5 July [1916][1]
ALS: Dalhousie University

Bateman's July. 5.

My dear Aunt Louie,

How kind and sweet of you to think of it. '51 Port[2] is *not* the kind of drink one finds flowing through the public conduits, these days. I will be very good to it and invite none but worthy and educated tastes to help me finish it.

Our village has been sent clean off its head by æroplanes – five or six of them – flying from Dover to Brighton and falling into the fields near by.

Yesterday we had two disabled machines, squatting like wounded birds, in the fields and *all* the village ran to help. Only the invalids were left. When they reached the scene of action they all took out pencils and wrote their names and addresses on the wings of the thing!! But why? What instinct is it that makes us do that? Dear love from us all.

Ever lovingly
Ruddy.

Notes
1. The letter has been endorsed "1916", and there is no internal evidence to contradict that date.
2. Doubtless from the great cellar of RK's late Uncle Alfred Baldwin: see 8 October 1898. George Saintsbury says of '51 Port that it was "the finest port, of what may be called the older vintages accessible to my generation, that I ever tasted; it was certainly the finest that I ever possessed" (*Notes on a Cellar Book*, 1920, p. 31).

To Andrew Macphail, 15–17 July 1916
ALS: Photocopy, National Archives of Canada

Bateman's / Burwash / Sussex / July. 15. 1916
(And the first fine day we've had in ever so long)

Dear Macphail

Bless you for your letter: and specially the news about Geoffrey. But why can't the boy get even a month back here? It means ... but then he wouldn't shift, I suppose, unless he were hiked out by the slack of his trousers. I wish he'd pick up paratyphoid and be slung home like a young friend of mine was the other day. Lord! What a world when *this* is the sincere wish of friendship!

If you were here now you'd see us in the agonies of hay making which, for us, is vital. Our weather has been of the Devil. One opens up and wind rows all day and at evening comes the rain. The wife – who is Executive Ability Its Very Self – has gone in for Female Labour; and has attracted some twelve women and three small babies to our fields. Our transport is one cart borrowed (when we can get it) and our own much astonished pony. But Female Labour has its draw backs. Our one solitary stockman, an unlovely man but skilled in his job, is wedded to a widow manifestly older than himself with a taste for drink and the more facile emotions. She is a-moral and *therefore* (as I have noted in many cases) very jealous. And, among our women is the wife of a man now at the Front: with no figure, a good worker and I imagine highly vitalized. She and the Stockman have worked together for some weeks this summer at cleaning beans etc. etc.: always in company with another woman, sometimes two. (We do not concern ourselves with what they do when *not* in our employ: for we are modest folk.)

Well – that fell which fell!

Some days ago, being at work, I heard the high shrill note of the Agitated Female ('tis a sex note there's no mistaking) in the garden. It was the wife of the Stockman, explaining to Carrie, without *any* circumlocutions, that her husband was not to work for us any more on account of his carryings on with the wife of the soldier. C. met her with frigid and calculating calm: which naturally wrought her on to the verge of hysterics. After she had well boiled over C. laid on lashes, knowing – as all our world does – that the virtuous wife had had a babe by her husband before she married him and that two of her daughters had each had one unedited baby. The troubled waters were just subsiding. The injured wife, moderately sane, was going out by the back gate when she ran into the Hated Rival who, by the way, was carrying a hayfork. There were words – Greek, Ancient, unquotable – which C. heard. Again she flung herself on the injured wife who said there would be murder done. The hated Rival fled into Bateman's hall, clinging to her pitchfork, and leaned against it panting and crying: – "That dirty woman!" *da capo prestissimo.* C. led the injured wife clean out into the landscape and dismissed her.

(End of Chapter I)

Well, I won't go on. There were a lot of other developments including the breakage of all the Hated Rival's windows by the injured wife. But this happened in the village outside our jurisdiction. We kept our Stockman: we kept the hated Rival (she being a good worker) and the injured wife has not done murder. What struck me was the fury and sound and passion of this little affair in the front-garden, the utter self-concentration of the parties involved – and behind the figures and between the pauses, the far notes of your guns.

(Here was a break of an hour when I went out and turned hay. It's clouding over and – ten ton are involved!) I've just finished doing a series of letters from Indian troops.[1] I told you didn't I, that the one thing all our Indian soldiers were united upon was the necessity of education for their women. By "education" they mean mere knowledge of how to handle the material appliances of civilization such as washers, wringers, churns, improved brooms etc. etc.[2] It's *very* [ ][3] the reverse way to the civilization of the Boers whose women we put into concentration camps and introduced to the Army and Navy store-list. That was enough. *Now*, it is our natives at large among all the wonders of Europe clamouring that their women shall work.

Also I am trying to write a preface to André Chevrillon's estimate of England and the War which is to be translated into English. Also, I have had an answer from Frank Doubleday, my publisher, to the letter that I wrote him[4] and read to you on the sofa. It's merely a fatuous repetition of general excellent and quite useless sentiments coupled with a desire that "the two countries shall understand each other better" – that's US and the U.S.! What *can* one do with such a mood of mind? I remember once running into a sudden gale, in the Bay, on our way up from South Africa. It came on at teatime and knocked crockery, and electric light fittings about. The women and children in the saloon were naturally impressed and the stewards were very busy. But I remember the single saw-like voice of one child through it all: – "*I* want to pee-pee!" again and again.

I wish I could think of the U.S. in any terms that connote dignity. Now they go down to the sea to look at – the type of boat that sunk the *Lusitania* and they decide it's a merchant ship!![5]

Somehow that seems to cap the horror of it all. I've had the head of the Northern End of the Nigerian show down for a night.[6] He's a general and was a schoolmate of mine and an intimate friend of one "Stalky" who is also a general in India. The man who guards the Khyber pass, with whom "Stalky" has to work, is also an old schoolmate.[7] (He appears in a tale called "A Conference of the Powers"[8] under the title of the Infant.) You can imagine what a funny mix up our conversation was – Nigeria, Westward Ho! India and all the rest. Nothing gives one so appalling a notion of the vastness of the fight as to come across men who for a couple years have been waging war across thousands of miles utterly out of touch with the main war. My friend's heart and soul were bound up in getting a certain quantity of native troops (West Africans) over to help Smuts clean up in British East Africa.[9] Think of the distances. He told me one nice tale. After the Cameroons were taken, the French and English divvied up the prisoners on a list – 1 and 3 for the French, 2 and 4 for the English and so on. A German general fell to the French lot. He came over to my general and besought him that he should be added to the English bag – on account of the damnable nature of the French. My friend said: – "No. We will abide by the apportionment." Upon which the Hun first wept then got down on his knees. My friend, nearly vomiting, passed him over to the French. Three or four days later came the French general to him and says: – "Well you *have* landed us with a sweep in the way of German general." "I know it" said my friend. "What's he been doing?" "Spending his whole time telling us what unadulterated blackguards you English are and how glad he is to be with *us*.". ... But later that German general was not in the least glad for the French do not coddle or cosset their captives.

It was queer campaigning – in the shadow of endless forest, sweating and dark with no news, no wireless and columns to co-ordinate *by runners*! – a hundred miles apart. We have given the French practically *all* the Cameroons including the best sea port.[10] Allah knows they deserve it. Other news we have not – nothing except the noise of your guns which, the other night in the stillness, shook our windows. They come between the mind and all thought – like a thorn in the conscience.

Sunday. Got all the hay in last night but the rick ain't thatched and now it looks as though it were going to rain. Anyway yesterday (Sat) was St. Swithin's and it did not *rain*. Per contra. It rained for forty days, more or less, before.

Monday. Whereat it rained consumedly *all* yesterday and my rick is wet – wet! Also two loads of hay that were overlooked are like mint sauce. As a compensation there blew in, in the afternoon on a motor byke, an enormously fat Navy Lieutenant[11] – a complete stranger so far as any man is a stranger these days – full of immortal tales all told in the amazing Naval Tongue. Had been blown up in the *Amphion*:[12] and had been in four or five naval actions, as well as having had to take a German trawler home with a mutinous Hun crew. He was all Marryatt translated into steam and petrol. He held us breathless or weak with laughter and then, after supper, disappeared in his roaring 7. h.p. Indian into the warm descending rain. I thought I knew most navy types but this was strange in my experience. He was a destroyer boy by profession – what he called "The Black Navy"[13] which is a brand apart. They do not like submarines and will not be cruisers or battle-ships. They are just "The Black Navy." Here my paper comes to an end. I have merely drivelled and drooled but you'll understand.

God bless and keep you and the boy.

Love from us all.

Ever affectionately,
Rudyard

Notes

1. *The Eyes of Asia*, which he sent to Dunlop Smith for approval on 13 July. These were, RK wrote, "evolved" from actual letters written by Indian soldiers in France, sent by Dunlop Smith to RK. In transmitting the results to Dunlop Smith, RK wrote: "You may urge that I've taken large liberties with the material? I reply that I certainly have: but an immense amount has been textually lifted from the original documents; and for the rest I have somewhat amplified the spirit that I thought that I saw behind the letters" (to Dunlop Smith, 13 July 1916: ALS, Tyler Collection, Yale).
2. The point about the need for educating women is made in each of the four stories in *The Eyes of Asia*: see, e.g., pp. 18, 37, 70, and 99 of the American edition (New York, 1918: the stories were not collected in England until the Sussex Edition).

3. Word illegible.
4. 30 May 1916. RK's reference to reading this letter to Macphail is the only record of Macphail's being at Bateman's in May.
5. The German "commercial" submarine *Deutschland* arrived in Baltimore with a cargo of dyestuffs on 9 July; the State Department, over British and French protests, determined that the ship was strictly a merchant vessel and had the privileges of a neutral port. It returned with a cargo of rubber and nickel.
6. Colonel Cunliffe (see 18–27 February 1886). On 11 September 1916 RK wrote to Dunsterville that "Old Cunliffe (*Ma*) blew in the other day thinly disguised as a Brigadier and a C.B. – but just the same old 'Bull' as ever. He was en route between his beloved West Africa where he has trafficked with W.A.F.F.'s and Fans and cannibals, and Smuts' East Africa whither he intended to take a proportion of his black guards. He was in charge of the Northern Nigerian advance and had some very interesting yarns to tell" (ALS, Sussex). Cunliffe commanded the Nigeria Regiment, West African Frontier Force, 1914–18, and led it in the Cameroons campaign. RK mentions him in *Something of Myself* as "an old schoolmate of mine who became a General with an expedition of his own in West Africa in the Great War" (pp. 66–7).
7. Sir George Roos-Keppel (1866–1921), Chief Commissioner of the North-West Frontier Province, 1908–19, was at USC with RK. RK's statement would seem to settle the question of the identity of "The Infant", which has been disputed. See Harbord, *Readers' Guide*, III, 1197.
8. The story first appeared in the *Pioneer Mail*, 28 May 1890, and is collected in *Many Inventions*.
9. That is, German East Africa, now still being defended by the Germans against troops commanded since early 1916 by General Smuts (see 27 March 1906).
10. A settlement made in 1916 after the British and French campaign in the Cameroons gave the French nine-tenths of the country, the British taking the section adjoining Nigeria.
11. This was Lt. Beckett, from Sheerness, who called on 16 July; he was also at Bateman's on 3 September 1916 (Bateman's Visitors Book). He is probably Walter Napier Beckett (1893–1941), who served in the Harwich Force and Dover Patrol, 1914–16. RK might have met him during his visits to the east coast naval patrols when he was at work on *The Fringes of the Fleet* (see 9 October 1915).
12. The light cruiser HMS *Amphion* struck a mine and sank off the east coast of England on 6 August 1914, with a large loss of life. It was one of the first British ships to be lost in the war.
13. Because destroyers were originally painted black.

To André Chevrillon, 22 July 1916

Text: Copy, University of Sussex

Bateman's / Burwash / Sussex. / July 22 1916

Dear Chevrillon,

Yours of the 17th just in. Please take the whole d–d thing off your mind. I am doing the preface: I am going to give it to my agent. He will take it to

Hodder and Stoughton. H. & S. will pay for it and that money goes to the French Red Cross. There are wheels within wheels, of course, but I think you may take it that the publisher will not profit by his "smartness" more than is avoidable.

I think myself that it is the agent Gilmer[1] who is being smart, or trying to be so, at the expense of us both.

But these things are wholly immaterial. The point is, as you say, to get a preface which may serve in the U.S.A. I'm specially grateful to you for your note on the points of your book. The book raises so many and such big considerations that I find myself, expatiating, so to speak, all over the horizon – vaguely and formlessly. I've been agonizing over it for days: but you've given me the clear note – the drop that ought to precipitate my turbid mind.[2]

What you hint about the English ethical and religious idea is very curious – since it is what has forced itself on me most clearly: and seems to me to explain a great deal of our attitude of self-criticism. This, I take it, is the subconscious argument in our national mind: – "If it be true (which we are slow to admit to ourselves) that we are chiefly swayed in this matter by a religious and moral ideal then, precisely to the extent we are swayed, are we penetrated by the sense of our personal and moral unworthiness as compared with the ideal for which we strive." I've heard the thing stated, in the slang of the Army and sport, by wounded officers and men. I tried to make some verses out of it but they got too self-consciously "goody-goody" for any reasonable use.

As to the attitude of the U.S.A. *Merci!* We know *all* about it. *We* shall be the whipping boy of the U.S.A. for a generation or so – to restore her self respect. You see, they talk a dialect of our tongue. That is the horrible bond between us. They can appreciate exquisitely what we think of them and therefore – but I've explained it again and again, they *must* justify themselves on our shortcomings. "I was a coward and a liar. I know it, but, after all, what did the other man do?" It 's the same argument as Cain used tho' it doesn't appear in the Bible: I've just been doing – out of a mass of documents – a study of this war as it has affected our Indian Army. It's amazing how their French experiences have caused them all – Sikhs, Gurkhas, Pathans, etc. etc. – to insist on the education of their own women! I wish I could show you the original stuff but you'll probably see the articles some time. France seen through Indian eyes is not a thing which I ever thought I should live to see. Curious that no one – not even the impassive Oriental – can come in contact with that electric mother of all ideas, without being electrified.

And now I'll get to work, all over again, on your preface.

Ever
Rudyard Kipling

Notes
1. Not identified
2. The subject of Chevrillon's book is the psychological change in England that led from its confused unreadiness at the outset of the war to the "fusion of all tendencies into one collective will and movement" (*Britain and the War*, p. vi). RK, following Chevrillon, interprets this process as moral: having come to believe in the Germans as the devil, the English "addressed themselves to its overthrow in much the same sombre temper as a man self-convinced of sin brings all body, soul and mind to his struggle for redemption" (p. xi).

To John St Loe Strachey, 24 July 1916
ALS: House of Lords Record Office

Bateman's / Burwash / Sussex / July 24. 1916

private

Dear Strachey,

"Arising out" of the Spec's review of Agnes Repplier's essays:[1] and the very just point she makes of the effect of educating young U.S.A.'s by women, here is an extract from something I wrote, the year before the war, when I went to Egypt.[2]

I met a lot of neutrals in the Nile boats and they struck me, most of 'em, as talking and thinking in a standardized fashion – as standardized as the fittings of a Pulman car. The rest follows in type.

The trouble is that the United States have been literally "schoolmarmed to death" as my American woman said. The extract, which is from a set of articles called "Egypt of the Magicians" may come in perhaps as a rider or a paragraph if you think it's worth it. No need to quote my name except incidentally. With every good wish and love to Amabel

Yours ever
Rudyard Kipling.

Notes
1. A review of Agnes Repplier's *Counter-Currents*, *Spectator*, 22 July 1916, pp. 105–6. The reviewer quotes Miss Repplier's argument that American men under thirty are likely to be more "sentimental" because "the men over forty were taught by men; the men under thirty were taught by women" (p. 105).
2. The passage comes from ch. 4, "Up the River", of *Egypt of the Magicians* (*Letters of Travel*, pp. 244–5). It is a dialogue between RK and an American woman, who explains that American men are conventional and timid because they have been "school-marmed to death". Strachey used the passage in a "letter" signed "Z", *Spectator*, 5 August 1916, p. 157.

To Sir Robert Baden-Powell, 29 July 1916
TLS: Scout Association

Bateman's / Burwash / Sussex / 29th July 1916

Private

Dear Baden Powell,

I am in receipt of your letter of July 28th, and am forwarding to my publishers the article that you have made for the Scouts' Magazine from the Jungle Books.[1] If they agree to your using it, I will let you hear. My permission is gladly given, only it will be necessary for you to say that the extracts are from the Jungle Books and that they are quoted by the kind permission of the author and the publishers, Messrs. Macmillan and Co.

Believe me,

Yours truly,
Rudyard Kipling

Note

1. Baden-Powell's letter to RK of 28 July (copy, Scout Association) explains that "we are now encouraging a junior branch of the movement under the name of Wolf Cubs for youngsters between 8 and 11, and I want to enthuse them through your Mowgli and his animal friends in the Jungle Book. Would you have any objection to my introducing it to them on the lines of the enclosed proof." In *The Scout*, 12 August 1916, p. 978, under the heading of "To the Wolf Cubs", Baden-Powell duly published a paraphrase of the story of Mowgli and the Bandar-Log, with acknowledgement of the "kind permission of Mr. Rudyard Kipling and Messrs. Macmillan and Co." This was followed in the number of 9 September 1916 by a further note instructing the Wolf Cubs how to "dance the dance of Kaa" (p. 18). Hugh Brogan, *Mowgli's Sons: Kipling and Baden-Powell's Scouts*, 1987, p. 42, takes Baden-Powell's letter to refer not to an article in *The Scout* but to the proofs of the original *Wolf Cub's Handbook*, published at the end of 1916, which makes extensive use of the *Jungle Books* for its terms and symbols; but it seems clear that RK has in mind only an "article" for *The Scout*.

To André Chevrillon, 7 August 1916
Text: Copy, University of Sussex

Bateman's / Burwash / Sussex / Tuesday / Aug. 7 1916

private

Dear Chevrillon,

My letter[1] must have crossed yours of the 3rd. All right. I've told my business man to get ahead with the arrangements for prefacing Hachette's new editions with my preface.[2] We are settling with Hodder and Stoughton about the arrangements for England. I fancy my N. Y. publishers – Doubleday Page and Company ('curious that the U.S.A. Ambassador in England should be junior partner of my firm in America) are publishing it in the U.S.A.[3] So all goes well.

It won't have the *least* effect on the mind of the U.S. Their one preoccupation is to keep out of the war and to make money: it makes them sweat all over merely to think of the possibilities of real strife. By the way they smashed their last Army aeroplane on the Mexican border the other day![4]

I shall go over the preface in proof and see if I can make it better. Yes, what you say about the 3,000,000 men is quite true: *but* the nature of the English is that they work best when they are least praised. The time for telling 'em what fine fellows they are is when *all* the hay is gathered in. Occasionally, I permit myself to think that England has not done so badly but I don't want to say it aloud. You must remember that the breed has been untouched and unwasted for three, at least, well fed generations. It was bursting with energies that were being violently misapplied and when the war came it went – subconsciously – as a virgin of temperament goes to the marriage bed. The Hun on the other hand, though an expert nation in these arts, needed, and still needs, a certain amount of "working up". Low be it spoken a certain proportion of our people – and these till now the most respectable – enjoy the deviltries and the killings. All the new Armies are of the new respectable stock – bankers, clerks, grocers, assistants etc. etc. They are frankly delighted to be of the world: and like all converts to new creeds are most zealous. It is too early to write about this yet but I am full of material.

And, in addition, we have now got all the whole vast factory system under way. Our supply-factories ought to be delivering full strength in three months from now. In another half-year, if need is, they can double their output with less effort than they needed six months ago to increase production by 25%.[5] You see, there is some sort of infernal law of progressive acceleration which applies to moving bodies, avalanches and munition factories. But the test is that the old executive hands have largely retired – warn out – and their places are taken by young imaginative and untrammelled persons who are thinking out new mechanisms and plans with a joyous abandon they have never known before. It is a sort of martial Renaissance. I wish I could tell you of some of our latest audacities in the way of appliances and devices. I only wonder now when and how it will be possible to stop the momentum of this huge single minded movement. I never conceived it possible that *all* our people should move in one direction, as to a football match.

(Here is a small tale told, quite incidentally; by a New Zealand boy,[6] wounded at Gallipoli and now doing another kind of duty. There was a New Zealand doctor who came out with the forces and thought much and long of war. He went to France. There he devised a certain form of bill-hook – something like this [ ][7] – but more elegant. Then he gave lectures to men who were interested in such things, on the precise location of the temporal and jugular arteries. His pupils went forth against the Hun with the Bill-hook he had invented and instead of vulgarly brawling and scuffling with the enemy "nicked" at their temples and their throats, as he had recommended. It was very satisfactory. The N. Zealand boy told it to me as a thing hardly worthy of comment).

Best of all, the temper of our people is beautifully set now. They know what they want and I think they will get it. They really do intend the destruction of Germany complete and final. The Lille business[8] made them very sick. A year ago they would have wasted themselves denouncing it. Now they don't. They go on with their job.

A propos. My very last man on the estate has been called up. He goes, serenely and unquestioningly, exactly as my gardener went. He is just as silent, just as unperturbed as ever he was. But I gather that he "does not like" Germans. I don't know whether you have noticed that now we have got conscription, we are engaged actively in raising *volunteer* Battalions of men beyond military age. There are about half a million of them now: and they are rather well equipped and drilled. They run from 45 to 60 – sound but elderly persons who can walk and shoot. The Government has at last "recognised" them and I believe has promised to use them if required. It took a long time before that concession was made. Now they are quite happy.

I don't think the process of breaking down the Hun will be as long as we think. He really *is* beginning to understand that he is not wanted upon Earth which is very sad and depressing for a parvenu. The new screams of hate, therefore, are quite justified: and they will not make the least difference to his future.

With every good wish

Yours in the Fraternity
Rudyard Kipling

Notes
1. 22 July 1916.
2. The 4th edition of *L'Angleterre et la guerre* (Paris: Hachette, 1917) carries the "Préface de Rudyard Kipling".
3. It appeared as *England and the War, 1914–1915* (New York: Doubleday, Page & Co., 1917).
4. In an episode of the protracted Mexican civil war the Mexican revolutionary Pancho Villa had, early in 1916, massacred eighteen American miners and then raided Columbus, New Mexico. President Wilson sent an expedition on an unsuccessful pursuit of Villa. I cannot find any account of the loss of the "last Army aeroplane" in this connection.
5. The English success in boosting war production was to a large extent owing to the work of RK's *bête noire* Lloyd George, Minister of Munitions from May 1915 to July 1916.

6. Perhaps the Mr Ross of New Zealand, now on *The Times*, who was at Bateman's for lunch and tea on 3 August (Bateman's Visitors Book). I cannot identify him further.
7. A space appears in the copy at this point, no doubt to indicate a sketch in the original.
8. It was reported that young men and women in such cities as Lille were being separated from their families and put to forced labour in the fields (*The Times*, 29 July, 3 August 1916).

To Alexander Pelham Trotter,[1] 17 August 1916

ALS: Syracuse University

Bateman's / Burwash / Sussex / Aug. 17. 1916

Dear Trotter,

I wish I could get up to town on any named day but I can only come when I have to and I don't know when I'm free. But I've booked Burn's[2] address (for which many thanks) and I'd like to have a talk with him some time.

How think you of our friend and fellow-member the Hon. B. Russell[3] of the U[nion of]. D[emocratic]. C[ontrol].? He says pretty things about soldiers and conscription for which Cambridge relieves him of his office at one of the colleges but the Athenæum committee see no blame in him.

Ever yours
Rudyard Kipling

Notes

1. Trotter (1857–1947) had been government electrician at the Cape, where RK had known him and his wife (see 25 December 1898). He was electrical advisor to the Board of Trade, 1899–1917.
2. Not identified.
3. Bertrand Russell (1872–1970), 3rd Earl Russell, mathematician, philosopher, and reformer. He had been convicted and fined under the Defence of the Realm Act in July 1916 for publishing a pamphlet held to be damaging to recruiting. Trinity College, Cambridge, thereupon deprived Russell of his lectureship and a special committee of the Athenaeum, to which Russell had been elected in 1909, met to expel him on 18 July 1916. RK evidently did not yet know of this action. In 1944 Russell was again appointed to a Trinity lectureship, and in 1952 he was again elected to the Athenaeum, whose members were apparently ignorant of his expulsion ([F. R. Cowell], *The Athenaeum: Club and Social Life in London 1924–1974*, 1975, p. 138). Russell was an early member of the Union of Democratic Control.

To Anna Smith Balestier, 8 September 1916
ALS: Dunham Papers

Bateman's / Burwash / Sussex / Friday: Sep. 8. 1916

Dear Mother

It is about a century and a half since I wrote to you but I have been follow-ing the course of your last adventure with breathless interest: and today at breakfast Carrie read me your triumphant account of getting rid of the sling and being able to do up your own hair[1] – with the nurse as audience and critic. I can't think of any one except your eldest daughter who would be more annoyed and put out by breaking her wrist; and no one (eldest daugh-ter always excepted) who would deal with the situation more sternly.

And that reminds me. Yesterday C. went to her jam cupboard to fight wasps who come in through cracks in the door and eat her jam. The cup-board was full of wasps and C. – exactly as you would have done – shooed them off with her hands while she tried to paste paper over the cracks. Result – two stings, one on the upper left eyelid and one on the cheek just below. Today one side of her face resembles that of a learned pig or pig-faced lady and she has a patch over her eye. To make everything quite comfortable five wounded officers whom we have never seen, are coming from a hospital to lunch at Bateman's at one o'clock.[2] I think I shall tell them that it was sharp-nel picked up in the last Zeppelin raid.

Elsie has gone away for a little visit to Isobel Law[3] – Bonar Law's daughter – at Thanet. You heard, of course, how she and another girl visited Lord Milner at Sturry and entertained the wounded Canadians at a tea party. The war has deepened and strengthened my small daughter's character most wonderful. She has many chores to do in the way of looking after people that we have to look after – children of poor or unlucky parents – and though she naturally does not like it she does her work very splendidly and patiently. She is also our chauffeuse and practically her little car which she washes herself is our only means of communication with the outside world. Then she helps housekeep and sews and knits and packs for wounded.

Now that she is a woman too, you can imagine that between her and C. I am *very* well governed and corrected.

As a revenge, some time ago, I told Elsie that the only living thing her mother went in fear of was *you* which I believe is true: and I described to her how when C. used to argue with you or suggest plans you just went on taking no notice whatever. This cheers Elsie, and when C. is laying down the law to us both or administering us with a severe hand, Elsie says to me: – "Tell me again how Grandmummy sits on Mummy. She wouldn't dare behave like this if *her* mother were here." Elsie is absolutely one of the two dearest things God ever made and I fancy, if the truth were known, she rules us both. She has a lot of social tact and is used to dealing with boys.

We had an invasion last Sunday of six Naval officers on five motor bicycles and one side car, from about fifty miles away.[4] I had told one of them who blew in some weeks before[5] that he could bring friends here if he wished to. And he took me at my word. They were a wonderful crowd of boys and their motor-bykes were more wonderful still. Elsie took three of them into the garden – boys not bicycles – and set them climbing trees for apples and eating plums off the wall. We got them away by nine o'clock in the pitch dark, with no lights and, as far as I could make out, their bikes tied up with wire and string. I expect they got back to their ships somehow but I haven't heard how.

Yesterday – in case we should feel dull – we added a large grey English sheep dog to our establishment to help us look after our sheep of which we have nearly two hundred. His name is Roy. I haven't seen him yet. The young lady in charge of our chicken farm went down to the station to meet him. She will make a pet of him and he will be ruined for shepherding. All our life now is concerned with the farms and getting as much as possible out of the land. Carrie handles 200 acres; 2 men; 26 head of cattle; two milch cows and Lord knows how many poultry with the help of two women who don't help and a sprinkling of female labour. I hope she tells you of her experiences. They are more comic than any play.

We have got in our wheat and our beans and are now deep in the sheep feeding which is the custom of the country in the autumn. We take in flocks to feed till the spring. I hate sheep. Also we, (C. that is) has sold all the timber she cut this spring and it has just been removed by five wise horses and two fool men who have cut the fields up a good deal. We have a lot of hedges to cut and clean up but, considering we have had *no* labour, we're as well ahead as any other farms. *How* I wish you could see your eldest daughter in charge of this little kingdom!

I don't know whether the war interests you much. We are getting the situation in hand a little: and the Hun is beginning to realize that he is not quite happy. But this is only the beginning. By the time he has spent another winter in the field he will find out where he is: He will begin to squeal long before that date but it won't make any difference. He has taken two years to teach the English how to hate, which is a thing we have never done before, and it will take us two generations to stop. It is curious to notice how the neutrals still seem to think that this is an ordinary war and not a general clean up.

Now I will get back to my small jobs and go over to the farm and see Roy the sheep dog.

Ever your most loving son
Ruddy.

P.S.   I quite sympathize with your annoyance and anger, after having run the U.S. transatlantic mail steamers for thirty years, to find them so irregular and casual. We shall put them straight for you in a little time but at present, your feelings must be beyond words. I've just had a batch of U.S. mail of *two* dates all at once.

R.

Notes

1. Mrs Balestier had broken her wrist in getting out of her bath (CK to Mrs Balestier, 6 August [1916]: ALS, Dunham Papers).
2. "Matron, Major Williams: Lt Massey, Needham and Gale from Crowboro hospital to lunch" (Bateman's Visitors Book, 8 September 1916).
3. Isabel Law (1894–1969), elder daughter of Bonar Law. She married General Sir Frederick Sykes (1877–1954) in 1920. According to her brother, Richard Law, Lord Coleraine, "Kipling had a particularly soft spot" for Isabel Law because "she reminded him of his elder daughter Josephine" (Bonar Sykes, "Memories of the Kiplings", *Kipling Journal*, March 1996, p. 39). RK was godfather to her first child, Bonar Law Sykes.
4. "Lt Beckett R.N.: Lt: Spencer: Lt Reid, Bowlby and two others all on motor-bikes from Sheerness (tea and supper)" (Bateman's Visitors Book, 3 September 1916).
5. See 15–17 July 1916.

To Andrew Macphail, 11–13 September 1916

ALS: Photocopy, National Archives of Canada

Bateman's / Burwash / Sussex / Sep. 11. 1916

Dear Macphail,

Your most welcome, and by-war-entirely-unaffected-in-caligraphy letter, just in. Even more welcome, if that were possible, is what you say about the new machine being keyed up.[1] That squares with what everyone tells me, by word of mouth or in letters. It was a portentous – an inconceivable – development – on our part and now it is under way, one dimly realizes a little of what has gone to its making. *You*, who saw and suffered through the original chaos, must realize it more livelily than any. Here, at the munitions and output end of the thing, it is almost stupefying. The whole land is on the move and concentrated on its one end: and I don't see, myself, how the deuce the momentum of the mass is to be checked. It seems to operate like that infernal sum of the multiplied nails in the horse-shoe: each month – week almost – squaring and trining the output of the month before.

And whenever there is the least chance of slacking or danger of pacificist discussion, the ever-careful Hun (to whom we owe our salvation) sends

Zepps to stiffen Organized Labour and confirm Resolutions in their congresses.[2] The drama of the last raid was very fine.[3] The great city saw the blazing star fall from Heaven and cheered as one voice. I heard of one woman whose house was a mile or two from where it fell. She and her husband slipped into their coats, started up their little car and raced to the scene, and knowing the local police were "accomodated with seats on the Bench" so to speak, she reported that the smell of the burnt Huns was extremely pungent and that she sniffed it with the deepest satisfaction. But was that what the Hun intended should be the effect on civilian morale? Which things are an allegory.

Last week for the first time in months I spent with an Anglo-Indian friend in his country house.[4] He was a bachelor – the only one of the house party who had not either lost or was in position to lose a son. In one case two were gone. And one listened to the quiet kept down English voices above the decent table cloth and under the shaded lights talking and taking for granted things inconceivable two years ago. *Inter alia*, there was among 'em the man who edits the literary supplement of the *Times*[5] and he talked not of literature but of certain [of] his colleagues at the front – men who had come straight from much ink and had discovered themselves to be much more than inksters. And he took *that* for granted too. We've got it in our bones and our marrow now. By a side wind I came upon the average English opinion of the U.S.: they have written it off, finally and politely in the irrevocable English way. It don't interest 'em any more than a man who has been caught cheating at cards. Did you hear that a U.S. Cruiser months ago was wandering about the East end of the Mediterranean picking up refugees from Smyrna or something and incidentally using all our Ports to put in at?[6] 'Twas at Alexandria I think, that one of their officers at a dinner wanted to drink the health of the Kaiser. Only it happened to be an Australian crowd at that meal and not English. Whereby, the toast finished in a pond and the drinkers with it. I'm glad it was Australia that took the matter in hand. One man told me (at this same week end party) of an "American" woman who confided to him that she was not "quite sure whether the national honour had been tarnished or not." That's a wonderful attitude and confirms my view that Wilson is the only person who could explain away the loss of a maidenhead. And when the war ends all that people will have to come out into a new world from under their beds where they have lain in company with their chamberpots.

I have just finished some stuff (I hope the censor will pass it) about the work of our destroyers at Jutland, on reports of the same destroyers.[7] It was magnificent material to which no one could do justice, but what struck me was the way in which the doing of great deeds caused, as a bye-product, a style of expression that was pure Homeric Greek. I begin to understand now the nature of the crowd that Jason signed on for the Argo: and that Ulysses worked with. Otherwise, my insides have been afflicting me at intervals[8] so that I couldn't keep up working – and what is *much* worse, couldn't work really in the fields where the thistles are growing like all the original sins. But we've got in our wheat and our beans, and have taken in 160 sheep which is our winter allotment of paying guests. *Your* geese (they are inseparably connected with you now by reason of the remark you made about the best people pluckin' 'em) had sixty sheep in their paddock. They faced the situation like school marms. It was a question whether they ran the class or the class ran them. So – I saw all this with Elsie hanging on the gate, in shouts of mirth – they, the geese, proclaimed one end of the field as their own room – a sort of "Janet! Donkeys!"[9] reservation. Here they abode till it was time to see what the children were doing, and tell them not to. Then they got up and went through the flock, line ahead, pecking a woolly bottom here and tweaking a foolish ear there, till the whole flock were aroused and attentive. Then – believe me – those three old virgins halted and shrieked at them and when the lesson was ended retired to their own end of the field – to repeat the operation half an hour later. It was like the whole question of education, as now comprehended by the Government.

Sheep, you know, must have a sheep dog. We've got one. He came from the Army and Navy Stores – a bluish grey person with topaz eyes, full of the cardinal virtues and tee-totally covered with lice which are being removed by quassia chips, kerosene and manual labour. The young lady from Tasmania who is in charge of the cows and chickens (this is one of the developments of women on the land) went down to the station to meet him. She is not much of a farmeress but she has the gift with animals. That was three days ago. Today, Roy has completely forgotten he was ever a sheep dog and announces he will live and die in her service as, I think, a devoted Pekinese. And thus administration is ever defeated by sentiment. Then the wife having cut down trees, even as you saw, when you were last here, sold 'em to the saw mills and – equally at last, the mills sent to take 'em away and most damnably cut up our poor meadows as they hauled them about. No thanks to them they didn't smash one of my more doubtful bridges. I told 'em, on *no* account, to leave the great Timber tug (four tons) on it. Wherefore they placed it exactly on the crown of the weak brick arch and went off to do something else. But oh, how I wished you had been with me to watch the quiet, cool science of the two small men and the five big horses dealing with those trunks! The mills themselves who have never done anything except the roughest of gate, plank and post work, are now making details of aeroplanes – struts and chassis I suppose. All the charcoal burners have revived and are at work. They are aged men coeval with the chap who attended to William Rufus his corpse:[10] and their pride in their resurrection is very fine. The charcoal is made and goes straight out to France "for our boys there." So if you get a whiff out of a brazier that reminds you of Bateman's you'll know why.

The very very last of our most reluctant and crafty service-dodgers have been combed out of our village and taken for the Army. They gained nothing by their delays except that they went amid the cheerily expressed hopes of childless mothers that they might "damned well die": that isn't a cheering send-off.

Our cottage for sick officers has been in full use till now when there is an interregnum. We expect a navy man shortly there:[11] I'm glad of that because when the brook floods he'll be all at his ease.

Also, several of our young stock have got the "husk" which is a cough, and have to be drenched out of a bottle. They know all about [it] by now and when they see their kindly physician approaching they scatter and dodge round the trees in the orchard. It is all grey still weather in the mornings now which burns off by noon to mellow heat – not live autumn yet but the prophecy of it. I love to think of you lying out in the dark and hearing the night noises once more as they were in time of peace. We haven't heard your guns in quite a while now – whether this is a trick of the wind or whether you are moving on I don't know.

Nor do I know whether the Hun is going to put up that fight, you hint at, in the Spring. He *may*, of course but on the other hand, what does he gain by it: and after a winter's reflection he will have time to calculate his losses. He has already made quite recently a most seductive offer to France for an armistice and was told, in the language of Molière, to go to Hell.[12] Then, again, he has to consider how much money his lost war is going to fetch in. Even he has, in the last resort, to be guided by Realities: and now that the neutrals nearest him see that the game is near its end he will feel the reaction. But what a true Hell on earth it will be for him when he realizes that his own gods and his own gospel of salvation have failed: that might *is* right as he always says: only that the might is not his. To have laboured for two generations at one's own damnation: and to have achieved it, artistically, philosophically, belligerently and in every other conceivable way, is a wonderful thing –

Sept: 13th. Here's a voice out of your forgotten past for you! Peterson[13] writing from the Savile Club wants to know if I have anything by me for the *University Magazine* adding "one of the minor horrors of war is that I have to edit it while Andrew Macphail is at the Front," adding also "you will be interested to be told that the medical unit equipped by your Alma Mater MacGill was described by the very highest authorities as 'the best unit in France.'" Well, I can believe that too. I only wish I had something by me that would fit the *University Magazine*. It's too dam' respectable for my profound psychological study of the effects of war on a population of Purely Civilian antecedents: but *you*, as a medical man, will see the scientific accuracy of the little gem. As thus: –

> "The sons of the Suburbs were carefully bred
>   And quite unaccustomed to strife:
> For the lessons they learned in the books that they read

Had shown them the value of life:
From Erith to Ealing They cherished the feeling
    That slaughter and bloodshed were sin:
From Hendon to Tooting They didn't like shooting,
    And didn't intend to begin. …

Chorus (con. molt. exp.)
    When the clergyman's daughter
    Drinks nothing but water
    She's certain to finish on gin! (*bis*)
(*mf.*) We've proved it again and again!
(*p*)   If the child of the vicar
       has never used liquor
(*ff*)   Look out when he finds the champagne!! (bis)
       Beware of all virgins, be*cuz*
       If the archdeacon's clerk
       Never went on a lark
(*fff*)   Why, it's Bow Street and bail when he does![14]

And so on, the rest becoming too technical. No one has yet developed the significance of the fact that when circumstances force the Innocent and Decently Conducted into Lawful Excess, they take to it with an abandon and a sincerity that leaves the Regular Practitioner far behind. Hence the amazing deeds of our peoples in this last push.

As I wrote you at the beginning of this letter, all you write me of hope and good cheer is abundantly confirmed by other men from various parts of the Line, even in this day's mail.

Also comes in a letter from a Brigadier General on the Indian Frontier – none other than the original of my "Stalky" – who lies in hold at Peshawur and watches his life long friends and faithful enemies the Mohmunds. (He had one battle with 'em already last year). He likes them immensely: recruits his men from them and in the intervals of campaigns they come and discuss things with him. Just now they are very peaceful – have been for a long time all down the Border. It was the mixture of High Explosives and aeroplanes that soothed 'em. They "didn't know Sahibs fought so bitterly." You see, we'd always handled them economically up till now, and they imagined war was a romp between sportsmen – not an affair of mere killing.

Another letter comes in from Nigeria telling me of the Black West African troops who went to war on the 5th of August 1914 against the Hun in Togo land: were broken to white men with Maxims; fought them all up and down the Cameroons and three months ago returned to their headquarters with £20,000 back pay distributable among 1200 of 'em. *And no crime whatever.* They drew breath for six weeks and are now grinningly away to the other side of Africa to help Smuts in the German East Africa round up.

D'you know there are times when I'm almost inclined to think that we are a Superior Breed, though very poor advertisers. You see, the Hun and the U.S. do that so much better.

But I become senile and tedious and will now conclude. Send us Dorothy's present address for she is not at Folkestone any more and I'd like to get hold of her and Geoffrey – if they'd care to come down for a while.

With unalterable affection and all our keenest good wishes

Ever Yours
Rudyard Kipling.

Finished 6 p.m. September 13th.

Notes

1. RK means the British war effort generally: as he wrote to Dunsterville on this day, "our tremendous machine is doing its job" (ALS, Sussex). The Somme offensive had been in progress since July, with only very limited success and with appalling losses: it was, however, the "first great action by a British army of continental size" (Taylor, *English History 1914–1945*, p. 59).
2. The Trades Union Congress meeting at Birmingham had rejected an invitation from the American Federation of Labor to an international conference to be held together with the peace conference, whenever that might be, in order to give Labour a voice in the negotiations. The Congress rejected the idea that delegates from the enemy powers should advise on the terms of peace (*The Times*, 6 September 1916).
3. One of thirteen Zeppelins, the L 21, was shot down during a raid on 3 September, the first Zeppelin to be brought down over England, with the loss of her sixteen-man crew. "Her wreckage was found at Cuffley, near Enfield, with the half-burned bodies of the crew. ... The people watched the attack on the Zeppelin in silence; but when she was seen to be on fire cheer on cheer was raised and repeated again and again" (*The Times*, 4 September 1916). The next day it was estimated that 10,000 people visited the field (*The Times*, 5 September).
4. Not identified. Perhaps the younger George Allen, of Free Chase.
5. (Sir) Bruce Richmond (1871–1964), editor of the *TLS* for 35 years, from shortly after its founding in 1902 until 1937.
6. The American armoured cruiser USS *Tennessee* spent eight months in Turkish waters in 1914–15; it conveyed "several thousand" refugees from Jaffa to Alexandria during this time (*New York Times*, 8 August 1915).
7. "Destroyers at Jutland", collected in *Sea Warfare*, was first published in the *Daily Telegraph* and other papers, 19, 23, 26, and 31 October 1916. It was written at the request of Sir Douglas Brownrigg, Chief Naval Censor (see his *Indiscretions of the Naval Censor*, 1920, pp. 58–9). RK began work some time after 19 August, when Brownrigg brought to Bateman's the "report of Jutland Battle for Rud to work over" (CK diary).
8. RK saw Bland-Sutton on this day and was "in pain and off work from the 11th till the 22nd" (Clinical History).
9. *David Copperfield*, ch. 13: Aunt Betsy Trotwood's "little piece of green" is kept sacred from the intrusion of donkeys.
10. William Rufus was killed by an arrow in a hunting accident in the New Forest in 1100. His corpse, abandoned by his companions, was carried to Winchester by peasants.

11. The house at Dudwell Farm was occupied on 20 September by a Mr Warburton and his wife. He was not a navy man but a Canadian "fighting in a Manchester regiment" (Rees extracts).
12. I do not know what specific occasion RK may refer to: there were many rumours of offers to negotiate at this time.
13. William Peterson, now Sir William, Principal of McGill University: see [1 May 1899].
14. An early version of "Sons of the Suburbs", a poem that RK wrote for a magazine called *Blighty* published for the troops. The editors were said to have been "composed largely of clergymen and ladies" (Stewardt-Yeats, *Bibliographical Catalogue*, p. 451). Offended by the clergyman's daughter and gin, they asked RK to alter the poem. He refused; in consequence it was not published during his lifetime, and it remains uncollected. The poem was published after RK's death in the London *Sunday Pictorial*, 19 January 1936, and in the *New York Times*, 6 February 1936.

To the Secretary, War Office, 18 September 1916
TLS: Public Record Office

Bateman's / Burwash / Sussex / 18th September 1916.

The Secretary
  War Office
Alexandra House
  Kingsway. W. C.

Sir,

In reply to your letter, No. 125146 / 1 (C. 2 Casualties) of the 14th September, I should be glad if you would postpone taking the course you suggest in regard to my son Lieutenant John Kipling. All the information I have gathered is to the effect that he was wounded and left behind near Puits 14 at the Battle of Loos on September 27th 1915. I have interviewed a great many people and heard from many others, and can find no one who saw him killed, and his wound being a leg wound would be more disabling than fatal.[1]

May I draw your attention to the fact that in your letter you state my son's rank as 2nd Lieutenant, whereas he was Lieutenant.[2] Also in the published casualty list, he was incorrectly report as "Missing" instead of "Wounded and missing."

Yours truly,
Rudyard Kipling.

Notes
1. This letter replies to a form letter saying that John Kipling must be officially presumed dead unless further information about his fate has been received (file WO 339 53917, Public Record Office). RK *had* found survivors of the engagement

in which John was killed saying that they had seen him dead – if not literally that they "saw him killed". But there were contradictory reports that allowed them to continue to hope. CK's diary for September 1916 records that they were writing to Switzerland for possible news of John.

2. John's promotion to lieutenant was gazetted on 9 November 1915, but since he was dead before that date he could not be promoted. In *The Irish Guards in the Great War* RK refers to him as a second lieutenant (Outward Bound Edition, II, 16).

To Oliver Baldwin, 3 October 1916

ALS: Photocopy, University of Sussex

Bateman's / Burwash / Sussex / Oct. 3. 1916

Dear Sir

I am much indebted to you for your kind thought in sending me your latest work "Platoon drill"[1] which I have read with great interest. The style strikes me as crisp and well-balanced though here and there a little staccato. The plot fascinates me immensely in spite of the absence of the feminine element. There is a vigor and movement about it which never flags and the interest continues to increase up to the end where No. paces the Interval. This scene is conceived with masterly grip and insight and the sudden disappearance of Interval after being paced held me breathless. I should be happier if you had not left your readers in doubt as to the fate of Remainder; or, may we, haply, look for a sequel in which he married Double March. But enough of Literature, however good.

Buttons, my dear,

We were rejoiced to get your letter on the typewriter that pretends to be a pen. We really *are* coming to see you if we can ever get away from our jobs here. And *what* tales of absurdity and complications we have to tell you! I am trying to imagine you as an Instructor. You probably do it very well since you have a false air of never being shocked or upset – which is the whole essence of wisdom and success in this world. Also, you ought to have filled out a bit on the square.

Dudwell is re-occupied and – O Gawd! Tisn't he (he's a Canadian with a soft hole in his forehead from a Turk bullet at Gallipoli) it's Her![2] She's our old Vi[3] – dear old Vi – fifteen steps lower down and fresh from the *Utter* Bar or I am a Hun. Not an h – peroxide locks; odol teeth but I believe at heart very fond of him and I doubt not, in her queer way, a good sort. He is keen on the axe and the shotgun – has already fraternized with the local poacher. They talk as tho' they intended a long stay. There are (so far as I can see) no signs of a Baby. This shows that we have always something to be thankful for, but then again it may be twins.

I have understood from several quarters that Cambridge is a sink. The kind of animile now being recruited can't hold his liquor as a rule. As to women, I imagine there is more and more variegated venereal now in England than at any time of her rough Island story. So for the love of Goodness look out! They ought to be inspected.

Do you ever get any leave? If so do you always spend it in town? If so why not let us know? And further if otherwise why not come down here for a week end. It's long since we've had a rag together and the billiard table is simply mildewed from lack of use.

Dear love from us all. You'll make a really a. 1. Officer in time and I daresay you feel it.

Ever your affectionate old
Uncle Rud.

Is there anything you want that there is at Bateman's that we can send you? Rough socks; mitts, etc. etc. are plentiful just now.

Notes
1. Oliver Baldwin had joined the Cambridge Officers' Training Corps in May 1916, and was now a corporal training recruits. Baldwin wrote that a new method of company drill having come out, he published "a small, talc-covered card with the new orders for company and platoon drill on it. This was very useful for instruction, and I allowed the cadets to hold it in the left hand under the rifle butt while they were learning" (*The Questing Beast*, p. 51).
2. Mr and Mrs Warburton, who came to Dudwell on 20 September: see 11–13 September 1916.
3. The wife of the officer named Savill who occupied Dudwell in May 1916: see 22 June 1916.

To Ian Colvin, 5 October 1916

TLS: Syracuse University

Bateman's / Burwash / Sussex / 5th October 1916.

Private.
Dear Colvin,

In the first place, thank you for The Birthright in the National Review.[1] You've done some useful things in your life, and I don't think that that is the least of them. It's a thing to keep on hammering at mercilessly because, among other facts, F. E. Smith[2] is a funk[3] and it rattles him.

Now, arising out of that, can't you take Bryce's address to the Congregational Union and attend to its doctrine *without* bringing in the old fool's name?[4] (Our mistake is to treat these ga-ga relics of a dead world with misunderstood respect. Combat their arguments: drop their dignities.) B. talks about the danger of a trade war after the war as likely to revive "hates" better left to die. Go for him scientifically and philosophically – as the Hun would – and the more detached you are the more will the Hun quote you.

Here is my suggestion for attack: –

There is no question of "hate" involved now in our relations with the Hun, whatever may have been the case at the opening of the war. One hates people whom it is conceivable that later one may care for – people, at least, of like passions with ourselves. The Hun is outside any humanity we have had any experience of. Our concern with him is precisely the same as our concern with the germs of any malignant disease. We know by experience of death and physical impairment that where these germs get foothold, they are inimical to human life. That is the law of their being. Therefore, we clean out, sterilize, flush down etc. etc. all places where they can get a foothold. In the case of sleeping sickness we cut down a belt of jungle 200 yards wide round villages and beside roads to prevent the tsetse fly carrying infection. It is monotonous and expensive work, but we have no animus against the germs or the flies. They are merely scientific facts. We only do not desire to die or be crippled. Therefore, we have to take certain precautions which have been proved efficacious. If the Hun trades with the Empire, it means the presence of Huns on some pretext or another within the Empire. A Hun inside the Empire, in any capacity has been proved hurtful to the lives and peace of our Empire's human beings. Therefore, it is inexpedient to trade with the Huns: *not* because trade *per se* is evil, but because trade furnishes the medium for conveying the danger.

So for the metaphors of infection. Now for the military comparisons. Where the Hun enters a land he instinctively goes underground commercially as he does in war. He has then to be bombed at vast expense of energy out of his commercial Thiepvals.[5] We cannot afford to leave a single commercial Hun machine-gun behind us in the advance of our Empire, however skilfully the weapon may be disguised; however deeply it may be buried. You see? We have the complete revelation of Hun character in his military operations.

There is another matter to be hinted at. The policy of the Empire will in the long run be decided by the men who have fought for it. Is it wise then, for anyone, to advocate a policy which, if put into effect, would be extremely unacceptable to some millions of armed males, of whom a large proportion have been dealing or facing death in the most public and revolting forms, for several years? Might not such a policy be violently revised by these rude men, to the scandal of our good name?

e.g. Imagine the emotions of a disbanded army of three millions and a half – to put it no higher – when they found the Hun had been allowed free return to his old haunts. What price riots of the gravest, conducted by men who were not in the habit of noticing death? Conceive further, juries, displeased by bombs being dropped on their heads out of Zeppelins, who refused to convict; and behind them, a public opinion of, say, four or five million persons who had lost relatives in the war, saying: – "Thank goodness, the boys did it"?

And all this would, humanly speaking, be inevitable if the Hun were allowed in England. I omit Canada, where they remember their crucified officer.[6] All these outbreaks would pain and shock the Hun; as well as people like Bryce, and – worst of all – it might show that the effective government of this country was not in the hands of the Government – or even of the trade unions. You see?

I think if you went coldly and judgmatically along these lines, in a leader or two you would get your reward in the discomfort and uneasiness of the Hun. *He* doesn't realize, any more than our Government, the passion of loathing with which he is regarded in quiet muzzled England. In his own interests, there ought to be a moratorium of a generation before he is allowed to risk his precious life at peddling and trafficking in England. The goods will, I fear, get in from neutral countries, but I see no need why the Hun himself should accompany them here in *any* capacity.[7]

Ever yours,
Rudyard Kipling

Notes
1. "The Birthright", *National Review*, October 1916, pp. 223–33, after praising English "insularity" and reviewing the history of naturalisation in England, develops an attack on the "overgrown German element, naturalized or unnaturalized", in England (p. 231). Colvin asserts that it is against the English interest to admit foreigners to the privileges of nationality – that is, to markets, land, and government.
2. Colvin singles out Sir Edgar Speyer's appointment to the Privy Council for special denunciation and wonders why a person so unfit should be defended by such a person as F. E. Smith (p. 233).
3. The word means "coward" in the schoolboy slang of RK's generation.
4. Lord Bryce (see 19 April 1910) addressed the Assembly of Congregational Union in Birmingham on the conditions of peace, 3 October. He said that "nations cannot hate one another forever, and the sooner they cease to do so the better for all of them"; and that severe terms of peace would "end by relighting the flames of war" (*The Times*, 4 October 1916).
5. Thiepval had just been taken in the fighting on the Somme, 27 September, and was entirely in ruins. In their two years of occupation the Germans had constructed extensive underground defences and installations.
6. The story that a Canadian soldier had been found crucified against a Belgian barn door was reported by *The Times*, 15 May 1915, after it had gained currency at the front. "The story was never verified, and it was almost certainly untrue" (Martin Gilbert, *The First World War: A Complete History*, New York, 1994, p. 162). RK wrote on 18 May 1918 to Milner, then Secretary for War, asking for "details of the case of

a Canadian soldier crucified by Huns early in the war. The case was reported at the time in the papers but, is now being used by Hun agents in the U.S.A. and Canada as a sample of the lies forged by the Entente against Germany. A certain amount of trouble has already arisen: and Ottawa has asked me if I could get the facts of the affair for propaganda" (ALS, Syracuse).

7. An editorial attacking the "free trade party" appears in the *Morning Post*, 20 October 1918: "Their argument is that to keep out German manufacturers would tempt the German to continue to hate us and prevent us from again loving the German. ... Only fools and old women – and Lord Bryce – could indulge in such inane speculations. ... And if we shut our doors, is it to be called hate? Or is it not rather a reasonable measure of precaution? When we sluice our drains with carbolic, it is not because we hate the microbes; but because we want to guard ourselves against their ravages. We know by experience that they are dangerous. And the Germans are more dangerous than the deadly microbe. ... They have their commercial Thiepvals holding out stubbornly in this country to-day."

To Andrew Macphail, 6–7 October 1916
ALS: Photocopy, National Archives of Canada

Bateman's / Burwash / Sussex / Oct 6. 1916

Dear Macphail

Your two letters came tumbling in atop of each other to my great job: for they give me the best news, (almost) about yourself that I could desire. God being good, that means you will be able to come down to Bateman's with Dorothy and exercise a Commanding voice in the Agricultural policy of the Estate.[1] Now as to Clubs. This is a grave matter. It is easier to recommend a man a wife than club for the one – but I will not pursue the parallel.

Much – most, I think, – depends on your geographical position in town. For example Victoria for many years was my station and the Savile 107 Piccadilly was my club. The Savile is grossly literary but comfortable and in a way sociable. There is a little card-playing upstairs and the liquors are decent. Later on, Charing + became my station and I never set foot in the Savile for so many years that out of shame and economy, I at last resigned[2] and kept only to the Athenæum. That extra half mile westward was as effective as a barrage. I don't know whether you'd care for the Savile – now. Ink's a fine thing in its place but after blood it is sometimes flat – or flatulent.

I have a notion that the Bath[3] would somehow suit you. It's cock and hen but you needn't associate with the hens: it is social which in these days means a flux of men on leave with the latest news: it has its Bath, rackets, squash gym etc. etc. and lots of quiet corners and you can have Dorothy to lunch. Everybody seems to use it. You can generally catch what's going on there at the front and the grab is fairly decent. It's initiation fee and annual subscription were absurdly high but now, I believe, they make, like many other clubs, special terms for men who are passing through. Shall I find out for you? And if the prospect allures shall I see if I can get you put up. I ain't a member but that is a detail.

If you want something remote from the war I'd suggest the Savile but the purely literary bird might irritate. Anyhow, give me your views and predilections and 'tis I will be more than proud to do all I can for you. I haven't the full range of your personal vices so I hesitate to open up on night and gambling clubs. I rarely go to Clubs now: my hostel being Brown's Hotel in Dover Street almost exactly opposite the Bath. But expatiate at large, please, and let me know exactly what your needs bodily and mental will be.

I told you, I think, of my Ex-Gallipoli-wounded Canadian-trephined-officer-with-a-soft-hole-in-his-head who is at Dudwell farm.[4] He sat under you at Macgill as a student. I was talking to him yesterday while he, beaver-like, was laying up a supply of wood. Said he never felt happy when winter was coming on, without a wood-pile. Suddenly, while talking of you and his father, the doctor in P.E.I. he says: – "And where's Geoff?" I told him where your boy was. It seemed to bring things very near.

He is a good boy but developed epileptic fits after they thought they had got out all the bits of the Turkish bullet. Hence the trephining and second convalescence. He must have got married in one of his fits for his wife. … there ought to be a society headed by the Public Hangman to prevent wounded officers being wedded. Doubtless she is kind to him and an help meet but the glitter of her peroxide hair and the absence of her h's shows up in this still green landscape like a set of false teeth dropped on a billiard table. I fawn on her because I want her to stay here because it is doing him good. She looks at me and the wife with hard, wary barmaid eyes under blacked eyebrows – suspicious and ready to see unkindness. I wonder! And so for Dudwell.

Have we had trouble at Rye-Green?[5] Who hath red eyes? Who blasphemes? Who is let down with a wop? He who employeth "ladies on the land." You see, as I hinted, she was a Tasmanienne with a certain timbre of voice and twist of feature which should have warned me. You might have called her kittenish out of her smock and gaiters. She was multitudinously incompetent and attended *one* cow and some fifty chickens *and* her young man somewhere in England *en route* for the front. To help her exist she invited to Rye Green another female, an old Tasmanian friend who was afraid equally of kine and Zeppelins. The she-friend used Rye Green as an hostel and a refuge for weeks on end. (There was also, to help her work (but she doesn't come into the story) a woman from South Africa whose husband was in the Flying Corps and she had a weird gnome like child of nine who danced among the chickens and chased sheep.) Well, Allah who made women Alone knows what happened but the Tasmanienne of a sudden announced that she just had to go. She didn't argue any more than an incontinent child. She only sulked and stormed. Go she must from Rye Green at once.

That there were contracts concerned her less than the east wind. And a date was fixed upon which she could go. Though it was foul confusion to all the farm. Nearly a week before that date, she, and her friend, fled privily across the fields in the morning to the railway station – levanted, bolted, were not! – leaving the kine and the poultry *and* the dog whom I have mentioned before – all as they stood or lowed or yapped. No explanation: no address (the wife had advanced her money too) just the eternal woman soul vanishing into the Ewigkeit. And now – so small is human nature – nothing will move me from my passionate conviction that when the Empire, Sir, is Federated, the Island of Tasmania should be left out, to howl among its apples and its Eves. I believe too, that the whole thing hadn't an ounce of intended crime in it – mere mental impotence, indiscipline and temperament. But we have had one Hell of a time overtaking the situation she left on our hands. Her successor is another lady originally an Art Student and wood carver – also with a husband in the army. I fold my hands and wait upon the dispensations of God who Alone knoweth what He hath made. There is nothing to astonish me under all the Heavens of Sussex – except a woman who works.

It's a sickening hot day with a high Sou' Wester and gouts of almost hot rain – unwholesome airs. The grass all filled between its blades with a blueish light from the heavy clouds and the roads a muck of dirt. It's no play trying to shove and boost a farm along as the wife is doing; and I am almost grateful for any weather that forces her to rest.

Saturday. And today fine: glory be for *your* sakes. Curious how everyone in England considers the weather first from the point of view of the Armies. Women working in the fields in the wet speak always of the wet with a venom they didn't show in the old days when it merely discomfited themselves. "It's bad for *them*" is their first word now. And we haven't heard your guns for some time – i.e. four days. Last week they broke in on us in a clap of noise that almost shook the valley. One of our old men – an expert, quick, surgeon of a wood man, (he cleans up round his work as though it were an operating table) has just had his boy reported missing. He goes about in dumb pain like an angry ox. We are trying to get details out of the W.O. He has another son almost of military age. Indeed the boy *did* sneak into the Army a year ago, was discovered to be an infant, and was turned out again to ripen. The father, implies, in the still Sussex way, that upon this youngster the family vendetta will descend. And from among your Canadians, came a word from a brother of one of our maids who was working in a mine. It struck him, he says, down in the dark, that he owed something extra for *our* boys's death – his sister having waited on my child almost since birth. They *do* hate now. I don't know whether the younger Nations are, au fond, as vindictive as the Englishmen. They can't approach the English women in the fervour of their hate. We had to abandon burying grilled Zepp crews publicly. Now we have a military escort at the funeral, ostensibly to pay honour, actually to discourage the crowd who love not to hear the Church of England service used for these purposes.[6]

Lloyd George's pronouncement[7] has done great good to us all here – because for once in his imaginative life he has expressed our true desire and intention. I am told too that it came as great discouragement to the Hun who has not yet understood that he is hated. That's a curious point about all human nature. Very, *very* few characters ever realize that they are actually disliked for themselves. Envied, yes: objected to on account of their higher standards and morality – yes: but – even with condemned murderers – the mind scarcely admits that it is an outcast. When I was a newspaper cub I knew a man condemned to death who expressed himself on this. It was the moral loneliness, the absolute shock of being loathed that hurt him. And he had so many just reasons too (if the world would only have let him explain) for killing his victim.

What will the Hun's state of mind be when, atop of physical hopelessness, comes that sick sense of moral isolation?

You say that the heaviest fighting is due in the Spring.[8] Certainly all preparations are being made for it – you know I expect, what number of troops are training in France behind you – but are you sure that the Hun will be given much rest through the Winter? And did you (as a moral revelation) see the Crown Prince's interview with the Neutral Reporter – a worthy address it seemed to me to a worthy audience.[9] "Rancid" isn't exactly the word but it comes near it. And I expect it will please the Uneutral States! I am busy with small things and small pains in my innards, but these last are better of late though they crimp one up at the time.

I would that your return to England came before mid November. I met Bruce[10] – your inspector of Hospitals the other day, with Sam Hughes.[11] Will you have an inspectorship or a hospital post under him? I wish you would let me know, roughly, what your new work would be. Sam Hughes interested me a lot as a man for a job which he has achieved, I think, to admiration. Anyhow, no one else could have done it.

Now, think well over your chosen type of Club and let me have your opinion.

With all affection and every good wish to you both

Yours Ever
Rudyard Kipling.

Notes

1. Dorothy Macphail was at Bateman's, 21–5 November, but her father was not there until 15–16 January 1917, when he came with Dorothy (Bateman's Visitors Book).
2. In 1905.

3. The Baths Club, 34 Dover Street, offered swimming to its 2,000 members, 500 of whom were women. RK and John visited the Club on 11 August 1915 when "John swims" (CK diary).
4. Warburton: see 11–13 September 1916.
5. Part of the Bateman's estate: see 2 August 1910.
6. The funeral of the crew of the Zeppelin L 21 (see 11–13 September 1916) had turned ugly: "The whole bearing of the crowd was unpleasant to see. ... One woman did not confine herself to remarks: she threw eggs at the trailer bearing the last remains of the dead German officer, and her language gave nearly as much offence as the act" (*The Times*, 7 September 1916). The crew of another Zeppelin, brought down over London on 1 October, was buried on 5 October. The Royal Flying Corps was in charge of the funeral, "and a large force of police and special constables attended, but there were few other spectators beyond a little crowd of villagers" (*The Times*, 6 October 1916).
7. Against any neutral interference, in a statement made to the American journalist Roy Howard of the United Press; such action, Lloyd George said, would be regarded as an "unneutral act" (*The Times*, 29 September 1916). This stirred up an angry response in Germany.
8. Plans for a breakthrough in Champagne in the spring of 1917 were frustrated by the German withdrawal to the Hindenburg line. The campaign on the Aisne that began in April soon failed, with the usual heavy losses.
9. The Crown Prince, in an interview with the American journalist William Bayard Hale, of the Hearst papers, invited American mediation and deplored the war's destructiveness (*The Times*, 3 October 1916). The interview was met with disgust in England. Hale (1869–1924), originally a clergyman but a prominent journalist for many years, and the author of President Wilson's campaign biography, had been in the pay of the Germans since 1915 to serve as an American apologist. When this connection became known in 1918, Hale was driven into permanent exile.
10. Herbert Alexander Bruce (1868–1963), Toronto surgeon, was Inspector-General of the Canadian Army Medical Corps, 1916. He was afterwards Professor of Surgery at the University of Toronto, Lieutenant-Governor of Ontario, 1932–37, and Member of Parliament, 1940–46.
11. Sir Samuel Hughes (1853–1921), Canadian politician and militia officer, was Minister of Militia and Defence for Canada, 1911–16, responsible for the organization of the Canadian Expeditionary Force. Hughes was a difficult colleague, impetuous and undisciplined, and in November 1916 he was compelled to resign by Borden, the Canadian Prime Minister.

To Stanley Baldwin, 22 October 1916

ALS: Dalhousie University

Bull Hotel / *Cambridge* / Sunday night / 8.30 p.m. / Oct. 22. 1916

Dear Stan:

We came down to spend a week end with Corporal Instructor O. R. Baldwin. He's just gone off to coach someone in platoon drill. He dined with us last night also he lunched and has been with us all this day since he got up. We've explored his sumptuous digs in Fitzwilliam Street and we have fairly exhaustively discussed the service in all its relations.

When we got in yesterday at 1: I went hunting for him and found him behind a typewriter in the Corps Orderly Room – serene and adequate as a cucumber. Never having connected Ollie with a typewriter, I refrained with difficulty from swooning – especially as the stuff he was turning out was a complex and elaborate schedule of the next week's company work. That was but the first of about 2,000 surprises.

I had had an idea that, unless I was absolutely out in my eye for form, Ollie would do well, but I hadn't the ghost of an idea *any* child could come on as he had done. It's simply beautiful to see and hear and watch. He's found his life; has a clear idea of what he wants to make of it and has for himself, grasped The Secret – that he who saves the other fellow trouble is the other fellow's master. Herein is the whole Law of Success: and if he does not go *very* far indeed, I am a Dutchman. His natural instinct is for the theory and practice of drill which he loves and he can make his lectures (he'll lecture on anything on God's earth at a minute's notice) interesting to his equals. He *knows* – and he makes it his business to know because knowledge is power. And when he says that a thing is correct or to be done, it is both correct and feasible. I saw him today with his Lieutenant, and it was very funny to notice how Ollie had the run of the company arrangement etc. etc.: and the clarity with which he set out what was to be done this coming week. I fancy, too, that the Regular Sergeant Instructors know that the boy knows. Otherwise he would have spoken to me about them on points of the new drill which has just come in and on which as you know he has "written a book."[1] We all went to the shop where it was exposed for sale. Fancy his being made Instructor at the mature age of 17.7! He looks very fit indeed and – as to smartness I went out with him in his british warm[2] this afternoon and he was several times saluted, as an officer, by other soldiers – including a Colonial and a Regular. This is the surest sign that he *looked* an officer and, walking behind him, I didn't wonder. He has it all and I think his sheer determination to get on and his keen interest in the drama and the human nature of it all will give him all the diversion he wants. We're both pleased beyond words to see him so happy and so rejoicingly abreast of his job. Our hearts go out to him a good deal, as you know.

Yesterday was a divine evening and I took Elsie to the Backs, winding up with the chapel of Kings at dusk. This morning at 10, in brightest sunshine, we made another trip winding up at Magdalen. Elsie was immensely funny about it. The burden of her indignant song was "why have I been deceived throughout my innocent youth? why was I not told these things?" She has written a letter to Landon telling him a few things about Cambridge *v* Oxford that will not soothe his pride.[3] And it *was* lovely beyond words.

We go home tomorrow after seeing Ollie start for a day's trenchery with his battalion.

Love to you all from us both.

Ever
Rud

Notes

1. See 3 October 1916.
2. A short overcoat worn by officers. RK uses the term in "The Janeites" (*Debits and Credits*, p. 179) and "The Debt" (*Limits and Renewals*, p. 215).
3. Landon had been an undergraduate at Hertford College, Oxford.

To John St Loe Strachey, 26 October 1916

ALS: House of Lords Record Office

Bateman's / Burwash / Sussex / Oct 26. 1916

private

Dear Strachey

I've been away from home and have only just got your letter. I'd very much like to come up and meet Kindersley[1] but, as things are at present I am not clear. However, I've "duly noted" your days given for lunch and dinner and when I'm up I'll wire or telephone to Wellington Street. Will that be all right?

Look here – you *must* have an account of the Varsity O[fficers']. T[raining]. C[orps].'s These are now largely made up of men (privates n.c.o.s.) recommended for commissions after actual work, who are sent home for an officer's course. They are then decanted into the colleges, where they dine in Hall and – in lieu of military police – have their names taken by the porters at the various gates if they are late o' nights! Never was such a game. After months of bloody war, this to them is joy and rest and relief – and a great deal more.

They say simply after a while: – "Oh! I'm Christ's – or Corpus or Clare" – as the case may be: and, in wonderful fashion, they are. You can hear the ages and the architecture and the aura working on 'em: and you can see the Master of Trinity[2] taking off his mortar board to acknowledge the salutes: and you can observe hairy fearless men of the Dominions in a blue funk because they have pinched, after lecture, some Dean's bicycle!

Not being of the colleges, this ain't my job but it's flying in the face of providence for *you* not to have Graves[3] or Lucas[4] write an adorable middle about it.[5]

There's my Rowland for your delightful Oliver about the "trained men." Our love to all of you.

Ever sincerely
Rudyard Kipling

Notes
1. Robert Molesworth Kindersley (1871–1954), 1st Baron Kindersley, merchant banker and in 1916 chairman of the War Savings Committee.
2. Montagu Butler (1833–1918), Master of Trinity, 1886–1918. Oliver Baldwin states that "the Master of Trinity … used to take off his cap to every soldier he met in his College" (*The Questing Beast*, p. 48). Perhaps RK actually saw this during his weekend at Cambridge.
3. C. L. Graves (see 9 November 1906), as well as writing for *Punch*, was assistant editor of the *Spectator*, 1899–1917.
4. E. V. Lucas: see 9 November 1906.
5. I find no such thing in the *Spectator*.

To Humphry Ward[1], 30 October 1916
ALS: Dalhousie University

Bateman's / Burwash / Sussex / Oct. 30. 1916

Private
Dear Humphrey Ward
   I've been away from home or I'd have answered sooner. I'm afraid I can't be of any use about Adam Lindsay Gordon.[2] In the first place it's altogether out of my line, as I've never done a critique in my life: in the second I am tied up with work of sorts, not on my own account, that I must clear off, and that is going to be a long job.[3]
   In the third place, any one who wants to get at the innards of A.L.G.'s work would have to go through the files of the Sydney Bulletin since it was started: for *he* was the man who set all those young 'uns singing. His is an extraordinary case of strongly localized influence springing from a transplanted origin. Had he stayed in England he might have ranked with but after Whyte-Melville,[4] so to say. Down under, he expanded and left a mark on Australian verse which really ought to be dealt with by an Australian. I don't know where "Banjo" Patterson[5] who wrote "The Man from Snowy River" is at present but, I think it's that sort of man you want to give his full value which *is* Australian. "Ashtaroth"[6] is not much use, as far as I remember. He stands by "Bush ballads and Galloping Rhymes"[7] which

went into the heart of a people of horsemen. You might try some Australian professor.

Ever sincerely
Rudyard Kipling.

Notes
1. See [16 August 1897]. Ward was preparing a new edition of his *The English Poets: Selections with Critical Introductions by Various Writers*, first published in 1880 with a famous introduction by Matthew Arnold. In the new edition, 1917, the (very brief) section on Adam Lindsay Gordon is introduced by Ward himself.
2. Gordon (1833–70), an Englishman exiled to Australia by his family, was famous as a horseman of great daring, and , afterwards, as a poet. He committed suicide the day after the publication of his *Bush Ballads* (see note 7, below). RK's "The Dying Chauffeur" in "The Muse Among the Motors" (originally published in the *Daily Mail*, 23 February 1904) parodies Gordon's "The Sick Stockrider".
3. This is perhaps a polite formula. RK had finished his work on *The Eyes of Asia* and "Destroyers at Jutland" and there is no evidence that he had anything else at all extensive in hand.
4. George John Whyte-Melville (1821–78), historical novelist, specialising in scenes of hunting, author of, e.g., *Holmby House*, 1859.
5. Andrew "Banjo" Paterson: see 22 November 1901. His *The Man from Snowy River and Other Verses* was published in Sydney, 1895.
6. *Ashtaroth, A Dramatic Lyric* (Melbourne, 1867).
7. *Bush Ballads and Galloping Rhymes* (Melbourne, 1870).

To Andrew Macphail, 3 November 1916
ALS: Photocopy, National Archives of Canada

Bateman's / Burwash / Sussex / Nov. 3. 1916.

Dear Macphail

I am sending you a map of the battle of Loos (Sep. 27 1916).[1] John's platoon of the Irish Guards dug in in Chalk Pit Wood and then advanced towards the Hulluch road in the direction of Puits 14 bis which were full of machine guns. John was last seen, wounded, going into a building close to what is marked on the map as the Keep. There was at that time heavy machine gun fire from the Bois Hugo. The presumption is that the body would be somewhere between the building by the Keep and the dotted road marked "metalled but poor road." He is thought to have been with Captain Cuthbert of the Scots Guards who is also missing and of whom news is anxiously sought. We are doubtful whether John wore a disc. He had written home for one which did not reach him in time: But his clothes were all marked and he wore a small signet ring on his little finger marked J.K.

I have a feeling at the back of my head that you above all will find some trace of him that may give us the certainty we long for.

Ever affectionately
Rudyard Kipling.

Note
1. Thus in MS, for 1915.

To Sir Max Aitken, 9 November 1916
ALS: Harvard University

Bateman's / Burwash / Sussex / Nov. 9. 1916

private
Dear Max,

I want you to rescue a man who has given himself to the war and is now very nearly used up.

He is Captain Andrew Macphail No. 6. Field Ambulance No. 2. Canadian Division. He was, as you know, before the war Professor of Medicine at Macgill, Editor of the University magazine: a man of almost international reputation and certainly one of the leading intellectual lights of the Dominion.

He came over with the ambulance (a horsed one) about two years back: being then 53 or 54.[1] He has worked and suffered like a devil ever since and lived in every Hell that your Armies have endured. *You* know what a Field Ambulance means.

Now he is finished – used up – worn out and can you wonder. (His son in the Canadian Engineers came over with him and to his own burden has, of course, been added *that* anxiety. The boy, after months of barrage-dodging is equally worn out but he is young and will recover).

What I want you to do for me is to exercise your long arm and fish, pull, extricate Macphail from France and give him some Canadian Hospital in England to look after before he collapses altogether. *How* you'll work it I don't know but I *beg* you not to reveal in any way that I've approached you in the matter. Let it come about in the official course of events but let it come quickly. He's an old friend of mine and one I'm very fond of. If I didn't do what I could to get him out I'd feel I had his blood on my head. *But* – (it's that damned stiff-backed Scots blood again) if he knew I was working to get him out I might lose his friendship. You see.

I believe he was under orders for England a little while ago but a change in the Canadian Medical Command altered all orders.

Fetch him out and land him in England for at least half a year and he'll go back a new man – and I'll bless you.[2]

Ever
Rud.

P.S.   Except that she lacks a white spot on the shoulder Cherkley Elsie[3] is the spit and image of Dene Song Thrush – might be her sister. She's as graceful as a fawn and as nervy as a woman.

I left her alone pointedly after she came and patted the other two under her indignant little nose. She stood it for three days and then pushed in to have her ears scratched too. She's going to be the jewel of the bunch I think – and that's saying something.

R.

Notes
1. Macphail was 50 in 1914, a year older than RK.
2. Macphail was transferred to the London Headquarters of the Medical Services, but not until May 1917 (Robertson, "Macphail as Social Critic", p. 256).
3. A cow, evidently from Aitken's herd, hence Cherkley. RK identifies Dene Song Thrush, who produced a calf called "Bateman's Baby" in December, as "widow of the late John Cherkley of Cherkley Court, Leatherhead" (to Aitken, [10 December 1916]: AL, House of Lords Record Office).

To Andrew Macphail, 26 November 1916
ALS: Photocopy, National Archives of Canada

Bateman's / Burwash / Sussex / Nov. 26. 1916

Dear Macphail

Comes yours of the 22nd almost on the heels of Dorothy's departure; she having come down here on Wednesday and being gone Saturday noon[1] after continuous (I heard it) talks with Elsie in which – this I did *not* hear but am sure of – they travelled over the minds of their respective parents. A dangerous thing to let the young get together and compare notes. But I heard all about Orwell[2] and the house and the farms so that I think now I could almost draw a plan of your literary-attic. And D and I went for a walk together in the which I introduced her to one of our village women and six weeks old baby. She has her father's zest for Humanity and when the proud mother said to me – in reply to a question about warming bottles of baby food o'nights: – "The bottle's *me*" at the same time smiting her breast, D's joy was on a par with yours (and God knows I didn't mean the pun).

For the rest the two young things talked and we managed to get some laughs out of things. It's a most Sweet Maiden and she'll come again. She looks very fit and eats and sleeps well. I want to know when you're coming that I may put the clubs in Hand. If you're over for long you may want a pair.

Thank you for what you tell us about the ground by Loos. No, I thought we hadn't reoccupied it and when we do it will be all a new palimpsest of mortality. By all the best evidence we have *Captain Cuthbert* of the <u>*Scots Guards*</u> was with him at the last[3] – so evidences of one may guide you to the other. You know best how long such evidence is traceable in that ground. Meantime bless you for your kindness.

The University Magazine (edited D. tells me by a committee) becomes progressively more loosely knit and unrelated but I take it you have long ago forgotten you were ever an editor.

With all our loves

Affectionately
Rudyard Kipling

Notes
1. 21–5 November (Bateman's Visitors Book).
2. On Prince Edward Island.
3. See 5 October 1915.

To Sir Max Aitken, 19 December 1916
ALS: Harvard University

Brown's Hotel, / London. W. / Dec. 19. 1916

Dear Aitken

Congratulations![1] What gratifies *me* most is that my Godson is now the Honourable Peter,[2] which fact I hope is duly brought home to him when he is bad.

It's a most marvellous career of yours and the best thought is that it's no more than beginning.

We're both immensely pleased and this brings our best love and good wishes to you two.

Ever
Rud.

For goodness sake take a little trouble in working out your coat of arms. You're entitled as a peer to supporters. I suppose they will represent Canadians – one soldier figure and one habitant?[3] As to your motto. It ought to be *"Res mihi non me rebus"*[4] – *literally* "Things for me not me for things": or, more expandedly "I would rather control things than be controlled by them."

It's a quotation from Horace and I don't think there is any coat of arms that carries it.[5]

R.

Notes
1. The King's approval of Aitken's peerage as Baron Beaverbrook was published in *The Times*, 18 December; the official date of the creation was 2 January 1917.
2. Peter Rudyard Kipling: see 16 October 1912.
3. "Kipling devised Beaverbrook's coat of arms for him" (A. J. P. Taylor, *Beaverbrook*, p. 127). It would perhaps be more accurate to say that RK took a keen interest in the matter and gave much advice, e.g., in letters of 12 and 28 April 1917 (ALS, University of New Brunswick, and ALS, Harvard).
4. Horace, *Epistles*, I, i, 19: "et mihi res, non me rebus".
5. Aitken adopted it as his motto.

To Sir Almroth Wright,[1] [1916?]
ALS: Mr Josias Cunningham

[Bateman's?]

private
Dear Sir Almroth Wright
   Forgive a layman, and an ignorant layman at that, trespassing on your time in these crowded days: but it has occurred to me that there is at least one aspect of the attitude of our pacificists and their friends who are assisting the enemy which might be dealt with, to the advantage of the empire, on scientific lines. The one certain note of the German character under stress, is its unfailing beastliness and its use of certain well known forms of perversion and degeneracy. This conforms to its character in normal times. We have, in

private

the reports of the atrocities, most ample proof that the sadism inherent in The Animal has been used, as all its qualities have been used, as a means to power. We don't republish the atrocity reports in full: and we certainly do not emphasize the foulest and most significant side of 'em – the mixture of blood and lust which is best calculated to break up the self-respect of the victim, and so to destroy his will. It is extremely difficult to make this clear to a people who cannot conceive yet the existence of another people to whom the Moral Law is not. I tried once in a speech to point out that the German game was to bring the conquered to such a condition that they would not be able to look at each other afterwards: but that was too general to be understood.[2] Also I am not a man with scientific knowledge of mankind. I only know them in the way of my business.

But I believe that, with certain temperaments, the fact or the report of a specific type of abominations being committed, wakes, consciously or unconsciously, a certain perverted interest which may increase to sympathy. It is deep calling to deep: passive responding to active. I have been at some pains to try to puzzle out the instinct underlying the words and works and publications of our pacificists as the war has gone on; and nothing has struck me more than the recrudescence of the mixture (ancient as Humanity) of luxury of sentiment and cruelty, and the scarcely veiled attraction towards a race that unites these qualities. Also, in some cases, the evident enjoyment of what they call "martyrdom" – i.e., the kicking, cuffing and knocking about of recalcitrant "objectors" to all forms of military service, by their indignant fellow soldiers. This nicks in exactly with a peculiar religiosity which finds solace in the physical details of the Crucifixion, and a persistent hysteria – made worse by the riot and confusion of actual war all around, – which expresses itself in terms of indiscriminate love for mankind and – unless I am very badly mistaken – merges into particular (or unparticular) love for the individual. One notices this last, most clearly, in some of the Socialist-Brotherhood papers and pronouncements.

As I see it, then, this class represents a shade of temperament which exists in all lands and which needs only the strain of excitement to reveal itself. If I am right, you know better than I do, the springs and the bases of such temperament and how far removed it is from its ostensible *raison d'etre*.[3]

Further (as I think you yourself have pointed out) there has, of late years, been an outbreak of intellectual lawlessness where, whatever the original texture of the mind may have been, the habit of the mind affected was to make light of all moral restrictions simply because they were restrictive. That movement had many names – "toleration", "the larger outlook", "self-realization" (you know all the labels) and it led, naturally and inevitably, to mental and moral slackness. Where the mind, for any cause, slacks off or ranges out too far the body sooner or later will follow if it can. (Forgive me for laboriously setting down all these platitudes. I am merely handing up my notebook for revision). And the end of it all is, equally naturally: – "To Hell with

private
contracts!" whether those contracts be with God, Nature, or Man. (The Hun has broken all three bonds). Also, the type of mind which counts what it calls "Humanity" as a thing worthy to be worshipped *per se*, differs very little from the type of mind which adores "the State above the Law."

This second class, as I make it out, recruits itself largely from the undisciplined, and therefore unhumorous and arrogant, intellectual mind; from the more arid socialist, who is temperamentally the impotent deviser of forms: from the more aggressive labour leader who has been used to employ physical cruelty in his scheme of Government, and the more rabid sectarian equally used to employ mental tortures and the fear of a jealous God in his more limited dominion – i.e. from all types with an abnormal desire to exercise control over other people in private life, chapel, bed etc. Class II may melt into Class I and *vice-versa* but, I hold, that both are sympathetic by bodily or mental instinct with an enemy who has scientifically co-ordinated luxury, cruelty and arrogance and who, since he really *does* know something of the triple Devil he serves, exploits both these classes in England because both these classes have power.

We in England persist in looking upon our pacificists as sports of nature developed by the play of "politics" or as sincerely conscientious idiots. I think we make a bad mistake. It is not schools of thought we have to deal with, but temperaments whose roots go down to the dirt: brains with lesions unnoticeable or masked in time of peace, and every form of mental or physical impotence x-rayed as it were by the light and heat of war.

(There was, to my mind, a beautiful illustration of induced hysteria rising to mania in the Irish rebellion at Easter,[4] which I was hoping some one would handle scientifically. Here was a race "misunderstood" for 800 or 1000 years by all the world and for all that period incapable of accommodating itself to any known form of rule. It found itself baulked, through religious pressure and the withholding of conscription from satisfying its natural instincts at a time when all the world round it was enjoying them openly and with every circumstance of publicity and appeal. Can you wonder that Ireland exploded? You can witness much the same sort of nervous crisis among the maids in a household where there has been a succession of marriages or funerals. And that there might be no doubt as to the diagnosis, the central figure of the rebellion was – precisely of the type one would expect.[5] But Ireland does not concern us. I merely submit her case as collateral proof.)

Here then, my case rests. Boiled and peeled, of course, it comes to this – that when the normal human being says, in his haste, of the Pacifists: – "Oh! They are all b—s together!" he is nearer the scientific truth than he thinks.

Now, it is along these lines, it seems to me, that the Pacifist might be dealt with – kindly and sympathetically but, above all, scientifically – just as you would deal with a patient at a clinic. I don't for a moment imagine he

private
would appreciate your kindness but patients, I believe, are proverbially ungrateful.

I have neither the knowledge nor the standing to develop the thesis properly. Even if I had, I am only a layman and the issue might be obscured by temper on the part of those who differed from me, thus reducing what ought to be a dispassionate discussion to vulgar ink slinging.

But, seriously, I believe the thing ought to be done with weight and with authority and I believe that the public mind is ready for it as the public mind would not have been even a year ago. The constant flow of men coming home with details of what the Hun has done have changed and hardened public opinion. Apart from this, the most important consideration, such a scientific treatment as I have suggested would give pain to the Hun which is always a good thing.

Would it be asking too much of you to let me know your opinions on the subject – just as regards the accuracy of my deductions and next as to the possibility of your taking up the whole question on the lines which I have very roughly sketched?

With renewed apologies for the inordinate length of this letter / believe me

Very sincerely yours:
Rudyard Kipling

Notes
1. Wright (1861–1947), bacteriologist, Professor at St Mary's Hospital, London, specialising in the problems of immunisation. He was currently serving with the Army Medical Service in France studying wound infections. In 1912 Wright published a letter in *The Times* on "militant hysteria" among the Suffragettes in which he affirmed that "the mind of woman is always threatened with danger from the reverberations of her physiological emergencies" and that "there is mixed up with the woman's movement much mental disorder". The disordered types were the "violent", the "sexually embittered", the "incomplete", and the "intellectually embittered" (28 March 1912). The letter appears as an appendix to Wright's *The Unexpurgated Case against Woman Suffrage*, 1913, a copy of which is in RK's study at Bateman's.
2. RK's speech in support of recruiting, Southport, 21 June 1915, in which he said that the British, if defeated by the Germans, would "be degraded till those who survive can scarcely look each other in the face" (*Southport Guardian*, 23 June 1915: uncollected).
3. Thus in MS.
4. The Easter Rising, as it is called now, 24 April 1916. The original plan for a rising, which counted on German support that did not materialise, was called off, but the Irish Republican Brotherhood occupied the Dublin Post Office and proclaimed the Irish Republic; several days of fighting and many deaths ensued.
5. Patrick Pearse (1879–1916), poet and Irish nationalist, led the uprising in Dublin. After proclaiming the Irish Republic, he surrendered on 29 April, was sentenced by court martial, and executed by a firing squad on 3 May 1916. It is not likely that RK has Pearse's homosexual inclinations in mind, since these were not known outside a small group of friends (Ruth Dudley Edwards, *Patrick Pearse: the Triumph of Failure*, 1979, p. 127); more likely he means Pearse's exaltation of death and martyrdom in the Irish cause.

To Stanley Baldwin, 29 January 1917

ALS: Dalhousie University

Bateman's / Burwash / Sussex / Jan. 29. 1917.

Dear Stan,

Your news is splendid![1] I had an idea that it might be necessary for some one to go to New York just now: but I wasn't expecting – what I ought to have expected if I'd thought for a minute. It's better by all odds than the Board of Trade because I fancy it may serve as a stepping stone to that – if you care for it – later on.

Also, it's great for Oliver. We are only useful, remember, as we serve our young. And with a Papa in the Government Oliver's horn is exalted.

I can't tell you how pleased we are at the reward of virtue and knowledge and a few other trifles. I am borrowing a year's income from an immoral Bank, to pay to the War Loan, on the strength of it – just to show my confidence in the family.[2]

Isn't there any way of vending £5 W.L. certificates over the counter? This signing of forms scares the small investor besides taking up his time. You see Ll. George about sickened the country of forms[3] before this little war began.

Ever yours joyfully
Rud.

Notes

1. Baldwin, having been Parliamentary Private Secretary to Bonar Law as Chancellor of the Exchequer, had just been appointed a Junior Lord of the Treasury, a post in which he would continue to assist Law. Baldwin did not go to New York, but one of his counterparts was sent there to look after British financial interests.
2. The reason given is a joke, but RK did make this arrangement: see 3 March 1917. The terms of the 3rd War Loan were announced on 11 January 1917: there were two issues, one at 4% and one at 5%. The minimum subscription was £5 at post offices, £50 at banks.
3. The forms, e.g., required by the National Insurance Act: see 18 June 1912.

To the Secretary,[1] the Society of Authors, 29 January 1917

Text: Society of Authors, *Annual Report* for 1917, [1918], p. 7

Bateman's / Burwash / Sussex / January 29th, 1917.

Dear Sir,

I see from the last number of *The Author* that the resolution requiring authors not to contribute to any charity books which have not been previously approved by the Society of Authors and Publishers' Association has been upheld with only two dissentients, of whom I am one.[2] This proves that I am altogether out of sympathy with the present views of the Society. I must ask you therefore, first, to accept the enclosed cheque for £100 for the benefit of the Pension Fund, and next, to accept my resignation from the Council and membership of the Society.

Yours faithfully,
Rudyard Kipling.

Notes

1. The Secretary of the Society of Authors had been, since 1892, George Herbert Thring (1859–1941), who continued in office until 1930.
2. The resolution of which RK complains appears in the January 1917 number of *The Author*, pp. 97–8. RK at once responded, saying: "I hold no brief for [charity] books, but I find myself unable to subscribe to an undertaking which invests in a committee the right to say what I shall or shall not do with my work" (*The Author*, February 1917). The other dissentient to the resolution was John Galsworthy (*The Author*, February 1917, p. 119). RK had been a member of the Society since 1890 and a member of its Council since 1892. In reply to a letter from the historian Stanley Leathes, remonstrating on behalf of the Society, RK reaffirmed his position: "The Society of Authors has decided by large majorities on a course of action which, to my mind, is not only unwise and unfortunate but is also a grave departure from the principles on which the Society was founded" (12 February 1917: ALS, Sussex).

To Andrew Macphail, 3 March 1917

ALS: Photocopy, National Archives of Canada

Empire Hotel, / Bath. / March 3. 1917.

Dear Macphail

Yours of the 27th Feb on the eve of our departure from Bath where the wife has been very ill.[1] She is better now, however, and we hope to get up to town on Monday, where we must wait for ten days or so.[2] Altogether *not* a cheerful experience but it might have been worse.

Bless you for what you tell us about what you have been able to do.[3] One can't expect anything really till our men are actually on the ground and free to look.

I don't know whether the loan cheered you: but it wasn't a bad little effort. You must always bear in mind that owing to the psychology of the English there is at least that much more available to be drawn upon. What impressed me was the evenness of the distribution of wealth through whole strata that never utter on the subject. E.g. our housemaid weighs in with £150: and every one of everybody's servants seems to have gone into unsuspected stockings. For myself I am pledged to the Bank for my next year's earnings: wherefore I am a person of consideration in my Bank Manager's eyes. One curious effect of the thing has been to make the English talk about their wealth – as individuals, a breach of all canons!

I am still betting that the U.S. will *not* come into the game, but that Germany will declare war on *her* for sinking or talking about sinking Hun submarines.[4] That would I think be the deep beyond which there is none lower but I am disposed to believe that the U.S.A. will plumb it. Meantime her *amour propre* – has been hurt by the knowledge that Mexico and Japan were to have been inspanned against her: and now they are all giving tongue like so many agitated housemaids.[5] It makes a heap of difference which fellow's ox is gored.

I only hope you will stick to your plan of coming home after certain things have happened. There is no man alive better fitted than you to write the saga that is in your mind because you are a philosopher whose philosophy has justified itself. Such men are very few indeed.

We shall see Dorothy when we are up in town, at Brown's. She was furious at having missed what she did of Geoff's leave; but I never heard any rumour of scarlet fever – just ordinary infernal measles. She addressed eloquent words to Elsie on the matter.

I am not at the exact top of my form but there isn't anything to complain of – only I haven't been doing any work.

We are all in the dark here as to what the Hun matures but there is talk in certain circles that we have been astounding him with a new explosive which does things that leave Titans gasping. Forgive this scrawl and believe me as ever affectionately yours

Rudyard Kipling.

Notes
1. They went to Bath on 6 February and remained until 5 March, when they went to London (Rees extracts).
2. In fact they spent nearly a month in London, at Brown's Hotel, from 5 March to 3 April (Rees extracts).
3. RK had written to Macphail on 12 February about possible sources of information about John Kipling. He sent the names of certain Scots Guards, prisoners of the Germans, who might know something if the Germans would allow communication (photocopy, National Archives of Canada).
4. At the end of January 1917 the Germans announced the resumption of unrestricted submarine warfare. President Wilson at once severed relations with Germany and spoke for a policy of "armed neutrality". Two months later, on 6 April, the US declared war on Germany.

5. A German proposal for an offensive alliance with Mexico and Japan against the US should the US declare war on Germany was made public on 1 March 1917. This was the notorious "Zimmerman telegram", intercepted and decoded by the British and passed on to the US. The chances of such a proposal were not serious, but the episode helped to intensify the war spirit in the country: "No other event of the war to this point, not even the German invasion of Belgium or the sinking of the Lusitania, so stunned the American people" (Arthur S. Link, *Wilson: Campaigns for Progressivism and Peace 1916–1917*, Princeton, 1965, p. 354).

To Colonel Lionel Charles Dunsterville, 7 March 1917
ALS: University of Sussex

Brown's Hotel, / London. W. / Mar. 7. 1917.

Dear Old Man:

Your letter with cheque for £10 duly to hand and noted etc. etc. etc.: you're wrong. I *did* get a prize – I got it for an alleged poem on "Assaye."[1] It was a piece of shameless nepotism on Price's part: also it was bound in tree calf and I forget what its title was. So you needn't swank about *that*! But I always imagined mathematics was the one thing you *did* know something about in your youth. Anyway I have a distinct recollection of your letting me crib my "trig" from you till little Bossu[2] was unkind enough to ask me what "co-sine" meant. Then I collapsed and the shameful truth came out.

Oddly enough the other day I found myself remembering a certain walk up from the sea through the football field when, you having decided I was to join the choir, were trying to make me learn the tune of "I know a maiden fair to see." You weren't patient with my lack of ear because, by the old parallel bars under the tree, you began to kick me. D'you remember?[3]

We've just come to town from a month in Bath which is a large cold wet piss-pot full of the aged and overfed. The wife was taking a cure there but had to stop it as she broke down and was very ill. She's better now but it wasn't a cheerful experience for any of us.

You seem to be trying the Mohmunds pretty high with all your "resources of civilization." Where the deuce d'you expect you'll get your recruits from if you knock the simple tribesman about with H[igh]. E[xplosive].[4]

Here we are in the thick of the game – on the edge of big fighting and really taking it seriously at last. We shall be taught what war is before we've done and it won't do us any harm. I'm glad to have lived to have seen it. There is even a chance that the U.S.A. may be kicked into the game.

Give my salaams to Davies *mi*[5] and all O.U.S.C.'s and believe me as ever, old man, affectionately yours

Rudyard

P.S.   As regards cheap "Kiplings" – there ain't enough paper for these luxuries.

Notes

1. "The Battle of Assaye", written as a prize poem at USC in July 1882 and first published in the USC *Chronicle*, 2 July 1886. The poem was called "The Battle of Assye" in the *Chronicle* and in subsequent printings until the Sussex Edition. In *Something of Myself* RK writes that "At term-end [Price] most unjustly devised a prize poem – subject 'The Battle of Assaye' which, there being no competitor, I won in what I conceived was the metre of my latest 'infection' – Joaquin Miller. And when I took the prize-book, Trevelyan's *Competition Wallah*, Crom Price said that if I went on I might be heard of again" (p. 37).
2. As RK's mathematics master, Herbert Arthur Evans (see 9 May 1896), was called.
3. In *Something of Myself* RK writes: "when it was necessary to Stalky that I should get into the Choir, he taught me how to quaver 'I know a maiden fair to see' by punching me in the kidneys all up and down the cricket-field" (p. 27). The song is J. L. Hatton's setting of Longfellow's "Beware", adapted from the German.
4. An article in *The Times*, 9 January 1917, reports that 400 Mohmands had been rounded up for internment by British troops under the command of RK's old schoolfellow Sir George Roos-Keppel. The British methods included the use of aeroplanes and electrified barbed wire.
5. Colonel Charles Henry Davies: see 30 January 1886.

Part Three
The End of the War and After

April 1917–December 1919

INTRODUCTION

America's entry into the war in April 1917 was officially greeted by Kipling with the verses called "The Choice": "Bear witness, Earth, we have made our choice / With Freedom's brotherhood!" Privately, his response was more mixed. As he wrote to the Canadian Andrew Macphail, "The U.S.A. have a hell of a lot of lee-way to make up in public opinion: but they don't realize that yet and think that having girt on their armour is the same as having taken it off. ... But 'tis satisfaction to know that a trousered people speaking some variant of our tongue have at long last subscribed to the elementary decencies."

The long ordeal of the war had its predictable effect on one so implacable as Kipling: he grew steadily grimmer in his view of the enemy, more violent in his rhetoric. At the outset of the war, the Germans were sometimes "Teutons", sometimes (when Kipling is in France) "Boches": most often they were "Huns". Kipling thought that he was responsible for the currency of this name, borrowed from a speech of the Kaiser's and derisively turned against him and his troops. As the war dragged on, Kipling's language for the Germans moves from the barbaric or sub-human "Huns" to terms drawn from the non-human realm. The figure of "germs" appears as early as 1916 – "the German is typhoid or plague – Pestis teutonicus, if you like" (12 January 1916) – as does "animal" – "the sadism inherent in The Animal" ([1916]). The germ metaphor is developed at length in a letter of 5 October 1916. Later Kipling declares that "Hun" should always be spelled in lower-case letters and be understood as a neuter noun. He suggests to Theodore Roosevelt that perhaps the US should retaliate on its own German population "every Hun outrage committed on the U.S. and on France" (5 August 1917), and he tells with apparent satisfaction a cruel story of long-naturalised Germans in England who are characterised as "a dog and three dry bitches" (21 September 1918). Much, no doubt, may be allowed for the effects of long-continued strain towards the end of the war, but Kipling was never to relent in his view of the Germans. In 1921, when he made a brief foray over the border into Germany from France in the course of one of his motor tours, he was almost over-whelmed by the hateful spectacle of a flourishing countryside and prosperous towns: "*And they were alive!*" (Motor Tours, 28 April 1921).

In these years Kipling wrote only one more work in response to an official invitation. This was *The War in the Mountains*, the description of his tour of the Italian front in 1917, a tour that he again made in company with Perceval Landon. Probably Kipling had many other requests to do something with his pen for one interest or another in the struggle of the war; and probably he had begun to doubt that anything he might write could be of much use. There is some evidence that he undertook to visit munitions factories in England in March 1918 with a view to writing about them, but nothing came of it. He continued to make occasional speeches, to the cadets of the Household Brigade, to a meeting on war aims at Folkestone, and to American troops, for example. There was no great crisis in his health, but he suffered severe bouts of pain at irregular intervals. By June 1918, his weight was down to 123 pounds, and, as he confessed to Mrs Hill, "I haven't been doing much of anything lately, as I have not been very well for close on to a couple of years" (18 July 1918).

The end of the war, when it came, was anticlimactic: there was relief, but no rejoicing. "Glad you escaped the peace celebrations", Kipling wrote to a friend: "I bolted home from town and had my dark hour alone" (18 November 1918). The relief was mixed with anxiety that the Germans would go unpunished and the victory betrayed: such is the burden of Kipling's "Justice", published at the end of October 1918:

> But now their hour is past
> And we who bore it find
> Evil Incarnate held at last
> To answer to mankind.

Kipling was deeply suspicious of Woodrow Wilson ("arid and first last and all the time a schoolmaster") and the officious idealism of the "Fourteen Points" ("Wilson's idiotic Fourteen Points"). He hoped that Theodore Roosevelt might again turn the US in the right direction, but that hope was extinguished by Roosevelt's death in January 1919. It was soon clear that the US wanted nothing to do with picking up the pieces of a shattered Europe, and Kipling again had the unhappy satisfaction of seeing that his gloomy prophecies about unreliable Americans were correct (22 April, 22 November 1919). For two years he worked on a poem, never published, called "Ed Baker", apparently an effort to sum up all that Kipling thought and felt about the political behaviour of the US. But he could not satisfy himself: "the dam' thing doesn't hit hard enough yet" (27 August 1919).

Kipling could now return to his identity as a writer, though all that he did would continue to be marked by the experience of the war. In 1919 *The Years Between* appeared. This was the first new collection of poems since *The Five Nations* in 1903, and the difference between the two volumes shows clearly in what direction Kipling had travelled in the intervening years. *The Years Between* is much the darkest work that Kipling had ever published, filled with savage things like "Gehazi" or "The Hyænas", or bitter things like the

"Epitaphs of the War". There are also poems of grief without any politics: "My Boy Jack" and "En-Dor". The publication of the book led some readers to talk of a "prophetic" Kipling – the poet who saw that the war would come, that the people were unprepared, that their leaders were derelict, that the enemy was remorseless, and so on. But if Kipling had many opportunities to say "I told you so", that was cold comfort when the outcome was just what one desired not to see.

Kipling had now been, as he put it, a slave of the inkpot for half a lifetime; it is not surprising, then, that he began to show a wish to see the pattern of his career – the "figure in the carpet". He entered into a lengthy correspondence with the French critic André Chevrillon, who was preparing a study of Kipling, on the formation of his ideas and the aims of his career. Such a willingness not only to accept an effort to "place" him but to help with it was a new thing for Kipling. Formerly, he would have been too busy, too full of the pressure to get on with new things, to have taken the time for a retrospect. He also sent a set of notes to his American publisher defending and illustrating the various items in *The Years Between*, a modest sort of *apologia* that he would not have troubled to make earlier. In 1919 he brought out, in three handsome volumes, a collection of his poems called *Inclusive Verse*, as complete as he was prepared to allow any such collection to be. This was arranged according to Kipling's own ideas, but if there is a key to the arrangement no one has yet found it.

Except for his official trip to France in 1915 and to Italy in 1917 Kipling had been confined to England since 1914. He now made a tentative resumption of his touring life with a trip into the Scottish highlands in the summer of 1919; he would not return to his beloved France until the next year. Two new interests were added in these years: he was appointed a Rhodes Trustee in succession to Dr Jameson in 1917, and that year he also accepted appointment as an original member of the newly-founded Imperial War Graves Commission. He was a faithful and diligent member of the Commission, writing propaganda for it, consulting on the design, development, and administration of the vast cemeteries that were its responsibility, and visiting them officially and unofficially whenever his travels might take him into their neighbourhood. In this material way the war was always with him. So too was it in the major literary undertaking to which he now committed himself: a history of the war service of John Kipling's regiment, the Irish Guards. He accepted this job in 1917, a job, one cannot help thinking, that many lesser writers might have done as well as, or better than, Kipling. For the next six years it was his main work.

To D. H. Pilkington,[1] 12 April 1917
ALS: Mr Michael Pilkington

Bateman's / Burwash / Sussex / April 12. 1917.

Dear Pilkington

I hear that you have been shifted from Berkeley Square and that you are now at Bournemouth. I was in London a little time ago where between snow-storms, rain and unmitigated dirt, I sampled all the local microbes of that foul little village. London is without exception the most beastly place I know – and that's saying a good deal.

But what I wanted to write was, as usual, a request or rather a suggestion for you to do something for me. Have you ever noticed, by the way, that no one ever writes a letter to any one, more than a page long, unless it contains a request of some kind or another? My request is this. My new book called "A Diversity of Creatures" ought to be out next week.[2] It is "embellished" as you will see for I'm going to send you a copy, with fourteen alleged "poems." Some of 'em I honestly believe would be singable if one could only get the proper *sympathetic* treatment of them. I'm not going to say which ones I think they are because that may prejudice your mind in advance. One of them has got rather an odd metre which seems to me to have possibilities of tone colour – like horns and wood-wind in the back ground.

I can get bushels of people to set the thing *but* (and it's a big but) none of these people have had any experience of the war: and I have an idea that our music in future is going to be profoundly affected both directly and indirectly by this same experience. I believe that in Music too there will be such a Renaissance as is now just beginning to show itself in Letters and Art. The poetry of the young men who have been through the mill is quite different, to my mind, from anything that has gone before. So I believe it will be with music.

I'm no musician myself: but talking with your father once after I had left Berkeley square, I gathered from him – what you hadn't told me – what a keen and devoted musician you were. Assuming that to have been the case before the war, you ought to be now, by the very virtue of your own grievous experiences, something much more than merely keen. I do not believe that sufferings such as yours can lie upon a man without sensitizing and in a way sublimating every talent that he has in his possession.

At any rate, when the book comes will you look over it with an eye to setting some of the songs that may strike you as fitting to music. I hope you'll pick the ones that I like best though, as I've said, I'm not going to hint what they are. I'd be awfully grateful if you could see your way to doing this. Then we'd see if a publisher would take 'em. I know it's asking a good deal of you – and you can see that I'm doing it for selfish motives because I believe that if you can do it you'll do it uncommonly well. I want genuine feeling – not the usual trash that is turned out by people who haven't had the experience. I don't care so much about absolute accuracy in technique. That's a thing that can be put right by learned Doctors of Music – and it really doesn't matter as much as they pretend, after all. Let's get the essential innards of the things first.

Do you think you can manage it? I suppose you'll say that you aren't a composer or something. That again is a detail which you can learn while you're setting the songs. Being an invalid you'll probably break into a cold sweat and say that you can't. I shan't mind *that* either, as I shan't believe it.[3]

I hope you're pulling up the hill a bit. It's infernally slow and heartbreaking work but it *does* come straight in the end. I have just heard from a man I used to know who had a 28 months Hell of it (it was legs and cut sciatic nerve) but he has come out all right and is now bossing coolies in India again. Get some one to send me a letter and give me your news and believe me

Yours sincerely (but selfishly)
Rudyard Kipling

Notes
1. Pilkington (1892–1981) had joined the 4th Suffolk Regiment on the outbreak of the war, had been wounded on the Somme, and had lost his right hand. He was afterwards a clergyman of the Church of England, serving parishes mostly in Sussex, and a composer of music for the church.
2. *A Diversity of Creatures* was published on 17 April.
3. Pilkington's son, Mr Michael Pilkington, informs me that he has been unable to find any evidence that his father attempted to set Kipling's verse.

To Andrew Macphail, 14 April 1917
ALS: Photocopy, National Archives of Canada

Bateman's / Burwash / Sussex / Ap. 14. 1917.

Dear Macphail
Yours of the 9th and a glad household we were to get it with the news of Geoff and your brother. Verily the battle[1] was real *and* complete: allowing no loophole for the Hun to advance arguments other than that it was carried through "by a brainless assembling of guns." You saw that I suppose? Physicians do not take their own medicine. And Canada has Vimy on her

colours for ever more! I haven't seen any one yet as I've been down here cherishing a fool throat but they tell me that the Dominion beat herself. And her standards are reasonably high. One has read and reread and treasured up every word that one can get, but – as with everything else – we are jammed with flat noses so close to the event that we can see nothing. What asses our grandchildren will think us not to have "grasped the significance" of things. I understand now why each generation patronizes its predecessors.

Was it you or that other dry cynic Jim[2] who said to me: – "When the U.S. comes in I shall know the war will end in three months." And now she has[3] – with all the pomp and pedantry of style and prose. (*Collier's Magazine* the other day wickedly compares Wilson's style to "A. C. Benson trying to write like Lincoln,"[4] which strikes me as happily unkind.) I've done verses – of sorts – on the matter which, though verses, have a certain hint of truth in 'em.[5] The U.S.A. have a hell of a lot of lee-way to make up in public opinion: but they don't realize that yet and think that having girt on their armour is the same as having taken it off. All my haut financial friends are smiling comfortably over the relaxed money situation. Do you suppose that the great Half million Army of Americans will ever mature? Somehow, in spite of the clamorous Roosevelt,[6] I have my doubts. But 'tis satisfaction to know that a trousered people speaking some variant of our tongue have at long last subscribed to the elementary decencies.

And now when do you think of coming back here for awhile? That is what lies nearest my mind just at present and I desire to know how I may help in it if possible. I want you down here for awhile alternating drowzily between the bed in the dimity room and the sofa in my study.

Our spring has fallen upon us with swords (and what it must have been to *you*!) and we see no signs of repentance. Today is officially sacred to the cuckoo's return (being Heathfield Cuckoo fair day) but the bird has not yet been heard. Tonsilitis I suppose. And I have to wander out under steely skies to find out the address of a certain Guernsey Bull – to make happy one of our cows. "That we should call these delicate creatures ours, And not their appetites" as William puts it.[7]

Send me a line if ever you have any time. We live in the dark here and can arrive only partially at results.

With all our loves

Yours affectionately
Rudyard

Notes

1. The Battle of Vimy Ridge, 9–14 April, part of the preparation for General Nivelle's offensive on the Aisne: 30,000 Canadian troops stormed Vimy Ridge, between Arras and Lens. After six days of fighting they had advanced 4,500 yards at a cost of 10,000 casualties, without making the always-hoped-for "breakthrough".

2. Macphail's brother.
3. The US declaration of war against Germany was made on 6 April.
4. I have not found the passage in *Collier's*. Benson (1862–1925), Master of Magdalene College, Cambridge, was a prolific essayist, critic, editor, and biographer in the genteel mode.
5. "The Choice", *Daily Telegraph* and *New York Times*, 13 April 1917 (*The Years Between*).
6. Even before the American declaration of war Roosevelt had announced that he hoped to raise a division for "immediate" service at the front; Wilson, however, refused to authorise such a plan. The "Half million army" was proposed by Wilson in his speech to the new Congress on 2 April.
7. *Othello*, II, iii, 269–70, slightly misquoted.

To D. H. Pilkington, 17 April 1917

ALS: Mr Michael Pilkington

Bateman's / Burwash / Sussex / April 17. 1917.

Dear Pilkington

I don't know whether you know your Stevenson as you should. If you do you will remember that in the *Wrong Box* (which you *must* read if you haven't already) a young solicitor who has "done himself well" in the course of the day explains to a lawyer: – "In case I don't make myself perfectly clear it's perhaps best to tell you candidly that I've been lunching. It's a thing that may happen to any one."[1]

And that's the case with you and the morphia. It happens to a certain number of men in hospital who've had long and painful wounds that they get to lean too heavily on drugs. Then they panic and say to themselves: – "Oh my God! I've got the drug habit!" and in that belief imagine 'emselves predestined to the Devil etc. etc. etc. All of which in the language of the Vulgar is – Tosh! What one mistakes for the motions of one's soul is no more than the inevitable reaction of the racked body and as the body builds up the morbidities pass away. But I *do* know from what I've seen that it's a bad time while it lasts. Let me know how you come on. I needn't tell you how fully you have my sympathy – though I keep a little of it for the officer who is your escort. I had to look after a man once who was off his head after long wasting fever. I didn't so much mind him cursing me; which he did with positive genius, but what I barred was that when he got all right he absolutely denied he had ever even addressed a harsh word to me.

But now to business.

My book goes off to you today all new and hot. I want you to sit upon it and consider it in cold blood without any adventitious aids: and to see for yourself which verses most appeal to you on the musical side. Get 'em by heart and hum 'em at the melancholy ocean – like Demosthenes.

I'm afraid you'll find that the trouble with my stuff is that it carries a very pronounced "beat" or pause – notably in the long lines. I have had many musicians complain of this habit of mine because, they said, the structure of the lines prevents 'em from shifting the musical accent. So you see, that's another limitation that you will have to get round in the practice of your art.

I don't know what your "school" is or what your affinities may be and I don't wish to hint at my own more than to say that I am *not* much in love with Germanic ideals of "tone-colour" and discords. It occurs to me that all the stuff is meant for male voices but there may be exceptions. I don't recall that I have done any decent song for contralto or soprano.

And so – there you are. You'd much better devote yourself to making a fool of yourself over these verses than over preparations of the chemists shops. Take your "escort" out along the undercliff and try your tunes on him! I foresee a cheerful set of walks for both of you.

Finally, disabuse your young mind of the idea that you are going to fail. You won't – at least not more than four or five times and that's nothing to make a song about. You'll get it all right in the end and perhaps with luck you'll do one or even two, songs that'll almost satisfy yourself. I believe the musical temperament is the most exacting of them all.

> Very sincerely
> Rudyard Kipling

Note
1. *The Wrong Box*, ch. 8. Pilkington has written at the head of RK's letter: "In answer to a letter telling him I was under open arrest for attempted suicide."

To Cameron Forbes, 21 April 1917
ALS: Harvard University

Bateman's / Burwash / Sussex / April. 21. 1917.

private
Dear Cameron Forbes,

I didn't answer your cable because I knew the censor would have fits over a reference to one of your grandfather's poems which held the nub of the whole proposition. Imagine a censor's feeling at this: – "*Yes. Concord Townhall Ode. Last verse.*"[1] But it's a huge weight off every one's mind this side the water. I imagine that the basic reason of this must be the sense of shock that people who talked our tongue (it's a potent bond after all) should, in our own tongue, write and say that they had no concern in the matter. One felt that sense of – horror almost – underlying what little talk men dared to permit themselves. However that's ended – glory be to God!

We are in for a most cheery and exciting time the next few months and I fancy that America will learn – as we have had to learn – that the Hun in *any* capacity or position – is essentially and irredeemably beyond the pale. We took years to grasp this fact. I hope your enlightenment will come quicker. I see Roosevelt wants to head an army corps or something.[2] He ought to have a look at the job close to. Then he would understand that the front is no place for an old or even a middle aged man. It's a young fellow's job, exclusively. The French and we are doing a little hammering just now which will not be without good results. It's a queer war in that the bulk of our killing is done by the guns, day in and day out; and the earth covers the dead six to eight feet deep – so that we not only slay but obliterate.

We want æroplanes and steamers I fancy, as much as we want most things. It's rather good to be living in these days – though we shall never know what these days actually are. That will be reserved for those of us who have children.

I'm very happy that the U.S.A. has taken her part before mankind and that I can sign myself

Yours in the fraternity of civilization[3]
Rudyard Kipling

Notes

1.
> "For He that worketh high and wise
>> Nor pauses in his plan
> Will take the sun out of the skies
>> Ere freedom out of man.

  Ralph Waldo Emerson, "Concord, Ode Sung in the Town Hall, July 4, 1857".
2. See 14 April 1917.
3. RK uses this closing in a letter of 3 March 1917 to Victor Giraud, writer and editor of the *Revue des Deux Mondes (Revue de la Littérature Comparée*, XL [1966], 291).

To C. R. L. Fletcher, 21 April 1917
ALS: University of Sussex

Bateman's / Burwash / Sussex / April. 21. 1917.

Dear Fletcher,

There goes to you today a copy of my new book "A Diversity of Creatures" not for any of its own merits but that you may kindly supply me with the original of that Horatian Ode which I have so inadequately translated.[1] As a matter of fact I only came across the second (Urbino's) copy of the missing

Fifth Book in the Library of the Vatican a few years ago quite by chance and transcribed the Third Ode, in haste, by very indifferent light, in the crypt of the Dogali Gallery. There is another copy of the Fifth Book at Upsala as you of course know but it is in a bad condition and the marginal notes of Claresius add nothing to its value.

The third copy – if Sir James Urquhart's statement to the Spanish Ambassador can be trusted – should be in the Bodleian and – again we have to depend on Urquhart – the text is reputed to be by far the least corrupt.

However this may be, I should be deeply in your debt if you would look it up and let me have your transcription, as I am doubtful whether I have given the precise shade of meaning implied by the words "clients of our body."

My excuse for troubling you is that I have already been attacked, in a private letter, by a so-called scholar who asserts that no such book as the Fifth ever existed: and I wish to confute him.

Very sincerely
Rudyard Kipling.

Note

1. "A Translation", identified as "Horace, Bk. V. *Ode* 3", following the story "Regulus" in *A Diversity of Creatures*. This "translation" from the non-existent fifth book of Horace's *Odes* is the first of a series of such exercises by RK. In subsequent years all of the following were published as from Book V of the *Odes*: "Ode XIII" ("Lollius") in *Q. Horati Flacci Carminum Librum Quintum*, and a series of four "Odes" to accompany stories in *Debits and Credits*: "To the Companions" (with "The United Idolaters"); "The Survival" (with "The Janeites"); "The Portent" (with "The Prophet and His Country"); and "The Last Ode" (with "The Eye of Allah"). RK's "The Pro-Consuls" (1909) was also included in the *Q. Horati Flacci Carminum Librum Quintum* collection. See also the summary in the note to the letter to Fletcher, 5 December 1920. The rest of this letter is a learned joke.

To Andrew Macphail, 21–2 April 1917

ALS: Photocopy, National Archives of Canada

Bateman's / Burwash / Sussex / April 21. 1917.

Dear Macphail,

There goes to you today a copy of my new book "A Diversity of Creatures" – in the hope that some at least of it may make you laugh for a little.

I'm glad your latest letter talks of coming to England but I *do* hope and pray before June. Anyhow I come to the Cavendish lecture[1] – on all fours if necessary: but I come. Make up your mind that *we* of this generation cannot overtake the war as it is. That will be done by the "emotion recollected in quietude"[2] of our children – or our grandchildren. Even for us at the back emotion and passion is overlaid like a crazy cinema on passion and emotion till the whole thing is a blurr of white lights and flying faces.

I think one point that sticks out in my mind is – the model in plasticine of Vimy Ridge[3] – the equivalent of vivisection in surgery; as who should clamp up a dog or a guinea pig on the board to make sure of the effect of certain excisions on the human!

(Now I go out to chaffer with an agent of Government for the disposal of certain felled alders and willows. Were you with me I'd get a higher price because you could talk to him learnedly of timbers; whereas I shall take what he offers if he will only send lorries and haul the logs off my innocent grass where they lie and encourage nettles).

And that's all right! They came – two men, and saw and were not in the least impressed with my little offering but they lifted up their eyes to my neighbour's woods (you remember 'em?) and forthwith went to investigate his larches and scotch firs. 'Must be very nice to be a sort of official beaver.

Today (Sunday) is a God's own day of sunshine and clear wind which I rejoice to think must be drying up your ground and giving visibility for the machines. The more one gets the wholly inadequate story of Vimy the more marvellous it is. But now life has drained all meaning out of words. I don't see how in the future men will write with any adjectives at all. We shall be cut down to the mere noun and verb of the earlier Latin exercises. Anciently, one used the phrase "praise would be an impertinence" or something of the sort and then proceeded to lay it on with a butter knife. But now mere praise *is* an insult. Have you ever considered that from the literary point of view?

We are all much sickened (Europe and Asia alike) with the accounts of the Hun Dead bodies factories where they turn cannon-fodder into pig food glycerine and fats.[4] There's a touch of loathesomeness about it that beats – and here again words are not. Naturally, I though of Thackeray's version of the Sorrows of Werther.[5] The final verse which I present to you for camp consumption runs thus in my revision:

> "Charlotte when she saw what Hermann
> "Yielded after he was dead,
> "Like a well-conducted German
> "Spread him thickly on her bread."[6]

A little after this reaches you I may be passing to the south of you, bound eastward for a while.[7] Whereof more later.

My best salutations to Jim and Geoff and with all our love

Affectionately
Rudyard

Notes

1. Macphail gave the Cavendish lecture on 22 June 1917 to the West London Medical and Chirurgical Society on "A Day's Work", an account of the organisation and preparation required for the battle of Vimy Ridge. It is incidentally an attack on German "scientific" education. The English, he says, require no alien teachers: "Trust your own. … Trust your Chaucer, your Shakespeare, your Dickens, your Kipling" (*The Lancet*, 30 June 1917, p. 982). RK does not appear to have attended the lecture, but he made efforts to publicise it (to Macphail, 24 June 1917: ALS, National Archives of Canada).
2. Cf. Wordsworth: "poetry is emotion recollected in tranquillity" (Preface to the 2nd edn of *Lyrical Ballads*, 1800).
3. This was presumably used in the preparations for the battle. I have found no other reference to it.
4. *The Times*, 17 April 1917, reported the existence of a German "corpse exploitation establishment" north of Rheims. Here, the story ran, fats were rendered into lubricating oils and all else ground to powder for pig food and fertiliser. The operation was alleged to be a private, profit-making venture. The description of the production methods is detailed, circumstantial, and fantastic. The "Asian" response was given by the Chinese Minister in London, who is quoted as saying that the Chinese regarded the "German desecration with a very special horror" (*The Times*, 20 April). *The Times* continued to maintain the truth of the story.
5. Thackeray's "The Sorrows of Werther", 1853, concludes:

> "Charlotte, having seen his body
> Borne before her on a shutter,
> Like a well-conducted person,
> Went on cutting bread and butter."

6. These verses are not recorded in any of the bibliographies. They are printed in Dorothy Ponton, *Rudyard Kipling at Home and at Work*, p. 26, and, in the version given in 29 April 1917, by Birkenhead, *Rudyard Kipling*, p. 273.
7. On his trip to the Italian front: see 2 May [1917].

To C. R. L. Fletcher, 24 April 1917

ALS: University of Sussex

Bateman's / Burwash / Sussex / April 24. 1917.

Dear Fletcher,

Ever so many thanks. What I want for my own purposes (and it's a tale that has long been hanging in my head) is that there shall be somewhere in the world a hint or a recollection somewhere of a fifth book of Horace's Odes. Not the Epodes but an indubitable Fifth Book of 'em. Sometime or other, years ago, I gathered from a man – it didn't interest me at the time – that there was in history some allusion or reference to that book. If my memory serves me it appeared and vanished; or, he who came across it lost track of it.

But if it was simply a rumour and there is no chance of – not finding the thing, but unearthing some report that such a book was once written – then my little tale falls to the ground for lack of materials.[1]

You'll see when you read my "translation" in the Regulus Tale that I went in boldly and invented an ode out of that book: but that's a minor item. What I'm after is some reference, direct or indirect in fact or on record, to the existence of a Fifth book.

Claresius and the rest were simply to "lend verisimilitude etc." It *may* for aught I know be in the purlieus of the Vatican: or, there may be somewhere (and here's a point that I want to know) Odes *ascribed* to Horace – or deliberately forged by the Middle-Agers. Is there any record of that anywhere?

I'm vexed about Fabulet: but he was always full of temperament. I can't understand why on earth he should object to maids waiting on students.

But nothing is quainter than the morality of the other nation. Thoreau – about *as* detached a person as ever set out to evade taxes and work of all kinds – doesn't seem to me a vital necessity these days.[2] But everybody is on edge.

I've got a big job ahead of me shortly which will give me all the work I want for some time: and, more by token, I'm not at the top-notch of health. The wife – thank God! – came back to much better health after Bath and then felt the good of her treatment but she is not yet well by a long bit, and the cares of housekeeping and farming these days, lie heavy on every one.

I was rereading our history the other day and alternately patting you and myself on the back for our perspicacity. Go now and do a rhyming geography. It's a needed want. I suggest a catalogue of natural products of various lands in the metre of Dryden to be followed by distances, for steamer, between ports and ports in the metre of "Marmion".

What do you think of the entry of the U.S.A.? Long delayed but I hope they'll take it on in good shape.

Ever sincerely
Rudyard Kipling

Notes
1. Apparently the story remained unwritten: see 29 April 1917.
2. Louis Fabulet's translation of Thoreau's *Walden* appeared in 1922.

To C. R. L. Fletcher, 29 April 1917
ALS: University of Sussex

Bateman's / Burwash / Sussex / April 29. 1917.

Dear Fletcher

All right. If you say so so it must be. I'm sorry because it knocks the bottom out of a promising little tale and incidentally (for I believed the legend) makes me out an ass. But both these things have happened before. Anyhow, I purr over the praise you give to my "Horatian Ode."

What sequel was there to Regulus? I remember reading you the tale and by the same token you corrected a howling false quantity in it, but I don't recall any continuation. Enlighten!

"The village that voted" ain't any sort of fooling though, I admit, it may look like that. It is a sanguinary allegory of an iridescent "civilization". Hence the music hall which together with Northcliffian journalism is a force, Sir – "a Force to be reckoned with."

My own idea is that Bat Masquerier (who is, after all, but the Eternal Crummles)[1] was an Hebrew. Otherwise he wouldn't have been so vindictive about the beak's references to Jerusalem.[2] Read "the Village" in alternate strophes with "As Easy as ABC" (for they are both allegories) and you'll see how the music hall purveyors of mirth end up in both.[3] You can't defeat the Jew – or the pimp.

Your dog Harvey hasn't got the evil eye. I know the fellow to him. It's just senile curiosity and the immense boredom from which dogs suffer. Being half human, if they find you don't like it, they set out to rag you. Take your friend and tell him that if he goes on glowering you'll belt him. He'll understand perfectly. If he doesn't take him and put a ham-frill round his neck or otherwise make him ashamed of himself and he'll become dog again. Pepper is another solvent.

Did you send me "Translations" by S.C. "found in a common place book."[4] It's interesting me no end. There's Greek intilt, I suppose, and there's Japanese intilt and how the dooce he gets his atmospheres beats me.

I agree with you about the utter inadequacy of any expiation that can be taken but I think you underestimate the power of the Army returned. There was a Parliament once that did much the same thing, didn't it? Only now the army is about four million – and it hasn't yet expressed itself on any subject except the immediate work in hand.

And talking of armies – the latest about cannon-fodder being turned into pig-food is very interesting and wholly logical. This is the last verse of an otherwise unprintable set of verses dealing with the subject: –

> Charlotte, when she saw what Herman
> Yielded after he was dead,
> Like a well conducted German,
> Spread him lightly on her bread.

And now farewell.

Ever sincerely
Rudyard Kipling

Notes
1. Vincent Crummles, the theatrical manager in Dickens, *Nicholas Nickleby*.
2. The magistrate makes an insulting reference to Masquerier's "home address at Jerusalem", and the recollection of the moment helps to sharpen Masquerier's desire for revenge ("The Village that Voted the Earth Was Flat", pp. 165, 167, 191, 207).
3. Bat Masquerier's equivalent in "As Easy as A.B.C." is Leopold Vincent, "who had purveyed all London her choicest amusements for the last thirty years" (p. 35). He exhibits the rescued "serviles" from Chicago as freaks from a vanished era.
4. *Translations (found in a commonplace book)*, edited by S.C. (Oxford, 1916), was by Maurice Baring; the book was reprinted, with the author's name, as *Translations, Ancient and Modern*, 1918.

To Caroline and Elsie Kipling, 2 May [1917]
ALS: University of Sussex

Hôtel Brighton / 218, Rue de Rivoli / Paris[1] /
(before every one is up) 6.30 a.m. / May. 2.

Very dearest both –

Our channel passage (hope you got my wire) was in perfect weather with hardly a ripple. We were a sort of convoy – us; a hospital ship: another hospital ship I think Belgian, and a fringe of destroyers. 'Don't suppose there was more than two destroyers but they produced the impression of a fringe. And we got in at 6.30. to find the Paris train started at 9.6. p.m. We were met by kind and adequate officers in the R[ailway]. T[ransport]. O[fficer]. line who took charge of us and told us that we should find *lits couchettes* (!) reserved for us to Paris. It all went on wheels.

Mrs. Kinnard – a youngish woman, very tired with hospital work, came down to the quay in a car, took us up to the ramparts of Boulogne, then through square miles of hospitals into the country to see the cowslips and then to a little square court yarded inn at the back of the town (La Bourgogne) where we had a very nice little *French* meal among French folk. It's too far from the quay for most officers. At 9. o'clock we went to our train; found all baggage in the *lits couchettes* (remember that trip to Vernet?)[2] and the R.T.O. very apologetic for the presence of a senior French flying officer who had taken the 3rd Lit (the compartment was ours). But we said it was his country and wouldn't have him ejected. I spent a most comfy night (slept like a dormouse). Landon didn't – he says.

Got into Paris in clear dawn at 5: 45: went to Ritz which was asleep, (all except one porter). Ritz was full. So round to the Brighton where one much overwhelmed person was sweeping out the dining hall. He has gone for coffee – tout de suite – I am writing in the little hall. L. is reading the paper and it's Paris – Paris, all divine in the morning light! Now when I get my room, I wash and shave and go to bed – *not* because I need it but it's a fine safe place to keep unbeknownst in. Then the Rome train tonight. I do *really* think this is going to be a comfy journey. L. swears the French flying officer – who was enormously fat and thick – kept him awake with snoring. I never heard a sound twixt 10. p.m. and five. Our train was about 300 yards long and progressed about 15 miles per hour.

And I am ever and always

Your beloving
Rud

Notes
1. The Italian trip was made at the instance of the English Ambassador, Sir Rennell Rodd, who wrote to RK as early as 15 May 1916 to ask if he would not write something about the Italian front to give the English a better understanding of the fighting there: "the idea is very prevalent in England that the Italian army is not doing much" (ALS, Sussex). Rodd repeated the invitation in 1917, adding that he wanted d'Annunzio to write an account of the western front while RK was doing the Italian (20 March 1917: ALS, Sussex). RK's response was evidently favourable, and General Delme-Radcliffe, chief of the British military mission in Italy, wrote to RK on 3 April 1917 to say that they were prepared to receive him in Italy at any time (ALS, Sussex). RK invited Perceval Landon to accompany him, as Landon had done on RK's French tour in 1915, and the two men left for France via Folkestone on 1 May. Their itinerary will appear in detail in the notes to the letters following but may be outlined here. They were in Paris on 2–3 May; in Rome, 5–8 May; at Udine, Cortina d'Ampezzo, and other points between 9 and 14 May, when they took the train for the return to London. RK returned to Bateman's on 17 May. The result of the trip was RK's *The War in the Mountains*, published in the *Daily Telegraph*, 6, 9, 13, 16 and 20 June 1917; it was not collected until the Sussex Edition.
2. From Paris to Vernet, 16–18 February 1911: see 23 February 1911.

To Caroline and Elsie Kipling, 2 May 1917
ALS: University of Sussex

Hôtel Brighton / 218, Rue de Rivoli / Paris / May. 2. 1917. / 6.30: p.m:
No. 302 (the room in the middle of the landing going to 301 which John had)

Dearest and most Dear:
There is but one mail, as far as I make out, to England and it leaves Paris at 7:30. a.m. which means that, early as I wrote this morning I must have missed

it. So I write again to explain ourselves and our movements. It was an interminable morning. We arrived before the milk. Never do that because you can't have your coffee before eight anyhow: and we wanted coffee. And when we had got it, and were clean – or at least cleaner – we telephoned to the Gare de Lyons to know what berths had been reserved for us for Rome tonight. After much delay the reply came there were none. So off we went en auto to the Gare de Lyons at 9: a.m. and there we were, as usual, herded into an interminable file of people waiting to reserve places.

It was all laborious and official and teasing but suddenly – it was Landon who subjugated her – a bare headed female employée of the company took us in charge and steered us by ways we should never have found out for ourselves, all across the gigantic station to the Wagon Lits offices, where she stood over us basking in our reflected glory – such as it was. The Wagons Lits people knew nothing of any reservations – no one had been to them – and were rather doubtful as to our getting any places to Rome inside of several days. Then I played Paul Cambon's[1] letter which broke the ice into large pieces. There was no possible place for tonight but if we went to the Head Office 5 Bld. de Capuchins – we could get places for tomorrow night. And that is exactly what we had to do. Evidently there is a sort of no-man's land between the kind offices of the British Foreign Office and the Italian administration and till we reach the Italian frontier we must fend for ourselves. Neither of us object in the least to the extra day here tho', of course, it would have been better to have gone on. We had a nap after lunch – an exceedingly good lunch – and tonight we go and take dinner at the Ritz, at 8 o'clock.

The old concierge is still here. The head waiter calls himself an Egyptian but he really comes from Assiout and talks both French and English. He is a Berber or a Soudanese. Today has been deliciously warm throughout. The leaves in the Tuileries gardens are out and spring seems a fortnight ahead of us in England. Paris is fuller than I have seen it – more people, more taxis and a general air of business doing. Food restrictions do not seem to exist: the bread is extremely good and the amount of green vegetables on sale in the streets is very astonishing. But the blackness of the garments strikes one more and more. More shops are shut but those who do business have more business *and* there appear to be ever so many more English officers in Paris than last time. The Americans are out in force too; holding their heads high and talking loud in the Rue de Rivoli, the Rue Castiglione and the other places that they inhabit.

I got my article in the Revue de Deux Mondes which I am posting to you.[2] It reads very well. I have, honestly, reduced my consumption of tobacco to an extent which would astonish you. I find every conceivable want and thought of mine, anticipated and cared for in my packing at every turn and now I will, *very* gingerly, extract a white shirt from bag no. 1: and get into it, that I may not disgrace Bateman's at the Ritz.

This goes – I am afraid – with the letter that I wrote you in the dawn of today, at least a century ago. It takes enough affection for several and I'll send you a line tomorrow on the eve of our departure. I don't know whether our letters are censored from the French side. If so I can confirm – what I have long suspected – that they keep a special brand of officer to be Censor.

Ever your
Rud.

Take note.   In the wire Landon sent, the Telegraph sent it back asserting that there were *two* Burwashes in England and therefore the county also must be indicated![3] You can't get ahead of the official mind.

Notes

1. Paul Cambon (1843–1924), French Ambassador to Great Britain, 1898–1920.
2. The first of three parts of *The Eyes of Asia*: "Les Fumées du Coeur", *Revue des Deux Mondes*, 1 May 1917, pp. 5–12. This was in advance of English publication, which did not begin until 10 May. The following two items also appeared in the *Revue*: "La Lettre du Cavalier", 1 June 1917; and "Un Compte Personnel", 15 June 1917.
3. There is a Burwash Common but no other Burwash in England. Burwash and Burwash Common are both in Sussex, only a few miles apart.

To Caroline and Elsie Kipling, 2–3 May [1917]

ALS: University of Sussex

'Brighton. / May. 2. / Wednesday / 10: p.m.
(I will *not* write at the wrong end of the paper)[1]

Just back from the Ritz. I was wrong when I said there were no food restrictions. It was meatless dinner at the Ritz. So we had hor d'œvres: boiled turbot with a sauce rightly named Divine: eggs in small pots (*en cocotte*) with asparagus tips: eggs were fatigued but asparagus was quite young: then a beautiful cauliflower *au gratin* and black coffee. The whole 33 francs which I don't call excessive. The Ritz is chock full of soldiers but they mostly dine at cheaper places.

We met there – he came over to speak to me – Major Rock and his bride.[2] She is a small, rather flat-faced very composed and very eloquent American child of the type who has had her lightest word much hung upon. She is extreme cosmopolitan, and I should imagine believes herself to be serious. There were touches of the L[adies']. H[ome]. J[ournal]. about her as she expounded the Italian situation to me and she was good enough to approve of the general efforts of the English. It amused me a good deal. Rock is not yet past the stage when his eyes sought hers. Landon, whose evil acquaintances are unlimited ran across Mrs. Elinor Glynn[3] who was just going out. So – Allah be praised! – I was not introduced. After dinner we met (*I* didn't) A'Court Reppington[4] and a F[lying]. C[orps]. man called Lygon[5] who was a friend of young Hartington's[6] and said he was most charming. Got out at 9.45 into a still warm night and so home and to bed.

Thursday. 10. a.m.

A splendid night's sleep till 8. a.m. which, after three hours solid "doze" in the afternoon is not so bad. Since then I have devoted myself to packing with a single mind and the intelligent help of the chambermaid. The white shirt which I wore last night goes back into the suitcase quite fit for fresh adventures at the Vatican: and nothing has been left behind. You were quite right. Everything that my wildest desires could conceive has been met and forestalled in my suit cases and, if you could see how they have been repacked you would admit, I think, that now and then, I really have my mind about me.

Yesterday L. complained of not feeling quite the thing – "queasy" was his word. So I got him one calomel tabloid which has been blessed unto him. On such occasions as these a man's chief pre occupation in his innards. The concierge – who desires to be remembered to you and to Ada – advised us to do, what we had already decided upon – i.e. to go down to the Gare de Lyons at 6.30, get our dinner there in comfort and ascend into our waggon lit in ample time. There are plenty taxis in Paris but as evening comes they do not like to take long fares but prefer to frisk about from restaurant to restaurant. I honestly don't think there is anything else to tell you my dears; except that I saw this morning, a little bevy of maidens going to their confirmation in white robes followed by male relatives in uniform and female relatives in mourning. A sharp three colour contrast down the bright street.

It's a beautiful warm day with never a cloud in the sky and I hope and pray it has reached you.

L. who looks out for coincidences, says he wouldn't in the least be surprised if Lloyd George were in our train for Rome. He is somewhere on the continent I believe.[7]

Now I will go provide myself with postcards which I can shoot off at you at the various stations. Allah knows if they will arrive in less than three or four days.

Write me *all* your news to the Embassy at Rome.

Ever and always
Rud.

Notes

1. RK apparently objected to the way in which the hotel letterhead paper was folded. He has left the side bearing the engraved name and arms of the hotel blank.
2. Major (afterwards Colonel) Cyril Rocke (1876–1968), of the Irish Guards. He served with the 2nd Battalion but was now about to take command of the 1st Battalion. His wife was Betty Iddings, daughter of an American foreign service officer.
3. Elinor Glyn (1864–1943), popular romantic novelist, notorious for her *Three Weeks* (1907), and admired by such men as Milner and Curzon.
4. Lt.-Colonel Charles A'Court Repington (1858–1925), soldier and journalist, who had served in Afghanistan, Burma, the Sudan, and South Africa, and was now military correspondent of *The Times*.
5. Major Henry Lygon (1884–1936), son of the 6th Earl Beauchamp, was with military intelligence in Rome and Paris after suffering serious injuries in an aeroplane crash with the Royal Flying Corps.
6. RK presumably means Edward William Spencer Cavendish (1895–1950), Marquess of Hartington, afterwards 10th Duke of Devonshire, who served in the war as a lieutenant of the Derbyshire Yeomanry. He had been married just two weeks before, on 21 April, which may have been a reason for RK's having him in mind.
7. Lloyd George went to Paris on 3 May to confer about what measures to take following the failure of Nivelle's campaign on the Aisne.

To Caroline and Elsie Kipling, 5 May 1917

ALS: University of Sussex

> *Grand-Hôtel / Rome /* Saturday May 5th 1917 / 10:15. a.m. to 11:20 a.m.
> grey: warmish and sticky.

We got in on time from Modane:[1] after a *very* good buffet dinner at Turin which we shared with a young Russian Naval officer (six feet six long) whom we met in our train. Certainly no food restrictions seem to worry Italy. Our other companions were a doctor from Salonika who had been in the Cameroons show; a major of Engineers who knew Greece and the Near East, and a fat cherry cheeked Colonel of Cavalry who seemed to know pretty well all the rest. They were going on their way towards Salonika.

At Modane there was a strong detachment of our sailors – mostly "hostility"[2] men on their way to Mediterranean ports. One of them found a rubber ring and began to throw it at a hook in the wall. Some one stuck up a 1 lira note as a prize to the man who first made the ring stay on. In less time than you could think the affair developed into an orderly game: with a bright eyed petty officer in charge, regulating the distance thrown, seeing that no one threw out of his turn and so on. *Very* occasionally some one made the ring stick on the hook. Then either L. or I put up another Franc as prize and the winner bored solemnly through the crowd to shake us by the hand. It kept 'em quiet and amused for nearly an hour. No one could have been kinder to us than Clarence the Railway Transport Officer and he is prepared to make everything comfortable for us on our return.

Once through the Mont Cenis we were in the full flush of spring – pears and almonds together in bloom; the young wheat nearly a foot high beneath and all the mountain sides pencilled and splashed with every shade of God's own greens. It began to rain there – a warmish growing rain – the kind that we could do with in the valley at home. I have seldom seen such beauty.

The campagna in the morning (oh how it reminded me of our trip!) was all grey and green with solemn silky white bullocks watching us. We got in punctually found Rome much as she always is and have since been washing ourselves and arranging our baggage (you'd be surprised at my system and neatness) in the palatial suite of rooms which they have given us at 65 lira per diem. I can't see myself that there is any one staying here particularly now. I have just telephoned to the British Embassy and am awaiting their reply. More anon.

6. p.m. So we went to the Embassy on foot in this heavenly warmth, with roses and wistarias full out on all the walls and Rome at large looking as though it hadn't heard of any war. Rodd was out, but sent us a note later asking us to dinner at 8:15 and we're going.

Then to dejeuner – extraordinarily good omelette and grilled chicken – a broiler. After that I went to the Borghese palace to leave my card upon Count de Salis[3] with a note, in case he was out, asking him to see me. Landon was off on excursions of his own so when I came back I got into my – got out of my clothes and had a luxurious snooze of an hour before he came back. Then came a newspaper correspondent of one of the London papers *not* to see me at all but to give me some information about positions and attitudes here (I've got an idea that all letters are pretty carefully censored or at any rate pried into so I won't give you details except to say that I was glad – and so was Landon – that he came). Then we went to our palace like sitting room (glad we were 'twas so palatial) to box a cup of cocoa and after that there came a Cardinal – hat and all – an English gentleman of the most charming that ever was,[4] accompanied by his secretary[5] also an Englishman but notably unlike a priest in that he contradicted his Eminence on certain matters. Well, conversation turned on a ceremony tomorrow at St Peter's where they are Beatifying a certain Carmelite Nun who died 150 years ago and now is to be made the Blessed Anne of somewhere or other.[6] His Eminence gave us the whole business of beatifying – how it's done and how long it takes and who decides on the evidence (there must be at least *two* proven miracles) and all the rest of it. I'd never heard it all told from the inside by an expert. The Cardinal is on the Board of Examiners or Committee of Admission for Blessed Ones. We talked of other matters too – very sensibly and humanly but somehow this detailed and serious account of a Beatification struck me as very-very wonderful indeed.

And he left amid bowed bared heads like a Prince of the Church which indeed he was and the Hotel management humble before is now on its tummy.

Then for a stroll with Landon among the shops. I wish I had the size of Ada's hand and I'd get her some gloves as I know she likes 'em. It was a sticky, grey homesickish evening and I drifted up (L. was going to the Excelsior)[7] to the Albergo Savoia[8] whose face has been washed and looks wondrous clean: and I thought of you and the Bird and her measles long ago and grew sentimental. Then I returned and that is all my account of the day. I lunch with the Cardinal on Monday. He came to ask me. He'll be worth a wilderness of smaller folk for instruction. If I have anything special I'll send it in the Embassy bag.

With a heart's love.

Ever
Rud.

Notes
1. Leaving Paris in the evening of 3 May they were at Modane, near the Italian border in Savoy, on the morning of 4 May; they left that afternoon to arrive in Rome on the morning of 5 May (RK to CK, 4 May 1917: ALS, Sussex).
2. Men who joined the navy "for the duration of hostilities only" (Partridge, *Dictionary of Slang*, 8th edn).
3. John De Salis (1864–1939), 7th Count De Salis (of the Holy Roman Empire), of the Foreign Office, was Envoy Extraordinary and Minister Plenipotentiary to the Pope, 1916–22. His eldest son was in the Irish Guards.
4. Cardinal Francis Neil Gasquet (1846–1929), an Englishman, was educated at Downside, where he was afterwards Prior; he then devoted himself to historical work in London, where he was a fellow-member of the Athenaeum with RK. He went to Rome in 1907 to superintend the revision of the Vulgate text of the Bible, the work to which the rest of his life was given. Created Cardinal 1914; archivist of the Holy See, 1917; librarian of the Holy Roman Church, 1919. The *DNB* calls him "the centre of English life and influence in Rome".
5. Father Philip Langdon (information from Mr Peter Lewis).
6. Anne of St Bartholomew (1549–1626), a Spanish Discalced Carmelite, companion of St Teresa and co-worker with Anne of Jesus in founding convents in France and Belgium. She was declared venerable in 1735 and blessed on 6 May 1917.
7. The headquarters of the British military mission.
8. Where RK, CK, and Elsie stayed in March and early April 1909.

To Caroline Kipling, 6 May 1917
ALS: University of Sussex

Grand-Hôtel / Rome / May. 6. 1917 / 7. p.m.

Very dear,

Just my usual daily line to let you know that I am but this instant returned from the Beatification of Anne of St Bartholomew – a carmelite nun. The

Cardinal sent us places which were good enough in themselves but – talk of coincidence – as I looked at the blaze of splendour of the altar of St Peter I saw on the next block of seats, reserved for diplomats, a chamberlain of the pope (there are scores of 'em all about the place) in ruff, hose, sword etc. etc. who, for the moment, struck me as one of the finest Rembrandts I'd ever seen. Then slowly through my mind as I stared passed the words: – "I *am* so sorree!" (Elsie will understand) and as I looked and looked he turned and saw me and flashed into smiles. 'Twas Spinola![1] Dressed in the costume of his office. No wonder we thought he looked well at the Engelberg fancy Ball! He came to us at once and said: – "The moment the Pope has come you come into my tribune – or block of seats." Which we did. Result was we had *absolutely* the finest view of the ceremony any one could by any means get. I saw De Salis among the diplomats but all my eyes and ears were for the ceremony which was beyond belief – in splendour, mass, colour and every grandiose appeal. There was only one hour of it. The main proceedings as far as the legal position of the Blessed Ann went having been got through in the morning where they read out her record for two hours I believe. The Pope[2] entered in his chair – a little dark man with glasses. *Very* petite all over but with an interesting face. He said not a word, of course because Popes do not lightly speak. The prayer for peace was read almost at the beginning but most of the rest of the service was merely singing – I didn't much care for the singing. There were the Noble Guard – 12 of 'em in helmets; the Papal Guard in their uniforms, helmets and halberds; there were nuns and friars of every known description; Cardinals, Bishops and dignitaries of the whole hierarchy and about – well Spinola said 60,000 people but L. and I thought it might be 20,000. In that marble sea of a place you can't tell to a thousand or even five thousand.

I can give you no idea of the actual ceremony for several reasons but chiefly because I'd never seen anything like it. My impressions I will tell by word of mouth. At the end when the golden litter had left through a far door the whole crowd liquified and flooded the Cathedral. L. and I were borne along in a stream of people who ceased to interest us – they squeezed too much – so we turned aside through a gap in a barrier, found a little door and ran literally into the arms of our Cardinal who very kindly took us home in his car! *Nota.* Cardinals' cars have an arm cushion like first class railway carriages so that you shan't jostle the Cardinal. I approve of that. 'Fact is I think Cardinals' motors are the only cars worth taking in Rome. I lunch with the Cardinal tomorrow – and I don't think it will be time wasted.

So here I am at 7: p.m. in evening dress (how useful that evening dress will be none but you will know) the grey scirocco sky has cleared there is a divine sun and the spectacle of the whole enormous crowd vomiting out of the steps of St. Peter's in the afternoon light will remain with me till I die.

This is but a scrawl in haste to catch the post. I don't know what I do tomorrow but I *expect* it will depend on the Cardinal. Sorry! If he has arranged aught I shan't be told of it till the actual moment.

Meantime I am still humbly

Yours ever
Rud.

Notes

1. Evidently an Engelberg acquaintance. RK identifies him as a 36-year-old, "head of a factory for making measuring instruments" (to CK, 8 May 1917: ALS, Sussex).
2. Benedict XV (1854–1922), elected Pope in September 1914; his policy was strict neutrality for the Vatican, and he made several attempts to secure a peace.

To Caroline and Elsie Kipling, 7 May 1917

ALS: University of Sussex

Grand-Hôtel / *Rome* / May. 7. 1917: / 6:30. p.m.

Dearests

And – after seeing the Embassy this morning, in the course of which I bought a trifle for Keene's child and some tortoiseshell combs for you – Landon and I went to lunch with our Cardinal in his palace[1] which was part of and built itself into a Benedictine monastery. It was across the river (d'you remember our drives on cold spring days in that direction?) near St. Maria Calista,[2] a bit of Papal Rome that I never knew before. Also it was like a scene out of all sorts of novels. There was the quiet brooding inner court facing a square of hot sunshine; a covered cloister, a climb up four flights of feet worn stone stairs and at last a long, long suite of rooms, rather like a little Versailles, one opening out of the other till the final one was all upholstered in yellow silk with a portrait of the Pope (who, I maintain, resembles Woodrow Wilson facially) and in front of it a tall golden chair back facing us, specially reserved for his Holiness when he calls. (But I don't see how he can get out of the Vatican *to* call!) Then, Our Cardinal emerged and said: – "Come into my den. I can't live up to those yellow chairs" – and we went into a little wonder of a study full of priceless old prints and a genuine Holbein. Then lunch – artichoke omelette; beef; chicken and marvellous ice-cream, with many curious wines whereof I did not drink. There was only L. and I and the Cardinal and his domestic chaplain who was also general secretary. This latter was of *quite* a new type to me. I never knew before that domestic chaplains contradicted Cardinals. Well, we talked and we talked (the Domestic Chaplain talked most) for about two hours. I am a low-minded beast and I suspected from the first that we had not been asked out for nothing. We hadn't: but that is a matter which I must tell you *viva voce* when we meet. (This land rightly or wrongly gives me the impression of being more full of eyes and ears than a peacock's tail). Finally, we were shown some priceless reproduction of ancient Bible texts (there is a most learned committee revising the Latin Bible in a long room off the Cardinal's study.)[3] Also we were shown his private chapel which he and the domestic chaplain made by luck and spoliation and the picking up of bargains – such as a set of priceless XVth century choir stalls and a 16th century entrance door and a few other trifles. It was the Cardinal's Bateman's to him and I think he really liked our delight. It was a gem of colour and design under a barrel-vaulted roof – a mixture of greys, greens and golds lovelier than aught Uncle Ned had conceived.

And so we got away – much – oh *much* interested! This is the d—dest queerest trap-doorest world I've ever got into. Nothing resembles its external appearance in the least and when you are told to go northwest it means you ought to steer sou'east. I shall be main glad to meet real plain soldier men again.

And tonight at 8:15. I dine with DeSalis *really* to see Tony[4] but Gawd alone knows what new signs and wonders I shall wander into or what what is said to me will really signify. Finally, tomorrow morn I meet a minister without a Portfolio who is in charge of Publicity and Allah alone can say what *he'll* want. Tomorrow even God be thanked, we leave for the Udine front. Three days in Rome are ample and too ample for me. I wouldn't have missed the Beatification I wrote you about for anything in the world but all the rest I can resign without a sigh.

It's divine weather today. Scirocco has vanished and the skies are blue and fresh. I've been for a meditative stroll on my own getting my ideas into order. If I only had *you* to discuss 'em with! However, the straight road is always the best. I am here I take it to describe some aspects of the Italian Campaign against the Austrians and *not* anybody else's campaign against anybody else. Landon is enjoying himself hugely over the drama of the whole thing. *His* account of the Cardinal's lunch will interest you. He's off now on some job of his own and won't come to dine with De Salis; alleging that he knows quite enough.

We have got seats in the sleeper for Udine tomorrow night. There is also a restaurant car on that train! Amazing land, which has not yet interfered with the Wagon Lits Company. The streets are filled with more strong handsome well set up young knuts[5] in civil dress than I can ever remember to have seen in the past three years.

Not a letter of any kind has come in from you but, on thinking things over, I can see that unless you wrote at once on my departure there is scarcely a chance as the mails are sketchy. However there may be something tomorrow in which case I'll acknowledge by wire: *but* I am always

Your loving
Rud.

Notes
1. The Palazzo di San Calisto in Trastevere.
2. Presumably RK means Santa Maria in Trastevere, next to the Palazzo di San Calisto.
3. Work on the revision of the Vulgate was suspended during the war. The first volume of the revised edition appeared in 1926; it is still in course of publication.
4. Anthony Denis De Salis, a captain in the Scots Guards, second son of the British envoy to the Vatican. He was a visitor at Bateman's, 23–7 January 1918, when RK identifies him as of the Irish Guards (Bateman's Visitors Book).
5. Swells, dandies.

To Caroline and Elsie Kipling, 9 May [1917]
ALS: University of Sussex

Udine: May. 9: 2: p.m.

... and so we arrived a little after noon at Udine[1] Which is large and scattered among green crops and has avenues of chestnut trees whose blossoms are already falling! There was a fatted ease about our progress in the wagon lit which more or less prepared me for the two cars (one shut t'other open) which greeted us. General Delme Radcliffe:[2] an Italian Colonel[3] in charge of the pressmen; a young Italian captain who spoke exceeding good English were on the platform and we moved so to speak on red carpets to this house which is marked in large letters as "a hospital for nervous diseases." I expect that was its walk in life before the war. It has been visited by an Austrian bomb which has cracked a wall a little bit but otherwise it has the air of immense peace which seems to brood over the entire landscape. It faces an immense circle of roughly pebbled ground from which roads and avenues radiate. There are railway lines down the roads and occasionally a friendly train load of low trucks goes roaring along or an officer on a spitting motor byke flees to some job or other. One avenue is bordered by a rushing canal of milky water on one side of which women wash; on the other there is a hospital for the wounded who lie about in the healing soft sunshine. All the rest is cultivation, stone-pines and mounds on mounds of flowering chestnut, with roofs of deep fluted tiles emerging, and here and there a factory chimney. My quarters are a bedroom with a weird teutonic sort of bed: a real sofa and everything else in the way of luxury and as the warm idle wind walks – or rather strolls about this town – it bangs my shutters. There never was a shutter in Italy yet that didn't bang. Delme-R and his next in charge Alexander[4] have gone off on their dejeuner (we had ours in the train) and we have tea at four. When I have expatiated a little more I purpose to do a snooze. I have to see the King[5] and Cadorna[6] but whether today or tomorrow I know not. I resign myself into the hands of the Military which is a dam sight better than trying to fuss. Moreover, there are no hosts in the world like soldiers. Think of the pure boredom of having to meet civils of all kinds and temperaments, to take them around to try to put some idea of the situation into their thick, opinionated heads.

3.45. And then came General D-R. to tell me things and then we talked and discussed future arrangements. It appears that I see Cadorna today at 5.30 and the King tomorrow. I can't give you any idea of the excellence, or the amplitude or the smoothness of the arrangements. We just came back from a visit to the local Bank – which is a portion of a wondrous old palace. All the town is full of most adorable architecture chucked about in the lavish Italian style – arcades, loggias, campaniles and everything else you choose. It appears that we are – very much so – the guests of the Italian Government who have a breadth of vision as to the duties of a host which fairly takes the breath away.

And now I close this to go to tea: more tomorrow but as ever

R.

I enclose Miss Jay's letter which I had ought to have sent you yesterday. I thought any kin of Martha McCook would interest you.[7]

P.S.   This goes in the special bag and is posted from London: Hence the penny stamp and my dearest love.

Notes
1. Udine lies 84 miles north-east of Venice. RK and Landon left Rome in the evening of 8 May for Udine via Venice.
2. Brigadier General Sir Charles Delme-Radcliffe (1864–1937) had been military attaché in Rome, 1906–11, and was now chief of the British military mission in Italy.
3. Colonel Pietro Andrian (information from Mr Peter Lewis).
4. Colonel (afterwards Major-General) Henry Lethbridge Alexander (1878–1944); he was Quartermaster-General to the British forces in Italy.
5. Victor Emmanuel III, who had appointed a regent to carry out his civil duties and spent the war at the front.
6. General Luigi Cadorna (1850–1928), Chief of the Italian general staff until relieved in November 1917, after the defeat at Caporetto.
7. Miss Jay and Martha McCook were sisters (RK to CK, 8 May 1917: ALS, Sussex); I know nothing more about them.

To Caroline and Elsie Kipling, 10–11 May [1917]
ALS: University of Sussex

Udine / May. 10. 6. p.m.

Dearests –

I don't quite recall where I left off. There were so many things to record. Anyhow my last letter to you must have gone into the bag here just before I went to see Cadorna at the Supremo Commando on the evening of the 9th. He was in a smallish, (as palaces go) palace scrupulously clean and austere, sitting so to speak in a large cool silence with very few visible members of staff around him. He was extremely nice and polite to me, and talked – as one in his place must – sonorous generalities to which I responded in my best field-french. The main point he bore upon was the creation of the new Italy unified – as up till now it has not been – by sacrifice. Then after that at 8.p.m. we dined in a little restaurant with General Delme-Radcliffe, and Colonel Alexander – just Landon and me. It was on the edge of moonrise just before ten when we walked back to the quarters here. Udine at night is lit – for obvious reasons – with a few lights all dark blue. It's a beautiful city in itself – with a main square, a cathedral and a few other old buildings all grouped together which are extraordinarily beautiful. The effect under the moonlight in the great square, dotted here and there with the blue lights was lovely beyond words. The town was silent; the moonlight slashed the fronts of the old buildings and the arcades and loggias showed like bits of blackness.

And so home and to bed in a room that somehow reminded me of pretty nearly every room I'd ever pitched my tent in in the East.

Next morning the 10th at 9.30. appeared Pirelli[1] our nurse – same as Pueaux in France – a cavalry officer and a millionaire being the son of Pirelli the motor-car tyre manufacturer. He and General Radcliffe accompanied us in a big closed car to see the country of the heaviest fighting of the campaign.[2] It was a vivid bright spring day; the roads were as white as bone and dry after days of wet. Every road was flanked by a little flashing water channel and lined with piles of limestone pebbles from which every few hundred yards a couple of men or a man and boy spread spadefuls of pebbles in every tiniest depression and worn spot and poured water out of a tin can at the end of a pole atop. The incessant traffic of motor cars, tractors and carts, ground the stuff down almost at once and the water made it bind: so that, the heavier the traffic the better the road. It was a miracle to watch. The Italians are Princes among Road makers. They make their roads save their vehicles instead of knocking the vehicles to pieces, and the whole land is seamed with new roads. Round Udine the land is flat and cultivated to the last inch – wheat, vines and everywhere the closely pollarded gnarled mulberry trees; for this is a great silk country. All round the horizon, with thunderstorms in their laps, lie the mountains just like the Himalayas. Some are white with snow others only speckled: but they are all dark and forbidding. The rivers with their shoals and reefs of white pebbles, are all milky blue green with snow water and they rise and fall without warning. The farm houses of any size; the country houses and the chateaux are all turned into hospitals – but one sees nothing of the wounded. And all along in the clean stone villages one passes masses of troops either at instruction or in reserve. These are much bigger men than you'd expect. They mostly wear tin helmets and carry themselves with the swing of Roman legionaries. They are made up of all sorts of Italians mixed together – North, South, Central and the Islands. This is so that the losses shall be equally spread.

Presently our car came to the old Austrian frontier – the fringe of level ground, before the hills begin. The houses here had been battered about a good deal but they were all rebuilt by the Italians who are as handy with stone and cement as the Canadians are with wood. Their neat-handedness impressed me enormously. Then we came to Gradisca on the Isonzo river[3] – a great scattered town of hutments, cemeteries, and all the rest and here the level ground stopped. Across the broad shallow river the land rose into ridges of a few hundred feet – say six or seven hundred – and the soil was red what there was of it – a sort of pocky conglomerate of stones, boulders, pebbles, stuck together with a little red dirt and covered with a false appearance of vegetation. But one knew without being told that that growth of green was only due to the wet and would wither away after a few days heat. A foot beneath the ground, the land seemed to be solid limestone either in chunks or layers or nodules – impossible to dig in with spades – impossible almost to describe. It reminded me of the Karroo at times, only the bushes were scrub oak and pine stumps destroyed by fire. Every few hundred yards there were huge hollows and sink-holes, some of them leading into caverns underground, which the Austrians had converted into shelters for whole battalions and all this inexplicable mess was scattered with battered traces of old trenches, bales of red rusted barbed wire, and all the wreckage and debris of battle that you could imagine. The road wound up among the wreck till we came to a few pale walls singing to themselves in the thin noon wind. That was all that was left of the village of San Martino – that, and a petrol pumping engine pumping water for the troops in the far off trenches somewhere on the sides of the further hills. There was a little firing of heavy stuff and now and again one saw the smoke of a shell through the heat haze, as it fell on the crest of a hill. Once we heard a big thing overhead going about its job – from the Italians to the Austrians. Then we reached a desolate quarry as it were of splintered stone on the very top of a stony ridge [sketch of hill, with points numbered 1 to 4]. That was St. Michael – which is their Ypres and their Hill 60 and all the rest. We were on the point no. 2. No. 3. point had been taken and lost six times before they could get a hold on the hill and, in one way or another, there were between 50 and 60,000 dead somewhere along there. The dead Italians had been carried down to the side of the River

Isonzo below us where they lay in mile long cemeteries. The Austrians had been simply buried under stones and stones and stones and tar and lime. You didn't need to be told it was a Golgotha. You felt it out in there in the clean sunshine under the blue sky – felt it as though it were midnight. It was a land apart from anything else – it was the Carso[4] and the Italians pronounce it with loathing. Unluckily 'tis the only open ground there is and they must fight down it on their way to Trieste. If the Karroo married the Matoppos the Carso would be the child of that union. Well we went; on foot, over these slivers of rent stone up to the top of the crest, picking our way among shell holes. A shell hole on stones is simply a funnel of finely shattered stone. There was a big gun speaking somewhere under the hill to the Austrians. No bombardment but a mere interchange of compliments before dinner. Suddenly there was an explosion in front of us, just like when Landon tried his blasting experiment at Keylands and the little rocks began to whizz. Then came another and another and yet more. They were excavating a position for a gun somewhere below us and the noon day assortment of blasts had just been touched off and they hadn't thought to warn us. So we turned back from that place and for half one lively minute I was sure it must be "pip-squeaks"[5] though common sense told me that nothing less than six or eight inch stuff could reach us where we were. I don't like stones flying.

Then we went down the reverse side of the hill and found enormous galleries where new big guns are coming in – a sort of T shaped tunnel eight or nine feet high full of rails and mechanisms. Then we came out into the dry glaring sunlight all among the stone again and got into the car and fled down hill and recrossed the Isonzo into Gradisca, picked up Radcliffe who was colloguing with a general, and went on to Cormons where we had a lunch with General Campello[6] who commands God knows what all on this front and will presently – I believe – launch a big attack.[7] It was a simple business like lunch – curiously *clean* in all its appointments – cleaner to my mind than the French idea.

After lunch, we went forth again – Pirelli, Landon and I – to see Podgora[8] over against Goritzia. Now Podgora is a Gibraltar of mud – even as San Michael was a Gibraltar of stone. The mud is now turned into hardest red earth but one realizes what a muck it must be when it is wet. Again the road left the plain and shot up and doubled and twisted for hundreds of feet till it reached the shoulder of this isolated Gibraltar. It is a hill shaped like this [sketch of hill]. We entered it by a boarded gallery of infinite steps that climbed up and up to the very top where there was an artillery operation post just under the letter a, above. We were told not to show ourselves too much up above as we were in plain sight of the enemy. Below us, not half a mile away as the eye goes, lay Goritza – apparently untouched, till you let your eye search a little – and certainly without much life. As we looked and wondered and watched the Austrians drop a shell on a convent just behind the town, we heard one of the gunner subalterns talking to a pal through a telephone. Even I, who have no Italian, could get the sense of the last sentence. It ran roughly: – "Congratulations. Then you'll dine with us tonight and you can pay for the drinks!" A youngster who was at that moment doing observing officer in the citadel at Goritzia below, had just got his commission as aspirant – i.e. sub-lieutenant and – very rightly – would celebrate the occasion by standing drinks at mess that evening. We heard the laughter of his companions rumbling in the mud galleries beneath us.

And when we had seen and discussed all the hot sullen landscape and the frowning hills close by we returned to our car and went into Goritzia – in order that we might say we had been there. Goritzia in its hollow is simply and thoroughly and plentifully dominated by the enemy guns. They pepper it every day – a few methodical 11 inch or even 15 in. howitzers. Hardly a house could I see that hadn't been shattered and pitted by shrapnel – the cathedral was in ruins; and house after house had been laid down. But the Italians mend and clean up as quickly as the Austrians destroy. There were no holes in the street and the rubbish was all carted away. There are about 1500 people left in Goritzia still as well as the troops. They have the same delicacy of movement as the inhabitants of Soissons. Half the roads are screened by hanging mats, from the observation of the enemy: but in the main place the full stately chestnut trees are all in flower and the wind goes through them lazily. We spent about half an hour there, during which the Austrians very kindly did not send in anything (*I* couldn't understand why they don't break up all the bridges every day) and then we came back to Cormons where I was taken to see a Radiograph hospital run by Countess Helena Gleichen[9] and Mrs. Hollis[10] which has been doing wonderful work. They have about half a dozen women assistants, including a Miss Hanbury Williams[11] who was at Rideau Hall when we visited the Greys there in Canada. They dress in khaki and their hospital – which was some sort of palace – has a garden full of irises and they have two cars to carry their apparatus and they are deeply grateful when they are allowed to go into Goritzia and practice their art there among explosions and gas shells. Certainly God made women most wondrously! Mrs. Hollis had lost her only boy and so took up this. Both she and Countess Gleichen have been affected by the X rays though I believe not to any serious extent *yet*. They have conducted close upon 6000 radiograph examinations. And we had tea and left them to their bravery and their simplicity.

We got back at 5: p.m. I had an hour's lie down and then went with the General to see the King who was good enough to express a desire to see me. I found him in a room a little better, because cleaner, than John's quarters, in the uniform of a full general in the field which isn't much more distinctive than that of a private. He is a man of amazing and elemental simplicity but every bit a man both of affairs and knowledge *and* guts. One felt that all through. He kept me over an hour during which he talked of the following, among other matters: the Army; the people; foreign travel; his visit in 100 ton yacht to Spitzbergen; the Ionian islands; apiculture; wolf-shooting and legends of wehr-wolves; artillery; his experiences in Shadwell Docks for a fortnight; his visit to the Emir of Bokhara; apple trees; agricultural development; American ploughs; classic literature and about ten other things. He's a *keen* man and I shouldn't imagine had many illusions. So we parted, with mutual esteems and then to dinner – Pirelli, another liason officer, Landon, D-R: Alexander and I – at the restaurant adorned with one of the hugest wistarias in full bloom that ever I did see. And so to bed comfily at 10.30. It wasn't a hard day.

(*May 11th*) Today we don't move out till after lunch. I didn't find any letter from you yesterday but I wish to state that your forethought in giving me tinted glasses made me *quite* happy all my trip. It's a strong hard light this Italian spring, and one has to treat it seriously.

Now I will close up. As I write you day by day, though I had to miss yesterday, there's no need to tell you my movements ahead. In the first place I don't know 'em for certain: being in the hands of the military who make changes from time to time. In the second, even if I knew 'em I couldn't be sure where to pick up your letters *except* at Modane where I hope the invaluable Clarence is sitting on a sheaf of 'em.

A heart's love to you and the Bird.

Ever
R.

Notes

1. Alberto Pirelli (1882–1971), of the Milan tyre manufacturing family; he was president of the company, 1956–65. An expert in international economics, he was also a flyer, a tennis champion, and a linguist. He appears as "the officer" in *The War in the Mountains*.
2. The substance of the following account appears in *The War in the Mountains*, I: "The Roads of an Army"; and II: "Podgora".
3. Gradisca on the Isonzo is some 15 miles south-east of Udine.
4. The Carso is a bare table land along the coast between Monfalcone and Trieste.
5. "A small German shell of high velocity" (Partridge, *Dictionary of Slang*, 8th edn).
6. General Luigi Capello (1859–1941), commander of the Italian 2nd Army. His career was ended by the defeat at Caporetto in October.
7. The 10th battle of the Isonzo was launched on 12 May. It is remarkable that RK was allowed to tour this front within hours of the commencement of a major offensive.
8. The heights of Podgora are just west of Gradisca, across the river Isonzo.
9. Lady Helen Gleichen (d. 1947), daughter of Admiral Prince Victor of Hohenlohe-Langenburg. Lady Helen, an artist from a family of artists, was joint commandant of the British X-Ray Section, Italian front, for two years.
10. Not "Hollis" but Nina Smyth Hollings (1862–?), younger sister of Dame Ethel Smyth and the wife of Herbert Hollings, of the Watchetts, Frimley, Surrey. "There was no more characteristic sight on the roads than the radiographic cars being driven by Mrs. Hollings and Countess Gleichen from hospital to hospital at the front" (G. M. Trevelyan, *Scenes from Italy's War*, New York, 1919, p. 108).
11. Major General Sir John Hanbury-Williams (1859–1946) was secretary to the Governor-General of Canada, Lord Grey, when RK was on his Canadian tour (see 12 October 1907). Hanbury-Williams had three daughters; I am unable to say which one RK means here.

To Elsie Kipling, 11 May 1917
ALS: University of Sussex

[Udine] May 11. 1917 / 7. p.m.

Oh Bird!

I've just received your note of the 4th on my return from war among the Alps. An inconceivable trip at the height of 4000 feet, in a country to which the Engelberg valley is tame and of no account, over roads like the creations of giants, and all the while, *above* us – 3000 feet above us, on the eternal snows one saw the trenches of the Italians on the edge of Monte Nero.[1] Conceive our Saint Louis trip[2] multiplied by 50 and you'll get some notion of it. We passed *miles* of ambushed guns and looked out through hidden casements over seas of mountains at villages of Austrians crawling beneath our feet thus: [sketch of mountains and valley]. And all the time guns were booming one against another lazily as they tried trial shots – they were 8" and 11" howitzers on our side: and when we climbed (or our car did) up to the very bare tops of mountains behold the grass was all pitted with shell holes. It's a war of giants among mountains. I looked into Tolmino and along 30 mile of Austrian front – wholly different from all I saw yesterday. The immensity of the landscape and the work dwarfs all comparison. I don't know how on earth or in the clouds I can described it.[3]

We go off early tomorrow into *real* Alps:[4] so I write this to give you all my love and to tell you how glad I am that Mother has (at last?) learned the habit of resting after lunch. Also the news about the Marks[5] is most cheering. This is a splendid climate but I will share it with you. If *only* you could be here to see the beauty of it all and to hear of my curious adventures all along.

Now I have to go to dinner. Dearest love.

Ever
Your daddy.

Notes
1. Just east of Caporetto.
2. I am unable to identify this trip.
3. RK describes it in *The War in the Mountains*, III: "A Pass, A King, and a Mountain".
4. The rest of RK's Italian tour appears in *The War in the Mountains*, IV: "Only A Few Steps Higher Up", and V: "The Trentino Front". He and Landon left Udine for Cortina on the morning of 12 May; the next day they visited the mountain troops at the front, perhaps in the vicinity of the massif of Le Tofane and of the Cinque Torre. On 14 May he and Landon began their return journey south past Asolo to Vicenza or Verona, from where the train would have taken them back to England. RK arrived at Bateman's on 17 May (Rees extracts). The fullest account of RK's Italian tour is an unpublished talk given by Peter Lewis to the Kipling Society in 1986; I have drawn extensively on the information in that. An abbreviated version

of the talk was published as "Italian Battlefields: May 1917", *Army Quarterly and Defence Journal*, July 1989, pp. 312–21.
5.   A Mr Marks and his wife succeeded the Warburtons in the farmhouse at Dudwell, arriving the day that RK left for the Continent. Marks, in the Royal Artillery, had been "an invalid since last September with dysentery" (Rees extracts).

To C. R. L. Fletcher, 4 June 1917
ALS: University of Sussex

Bateman's / Burwash / Sussex / June 4. 1917.

Dear Fletcher,

Back again! And what I've seen isn't to be told by any pen. I've seen the Exercitus Romanus,[1] reborn, all alive, same as it was under the Republic and the Cæsars at their best and, if you'll credit it, the same identical heads of generals – wide browed, bull necked devils, lean narrow hook-nosed Romans – the whole original gallery with a new spirit behind it.

Also, I saw a Beatification at St. Peter's which gave me the untouched untouchable Church all in one immense setting of lights, incense and mosaics and cardinals. When we meet I'll have to talk your poor head off. I've written something about it but only the barest fringe of the stuff. Italy in May was a thing to dream over. Do you know that a swine of a wealthy Italian returned from the U.S.A. has bought Browning's villa at Asolo and – *has surrounded it or enclosed it, in a house*!! I didn't see it with my own eyes but I was told it as we passed by the town.[2]

You are right about part II of Regulus. I only wish I could do it. Meantime I am being damned in heaps by "scientific" Johnnies who, much to my amazement, seem to understand that Regulus was an attack on their sacred doctrines. I never thought "science" had that much sense.

Now I'll go on with my work.

Ever sincerely
R.K.

"The flood strewed wrecks etc." is out of Jean Ingelow's "High Tide on the Coast of Lincolnshire"[3] – as perfect a thing as ever was. So is the song in The Dog Harvey that the woman sings.[4] I forget where the entire poem can be found but it's somewhere in Jean Ingelow's works.

Notes
1.   "Roman army". RK uses the phrase in *The War in the Mountains*, V: "The Trentino Front".

2. RK was either misinformed or misunderstood what was said. Browning the poet
    never owned any property in Asolo. His son Pen did. One of those properties was
    the Casa Torrecella, which was acquired in 1916 or 1917 by the American com-
    poser John Beach. He and his wife remodelled the Casa and lived there until the
    outbreak of World War II but they could hardly have "enclosed" it (information
    from Mr Philip Kelley).
3. Lines from the next to the last stanza of "High Tide on the Coast of Lincolnshire"
    are quoted (or misquoted) in three places in "My Son's Wife", which also takes its
    title from the poem (*A Diversity of Creatures*, pp. 340, 371, 373).
4. The first four lines of the poem and four lines from the last stanza of "Sailing
    Beyond Seas" are (mis) quoted in "The Dog Hervey" (*A Diversity of Creatures*,
    pp. 140–1); RK calls the poem "an almost forgotten song".

To Bonar Law, 2 July 1917

TLS: House of Lords Record Office

Bateman's / Burwash / Sussex / 2nd July 1917.

Private.

Dear Bonar Law,

Many thanks for your wire of Sunday about the Companions of Honour.[1] I
am sorry to have added to your work, but there is absolutely nothing in the
Acting-Secretary's letter to indicate that the matter was not irretrievably settled.

On the face of it, it looks as though the Prime Minister's prerogative
included recommending his fellow-subjects to the King's notice without consulting them beforehand.

This opens a way to a new form of frightfulness which I don't think people
should be called upon to endure – even in war-time. How would *you* like to
be waked up on a Sunday morning by a letter from the Acting-Secretary of
the Clerical Aid Society, informing you that your name was among the list of
Bishops that had been recommended to the King? Wouldn't you assume that
the Archbishop of Canterbury had landed you at last in his fold, and
wouldn't you at once collaborate with me and Swift MacNiel[2] in a Bill against
the imposition of arbitrary honours on the King's *loyal* subjects? So you see
how earnest was my appeal to you for help.

Very sincerely yours,
Rudyard Kipling

Notes

1. On 1 July RK received a letter from the office of the Privy Purse stating that he had
    been recommended to the King for the order of Companion of Honour. RK at
    once telegraphed Law to protest, asking him to remove RK's name from the list

(telegrams dated 1 and 2 July 1917: House of Lords Record Office). This was the third occasion on which RK had been offered and had refused official honours: he declined a KCB in 1899 and a KCMG in 1903. Now, in 1917, he was informed on 28 May that he could have "pretty much any honour he will accept". He declined to accept any. On 6 June he learned that he was on the list of knights for the new Order of the British Empire; he at once instructed Bonar Law's secretary that his name must be removed. This demand was evidently disregarded, and the offer was made on 1 July (Rees extracts, 6 June, 1 July 1917). For the history of the various honours offered to and refused by RK see Birkenhead, *Rudyard Kipling*, Appendix B, pp. 376–85.

2. John Gordon Swift MacNeill (1849–1926), Irish lawyer and MP for South Donegal, was sponsor of a bill then before Parliament to deprive peers and princes of hostile countries of their British titles and honours. The bill passed in October 1917.

To Theodore Roosevelt, 5 August 1917

ALS: Library of Congress

Bateman's / Burwash / Sussex / (Sunday) Aug 5. 1917.

private

Dear Roosevelt

We had the good luck to catch Kermit and his wife for a night (Aug 3rd.) while they were in town.[1] They came down on Friday evening leaving the man-child[2] behind and not even bringing his photo for which they were duly rebuked. However they are going to send us one.

The two of them looked well though naturally Kermit's spirited attempt to boil his son and heir on board ship had given them rather a shock. As is always the case in such matters it was the child who took the accident to heart least. We talked – you can imagine how we talked – but they didn't sit up much later than 11: p.m. Next day (Saturday) I took them up to the village to see our old Colonel Feilden who won his wife in your Civil War and was Lee's a.d.c. I daresay Kermit has told you about him on previous visits.

The old veteran and his wife discoursed of the South that was and the U.S. that are with the two young people. And at 2. p.m. on Saturday afternoon they had to go back to town. It was an all too brief visit but we're only thankful that they managed to squeeze it in.

Kermit, as regards raiment, is between hay and grass. He wears a Sam Browne belt over a U.S. army tunic neither of which is constructed for the other: but he is getting his staff uniform as swiftly as may be, at Burberrys. He didn't know the Army and Navy Stores as *the* place where officer's kit of every kind can be got, so we told him. Also we gave him a reserve medicine case no bigger than a cigar case filled with potent drugs. They're always useful. He thinks Mesopotamia will be "interesting." I don't know what his ideas of interest are but I told him what I believe to be the truth that he will be abominably uncomfortable in Mespot but he will live. In France all the comforts and luxuries are always at hand – and so also is Death. I like the boy's poise and modesty immensely and he has a splendid breadth of mind. It would be curious if he fetched up in charge of railway construction between Babylon and Bisra with a few thousand Tamils and Punjabis for workmen. But this is a world where every conceivable thing is possible.

I was specially interested in what he told me about you: and for once in my life I was thoroughly in accord with Wilson's attitude.[3] What his intentions and motives were don't matter but in keeping you back he is, as I see it, doing the best thing in the interests of the U.S.A. The present game of war is no show for a middle-aged man. It means collapse at the end of a few days. (We've had bitter and expensive experience in this line.) If you were held at the base you'd fret yourself to bits to get forward. If you went up you would go out – with no corresponding advantage to your country.

But, so long as you are in the U.S.A. there is always the element of strength sanity *and* drive for the world to rely upon in the days when (*as* will surely happen) your pacifists, doubters and general Slimers begin to bleat. *There* your power and prestige can save and steady and rally and keep your faint-hearts up to the mark. This is a service inestimably beyond any other that you could render to mankind. So, as I said, I applaud the Great and Good Wilson – though I don't know what was in his mind.

As far as I can make out, the U.S. contingent already in France will be *quite* keen enough without your being anywhere around. *Our* fear is that they'll simply use up the first two divisions out of pure devilment – and the Huns will rejoice over it.

I hear too that they purpose to take their flag with 'em. If that's so, they will simply be frizzled up. A word or a sign from you might stop it – if the rumour's true: but I can hardly believe it. We have a hard time ahead of us this fourth winter but our people's temper is hardening too, and we are more worried about our politicians than about the Hun, by a long way.

I fancy that before you've done, in the U.S.A., you will discover as we have that the really dangerous animal is the Hun in one's own country no matter what he pretends to be. You hold a good many hostages for his good behaviour and I sometimes wonder whether, if the U.S.A. took toll from her own unnaturalized Germans for every Hun outrage committed on the U.S. and on France, it wouldn't have a sedative effect. *Exempli gratia*: the drowning of so many U.S. citizens to be answered, *as a matter of business*, by the confiscation of so much German property in the U.S.: and, if that didn't work, by the wrecking of a German quarter in some of your big German cities. It's what the Hun comprehends perfectly. We have bled him badly in men, and if we can use up a decent percentage of his 1919 class this winter by exposure in the trenches as well as direct killing, he will feel it more. What he seems to funk more than most things is the stringency of the new blockade now that the U.S.A. is imposing it and neutrals can't feed him as much as they used to. We've got another twelvemonth of trouble ahead of us I expect but it won't be all on one side.

Ever sincerely
Rudyard Kipling

Notes
1.   Kermit Roosevelt (see 2 August 1910) had, through his father's influence, obtained an honorary commission with the motor machine-gun corps of the British forces in Mesopotamia. At the close of the campaign in June 1918 Kermit was awarded the military cross and then transferred to the American Expeditionary Force on the western front. He published an account of his experiences in *War in the Garden of Eden* (New York, 1919).
2.   Kermit Roosevelt, Jr, born 16 February 1916.
3.   His refusal to allow Roosevelt to raise a special division and to accompany it to the front: see 14 April 1917.

To Captain G. A. Robinson,[1] 29 August 1917
ALS: Berg Collection, New York Public Library

Princes Street Station Hotel, / *Edinburgh.*[2] / Aug. 29. 1917

Dear Captain Robinson
    Your note of the 30th July has been sent on to me here where I have been for the past few days in a climate rather like that of London in November – grey weather with small fine rain varied by heavy downpours. *You'd* appreciate it. Now, as to the Seven Seas, they are as under: –

North Atlantic
South "
North Pacific
South "
        Arctic
        Indian
        Mediterranean.

It's an unscientific system but it covers all the seas with which our Empire and Army is concerned. Some people have a slightly different list of seas but I prefer this one as most comprehensive.
    "Caviare to the general" is a quotation out of Hamlet,[3] as far as I remember. The meaning of course is a rare and unusual dainty (such as caviare) offered to the general public – which naturally doesn't appreciate it. I suppose

Russian caviare in Shakespeare's time was very much of a dainty. It may have been a common saying in Shakespeare's day or, what is much more probable, Shakespeare himself invented the simile. From what news reaches me you must be having one hell and a half of a time in your part of the world. If the Lord would only split the wet which he is now spilling all over Flanders and give your crowd their fair half of it life would be [   ]⁴ all round.

I've been seeing the ships here – there is quite a small collection – and looking at some of the new submarines. Edinburgh appears to be full of Australians and New Zealanders on leave, all of them (apparently) having just discovered long-forgotten female cousins in Princes Street. It is a beautiful sight!

With every good wish to you and your mess
    believe me

Very sincerely yours
Rudyard Kipling

Notes
1. According to a note from his daughter, Mrs D. M. Venn, Robinson was then serving with General Allenby in Egypt. He had written to RK in consequence of a discussion in his mess over the identity of the "Seven Seas".
2. RK and CK had left on a holiday on 17 August. They went first to stay with Mrs Harold Cuthbert at Beaufront Castle, Hexham, 18–21 August. Mrs Cuthbert was the widow of Captain James Harold Cuthbert, Scots Guards, who was killed in the same action as John Kipling (see 5 October 1915). She married the 4th Baron Rayleigh in 1920. On the 21st the Kiplings went to Edinburgh, where they remained until the 30th. They then returned to London and were at Bateman's on 1 September (CK diary and Rees extracts). While in Edinburgh they arranged for Trix to come to Dudwell Farm with a companion. The trip was marred for RK by a recurrence of stomach pains.
3. *Hamlet*, II, ii,.457.
4. Word illegible.

To John St Loe Strachey, 26 October 1917

TLS: House of Lords Record Office

Bateman's / Burwash / Sussex / 26th October 1917.

Private.
Dear Strachey,
    I know the war has a demoralizing effect, but I never expected the Editor of the *Spec* to succumb to the poetry streptococcus. Send along the Message, and I'll give it what-for!¹

As to Ireland she doesn't matter if we win the war. I expect the Government is playing up to the U.S.A. opinion just now and treating her with special tenderness. But it makes no odds in the long run. Ireland has done what the Pope and Divine Right did long ago – made herself a bore to all the world. Among the Canadians and Australians the mere word "Ireland" is almost as sure to raise a grin as the word "M.P." among the English. And, of course, the vulgar English opinion is "why on earth should the Irish not die and what *does* it matter if and when they do?" And that's a long way from Home Rule. The most amusing thing will be when it becomes necessary to kill a few of her rebels, and Ireland makes an outcry about it and finds that everyone is quite fed-up with her and her tantrums. Remember, she hasn't been hurt for forty years, and she must pay like the rest of us.

I send along the enclosed, which I did to amuse myself the other day, and if you care to use it, either as correspondence or as a middle – *without my name* or hint of origin – it's all at your service.[2] I think, and I hope that it may lead to discussion. (It's high time we did something for our Imperial post-war Heraldry), but I particularly do *not* want the discussion in my correspondence. It may be rather fun to see what it draws in the *Spec.* If you don't want it send it back. Guillem[3] was a sound man, and he ought to be at the College of Arms now.

Ever sincerely yours,
Rudyard Kipling

Notes
1. Not identified.
2. RK's article called "A Displaie of New Heraldrie", published in the *Spectator*, 3 November 1917, pp. 484–5, signed "Z". This was not acknowledged until it was collected in volume 30 of the Sussex Edition.
3. The article is headed by a text attributed to "John Guillem, Late Rouge Croix Pursuivant at Armes and formerlie of Brazenose College, Oxford". Guillim (1565–1621), a herald employed at the College of Arms, was made Rouge Croix pursuivant at arms, 1619; he published *A Display of Heraldrie* in 1610, a standard work in its time. RK's article is written in the idiom and spelling of the 17th century.

To Lord Derby, 1 November 1917

TLS: Commonwealth War Graves Commission

Bateman's / Burwash / Sussex / 1st November 1917.

Private and Confidential
My dear Lord Derby,

I have your letter, with enclosures, of the 30th October.[1]

In reference to your suggestion that General Fabian Ware should be permanent vice-chairman of the Imperial War Graves Committee, I entirely agree.[2] This strikes me as the obvious and workmanlike solution of the question.

As regards Sir F. Kenyon[3] being appointed Advisor on the question of the artistic treatment of the cemeteries etc. I have had some knowledge of the differences of opinion among the informal Committee of Artists[4] to which General Ware refers in his confidential memo. It seems to me expedient on all grounds that there should be an arbiter in artistic matters to adjust and compose the many differences of opinion that are sure to arise. I think that Sir F. Kenyon's appointment in this capacity would be a sound one, and that no time should be lost before he goes to France to collect views and data for the work required.

What knowledge I have of the feeling among officers and men, dead and alive, convinces me that their chief desire would be for *distinctive regimental* headstones which could be identified in every quarter of the world where a soldier of their regiment may be buried.[5] After all, whatever his individual position as a civilian may have been, when a man is once in the Service, it is for his regiment that he works, with his regiment that he dies, and in his death he wishes to be remembered as one of that regiment. I think, therefore, that any regimental suggestions for the design of the headstones should be considered sympathetically. Any artistic shortcomings in this respect seem to me of less importance than readiness to meet and, as far as possible, to carry out, a regiment's wish as to the headstone to be placed over their dead.

Yours very sincerely,
Rudyard Kipling

Notes
1. Regarding the work of the Imperial War Graves Commission, afterwards the Commonwealth War Graves Commission, created in May 1917, to record the war dead and to build and maintain cemeteries and other memorials. Early in September 1917, RK had accepted the invitation of Lord Derby, the Secretary of State for War, to join the newly-established Commission (Rees extracts, 6 and 7 September 1917), and he took an active part in its work until his death. The administrative appointments discussed in this letter were made at the Commission's first meeting on 20 November 1917. RK's best-known contributions to the work of the Commission are the text that he chose to be used on the "stone of remembrance" placed in every cemetery (see [*c*.19 November 1918]), the two booklets publicising the Commission to which he contributed (*The Graves of the Fallen* [1919], and *War Graves of the Empire* [1928]), such poems as "The King's Pilgrimage" (1922), and such stories as "The Gardener" (*Debits and Credits*) and "The Debt" (*Limits and Renewals*). The records of the Commission show that RK was regularly invited to compose or to revise inscriptions, and on his death a resolution of the Commission affirmed that all of the "inscriptions on the memorials erected by the Commission throughout the world were written, approved or selected by" RK (191st meeting, 12 February 1936: Commonwealth War Graves Commission). The inscriptions used by the Commission were frequently the results of a complex collaboration, but those on the memorials in Baghdad, Dar-es-Salam, Delville Wood, Lagos,

Tower Hill (London), Menin Gate, Notre Dame (Paris), and Thiepval, to name no more, may be regarded as by RK.

2. The creation of the War Graves Commission was the result of Ware's work; he was confirmed as the permanent vice-chairman and devoted the rest of his life to the Commission.

3. Sir Frederic Kenyon (1863–1952), Director of the British Museum, 1909–30, accepted appointment as head of a committee to determine questions of design and ornament in the cemeteries maintained by the Commission; he was called the Architectural Adviser.

4. Sir Edward Lutyens, Sir Herbert Baker, and Charles Aitken of the Tate Gallery had been invited by Ware to visit France and "advise on the general architectural treatment" of certain cemeteries. They were unable to agree, so that the post of artistic arbiter was invented for Kenyon: see note 3, above (Philip Longworth, *The Unending Vigil: A History of the Commonwealth War Graves Commission, 1917–1984*, 1985, p. 33).

5. It was soon agreed by the Commission that headstones should be uniform in size and shape and that each would be inscribed with the appropriate regimental badge as a distinguishing mark (Longworth, *The Unending Vigil*, pp. 35–6).

To Theodore Roosevelt, 12 November 1917

ALS: Library of Congress

Bateman's / Burwash / Sussex / Nov. 12. 1917.

Dear Roosevelt:

Thank you very much for the book[1] and the letter with it. Like you, I am rather aghast at the psychology of the Pacificist – and I should be more so if I did not know how long and how effectively Germany has worked upon them all over the world. If you go back far enough you'll find that Marx – a Hun – was at the bottom of the rot. There must always be, I suppose, a certain percentage of the perverse among mankind to whom cruelty and abominations make a subconscious appeal. They represent the "passive partner" in certain forms of vice: and few things are more curious than to study the forms which their mental perversities take. We have a reasonably large stock of them in England as well as the people who are, for financial reasons, working for the Hun. Someday the U.S.A. will awake to the fact that she too has been exploited psychologically by the world's enemy.

I read, of course, several of your pronouncements, when they appeared in magazine form: and I reread them with intense appreciation. As one of our journals says you are not a citizen but an institution of the U.S. now and more and more do I perceive your value in being where you are instead of at any of the fronts.

I hope you have got some news from Kermit. The young villain hasn't sent me a word since he went East so I am sending a chaser after him. I hear very good accounts of your men at the front in France. They are not penetrated with any excess of love for the Hun: and I expect that by the time they have had a few thousand casualties they will be even less affectionate. The Hun has a holy dread of the U.S. – not only on military but on economic grounds – and it is just dawning on him that if he gets the U.S. seriously engaged against him, he will have no place for penitence in all the world. Hence his desperate whack at Italy – and all the propaganda that made the break in the Italian Army.[2] It's a long, long, and peculiarly bloody business that we are in for: but I maintain that the Hun's temperament will impose his own destruction upon him. Looking back these three years I find I have lost nearly everyone that I ever knew: John's death gives one a sense of superfluous age and impotence. I hope you'll not have to go through that furnace. With all good wishes and sincerest admiration believe me

> Yours ever
> Rudyard Kipling

P.S.   If I could meet you I'd tell you what I think of your handling of Wilson. It won't do to write it at large.

Notes

1. *The Foes of Our Own Household* (New York, 1917), a selection from Roosevelt's speeches and writings during the war. A major theme is that "the Hun within our gates … is our dangerous enemy; and he should be hunted down without mercy" (Foreword).
2. The combined German and Austrian attack on the Italians in the battle of Caporetto, beginning on 24 October, succeeded beyond all expectation: the Italian centre was broken, and by 9 November the front lay on the Piave, many miles to the west of the Isonzo. German propaganda directed at the Italian troops in preparation for the battle was, at the time, credited with a large part in the defeat.

To Sir J. R. Dunlop Smith, 12 November 1917

ALS: Syracuse University

Bateman's / Burwash / Sussex / Nov. 12. 1917

Dear Dunlop –

With regard to the story of a flight by æroplane in the Maldives – Lt. Duncan Smith – that you sent me: I've done it in rather dressed up form as a tale, and called it "A Flight of Fact"[1] – suppressing of course names, dates and place. Also I've destroyed the original confidential memo.

> Ever yours
> Rudyard.

Note

1. *Nash's Magazine*, June 1918 (*Land and Sea Tales*). Flight Lieutenant Guy Duncan Smith, flying a biplane attached to the parent ship HMS *Raven*, had made a forced landing on Malé Island, among the Maldives, on 21 April 1917, and was later rescued. What happened in the interval is the substance of RK's story, "dressed up", as he says. Dunlop Smith, in his position as political advisor to the Secretary of State for India, would have had access to reports of the episode. Dunlop Smith had earlier provided RK with the information that he used for *The Eyes of Asia*: see 9 June 1916.

To Stanley Baldwin, 1 December 1917

ALS: Dalhousie University

Bateman's / Burwash / Sussex / Dec. 1. 1917

Dear Stan,

We're sorry. It would have been nice to have seen you. However, perhaps you may be able to get away later.

As to Lansdowne's letter to the D. T.[1] I fancy it appeared there because the proprietor is a Hebrew[2] and was suffering from cold feet. It *is* a Semitic complaint.

But the origin of his letter must be much more interesting. I am, as you know, a low-minded soul and I expect the poor old bird (who is ga-ga) was worked upon as a "patriot and a statesman" by some one – female for choice – in the Liberal interest.

The Liberals have an idea – one gets at it now and again in queer places – that the war ought to be "drawn" because that, in some insane way, justifies their contention that the war might have been "avoided." It is all mixed up with admiration for Asquith and a lot of loose talk about "larger views" and "detachment." Brassey who is also vehemently ga-ga holds Lansdowne's opinions in advanced form and, I should imagine, may be engineered to lend his name to a letter following on the same side.[3] All these old Davids have their Abishags,[4] and every Abishag has some young man she wants to help forward. Of course, au fond – the whole fault rests with D. O. R. A.[5] who should have known that the old imbecile meditated these performances.

But it will pass over like the rest – after a few juicy questions in the House and it will add to the bewilderment of our enemies who never understand why we do all our mental toilette in public.

Ever thine
Rud.

P.S.   And the letter is a further proof of heredity. The founder of his family –
he himself said so many years ago – was a Hatter. Hence the madness[6] – but
D. O. R. A. wouldn't use so obvious and vulgar a retort.

Notes
1. Lord Lansdowne published a letter in the *Daily Telegraph*, 29 November 1917,
    arguing for a negotiated peace with Germany on the basis of clear war aims.
    Lansdowne was not now in office but he had been a member of the Cabinet war
    committee as minister without portfolio in the first coalition ministry, May
    1915–December 1916. He had long thought that in a war to the finish there could
    be no victor. The points that he now put forth in his letter he had earlier put
    before the government as a memo. The letter itself had been reviewed by Lord
    Hardinge for Lord Balfour, then Foreign Secretary, and no objection had been
    made to it. But after its publication, when it was widely though by no means uni-
    versally condemned, the government officially denied any foreknowledge of the
    letter. At a meeting of the Tory party on 30 November Lansdowne's letter was
    violently repudiated. But the collapse of Russia, the disasters on the Italian front,
    and the continued failure of all offensives on the western front, made efforts at
    peace particularly attractive at the end of 1917.
2. Sir Harry Levy-Lawson (1862–1933), 1st Viscount Burnham, managing proprietor
    of the *Daily Telegraph*, 1903–28. The letter appeared in the *Daily Telegraph* because
    The Times had refused to publish it.
3. I do not find any evidence connecting Lord Brassey with current peace efforts: he
    died early in 1918.
4. See I Kings 1:4.
5. The Defence of the Realm Acts, personified as DORA. These defined what the
    English could and could not do during the war. They established a censorship,
    control of labour, control of production, and many other powers, including the
    long-lived regulations on the hours of opening for public houses.
6. The deleterious effects of mercury, used in the manufacture of felt, had long given
    hatters a name for madness, as in *Alice in Wonderland*.

To C. R. L. Fletcher, 18 December 1917
ALS: University of Sussex

Bateman's / Burwash / Sussex / Dec. 18 1917

Dear Fletcher

"And upon you also be the Peace." Why should the Hun defile our
Christian feasts. Besides, we are at the point when as the late M. Tapley
observed "there's some credit in being jolly."[1] I have an idea now that Allah
means the Hun to finish himself up utterly, well knowing that the Allies
would never finish him if he chucked up his hands.

As to the lecture it's out of all question for me. I've got more than I can
hope to do now and more seems to be coming. I'm truly sorry because an

evening with you and your boys would be good and healing to the rags of my mind and the bones of my soul.

But if it's Horace you're after, there's an ode in the Fifth Book which might have been prompted by Selborne's speeches on the sale of honours,[2] *and which* (what a vile and useful phrase that is!) I shall be very happy to send you if you'd care to put it before your boys for retranslation.[3]

H. takes the view that money is the least dangerous thing that can pass in return for honours, since the cheque once paid frees the purchaser from further obligations towards the party of the day. It appears that Lollius had bought equestrian rank as a social investment; and H. sets out the advantages of the step, as they existed in the Augustan age, with his usual clarity, and, *I* think, fairmindedness. Also he acquits Lollius of any intention to interfere in State matters. The ode is curious, to my mind, because it is the only one that I know in which H. seems to have reached towards the idea of a pun[4] – impossible to render in English verse. Altogether a most interesting find and I should fancy might take a couple of hours to turn back into Sapphics.

Very sincerely
Rudyard Kipling

Notes
1. Dickens, *Martin Chuzzlewit*, e.g., ch. 5: the refrain of Mark Tapley.
2. Selborne had first spoken on the question in the Lords in 1914 and returned to it in speeches of 7 August and 31 October 1917. The object was to deny honours given in return for party contributions.
3. The rest of the letter described RK's "Lollius" ("Why gird at Lollius if he care"), published in the volume of parodies called *Q. Horati Flacci Carminum Librum Quintum* (Oxford, 1920), as from Horace's *Odes*, Book V, 13.
4. In the phrase "by the head of either George" in the sixth stanza, alluding to the King, to the coinage carrying the King's head, and to Lloyd George.

To C. R. L. Fletcher, 2 January 1918
ALS: University of Sussex

Bateman's / Burwash / Sussex / Jan. 2. 1918

Dear Fletcher,

That's an excellent notion! Yes. Keep him by you,[1] by all means and let's have translations both for him and for the one about Stinks at the end of a "diversity of Creatures".[2] That'll make a beginning for your great idea of Book V. I've got Horace on the motor-car somewhere or other:[3] and notions in the back of my head for some more. It would be great fun if we could eventually make a little collection of 'em – something to keep one's mind at play sometimes. Thanks for the note about "The Jesus of History."[4] I'll see about it when I go up to town.

It's curious how the war has stood us all on our financial heads and given us– what nothing else would have done – a distinct pleasure in the business of "œconomy".

Misering is a distinct game and one that grows on one. We've done it and it develops as one goes on.

Here's to the new year.

Ever yours
Rudyard Kipling

Notes
1. The pseudo-Horatian ode, "Lollius" (see 18 December 1917). This letter evidently marks the first idea for the book published in 1920 by RK, Charles Graves and A. D. Godley as *Q. Horati Flacci Carminum Librum Quintum*. Fletcher is not acknowledged in the book as published, but from the evidence of this and other letters he appears to have had some part in the Latin translations of RK's Horatian poems. Graves himself gave a different account of the origin of the book, making no reference to Fletcher: "The genesis of Horace Odes, Book V, was in the brains of Kipling. It occurred to him about the blackest time of the last war, end of 1917 and early months of 1918, as a means of keeping up one's spirits and distracting our thoughts from present troubles, and he wrote to me outlining his plan and making many admirable suggestions for subjects of the sham odes" (letter of 10 September 1941, in *Kipling Journal*, December 1945, p. 21).
2. "A Translation: Horace, Bk. V., Ode 3" following "Regulus" in *A Diversity of Creatures*. It is included in *Q. Horati Flacci Carminum Librum Quintum* as Ode 1.
3. "Carmen Circulare", first published in the expanded "Muse Among the Motors" in volume 25 of the Bombay Edition, 1919. It does not appear in *Q. Horati Flacci Carminum Librum Quintum*.
4. T. R. Glover, *The Jesus of History*, 1917.

To Sir Andrew Macphail, 4 January 1918
ALS: Photocopy, National Archives of Canada

Bateman's / Burwash / Sussex / Jan. 4. 1918

Dear Macphail –

We saw It in the Honours List[1] all of a sudden and we had hardly done cheering over it when your letter out of the belly of the deep came in which you wrote on Xmas day, with your secret in *your* belly! Dramatic as you please, and satisfying all my notions of why the accolade should be given. It isn't often that human nature is genuinely and unreservedly delighted with another man's merit coming to its own. But Bateman's stood up and bayed with approval and content and satisfaction and a warm sense of the Decency of Things and I've been hunting my Horace for a good motto for the Arms. Whether you be armiger or not I cannot say: but if you are you must have an augmentation of some kind to your existing coat.[2] And anyhow you'd like old Scott-Gatty[3] (Garter King) at the Athenæum.

And another thing that makes me most happy and warmed is your Mother, and *her* joy. Altogether, it's very perfect and consoling in every aspect.

You must have had a very Isaiah's time of it in the Dominion![4] I didn't dare to think that Canada would apostasize but I put in my little appeal from this side.[5] There was no need to appeal to the men here. They and the nurses were all right – savagely so. I want to see some of your speeches now. I saw what you wrote in the last number of the University Magazine – "*In this our necessity*."[6] I think Canada's decision – now, after the three and a half years cold strain – has been the biggest thing yet in the Empire: and for the world.

So far had I written, when, as Pepys says, I took medicine – my innards being still of the Bolshevik order and now I am a worm and no man.

You'll be coming down here of course but you must advise us *well* ahead on account of our transport which gets less and less.[7] I don't know why I feel cheered: – as I do: possibly because you're this side the water again: possibly because it looks as if the Muscovite were beginning to doubt the integrity of the Hun. My friend Trotsky seems perturbed about something or the other.[8] In which case I do not envy the Hun as much as I did. I thought he was only chained to a corpse which would smell and waft microbes over all the earth. It may be that the corpse may have convulsions as well as microbes. In which case it will be demoralizing for the Hun. We're all very glad you've left Dorothy behind and we charge you send her our love.

Ever affectionately
Rudyard Kipling.

This to your old address in Oxford Street.

Notes
1. Macphail's knighthood was announced in the new year's honour's list.
2. Macphail was not "armiger" at the time of his knighthood nor did he acquire a grant of arms (information from the College of Arms).
3. Sir Alfred Scott-Gatty (1847–1918), Garter King-of-Arms from 1904. His mother published *Aunt Judy's Magazine*, important in RK's early life, and his sister was the Mrs Ewing whose *Six to Sixteen* RK knew "almost by heart" (see *Something of Myself*, p. 7). Scott-Gatty was also a prolific composer of songs.
4. Macphail had returned to Canada on leave in early November.
5. The issue was conscription in Canada; the Union government had passed a conscription law in August 1917, which was solidly opposed by the French-speaking

population. The general election of December was a victory for the government. Men began to be called up in January 1918, but there were demonstrations and riots in Quebec. At Beaverbrook's urging, RK had contributed to the campaign a letter widely published as "Kipling's Message to Canadian [or "Dominion"] Electors"; this appeared in Canadian and English papers on 1 December 1917 (uncollected). "If reinforcements are not forthcoming", the letter urged, "Canada, after all her sons' mighty sacrifice in the last three years, must gradually go out of the war. The enemy will be encouraged, the war for liberty will be prolonged, the world's misery will increase" (*The Times*, 1 December 1917).

6. *University Magazine*, December 1917, pp. 476–83, in support of conscription: "This war has been carried on by Canada's help to the present point in which success every day becomes more certain. By Canada's help we shall have our desire upon our enemy. That desire will be accomplished the sooner if Canada continues. It will be accomplished even if Canada refrains. But if Canada does refrain, and holds back a part of the price, Canada will then lie down dead as a Sapphira among the nations" (p. 482).

7. RK wrote in 1916 that "we have put down our cars" (to Cameron Forbes, 2 April 1916: ALS, Harvard). Macphail came to Bateman's for lunch on 20 January 1918 (Bateman's Visitors Book).

8. On 20 December 1917 the Bolsheviks and the Central Powers had begun the negotiations that led to the treaty of Brest-Litovsk. The Russians had little hope except in delay and obstruction. *The Times* reported on this day, 4 January, that Trotsky had condemned the German conduct of negotiations and asserted Russia's determination to defend its front if necessary. When the Germans renewed military action, the Russians were compelled to accept the terms of the treaty, 3 March 1918, by which Russia lost the Ukraine, its Polish and Baltic territories, and Finland.

To C. R. L. Fletcher, 12 January 1918

ALS: University of Sussex

Bateman's / Burwash / Sussex / Jan 12. 1918.

Dear Fletcher:

I am, as you know, no scholar when it comes to the Latin but *I* think it's lovely. "Docta curandum jecur"[1] makes me happy: So does "Quisquis est uni"[2] etc. and specially the last verse but one where one sees the hook-nosed social climbers. I think this is going to be glorious larks!

As to "the head of either George –"[3] Lollius means to say that having once paid for the Honour, he, by George! won't pay twice, as many politicians do who hold Honour on the understanding that they prostitute themselves as requisite to party ends. The Georges by whom he swears are obviously the P.M. who "recommended" the honour to George Rex: Also he probably had in his mind the King's image and superscription on the gold coins which were duly paid for the Honour. I hope I've made it clear because it's the nub of the argument. See the next two verses.

I'm bringing out "Twenty poems"[4] price one bob and have asked leave to include from our book (which will yet come into its golden own) Big Steamers, The Dawn Wind and the Secret of the Machines. It's what you might call "issued by request."[5]

Also, I've got a new Fifth Booker whereof Hankinson Ma.[6] is preparing the translation. It came out in the Times ever so long ago under the title The Pro-Consuls but I perceive now that Horace wrote it.[7] Rather a big effort for him and on a higher plane than usual – unless he'd been deliberately flattering some friend in the Government. I'll send it along.

Ever yours
Rudyard Kipling

Notes
1. From the 4th stanza of "Lollius" as translated for *Q. Horati Flacci Carminum Librum Quintum*: roughly translatable as "Learned [throngs of Aesculapians] [will yearn for] the care of his liver."
2. From stanza 7 of the Latin "Lollius": "Whoever is to himself alone [bountiful of honours not unpurchased]".
3. See 18 December 1917, n. 4.
4. *Twenty Poems from Rudyard Kipling* (Methuen, 1918), published in May. The selection included all of the poems here named from *A History of England* as well as "The Glory of the Garden".
5. J. H. C. Brooking had been urging RK to bring out a cheap selection of his poems (e.g., to RK, 31 December 1917: Copy, Yeats Collection, Texas A&M); *Twenty Poems* may possibly have been RK's response.
6. Invented by RK as the "translator" into English of RK's Horatian imitations. RK wrote to Fletcher on 25 December 1917 that he was sending the text of "Lollius" with "a translation alleged to be literal, and indubitably conscientious, by one Hankinson *Major* who assures me that he has looked out every word" (ALS, Sussex).
7. Published in *The Times*, 22 July 1905, on the occasion of Lord Milner's return from South Africa. It is included in *Q. Horati Flacci Carminum Librum Quintum* as "Ode VI", where it is accompanied not only by a verse translation into Latin by A. B. Ramsay but by a comic prose "translation" into English by RK alleged to be a "fragment of unknown origin". See 5 December 1920.

To J. H. C. Brooking, 19 January 1918
TLS: Kipling Society

Bateman's / Burwash / Sussex / 19th January 1918.

private.
Dear Mr Brooking,

I have been away from home, or I should have answered your letter, with enclosed series of your firm's advertisements,[1] before this.

I have had some experience in the unauthorized use of my verses, but I confess that what you have done is outside all my experience. I send you with this a copy of a letter from my lawyers to me which will show you to what extent you have infringed the law of copyright.[2] You have been using my verses in order to draw attention to your firm's goods. Obviously, unless you believed that people would have been attracted by the verses you would not have used them. I do not know how long it has taken your firm to make, perfect and popularize its output. It has cost me close on thirty-five years to build up the goodwill and connection of my business which you have used for your firm's advantage, without my knowledge or consent.

To reverse the situation for a moment, conceive what my position would be if it came to your firm's knowledge that, for over a year, I had been appropriating portions of their apparatus and presenting them gratis to the public in order to help the sale of my books. It has been repeatedly established that an author's writings cannot be used for the purposes of advertisement without his sanction. Were this not so, you can easily see that a man's work might be used to forward most objectionable purposes.

But I hope you will agree with me that you are lucky in having chosen me for the subject of what, in your own interest, I trust is your first experiment in this line. I say this because the letter in which you refer to having "taken my name in vain" (i.e. taken my property) and enclose the advertisements which establish the case against yourself, seems to prove that you acted in good faith – perhaps on your own responsibility – and without knowledge of what you were laying your firm open to. This makes me less inclined to move against your firm till I have written to ask you if you can see your way to give me an undertaking that you will not use any further extracts from my writings in your firm's advertisements.[3]

Yours faithfully,
Rudyard Kipling

Notes
1. Brooking had sent RK copies of advertisements placed by his firm in such trade journals as *The Electrical Review* and *The Electrical Times* carrying passages from RK's poems, intended, as Brooking said, to "help the patriotic feeling among readers". Brooking allowed that, in making use of the poems, he had been "taking your name in vain during the past year or so", but evidently he had no idea that RK might object (to RK, 6 January 1918: copy, Yeats Collection, Texas A&M).
2. The solicitors advised that "every one of these insertions constitutes a flagrant infringement of your copyright" and that if RK brought suit he "would obtain a substantial sum by way of damages in each case" (Field, Roscoe and Co. to RK, 18 January 1918: copy, Yeats Collection, Texas A&M).
3. Brooking replied that he was "greatly surprised" by RK's response; he at once agreed to desist, but argued that the intent had never been to advertise his firm's products, only to "arouse a stronger feeling of patriotism in our Country" (22 January 1918: copy, Yeats Collection, Texas A&M). RK then allowed Brooking

to print extracts from his verses without any accompanying advertising "(but not more than two-thirds of any set of verses)" (to Brooking, 21 February 1918: TLS, Kipling Society).

To Colonel H. W. Feilden, 1 February 1918
ALS: Syracuse University

Bateman's / Burwash / Sussex / Feb. 1. 1918.

Dear Colonel –

I ought to go up to London tomorrow for the week end as I have a good deal of important business there. But I understand that some sort of "demonstration" with regard to the food question[1] is being planned by some of the women in the village, for Saturday night, which is not the sort of thing to leave behind one as it might easily end in window-breakings and other things that would upset our maids.[2]

I should be very glad if you would let me hear what you know on this subject and whether any arrangements have been made for dealing with it so that one could be able to go to town and leave the house and servants as usual. I ask early because otherwise I must cancel all my engagements by telegraph.

There has been in our service a Mrs. Smith – sister of Pennels – who has been here as charwoman. She has suddenly given notice for no reason though she has no other work and has been carried by us through hard times; and I understand that she is among the women concerned.

This seems to point to Bateman's as one of the objectives in the "demonstration."

Very sincerely
Rudyard Kipling

P.S.   Whether any thing actually happens or not, the notoriety of the affair will be seized upon by the Press everywhere and the result will be unpleasant nationally as well as parochially.

RK.

Notes
1. Shortages of food, particularly butter, margarine, and tea, and the absence of any national scheme of food rationing, had produced long queues at shops and charges of hoarding and unfair distribution. But there were no serious shortages, and the popular alarm that swept the country early in 1918 was, as A. J. P. Taylor has put it, "war psychology at its most mysterious" (*English History 1914–45*, p. 95).

2. I find no report in local papers of any disturbance at Burwash, nor is there any mention of such a thing in CK's diary.

To Charles Plumptre Johnson,[1] 17 February 1918
ALS: British Library

Bateman's / Burwash / Sussex / Feb. 17. 1918

Dear Johnson

Thank you for your note and the sporting way in which you back your interest in the speech.[2] I'm very proud. But, as things are now, unless the Propaganda depts[3] take it up and circulate it I don't think – in the present scarcity of paper – that it would be an easy thing to circulate it largely. They have all the controls. I hope however it may be quoted here and go to America. With every good wish from us all

Very sincerely
Rudyard Kipling

Notes
1. Johnson (1853–1938), an insurance executive and bibliophile, was a fellow-member of the Athenaeum with RK.
2. At Folkestone, 15 February 1918 (uncollected). The speech was made in the interest of the war loan and argued that, since there could be no thought of peace with the Germans, the war was the only activity worth supporting. It was published in a penny pamphlet form by W. H. Smith in London as "Kipling's Message", 1918, and by the American YMCA, Paris, 1918.
3. The direction of British propaganda had just been taken over by Lord Beaverbrook, who was appointed Minister of Information on 10 February. Beaverbrook then offered a post in the home propaganda department of the ministry to RK, who refused on the grounds that "he would be a failure at office organisation" (Rees extracts, 19 February 1918).

To C. R. L. Fletcher, 17 February 1918
ALS: University of Sussex

Bateman's / Burwash / Sussex / Feb. 17. 1918.

Dear Fletcher

I've been busy and moving about lately: and tomorrow (D.V.) we go to Bath[1] where I expect I shall have to move about some more.

Now I have left all the translations up to date sent in, together with R's[2] "pro-consuls" (the first verse of which strikes me about as good as it can be made: opening like an organ) with my secretary, to type in triplicate and when done to send on to you at Eton so as you can distribute.

God knows with how many errors she will do it; but if you'll revise the stuff and return to her she will make you a clean copy. And that will be all right, won't it?

I think highly of any good "fake" and the idea of the original M.S. – of a decent rich brown tinct – is very fine indeed. Thus are Immortal Works built up! 'Only hope we'll have some paper left after the war! Facsimiles cost like sin: but I foresee an edition de luxe in the years to come!

And I think too the notion of fresh hands in the game is fun. We oughtn't to keep the fun to ourselves. I'll write Graves[3] and see if he'll play. That pro-consuls of R's is *fine*!

All good luck be with you.

Ever
RK.

P.S.   How does this go into Greek. It's out of the sepulchral unchristian epigrams of the missing parts of the Anthology:

On an R. A. Subaltern

Death fell upon my Son from out of the skies while
he was laughing, they tell me, at some jest. Would
I had known what it was. It would serve me through
the years when I shall not laugh.[4]

(The grammar is mixed I think.)

On a poacher shot in No-Man's Land.

Tom Airos the free hunter owed his country no more
than imprisonment in several gaols. In return for this,
he gave her all his skill in catching rabbits and, at the
last, his soul that abhorred imprisonment.[5]

Notes

1. They went to London on the 18th and to Bath on the next day, where they remained until 15 March. They went then to London, where, on 18 March, they attended a "matinee" for the Irish Guards at which RK's poem "The Irish Guards" was recited (Rees extracts).
2. Allen Beville Ramsay (1872–1955), who did the Latin translations of RK's "The Pro-Consuls" as well as of the other two RK items published in *Q. Horati Flacci Carminum Librum Quintum*. Ramsay was then assistant master at Eton, where Fletcher was teaching during the war. Ramsay was appointed Master of

Magdalene College, Cambridge, in 1925, and was Vice-Chancellor of the University, 1929–31.
3. Graves (see 9 November 1906) records that RK "wrote to me outlining his plan and making many admirable suggestions for subjects of sham odes" (*Kipling Journal*, December 1945, p. 21). Graves responded with twelve "odes" for the book.
4. An early form of the lines later published as "A Son" in "Epitaphs of the War" (*The Years Between*).
5. This is not known to have been published.

To Lord Beaverbrook, 25 February 1918

ALS: Harvard University

Empire Hotel, / Bath. / Feb. 25. 1918.

Dear Max:

That announcement in the papers unchained a lot of correspondents who have been telling me ever since what to do.[1] I've been among some factories round here.[2] It's the munition worker who needs propaganda the worst way. He and she is too tired or lazy to read about anything that requires thought after the work is done: they want something exciting – and the Labour papers supply it. But our strong hold will be the cinema. They are trained to go to cinemas: and they can be made to think through their eyes. I am sending you in a day or two my list of recommendations. They aren't all practicable just now, but they are all sound. I think newspaper propaganda for the munition workers is dead – if it ever had any life. The *spoken* word and the *picture* is the game.

I have about twenty requests (daily) orders and demands to reprint my Folkestone speech. If you don't do it I'll send all the letters on to you.

Rud.

Notes
1. The papers on 20 February reported that RK had been appointed director of propaganda at home; Beaverbrook had in fact offered the position but RK had refused it: see 17 February 1918. The mistake is perpetuated in A. J. P. Taylor, *English History 1914–1945*, p. 107.
2. I have no particulars about these visits. RK wrote to Beaverbrook on 5 March that "I am speaking to factory hands and cadet-corps" (ALS, Harvard); on 13 March he spoke at a munitions works in Bristol: "over a thousand workers and the speech a great success" (Rees extracts). I have not found any published account of this speech. Probably it was connected with a plan for RK to write a series of articles on munitions workers. Winston Churchill wrote to urge RK for a series of such articles on "the supply of munitions from the factories to the field" (27 January 1918: ALS, Sussex), and there is a correspondence with Sir Roderick Jones on the subject (Sussex).

To Sir Andrew Macphail, 10 April 1918
ALS: Photocopy, National Archives of Canada

Bateman's / Burwash / Sussex / April 10. 1918.

Dear Macphail:

What a great and sure prophet was Isaiah, when he wrote "their webs shall not become garments."[1] The cloth was magnificent – such stuff as now is not to be found – and I was congratulating myself aloud on breeches: a coat maybe; and so forth. Then said the wife and daughter, with the awful finality of women: "Yes, there's enough there for two skirts," and fell to measuring up!! But you must have forseen that from the minute the splendid gift was sent. They are loud in their thanks and praise. It's splendid honest stuff.

I don't think the Integer vitae – which I return – could be translated with any greater economy of words and certainly couldn't be more beautifully inscribed.[2] It's scriptorium work. But – qua ode – I love it not. I "potted" it once this way:[3] –

> The pure and perfect bore
> Walks scatheless evermore
> Arrows and poison never yet destroyed him.
> Such is the mantle thrown
> By Dullness o'er her own
> That when he talks the very beasts avoid him.
>
> So he pervades the earth
> Absorbed in his own worth
> No tact restrains – no sense of humour moves him.
> And yet – Oh womankind! -
> This Gods Own Prig can find
> Some much enduring Lalage to love him!

There's my Roland for your Oliver.

We'll all be delighted when you bring down Geddes.[4] We are here for the most part but, fate being what it is, if you don't send a wire to say you're coming that might be the one time we'd be away. And the unfeeling Spring makes everything lovely. *Do* come along!

My love to Geoff and your brother. (*Doesn't* one understand why he should be interested in what are called trifles! –)

I'm busy at all sorts of stuff which doesn't seem of any use and the wife has been up to town enlarging yet once more the accomodation of the Maple Leaf clubs for her beloved Canadians.[5] I think soon they will be able to take in 1000 a night. I was up the other day going over some of them – a complete cross section of Canada, even down to the barber's chairs.

All our best wishes to you and yours

Ever
Rudyard

Notes

1. Isaiah 59:6.
2. A translation, presumably Macphail's, of Horace, *Odes*, I, xxii ("Integer vitae") written out in calligraphic penmanship accompanies this letter.
3. RK's "translation" is included, with slight variants, in *Selections from the Freer Verse Horace*, a copyright pamphlet issued in New York, 1932; it also appears in Carrington, *Kipling* (p. 482) and in Carrington, ed., *Kipling's Horace* (p. 7) but remains uncollected.
4. Sir Auckland Geddes (1879–1954), trained as a doctor, had taught at McGill with Macphail, 1913–14; he was made director of recruiting for the War Office in 1916 and was now Minister of National Service. After the war he become Ambassador to the US. No visit from Macphail is recorded in the Bateman's Visitors Book after January 1918.
5. See 4 August 1915. CK had resigned from the Club on 28 November 1915 (CK diary) but had resumed the work by November 1916 (Rees extracts, 7 November 1916).

To Lord Beaverbrook, 11 April 1918

ALS: Harvard University

Bateman's / Burwash / Sussex / Ap 11. 1918

Dear Max,

I've had my time in town and I've got down to work again: hence my answer to your wire. Also I am being chased up by the Agricultural Dept.'s understrappers who, instead of doing their job, deliver political lectures to poor land owners.[1] They seem to have appointed Radicals for this purpose. My fields are full of German prisoners,[2] under *unarmed guards*, and I am trying to get the authorities to instruct the small tradespeople in villages *not* to sell things to prisoners. There's a mess ahead unless the whole prisoner-treatment is stiffened up. They'll rape some women before they're done.

This goes to Cherkley. Let me have your London address and (I won't betray it) a telephone number that will find you personally.

Ever yours
Rud

Notes
1. "Carrie much ruffled by a visitor from the Min. of Agriculture who tells her how to farm her land" (CK diary, 10 April 1918).
2. These are first mentioned on 26 March 1918 (CK diary).

To Theodore Roosevelt, 21 April 1918
ALS: Library of Congress

Bateman's / Burwash / Sussex / Ap. 21. 1918

Dear Roosevelt:

I've been trying to write to you several times since your long and immensely interesting letter:[1] but though I made several beginnings circumstances, so to speak, overtook the facts and I found what I had written was already out of date.

What you wrote me about W[ilson]. was in my own mind and – to tell you the truth – had been there from the first. But naturally that wasn't a sentiment one would avow even in a whisper. None the less a great many people share it: and now that the past month has gone over and our position is what it is,[2] very many people see what his initial delay – and (worse still) his neglect to make any preparations in the 2 years and 7 months before he moved – actually mean. This war is damned hard on liars! One sometimes wonders how much blood that man might have saved while he was so busy saving everybody's soul.

And God and the government alone know how much he is hampering us in regard to Japanese action in Siberia[3] and our own in Ireland![4] As you are perfectly aware, civilization's great enemy is the Papacy.[5] Not the R.C. religion of course but the secular political Head, unaltered in essence since the beginning. In Canada, in Australia, and above all in Ireland, every place where there is allegiance paid to the Papacy, there is steady, unflinching and unscrupulous opposition to all that may help to win the war. Obviously there must be: because the defeat of the Central Powers means ruin for the Papacy materially and morally. Austria and Spain are St Peter's last hopes: If one breaks, the other goes and – a consideration that has been in Rome's mind for many years past – the Modernists among R.C.'s will get a free hand. The revolt against the Papacy – as distinguished from the tenets of the R.C. church – is of course spreading and widening by reason of the Pope's attitude towards the moral issues of the war. These things are elementary – you knew them long before I did. I only repeat them for my own satisfaction.

And now, at the eleventh hour we in England are constrained – in order to please an immensely ignorant intellectual – to consolidate and confirm the power of a hostile Papacy in Ireland. For that is what Home Rule means. That is one aspect and one only of our present position! But, whatever the price we must pay it for the help of the U.S.A. My grief is that the head of that country is a man unconnected by knowledge or experience with the facts of the world in which we live. All of which must be paid for in lives of good men.

Now I'll stop growling for the moment. I've just been seeing one of our naval officers[6] for a day or two and he brings me, at first hand, news, which I have often heard at second hand, of the almost comically good and close relations between the two Navies. You know, of course, how mixed up both fleets are but I don't think that even you know how entirely both sides accept and rejoice in the situation. Admirals take over each other's squadrons and flotillas, lend borrow and dispose of destroyers and battleships in a way which reminds one of boys at school or sub-lieutenants in the Navy "having all things in common."[7] Your destroyers shine specially in convoy and anti-submarine work. Both sides groan together over the enormous amount of unnecessary paper-work on trivial subjects which is exacted from them by their superiors: the American reports – i.e. destroyer and convoy reports – are held up to our people as models of what concise and accurate reports should be. Your people, in reply, say that they are burdened with more paper-work than we are, a good deal of which, under stress of war, finds its way into the waste paper basket.

All our navy men speak very highly indeed of the U.S.N. and are getting on with them as sociable as "a basket of kittens" to quote Uncle Remus.[8] I've heard a good deal too about your Air men – their competence, modesty and insatiable zeal. I haven't come across many of the U.S. Army yet. They have been having their own experiences in the front line – including a lot of High Explosives which is awfully trying for new troops: and the Hun has been treating American prisoners with his usual "frightfulness" in order to put the fear of Germany into your people.[9] I'm willing to bet that, as I wrote you some time ago,[10] you will have to go in for some healthy reprisals on American-Hun "citizens" before you are through.

We have had a lively month of it since Mar 21st – any amount of trouble and fairly heavy losses. Theoretically, I presume, we ought to have been utterly knocked out but, being an illogical and unimaginative race we couldn't see that we had been. We've killed a reasonable sufficiency of Huns on the ground given and our Air arm have had rather a good time. We shall have one cheery hot summer, during which I expect, the Hun will win lots of victories and will get progressively more annoyed because he doesn't win a war.

Even now, I confess I don't trust W: and shall not till your people are so deeply committed in casualties etc. that they can't be prised off. We want every ounce of help that you can give us and we want it quick. I was reading your last book[11] the other night – on the dangers of delay in preparation. Every word is cold truth: we are paying for it now. Every lie, every bit of camouflage in the past, is being paid for – not by the politician who was responsible for it but by the young, and as the young are used up the inefficient and the compromiser takes heart and begins to talk.

It is in this direction that your help and leading will be of priceless value to us all. You say it's no use to be always in the vocative – that you are tired of talking. So is every one except the Pacifist whose trade it is: that is the very reason that one must go on and on even though the sound of one's own voice and the sight of one's own words makes one sick. The forces of Ineffectiveness *never* let up – precisely because one can be ineffective at the minimum expenditure of energy and mind.

I beseech you, therefore, to continue to testify. I know exactly what your reward is. I heard it the other day from a U.S. journalist whose mission in life seems to be to get the Bolsheviks "recognized" by the Powers. It ran on the familiar lines. "Of course no one – W. least of all – objects to fair criticism but R. is impossible. He's a crank you know etc. etc." And there you are! It might have come out of the mouth of any one of our ministers. But the more I look over the past years the more I see how right you were – even tho' you used the anti-English lever to get the beginnings of the U.S. Navy started in '96.[12] You *must* go on in the position of a gadfly – for the hide that you have to deal with is thick and complacent beyond belief. No one knows that better than you. In season and out of season keep your folk up to the *facts* of the case. You are about the only one who has seen the facts from the first.

And now I'll bring my infliction to a close. We've got to the state now where Death and loss somehow don't bite any more – a sort of anæsthesia which is very curious – as far as one's own soul is concerned. *Pari passu* one is livelily concerned for other people and all our keenest sympathies are with you and especially the womenfolk, for the boys. I haven't heard how A.[13] is coming on after his wound. I hope it was a reasonably disabling one because life is very hard for a wounded man returned to the front. Kermit seems all right in Mesopotamia so far though the young villain hasn't had the decency to send me a line. You might paternally reprehend him next time you write. We had a photo of the Grandchild from Spain (you've got one of course) which looked like a strayed cupid. It's something if one has grandchildren, in these days. You ought to encourage 'em. Now I will really stop with every message unwritten that affection and admiration can prompt.

Ever sincerely
Rudyard Kipling

Notes
1. This does not appear to have survived.
2. The final German offensive on the western front had been launched on 21 March in the battle of St Quentin. The offensive had great and alarming initial success; after some days of crisis and near-panic the French and British recovered, and by early April the German momentum was gone. The intensity of the crisis,

however, was matched only by that of the Battle of the Marne at the outset of the war.

3. The Japanese had sent a small force of marines to Vladivostok in early April in order to protect their nationals in conditions of civil war. *The Times* of 20 April reported the US Ambassador to Russia as saying that the situation was of no political significance. This was the beginning of what soon became a considerable international intervention in Siberia in the chaos of factions there.

4. The new Military Service Act, passed on 18 April under the sense of emergency created by the German offensive of March, extended conscription to Ireland. The government attempted to offer Home Rule in return for agreement to conscription, but the deal failed. The Irish MPs walked out of Parliament, the Catholic hierarchy in Ireland denounced the Act, and a general strike shut down Ireland on 23 April. All of this was treated as a "German plot" (see 21 May 1918). The government did not apply conscription in Ireland but the damage done by the Act was irreversible. The Pope was inevitably suspected of a hand in all this. Wilson, who was subject to pressure from the Irish in the US, managed to evade any action.

5. The determination of Benedict XV to take no side, and his effort to initiate a negotiated peace in 1917, were inevitably seen as hostile by partisans on both sides. He was simultaneously "der französische Papst" and "le pape Boche". It was about this time that RK wrote "A Song at Cock-Crow", attacking the Vatican policy (*The Years Between*). He recited it to Rider Haggard on 22 May 1918 (D. S. Higgins, ed., *The Private Diaries of Sir H. Rider Haggard 1914–1925*, 1980, p. 136).

6. A "Mr Robson, R.N." appears in the Bateman's Visitors Book, 20–22 April 1918.

7. Cf. Acts 2:44.

8. See, e.g., "Why Mr Possum Loves Peace" in *Uncle Remus: His Songs and Sayings* (New York, 1930), p. 12: "ez sociable ez a basket er kittens".

9. *The Times*, 20 April 1918, reprints an article from the *New York Times* on "Cruelty to American Prisoners. Examples of German Barbarity".

10. See 5 August 1917.

11. *National Strength and International Duty* (Princeton, 1917).

12. Roosevelt did not become Assistant Secretary of the Navy until 1897, under McKinley. See RK's account of Roosevelt's policy in *Something of Myself*: "It was laid on him, at that time, to furnish his land with an adequate Navy; the existing collection of unrelated types and casual purchases being worn out. I asked him how he proposed to get it, for the American people did not love taxation. 'Out of *you*,' was the disarming reply" (p. 122).

13. Archibald, the third of Roosevelt's four sons, was with the American army in France. He had been severely wounded by shrapnel and was invalided home in consequence.

To Sir Herbert Warren,[1] 2 May 1918
Text: Copy, *The Times*, London

Bateman's. / Burwash. / May 2nd. 1918.

Dear Sir Herbert Warren,

I have read and re-read your splendidly generous review in the *Times*,[2] and make haste to thank you most heartily. It is beyond all desert. But your estimate of the usefulness of my work in the lump gives me new courage and makes me very proud indeed. I do not mind confessing now that I have worked for the last thirty years very much for one end in everything I tried to do whether prose or verse. That is why it specially delighted me to see how you have pierced my camouflage of dialects etc. The French got on to it some years ago, and the damned Hun of course saw what I was driving at much too soon.[3] But to the best of my knowledge you are the first man on this side to have seen it and said so authoritatively. I wish I could accept the implication that I am a scholar,[4] but alas! my own conscience tells me that it is not true. I am very glad you liked the selection. Everyone is writing me now to tell me what I ought to have included. So far I make out that I have gone wrong in twenty specified items. But for the better prevention of indecent pride I have just gone through an obscure and out of date monodrama called "Maud"[5] not by any means some say the best.[6] My word!

Ever sincerely yours,
Rudyard Kipling.

Notes
1. Warren (1853–1930), President of Magdalen College, Oxford, 1885–1928; Vice-Chancellor of Oxford, 1906-10; Professor of Poetry, 1911–16; a scholar of Virgil and of Tennyson.
2. Warren's review of *Twenty Poems* in *The Times*, 1 May 1918, entitled "The Poet-Prophet of Empire" by "Our Oxford University Correspondent" (Warren's identity as Oxford correspondent of *The Times* was well known, but if RK had been in any doubt his friend Fletcher, a fellow of Magdalen, could have informed him). Warren calls *Twenty Poems* the "quintessence of Kipling". "What does it say and sing to us? To be of good cheer. To hold our head and our heart high. For it is verily the war of 'Mansoul'. That is the true meaning of our Empire, if it is worth anything. We ought always to have known that we must fight for it."
3. RK returns to this subject in a letter to Chevrillon, 14 January 1919; his remarks there perhaps explain what he means here, which seems, in general, to be the imperial theme.
4. Warren's review observes, "What would surprise most is to be told that he is a scholar. Yet so it is." On receiving RK's letter, Warren replied: "As to your not being a scholar, a man who can read Horace and love him and enter into his spirit as you do *is a scholar*" (3 May 1918: ALS, Sussex).
5. Tennyson, *Maud, a Monodrama*, 1855.
6. Thus in copy.

To Lord Sydenham,[1] 5 May 1918
AL: Cornell University

Bateman's / Burwash / Sussex / May. 5. 1918

private

Dear Lord Sydenham,

Thank you very much for your letter of the 4th.

I had just written the Indo-British association[2] to say that I didn't know that they were forming themselves into a company (which is an extension of liabilities that is beyond me) and, for that reason, asking to be excused from joining.

But that, of course, doesn't in the least affect my interest in the present situation in India which we owe, in no small part, to Mrs. Annie Besant.[3] The very beastliness in which that pestilent woman has been involved is her protection: and one can't – or under our racial codes of decency it's impossible – to explain what she has been mixed up with. Again, a certain amount of the Home Rule Movement must be part of Hun-propaganda and there again, we shan't get any help from the Indian Government. They must be spending a lot of money and one would like to know where it comes from.

As to the list of writers you gave me, it seems to me that, like myself, they are rather old game. Except, perhaps in Chesney's[4] case, it would be open to the enemy to say: – "Oh yes. These people are a generation removed from the new ebullient India etc. etc. We have advanced since then." We want younger folk if we can get 'em. I suggest young District Officers of the kind who can make a good story out of the cases of *Zoolum*[5] and oppression that came before them and can present to the public the unaltered India of the present – where the high caste man, or official, grinds the faces of the poor in the old sweet way. There are generally a few writers from the I.C.S. who contribute to the *Bombay Gazette, Englishman, Pi*[*oneer*] etc. etc., articles on rural life and perhaps Chesney might be able to give you the names of some of them. (W. W. Hunter[6] made his mark as a young man in Annals of Rural Bengal, very much on these lines, I believe). Again, you have the Indian Law Courts with their cases of Temple rights and caste privileges which, properly handled, would be a mine of instances giving the *true* picture of India.

There isn't money enough, I presume, for films of Indian life – presenting the mass of cultivators in contrast to the very few of the "educated." I am a great believer in the film as propaganda among "Labour."

I know the Home Rulers are trying for Labour and it occurred to me some time ago that a series of lectures – really interesting ones – on "India as it is" among the big manufacturing towns would be worth trying. The note to strike *always*, it seems to me, is that India is the land of privilege – the stronghold of it. People forget now, under this mass of words, [how ent]renched Caste has become: how [   ][7] continue; how [   ] touch with the India of today, it is work I should love to be doing now; but unluckily, I wrote my propaganda a generation ago. There is a tale of mine called "The Enlightenments of Pagett M.P."[8] which stands perfectly good now but – after 25 years who would believe?

Summa. If you want to counter the Indian Hun-paid agitator among British Labour, lean rather on lectures and cinemas than magazine articles which either appeal to the converted or are wasted on the "intellectual" impenitent. And forgive me for the length of this letter.

If there is any way in which I can be of any use with suggestions, pray [   ][9]

Notes

1. George Sydenham Clarke (1848–1933), 1st Baron Sydenham, began life in the Royal Engineers and served on many agencies and commissions having to do with military administration; Governor of Victoria, 1901–3; of Bombay, 1907–13.
2. Recently formed, under Lord Sydenham's leadership, to "foster the unity and advancement of the Indian peoples under the British Crown, and to resist the agitation of a small body of extremists for immediate Home Rule" (*The Times*, 22 May 1918). The agitation for self-government in India had intensified throughout the war. In response to this pressure the Secretary of State for India, Edwin Montagu, had already declared (20 August 1917) that the government was committed to "the progressive realization of responsible government" in India. Sydenham's association was a die-hard response to any such development.
3. Mrs Annie Besant (1847–1933), the founder of the Home Rule League in India, the sister-in-law of RK's old friend Sir Walter Besant. She had been notorious in public life since the 1870s, when she was associated with Charles Bradlaugh in the causes of free-thought and birth control ("certain of her proteges started what might be called Shrines to Onan", as RK put it: to Lord Sydenham, 9 May 1918: ALS, Cornell). She joined the Fabians in 1885, and then took up Theosophy under Madame Blavatsky, whom she succeeded at the head of the movement. From 1895 the scene of her activity was in India, both as Theosophist and as a friend of the Indian National Congress. After the Home Rule campaign had begun, she was interned by the governor of Madras from June to September 1917. Though she became head of the Congress in 1918, her political influence faded after the rise of Gandhi in 1919.
4. The former editor of the *Pioneer*: see 30 April 1886.
5. "Tyranny, extortion, oppression" (Ivor Lewis, *Sahibs, Nabobs and Boxwallahs*, 1991).
6. For Hunter, see 25–7 May 1888: *The Annals of Rural Bengal*, 1868.
7. The lower third of this leaf of the letter has been cut away for the signature, taking away about ten lines on this side of the leaf and the bracketed parts of the two lines above the missing section.
8. First published 1890; collected in *In Black and White*, Outward Bound Edition, 1897.
9. About ten lines, and the signature, on the lower third of the leaf have been cut away.

To Edward Lucas White, 18 May 1918
TLS: Cornell University

Bateman's / Burwash / Sussex / 18th May 1918.

Private.

Esteemed younger Brother,

Many thanks for "The Unwilling Vestal".[1] I have read it all with very great interest. My criticism – for what it is worth – is only that it seems to me that with that highly-specially[2] active life of Rome to deal with – and you have chosen an almost unworked mine – it might, perhaps, have heightened the illusion if you had *paralleled* the slang of the age – that it to say, given the idea that they talked slang, which they most certainly did – instead of giving modern equivalents for the slang.[3] It is an awfully difficult job to produce the impression of slang without actually committing oneself – as I know: and my feeling was that the stuff was so good that the modern phrases held one back. That is my only comment. It is easy to sit back and advise. You have got the character of the girl and the study of Commodus and his administrative problems most enviably. It is only the modern slang that pulls one out of the picture.

The war here continues on the old lines. Pharoah's heart is being hardened by the Almighty to his own perfect destruction.

Rudyard Kipling.

Notes

1. White's *The Unwilling Vestal: A Tale of Rome Under the Caesars*, New York, 1918.
2. Thus in original.
3. A "publisher's note" at the beginning of *The Unwilling Vestal* warns that readers "who are not acquainted at first hand with the lighter and more intimate literature of the Romans may be surprised to discover that the lights of Roman high society talked slang and were interested in horseracing". Brinnaria, the unwilling Vestal, says "Why, Daddy, I'd marry a boar pig rather than be a Vestal" (p. 5) but determines to "stick it out here in Rome" (p. 36) and "take the licking" (p. 96); she gets her own back, though, on the man who punishes her: "I beat him till he is just a lump of raw meat, eleven-twelfths dead, wallowing in his blood like a sausage in a plate of gravy" (p. 106). The Emperor remarks, "a juicier story I never heard" (p. 240).

To [Major Ernest?] Helme,[1] 21 May 1918
ALS: Cornell University

Bateman's / Burwash / Sussex / May. 21. 1918. 11: a.m.
(and it might be mid August from the heat)

Dear Helme

We were all awfully glad to get your letter with its news of the Red Dragon – bless him! Just at the present moment we are wrestling [   ][2] Shinn Feinner who seems at last to have been run to earth and revealed as – one isn't surprised – an ordinary Hun agent.[3] It's curious that a certain type of Irish seem unable to exist unless they are taking money from some one or other to commit crime. The last round-up of traitors has produced, for the time, an excellent effect.[4] Whether it will end in our Government weeping on their necks yet once more and releasing them, remains to be seen.[5] Personally, I wish to goodness we would do without Irish conscripts of any sort – carry on with common white men. A friend of mine has just been over and describes the land as exceedingly happy and rich and without any intention of taking part in anything except feathering its own nest. Meantime the unregarded general public is being rather fed up with the breed.

Elsie has been up to town, greatly enjoying herself and, incidentally, meeting Lloyd [George   ]. It was at the Bonar Laws. Oliver Baldwin on final leave comes down here on Thursday:[6] and we expect Rider Haggard tomorrow if there is any transport from the station available for him.[7]

Meantime – as you know – the heat is hurrying the procession of summer forward at railway speed. Iris, lilac, may, guelder rose, rhododendrons all blazing away together and the sun hot enough for hay-making. We've got a wounded officer and his wife at one of our farm houses.[8] They are town people unused to country life: and a large and industrious community of bees have set up housekeeping under the tiles on the side of the house just beneath their bed-room window. A local expert has promised to come and "take" them. I expect circuses when he does: but what amuses me is the swiftness with which these two town-birds are adapting themselves to the country life – bees and all: though they still speak of our harmless fat bullocks as "bulls." The man has discovered the whole art of fishing (I can't forbid worms during the war) and is extraordinarily happy with [   ] accomplishment.

Hun prisoners [   ] leisurely-enough) cultivating the [   ] grain growing country but a furiously energetic agricultural committee has us in charge, and seems to be quite content if we break up old pasture for the benefit of the young and voracious wire-worm. The Huns will be perfectly useless for German purposes when returned. They have learned to work the

English stroke and evidently approve of the genteel life they lead. Foxes are getting bold too as I've never known 'em before and – how do you explain this? – a few weeks ago, in calm weather, a large flock of seagulls settled down in one of our fields. Zeebrugge?[9]

The glimpse that you give of your affairs makes me – it's impossible to admire more than I do – wonder and marvel at the Spirit of Man. And knowing what one knows of the Hell of it – one has no fit words. Not that words are much good these days. The picture of your R.T.O. piling chaos on confusion goes home to one. I once had a brush of the same experience, when no one knew anything – not even the points of the compass – and it rained, *and* it rained. I think that's the way the Powers Above express their contempt for R.T.O.'s — pee on 'em!

Your Welsh stories remind me that I was taken [   ] Hall [   ] the first time I heard a woman sing a song in Welsh. As you know, I'm a babe unborn in these matters but I thoroughly realized that Welsh is an absolutely *glorious* tongue to sing in. Liquid and yet firm with a marvellous range of expression communicable even to a heathen like myself. Now I want more Welsh songs. Where can I get 'em? And who is the best Welsh singer?

This scrawl takes with it all our best wishes to you and to the Sons of the Red Dragon. I am told that the U.S. shipping situation has very greatly improved and that more stuff is coming over. Also that the U-boats are having a progressively thin and awkward time of it.

Ever yours
Rudyard Kipling

Notes

1   Probably the Major E. Helme, a letter from whom dated 28 March 1917 is now at Wimpole Hall. This says that Helme is then waiting to be sent overseas from the camp at Redcar where he is with the 3rd Battalion of the Welsh Regiment. Helme later commanded the Battalion. On 1 March 1918, when they were at Bath, CK recorded that "Major Helm plays the Edward German setting of the Irish Guards verses" (Rees extracts).

2   The letter has been folded so often that it has fallen apart and the parts have been pasted on a piece of backing paper. The words written on the folds are now mostly irrecoverable. The bracketed spaces in this letter give an approximate idea of the length of each illegible passage.

3   Probably RK is writing about the "Pro-German conspiracy" in Ireland that Lord French, the newly-installed Lord Lieutenant of Ireland, officially declared to exist on 18 May. The Germans, it was said, were to land arms in Ireland in April to coincide with the German offensive in the West. A Corporal Dowling, who had been a prisoner of the Germans, had allegedly been put ashore on the west coast of Ireland from a German submarine. He was arrested and condemned to death, the sentence being commuted to life imprisonment (*The Times*, 5 August 1918). The assertion that a plot existed had no basis in any evidence but was an episode in the government's struggles with the Irish over the conscription débâcle.

4   150 Sinn Fein members, including Eamon de Valera, had been arrested in connection with the "conspiracy" not on any concrete charges but under the powers of the Defence of the Realm Act.

5   The conspiracy charges were not followed up and the "traitors" were quietly released early in 1919. De Valera had already escaped.

6.   Oliver Baldwin was with them from the 23rd to the 30th, when he left for the front in France (Bateman's Visitors Book). CK wrote that "he goes with a lion's heart but won't return unless wounded. They never do in the Guards Regiment" (Rees extracts, 30 May 1918).

7   Haggard's account of this visit, on which he found RK looking "thin and aged and worn", is in Cohen, *Rudyard Kipling to Rider Haggard*, pp. 98–101. RK read "On the Gate: A Tale of 16" to Haggard on this occasion.

8   This was a Lieutenant White and his wife, who came to Dudwell Farm on 19 April and left on 4 June, he being "much improved by his six weeks in the country" (Rees extracts).

9   The British made an attempt on 22–3 April to block the harbours of Ostend and Zeebrugge, both used as German destroyer and submarine bases, by sinking concrete-laden ships in them. The attempt failed at Ostend but succeeded at Zeebrugge, where two old cruisers were sunk.

To Basil Thomson,[1] 3 June 1918

Text: Copy, University of Sussex

[Bateman's] 3rd June 1918.

Dear Mr. Basil Thomson,

Mr. Smale, the "Times" enquiry agent, tells me that he is working in conjunction with you over the "Old Volunteer" forgery in the "Times".[2] The plot thickens. I received yesterday (Sunday June 2nd) a communication bearing the Chelsea post-mark which I at once forwarded to Mr. Smale and on which I should be grateful for your opinion.

As far as I recall the original effort which Mr. Smale showed me, this second one seems suspiciously from the same hand both as regards the envelope, the method of placing the two half-penny stamps and the half-printed hand-writing. And it was also posted to be received on a Sunday, as the "Old Volunteer" was. The signature of I. Zangwill[3] which I have compared with a genuine one is very badly copied.

I have explained to Mr. Smale what I thought is meant by the allusion to "our Society".[4] It begins to look to me that Old Volunteer is enjoying his joke so hugely that like many jesters he does not know when to stop, and so ends by being caught.

Yours sincerely,
[no signature in copy]

Notes
1. (Sir) Basil Thomson (1861–1939), assistant commissioner of the Metropolitan Police in charge of criminal investigation.
2. On 27 May *The Times* published a poem called "The Old Volunteer" over RK's name. It is a remarkably feeble forgery, and that, coupled with the fact that *The Times* had accepted the poem without question, infuriated RK. He demanded an investigation. *The Times* sent a London private investigator named H. Smale to Bateman's to interview RK and carry out a search for the actual author. This proved wholly unsuccessful. RK entertained many suspicions, and seems to have attached an exaggerated importance to the episode. He twice called on Basil Thomson at Scotland Yard about the affair (CK diary, 8 and 21 June 1918), though this seems to have been at Thomson's instance, not RK's. RK's final view appears to have been that the poem was "a Hun trick meant to discredit and annoy' (to Ian Colvin, 2 July 1918: ALS, Syracuse). For a full account of the episode, see Gordon Phillips, "The Literary Hoax that Fooled The Thunderer and Did Kipling Down", *The Times*, 1 August 1977.
3. Israel Zangwill, the novelist, and an officer of the Society of Authors. His name was signed to the second letter.
4. "The allusion to 'our Society' is, I take it, a reference to the Society of Authors from which I resigned last year" (RK to H. Smale, 2 June 1918: copy, Sussex).

To Oliver Baldwin, 17 June 1918
AL, Incomplete: Photocopy, University of Sussex

Bateman's / Burwash / Sussex / June. 17. 1918.

Dear Old Man,

Aunt Carrie and the Bird at once and immediately and seriously tackled your suggestion for food. I heard words like "cake" and "candied fruit" and saw them flapping Harrod's catalogues about: and your Aunt is in town today where I expect she will keep an eye on your interests – stomach, I should say. So I think *that's* all right.

I don't know whether Elsie told you how "old volunteer", the Sunday after his first achievement, sent me – from Chelsea this time, a cheering or rather jeering note signed by the name of a fellow author – a dam' poor tracing it was. I had hopes he would keep it up but he has been silent since.

I went up and saw Basil Thomson at the C. I. D. sitting in a room whose walls were delightfully ornamented with revolvers, centrebits, jemmies and other burglarious weapons. He is a most interesting man and we got to talking about a lot of things – from the Billings trial[1] to the refinements of the late Roger Casement.[2] *But*, the main point is that, so far, we don't seem to have hit the trail of "old volunteer." Oh, I nearly forgot. *All* the postmarks on the first envelope (the one with the four stamps that you evolved such a fine Sherlock Holmes theory about) were faked! The envelope must have been dropped into the Times private post box. There's Crime for you! It makes detection even more difficult. And now you are as far abreast of the Affaire Kipling as I am.

There is no news in the valley except that, the other day, going over Dudwell after the Whites had left, just to see that the house was all right I discovered a STINK of amazing strength and colour. The cleanly charwoman had – shall we say overlooked? – the earth closet and had also filled the bucket with corrupting slops. My son, if you had seen your Noble Uncle wrestling with this situation you'd have respected him. I howked the reeking and pestilential bucket into the open (it weighed tons!). I sweated it over to the potato garden. I dug a hole in the iron ground and – I tipped out the contents! Oh Lord! Then I had the dismal job of cleaning the bucket which I intended to do in the mill pool, by tying it to a rope and letting the little waterfall play upon it till it was washed out. But, down in the pool itself, busy fishing was Colonel Feilden! So I slank off hastily with the bucket. The Colonel was full of curiosity. "Is the house on fire?" said he following me up. *Then* he found out what the trouble was ('twasn't difficult to guess) and laughed. *I* didn't laugh at all. No one would with a Bucket that beat a regimental latrine, perfuming the whole landscape! But, at last, with water and gravel and groans and sweat and retchings I had the dam thing tame. Now all is well. The other day a slightly insane and I believe slightly consumptive Naval officer turned up here – to look at Dudwell! He had thoughts of coming down to reside there with his Mother and Sister. He went sick after Gallipoli. He was a queer card. He doesn't know his Mother very well: he didn't know whether she'd like being in the country and I think he thought us all mad. This is the first time we ever had any one look over Dudwell and we didn't like it. ('Shouldn't look a gift house in the chimney so to say) [the rest is missing]

Notes

1. Noel Pemberton Billing (1881–1948), aviation pioneer, M.P., inventor, entrepreneur, had been sued for criminal libel by the dancer Maud Allan over a paragraph in the journal *Vigilance* about a private performance of Wilde's *Salome*. "With his usual flair for publicity, Billing conducted his own defence, amusing and scandalising the nation with his claim that the German government was in a position to blackmail 47,000 prominent British 'perverts', among them Mr and Mrs Asquith … whose names, he alleged, figured in a 'black book'"(*DNB: Missing Persons* volume). Pemberton was declared "not guilty" on 4 June 1918. *The Times* called the whole thing "deplorable" and declared Billing's accusations to be a "monstrous libel on the nation" (5 June 1918).

2. Sir Roger Casement (1864–1916), of the British Consular service, knighted for his reports on abuses in the Congo Free State, 1903, and in the Peruvian Amazon, 1910. On the outbreak of the war, Casement, then retired, worked to secure German help for the Irish independence movement. Returning to Ireland from Germany in a German submarine, Casement was captured, tried at the end of June, and hanged on 3 August 1916. Casement's homosexuality – perhaps what RK means by his "refinements" – was publicised by the British authorities.

To Andrew Macphail, 23 June 1918
ALS: Photocopy, National Archives of Canada

Bateman's / *Burwash* / *Sussex* / Sunday / Jun. 23. 1918.

Dear Macphail

I saw the verses in *Punch* when they came out and they have stuck.[1] They are perfect in form too. I wonder if they came suddenly in one heat. I'm *very* glad to hear about Geoffrey. He should be *emeritus* by this time: and it will be joy and relief to Dorothy, over there as well as you here, to know that he is at least resting a while. But what searing marks this will leave on all youth for the rest of their lives.

My interior has been skiagraphed[2] and I was told interesting things about it but, for the time being, it has ceased to double me up – on condition that I don't knock about. We have begun hay making: have 20 acres arable and 30 head of stock with three acres of potatoes. *Therefore* – thanks to Ireland[3] – the tribunal tomorrow will take my head outdoor man – general factotum, gardener and organizing head – aged 47 with double rupture, to do God knows what, but it means knocking out all the autumn work. *Per contra* his wife, a hard shrew and till now ignorant as only peasants can be, has completely grasped the inwardness of the Irish Question and clamours for Justice on Ireland. And she is one of the six million odd females who will have votes![4] Curious thing how Fate works out – the kept woman of the Vatican having her fate settled for her by ignorant women!

The American mentality is getting worth the study, but nothing except the pressure of facts will reveal them to themselves – precisely as that pressure revealed the Dominion to itself. *Au fond* it is a hard and a cruel race which makes a business of every thing in life and by the time it has put an edge on the business of killing it will be the hardest and least amenable race under Heaven. What I hear now about the submarine campaign cheers me more than anything else. The Americans are really showing up gloriously in their sea-hunting and convoy work. You know, don't you, that our mercantile mariners have been equipped with a big bomb howitzer – practically a depth-charge – of 1000 yards range which they are using with joy and great effect. I believe it's nearly an eight-inch sphere of enormous potency.

I am inclined to agree with you that the end is nearer than it is good for people generally to believe: But then comes the fear of our being sold back to intercourse with the Hun. *That* is the thing I lie awake over. Meantime I am doing stuff of sorts about the U.S.A.[5] and striving, day and night, to get food out of the farm and live up to the mandates of the Agricultural Committees, and the absence of all labour. Fifteen ton of hay down and the skies darkening above it!

But when you come down these things shall be shown you. Meantime ever yours, affectionately *and* – glory be! – quite a good deal better

Rudyard Kipling

Notes

1. Presumably something by Macphail is meant; I cannot find any likely verses in *Punch*.
2. I.e., x-rayed. This was done on 14 May by Dr Ironside Bruce after RK had suffered many days of pain. The report was that there was "no tangible evidence of disease but great irritability of the stomach" (Clinical History, 18 May 1918). RK's weight was now 123 pounds (Rees extracts, 19 May 1918).
3. RK means the refusal of the Irish to accept conscription: see 21 April 1918. The new Military Service Act extended the age of conscription, in some cases, up to 55 years.
4. The vote was given to women by the Representation of the People Act, 6 February 1918, which allowed women over 30 to vote if they were married, or were house-holders, or were university graduates. The number of women so eligible was esti-mated to be about 6 million but turned out in fact to be around 8.5 million.
5. "The Second Sailing of the 'Mayflower'", *Daily Telegraph*, 17 August 1918 (uncollected); and perhaps the speeches delivered at Winchester: see 18 July 1918.

To Stanley Baldwin, 2 July 1918

Text: Copy, University of Sussex

Brown's Hotel, / London, W.1. / July 2. 1918

Honoured Sir,

Such a Pipe as your graceful Hand transmitted to me yesterday cannot be purchased, or even stolen, in our distressful country at the present moment. You have indeed enriched me beyond the Dreams of Avarice for mere Wealth, as your department seems to be aware, is dross.

But at the same time, Honoured Sir, may I urge you alike in your own and the national interests to desist from smoking, as I perceive you do, tobaccos which, though doubtless to you as of the most delicate, are in fact and essence nothing better than chopped tarred twine, ensilage and cinchona bark, with traces of valerian.

I am now taming and educating your gift by means of blander and more aromatic mixtures to become such a pipe as may without offence be used in the presence of the Sex, Royalty and the medical Profession.

None the less, honoured Sir, I am gratefully yours

Erasmus Hogan Polewhale.

P.S.

It's perfect beauty, but you *do* smoke much stronger tobacco than I dreamt of.

To Edmonia Hill, 18 July 1918
Text: Copy, Cornell University

⌐ Bateman's / Burwash Sussex July 18, 1918.

Dear Mrs. Hill:

It was very pleasant to see your handwriting on the envelope again, and to be told that what I write still interests you, after more than thirty years, if we count from '87. I'm specially glad you liked the "Eyes of Asia" because I loved writing it. The main outlines – the insistence of all castes of men on female education – are quite true. From Gurkhas to Bombay Siparis, all the soldiers who served in France are united on this point.

The capacity of the French women carrying on business alone struck them enormously. A wounded Sikh farmer from Amritzar way – the Fumes of the Heart man – was simply lyric on the subject as he lay under the big gilt dome of the Brighton Pavilion. "Our women," he kept repeating, "Fools! All fools and the mothers of fools, Sahib."

England is filling up with your troops now, as you are keeping a lot of your hospitals and administrative bases here. This gives the last touch to London.

We could not be more cosmopolitan until Allah invented a new race to go listening to the bands in the Park. You meet Fench, Belgians, Italians and Czecks, with an occassional Cossack officer without a regiment as a matter of course. The Canadian, and Australian, New Zealander and South African have long owned the place, and now the sidewalks are thick with all the U.S. The effect of all this collection of variegated slangs on London's vernacular is beyond belief. Our bus and tram conductors are women – so, for that matter, are a great many of our railway porters, lamp-lighters, and municipal employees, and it is from their lips that one generally picks up the latest phrase or piece of chaff. London takes kindly to your army.

I gathered from a young man from Wisconsin, whom I sat next to on a penny chair in the Park the other day, that he had no complaints to make about the English "aloofness" of which he had heard so much. "I didn't know there was a city like this in the world," he said. "It's as much as a man can do to pay his expenses." There wasn't any need for me to draw him out. He opened up at length and at large on the hospitality of the land, and assured me that the theatres in the "city" (by which he meant London) were equal if not superior to anything in New York.

They have a free entertainment for the boys once a week. I wish you could have heard his unabashed delight and surprise over the English.

Yet the boys are as good as gold and neither make nor find trouble. My only anxiety is how they will stand the winter, for damp cold is trying to the young. But if you could see them you would be proud. Of course, it is impossible for you, at your distance, to visualize the constant background to our life here – the unending frieze of blue-clad wounded, legless, armless, crippled young men in every street and public place. Then too many of the officers at home have been wounded and limp to their duties. I find this crippling of youth harder to bear even than death – or I think I do. But I daresay I would have been glad to get the boy back even with both legs gone. The constant spectacle reminds us duly and daily of our bill against the enemy. To-morrow I have to do down to[1]—see how cautious one becomes through habit and fear of D.O.R.A. who is God, you don't know. I go down to one of the U.S. camps to open an officers' hut there.[2] It ought to be rather interesting.

I haven't been doing much of anything lately, as I have not been very well for close on a couple of years. However, I am better now. In these days something has got to go, and as my trouble wasn't in my head I don't much mind. But after all, I shall be fifty-three in a few months – which is a long way off twenty-two[3] – and the incessant pressure of events and accidents wears on me. I see to-day that poor young Quentin Roosevelt has been killed flying.[4] One doesn't mind these things so much for oneself as one does for other people. I know Kermit and like him immensely but I believe Quentin was a great favorite of his father's and a most promising man. His mother will feel it – and more as the years roll round.

Can you imagine such a life as it is with us here now – where there are no young men left among the people one knows, within eight visiting miles of us, every house has lost its son. Now my young second cousin[5] – younger than John – has just gone out to take John's place in the Irish Guards, and I'm praying that he'll get one good satisfactory deep-seated wound that will keep him quiet for six or eight months.

We had a boy staying with us one Sunday night. He had just recovered from a wound and was off on Monday morning. By Thursday he was wounded and back again in hospital. Now he is out once more at the front twice wounded and a Major at the age of twenty-three! Another friend of mine is a Brigadier General, aged twenty-six! which when you remember the ancient Generals in the East seems revolutionary.

However, I think that now we are really working towards the end. There will be some bad work yet, but it looks to me that the sting was out of the German. One's only fear is that unless your people stiffen us at the conference we may be tricked into making a bad peace. But here again I have a large confidence in the U.S. They are a hard people with a very clear sense of what life means, and I do not think that a wilderness of German chancellors will pull the wool over their ears, or make them stop till they have done what they think is required.

Forgive this unconscionably long letter – but it is chiefly about your people, and I hope, perhaps, it will interest you. They fight, I hear, like fiends on the front, but of course, they are too impetuous just at present which, till they learn caution, means death.

Very sincerely yours,
Rudyard Kipling

Notes
1. A note on the copy here says "scratched out".
2. This was at the American rest camp on Winnal Down, near Winchester, not on the 19th, as this letter seems to say, but on the 20th July. RK had already been asked to speak at the opening of a YMCA "hut" for American officers; now he had been asked to address an open air assembly of 7,000 American men and officers as well (Rees extracts, 20 July 1918). He thus gave two speeches on this day. They were published in pamphlet form as *To Fighting Americans by Rudyard Kipling*, YMCA, Paris, [1918] (uncollected). RK wrote to Moreton Frewen of this occasion that the Americans were "marvellous simple and modest, and they say, quite sincerely, that their desire is to 'kill Germans.' Now we've been at war four years and it isn't good form to say that yet. By which you may judge the essential differences" (24 July 1918: ALS, Syracuse).
3. As he was – almost – when he first met Mrs Hill in Allahabad in 1887.
4. Quentin (1897–1918), youngest of Roosevelt's four sons, was shot down behind the German lines on 14 July 1918.
5. Oliver Baldwin.

To Oliver Baldwin, 2 August 1918
ALS: Photocopy, University of Sussex

Bateman's / Burwash / Sussex / Aug 2. 1918

Dear Old Man –

Come to think of it, for comfort and real ease there is nothing to beat a latrine seat. The idea ought to be popularized in the Halls – only, of course, – well, you can see the objections for yourself. On the other hand applause might be "registered" by slamming down the lids – same as in the Austrian houses of Parliament the members rattle the lids of their desks.

Lorna was down here for the inside of a week.[1] Only wish she could have stayed longer. She kept us very happy and bucked up Elsie no end.

What you say about the Americans has been very much what I expected. They'll get the discipline all right but I'm glad you find 'em humble. They struck me at Winchester, as most meek. Mistrust the meek man, Ollie. When his time comes he develops into a devil. I'm writing an article about 'em which will be out before long.[2] Mummy and Elsie were the only two women visible among 9,000 armed warriors at Winchester. They liked it: and E. got boxes of candy (splendid stuff) from their canteen. *I*, my son, had a company called to attention as I passed 'em – in the close of Winchester Cathedral which they persisted in calling "a church"!! From what I saw of 'em they look a dam' awkward crowd to tackle if excited.

We have a sick officer, his wife and 7 yr old boy (with giglamps) at Dudwell.[3] She has been a nurse in the Army but oddly enough, didn't quite seem to understand the workings of the vast earth-closet which you and I know. Also, we have three tired Army nurses in retreat at Rye Green.[4] They come for a fortnight or three weeks. One of 'em would interest you immensely. I said, the minute I saw her that she was "gifted" in odd ways and, later, it turned out she was more or less of a clairvoyant with mediumistic leanings – a fortune teller, visionary and so on. There's no mistaking those queer eyes and curious tints to the eyeballs. The other sister is – Scoortch – with a Perth accent that takes the skin off your hand.

I'm hellish busy with the inkpot. Also, I've had dinner at Buckingham Palace.[5] Rather fun. Nothing to drink but lemonade, gingerbeer, barley and Malvern waters[6] – and when we all went away the enormous red official at the head of a vast red and marble and gilt double staircase said: – "You can go down by either way gentlemen." That would have been all right if we'd been tight but – after Malvern water and cigarettes, it struck me as superfluous.

I expect the Bird will be writing you anon and telling you what news we have – which is none.

Bless you, my son, and here, as usual, is all our love.

Ever your affectionate
Uncle Ruddy

Notes
1. Lorna Baldwin was at Bateman's, 24–30 July (Bateman's Visitors Book).
2. "The Second Sailing of the 'Mayflower'", *Daily Telegraph*, 17 August 1918 (uncollected).
3. I have no further identification of these guests.
4. The first, a Sister Meadley, arrived on 18 July; she was followed by one unnamed, and by a Sister Watson on 26 July (Rees extracts).
5. 12 July. The guests included W. H. Hughes, Prime Minister of Australia, W. F. Lloyd, Prime Minister of Newfoundland, Sir Joseph Ward, Minister of Finance, New Zealand, and other officials from the Dominons, Lord Salisbury, Lord Selborne, Admiral Jellicoe, and Asquith.
6. George V had determined to do without liquor for the duration of the war.

To Frank N. Doubleday, 21 August 1918
ALS: Princeton University

Bateman's / Burwash / Sussex / Aug 21. 1918

Dear Frank

Yours of the 29th – Bless you for it – and to find that you are up to your eyes in different works. There is no other drug fit to take – but the loneliness in between times, is Hell.[1] The Papal propaganda just now is *very* busy.[2] The Vatican seems at last to comprehend that we are really going to win and the Holy Father is shifting uneasily on his fence, preparatory to descending into our embarrassed arms. But he has knocked the bottom out of the really *devout* Catholic churchman, and, were it conceivable for such a thing as congregational Catholicism to exist, I'd say he was on the way to make it possible. Ireland's attitude has been another eye-opener to the Catholics from the U.S.A. who at last are seeing that poor tortured persecuting land at close quarters and are realizing what a dam' pernicious little bitch of a country she is and always has been.

I've been seeing your troops at Winchester – such a splendid revelation and so keen and yet so simply humble. They haven't had anything like a casualty list yet but I observe that they do religiously keep accounts of their dead and pay back. They don't like the huns' booby-traps in abandoned villages – wires and mines and blow-ups in apparently innocent villas and churches. So, being used to imported labour, they make their hun prisoners take down the pictures, lift up the tables and shift the furniture where there is the least ghost of a chance that a bomb may follow the rearrangement. Practical kids! I found a couple in one of my fields t'other day – on a visit to Burwash! One was from Seattle: another 12 miles west of Rochester N.Y.!! I gave 'em "flowers for mother" out of the garden. I tell you, old man, that even tho' it is Hell, it is a dam' interesting world still, and your crowd are going to make it yet more interesting for the hun. (By the way I suggest that in all publications controlled by F.N.D. the word hun be set up *lower case always* – never capitalized: and in referring to the animal it be spoken of and written of as neuter – not "he" "his" "whom" etc. but it, its and which. Besides absolutely covering the truth of the case, I know that in its present mood the hun feels that sort of thing worse than it ever did before. It is just beginning to realize what sort of a hell of a sort of Hate it has created for itself).

Glad my Indian letters amused you. They are, as I know, *very* close to the truth.

I've just done the first lot of proofs for my verses[3] but, for the life of me, I can't get a decent title so please excuse 'em coming unnamed. I'll send later when I arrive at a good phrase. It's a red hot day – has been ideal harvest weather for some time. We've got the self-binders going all round us. I've got 40 acres under crop at Bateman's and with any sort of luck we'll get it all in.

One of our farm houses is full of sick nurses resting: another is for wounded officers and their wives. It don't stay vacant long. C. is as busy as ever. I'm up to my eyes in useless stuff of sorts but I'm specially keen on having all huns hunted back to their own pen as soon as the war is over. You'll have to do it too: but when you read the full tale of the horrors the huns have done I don't think you'll take it as quietly as we have. Now hurry up your Liberty air machines[4] and let's get to the bombing of Berlin on long and continuous lines. Give my sincerest love to Roosevelt (I sent him a line when Quentin died) whom I respect more and more and with all love from us three

> Affectionately ever thine
> Rud

Notes
1. Mrs Doubleday had died from undetermined causes in February 1918, in Canton, China, where she and her husband were on a special mission for the American Red Cross.
2. One can only guess at what RK may mean. Since the failure of its peace initiative in August 1917, the Vatican had backed away from political action.
3. *The Years Between*, published in April 1919. RK had begun arranging his poems for this collection in March (Rees extracts, 28 March 1918), but the idea was older than that: CK recorded on 12 April 1916 that RK was "busy polishing his verses which he will publish in a book directly after the war" (CK diary). According to Flora Livingston, the title as first announced in the *American Publishers" Catalogue* was "Gethsemane" (*Bibliography of Kipling*, p. 388).
4. Production of the Liberty engine, developed as the standard engine for American planes, had suffered long delays.

To John St Loe Strachey, 22 August 1918
ALS: House of Lords Record Office

> *Bateman's / Burwash / Sussex* / Aug. 22. 1918

private
Dear Strachey

If you have any reason to suspect that I have committed embezzlement, forgery or murder you have only to tell me so directly, and I will do my best to send you some sort of explanation or excuse, not necessarily for publication but as a guarantee of good faith. But even if I had been guilty of noxious practices I have my own point of decency and – I am *not* a friend of Montagu.[1] It's an awful suggestion to pitch in on a red-hot August day with the harvest coming in.[2]

But I forgive you for your luminous diagnosis of the Yid mind under pressure or released from it. Blackmail or Dane gelt it always is: and one sees it working through the most casual social relations. But your evil habit of qualifying makes you assume that this particular Yid wants to save the British Empire. Racially, he does not care for it any more than Caiphas[3] cared for Pilate: and psychologically he can't comprehend it.

There are no words to describe Curtis:[4] and his works are mixed up with all sorts of queer devildoms that ramify all over the place. I thought you'd like to see the Christian Science Monitor for that reason.[5] You'll observe that P. Kerr[6] is mentioned too: and a Roman-Catholic faith-healer is an unsavoury combination.

Thank you for your article on the Godfrey Isaac dirt.[7] The shocking thing about it is that it's true. We *can't* do anything because we didn't do anything at the first onset. And remember always that is another debt we owe to Israel.

Ever yours
Rudyard Kipling

I have no word of my God-Daughter Susan.[8] Is she christened yet?

Notes

1. Edwin Samuel Montagu (1879–1924), Secretary of State for India, had just issued (6 July) the *Report on Indian Constitutional Reform*, known as the Montagu–Chelmsford Report (Lord Chelmsford signed the report as Viceroy of India). As a very modest start towards self-government this recommended that some powers be transferred from the Governor-General to newly created provincial governments.
2. RK's remarks do not seem to refer to anything that appears in the *Spectator*; perhaps to a letter from Strachey?
3. Caiaphas, high priest of the Jews: Matthew 26:3; John 11:49. Montagu was a Jew, the son of the 1st Lord Swaythling, who had been a leader of Jewish causes in England.
4. Lionel Curtis (see 27 February 1906); on his return from South Africa Curtis started the "round table" movement to federate the self-governing countries of the Empire. He founded the Institute of International Affairs in 1921 and devoted himself to the cause of world federation. In June of this year he had published *Letters of an Englishman to the People of India on Responsible Government*, arguing that the Indians could learn responsible government only by being allowed to exercise it. Curtis was supposed to have had a hand in the Montagu–Chelmsford Report. The *Spectator*, 13 July 1918, p. 36, wrote that "now the gossips tell us [the Report] was thought and written by Curtis, camouflaged by Montagu, and signed by Chelmsford".
5. "Definition of Policy in India", *Christian Science Monitor*, 19 July 1918, reviewed Curtis's political career and gave a favourable account of his views about Indian self-government. A further article appeared in the issue of 25 July 1918. RK sent this material to Lord Sydenham with the following note:

   > This is from the *Christian Science Monitor*, U.S.A. and strikes me as interesting. Its origin I take it is from Clieveden: Mrs Astor being an energetic Faith Healer and Christian Scientist. The devil of healing-systems is that their exponents *will* extend 'em to the body politic.

You might pass it on to Strachey for information in the *Spec* as I think Curtiss has rather denied he had much to do with the Montagu scheme ([*c.*20 August 1920]: ALS, Cornell).

Two further articles appeared in the *Monitor*, 15 and 17 August, approving the Montagu–Chelmsford Report and the opinions of Curtis, "the well-known authority on India" (17 August).

6. Philip Kerr (1882–1940), afterwards 11th Marquess of Lothian, had been, like Curtis, a member of Milner's "kindergarten" in South Africa and held administrative posts there; he had been associated with Curtis in promoting South African union. On his return from South Africa he became editor of *The Round Table: A Quarterly Review of the Politics of the British Empire*, the periodical devoted to the support of Curtis's ideas of commonwealth federation. He was now private secretary to Lloyd George, and was to be credited with a large part in the construction of the treaty of Versailles. In 1925 his appointment as secretary to the Rhodes Trustees precipitated RK's resignation as a trustee. Reared a Catholic, Kerr was a convert to Christian Science.

7. Godfrey Isaacs (d. 1925), managing director of the Marconi Company, 1910–24, and brother of Rufus Isaacs. it was Godfrey Isaac's offer of American Marconi shares to his brother that grew into the Marconi scandal of 1912 (see 22 December 1912). Godfrey Isaacs had brought suit for libel in July 1918, against Sir Charles Hobhouse on account of remarks concerning the Marconi business. On 25 July a jury decided the case in favour of Hobhouse. The *Spectator* approved the verdict but concluded that the truth of the Marconi scandal would never be arrived at, for the truth "might have results highly injurious to the national interest" (3 August 1918, p. 117). Isaacs appealed for a new trial, but this was denied in December. In that month, by coincidence, Isaacs invited RK to write a book celebrating the contribution of the wireless to the Allied victory: "All of the Marconi Companies' existing records and the fullest facilities for obtaining the material for the volume would be placed at your disposal by us" (4 December 1918: ALS, Sussex).

8. Daughter of Amabel Strachey (see 6 October 1902) who had married Bertram Clough Williams-Ellis, of the Welsh Guards, in 1915.

To Stanley Baldwin, 21 September 1918
ALS: Dalhousie University

Headland Hotel, / Newquay, Cornwall[1] */ Sep 21. 1918*

Dear Stan,

We've had ten days here of mixed and rather ferocious weather but there's no denying that all three of us have fallen in love with the place and we are laying plans to come again.

The only drawback, from a tripper's point of view, is that Newquay harbour is the mortuary for the locally drowned crews. Since June there have been over a dozen – sixteen to be correct – torpedoings off this part of the world. I saw a few corpses landed off an M. L.[2] boat the other day, and hauled up from the quay through the town on a wheeled stretcher. Not a pretty sight.

Oddly enough, this sort of thing has been rather too much for local patience; and there has been a small riot. A party of Huns – dog and three dry bitches – occupied a boarding house, or most of a boarding house, kept by a man called Butler on the Island Estate. It commanded lovely views up to Trevose head, all over the harbour etc. etc. and there they lived for *fifteen months* slam *on* – but you know the geography better than I do – the sea front of an M.L. base and with full views of passing traffic.

They are a long suffering breed in Newquay. They didn't begin to petition for the removal of aliens till a few weeks ago (I can't find out yet what happened to the petition but it was numerously signed). Then they tried, I'm told, to pass a resolution in the Town Council but that was side-tracked by a tactful town councillor. But even that masterly inactivity didn't prevent the corpses coming in (all wet and twisted under Union Jacks) and very naturally the report went that the Huns from their eyrie felicitated each other on each fresh haul. Also, they were supposed to drink champagne together on special occasions.

At last – if you'll believe it – there was actually a "demonstration" opposite the boarding house – longshore men, and visitors combined. They hove stones and smashed windows and tried to get in with the very laudable intent of heaving both the Huns *and* the boarding house keeper (which is a joyously significant sign) over the cliffs. But being inexpert in the detail of lynching, they were dissuaded by a local town-councillor who managed to get the Huns out of a back door in a car (the dog was between 60 and 70 *and* an "invalid") and they fled to St Columb Minor police station[3] where they rested a night under police protection and are now disappeared. Four youths who "rioted" are under arrest and will shortly be tried when there is reasonably sure to be a procession to the courthouse and there ought to be a riot. But that will come later.[4]

It's most cheering to find that, as I foretold,[5] the Aliens Committee[6] are forcing people to take the law into their own hands and if there is much more torpedoing here I shouldn't be surprised if a wandering Hun visitor were actually killed!

Did you know that in the "politer" walks of life proctective measures have been reduced to a system? For example, a Hun of the name of Waechter[7] with a bitch, came here to stay at this hotel. The guests explained what was necessary to the manager, who in turn explained to the Huns adding, quite truthfully, that *he* couldn't protect 'em in event of trouble and they evaporated. I'm told that this Waechter is related to Cave[8] through the latter's first marriage but an old *Who's Who* (1915) doesn't mention this point which seems to be held as an article of faith by the town at large. I think if I were Cave I'd disclaim it very quick and very clear. Otherwise if he wandered into Newquay investigating he might get drowned.

So, there you are! It's all beautifully unnecessary and I dare say it is due to nothing more than mere incompetence or swank on the part of the official mind. But, everything has a bright side and if the Aliens Advisory Committee[9] will teach our people to kill Huns and incidentally pro-Huns, they deserve well of the country.

We come up to town on Monday so I shall miss the trial at St Columb Minor: but, you might let me know at Brown's whether Cave *is* connected with Waechters and such like.

Ever affectionately
Rud

Notes

1. They left for Newquay on 10 September and stayed until 23 September; they then went to Brown's Hotel in London before returning to Bateman's on 2 October (Rees extracts).
2. Mine layer?
3. St Columb Minor is two miles inland from Newquay.
4. Six young men were brought before the magistrate at St Columb petty sessions on 24 September for their part in damaging Waverley House, Island Estate, Newquay, on 5 September 1918, to which they had attempted a forced entry. A Mr and Mrs Harding, German-born and long naturalised in England, had resided in Waverley House since July 1917. The residents of Newquay had petitioned the authorities in June regarding Germans in coast-facing rooms and alleged cases of "signalling"; when no response to the petition was received, a crowd of about 2,000 people took popular action. The six men pleaded guilty but affirmed that they had no regrets for their actions. The court concluded that "general circumstances" did not justify fine or imprisonment but the defendants were bound over to keep the peace for six months. Four other young men were summoned for breaking the windows of Waverley House; they pleaded guilty and were ordered each to pay 10s towards the cost of the windows (*West Briton and Cornwall Advertiser* [Truro], 26 September 1918).
5. In, for example, the letter that he wrote to be read at a public demonstration in Trafalgar Square, 13 July 1918, to protest against the presence of "enemy aliens" in England and to demand their immediate internment: "I have long realized that the great body of public opinion will boil over in regard to this matter, and I am very glad that steps are being taken to convince those in authority of the state of public opinion on this question" (*The Times*, 15 July 1918).
6. A committee appointed by Lloyd George in June 1918, to advise him on how to treat the "enemy alien peril", about which an increasingly violent agitation developed in the course of 1918. The committee's report recommended, among other things, the internment of "all male enemy aliens over eighteen", the repatriation of "alien women of enemy origin", the immediate discharge from government office of all persons "of enemy origin", and the immediate closing of "enemy" businesses (*Annual Register*). The question was debated in Parliament on several occasions in July, and in August an Act on the "status of aliens", more stringent than the government had asked for or desired, was passed.
7. Sir Max Waechter (1837–1924), a merchant and active philanthropist. A native of Stettin, he had come to England in 1859 and had been naturalized in 1865. He was a magistrate and served as High Sheriff of Surrey. Waechter devoted his later years to the cause of a federated Europe.

8. George Cave (1856–1928), afterwards 1st Viscount Cave, a lawyer and Unionist MP, was Home Secretary, 1916–19; Lord Chancellor, 1922–4; 1924–8. As Home Secretary, Cave was responsible for the control of aliens in England and had had to defend the government's policy against the public outcry for summary treatment of "enemy aliens". RK has got the relationship between Cave and Waechter backwards: Waechter's first wife, who died in 1910, was Cave's sister.
9. An Aliens Advisory Committee, first appointed in 1915, had now been given increased powers and charged with reviewing all cases of "enemy aliens" still at liberty. This was evidently not enough for RK, who seems to have agreed with the simple view that all enemy aliens should without exception be interned.

To Sir Herbert Baker, 7 October 1918
TLS: University of Sussex

Bateman's / Burwash / Sussex / 7th October 1918.

PRIVATE
Dear Baker,

Many thanks for the Rhodes Notes which I return herewith. They are very interesting, and bring out the large artistic side of his nature very completely – and give also a hint of the vast range of his interests. But do you think the anecdote about the blood on the marble looking well, is a sound thing to release in a world still populated by little people who hate? It might be twisted to do harm.[1]

One other point, l have had a good deal of publicity in my life, and love it not. "The Woolsack" has come to be very closely associated with my family life, and we look forward to returning there after the war. So l would be grateful if you could cut the note about it down to the fact of your designing it.[2] l always maintain – cottage or no cottage – it was one of the best designs even you ever made.

Yours very sincerely,
Rudyard Kipling

Notes
1. This must refer to notes for the book that Baker later published as *Cecil Rhodes, by His Architect* (Oxford, 1934), which emphasises Rhodes's interest in art and architecture. I do not find any reference to "blood on the marble" in it. It is possible that Rhodes may have made such a remark about his planned but unbuilt lion house: "he was quite unperturbed, when warned of the sanguinary fights which would ensue" (*Cecil Rhodes: by His Architect*, p. 46).
2. Baker's account of The Woolsack says only that Rhodes had invited Kipling to use it, and "this the Kiplings did for many Cape Summers" (*Cecil Rhodes, by His Architect*, p. 45).

To Demetrius Caclamanos,[1] [8? October 1918]

Text: Draft, University of Sussex

[Bateman's]

Dear Sir

I am very glad to learn that my rendering into English of the Greek National Anthem[2] meets with your approval and I shall feel honoured if you publish it, as you say, along with the music.[3]

As regards my sending it first to the press for publication I will take a few days to consider the matter and will let you hear from me later.

Notes

1. Caclamanos, or Kaklamanos (1872–?) was the Greek minister in London. He had written to RK on 7 October 1918 acknowledging receipt of RK's translation of the Greek national anthem, saying that the Legation would like to publish the poem "along with the music", and asking whether RK wanted to publish first? RK's draft response is written on the letter from Caclamanos.
2. A translation from the original of Dionysios Solomos, first published in the *Daily Telegraph* on 17 October 1918, and collected in *Verse, Inclusive Edition*, 1919. It was made apparently at the request of Caclamanos: an entry in CK's diary, October 1918, says "Rud writing his Greek Nat. Anthem for the Greek Minister."
3. No printing of the poem for which Caclamanos might have been responsible is known. RK sent the *Daily Telegraph's* payment of £50 for the poem to the Greek Legation for the Greek Red Cross (Caclamanos to RK, 12 October 1918: ALS, Sussex). On 22 January 1919 Caclamanos wrote to say that the Greek government, in thanks for the poem, had presented RK with "a gold medal of Alexander the Great" and added that "your rendering was reproduced in many Greek papers and commented on as an important step towards spreading a knowledge of Modern Greek poetry abroad" (ALS, Sussex). RK received the "medal" (that is, a coin from the era of Alexander the Great) on 4 February 1919 (CK diary).

To Major-General Lionel Charles Dunsterville, 2 November 1918

ALS: University of Sussex

Brown's Hotel, / London. W.1. / Nov. 2. 1918.

Dear Lionel

Yours of no date worth mentioning, from Nowhere in particular, has just come in with cheque for £260 clearing off the whole £500 with interest.[1] I don't remember about the guineas. If so hang on to the £25 till you get home and we'll have a dinner on it – with a few select friends and – if it be possible at our time of life we will try to get drunk.

I have been following the Baku affair,[2] naturally with the most intense interest. I guessed it was you even before I was told and I knew it was absolutely *the* one job that you would love. Likewise I knew that, if possible, you would be let down over it by (a) lack of troops and (b) instructions that covered your General and left you exposed. Then I saw how you evacuated your force at Baku after raising general Hell and I chuckled again. The W[ar]. O[ffice]. – into which I stray occasionally – wanted to know what manner of man you were. I gave them a lurid but, on the whole, not untruthful, summary of your character and nature. What *I* want is for you to get a district or a frontier to play with – Caucasia or Trans-Caucasia or Hell or somewhere on the Persian border which is much the same. You're only at the beginning of your career: and you may finish yet as Governor of the Urals. Which reminds me. I've just met a Colonel Lawrence[3] – he is an Oxford Don really – who is an Emir of the Arab Empire and has made more Kings than anyone since Warwick the King-maker. He is aged 29 – has been warring from Medina to Damascus against the Turks with armies of Nejd Arabs: and blowing up Turkish troop trains in the intervals of camel-charges. The Arabian Nights are tame and unconvincing besides his adventures: and having made his Kings he is now going back to teach history at Magdalen College, Oxford!

We here in England at present are sitting stupefied, like children at a cinema, among the wrecks of Empires. It has all come down in one gigantic landslide – Bulgaria, Turkey, and Austria[4] and – Lord knows what else to follow. The last four years have slain all our faculty for emotion and there isn't a sign of jubilation anywhere. Of course Europe is back where she was in the 8th century when the Roman Empire finally smashed,[5] but *our* main preoccupation now is that the Hun shall be made to suffer. The process is beginning but it hasn't more than begun. The Versailles Council[6] seems to be holding its hands quite quietly till it can find out what the situation really is: and as the situation changes (badly for the Hun) every 48 hours I think the final terms for him will be drastic to admiration. And *after* justice, he is exposed to the hate of the whole world – a little thing in which, even now, he cannot believe. The Army wants him to shut up – with their help and Foch[7] of course wants his super-Sedan.[8]

Altogether, life is a queer job just now and nothing more characteristic than the "phlegm" of the English. Not a flag waving or a bell wagging anywhere and – for a wonder – every one hoping that the terms will be complete enough to finish the Hun. Of course, we are all too near the facts of the case to realize what they mean. I am trying vainly to comprehend what the collapse of Turkey implies. So far, I have only got as far as the brilliant idea that we should hand Constantinople over to the U.S.A. They haven't had much of a show up to the present and it might amuse them.

By the time this letter reaches you, Allah alone knows what may have happened. You may be in charge of half Persia. But whatever and whichever it is, old man, be sure you have my abiding affection and loud cheers in the background.

Ever thine

R. K.

Notes

1. The loan that RK had made to Dunsterville in 1914: see 24 February 1915. In sending his check for the sum, RK wrote: "You will observe that I have made it guineas ... because it is Spring and the shops are full of pleasing confections and it is good for the health of our betters to shop" (to Dunsterville, 17 February 1914: ALS, Sussex).
2. Dunsterville had been sent to northern Persia at the beginning of 1918 to patch up some sort of defence against the Turks in country left undefended since the Russian withdrawal and now swarmed over by every sort of hostile force. His command, known as "Dunsterforce", never amounted even to brigade strength. In June he was directed to attempt the defence of Baku, on the Caspian, against the Turks, and he succeeded in reaching the city in August with a small force. By mid-September, after fighting without support, Dunsterville withdrew his force to Persia. He was then returned to India. On 22 November he was decorated with the Star of India.
3. T. E. Lawrence (1888–1935), "Lawrence of Arabia". The date of RK's meeting with Lawrence is not recorded but it must have been shortly before this letter was written. Lawrence had held a Magdalen scholarship before the war but did not return to the college; he was elected a research fellow of All Souls in 1919. For some further account of RK and Lawrence, see F. N. Doubleday, *The Memoirs of a Publisher*, pp. 254–63.
4. Bulgaria signed an armistice on 28 September, Turkey on 30 October, and Austria on 3 November.
5. RK repeats this idea in a letter to Rider Haggard of 6 November: "We're back in the 8th Century after the Holy Roman Empire turned in its hand" (Morton Cohen, ed., *Rudyard Kipling to Rider Haggard*, p. 105). Since the Holy Roman Empire was not established until the 10th century, one wonders what he means.
6. The Supreme War Council, sitting at Versailles, composed of the Allied prime ministers and advisors, intended to coordinate the conduct of the war. It had been established in November 1917.
7. Ferdinand Foch (1851–1929), Marshal of France, the supreme Allied commander since April 1918.
8. That is, revenge for the Prussian victory over the French at Sedan, 1870.

To Theodore Roosevelt, 7 November 1918
ALS: Library of Congress

Brown's Hotel, / London, W. 1 . / Nov. 7. 1918.

private and confidential
Dear Roosevelt

In the very first place congratulations on the recent Republican gains[1] which, as we see it from here, strengthen the cause of the ultimate decencies by keeping W. up to the mark.

The guts of Europe are sliding into our laps day by day but, at the one moment when we Allies ought to have our hands free to deal with a hemisphere *in extremis* we are tied up by W's idiotic Fourteen Points.[2] The only word of truth the Huns have spoken since the war was when they called them "theses." They open the door to every form of evasion and quibble from the Huns and their friends all over the world.

It's trying the Nations who have lost a million dead apiece, rather high when at the eleventh hour they have to explain to the Hun, who has brought mankind within sight of starvation, that they – reserve to themselves the interpretation of the "Freedom of the Seas" phrase.[3] To put it bluntly the U.S.A. has grown up and thriven for 142 years under the lee of the British Fleets and but for those fleets would have gone with the rest of us into servitude two years ago. An ape looking down the palm tree on which he sits is reasonable compared to – but I needn't tell *you*.

Similarly, as to indemnities, the 14 P's have no word about those. All earth it seems must bear the cost of the war that was forced upon it – a war that would hardly have been begun or if begun would have ended in a few weeks, if the U.S. had entered with the rest after the *Lusitania* was sunk. But I can hardly conceive that the nations will abide to be taxed for generations while the Hun recuperates – any more than I can imagine that our Dominions will consent to the "most favoured nation" clause[4] in their trade relations with these dogs after the war.

Hughes[5] of Australia has already opened on that point and I don't think he'll be the only one of the Premiers. Yet, all these points of friction might have been saved if only that egregious dominie had kept his stylo off paper, and refrained from lecturing both sides.

In the meantime the U.S. Armies before Sedan etc. have through sheer lack of organization had the devil and three quarters of a time.[6] All their discomforts and a large proportion of their losses have been *absolutely* unnecessary and are due only to the staff's incompetence. You will get ample details later but it's heartbreaking to have the boys wasted and messed about in this way. The material is beyond praise: but the handling of it simply awful: and a grain of imagination or an hour's reading of history, should have saved the U.S. army from entering Sedan before the French – even if it had been no more than a corporal, three poilus and a tricolour. We pulled up outside Lille to let a French regiment go in ahead and compared to Sedan Lille is nothing.

All this is my private grumble in your private ear and I come back to where I started – my enormous satisfaction in the Republican gains and your acknowledged return to the leadership – if you choose – of that party, which means that "politics" would not be allowed to interfere with the combined work before our two nations.

It's a queer thing to live through these days and to realize that we can't realize 'em. England takes her victories very grimly.

With every good wish, sympathy and affection

Ever yours
Rudyard Kipling

Notes

1. As *The Times* reported on this day, the Republicans gained majorities in both the House and the Senate in the election of 5 November.
2. The "fourteen points", President Wilson's plan for a peace, were first put forth in Wilson's speech to Congress, 8 January 1918. They aimed at a generous peace and at idealistic provisions for political and economic freedom, including a league of nations. They were at once the main point of conflict between the US and the Allies on the question of peace. The Germans were glad to accept them but the Allies did so reluctantly and then only because they had no agreed war aims of their own.
3. "Absolute freedom of navigation upon the seas" was the second of the Fourteen Points.
4. Wilson wished to get rid of the "most favoured nation" arrangement: the third of the Fourteen Points was "removal as far as possible of all economic barriers". I suppose what RK means is that the Dominions would not readily give up such trade advantages as they already had.
5. William Morris Hughes (1862–1952), Prime Minister of Australia, 1915–23, had been in England since June 1918 to participate in the Imperial War Cabinet and had been campaigning for imperial preference and the exclusion of Germany from the trade of the British Empire.
6. Ignoring the obvious symbolic value of Sedan to the French, General Pershing, on 5 November, ordered his American troops to capture the city. The American commanders scrambled for the honour and so created a very unprofessional confusion of troop movements as well as insulting the French. On 7 November American troops reached Sedan but were ordered to halt; the French, after all, were first officially into the city which had been the scene of their humiliation before the Prussians in 1870.

To John Powell,[1] 7 November 1918
ALS: Columbia University

Bateman's / Burwash / Sussex / Nov. 7. 1918.

private

Dear Mr. Powell

I shall feel very honoured if you care to translate my "Justice" into Greek.[2]
What I meant by

> A people with the heart of beasts
> Made wise concerning men

was a people with such an outlook on life as would be possessed by animals who had been laboriously instructed in the baser side of humanity and also the higher – a sort of were-wolf people in fact. (And it's curious that out of the Hun country comes the best and fullest story of the were-wolf who disguises itself as man or woman, begs for charity, or works on the trust of men and, biding its time by the fire or in the bed, at last kills its host and his wife and children. Every race betrays itself in its legends, don't you think?)[3]

I am no scholar so I can't get at the Greek word that I want but, if I were translating, I should lay the emphasis on *made* wise – i.e. educated, preached and drilled into this dreadful knowledge by the schools, the priests and the kings. The whole gangrene comes out of a false education which till practically a few minutes ago, we were loudly called upon to admire and copy.

I don't know whether what I've written has made the lines any clearer but if there is anything I can do to help I'll be very pleased.

Sincerely yours
Rudyard Kipling

Notes
1. Powell was tutor and lecturer in classics at St John's College, Oxford. As an undergraduate he had won the Gaisford Prize for Greek verse. Powell was one of the contributors, with RK, to the learned joke called *Q. Horati Flacci Carminum Librum Quintum*: see 5 December 1920, to Fletcher. RK's "Justice" was published 24 October 1918 (*The Years Between*).
2. Powell's translation appears not to have been published. RK authorised Powell to use it as a Christmas card (to Powell, 6 December 1918: ALS, Columbia).
3. This is the theme of RK's speech at the banquet following the award of an honorary doctorate at the Sorbonne, 19 November 1921. Arguing that "the folk-tales of a race never lie", he then presents the stories of the werewolf as "the forecast of a modern philosophy of Absolute Evil which has since been made plain in the face of all mankind" ("A Thesis", in *A Book of Words*).

To Sir Hugh Clifford[1], 18 November 1918
Text: *Notes and Queries*, XXXIII (1986), 180–1

Bateman's / Burwash / Sussex / Nov 18 1918

private

Dear Clifford,

By my early training blue books are meat and drink for me: for that's where you find all the uncut jewels. I've taken the record of the Gold Coast Regiment and that amazing – only nothing about the Hun is amazing – story of the Stolen Sacrament and sent it to a paper.[2] I *love* an administrative report and envy the administration always. In crelly[3] I've always longed for the Seychelles, to grow vanilla beans and improve the harbour facilities; or else the Falklands with a ship of my own.

I can't make out your road problem or why – I suppose it's local metal— the surfaces pound up so Ford ought to be grateful for the *chit*[4] you've given his lorries – half-ton converted F's I presume.

Now you've got to lay out your overhead mail routes. I've just seen the new Indian aerial mail line[5] – 36 hours to Cairo and [deleted] approximately, 78–80 to Quetta via Jerusalem, Damascus, Hit, Bagdad, Bushire Brendes abbas,[6] Australian extension not yet outlined.

And here we are in England – dazed and stupefied with the guts of Central Europe trailing round our legs so to speak – the whole shoot collapsed like the last scene of some Wagnerian opera.

We shan't know for many years *why* the Hun was let off his Sedan[7] on the West Front where we had him at our mercy. I suppose it was the Jews. But, humanely speaking, the Hun is down and out. Our folly may recreate him. So I expect we shall try.

The moral surrender[8] has filled our boys with most curious puzzled disgust. They *can't* understand the psychology of it all. I've got several letters from youngsters who were at the handing over of the Hun ships.[9] They all write as tho' it had been a personally defiling affair. We are whirled now, breathless, into an insane election[10] – rather like making a typhoid convalescent drunk, by way of keeping up his interest in life. The Army which did the work can't, for physical reasons, vote to any effect but every dam' Bolshevist can, and will. It's all too near to be believable: but for you and I who belong to the old, old days – doesn't it seem ages since your boy died?[11] When the youngsters were making the road over which these armies are walking to the Rhine, we feel the loss of our young 'uns more bitterly now in peace, even than we did in the heat of the war of the early years. Glad you escaped the peace celebrations. I bolted home from town and had my dark hour alone.

Ever sincerely
Rudyard Kipling

Notes
1. Clifford (1886–1941), colonial administrator, had served in Malaya, Trinidad, and Ceylon; he was now governor of the Gold Coast, and was afterwards governor of Nigeria, of Ceylon, and of the Straits Settlements. He was a prolific writer on imperial topics and of fiction. He was, like RK, a member of the Athenaeum.
2. I can find no reference to this story in the Blue Books for the Gold Coast or in the Reports of Commissioners for the relevant years. Nor does a search of the London papers yield anything. The Gold Coast Regiment is treated in Clifford's *The Gold Coast Regiment in the East Africa Campaign*, 1920, but that contains nothing about a stolen sacrament either.
3. Thus in printed text: In secret? Incidentally?
4. In this instance, apparently it means "testimonial", "recommendation".
5. This was perhaps the occasion of which RK writes at the end of *Something of Myself*: "Left and right of the table were two big globes, on one of which a great airman had once outlined in white paint those air-routes to the East and Australia which were well in use before my death." The airman is identified as Sir Geoffrey Hanson Salmond (1878–1933), a pioneer Royal Flying Corps aviator. In December of this year he made the first flight from Cairo to Karachi, following the route that RK outlines in this letter (*The Times*, 13 December 1918). There was at this time much discussion of the importance of air transportation to imperial communications.
6. Thus in printed text. Bushire is in Iran; for "Brendes abbas" one should probably read "Bandar Abbas", in southern Iran on the strait of Hormuz.
7. There was nothing to correspond to the abject capitulation at Sedan. The Germans were required to withdraw within their own borders, but that was not accomplished till after the Armistice. The British, however, got their main purpose fulfilled by the handing over of the German fleet (see note 9, below).
8. Presumably that of the Germans.
9. Officially the surrender of the German submarine fleet did not take place until 20 November, at Harwich; the surrender of the surface fleet was on 21 November, at Edinburgh. RK must refer to some preliminary meetings.
10. The current Parliament had already outrun its legal life by three years. A general election was announced on 14 November; polling day was 14 December.
11. Clifford's only son, Hugh Gilbert Clifford, was reported missing in July 1916.

To [Imperial War Graves Commissioners], [*c.* 19 November 1918]¹

Text: *The Times*, 28 November 1918

It was necessary to find words of praise and honour which should be both simple and well known, comprehensive, and of the same value in all tongues, and standing, as far as might be, outside the flux of men and things. After search and consultation with all ranks and many races in our armies and navies, as well as with those who had given their sons, it seemed to me that no single phrase could better that which closes the tribute to "famous men" in Ecclesiasticus: – "Their name liveth for evermore."

Note

1. The Imperial War Graves Commissioners met in London on 19 November, with the Prince of Wales, "very keen about it all", in attendance. On this occasion RK proposed "the Text for all altars in the cemeteries which is accepted" (Rees extracts) – that is, the text to be engraved on the "stone of remembrance", designed by Sir Edward Lutyens, placed in every British cemetery. The text is from Ecclesiasticus 44:14, the end of the passage whose beginning furnishes the text for "A School Song", the prelude to *Stalky & Co.*

To Dr W. S. Melsome, 25 November 1918

Text: Copy, University of Sussex

Bateman's / Burwash, / Sussex. / Nov. 25. 1918.

private.

Dear Melsome,

It's come at last: and the thing I find so bitter is that the men who helped to bring it about – your John Maxwell,[1] our John and the other thousands – never lived to see it. One feels as if one were just coming out of an anaesthetic – before things had adjusted themselves to sight and hearing.

The wife has to come to Bath again this spring or she won't be able to carry on. She, like all the rest of us who have suffered, feels the reaction. But the trouble is that apparently one can't get accommodation. I've written to the Empire Hotel asking for rooms for February. They reply that owing to their residential guests they can only offer us rooms for three weeks in January (the first week). This is impossible. Is there *any* way in which you can of your kindness help us? I know Bath is scandalously full of people who have chucked housekeeping and dodged their responsibilities for the war, but it is too damnable to have these people interfering with the legitimate cure business. Nor is it sound policy for hotel keepers to give them preference over the regular trade since the "residentials" will promptly abandon Bath the instant that travelling is made free again.

I've written again to the Manager of the Empire asking him for a definite statement of what he can really do. I haven't tried the Pump Room because it's too dark for an invalid and the Spa is too far from the Baths.[2] I'd be more than grateful to you if you could make or find a way for us into the Hotel this February. I don't suggest your poisoning anyone in particular, but short of that there may be other ways.

I'm desperately busy and the daughter has had the 'flu – no complications thank goodness. *You* are probably run off your legs.

With our united best greetings,

Ever sincerely,
Rudyard Kipling.

Notes
1. Unidentified: no John Maxwell Melsome is among the casualties of the war.
2. In the event, they stayed at the Grand Pump Room Hotel, 10 February–2 March 1919.

To J. H. C. Brooking, 28 November 1918
TLS: Kipling Society

Bateman's / Burwash / Sussex / 28th November 1918.

Private.

Dear Mr. Brooking,

Thank you very much for your letter and for the very complimentary idea conveyed in it.[1] To the best of my knowledge there has never been a Kipling Society in England, and I think it is best not to have one. Work, to do any good, must win its own way *quietly.*

> Yours sincerely,
> Rudyard Kipling

Note
1. For the formation of a Kipling Society. Brooking was not to be discouraged. On 12 February he called on RK at Bath "with proposals to start a Kipling Society on a large scale" (Rees extracts). The Society was not in fact established until 1927, over RK's steady objection that such a thing was unseemly for a living author.

To Sir Andrew Macphail, 29 November 1918
ALS: Photocopy, National Archives of Canada

Bateman's / Burwash / Sussex / Nov 29. 1918.

private

Dear Macphail

It had to be Ecclesiasticus – hadn't it?[1] And also, it is about the only thing of which one can be certain, in this world.

Conceivably what they fought for may be lost, stultified, jeered down and variously defiled in the ages to come: but certainly – and it will grow as our children get further from it – the memory of all that crowd of demi-gods will stand. But already my mail groans and sweats under alternative suggestions. But don't let McCullough[2] make it names. It's name – *nâm* – honour reputation fame etc. Nor, as I see it, does it beseem any man to use his own words in this matter. I've been away for a few days: and so has, and is, Elsie so the household is out of gear *pro tem*. You've got to come down soon though and consider all our miracles over the Pre war whiskey.

The sense of loss and a life missing becomes acuter when the pressure of war-facts are removed, we find: and so I notice do most parents. I've presented my two year old bull to the Devastated Areas Relief Committee and expect that, anon, he will be repairing ravages in Picardy. It's a funny idea some how: because, of course, we ought to have raided the cattle out of Germany.

I am very uneasy about the Peace Terms – and over the mystery of the Armistice and the desperate Hun peace-offensive. I suppose one can't get out of the custom of worrying. The Wet Night's a splendid piece of work;[3] transferring almost the mortal physical discomfort of it all to the reader. What was the case with "designation marks" that gave "two ounces apiece" – whiskey? I even hope so.

Maybe later we'll go a trip into Germany. Maybe too, later still, we'll find that our people will have to sit in Germany for a long long time. That's if we mean ever to get any of the expenses of the war back. But now we are lured aside by promises of superior plumbing and cottages with WC's for all.[4] Curious, ain't it!

Ever
Rudyard

Notes
1. For the inscription in military cemeteries: see [*c*.19 November 1918].
2. Not identified.
3. Not identified.
4. "Homes for heroes had been a universal promise during the general election of 1918" (A. J. P. Taylor, *English History 1914–1945*, p. 147).

To Sir J. R. Dunlop Smith, 21 December 1918
Text: Copy, Macmillan Papers, British Library

Bateman's, / Burwash, Sussex. / 21st December 1918.

PRIVATE
Dear Dunlop,

When it comes to business you can't beat a babu's style. The enclosed will show you what I am after.

It's a Major Tallents,[1] Irish Guards, aged 24 with double D. S. O. who wants an administrative job in Egypt, Mespot, or anywhere else (including Turkey) and I don't know whom to approach in the matter. My geese are very rarely swans, but I have a sort of idea, from what I've seen and known of the boy, that he is that rare animal a dark horse of promise. I'd be awfully grateful if after reading the babu's letter you'd tell me whom I ought to begin upon in his behalf.

We can wish each other Merry Christmas and a happy New Year now. Long may you and yours know 'em. Mine have finished.

Ever yours,
Rudyard.

Bateman's / Burwash / Sussex / December 21 (Shortest Day Anno Dom. 1918)

Graceful sir and Most Eminent Companion,

At present period of rapidly approaching dissipation of His Majesty's awful armies and consequent Necessity for all and sundry to *puckrow*[2] Civil Job. Your Honour shall not be astonished with any amazement to find me supplicating at Your Honour's Noble Feets on behalf of young officer of unblemishable ancestry, and also personal friend of My own as *per* under: –

Major T. Tallents, D. S. O. (In duplicate issue with bar attached and also I am believing one (1) M. C.) who is and was member of His Majesty's Regiment *Irish Foot Guards* but now commanding *No. 2 Company 4th Battalion Guards Machine Gun Regiment.*

This warrior have begun operations in civil life 1914 a.d. as Head Boy of Harrow but on supercession of Horrida Bella instantly forsook proposed University Career for Irish Guards aforesaid and have since battled in continuity without cessation since 1915 and accumulated several wounds but none of nature to impose physical limps or mental dittoes.

Surely to God, Honoured Sir, if Major at 24 years approximate age, such a child shall not be without capacities in leadershipping of mankinds and acquaintance essential administrative details of Life. Regimentally also he enjoys efficiency Reputation Mark I and personal Popularities. His family on both generations for some distance back into Posterity is quite the gentlemens and ladies.

Now his desire is earnestly to assist in Administration – subject to your kind Honour's assistance to put him up to who to ask – if any part, provinces, pergonnas[3] or teksils[4] *et hoc genus omne*, of Holy Land recently acquired, Egypt, Arabia, or Mesopotamia in Civil or Military or Civil and Military Gazette situations or employment officially, Honoured Sir Dunlops, I am of opinion that Arabia owing to ideosinkracies of Arab tongues and peculiarities of inhabitants is not so good for this Officer as Holy Land, Syria, Smyrna or Turkish territories, but in this matter am materially anxious not to hide these tallents under any bushels and from personal knowledge of same extending over four (4) years when he was leave-takings in England or in hospitals, can vouch for Character and integrity *plus* unusual endowments in Mind and such Intellectual things, &c. And now, Honouredest Sir; Question is who the Devil for me first to Approach on behalf this Veteran of tender age and so this shall be my excuse for impinging on your Asiatic Office and Kind Goodwill to supply me with outline of Plan of Campaign stating whether I drag myself before Footstool of Foreign Office (Egypt?) or pray to Indian Office Gaddee[5] (Mespot?) or whether some heretofore Uncreated New Department looking after Mespots. Everything now being in melting Pots and God He Alone officially informed who gentlemens in control of which. My path is beset with Thorns and Briars.

And if Multitudenous Honour kindly condescending furnish me with details on same, including names of Eminent Potentialities with strings in hands, so that I shall see how if possible this Major Tallents D. S. O., shall demobilize from Guards into Administrative Service, with possibility of Career. Your Honour, as in Duty bound, shall hear me praying through all Eternity for Your Honour's salubrity, Sanctity and Longevity,

and have Honour to be permanently

Yr. Honour's Attached Petitioner
Rudyard Kipling.

P.S.   If Civil Post of Administrative nature does not mature there is horrible chance of Reversion to Balliol College, Oxford, for Major Tallents which besides Derogation to King's Uniform as Undergrad, is as though Rose should shut up and resume antenuptial formation of being Bleeding Bud.[6]

Notes

1.   Thomas Francis Tallents (1896–1947) entered Harrow in 1909 and was Head of School, 1913; his elder brother was (Sir) Stephen Tallents, also of the Irish Guards and associated with RK later through film work for the Empire Marketing Board: see 10 October 1927. RK devotes a couple of pages of *The Irish Guards* to an account of the raid, following the Battle of Loos, in which T. F. Tallents was first wounded (Outward Bound Edition, II, 36–8). Tallents was afterwards prominent in the shipping industry as a director of Anderson, Green and Co., Ltd, and chairman of the New Zealand Shipping Company. He was a governor of Harrow School from 1943.

2.   To seize, lay hold of.

3.   A *pergonna* or *pergunnah* is a sub-division of a district.

4.   Thus in copy, for *tahsil* or *tehsil*, village or administrative district?

5.   Throne, or seat of power.

6.   RK wrote again to Smith on 31 December 1918: "You are a brick! … I fancy he's a boy that would do credit to a career and of course the I. C. S. is, of all, the best. I can't tell you how grateful I am" (ALS, Tyler Collection, Yale). But this prospect, whatever it was, evidently did not work out: Tallents was at Balliol, 1919–20.

To Lord Milner, 24 December 1918
ALS: Bodleian Library

Bateman's / Burwash / Sussex / Dec. 24. 1918.

private
Dear Milner:

I send you the enclosed,[1] which only reached me today, because Roosevelt is again by force of circumstance and character leader of the Republican party whose recent victory at the elections has forced, and is the only force which is keeping Wilson to a stronger line with the Hun and an easier line with us.

In all human probability R. will be President again[2] when W's term ends and, leader or President, he is the one man who can swing and influence the U.S. by his own personality without engineered Press aid.

He is as usual blazingly indiscreet and a little sore: but he does not tell lies and he is quite right in his contention that it was our adulation of W's "statesmanship" and our excusing of all the terrible delay that was called "statesmanship" which crippled R's efforts to help us, and to that extent played Wilson's game against us. Roosevelt hasn't got his values of British "statesmen" or he wouldn't drag in Bryce, Lansdowne and Co but otherwise he sees clearly enough what we have done.[3]

Au fond W. is strictly neutral to everyone except himself, and the Democratic party leans heavily on the foreign vote. But Roosevelt's people – and R. is the Republican party – have now the whip-hand in the Senate and in Congress and Wilson is afraid of what Roosevelt has behind him. In October Wilson was *not* afraid. Hence his attempt to deal with the Hun.[4] (I have other reasons for crediting R's statement in this respect).

I send you the whole letter because you will easily wash out what is immaterial and I think you will find his statement of his past naval policy and his general feeling towards England[5] – which I had to draw out of him – very interesting. What he writes and hints about W's change of attitude since the election is confirmed by a friend of W's who came over by the last steamer and with whom I had a talk directly he landed.

W. is now squeezable and anxious (unless he gets a flaming endorsement from us) and I thought you might be interested, at just this minute, to have, on good authority, the nature of his vulnerable points.

Please let me have the letter back by registered post when you've done.

Ever sincerely,
Rudyard Kipling.

Notes
1. A long, two-part letter from Theodore Roosevelt, dated 23–30 November 1918 (published in Elting E. Morison *et al.*, eds, *The Letters of Theodore Roosevelt*,

Cambridge, VIII [1954], 1403–10). RK thought it so important that he had it delivered to Milner, now Secretary of State for War, by Maitland Park, who had been staying at Bateman's: "Maitland to London for RK to deliver a letter to Lord Milner written R by Mr. Roosevelt on the American situation in regard to Wilson – and being important at this moment of the start of the negotiations with President Wilson here" (CK diary, 26 December 1918). Wilson arrived in London from the continent two days after RK's letter was written. He was entertained by King George at a state banquet at Buckingham Palace, the first such event since the beginning of the war. The guest list was overwhelmingly official and military, but Gilbert Murray, John Singer Sargent, and RK represented arts and letters. RK found Wilson to be "arid and first last and all the time a schoolmaster" (CK diary, 28 December 1918).

2. Roosevelt died on 6 January 1919.
3. Roosevelt wrote that "continually your statesmen, like Asquith, Grey, Bryce, Lansdowne, even occasionally Lloyd George and Balfour, would praise Wilson for taking one of the very attitudes which he summarized in his Fourteen Points; and again and again, when I was attacking those attitudes or attacking his neutrality, Wilson's defenders quoted with unction the seeming English endorsement of his position as to a League of Nations, or as to neutrality and the like" (Roosevelt to RK, 23 November 1918).
4. "At the beginning of October he started a private negotiation with Germany on the basis of his fourteen points of peace, all of which Germany eagerly accepted; his theory was that he could still fool our people with fine phrases and get them to accept a negotiated peace – a peace without victory – with the United States sitting at the peace table, not as one of the allies, but as an umpire between the allies and the Central Powers" (Roosevelt to RK, 23 November 1918).
5. Roosevelt denies that he ever depended on the support of the British fleet (as RK had asserted: see 7 November 1918) but agrees that "Britain's position is such that she should have the largest fleet in the world." He adds that "I have come out of this war with a greatly increased sense of admiration and good will to the British Empire" (Roosevelt to RK, 23 November 1918).

To T. E. Lawrence, 7 January 1919

ALS: Syracuse University

Bateman's / Burwash / Sussex / Jan. 7.1919.

private

Dear Lawrence,

I wanted very much to get a word with you – after we met at Doubledays rooms[1] – about your U.S. Asia notion:[2] and to tell you that the only American who could visualize it was Theodore Roosevelt. Today (we being shadows) he is dead[3] and the loss on all counts is not to be reckoned.

But my meaning is that it is to the Republicans – not to the Democrats now in a minority in both Senate and Congress – that you must look for the furtherance of your idea. Wilson's most human and most politic notion is to give lofty advice and return to his national fire side: and the men he has appointed – such as Davies[4] – Ambassador are, most like, of the same mind – against taking "responsibilities" in the face of a critical world.

But (you probably know all this) a good many Republicans have come over to keep watch on Wilson. I don't know their names but you will, and Davies' ear is to the ground to learn what these men are doing. That being always an Ambassador's first job. Incidentally Doubleday is in the Wilson interest, though friendly to Roosevelt. It might serve your plans were you to approach these Republicans *if* – which I believe to be the case – the star of Wilson is on the wane.

I have lived for years in the U.S.A. and though I have not been back for a long time I have a large circle of American correspondents. I had a very full letter from Roosevelt only last week[5] and I know from that the drift of what the Republicans meant to do, under his guidance, in Senate and Congress when they come in, with their majority, in March. Remember that then will be the first time that Wilson will be subjected to any political pressure from the opposition. Cabot Lodge[6] – an old man unluckily – but always in charge of foreign affairs in the Senate – is one of the most important men now to be considered in the U.S.A. This at least is how it seems to me. What says the perspicuous Lebíd?

> 'Strangers at the king's court come thirsting for booty. ...
> Our fathers held power as it came from their fathers
> We give Law to the nations, our promises bind us
> And what God hath given us *we* deal it equally.[7]

Ever sincerely
Rudyard Kipling

Notes
1. This was on 3 January, when RK "met Col. Lawrence 'again' in FND's rooms" (CK diary). "Kipling and Alan Bott were there, and I never heard more brilliant conversation" (Doubleday, *The Memoirs of a Publisher*, p. 255).
2. *The Times*, 27 January 1919, reports: "A proposal is to be submitted to the Conference suggesting the formation of a federation of all Arab States from the Red Sea to the Persian Gulf under the protection of the United States." Lawrence may have been responsible for the suggestion. He actively sought to achieve an Arab "settlement" and succeeded in becoming a member of the official British delegation to Paris. Lawrence particularly hoped to exclude the French by persuading the US to take over Syria and to support an independent Arab state under Feisal. He thus carried on a "campaign in favour of America cooperating in the East" (*The Letters of T. E. Lawrence*, ed. David Garnett, 1938, pp. 273–4).
3. Roosevelt died on 6 January: RK was "greatly distressed by Mr. Roosevelt's death. A friend of 25 years and a constant correspondent" (CK diary, 7 January 1919).
4. John W. Davis (1873–1955), newly appointed Ambassador to England, had taken his post in December.

5. Probably the letter of 23–30 November 1918, not received by RK until 24 December.
6. See 23 November 1895. Lodge was now chairman of the Senate committee on foreign relations, from which position he led the successful fight against ratification of the peace treaty and the covenant of the League of Nations.
7. From the "Ode" of the pre-Islamic Arabic poet Lābid ibn Rabī'ah, preserved in the anthology called *al Mu'allaqat*. I do not know what translation RK is using.

To Frank N. Doubleday, 14 January 1919

ALS: Princeton University

Bateman's / Burwash / Sussex / Jan 14. 1919.

Dear Frank

You were saying the other day that you wanted a Kipling "fou" for advertising purposes. There is one. Her name is *Katherine Fullerton Gerould* and she has written an article in the January *Atlantic Monthly* called "The Remarkable Rightness of Rudyard Kipling."[1] She seems to know her author tho, in this case, she has only stuck to one book of his and I think she might be useful to do the article which you were proposing.[2]

Best love.

Ever
Rud.

I have <u>done</u> the collected verse[3] (it's a hell of a handful!) and the copy has gone to Watt. It's all of 600 p.p. on the lowest estimate. The sooner it is started the better because *I must correct proof* and for de Lawd's sake tell your people to set it up carefully and *send me the proof in a block*!

R.

Notes
1. *Atlantic Monthly*, January 1919, pp. 12–21. Mrs Gerould (1879–1944), wife of a Princeton English professor and herself a writer of stories, essays and verse, focuses on *The Five Nations* as the book that alienated the "intellectual" and "liberal" public; yet, as she says, RK was "right about preparedness, right about demagogues and 'labor,' right about the elderly politicians, right about the decent British code, right about patriotism and the human heart – right about love" (p. 21).
2. Mrs Gerould's article is reprinted in *The Kipling Index* (Garden City, NY, 1919), a promotional volume put out by Doubleday.
3. *Rudyard Kipling's Verse, Inclusive Edition, 1885–1918*, published in 3 volumes by Hodder and Stoughton, London, 1919, and in one volume of 784 pages by Doubleday, Garden City, NY, 1919.

To André Chevrillon, 14 January 1919
Text: Copy, University of Sussex

Bateman's / Burwash / Sussex / Jan. 14 1919.

Dear Chevrillon,

Yours, of no date, crosses mine about *Près des Combattants*.[1] Peace congresses play the devil with mails.[2] I have met Wilson.[3] I pray that the Tiger[4] may swallow him but I can imagine nothing more calculated to give the Tiger indigestion. I think we deal with the Bolsheviks in the Spring – from overhead – and I do not imagine that we shall say much about it. We have so many machines that are only waiting to be tried. The Armistice stopped them when they were quite ready. Our Labour party is just now badly defeated at the Polls[5] and is making itself a face. What it fears more than anything is Responsibility; and now everyone is saying: – "You can cut off our light and stop our transportation. *Please* let us know to whom we owe these inconveniences". Naturally, they take refuge in long words and programmes.

Meantime 'tis curious to see the demobilized men joyously returning to their old stuffy town jobs or their gardening in the country. The smoking room waiter at Brown's Hotel – a sergeant of machine guns in the Flying Corps – has come back. He is not an imaginative youth. But all he desires is to "forget the whole dam' show". His views about the men who didn't fight are very coarse.

As to young Castiers[6] – it's very funny but it's very natural. The only thing that matters is your preface – but he does not know that. After all, if a man can get comfort out of translating verses in a Hun prison, he is entitled to his little amusement when he comes out. And was there ever a Gaul yet without a theory of Art? Let him do his experiments. So long as he doesn't put MacAndrew into a Zouave's fez or make a Moghsabin[7] of Sir Anthony Gloster. If you don't mind it, I don't, and maybe, in the long run he'll strike out a note for himself and end by being a poet. What did Allah make old people for except that the ungrateful young should practice upon them. I'd give a good deal to see your face when he explains to you – as he surely will – his theory of Poetry. I've just suffered in that way myself. I wrote to him strictly enjoining him to take your advice. Your simile about copying cartoons in colour would be perfectly right if the boy had had a better picture to copy.

Now as to what you ask about my "work".[8] I have an idea that you know what my game is as well as I do. You saw it, twenty years ago.[9] My respected compatriots have not seen it yet, which on the whole is perhaps as well. You know that all I tried to do was to open certain gates into new fields and to interest men who worked in each other's work all over the Empire. I shall not live to see the young horsemen who have ridden through the gates I have opened come to their own twenty five years hence: but at least I have helped to make men interested in each other.

But here is a curious thing. You might see if there is any use in it as a side light. The Hun – blast him! – with his usual devastating thoroughness got onto my game during the Boer war which, of course, was his first move in the long game against *us*. (And *we* were quarrelling over Fashoda,[10] of all stupid things!)

The Hun's first step, as far as I was concerned, was an account in a Swiss paper (that harlot of Europe was in the propaganda business then, as now) setting forth how an English officer and I were at a certain farm-house after a certain battle. Time and place were quite correct. It went on to say that we found some Boers *and* Boer women under a bed; that we dragged them out, gave them a few hundred yards start across the veldt and then shot them down with rifles![11] At the time, I remember, I laughed: but it reads grimly enough now – doesn't it? That was in 1900: and from then on the Hun began to mobilize in England and the U.S.A. – specially in the U.S.A. – a very cleverly worked intellectual pressure against me. The *motif* was that I was written out – used up – *mafeesh*.[12] I couldn't understand it because by the vulgar test of the market, here were my sales going up all the time, and here was this concensus about my being done. In 1902 I was rude to the Holy German Nation – called 'em in fact, Huns on the strength of the China expedition.[13] That got me a whole storm of letters from all over Germany most of them (and this is the characteristic Servile touch) pointing out my base ingratitude to the Kaiser who had honoured me with a telegram when I was ill in New York in '99!! That, I grieve to say made me suspicious, but, like a fool, I didn't keep (I hadn't the time, indeed) the mass of evidence that kept accreting, of my general depravity, unimportance and immoral outlook on this peaceful kindly world through which I was beating on a foolish war-drum. That was about the gist of the thing.

A few years before the war there was a general tendency in the U.S. to point out that war was obsolete, foolish and the rest; and among those who used this "fact" against me was a Columbia professor with a most tender regard for my "literary reputation". In a lecture, he announced that it would have been better for me as artist had I died in '99 in the odor of sanctity. That was taken up, especially in the U.S.A. as the note: and I got quite used to journals imploring me to have died, as one might put it in '99. The English crowd – I don't blame 'em in the least, I was in their way – echoed the idea and it's now very firmly established in the pro-Hun quarters.

But, when the war at last broke out in American one of the first persons removed by the U.S. Government from his chair of English at Columbia was this very professor who was so keen on my dying at the proper time. He was shown to be practically a Hun agent.[14]

Now this is curious: because rarely in literature does one come across a general expression of (in his life) the abstract idea than an author should have died at a particular time. *My* time was the Boer war and afterwards California, the Argentine, the Southern States, and here and there a Canadian–American journalist were agreed in this.

I only wish now I had kept the evidence with the writers' names and had watched what became of them during Armageddon. It was all beautifully worked and controlled and since it did me no harm I was much interested. I don't know whether it is worth while pointing it out – perhaps it isn't – but certainly I've caught it more hotly for what are euphemistically called "political reasons" than most men in England in my trade. And all the "reasons" trace back directly or indirectly to the Hun. I can't for the life of me comprehend why Sweden was allowed to give me the Nobel in 1907.

Lord! How a man does gas about himself when he is given a chance!

When do you come over and where go you when you come and how long do you stay? I ask because we have to go to Bath from the 10th February to the end of that month and then we are in town for a few days. Let me know your dates as soon as may be: so that we can get you down here for a night or two. The country at present is fluid mud, rain, mist, fog and frost but it can't continue in that state.

I have told Frank Doubleday, *our* publisher about *Près des Combattants* for the U.S. market.[15] He is now in France – Paris – where his address is c/o the U.S. Embassy. I told him that the book was good for propaganda. By the way – p. 136, you make two tiny slips: the only ones I could find: "*midships*" for "*midshipmen*" and "*middie*" for "*middy*".

> Ever yours
> Rudyard Kipling

Notes

1. Chevrillon's book of personal impressions of the war, Paris, 1918, with a long section called "Sur le Front Anglais".
2. Paris was now filling up with the delegations to the peace conference, the first plenary session of which was held on 18 January.
3. See 24 December 1918, note 1.
4. Clemenceau.
5. In the general election in December Labour received 58 seats against the coalition majority of 478.
6. Jules Castier; his translation of *The Seven Seas* appeared as *Les sept mers* (Paris, 1920). In the preface to his translation, which is dated from the "Prison de Magdebourg, décembre 1917", Castier explains that he has given not merely a rhymed verse translation, a rare thing in French translation from the English, but has aimed at retaining the accentual feet of the original and its elisions, "généralement prohibée dans la poésie française". Castier also published a translation of *The Five Nations* (Paris, 1920), this with a preface dated from the fortress of Spandau, March 1918. Castier made further translations of RK's work in later years. In 1954 he was made a vice-president of the Kipling Society.
7. Thus in copy.
8. Chevrillon was at work on his study of RK published in *Trois études de littérature anglaise: La poésie de Rudyard Kipling; John Galsworthy; Shakespeare et l'âme anglaise* (Paris, 1921).
9. In Chevrillon, "Rudyard Kipling", *Études anglaises* (Paris, 1901), pp. 155–246 (essay dated March 1899). Chevrillon sums up all the varied types of empire that RK has presented and says that they came together on RK's return to London: "à Londres,

dans la monstrueuse ville obscure où il s'isolait pour rêver et travailler, tout cela venait se ramasser et se concentrer en lui. Pour la première fois, ce vaste domaine interrompu, dispersé sur la planète, se réfléchissait en une seule conscience, et il l'apercevait, non plus comme une série de colonies ratachées à la mère patrie par un lien plus ou moins solide et qui demain sera brisé, mais comme la patrie elle-même, comme la véritable patrie anglaise, 'terre du palmier autant que du sapin'" (p. 235).

10. On the White Nile, the scene of a confrontation between the French and the English in Africa in 1898 just after Kitchener had retaken Khartoum.

11. RK retells this story in *Something of Myself*, p. 162. A clipping from *La Tribune de Genève*, 18 January 1901, among the Kipling Papers at Sussex, must be the account referred to. In it, RK and a group of officers are shot at as they pass a Boer farmhouse. The officers enter to find only women and children in the place, but on searching they discover a young man hiding under a bed. Without further inquiry, they make him mount a horse and ride for his life; then, at a distance of three hundred metres, they bring him down with their carbines.

12. "Dead", "useless" (Arabic).

13. In "The Rowers", written, as the headnote to the poem explains, "when Germany proposed that England should help her in a naval demonstration to collect debts from Venezuela". The poem concludes:

> "In sight of peace – from the Narrow Seas
> O'er half the world to run –
> With a cheated crew, to league anew
> With the Goth and the shameless Hun!"

The name had been applied by Kaiser Wilhelm himself in a speech to German troops about to sail for China, 27 July 1900: see the *OED*. "The Rowers" was first published in *The Times*, 29 December 1902 (*The Years Between*).

14. RK presumably means Henry Wadsworth Longfellow Dana (1881–1950), who taught English at Columbia and was, with another Columbia professor (of psychology), fired by the University trustees on 1 October 1917 for opposing the war. But I cannot find that Dana ever made the remark that RK ought to have died in '99, or even that he had anything to say about RK. Dana was the grandson of both Henry Wadsworth Longfellow and Richard Henry Dana; after his departure from Columbia he several times visited the Soviet Union and published on the Soviet theatre. He ended his days as a resident in and guide to his Longfellow grandfather's home, Craigie House, in Cambridge.

15. "Our" publisher because he had published Chevrillon's *England and the War* with RK's preface, 1917: see 7 August 1916. I find no record of any American publication of *Près des Combattants*.

To Stanley Baldwin, [19? February 1919][1]

ALS: Dalhousie University

Grand Pump Room Hotel, / Bath. / Wednesday.

Dear Stan

The weather here is of a vileness beyond words but your Daughter,[2] so far as may be, makes us forget it. She is, in all ways, immense – of a serenity and a joyousness and an essential goodness beyond words. And talking of words I know now what a "sheeted pig"[3] means. In an agricultural paper lately I saw that particular variety recommended to the small holder. Naturally, I asked Margot what it might be. She said she didn't know; Worcestershire not producing 'em. But this morn at 8:30 I was bidden to urge the maidens to rise. They sleep in a bed and a cot side by side in a minutish room. They do not wake easily, spontaneously, or even gratefully. But I saw what sheeted pigs are and how they behave when roused.

She and Bird skirmish about Bath on their innocent errands, varied by Naval Cinemas ("Surrender of the German fleet") to which they take me. If I may say so M. has salted herself all over – so marine is she: but she owns to having seen nothing bigger than a celluloid swan in a bath-tub or words to that effect.

We are *all* giving her advice which she takes like a Duck. Carrie tells her how to run Tompkins's Rents when she starts housekeeping in Cambridge: I enlarge on the psychology of husbands and Bird fills in any available interval. M. has produced her usual Baldwin effect on Bird. She was perfectly neat-handed till M. came but, last night – I merely said: – "Bird ring the bell" – she plunged at the wall of the room, swept off the electric lamp to the floor and all but pulled out the fire-place – in one lightning thrust quicker than eye could follow.

And talking of production Teddy Price has written me a letter all about his future and whether he shall volunteer for the New Army or not.[4] He pointed out that, it was possible, for a man later on to "meet the right person and settle down." Ominous! After which, he added "*A woman's natural instinct is to produce.*" It's a detached way of looking at it but it broke me wide open. This generation grows up all too fast.

Carrie is being conscientiously boiled to rags and does not go out. The bath treatment is meant to half-kill one, of course; but it is not pleasing to watch. I've got a return of my "curious old vatted" stomach trouble,[5] which is currently reported to be wind but sounds much worse – and we'd all give a year to see the sun for a week. But Margot is a great prop and stay – and I have yet to find the phrase that will get a rise out of her. When she is not with Bird she sits and writes letters to Morris. She is doing it now, with a pencil, I think, on the back of a book on her knee by the window. She sends you her love and asserts that she is behaving herself, and adds that she is coming home on Saturday in time for lunch.

Bless you old man.

Ever
Rud.

t.o.

There was a young parson of Wells
Who remarked: "Here is something that smells!

"As the Canon is out
"I haven't a doubt
"It's the Bishop and nobody else!"

Notes
1. They went to Bath on 10 February and remained there until 2 March, when they went to Brown's Hotel, London; on 23 March they returned to Bateman's (Rees extracts). They were thus in Bath on three Wednesdays: 12, 19, and 26; 19 seems the most likely date.
2. Margot Baldwin; she was just about to be married to Lieutenant Maurice Huntington-Whitely, RN (1896–1975), afterwards 2nd Baronet. The wedding took place on 2 April at St Margaret's, Westminster, with Elsie as one of the bridesmaids.
3. In livestock, "sheeted" means having a band of white around the middle, as, for example, a Hampshire pig.
4. RK replied that the questions both of enlisting and of marrying depended on what Price thought he could earn in civil life (27 February 1919: ALS, Lorraine Price).
5. RK had been troubled throughout February by the return of stomach pain; on 1 March Dr Melsome examined him to "confirm his theory that there is an adhesion of the liver and colon and this gives him his pain. He says it can be kept in order by medicine and the pills [RK] now takes give him great relief" (Clinical History, 1 March 1919).

To General Sir Fabian Ware, 22 February 1919
ALS: Commonwealth War Graves Commission

Grand Pump Room Hotel, / *Bath.* / Feb. 22. 1919

private
Dear Ware,
 Thanks for your letter. I'll send the correspondence on where it needs an official answer: but these damned mothers are too heartbreaking, sometimes, not to answer.
 The secret of journalism, as *you* know, being the para and the cross-heading, they're now panicking to know what will be done about the missing dead – whether their names will be recorded in the cemeteries "as a tribute of respect." When you send me the proof of the article for pamphlet purposes please let me know exactly, if possible, what the Commission want to do about these missing dead and I'll para and cross head it. If nothing has been decided on, I presume it will be all right if one says generally that the names of the missing dead will be recorded. They seem more worried about that than anything else and I want to make it quite clear to 'em.[1]

Having regard to the ineradicable human instinct of writing up its name somewhere, it mightn't be a bad plan, if artistic considerations allowed, to use the inside of the big bounding walls of the larger cemeteries as a sort of cloister, duly divided by buttresses, on which relatives could put marble, bronze, alabaster and compo memorial plaques and every other sentimental abomination after their own hearts. (Otherwise they'll keep on making a row). The effect would be vile at first but as the walls filled up it would all pull together.[2]

I've been writing to Strachey[3] trying to show him that, as far as inscriptions and letterings go [outline drawing of a cross on pedestal] is not equal to [outline drawing of rectangle] for advertisement purposes. I don't know whether he'll understand.

But a wall where people could spend their own money putting up plaques would, I think, smooth over the situation wonderfully. Even the suggestion of it would.

Hurry up with the government proof for pamphlet.

This is a foul town, full of wet and suddenly demobilized prostitutes. I'm sorry about the influenza and specially about Chettle[4] but we'll get no relief till the spring or strong March winds. It was bound to come and it's come along the old lines.

Ever sincerely
Rudyard Kipling

Notes
1. RK was at work on *The Graves of the Fallen*, published later this spring as an official pamphlet by His Majesty's Stationery Office. The question of how to treat the missing dead, of whom John Kipling was one, was not easily solved. In *The Graves of the Fallen* RK could say only that "the dead who have no known resting-place will be made equal with the others" (p. 12). In the event, the names of the missing were inscribed either on the main battlefield memorials (e.g., the Menin Gate for Ypres, Thiepval for the Somme) or on the walls of certain large cemeteries (John Kipling's name is inscribed on the Loos battlefield memorial, Dud Corner).
2. No private memorials were allowed in any of the Commission's cemeteries.
3. In an editorial in the *Spectator*, 1 February 1919, Strachey had argued against the War Graves Commission's plans for a uniform headstone and for allowing a cross instead. In the *Spectator* of 22 February, responding to RK's article on "War Graves" (*The Times* and other papers, 17 February 1919: uncollected) Strachey repeated his argument: "very many bereaved parents and relatives will not be satisfied unless they are allowed to have a cross as the actual headstone".
4. Major Henry Francis Chettle (1882–1958), Director of Records for the Imperial War Graves Commission.

To Brander Matthews, 4 March 1919
ALS: Columbia University

Brown's Hotel, / London. W. 1. / Mar. 4. 1919.

private

Dear Brander:

Sixty seven you may be and with gout to boot (which, of course, is where it mostly is) but I recognized your fine Roman hand from far off, and was glad to see it. We had just returned from a visit to Bath for "cures" – same as the Romans practised and, I doubt not, with about the same success. Bath is filled with Australians and New Zealanders which is quite natural: east of Swindon there is a large American contingent. The county of Hampshire was long ago annexed by the U.S.A. and I believe there is a forty ninth (or fiftieth is it?) Federal State somewhere in Lancashire. These things long ago ceased to move us but now that peace has come one can occasionally pull one's self back to pre-war perspectives and rub one's eyes over the Surpassing Madness of the whole mix up. And I once wrote that "East was East etc." whereas all thirty two points of the compass are apparently one and the same only more so.

I've been speculating – would you were here to assist – on what sort of effect and influence all this will have on literature and expression generally. For one thing Life has Fiction beat to a frazzle – so it's only a matter of selection. Has it occurred to you that never since the Elizabethans has there been more to write about than there are likely to be writers? For that reason I'm inclined to bet that our English fiction for the next five years will return to curates, roses and small talk. The lucky chaps will belong to the next generation when the picture has more or less retired far enough for them to see the general effect. But, of course, *any* minute may throw up *the* Dark Horse.

It's a queer sensation to be in and of a people who've been put through the whole mill of all available motion and have come out the other side – dazed, dumb, bewildered but still alive. It's rather like a nation returning to life after a long operation – things aren't adjusted on the eye-balls yet and the sides of the room look strange. I'm sorry for people who haven't had the experience – Hell though it is and has been. There is literally no one left of the next generation in one's own walk of life except a few of the boys who were sixteen when the war began and weren't sent out till they were nineteen. A young cousin[1] of mine is in the room now who at $17\frac{1}{2}$ years of age was a staff sergeant instructor to a cadet corps. At $18\frac{1}{2}$ he entered the Irish Guards: had seven months fighting including smashing the Hindenberg line, helped to occupy Cologne: ran a Hun steamer up and down the Rhine picking up English prisoners for three months, came home on his 20th birthday and is now demobilized! What the deuce must his mind be like.

II

private

And he is one of hundreds of thousands all fitted with new minds. But we old birds are rather lonely. There are no young men untouched and the next crop coming on is too young. Our girls too have been knocked out in every direction by nursing or by sickness or the accidents of war.

As to the anti-British propaganda in the U.S. that is of course a part of the war which was not stopped by the Amazing Armistice which let off the Hun: and we shall have to pay for our weakness for many years to come. There isn't any anti-U.S. propaganda here *except* – characteristically enough – among the Irish who, having stood out of the show, are now assailed by the gnawings of conscience which they mistake for political activity. I have observed that what the Hun agent hates most is being made fun of, and I recommend the practice to you on your side the water. We can't tackle 'em here because they do not work in our press, but you can.

You ought to come over – age or gout not withstanding – in order to use the stage set for the New Age and all the present actors not in the least comprehending that new perspectives and conventions are coming in. Even William Himself of Stratford might be a trifle dashed at the size of the theatre. I've been reading Him anew these days. He had it all – as he has everything else. You won't have adjusted both sides of your head to Life unless and until you come along and take a look at it.

I haven't had anything from Lodge about Roosevelt.[2] Things seem a bit hectic with you politically and I hope to live till I can see for myself whether the great and good Mr Wilson can deliver the goods. I've never before seen the principles of Chatauqua applied to the practices of Armageddon: but I am long past being surprised at anything.

Yours with old affection
Rudyard.

Notes

1. Oliver Baldwin; he had just returned from the Continent and called "repeatedly" while they were at Brown's (CK diary, March 1919). According to his account in *The Questing Beast*, p. 76, he was not demobilized until June.
2. See next letter.

To Henry Cabot Lodge, 15 March 1919
Text: Copy, Harvard University

London, Eng., Mar. 15, 1919.

Private

Dear Cabot Lodge:

I've been away from home and have only just got your splendid tribute to Roosevelt.[1] He was the greatest of your people's line of great men but, because he did not pose for the part men will not realize it till later. He was too big to be "discreet" as little men reckon discretion but, looking back, one sees how seldom his confidence was abused. It was his knowledge of men and his humour served his country at all turns.

Your Mr. Wilson does not impress one as being consciously humourous. It strikes people now that if the world had settled first with the Hun and had considered the League of Nations later, it might have been a happier world than it is: and if the settlement had included Russia – which is the strength of Germany – things might have been very much better.

But I suppose one has to pay for Spiritual Luxuriousness as one pays for the bodily article. The chief thing that is worrying the powers of Europe now is whether Mr. Wilson has authority from the U.S.A. (who one gathers from the Constitution, though not from his language, employs him) to deliver any goods in her name.

At the present moment, he gives one rather the impression of the Labourer who entered the Vineyard at the Eleventh Hour and spent the time in a lecture on the Principles of Viticulture and the Horrors of Intemperance, instead of helping to clean up the winepress of the wrath of God.[2]

If you could only come over here and see the situation for yourself I think you'd agree with this.

With every good wish believe me

Very sincerely yours,
Rudyard Kipling.

Notes
1. A eulogy delivered before the Congress, 9 February 1919, and published as *Theodore Roosevelt* (Boston, 1919).
2. Cf. Matthew 20.

To Frank N. Doubleday, 18 March 1919

ALS: Princeton University

*Brown's Hotel, / London. W. 1. /*Mar. 18. 1919.

Dear Frank,

Here are my notes on The Years Between[1] – dealing with the verses one after another. There may be one or two things in them likely to be useful when making up ads or choosing quotations.

I hope you had a less than usually uncomfortable voyage across. You must have been hideously crowded!

Ever
R.K.

Notes: THE YEARS BETWEEN

p. 1.[2] *The Rowers*: originally published in the Times 1902[3] at the time when Germany wished to embroil England with the U.S.A. under pretence, as usual, of friendship: by the suggestion that England should jointly with Germany, put pressure on Venezuela for the collection of debts due by the latter to both England and Germany.

Verses excited an uproar in Germany and were very badly received in England; but are noteworthy for the first use of the word "Hun". This was based on the Kaiser's message to his troops when co-operating with the Allied Forces in China at the time of the Boxer Rising. He urged them to remember Attila and to make their name terrible among the Chinese.[4]

p. 5. *The Veterans*:[5] anticipation of the Day which came seven years later.

p. 6. *The Declaration of London*:[6] The refusal by the House of Lords to abrogate the Declaration of London which set out that the neutral flag did *not* cover neutral cargo, was, under Providence, one of the chief means whereby the British Navy was enabled to save the world.

p. 13. *The Covenant*:[7] Gives the situation as it stood immediately before the outbreak of the War.

p. 15. *France*:[8] Written on the occasion of the French President's visit to England the year before the War. A fairly complete prophecy in itself. "That undying sin we shared in Rouen market-place," is, of course, the burning of Joan of Arc.

p. 21. "*For all we have and are.*"[9] Generally adjudged at the time it was written as "too serious for the needs of the case" but in 1915 it was realised that it was the truth and was generally used, for propaganda.

p. 27. *The Outlaws*:[10] Forecast in 1914 of the German moral collapse. "Their own hate slew their own soul before the Victory came." Illustrated by the way in which the defeated Hun turned and rent his own land. "They plotted by their neighbour's hearth The means to make him Slave," gives the Hun's whole mental attitude in regard to commercial enterprise.

p. 28. *Zion*.[11] The difference between the spiritual attitudes of the Hun and his opponents. *Really* wicked people are never humorous and never dare to stand easy even for a moment.

p. 35. *The Choice*:[12] The italicized verses give a new version of the Doxology – "Praise Father, Son and Holy Ghost."

p. 38. *The Holy War*.[13] Note how thoroughly Bunyan understood the Hun and the Pacifist mind. Used as card-reprint for propaganda.

p. 42. *The Houses*.[14] This was originally published in the Navy League Journal twenty one years ago; Defines the relations of the Dominions to England and their attitude to her and to each other as proved in the War. On these principles roughly speaking the Federation of Free Peoples is based – No talk of "headship or lordship or service or fee" but merely friend comforting and councelling friend. Noteworthy as a prophecy that fulfilled itself within one generation.

p. 44. *Russia to the Pacifists*:[15] Written more than two years ago, but gives exact presentation of Russia's present conditon which was due to the intellectuals and pacifists whose efforts directly produced the disease called Bolshevism. It is practically a dirge over a dead Nation.

p. 48. *The Irish Guards*.[16] This Regiment traces its descent with more or less accuracy, from the Irish Brigades who fought for France against England in Louis XIV's time: and at Fontenoy very nearly broke up the attacks of the Grenadier Guards. The recruits who fled out of Ireland to join these corps were generally known as the Wild Geese. The great stand of the Irish Brigade at Fontenoy was made at Barry Wood, and Gouzeaucourt (1917) was one of the many great battles during this War in which the Irish Guards took a leading part.[17]

52. *A Nativity*.[18] Alfred Noyes[19] considers this an extremely good poem: and it is eminently singable. You will see that the Christmas Carol in italics is interrupted at every verse by the bereaved mother.

55. *Endor*.[20] A direct attack on the present mania of "Spiritualism" among such as have lost men during the war. It ought to be quoted extensively in the U.S. especially the third verse and the last. It will provoke a great deal of protest and discussion. A line or two such as "Nothing has changed of the sorrow in Store, For such as go down on the road to Endor" might appear in some Ad.

58. *A Recantation*.[21] A severely classical rendering of an experience common to thousands of parents whose sons admired one or other of our English music hall artists who, it must be remembered, did more to keep up the spirits and cheer the minds of our boys at the Front and on leave than will ever be known. (Hence the decoration of some of them.) It is the only direct tribute yet paid to this body of people who were at heart public servants who put aside their own grief and losses as Lyde[22] did, and worked without rest

to keep the boys amused and cheery. The incident of the music hall star going on with her work – "for the boys' sake" – on the very night she had received news of her own son's death is not fiction. The first and last verses of the poem convey the moral.

p. 61. *My Boy Jack*.[23] Sung at concerts, etc. all over England, and next to "*For all we have and are*" the most popular of the war-verses for quotation.

63. *The Verdicts*.[24] This applies, both in the U.S.A. and England, to all the judgments of this generation on the men who are supposed to have done the most important work in the war. That is a question which can only be settled by our children who will be far enough removed from the dust and heat and recrimination of the present strife to see clearly. The first verse gives the moral.

64. *Mesopotamia*.[25] This deals with the hideous scandals of the Early Mesopotamia expedition as set out in the official report on the same[26] and exactly describes the attitude of all officials implicated – not one of whom has been punished or even permanently degraded for their share in the debacle. You will probably have something of the same sort on your side when all your investigations are concluded, which in all likelihood will end exactly as ours did. The fifth verse is the quotable one, as illustrating the methods of politicians in tight places.

68. *The Hyenas*.[27] A parable of newspaper attacks on dead men who cannot defend themselves. Useful also in U.S.A.

70 *The Spies March*.[28] Written many years ago but useful at the present time of influenza epidemics to show that disease is a far deadlier scourge than any war.

75. *The Sons of Martha*.[29] Published many years ago in a newspaper and for some reason quoted all over the world since. A study of the two temperaments that make up mankind – the people who at all costs will work, and the people who trust that other people will work for them. It bears out the other poem "*Things and the Man*" (p. 93) as showing that "Things never yet created things – once on a time there was a man." It has nothing whatever to do with "Labour" as some people say, but with all Humanity. You will see Mary's type indicated in the following set of verses: *Mary's Son*[30] which when they first appeared in a paper were quoted all over the U.S.A.

76. *The Song of the Lathes*:[31] The employment on an immense scale and for a long time of female labour in the munition factories of Great Britain evolved, among other things, a type of grim, resolute and enthusiastic women most of whom owed a debt of blood to the Hun, who worked with a sustained energy that was almost terrifying. Mrs. Embsay may be taken as a fair type of that class who turned, gauged, filled or fuzed the millions of shells that were monthly turned out. The quiet heroism and sang froid of the women, all among the explosives, when the air-raids were in full swing above them, was beyond all praise. The last verse but one "Man's hate passes etc." contains the hub of the whole proposition, and woman's attitude toward the Hun in the future.

p. 85. *Gethsemane.*[32] Your own boys can bear out the truth of this – and of the horror that overtakes a man when he first ships his gas-mask. What makes war most poignant is the presence of women with whom one can talk and make love, only an hour or so behind the line.

p. 93. *Things and the Man.*[33] Another much quoted set of verses though it only appeared in a newspaper. The last verse but one has the moral, which may be very hotly contested by those who prefer to believe in things happening in obedience to the Time Spirit or whatever they call it.

p. 96. *The Benefactors.*[34] Covers the whole theory of strikes and in the last two verses gives the end of them.

p. 100. *The Dead King.*[35] Supposed to be something in the nature of a new departure in verse form and has been applauded by the French for that reason.

p. 106. *A Death Bed.*[36] This balances "The Dead King" and is a fantasy of the Kaiser on his Death-bed explaining his views and principles (in quotation marks) to the doctor who (in italics) attends strictly to the pathological aspect of his patient's case. The rest of the verses are filled with a consideration of the different kinds of death which the dying man had caused others to suffer.

p. 114. *A Pilgrim's Way.*[37] Another quoted poem specially the last line "The people, Lord, Thy people are good enough for me."

p. 121. *Natural Theology:*[38] One of the poems there is likely to be discussion about.

p. 125. *The Song at Cockcrow.*[39] the attitude of the Vatican in regard to Hun atrocities throughout the war. This will make more trouble than any of the others.

p. 128. *Female of the Species.*[40] Well known and likely to provoke some discussion but based on the facts of human nature.

p. 135. *Epitaphs.*[41] Note specially the first
   "Equality of Sacrifice"
   "The Wonder"
   And
   "Batteries out of Ammunition."
The general point of these epitaphs is that England who was in the thick of the war had more experience than most of the different sorts of deaths that men *and* women died. Illustrations of this in "Unknown Female Corpse" and "Bombed in London."

The City of Brass.[42] Wirtten over seven years ago – gives a careful outline of the state to which Socialism reduces a nation and has the curious line, which was humorously discussed by the press at the time: – "Out of the Sea came a sign, out of Heaven a terror." One of the English papers[43] in 1911 published a "comic" illustration of them in the shape of a sea full of submarines and a sky full of aeroplanes!

Notes
1. The typescript notes enclosed with this letter at Princeton were substantially published in two promotional volumes issued by Doubleday, Page and Co.: *The Kipling Index* (Garden City, NY, 1919), pp. 37–46, and *The Country Life Press: Garden City, New York* (Garden City, NY, 1919), pp. 173–9. In giving Doubleday permission to publish the notes, RK required that they not be identified as his (see 5 June 1919, to Frank N. Doubleday); in consequence they could not be known to the bibliographers. The prefatory note appearing in both volumes can only hint at the truth: "The material may be said to be authoritative and to state clearly Mr. Kipling's own ideas in regard to this book, which he considers his most important."
2. The page numbers are those of the English edition of *The Years Between,* published on 10 April; the American edition also appeared in April.
3. 29 December 1902.
4. See 14 January 1919, to André Chevrillon.
5. Originally titled "1857–1907", *Morning Post,* 24 December 1907. The poem is headed: "Written for the gathering of survivors of the Indian Mutiny, Albert Hall, 1907".
6. *Morning Post,* 29 June 1911. RK's description of the Declaration of London is obscure. The Declaration, issued by the Conference on Neutral Trade in Time of War, meeting in London, 1908–9, defined contraband; it was never formally ratified by any country but was practically accepted by all belligerents at the outset of the war. It soon proved unworkable and was quietly abandoned. The House of Lords had refused to accept (not, as RK puts it, to "abrogate") the Declaration in December 1911.
7. See 15 May 1914. "The situation" was the Ulster crisis and the determination of the League of British Covenanters to take up arms if necessary.
8. *Morning Post,* 24 June 1913; the poem was then used as a preface to *France at War,* 1916. President Poncaré's state visit to England was made on 24–7 June 1913.
9. *The Times* and other papers, 2 September 1914. The poem was "extensively used as recruiting propaganda" (Lloyd H. Chandler, *A Summary of the Work of Rudyard Kipling,* New York, 1930, p. 84).
10. First published in *King Albert's Book: a Tribute to the Belgian King and People from Representative Men and Women throughout the World* [1914].
11. First published without title in the third article of the "Destroyers at Jutland" series, 26 October 1916 (see 30 October 1916).
12. See 14 April 1917. The new person added to the Trinity is presumably "the God in man displayed" or "the Spirit that moves in Man". The last two stanzas, in which these phrases occur, were not in the poem as originally published but first appear in *The Years Between.*
13. First published *New York Times,* 6 December 1917. A leaflet version, 1918, is described in Stewart-Yeats, *Bibliographical Catalogue,* pp. 326–7.
14. *Navy League Journal,* 28 June 1898.
15. First published in *The Years Between.*
16. First published in a limited edition for distribution at a matinée in support of the Irish Guards, London, 18 March 1918 (see 17 February 1918, to C. R. L. Fletcher). Livingston and Stewart-Yeats state that the poem was published in *The Times,* 11 March 1918; Harbord says 18 March; but it does not appear in *The Times.*
17. RK describes the fighting at Gouzeaucourt in *The Irish Guards* (Outward Bound Edition, I, 361–3).
18. First published *Daily Telegraph,* 23 December 1916.
19. Noyes (1880–1958), poet, playwright, and novelist. I do not know where he gave his opinion of the poem.

20. First published in *The Years Between*.
21. First published in *The Years Between*.
22. From Horace, *Odes*, II, ii, 22. The singer RK had in mind has not been identified.
23. First published, untitled, with part 1 of "Destroyers at Jutland", *Daily Telegraph*, 19 October 1916.
24. First published, untitled, with part 4 of "Destroyers at Jutland", *Daily Telegraph*, 31 October 1916.
25. *Morning Post*, 11 July 1917.
26. The report of the commission appointed on 18 August 1916 to inquire into the operations in Mesopotamia was published on 26 June 1917. RK was writing the poem on 1 July; it was refused by the *Daily Telegraph* before RK sent it to the *Morning Post* (CK diary, 1 July and undated July).
27. First published in *The Years Between*.
28. First published in *The Literary Pageant*, 1911, in aid of the "Prince Francis of Teck Memorial Fund" for the Middlesex Hospital.
29. *The Standard*, 29 April 1907.
30. First published, untitled, with chapter 7 of *Egypt of the Magicians, Nash's Magazine*, December 1914.
31. *Sunday Herald*, 24 February 1917.
32. First published in *The Years Between*.
33. *The Times*, 1 August 1904, subtitled "In Memoriam, Joseph Chamberlain".
34. First published in *The Years Between*; two stanzas, untitled, appear as heading to "The Edge of the Evening", 1913.
35. See 16 May 1910. I do not known what French comment RK means.
36. First published in *The Years Between*.
37. Three stanzas published as heading to chapter 4 of *Egypt of the Magicians, Nash's Magazine*, September 1914; complete poem, *Red Cross Magazine*, March 1919.
38. First published in *The Years Between*.
39. See 21 April 1918. First published in *The Years Between*.
40. See 10 November 1911; first published *Morning Post*, 20 October 1911.
41. First published in *The Years Between*.
42. See 13 July 1909. Published *Morning Post*, 28 June 1909.
43. Not identified.

To Frank N. Doubleday, 27 March 1919
ALS: Princeton University

Bateman's / Burwash / Sussex / Mar. 27. 1919.

Dear Old Man –

This is a letter from the heart – or, rather, that much more important organ, the Stomach, to thank you both for all the good things we found waiting us when we got back to Bateman's.[1] It was a hard fight for me to get my fair share – specially with the grape fruit marmalade – but I did, and this morning I cheered my flagging muse with crystallized lemon peel. I found it improved the style besides being new to me for the past four years. The raisins I got a lot of too. There are other things – in the bacon line I believe – which will presently be revealed to me. Heaven reward you for your Benificence.

Oddly enough Freeman (Lewis R)[2] R.N.V.R. attached to the grand fleet for propaganda purposes was dining here last night and joyously identified the raisins as Californian – he being a rancher in those parts when he isn't writing first-class stuff for U.S. syndicates. I expect you know him. I think he's a good man to get hold of. His "Stories of the Ships" just published runs splendidly.

We got back to Bateman's on Sunday and since then have been stoving[3] ahead wildly to catch up with arrears and tidy things generally. Our infamous British Climate has at last turned a shade milder and it's possible to work in the garden and woods. I've been chopping faggots till ten minutes ago. That is why my fist is so angular. A sick officer from British East Africa with wife and child is coming to our rest-house at Dudwell in a few days. *He* is rotten with malaria. *She* (we have just discovered) will be confined in a few weeks – a fact which was *not* revealed to us when he asked to come down. Well, Well! We've had pretty near everything except maternity down at the rest-house and if it's a boy it's worth the trouble. Also, yesterday, one of our own cows calved. So, as the poet says, "Spring touches us all." The European situation is punk and smouldering punk at that; Wilson dunno where he are; the Huns are smiling and our Labour situation is something quite lunatic.

So we all send you both our love and I rest and remain as ever

Yours affectionately
Rud.

Do for pity's sake let us know if Bok is on or off the L.H.J.[4] What are empires compared to that?

R.

Notes
1. From their stay in Bath and in London.
2. Lewis Freeman (1878–?), Royal Naval Volunteer Reserve, attached to the fleet as a correspondent, 1917–18. RK had entertained him at Bateman's at the end of 1917 (Bateman's Visitors Book, 4 December 1917). After studying at Stanford, Freeman travelled as a journalist in Asia, Africa, and South America. His *Stories of the Ships* was published in 1919. Freeman published an article on RK in the *World's Work*, July 1919, in which he took RK's "The White Man's Burden" to be a call for an American mandate over Turkey. In 1920 a limited edition of RK's "The Feet of the Young Men", with photographic illustrations by Freeman, was published by Doubleday. Freeman was, with RK, a member of the Ends of the Earth Club.
3. So the word appears to be in the MS.
4. Bok left the *Ladies' Home Journal* in September of this year, on the thirtieth anniversary of his editorship.

To Frank N. Doubleday, 22 April 1919

TLS: Princeton University

Bateman's / Burwash / Sussex / 22nd. April 1919

Dear Frank,

Your good letter of April 10th. (Fancy getting mails again in less than 4–5 weeks!) to hand and duly noted.

Like you, I am hoping and praying that the U.S.A. will come into the game to stay. It isn't as if she wasn't being offered every inducement to do so. Never before in history has a people been tearfully besought to take over the keys of the world and jingle them on her chatelaine. I hear now, indirectly, that there is hope that she may make herself responsible for Constantinople.[1] But the main hitch of course is that there is no sense in making a League of Nations if you don't put down an adequate force of police to watch the chief offender, and up to the present the U.S.A. don't seem inclined to help police the Hun border, and the Hun is the last tiger in the world with whom paper safeguards are effective. That's why I liked your interview.[2] Every Hun and Bolshevik agency all over the world are now doing their very damnedest to divide civilization against itself and, since not more than 10% of "civilized" mankind trouble to do their own thinking, they are meeting with a certain measure of success. After all, they have the easy end of the job. It's so dead easy to start panics and confusion and hell about generally.

Now, as to your new campaign, it promises splendidly.[3] I was delighted with the "Jacket" and more than delighted with the way you re-handled Mrs. Gerald's article.[4] The notion of getting Stephen Leacock to weigh in with an article is immense.[5] After all, my stuff *was* right and thirty years have proved it line by line, almost letter by letter. *Therefore* (which is where human nature comes in) it is often handled as though it were "journalism". The same man reviewing the whole output since '89 will call it "ephemeral" and then quote something I wrote a quarter of a century ago. I see the reviews of "The Years Between" in the English papers take this line sometimes, or lament (in the face of a cannabalistic Russia and India aflame!) that there is no "enlargement" or development of my "Gospel".[6] Naturally there ain't. If a man sticks to the second line of the first chapter of the Multiplication Table – "twice two are four" – he isn't likely to develop the proposition that they make five or three. If you care to look up some of my old Indian work in the old Tales – "The Head of the District"[7] – , "One View of the Question"[8] and so forth, you'll see that what I wrote then covers what is happening in India to-day, just the same as "The Walking Delegate"[9] (Day's Work) covers what is happening with your (and our) present Labour movement, and it is the same thing with "The Mother Hive"[10] (Actions and Reactions) which gives all the history and development of the Socialism that wages[11] in Bolshevism. The great advantage of my not having ever been in "movements" and having had my early education in the East, where the facts of life are a little more apparent than they are in the West, is that they enabled me to watch the movements without violent prepossessions. Alec[12] tells me that "The Years Between" are doing well here, but I don't think Methuen has sold 100,000[13] copies. I fancy it is about half that figure, but have an idea it will keep on selling like the others as people get to read it. The impetus of more than half a million of copies of books of mine already sold helps any new work along.[14]

About "*School boy Lyrics*" for the W.D.T.[15] *No*, I hadn't ever thought of it for the Edition. It was work finished before I was sixteen and cannot be supposed to be part of collected verse. Otherwise, a man would begin to be "collected" from his cradle. *The Muse among the Motors*.[16] No, also. This in no sense belongs to a collected edition since it has not been published in a book (the same is true of Schoolboy Lyrics. They have both been printed in the Outward Bound).[17]

But I do re-consider the position about Greatheart[18] and am having Watt wire you to use it. It has not been published in book-form but I think it will be useful. This does not apply to *The Scholars*[19] as I can't keep on throwing in poems up till the time the work has gone to press. It must stop somewhere and the date I had set was when I completed the copy sent to you.

Anyway you've got some hundreds of poems – between 4 and 5 hundred if I mistake not – and you've got to work a miracle to get them in. I bet you will too.

With love
Rud

Notes

1. Among the many proposals for governing Turkey was that it become an American "mandate". Atatürk's campaign for Turkish independence, successfully concluded in 1923, put an end to all such schemes.
2. At an official lunch given in his honour in London, 26 February 1919, Doubleday said that propaganda in the US was being "systematically and insidiously employed by the Germans and their Sinn Fein allies" (*The Times*, 27 February 1919).
3. The immediate object of the "campaign" was the promotion of *The Years Between*, already published, and *Verse, Inclusive Edition*, to be published in December. As well as newspaper and magazine advertising, the campaign included reprinting several RK items in the volume called *The Country Life Press* (New York, 1919: see 18 March 1919) and a new edition of the *Kipling Index*, first published in 1911; it presented *The Years Between* as "the result of the master poet's mature inspiration".
4. That is, the article by Katherine Fuller Gerould: see 14 January 1919. The article was reprinted in the new edition of the *Kipling Index*.
5. This does not seem to have been written. Stephen Leacock (1869–1944), English-born Canadian author, was a colleague of Macphail's at McGill, where Leacock was Professor of Economics. He is best-known for his many humorous stories and essays, collected in, e.g., *Literary Lapses*, 1910, *Nonsense Novels*, 1911, *Moonbeams from the Larger Lunacy*, 1915.

6. This does not seem to have been a very prominent theme in the reviews, but may be found in the early notice in the *Athenæum*: "The simple creed we know so well is held with the old unhesitating faith" (11 April 1919, p. 188); or in the *Daily Telegraph*, 11 April 1919: "These were his ideals thirty years ago, and they remain his triumphing ideals today."

7. *Macmillan's Magazine*, January 1890 (*Life's Handicap*).

8. *Fortnightly Review*, February 1890 (*Many Inventions*).

9. *Century Magazine*, December 1894.

10. *Collier's Weekly*, 28 November 1908.

11. Thus in MS.

12. Watt.

13. Doubleday's ad for *The Years Between* in the *New York Times Book Review*, 20 April 1919, states that "the first edition of the book in England numbered 100,000 copies, and the second will reach 50,000".

14. This is a very modest estimate. In the next year Doubleday was proclaiming that "approximately 2,000,000 of the authorized editions of Kipling have been sold" (*World's Work*, March 1920, p. 390).

15. "Whole Damn Thing", by which is meant RK's *Verse, Inclusive Edition* (see 14 January 1919, to Frank N. Doubleday). A note by Doubleday on RK's letter of September 1919 (ALS, Princeton), explains that he had told RK that an "inclusive edition" would have to be "the whole damn thing". They always called it W.D.T. thereafter.

16. RK was not done with this series yet: the first fourteen items appeared in 1904, six more in this year, and six more in 1929. The whole series was first collected in *Poems 1886–1929*, 1929, a limited edition.

17. *Schoolboy Lyrics* appears in the Outward Bound Edition, XVII, but "The Muse Among the Motors" does not. Neither is in *Verse, Inclusive Edition, 1885–1918*.

18. RK's memorial poem on the death of Theodore Roosevelt, *Daily Telegraph*, 5 February 1919. It is the last poem in *Verse, Inclusive Edition*, where it is preceded by a note explaining that "all the poems in this volume belong to the period of 1885 to 1918 inclusive, with the exception of 'Great-Heart,' which was written after Theodore Roosevelt's death in 1919".

19. *Daily Telegraph*, 29 January 1919; RK had sent off the copy of *Verse, Inclusive Edition* two weeks before this poem was published (see 14 January 1919, to Frank N. Doubleday). It was first collected in *Songs of the Sea from Rudyard Kipling's Verse*, 1927.

To Brander Matthews, 29 April 1919

ALS: Columbia University

Bateman's / Burwash / Sussex / April 29. 1919

Dear Brander –

Just risen from browsing through your *"These Many Years"*[1] and (premising that any human being who spells "through" as "thru" *ipso facto* forfeits his right to the League of Nations) I delighted in it and bless you for it. It's a wonderful record and every word is interesting from at least two points of view – personal and national; and I don't known which fascinates me most. All about the old Savile (I wonder what it's like now!) and the Rabelais Club,[2] Brookfield,[3] Besant, Pollock and the rest, has been reviving my memories which took on just at the close of that period. One feels a few years older than the age as one realizes the clean cut that the war has made for everyone here between present and past. I expect your folk don't feel it as much; but with us it's in everything and everybody, and every point of view, in every household. When the U.S.A. visitors' traffic resumes in the next year or two, they will find themselves in a new world. (And there's a story to be written about *that*, too!)

By the way d'you remember your perfect title "The Parrot that talked in his Sleep".[4] Never have I forgotten it but never have I found the tale till the other day when I came across a Parrot of great age and devilish cunning who was being sent to Belgium to help life in the devastated areas. London was unsuitable for him because he had learned to imitate precisely the warning cry of "take cover" which goes before an air-raid and had shaken the nerves of establishments in the kitchen. And when peace broke out, he had mastered how to call and whistle for taxis (which is strictly forbidden) and so he broke the civil Law. A Bolshevik of a bird. The police used to ring at the door and demand his arrest!

I read your much too kind review of *The Years Between*.[5] It wasn't stuff written with any light heart and the temper of the present time doesn't make for lightheartedness later on. As a matter of fact, the world is in the state of the convalescent who insists on trying to get up and do work when he ought to be at full length on a diet of slops. What people call the "new age", is for the present, very little more than the hysteria of over-fatigue. You can see it in a tired woman when, by way of rest, she begins to tidy up things and put bureaux in order. Only, of course, with the world, there is no crisis which, after tears, restores the temper.

However we must go on and cultivate what has been left to us of our garden. Your Mr. Wilson is a source of marvel to the assembled Nations at Paris. He means well and is devoutly earnest, and does it all for the best I have no doubt. (I've seen a nurse with thick shoes and creaking corsets reduce a ward of malaria cases nearly to lunacy by her ministrations – and she couldn't understand what ailed the dear boys.)

I wish to goodness you'd come over and let us meet again. Reading "These Many Years" reminds me of a hundred things that I'd like to talk over with you over a pipe: and, as I've said, you'd get a new experience which is a rare thing at our time of life. Come along and enliven the solemn halls of the Athenæum for a few weeks and watch a world emerging after a deluge! Meantime, all good luck and happiness be yours.

Ever affectionately
Rudyard

Notes
1. *These Many Years: Recollections of a New Yorker* (New York, 1917).
2. The Rabelais Club was founded by Charles Godfrey Leland in the early 1880s and survived for a decade. Members had to declare on oath either that they had "diligently read the works of the Master" or that they had "not read them faithfully" (*These Many Years*, p. 282). Saintsbury calls it "that most delectable of dining-clubs" and lists its members, who included Besant, Henley, Lang, and Walter Pollock from RK's circle (*A Last Scrap Book*, 1924, pp. 203–4).
3. Charles H. E. Brookfield (1857–1913), actor and playwright; a member of the Savile, and earlier a writer for the *Saturday Review* under Pollock. He was the son of Thackeray's friends William and Jane Brookfield.
4. See 2 January 1894.
5. In the *New York Times Book Review*, 13 April 1919. A review of RK's poetic career as well as of *The Years Between*, in which "he here reveals once again that the poet is a prophet and the singer a seer".

To C. W. Hodell,[1] 30 April 1919
Text: Copy, University of Sussex

[Bateman's] 30th. April 1919

Private
Dear Sir,

I have to thank you for your kind letter of April 15th. in reply to my letter to you in regard to some painted plates which you understand that I had painted for Miss Taylor.[2] Since writing my last letter to you I have not been able to recall the circumstance of having decorated these plates thirty years ago.

I am, however, very anxious to help Mrs. Hill in her present circumstances which you report, and I propose that you say to her that you have a purchaser, and that I become that purchaser, and that the price fixed be one that she had hoped to raise for their sale. The plates can be carefully packed and forwarded to me.

I trust that this will seem to you a satisfactory way of giving Mrs. Hill the assistance she requires in a way that will be acceptable to her.[3]

Very truly yours,
[no signature]

C. W. Hodell,
The Finance Trust,
26 Exchange Place,
New York, U.S.A.

Notes
1. Charles Wesley Hodell (1872–1925) was professor of English at Goucher College, Baltimore, 1897–1912, and a Browning scholar. He was now treasurer of the Finance and Guaranty Company of Baltimore.
2. The six plates in question, decorated with paintings of fruit and hand-lettered verses by RK, were made for Caroline Taylor when RK was staying at Beaver, Pennsylvania, in July–August 1889. The verses – "Apples", "Berries", "Grapes", "Peaches", "Plums", and "The Watermelon" – are uncollected but are included in Rutherford, *Early Verse*, pp. 460–2.
3. The proposal was evidently not accepted. The plates were acquired by the Chicago collector W. M. Carpenter, who "discovered" Mrs Hill some time in the 1920s and bought a great many Kipling items from her over the course of years. The Carpenter collection, after Carpenter's death, went to the Library of Congress, where the fruit plates now are.

To Henry Arthur Jones,[1] 1 May 1919
Text: Copy, Texas A&M University

Bateman's / Burwash / Sussex / 1st. May 1919

Private.
Dear Arthur Jones,

I have read and re-read your letter to the address of Mr. Fisher,[2] but I don't expect it will have the least effect on that authority. As you point out,[3] it is all in Jack Cade's mouth and Shakespeare knew it – as he knew everything else. We shall probably re-acquire that knowledge by ways more dramatic than anything that Shakespeare wrote but it won't be a pretty Fifth Act. Meantime one has to carry on as best one can.

Very sincerely,
Rudyard Kipling.

Henry Arthur Jones, Esq.
c/o Chapman and Hall
11 Henrietta Street
Covent Garden W.C. 2

Notes
1. Jones (1851–1929), the popular dramatist, whose greatest successes lay in the 1890s. He and RK were fellow members of the Athenaeum.
2. *Patriotism and Popular Education ... the Whole Discourse Being in the Form of a Letter to the Right Hon. H. A. L. Fisher, President of the Board of Education*, 1919. This argues that popular education should be practical education and includes a diatribe against "internationalism" in favour of "patriotism".

3.   At the end of his polemic Jones gives a series of quotations from Jack Cade's speeches in *2 Henry VI* as illustrating the demagogue's promise of "an International paradise to ignorance and sloth and sedition" (p. 268). Jack Cade was part of RK's local tradition: see April 1904, to Filson Young.

To Otto Beit,[1] 1 June 1919
ALS: Library of Congress

Bateman's / Burwash / Sussex / June. 1. 1919.

Dear Beit,

I should like very much to be able to deliver an address at the West London[2] at their opening meeting in October next; because in the first place I am very greatly interested in post graduate medical work and its development in this country for Dominion sutdents; and in the second because I should like to do anything possible for Jameson's doctor.

But I cannot pledge myself as to dates, further than I already have, till the end of the year. I am writing the history of my son's regiment[3] – the Irish Guards – and this necessitates my interviewing and collecting information from its officers whenever and wherever I can find them and involves my going to France at uncertain dates to cover the ground used by battalions of the regiment during the War. Time is the essence of this work because the men are taking up civil billets and getting scattered all over the world; and I have put aside for them and for the work of writing all the spare time I have till the end of the year at least.

I am very sorry but you will see from this that it's simply impossible.

Very sincerely
Rudyard Kipling

Notes
1.   Beit (1865–1930), 1st Baronet, was the brother and heir of Rhodes's friend and associate, Alfred Beit. He was, after 1917, a Rhodes trustee with RK.
2.   The West London Medical and Chirurgical Society.
3.   The invitation to write what became *The Irish Guards in the Great War* came to RK from the headquarters of the Irish Guards on 8 January 1917 (Douglas Proby to RK: TLS, Sussex). RK at once accepted and had been intermittently engaged on the history since then; he seems to have decided to devote himself to it early in this year.

To Frank N. Doubleday, 5 June 1919

TL and *ALS*: Princeton University

Bateman's / Burwash / Sussex / 5th. June 1919

Private

Dear Frank,

Your letter of May 23rd. has come to-day and I have instructed Mr. Watt to wire you in regard to the Autograph Edition Yes.[1] We did not understand that this edition was as proposed but that it was conditional on the inclusion of SCHOOLBOY VERSE and ECHOES.

Now I am plodding away with the proof[2] which I find a very stiff job, and it will be necessary for you to get someone of intelligence and with a knowledge of the poems to go over the work after the printers have embodied my corrections to see that the thing is really done correctly. In several cases they have omitted whole verses in the poems, and even a casual glance at the corrected proof as returned will show you what an immense amount of illiteral[3] I have had to deal with.

Your new wrapper sounds inspiring and the line that you quote I congratulate you on. I also agree to the 25 poems from "THE YEARS BETWEEN" being used in the way that you propose.[4] It is, of course, understood that the notes on the poems are not published as my notes.[5] I have forwarded this suggestion of yours to Mr. Watt and asked him to make a note of the business arrangements in regard to it.

I have considered with care Mr. Page's memorandum that was forwarded to me from Watt some time ago in regard to a kind of biography of myself and my works and ideas, but I do not think the idea possible. Every man has his own way of working and I don't think this is mine, and frankly I do not think, in my case, it would be effective. So, since you forward me these notions as they come into your head, I treat them as they appear, quite frankly, and this time I do not agree.[6]

I think you mustn't work the "prophetic" idea too hard.[7] It was a good one while it lasted but you'll agree we mustn't overdo it; and we must get a new one to take its place.

I've been busy working entente-work on the U.S. students here (ex-army boys) whom I've seen in large groups at Oxford and in London.[8] *That's* the material that gives best results because they have all discovered for themselves that the English ain't "hostile" to 'em, as the Micks and the Yids would have them believe. And, being young, they are sincere and impressionable. But the work really lies with *you* in the U.S.A. Over here when you talk to our people you are preaching to the converted. You must convert your own folk.

Wilson has tied himself into double knots at the conference once more.[9] Send a battle ship and take him home and let's get to business.

With love

Ever
Rud

F. Doubleday Esq.,
    C/O Messrs Doubleday, Page and Co.,
        Garden City, New York

Notes
1. I have not identified this.
2. Of *Verse, Inclusive Edition*.
3. Presumably RK's coinage: in printer's jargon, a "literal" is a wrong character or wrong font or defective font.
4. I do not know what "use" is meant.
5. For their publication, see 18 March 1919.
6. From this point on the letter is in RK's hand, except for the address at the end.
7. Following the lead given by Katherine Fullerton Gerould (see 14 January 1919, to Frank N. Doubleday); the notes to *The Years Between* in the new edition of the *Kipling Index* are published under the heading of "Rudyard Kipling Prophet"; an ad for *The Years Between* in the *New York Times Book Review*, 27 April 1919, calls RK the "inspired spokesman of his people" who "speaks with the tongue of prophecy – much of which has become fact – in his new book of poetry". It was perhaps all such talk of his "prophetic" power that led RK to write, in August, the ironic "Gods of the Copy Book Headings", reducing prophecy to a common-sense notion of consequences (CK diary, 24 August 1919).
8. RK was at Oxford, 22–5 June, and met "25 of the Rhodes scholars" on 24 June (Rees extracts). I have no information about any such meetings in London.
9. I do not know what exactly RK has in mind: Wilson had made a major speech on 30 May at the military cemetery at Suresnes which was understood to be a shot in his campaign to get the League of Nations accepted in the US. Nothing remarkable appears in the affairs of the conference itself at this time.

To C. R. L. Fletcher, 5 June 1919
ALS: Oxford University Press

Bateman's / Burwash / Sussex / June. 5. 1919.

Dear Fletcher

Many thanks for your letter and the enclosure from the University Press which I return. I've been re-reading your chapter and thinking it over carefully.[1] As I told you, I still hold, that it is too soon for such a chapter and further I don't agree with all your conclusions *but* I don't want in any way to interfere with the chapter or to hold back the history.

What I propose, then, is that you go ahead and publish it at the end of the history but head it as written by you – "Final (or supplementary) chapter by C. R. L. Fletcher." This will relieve me of any responsibility for views that aren't my own and will enable the new edition of the History to go forward at once – and may it be prosperous exceedingly and may you be right.

Many thanks too for the quotations for the missing men.

Ever sincerely
Rudyard Kipling

Note
1. Even while the war was still being fought, Fletcher had wished to add a new chapter to the *History of England* in which "credit could be given for the war effort, slackers exposed, and the Irish further chastised" (Peter Sutcliffe, *The Oxford University Press*, pp. 161–2). Fletcher was now again urging the idea, but the University Press opposed it. The new chapter was never published, to Fletcher's great distress.

To George Saintsbury, 9 June 1919
ALS: University of Sussex

Bateman's / Burwash / Sussex / June 9. 1919

Dear Saintsbury,

I've had a superior sort of Whitsuntide holiday. My cousin who is Financial Secretary (Stanley Baldwin) came down from town, very tired, for a rest.[1] *He* bagged the 2nd vol of "the French Novel"[2] first because he wanted to know your faith about Balzac and I got the first (not without heat) to see about Rabelais. Then he curled up in the house and the garden, and I browzed in my room and we didn't do anything else at all on Saturday or Sunday except read and compare notes and most thoroughly clean out our minds and our readings in the past. I haven't had as good a time for years – nor has he. I liked the order, I liked the expositions, and the clarity and the sanity and, above all, the immense results of your work all spread out for me to use till I almost felt that I'd made my own researches. (Well! I *did* once bite pieces out of the *Grand cyrus*).[3] Then I went on to the second specially Maupassant and was struck by the justice of it all[4] and the result, as I have already said, was absolutely one of the very best holidays that I had ever enjoyed, added to an earnest resolve (which I shall never have time to fulfill) to renew my old French readings. For this and more I send you my best and most grateful thanks. I'm in the black heart of an historical job – mere collatings of evidence and the like – and the French Novel came to my help and comfort. For this once more gratitude.

Ever sincerely
Rudyard Kipling

P.S.   Specially Victor Hugo.[5]

Notes
1. Baldwin and his wife were at Bateman's 6–11 June (Bateman's Visitors Book).
2. George Saintsbury, *A History of the French Novel to the Close of the Nineteenth Century,* 2 vols, 1917–19. The second volume was published in May 1919. This was Saintsbury's last major critical work, the fruit of his retirement.
3. A romance by Mlle de Scudéry in 10 volumes, 1649–53.
4. "He was certainly the greatest novelist who was specially of the last quarter of the nineteenth century in France" (*History of the French Novel,* II, 514).
5. Saintsbury devotes an entire chapter of some thirty-six pages to Hugo, finding him no novelist at all but a "marvellous, magnificent" exception (*History of the French Novel,* II, 132).

To Stanley Baldwin, 13 June 1919
Text: Copy, University of Sussex

Bateman's Farm / June 13 1919

To Mr Staneley Baldwin Esq. M.P.
Sir,
     Just after you got home that Evening I rec'd enclosed from yr Mr Retrench But I think it is Walton[1] but I want to know why I have got to get such Things and be Woked up to be made sing songs re Lones even if I do it all comes to the Sam thing for yr Mr David[2] he takes it all 1 way or the other and It All goes up the Bang-hole Sir and you can tell yr Mr French[3] he can go to Hele and Shak Himself befor I do him Pouemns about Loans Sir if I pay Tacxis it is a oatrag to mak Songs re them and no Reply-Paid answer either and to wit when I want to be brod-cast and pressed I bless God can do it on my Own for cash rates myself and will now suscribe Myself hoping This finds you as it leaves me yr

Obedt Servant
J. N. Shoesmith

I oppen to Add it is Dr Brigdes's[4] work to sing re Lones and hes Propper Jobb as wel as he is paid Butts of Marlmesbury[5] for doing sam annually.

Notes
1. A "victory" loan was about to be promoted by the government; as Financial Secretary, Baldwin was concerned in it. "Walton" is Sydney Walton (1882–1964), a journalist who had been put in charge of publicity for the loan. Churches were asked to ring their bells to mark the opening of the subscription; cabinet ministers were to tour the country in decorated trains; shops would display signs advertising their participation, and airships were to drop leaflets. No doubt RK had been approached to write a "song" for the campaign.
2. Lloyd George?
3. Not identified.
4. Robert Bridges (1844–1930), an MD, poet laureate since 1913.
5. A butt of Canary or of Sack was the traditional emolument of the poet laureate. Shoesmith has confused this with the Duke of Clarence's "butt of Malmsey" (*Richard III*).

To Major-General Lionel Charles Dunsterville, 9 July 1919

ALS: University of Sussex

Bateman's / Burwash / Sussex / July. 9. 1919

Dear Lionel

I wish you'd told me before you had been attacked by the disease of book making,[1] and I would have handed you over to my own agent who has done all my work for me for thirty years and never put a foot wrong. As it is, you've gone and tied yourself up with a man who is most difficult to get on with[2] – either from the publisher's or the author's point of view.

I wrote to him at once asking him to let me have a look at the book. He wrote back and sent it to me with the suggestion that I should write a preface to it.

Well, I took half a day off and read both the typed vols. I can see what sort of thin ice you've had to skate over and I guess at the whole chapters that you must have had to cut out or suppress. But, for all that it is a splendidly interesting revelation, well told, full of character, humour, observation, statecraft and (what gets home with the public) grip. You may say that you had splendid material to work upon. Even so, unless you had had the gift for writing, you might have bitched the presentment of the whole show. The story of the camouflaging of that 300-mile hole in the front with a few motor cars and a screen of lies and bluff is immortal.[3] I'm very, very proud of you. I knew you could write but I didn't know you could pull it off so well.

Now, as to my writing any preface – the crab to it is this.

If I know anything of you, you have probably made your own enemies in the course of your career but I don't think it's likely that they came of the caste that can do you much harm on the literary side. Therefore your book ought to have a fair run for its money. But I have made enemies (Allah be praised!) for thirty years. And, just now, they are pretty thick upon the ground inasmuch as neither R.C.'s, Irish, Jews, "labour", socialists or Liberalism at large are penetrated with any great love for me. (If they were my work since 1890 would have been a failure).

Consequently, were I to write a preface to your book you'd be more than likely to draw a lot of fire which would be meant for me. Any man who wanted to get his knife into me would begin by explaining to the public that a book I gave a chit to must be wickedly militaristic, bloody and so forth. (Remember, that a large section of these people in England haven't learned anything from the war.)

Now, as things stand at present, particularly with regard to the Bolsheviks, that sort of thing is just what I do *not* want to happen to the book. So I won't write any preface – much as Heinemann or any other publisher would like me to do it. I have sent the book back to Colles without comment. When it comes out I'll do what I can to have it properly reviewed in certain quarters.[4]

The only suggestion I venture to make is that you might give us more anecdotes about the mentality of the Persian who is the same now as he was in the days of *Hajji-Baba,*[5] to which your book is a not unworthy pendant. Give us more, too, if you can, about the Bolshevik with his collar and pen and the dirt under his fingernails; and hint more clearly at the ghastly confusion of the whole affair and the divided councils that added to the mess.

Your young nephew[6] has been writing too. I don't think that he does it badly either but I only told him in general terms to go on and trust to his own cheek. I think he must be the man I met as a boy in my first visit to the old Coll when the prep-school was still flourishing up the hill. I identified him then as a Dunsterville by the way he wore his flannels!

I'm as busy as the Devil in a gale of wind at all sorts of jobs that don't seem to matter much. Nothing matters much really when one has lost one's only son. It wipes the meaning out of things. However, the war is officially over which means that it has only gone underground where it is waged more ferociously than before.

This is a cold, grey July day, temp. 55° and a raw S.W. blowing. No. I have *not* forgotten the Indian hot weather and even at this distance I can smell Agra in July[7] – *Kus-Kus,*[8] hot wind and the smell of the dust on the Mall. Good luck old man.

Ever affectionately
Rudyard

Notes
1. *The Adventures of Dunsterforce*, 1920.
2. William Morris Colles, literary agent: see [early August 1895]. "He had difficulties with all the writers whose dealings with him are known in any detail – Arnold Bennett, Eden Phillpotts, Murray Gilchrist, and Somerset Maugham" (James Hepburn, *The Author's Empty Purse and the Rise of the Literary Agent*, 1968, p. 56).
3. Dunsterville's mission was to reorganise the scattered Russian and Armenian units around Tiflis in order to meet the Turkish advance to Baku on the Caspian. He was unable to do this, but "by a kind of moral camouflage, the original party of twelve officers and forty-one men filled the gap left in North Persia by the evacuating Russians on 300 miles of road, and entirely checked all enemy enterprise on this line" (*Adventures of Dunsterforce*, p. 3).
4. The two London papers edited by RK's friends both published enthusiastic reviews on the book's publication in April 1920: "a fascinating narrative of adventure, brightened with brilliant character sketches and amusing anecdotes" (*Morning Post*, 12 April 1920); "The hero of 'Stalky and Co.' has fully lived up to his early promise as a leader of men" (*Daily Express*, 12 April 1920).
5. *The Adventures of Hajji Baba of Ispahan*, by James Justinian Morier, 1824.
6. There is no other Dunsterville in the *OUSC Register;* the nephew in question must have been the child of one of Dunsterville's five sisters. I have not succeeded in identifying him.
7. At the end of 1918 Dunsterville had been appointed commander of the Agra Brigade (*Stalky's Reminiscences*, p. 287). Agra is, according to a line RK quotes in "Home" (*Civil and Military Gazette*, 25 December 1891), "the hottest town in all this land of Ind."
8. A grass whose roots are used in cooling screens called "tatties" ("thermantidotes") in India.

To General E. M. Maitland,[1] 15 July 1919
ALS: Dalhousie University

Bateman's / Burwash / Sussex / July. 15. 1919.

Dear General Maitland:

The letter that you so kindly "flew" over for me in R.34. reached me from New York at exactly the same time as a letter mailed in London on July 10th.[2]

May I add my mite to the world-wide chorus of wonder and congratulation that has greeted R.34's passage? Later on, I suppose, we shall begin to realize that it was the most significant event of the century: but, at present, after the fashion of the English, the thing has been done so quietly that it is accepted, apparently, as part of the natural order of life.

I am sending you with this, if you will accept it, a book of yarns which contains a story of a dirigible a few years from now. I was pleased to see that

R. 34 hit Trinity Bay on her outward passage exactly as my "postal packet" did.[3]

Ever sincerely yours
Rudyard Kipling

Notes

1. Brigadier-General Edward Maitland (1880–1921), a pioneer in the development of lighter-than-air flight, was "Chief Observer" on the British dirigible R34 on its flight across the Atlantic and back, 2–13 July 1919. This was the first such flight ever made, though a west–east Atlantic crossing had been made in an aeroplane by Brown and Alcock in June 1919. Carrington writes: "When the first Atlantic flight was achieved, by the British airship 'R.34' in 1919, the crew took with them a single book, *Traffics and Discoveries* [i.e. *Actions and Reactions*] so that they could refer to his story 'With the Night Mail'. Then, autographed by each member of the crew, the book was presented to the author" (*Kipling*, p. 453). When Maitland's *Log of H.M.A. R34* came out in 1921 it was prefaced by a letter from RK (see 26 November 1920). Maitland died in the next year in the crash of the R38.
2. The R34 made the return trip in 85 hours, carrying a 25-pound sack of mail from New York (*The Times*, 11 July 1919).
3. "With the Night Mall", p. 137: "Westward, where no planet should rise, the triple verticals of Trinity Bay (we keep still to the Southern route) make a low-lifting haze." Trinity Bay is on the south- east corner of Newfoundland.

To Louisa Baldwin 19 [July][1] 1919
ALS: Dalhousie University

Bateman's / Burwash / Sussex / 19. Jun. 1919

Dear Aunt Louie

The tale is of the simplest[2] but interesting as giving the angle of an outsider's point of view and his estimate of Stan's personal magnetism.

Allah, for His own purposes, has created a Pig called Mond[3] Head of the Public Works and an 'Ebrew whose mere voice and presence is enough to put up the backs of any and every committee that he presides over. Consequently, when Mond is trying to get anything done or passed on a parliamentary committee he – just doesn't. That's all. Consequently, business is hung up and friction develops; specially when there is any question of the relations between the Board of Works and the Treasury.

Well, the story as I got it, was of a particularly dead deadlock between Mond and one of his Committees over some branch of Treasury accounts. "And then" said my informant – "we send for Baldwin if we can get him." It appears that Stan turns up in response to an S.O.S. signal, smiles upon the assembly, explains the situation in that wonderful voice of his, and smooths the whole show out, on his personal popularity: tells exactly what the Treasury would like to be done and – done it is! –

The tale was embellished with all sorts of Parliamentary detail which I don't understand but I have given you the substance of it: but it showed the power of the man and the interesting thing is the command over the House that that power gives him and it ought to take him, as I said, very very far.

We got through "Peace" day[4] all right and all the servants went out for the day to the sports and left us alone.

Ever lovingly
Ruddy

Notes
1. RK has written June but internal evidence makes July certain.
2. RK had written to his Aunt Louisa on 3 July saying, apropos of Stanley Baldwin, "I'll tell you a tale someday when we meet that will make you proud" (ALS, Dalhousie).
3. Sir Alfred Mond (1868–1930), afterwards 1st Baron Melchett, the head of those enterprises later consolidated as Imperial Chemical Industries, Ltd, was Liberal MP, 1904; 1910–23; 1924–8; First Commissioner of Works, 1916–21; Minister of Health, 1921–2. The *DNB* calls him "blunt, direct, sometimes rather blustering, and occasionally distinctly ill-mannered". He served with RK on the War Graves Commission.
4. 19 July was declared a bank holiday for the celebration of peace following the signature of the Treaty of Versailles on 28 June. In London there was a parade of Allied troops, illumination of public buildings, and a choral performance in Hyde Park followed by fireworks.

To [Osmund Airy],[1] 21 August 1919

ALS: Robert H. Taylor Library, Princeton University

Bateman's / Burwash / Sussex / Aug. 21. 1919.

private

Dear Doctor Airey,

I have received this morning your more than kind letter and will go through the points in order.

(1) As to *Mahbub* and *Kim*:[2] Mahbub was deliberately testing Kim's temper and fidelity by suggesting to Creighton that Kim should be made an orderly or soldier – this on the heels of Kim's loudly expressed detestation

of that work. (Hence Kim's vision of "barracks, schools and barracks again,") and his wrath that Mahbub should be talking in this strain to the very Sahib to whom he, Kim, had delivered the war-waking letter at Umballa. And yet Mahbub was telling Creighton as plainly as possible that this very boy in English uniform had been that very "low-caste Hindu boy" who had delivered the letter. This Kim, in his rage and fear, did not understand. He knew Creighton was the Sahib of the letter, but Creighton was looking at him "without a glimmer of recognition." He refrained himself from crying aloud: – "I was the boy in the garden at Umballa and a servant of your mysteries, Sahib and lo! this Afghan son of shame, who himself employed me in the matter, now wishes to hand me over to be a common white soldier!"

That is my explanation of point I. Kim might have appealed from the agent to the principal.

(2) Sitabhai and her child.[3] Kate's experiences in the Zenanas had shown her, what it shows all women doctors, that the childless wife of a king or an important man, or even of an ordinary citizen, is a little too prone to poison the child of her fruitful co-wife. (This by the way, as a Muhammedan friend of mine once told me, makes polygamy very interesting.) *A fortiori* a dispute between two Queens one favorite and one despised, – each with a child capable of succeeding – was, as Kate knew, almost certain to be complicated by attempts to poison. Nick tells her so after the Queen has sent a message to the same effect and she "already knew" what hate meant in the palace. So much for point II.

3. *0 Neil of the Black Tyrone.* It is quite true that in The Main Guard Mulvaney carefully distinguishes between the Ould and the Black Tyron.[4] At this distance, for the Ballad of Boh da Thone was written in 1889[5] – it looks to me like what is vulgarly called "dam' carelessness": though I see that in my Service Edition Mulvaney alludes to Crook as "him that I told you that tale of when he was in Burma." And there is also a footnote

> "Now first of the foemen of Boh Da Thone
> Was Captain O'Neil of the Black Tyrone."

All this, seems to me an attempt to pull together a piece of scamped work though, to any one but yourself, I would have pointed out that Crook, like M. himself, might have exchanged from the Tyrone into the Old. But alas! Even in fiction truth is the truth and I must have drawn in Crook for the Ballad of Boh da Thone without thinking of his "former rank and service."

And that is point III.

If this is of any service or interest to you it is I who am in your debt.

Very sincerely
Rudyard Kipling.

Notes
1. I conjecture that the "Doctor Airey" of this letter is Osmund Airy (1845–1928), an Inspector of Schools, author and editor of historical works, and an LL.D of St Andrews.
2. The reference is to chapter 6 of *Kim* pp. 153–4, the scene, full of indirections, in which Mahbub Ali introduces Kim to Creighton in a way that Kim perceives as "deadly insult" added to "deadlier injury".
3. At the end of chapter 9 of *The Naulahka* the Maharaj Kunwar, a child, delivers a cryptic message from his mother to Kate and Tarvin. Tarvin interprets the message to mean that Kate should look after the child: "Kate began to understand a little. Everything was possible in that awful palace, even child-murder. She had already guessed the hate that lives between childless and mother queens" (p. 121). The phrase "Sitabhai and her child" is a little confusing, since it is not Sitabhai's child that is in question but the child of a rival.
4. In "With the Main Guard", pp. 58–9, Mulvaney says that he was in the Black Tyrone regiment before coming over to "the Ould Rig'mint", in which Captain O'Neill served. Mulvaney then (p. 60) identifies O'Neill – "Old Crook" – as "him that I tould ye that tale av whin he was in Burma", and this reference is accompanied by a footnote citing two lines from "The Ballad of Boh Da Thone":

> Now first of the foemen of Boh Da Thone
> Was Captain O'Neil of the Black Tyrone.

RK has thus put O'Neill (or O'Neil) in two different regiments. The footnote that creates the confusion does not appear in the first edition of *Soldiers Three*.
5. "The Ballad of Boh Da Thone" was first published in the *Week's News*, 1 September 1888. "With the Main Guard" appeared in the *Week's News*, 4 August 1888.

To Dr Vaughan Bateson, 26 August 1919

Text: Composite of copies at Dalhousie, Kipling Society, and Texas A&M

"Bateman's" Burwash, Sussex. / 26th. Aug. 1919.

PRIVATE
Care Frater Vaughan Bateson,

In the first place forgive typewriting which is better than my proper hand of write. In the second, accept my heartiest congratulations at the end of your Odyssey.[1] I knew you were out somewhere East and I read of you in Palestine, but I had no notion you had held so much of "the gorgeous East in fee."[2] Now I look for a series of lectures before the College – specially on the Eastern Oases.

As to "THEY" I will try to answer your questions. You will observe that only those who had lost children themselves – i.e., the butler, who accepted the whole situation as quite natural – saw the childen whom the blind woman's longing had drawn to her. The draggle-tailed wench also "walked in the wood" – that is to say, saw the shade of her child, after she had lost it.

Evidently there was an atmosphere around the blind woman which made it possible for these things to happen to people who had lost; and the whole house and grounds were saturated with that atmosphere.

The farmer sweated with terror because he knew that, from his point of view, there was something wrong with this house full of ghosts – he had probably heard about he children's shades and did not like being there between lights. It was wrong for the man to return to the house because he had really lost his child and it was not his business to continue dabbling among the shadows evoked by the blind woman. But the whole tale is rather difficult to disentangle and I think it is susceptible of several interpretations according as the reader has or has not undergone certain experiences. I don't know that I should apply the word "clairvoyant" to any of the characters; as, in my mind, that always seems to go with "mediums" and suchlike. This is as near as I can get to an explanation and I hope it may be useful to you.

The last five years don't make people any younger, but they undoubtedly keep one busy; and I very greatly envy and admire you for all that you have gone through.

Fraternally always,
Rudyard Kipling.

Dr. Vaughan Bateson,
  Sonada,
    675 Manchester Road,
      Bradford,
        Yorks.

Notes
1. Bateson (see 29 July 1909) had served in the Gallipoli, Mesopotamia, and Palestine campaigns. He was medical officer of the 2/10th Battalion, the Middlesex Regiment, and commanded the 1st Mobile RAMC Convoy, Eastern Expeditionary Force. He was severely wounded in the shoulder during the Palestine campaign.
2. Wordsworth, "On the Extinction of the Venetian Republic".

To Frank N. Doubleday, 27 August 1919

ALS: Princeton University

*Bateman's / Burwash / Sussex /*Aug 27. 1919

Dear Frank

"The Years Between," Outward Bound[1] has just come – ever so many thanks. I don't notice save on comparison, the change in the paper of the covering and it seems to me every whit as beautiful a turn-out as its prede-cessors. I don't think that the Outward Bound *qua* edition will ever be beaten.

Things here are pretty much as you are except that I believe our Government has a fairly accurate knowledge of the criminal and treasonable relations of certain of our Labour "leaders" and their connection with the Hun and the Bolshie. I've been hearing some very interesting details about this of late which are not quite the thing to write down.

Meantime, everything possible is being done to poison the relations between you and us and the R.C.'s are really working like the Devil their master. I see only *one* way of stopping the fuss which is for the U.S.A. to come into the game *via* either Constantinople or Armenia. Once in, national pride in achievement would cure the flood of mean and irrelevant bosh that the Hun is putting up but so long as the U.S.A. has retired from the field into her own woodchuck hole just so long will she be liable to being infected by sus-picion and small thoughts.

I have tried to get "Ed Baker"[2] into shape for the cause, but the dam' thing doesn't hit hard enough yet. If I ever get it to my liking I'll send it along. *Please*, remember what I tried to say to you about "guying" the Hun agencies wherever possible. They *do* hate it. We're trying it now in some of the papers.

There isn't any news except that Carrie is better than she has been for some time and that we hope to get away for a holiday in the car at the end of the month to Scotland;[3] that we have got our oats in and a cow is due to calve and that we are awfully busy with small affairs generally.

Elsie is away on a visit to the Bonar Laws or she'd join us in the love we send you both.

Write me from time to time about the situation. It's the thing I'm keenest on.

Ever affectionately
Rud

P.S.   Isn't it about time that the World's Work explained that Page was one of the biggest Americans since Lincoln.[4] We shan't get his full record for about 25 years but there is enough available to give something like the size of the man.

Notes
1. Volume 27 of the Outward Bound Edition, 1919, containing *The Years Between* and the poems from the *History of England*.
2. This work, first mentioned in June 1918 (CK diary), is described as "verses which are about American affairs" (CK diary, 1 October 1920). RK eventually decided not to publish it (see 1 October 1920).
3. They left on 3 September and returned to Bateman's on 29 September; their route took them to Ascot to see Lady Roberts, to Oxford, to Astley and the Baldwins, to

Aunt Louisa at Wilden, and on to Dalclathic Lodge, Perthshire, where they spent from 11 to 25 September with Daisy Low (CK diary and Rees extracts).

4. Page, who had died in 1918, was the founder of the magazine called *The World's Work*, a publication of Doubleday, Page and Co. Page's son, Arthur, was now editor of the magazine. In a series of eight articles, 1921–2, *The World's Work* published extensive excerpts from *The Life and Letters of Walter Hines Page* by the associate editor of the magazine, Burton Hendrick, a work afterwards published by Doubleday, 3 vols, 1922–5.

To Frank N. Doubleday, 16 September 1919
AL: Princeton University

Dalclathic Lodge[1] / Comrie / Perthshire / Sep. 16. 1919

Dear Old Man –

I enjoyed it all right. It's priceless and the book, when it emerges from B's magnificent brain, will be finer still.[2] But Allah has deprived him of all sense of humour – else how could he have run the L.H.J. and he is persuaded that it is something of a credit to be Dutch. Over here, we are still divided in our minds as to whether the Dutch were absolutely the basest or only the most mercenary of the neutrals. I think you missed a chance in not taking it and running it serially – with photoes – under the title of "Suffering America."

We came up here by car a few days ago from Bateman's and are living in "lone Glenartney's hazel shade" (v. Lady of the Lake, W. Scott)[3] on terms of almost indecent familiarity with the stags. Day before yesterday, crossing a path, we slid down on a couple of 'em and had to stop to let 'em cross the road – which they did in one bound of what looked like fifty feet. It's breathless, burning blue weather – which has dried all the rivers so we get no salmon – but it's almost good enough merely to be alive. I wish to goodness I had you sitting up on these dried lumps of heather looking over what seems like the end of the world – Thus [sketch of barren hills]. As simple as that [arrow pointing to sketch].

Carrie has begun to get a little rest at last: Elsie is enjoying herself and eating enormously and I have done literally not one stroke of work for ten days! [the rest is missing]

Notes
1. The house where they stayed with Daisy Low from 11 to 25 September. It was on the 76,000-acre estate of the Earl of Ancaster.
2. Perhaps an outline or early version of Edward Bok's autobiography, *The Americanization of Edward Bok* (New York, 1920), which became a best-seller and, for many years, a standard item on the lists of books recommended for school

reading. Doubleday, who had known Bok since their school-days, evidently had an opportunity to publish the book; in the event, it was brought out by Scribner.
3. Canto 1, stanza 1.

To Stanley Baldwin, 23 September 1919
ALS: Dalhousie University

Dalclathic Lodge / Comrie / Perthshire / Sep. 23. 1919

Dear Stan

Unless all signs fail I'm beginning to think that we've found *the* spot in all the Highlands. It is true that the river at the foot of the garden produces no fish but that is because there hasn't been any water in it worth speaking of, till today; and it is equally true that one can't get leave to shoot a stag but somehow, I don't think that you and I would be worried by these disabilities. Likewise grouse, blackgame, pheasants and partridges and rabbits and snipe are simply jostling each other all round the landscape but, again, they belong to God and my Lord Ancaster and for my part, I'm content to watch 'em. But never did you imagine such mountains and moors. Glenartney Forest is its name and it's all gentle easy naked slopes running up to 2500 feet, with glens and corries and rifts in the mountain sides and burns with waterfalls and fairy caves and sweeps of heather and bracken – and an air that wipes the years off the back. Carrie and I went out yesterday and were misled by seeing shelties grazing far up the mountainside into the belief they were deer. (The deer are all round the place, anyhow). Whereby we walked about three miles after them and came home, skipping across rocks and stepping stones and disturbing all the game in creation.

It's five miles from a station (which in itself is a miracle) and within an hour and a half motor of all the Trossachs. It's within reach of Aberfeldy, Dunkeld, Pitlochry and the pass of Killiecrankie etc. etc. and every motor run we took was lovelier than the last. Moreover the house itself rejoices in Conveniences – three of 'em – and a bath with real hot water out of a tap and discreetly arranged bedrooms whereby the Sexes do not cross each other in pursuit of the Obvious. Much better than raw bracken in the face of nature, my cousin. Its provisioning and maintenance – thanks to the opulent and luxurious towns of Comrie (5) and Crieff (12) where they understand food – are direct, simple and easy. It is *not* descried by sportsmen since Ancaster reserves all shooting – bird and stag – and the River Ruchell which I have been flogging for a week only gives sea-trout and a *very* occasional strayed salmon. It has a triple garage capable of holding the largest and well-appointed servants offices; the supply of blankets to the beds is beyond the dreams of avarice; and the chamber toilette appliances are abundant and seemly. There is, further, a smoking room. The pictures on the walls though not inspiring are meritorious and the Factor of my Lord Ancaster (he always calls him "my lord") appears to be accomodating and is certainly affable.

I am in hopes of getting it for next August if it can be done without taking it for the season, and our hostess's arrangements permit. (She has a lien on it for the next few years I believe) but *if* the thing works out satisfactorily[1] I foresee rather a good time for a couple of deserving citizens whereof the most deserving is

>   Your affectionate cousin
>   Rud

P.S.   The end of the story about the powder is this.
>   The girl asked the chemist for five cents worth of powder.
>   He said: – "Face, tooth, gun, or bug?"
>   She said: – "Bug."
>   He said: – "D'you expect me to make up five cents worth of bug-powder?"
>   She said (opening her corsage the while) "Who asked you to make up anything? Shove it down!"
>   I knew the first part. The second has but even now been told me.

>   R.

Note
1.   It evidently did not.

To Dr F. A. Dixey,[1] [30 September 1919][2]
ALS: Bodleian Library

>   *Bateman's / Burwash / Sussex*

private
Dear Dr. Dixey:

I am only just home to find your kind little note and the copy of your Bournemouth address.[3] I am specially delighted that after reading "Hartopp v. King" you are inclined "on the whole to give the palm to King."[4]

Like yourself, I've often wondered if the Humanities couldn't be taught without so much Latin and Greek grammar; but the mind of a boy is a fluid and vagrant thing and I suppose the Wisdom of the Ancients early discovered that, it doesn't much matter what you teach a growing organism so long as the organism dislikes the task. Hence "the yoke in our youth."[5] We teach, of course, the unteachable since, at the time we call on the brain, the body is in a ferment: whereas the savage lets his young imitate his methods of getting food or plying a handcraft, and reserves "education" till the old men get together to recite or sing or paint the tribal History.

But I'm very flattered you liked "Regulus," which, as you have seen, is a Moral Tract!

Very sincerely yours
Rudyard Kipling

Notes
1. Frederick Augustus Dixey (1855–1935), fellow of Wadham College, Oxford; president of the Entomological Society of London and of the Zoological Section, British Association for the Advancement of Science.
2. A note accompanying the letter states that it is postmarked 30 September 1919.
3. In the first part of his presidential address to the Zoological Section at the Bournemouth meeting of the British Association for the Advancement of Science, Dixey recalled that his own training had been "the classical and mathematical routine". On the whole, he had no regrets, and went on to cite "the vividly truthful sketch of school life called 'Regulus'" as evidence of the utility of the classics. But he adds that "much of the time spent over the minutiae of Greek and Latin grammar" might be better employed and that natural science should be a regular school subject ("Presidential Address", Zoological Section, in *Report of the Eighty Seventh Meeting of the British Association for the Advancement of Science, Bournemouth: 1919*, 1920, pp. 200–1).
4. "I give on the whole the palm to King" (ibid., p. 200).
5. Lamentations 3:27.

To André Chevrillon, 6 October 1919

Text: Copy, University of Sussex

Bateman's / Burwash / Sussex. / Oct. 6. 1919

Dear Chevrillon,

Yours of the 27th Sep. has demanded some research and I send you the result typewritten for your information if you write the article.[1] You needn't quote what I say textually: but, so far as a man can judge of his own mind, I have given you the facts of the case.

I can't pretend to explain why the dedication to the Five Nations – "Before a midnight breaks in storm" – should have been so curiously apposite. As my memory serves me it began with the verse "Before the year's reborn behold etc."[2] and worked backwards from that point. I suspect I must have felt the ground-swell of events before the storm came and rocked to it. You'll find in "The City of Brass" in the "Years Between" written in 1908[3] another fairly close forecast of things already befallen in Russia and, it may be, about to befall else-where. My conscience smote me when I read your letter because I had not sent you any of my verse. So I have arranged now – so far as anything can be arranged in these days – for my publishers to send you over *The Seven Seas*; *The Five Nations*; *The Years Between* and *Songs from Books* which latter contains all the verse that I am in the habit of slipping in between, and on the tops of my tales. It's a book I'm fonder of than some of the others. The poem to France has not been republished in slip form but you will find it in *The Years Between*.

What a deuce of a time you must have had with young Castier[4] – and how angelically patient you've been about it. Myself, as an author, I cannot see why on earth McAndrew and Sir Anthony Gloster could not have been plainly and decently translated instead of transliterated into Apache and Poilu.[5] But, as student of psychology, I can comprehend that a young man full of his subject would be greatly tempted to decorate and generally bedevil (for his own glory) the stuff he was saturated with.

I've had something of the same kind happen to me with other translators and – perhaps I have done something of the same kind myself! It's very annoying and it's very ridiculous but – the boy was a prisoner among the Boches; and you are kindness itself in enduring his vagaries. Of course, he *would* flatly contradict your judgment and then claim your help. They always do. As to the German danger (I didn't write this in my typed sheet) I always held that this sad new world began in 1896 and that the first move in the war game was the Kaiser's wire to Kruger.[6] I may have been prejudiced by the fact that I was shouldered off the street pavement in Johannesburg in '98 by Boche officers who were superintending the mounting of heavy (Hun) artillery in the Pretoria forts and nearly got into trouble for a speech I made at a certain dinner in J'burg.[7] Say then in '98 I had a clear notion of the Hun peril and you won't be far wrong. But it broke my heart that people wouldn't listen or believe when I tried to interest 'em in military preparation. All those first years of the 20th century were a dreadful hypnotic trance among "civilized" peoples. The literature of it will be curious to read a few centuries hence.

And, at the present moment, in a land where all men and most women have the vote we are in the midst of a spirited attempt to govern the English by making them uncomfortable and frightening them. Nominally, it is the Railway men and the Trade Unions who are doing it. Actually it is the Hun, the Bolshevik and the Jew of Poland chiefly. In spite of their best efforts to speak and act like white men, one sees in the cruelty practised on the railway horses,[8] the hand of the Hun. Our people are very good tempered, but very "fed up" with the whole thing. It doesn't pay to deprive English folk of their few comforts or to try to oppress them beyond a certain point. For myself, I could wish the railway men had not chosen the fourth anniversary of Loos to open their demonstration. We were caught in Scotland and had to flee down the Great North Road in our car. 370 miles through fantastic surroundings and across dead railway lines and processions of buses and lorries carrying refugees as it might have been an evacuating back-area in France. And, near York, under hard sunshine we came on an elephant with two camels pulling a huge circus car of Wombwell's Menagerie. I took it for a good omen; the elephant being my token as well as the vahon[9] or incarnation of Ganesh the God of good luck.

Now I must finish. Forgive a long and boring letter but when a man begins to write about himself and his doings he babbles like a brook. We shall live and we shall live to see the world re-established – but *oh* we shall be tired, you and I.

With all greetings to you and your France
Ever
Rudyard Kipling

P.S.   You will find most of the verses referred to in the books I send. R.K.

Notes sent to Chevrillon[10]

(I)   "First idea of the Saga of the Anglo-Saxon. Chap XXXVI *From Sea to Sea*"[11]

I do not recall any direct intention on my part in writing that passage but in all likelihood the idea came to me after my voyage across the World that something on the lines indicated ought to be done. You will find a hint of the same idea in "My Great and Only"[12] out of *Abaft the Funnel*, a collection of stories published in the U.S.A. in 1909 without my knowledge or consent, composed of stories contributed ten years before to various newspapers.

(II)   There was no time at which any conscious vision of the Empire rose before me, but my daily life in India from my seventeenth year prevented me from looking at things from an insular point of view, even if I had not spent five years at a school largely composed of the sons of Anglo-Indians and Army officers most of them with youthful memories of the East and the greater part separated from their parents and therefore deeply interested in the arrival of the foreign mails. And how far that school's life impressed me you can judge from a set of verses written when I was sixteen and published in the school paper.[13] It seems to set the key for the rest of my writings.

As an Anglo-Indian journalist it was part of my duty to go through the newspapers which arrived at our office daily or weekly from all parts of India, from Singapore, Hongkong, Australia, New Zealand and South Africa – as well as the Russian Journals, such as the Novoe Vremya[14] (you can imagine how I studied *that*!) and French publications from Saigon and

Annam. In those days India newspapers whose supply of original matter was small, were greatly dependent on extracts from other papers – "the exchanges" as we called them. Even to this hour the shape, type and above all, smell of those papers is burnt into my memory. So you must imagine to yourself a very young man in the north of India after a voyage at the most impressionable period of his life, spending twelve hours a day in an office which vibrated with the news of the Empire from Aden westward to Quebec, and from Cape Town to Hongkong – all of which news it was his duty to search, condense, and reproduce for his readers' interest, and at the same time to try to comprehend and comment intelligently on the different views of the various cities and nations represented by those journals. Add to this, that I was occasionally despatched on tours and reporting expeditions, from the Himalayas to the Sea, where – holding no rank – I could mix with all classes, Army and Civilian. My commission as a journalist passed me everywhere. The esteem and affection in which my father was held throughout India secured me a toleration beyond my merits, and my youth permitted men to speak to each other before me without weighing their words. Apart from the friends of my family, there was the incessant come and go of travellers, savants, specialists, etc. on their way through India who sooner or later would stay for a time in my father's house (I mention Darmstetter[15] and Gustave LeBon[16] for examples) where, in that the sympathetic atmosphere they naturally talked at ease, and I, at the foot of the table, listened and absorbed. You will easily see how this atmosphere and these surroundings impressed and coloured my outlook without any effort on my part. In one aspect or another, the Empire was of the fabric of my physical and mental existence. So far as I can see that continued without any break from 1882 to the present day – a period nearer to forty years than I care to think of.

As far as "Imperialism" went, my only conception of it was that which I saw around me – men devoted to burdensome tasks under difficult conditions without much assistance or any immediate hope of reward, working for impersonal ends. In my own little world the first lesson that I learned was that of loyalty to my paper and the necessity to serve it whether I was hot or cold or well or sick.

(III)   *The Seven Seas* was first published in 1896. *The Five Nations* with the dedication "Before a Midnight, etc." appeared in 1903 or eleven years before the war. A large proportion of the verses in both books appeared originally in Newspapers and Magazines. For instance, in *The Seven Seas*

The Song of the English (English Illustrated Magazine, circa 1890)[17]
The Last Chantey (Pall Mall Gazette) 1893?[18]
The Merchantmen (Pall Mall Gazette '93)[19]
McAndrew's Hymn (Century circa 93)[20]
The Rhyme of the Three Sealers[21]
The Answer (Scotts Observer 1890)[22]

The Song of the Banjo (Scots Observer)[23]
The Sea Wife (in a foreword to a book – circa 1893)[24]
The Rowers[25] (Daily Chronicle circa 1892?)
The Last Rhyme of True Thomas (A Magazine circa 1892)[26]
The Three Decker (An English Weekly circa 1892–3)[27]
An American (St. James' Gazette circa 1894)[28]

I quote from memory, only, all appeared in newspapers, together with a number of the Barrack Room Ballads, in that book.

The Seven Seas includes all my verse, (with the exception of the Songs in the *First and Second Jungle Books*) written between 1889 and 96. Similarly *The Five Nations* includes all my verse between 1896 and 1903 excepting always the verses and chapter-headings in *Kim* and the *Just So Stories* and *The Rowers* ("The Goth and the shameless Hun") which appeared in the Times in 1902. A large amount of my verse has gone into my collections of stories etc, as you will see from the volume of *Songs from Books* which I am sending you.

The Five Nations (1903) has a great deal of verse which was published in English and American papers.

The Burial of C. J. Rhodes (1902)
The White Man's Burden (99) also McClure Mag.
Recessional (1897)
Kitchener's School (98)
The Old Issue (1899)
The Lesson (1901)
The Reformers (1901)
The Islanders (1902)
The Settler (1902)[29]
Our Lady of the Snows (1897)
Bridge Guard in the Karroo[30]
The Young Queen (1902 circa)[31]
General Joubert (1900)

All these appeared in *The Times*[32] and *White Horses* appeared in *Literature* (the present literary supplement to the Times in 97).

The Files in the Spectator[33] –
Destroyers in the Windsor Magazine '99[34]
Feet of the Young Men. Scribner's '97
Pharaoh and the Sergeant Illustrated London News 97[35]
M.I. in the Windsor Magazine about 1901 or 1902[36]
The Truce of the Bear, in the Times Lit. Supplement.

There are also others in the same book of whose original appearance and date I am uncertain.

Now as to the *Bandar Log*[37] this was written in 1894 and faithfully reflected, as it does today, my views on the Great God "Democracy". It had nothing whatever to do with the French, and as I think I have told you, that amiable theory must be a Hun-made one. But it *is* a reasonable presentment of "Government by popular opinion" in whatever part of the world that may be adopted. In England it was assumed to be a picture of the *Radical Party*, which did me no especial service. The U.S.A. journals thought it reflected on the Republic which is the inevitable result of any attempt at impersonal portraiture.

Notes

1. The notes that follow this letter: an entry in CK's diary for October 1919 notes that "Rud finding material for André Chevrillon." Chevrillon's article is the essay on RK called "Rudyard Kipling's Poetry"; it appeared in the *Revue des Deux Mondes*, 15 April 1920–15 May 1920, before being collected in *Trois études de littérature anglaise* (Paris, 1921; translated as *Three Studies in English Literature*, 1923). Chevrillon makes considerable use of the information that RK supplies in this letter and its accompanying notes, often in the form of direct quotation or of paraphrase.
2. The fourth stanza of "Before a Midnight Breaks in Storm": "in his more important poems, the warning note sounds continually. The whole Prelude to *The Five Nations* (1903) is a startling prediction . … What fulness and certitude of vision in these dedicatory lines!" (Chevrillon, *Three Studies*, pp. 112–13).
3. Perhaps (but probably not) written so early; not published until 1909: see 18 May 1909, to Leslie Cope Cornford.
4. See 14 January 1919, to André Chevrillon.
5. The character of Castier's struggles with RK's text may be briefly illustrated. These lines from "McAndrew's Hymn":

> Better myself abroad? Maybe. *I'd* sooner starve than sail
> Wi' such as call a snifter-rod *ross*. … French for nightingale.
> Commeesion on my stores? Some do; but I can not afford
> To lie like stewards wi' patty-pans – . I'm older than the Board.

are rendered thus:

> J'f'rais mieux à l'étranger? Peut-êtr' … Mais j'aim' 'cor mieux la crève
> Que d'naviguer avec des gens qui baragouin'nt sans trêve …
> Ou bien, la r'mise aux fournitur's? 'Yen a qui l'font – mais moi
> J'peux pas mentir comm' des larbins, – j'suis trop vieux dans l'emploi!

6. A telegram of congratulation following the failure of the Jameson Raid: see 8 January 1896.
7. The speech was that of 2 April 1898 at the Rand Club, Johannesburg (see [early April 1898]). Chevrillon handles RK's encounter with the German officers thus: "In 1898 he was in Pretoria, where German officers were superintending the mounting of heavy Krupp guns on the forts of the town. Here it was that he made acquaintance with blue uniform and spiked helmet, with the haughty stare of the monocle, the swaggering tread of heavy boot and spurred heel, the clank of trailing scabbards, the insolent elbowing that hustled an Englishman off the footpath" (*Three Studies*, p. 111).

8. A general railway strike was declared on 27 September and ran until 5 October. In the interval, 1,200 horses at King's Cross stables and 1,100 at Paddington were reported as "abandoned" and appeals were made to provide emergency care for them (*The Times*, 4 October 1919). These "railway horses" were used in making deliveries in London.
9. Thus in copy. A *vahan* is "the mount or vehicle of a god" (*OED*).
10. This is the title, in a secretary's hand, on the undated typescript, with RK's manuscript additions and corrections, at Sussex. I assume that a corrected typescript was sent to Chevrillon and this original kept as a file copy.
11. A passage apropos of American patriotism and its songs; RK writes that "there must be born a poet who shall give the English *the* song of their own, own country – which is to say, of about half the world. Remains then only to compose the greatest song of all – the Saga of the Anglo-Saxon all round the earth" (*From Sea to Sea*, II, 172). Chevrillon says of this passage that it marks the moment when RK "conceived one of the main ideas of his poetry" (*Three Studies*, p. 22).
12. *CMG*, 11 and 15 January 1890: see 8–16 November 1889.
13. "Ave Imperatrix", USC *Chronicle*, 20 March 1882: see 9 March 1882. Chevrillon writes: "The verses were called *Ave Imperatrix*. Now that nearly forty years have passed the poet is convinced that there and then, under the influence of "Westward Ho!" the general direction of his life-work was determined" (*Three Studies*, p. 13).
14. "An accursed Muscovite paper, the *Novoie Vremya*, written in French" (*Something of Myself*, p. 49).
15. James Darmesteter (1849–94), professor of Persian in the Collège de France, travelled in India, 1886; *Lettres sur L'Inde* (Paris, 1888). "La plupart des langues lui étaient familières" (*Dictionnaire de Biographie Français*).
16. Gustave Le Bon (1841–1931), doctor and sociologist, in India in 1884 to study Buddhist monuments: *Les Civilisations de l'Inde* (Paris, 1887). RK wrote a brief note in the *Civil and Military Gazette*, 6 February 1885, on the appearance of Le Bon's *La Civilisation des Arabes* with a reference to Le Bon's Indian visit. RK met Le Bon again in 1914: see [23 February 1914].
17. May 1893.
18. *Pall Mall Magazine*, 15 June 1893.
19. *Pall Mall Budget*, 15 May 1893.
20. *Scribner's Magazine*, December 1894.
21. *Pall Mall Budget*, 14 December 1893.
22. *Century Magazine*, November 1892.
23. *New Review*, June 1895.
24. In John Arthur Barry, *Steve Brown's Bunyip*, 1893.
25. Thus in MS, but RK must have meant "The Flowers", *Daily Chronicle*, 10 June 1896.
26. *To-day*, 17 March 1894.
27. *Saturday Review*, 14 July 1894.
28. *Pall Mall Gazette*, 19 July 1894.
29. *The Times*, 27 February 1903.
30. *The Times*, 5 June 1901.
31. *The Times*, 4 October 1900.
32. "General Joubert" did not.
33. It does not appear in the *Spectator* but was first published in *The Five Nations*. RK apparently did offer it to the *Spectator* (see [20 June 1900]).
34. *Windsor Magazine*, June 1898.
35. *Graphic*, July 1897.
36. *Windsor Magazine*, October 1901.
37. "Road Song of the *Bandar-Log*", first published in *The Jungle Book*.

To T. E. Lawrence, 8 October 1919
ALS: Syracuse University

Bateman's / Burwash / Sussex / Oct. 8. 1919.

Dear Lawrence

Naturally, if you didn't take what was offered you and do what you were wanted to do, you would – from the F.O. point of view – be the worst kind of crook.[1] They don't understand deviation from type. Later on, I expect, you will be accused of having been actuated by "financial motives" in all you did. Wait till you are cussed for being a "venal hireling" – as I was once – in a Legislature.[2]

But we are all sitting in the middle of wrecked hope and broken dreams. I tried all I knew to put the proper presentation of the American scheme[3] before men over there who, I thought, could help. But one can't expect people whose forbears went west to avoid trouble to stand up to responsibility in a far land for no immediate cash return. But you will not go out of the game – except for the necessary minute to step aside and vomit. You are young, and the bulk of the men now in charge are "old, cold and of intolerable entrails"[4] and a lot of 'em will be dropping out soon.

But it's impossible to write these things and it's hopeless to try in talk in town. Do you think you could manage to come down for a night or two next week?[5] There will be no one here of course, and you'd better bring some work down with you, because I'm at the grindstone in the morning (you've probably got a lot of arrears). Then we can have a talk *with* maps, which please bring. Mine are old. We're here for some time and any time next week would suit. If you will write your train the car will meet you at Etchingham and we'd all be delighted. *Do* see if you can fix it.

Ever yours
Rudyard Kipling

P.S.   I think the cinema man is the last and most perfect touch of beastliness.[6] What a lot Dante missed in his Inferno by not being abreast with "modern progress"!

Notes
1. Lawrence's activities in favour of the Arabs as against the French had made him *persona non grata* to the Foreign Office and he had been excluded from the negotiations over Syria: see Jeremy Wilson, *Lawrence of Arabia* (New York, 1990), pp. 616–20.
2. In the Canadian Parliament by Alexander Maclean: see 30 January [1913].
3. Lawrence's plan to have the US support an Arab state: see 7 January 1919.
4. *The Merry Wives of Windsor*, V, v, 162: "Old, cold, withered, and of intolerable entrails."
5. It does not appear that he did.

6. Perhaps a proposal arising out of Lawrence's current great notoriety. Lowell Thomas had been giving his illustrated lecture on "Lawrence in Arabia" in London to large and fashionable audiences since August. It was the sensation of the year and made Lawrence a national hero.

To Brander Matthews, 10 October 1919

ALS: Columbia University

Bateman's / Burwash / Sussex / Oct: 10. 1919.

Dear Brander:

What you say is just, true, impeccable and – a sight more important – interesting in every word.[1] What I liked best was "If William came back"[2] because it squares with my estimate of William's sanity and simplicity and humour. A great deal of the Shakespeare stage-traditions was new to me altogether. The Falstaff scene where he looks over the back of the chair was an inspiration.[3] If I could but put your and a few other authorities' principles into practice I'd perhaps be able to write a play: but – I don't know whether any drama comes up to the stuff that we have here to move in. I rather wonder whether it will react, in my time, upon the acted drama and swing us back into Elizabethan lines. Every conceivable thing and situation is not only possible now: but has taken place on the largest scale.

But, O Brander, why when God has given you gifts and "civilization" has dowered you with a printing press, and the gracious forests with paper, WHY do you spell after the manner of the Savage and the Insane? "I will not cease from mortal strife"[4] so long as you persist in this Moral Leprosy. How can we have any League of Nations when one person of one nation writes "thru" and "accomplisht" and "smackt" and "catalog" and all those atrocities? How can we go to the same Heaven? More important still, how shall we get on in the same Hell? What bond – even though William Himself signed it – can subsist between us? It hurts, it separates, it amazes; it distracts; it breaks all the Dramatic Unities and delays action. If yu want tu be fonetik, be fonetik al thru and dam the konsekwenzes but for pittee's sâk don't spangle yŭr bŏks wit small attem's at Krīm. *Pecker fortitur:*[5] and believe you

Yours ever affectionately
Rudyard.

Notes
1. In Matthews' *The Principles of Playmaking and Other Discussions of the Drama* (New York, 1919).
2. "If Shakspere Should Come Back?", *The Principles of Playmaking*, pp. 93–8.

3. "Shaksperian Stage Traditions", *The Principles of Playmaking*, pp. 113–14, describes the treatment of Falstaff's exposure by Prince Hal (*I Henry IV*, II, iv) as produced by Robert Taber and Julia Marlowe.
4. William Blake, "And Did Those Feet?", last stanza: "I will not cease from Mental Fight."
5. *Pecca fortitur* ("sin strongly"): Luther, *Letter to Melanchthon*.

To André Chevrillon, 11 October 1919

Text: Copy, University of Sussex

Bateman's / Burwash / Sussex. / Oct. 11. 1919.

Dear Chevrillon,

Yours of the 9th has crossed, I hope, my letter in reply to your queries in your first letter: sending you also some voLumes of my verse.[1]

Songs from Books as I think I wrote you contains all the verses scattered up and down my prose. In it you will find "If".

"For all we have and are" is in *The Years Between. NOTA*. When this poem first appeared in the papers in 1914 an American or Canadian journal said it resembled the lamentations of an old woman at a thunderstorm on the roof! That stuck in my memory through the years.

I don't know whether you have ever come across the verses I wrote for a child's History of England which was published in the Oxford Press, 1911. Anyhow I send it to you. I helped a little with the text also. See p. 29 and the verses at the head of chapter II with reference to the north east wind.[2] The last one "The glory of the garden" became a sort of school recitation piece: together with Big Steamers which had a vogue at certain stages of the war. The whole book however was too militaristic and imperialistic for the balanced judgment of the period and was denounced in Parliament by an Irish rebel who had fought against us under the Boers – whereupon the then Minister of Education (Pease, I think was his name) apologised for it and said it would not be used in Government schools.[3] I plead guilty to having written several of the poems in the book, with intention. Perhaps the French wars "Norman and Saxon", "Danegeld" and the verses about America's first rebellion may interest you.

As to Armageddon and the like, I've been looking through the books and I find them bristling with hints and forecasts. In the *Five Nations* for example all the following bear on the years to come.

Dedication
Bell Buoy
Dykes
Et Dona Ferentes v. the Puzzler (Songs from Books)
The Islanders
The Lesson (note verse 5)

The old issue
The old men
The Reformers (quite the clearest of the lot in prophecy)
Resamon[4]
The truce of the Bear (for which I caught it heavily from all sides)

In *Songs from Books* the following are the same sort of stuff.

The King's Task (p. 256)
Our Fathers also (p. 94)
(p. 98) a Pict song (and if that isn't Ireland's part in the war I'm a Shinn Feinner!)
A servant when he reigneth (p. 124) Labour
The Stranger (p. 100) Imported Bolshevism.
The Heritage (p. 130)
A British Roman song (p. 96)
The Puzzler (p. 73) English character v. Et Dona Ferentes

There may be some others but these are all I could spot at first going over. Thinking it over impersonally, I begin to be persuaded that, though I knew it not and none of my friends would credit it, I must have the mathematical mind which, given two sides and an angle, can say what the length of the third side of the triangle is bound to be. Or, perhaps, my intellect clings most closely to ancient fact – and the oldest fact in the world is that $2 + 2 = 4$. Evidently prophecy must be based on that fact. Therefore I am a Prophet!

Our Railway Strike as you will see, has ended; our people did not like being made uncomfortable and the neglect of the horses who were allowed to go without food or water was against our stomachs. The most interesting facts of the affair do not appear in the papers – notably the public anger and the zeal with which volunteers offer themselves for public service. I expect there will be more trouble anon, but I don't think the public will be at all pleased. Their psychology is very curious.

I see from the cartoons in your papers that you are reprehensibly frivolous with the Americans. They do not like being jested at – your laborious humourist seldom does. Revert to us, and let us crack jokes together. I see, too, that we are officially at issue about Syria etc. etc.[5] Let us take the Anglo-French commission and drive them up and down the devasted areas for a week. Some people have no sense of proportion.

Now I will stop. If there is any further information that may be of any use to you please let me know. There is no need to tell you that a man is least trustworthy and accurate when he is talking about his own mental processes.

Ever yours
Rudyard Kipling

Notes

1. See 6 October 1919.
2. "The Pirates in England".
3. See [late December? 1911]. When Cathcart Wason put his question about the *History of England* to Joseph Pease, then President of the Board of Education, Arthur Lynch (1861–1934), liberal MP for Galway City, remarked on the "low and vulgar tone" of the book. It was Lynch who was the "Irish rebel"; he was in fact Australian-born, but he had fought with the Boers, had been condemned to death and then pardoned after the war. Pease said on this occasion that he thought some parts of the *History* unsuitable for use in schools and hoped that local authorities might be alerted to the fact (*Parliamentary Debates, Commons* 5th Series, XXXII, 33: 27 November 1911).
4. Thus in copy, for "Rimmon".
5. The British were then preparing to withdraw their troops from Syria in favour of the French in the west and the Arabs in the east, an arrangement that the French had no intention of maintaining and soon overturned.

To André Chevrillon, 22 October 1919

Text: Composite, *Études Anglaises*, XIX (1966), 407–11 with partial facsimile, and copy, University of Sussex

Bateman's / Burwash / Sussex / Oct. 22. 1919.

Dear Chevrillon,

Yours of the 20th. Something must have gone wrong with the mails, for I have sent you, days ago, Songs from Books; Seven Seas, Five Nations, Years Between and the child's History of England for which I wrote some verses. One never is sure nowadays of anything arriving anywhere, and I will send you fresh copies of *Songs from Books* and the History of England.

You have in your last two letters asked me for information on certain details: Behold: –

(I) Mowgli's song is, of course, a direct crib from the war-chant of primitive humanity whereof Deborah's song in the Bible is the best exemplar. All that type of outpouring is only emphasis and copious repetition – to match the stamp of the foot with which the first singer originally accompanied himself.[1]

(II) The man whose name rhymed to "frail" was the late H. D. Traill,[2] an English critic of eminence some 25–30 years ago who said that I was a minor poet. It was quite as much as I deserved at that time, but – the young do not like being called minor in any respect so I suppose that I resented it as an impertinence.

Now for documentation of dates:

I was born in Bombay (*1865*) and there I lived till I was between five and six – those terrible first years of which the Jesuits know the value.[3]

It was a very primitive, unbuilt Bombay with vast green spaces inside and wonderful walks through coconut woods on the edge of the sea where the Parsees waded in and prayed to the setting or rising sun. I spoke English without enthusiasm for my natural speech to the servants, was the vernacular but, to my parents, English; and my nurse – a Roman Catholic native – was particular to tell me on going into breakfast "Now speak English. …" My body servant was a Hindu and among the house servants were some Mahommedans. With these of course I associated on terms of perfect equality for I was below the age where caste has to be considered; and I remember going with one or other of these people to the Bombay markets, in the early cool of the dawn to buy fruit and kneeling with my nurse before the Catholic shrines and crosses or assisting with offerings at some Hindu wayside temple where I could trot in and out without offence, and listening as a child will to the queer (unclean, I suppose) direct life-philosophy of the servants' talk among themselves or talking with their own children. Incidentally, I do not recall any time of my life at which the elementary facts of life so discreetly veiled from the young in the west, were not accepted by me as I accepted the facts of caste, food and play. That is to say, I was as wise as any native child of five years old, and on terms of complete accord with the gods of at least two religions – Mary and the Child, and certain vague Hindu deities with marigold garlands round their necks.

Can you imagine a better equipment for certain things than to be the first child of a sensitive English woman herself new to all the surroundings of the East?

Then in *1870* or '71[4] – I came to England – a child of six and was left on my people's return to India (where it was inexpedient and dangerous for a white child to be reared through youth) in the care of a bitter, narrow, bigoted, Evangelical woman who took in Anglo-Indian children. It was very hard on me in those years except that I had a sort of friend in her old husband, a Navy captain, who had fought as a midshipman at Navarino and with whom as a small boy I perambulated all Portsmouth, Gosport and Fratton – the old Portsmouth with its old ramparts and old houses. He died but the town remained to me and as I grew bigger I wandered all over it and to the mud-flats at the back among the old forts. At that time I was taught French by a strange black-bearded Frenchman who, I can now see, must have been some sort of refugee of the Commune. I understood little of what he said but I can see now the passion and wrath of the man subdued to the necessity of teaching boys his tongue for a living in a hostile land.

That was, as I said, an evil experience for me through those years of misery and discomfort and loneliness. Yet, once a year, I entered Paradise (*and knew that I did*) when I visited at Christmas the house of my uncle, Edward Burne-Jones in London and there – not knowing it, but conscious of the colour and the joy and the affection of the life that my aunt moved in – met as a child meets and accepts, artists and poets who stormed in and out of this house of wonders – such as Morris, occasionally Browning; Holman Hunt;[5] and others that I have forgotten. But Morris whom we called "Uncle" was a figure that remained. He was doing things incomprehensible to childhood – he and Burne-Jones together – talking and laughing and painting and drawing and playing with coloured glass and, in the background, my aunt reading us Scott's novels and happy children of William Richmond[6] and Morris: children coming in – a vista of rocking horses, magic lanterns, the Earthly Paradise[7] being published, Morris, in the schoolroom, telling us the plots of his future work *not* because we understood, but to get it clear in his own mind; de Morgan[8] who allowed me to play with his painted tiles (ages before he wrote a novel) and so on and so forth. One month a year of this. Then misery and Evangelical brutality and childish fears.

Then in '77 the return of my mother: a sudden lifting of the darkness and a return to warm life without fear, a wonderful summer spent wild as a colt in Epping forest among pigs on a farm and then at about eleven years of age[9] translation to the school at Westward Ho! (1878) under Crom Price, one of Burne Jones's most intimate friends and one of my numerous deputy "Uncles" in the Life in London. Those were in all, good days and some shadow of them is in "Stalky and Co". But I see now the wonderful kindness and forbearance of my master Price and the care and forethought with which, without showing it, he steered me towards my work. For the last two years of my school life I perceive *now* that I was practically set free, under pretence of studying Russian, to read at large in his library and, under some pretext of writing précis and summaries of what I had read, was left alone to write. I was Editor of the school paper which – I see now – he caused me to edit and to him I used, in all innocence, to bring my work for it. This he dismissed lightly but was very serious about verse and style. And *yet* – throughout – I can not recall one moment when he permitted me to imagine that I was anything out of the common as a boy with a taste for letters.

To balance this life, I was, in my holidays (my people having again returned to India)[10] in charge of three old maiden ladies of the mid-victorian type: one of whom was a now long forgotten novelist who wrote her novels on a pad on her knee in minute script in a drawing room by a fireside adorned with two clay pipes which Carlyle had smoked. They were beyond words, kind patient and loveable and, in their quiet lives they touched a gentle serious yet very humorous, literary circle whose names wouldn't interest you; and their sympathy and preoccupation with my "literary" work was adorable. Also, I had more and more the circle of my uncle's friends and the influence of his atmosphere to help me. Yet – being young I saw none of the guidance and took the help for granted.

When I was 16 years and nine months[11] I was responsible for a mass of "literary" effort – my school paper, a whole sonnet in the "*World*"[12] on which

I achieved one guinea (!) and M.S.S. beyond count. I did not want to do any-thing else. At Mathematics I was hopeless; my Classics were an abomination; my written French was an outrage *but* (I say this with proper pride) I read French as easily as English and in those days there was good French to read and one got drunk on the roll and turgid grandiosity of the worst of Victor Hugo. In those days I came across Béranger's stuff[13] and loved it; because, in one of his visits to England my father had taken me to the Paris exhibition of '78.[14] (That is another cycle of development – the realization of a new European bond and the fun and joy of Paris when a child. I visited Paris later on, on my return from India).[15]

Meantime, my people were in Lahore, in the Punjab, where an old, old friend of my father's[16] owned the *Civil and Military Gazette* in that town and the *Pioneer* in Allahabad 800 miles south of it. He had been shown my school work and was good enough, after an interview with me in London, to risk employing me as sub-editor of the Civil and Military Gazette at the salary of £100 per annum. (I shouldn't have taken a boy on those wages for such slight equipment). So I went to India in September 1882 and at Bombay found my way by myself through the enlarged, rebuilt city to the place where the house had stood where I was born. It was a strange experience because all that life returned to me with the sights and specially the smells: so that I found myself uttering automatically sentences and phrases of the meaning of which I was ignorant. It was a return to a previous existence. Then began for me five years of perfect felicity at Lahore – in a damnable climate. I lived with my people – father, mother and sister. I had my own work, my own servants, horse cart and dog, my Father's help and philosophy, my Mother's love and sympathy and a home life beyond compare. Outside was all India for me to write about and, when I had a holiday, or was sent reporting, to explore. I was half the staff of my paper – the Editor and I were the whole outfit – I had 160 natives in the office or in the composing room; a Mahommedan foreman, a great and wise old friend of mine; and all my father's friends and my own friends to meet and learn from.

I ought to have done ten times more than I did with so much at my dis-posal. The only drawbacks were heat, overwork and sickness, such as fever and dysentery but – when one is young, these things don't matter. And I wrote and I wrote and I played and I enjoyed myself and desired nothing better under Heaven and I achieved a small reputation by my verses and writings and then – in *1887* – the big sister paper – the great *Pioneer* herself – the leading journal of India ordered me to transfer to her. It was promotion: it was very good pay and – I hated it. It took me from my home, my club, my own province, my own known regiments and peoples and shifted me 800 miles to the northwest provinces, fat, hot, densely populated, smoking Delhi[17] (which to me was the limit of civilization) and – worst of all to a paper where I was only one of four instead of one of two in the direction. But it gave a new twist to my work and I was ordered to take charge, in addition to my daily work, of a weekly summary of the *Pioneer* called the *Week's News* which I embellished with most of the stories in my six little earliest books – Soldiers Three, Wee Willy Winkie, The Story of the Gadsbys etc. (I had already published *Plain Tales from the Hills* in the *Civil and Military Gazette*.) That was a comfort to me, because I *had* to write and in my spare time, I wrote verses and political lampoons – some of which got me into trouble and others didn't – and, being alone, there was nothing much to distract me from writing and seeing things and, when I was 23 years old, I was earning close upon £800 per ann.! I considered myself the equal of kings and potentates. I was known throughout our little India; even kings had spoken to me and Lord Roberts, my father's old friend, had conferred with me seriously about life in barracks and crime in the army.[18] I could go where I chose and, either for my verses or my Father's sake, or the prestige of my paper, I was accepted.

Then that chapter shut as it will when one is young. I wanted to know what my size might be measured against the door-sills of London. Friends at home who had known me when I was a boy said: – "Come and try your luck here". Also I had saved a little money so, in March 1889 being then 24, I embarked all my savings in a wander through the Far East and the U.S.A. and reached England in Sept. 1889[19] – seven years after I had set out and, by the miraculous good fortune that seemed to follow me the way was made smooth and all men were kind. And my Uncle[20] received me with joy, bade me go ahead and do my own work and not bother about doing what other folk thought I ought to do. So there you have ("you asked for it" as the slang phrase is) the documentation of the formative influences when I was a boy. You see how it all worked for one end – coerced me, almost, to one end – the literary use of the thing seen and the one conviction beneath it. You will find a key to a good many things in some verses called "The two-sided man" in *Songs from Books*.[21] One does not outgrow the first six years of one's life.

Naturally as one grows older the pen moves from the external world towards the internal. You'll find that, in "Simple Simon" in Rewards and Fairies. Drake in the midst of the Armada fighting argues that the outside life is not much as compared with the things that happen *to* a man – meaning inside him.[22]

I can't quite understand your being struck with my metrical work – the rhythm etc.[23] That always seemed to me unsatisfactory. I never yet have reached verse that contented my notions of sound and pulse. But no man knows his own work.

Ever sincerely
Rudyard Kipling

P.S.   I enclose the details of the posting to you of my books. Someone has evidently "pinched" 'em.

Notes

1. "One of his finest songs is the great triumphal chant of Mowgli over the corpse of his enemy, Shere Khan, the rhythmic repetitions of which (we seem to hear the trampling of the feet), the sudden movements, the cries of exultation and defiance, recall the wild grandeur of the Song of Deborah" (Chevrillon, *Three Studies in English Literature*, p. 52).
2. Stanza 6 of "In the Neolithic Age": "And a minor poet certified by Traill!" H. D. Traill (1842–1900), journalist, editor, and miscellaneous writer; he edited *Literature*, the predecessor of the *Times Literary Supplement*, 1897–1900. Traill published an article in the *Nineteenth Century*, January 1892, on "Our Minor Poets", enumerating the members of the category and arguing that there were altogether too many of them between the "great poets" and the "mere versifiers". In March 1892 he published a sequel – "Minor Poets – and Others" – which, among other things, apologised for having omitted RK, whose "splendid *Ballad of East and West* … would alone have sufficed to secure … a place in the list". Thus was RK "certified" by Traill. The poem in its first published form (*The Idler*, 2 December 1892) did not contain the reference to Traill.
3. See the epigraph to chapter 1 of *Something of Myself*: "Give me the first six years of a child's life and you can have the rest."
4. RK came to England to be left with Mrs Holloway in Southsea in 1871. See the first chapter of *Something of Myself*.
5. William Holman Hunt (1827–1910), first and most committed of the Pre-Raphaelite painters.
6. Sir William Bell Richmond: see [29] April 1882 and 8–16 November 1889.
7. William Morris, *The Earthly Paradise*, 1868–70. RK has evidently confused this with some other of Morris's publications: perhaps *Sigurd the Volsung*, 1876?
8. William De Morgan (1839–1917); after a career as a manufacturer of decorative tiles associated with the Pre-Raphaelites and the craftsman movement, he enjoyed a second career as a successful novelist, 1906–17.
9. In January 1878, when he went to Westward Ho!, RK had just passed his twelfth birthday.
10. Alice Kipling returned to England early in 1877; she was joined there by JLK on furlough in the spring of 1878; he went back to India in October 1879 but she remained in England until late in 1880. For some, at least, of his holiday-residences with the "Ladies of Warwick Gardens" his mother, too, was part of the household. The ladies were the sisters Mary and Georgiana Craik and their friend Miss Winnard, of 26 Warwick Gardens, Kensington. Georgiana, afterwards Mrs May, was the novelist. See the articles by Lisa Lewis in *Kipling Journal*, March, September, and December 1989.
11. That is, his age at the moment of his departure for India, 20 September 1882.
12. "Two Lives", published in the *World*, 8 November 1882.
13. Pierre de Béranger (1780–1857), poet noted for his political songs.
14. June 1878: see *Something of Myself*, pp. 24–5, and *Souvenirs of France*.
15. RK made two brief visits to Paris, October 1889 (see [22 October 1889]) and May 1890 (Carrington, *Kipling*, 3rd edn, p. 215), once in pursuit of Mrs Hill and once in pursuit of Flo Garrard.
16. George Allen. No record of his interview with RK in London is known.
17. Thus in copy: Allahabad?
18. See *Something of Myself*, pp. 56–7.
19. In fact, on 4 October 1889.
20. Burne-Jones.
21. "In Kipling the two souls co-exist, but remain independent. He himself is well aware of this duality, and thanks the gods therefor in one of Kim's songs" (*Three Studies*, p. 17).

22. Perhaps the passage in *Rewards and Fairies*, p. 300:

> "'But ye never foretold this'; he points to both they great fleets.
> "'This don't seem to me to make much odds compared to what happens *to* a man,' she says. 'Do it?'"

23. "Nothing could be newer or more varied than his metres, yet they never suggest research. The rhythm seems the result of a natural force" (*Three Studies*, p. 48).

To A. S. Watt, [*c.*2 November 1919]

Text: Copied in A. S. Watt to Sir Frederick Macmillan, 3 November 1919: TLS, British Library

[Bateman's]

Macmillan's letter to you regarding the falling off in my sales has annoyed me more than a little.[1] He takes the pre-war scale of sales as his standard of average and seems to accept the last six months drop in them as not only beyond his control but as almost beneath his notice.

During the war my sales increased. Surely then was the time for Macmillan to take advantage of the larger public which my books had attracted and to hold and increase this connection. But when you get down to the facts, my books were allowed to sell themselves and when any effort was needed to sell them neither the will nor the machinery to do so was put into motion.

Given a business even one third the extent of mine this would be unwise, but, as things stand, it is worse than unwise. For the last quarter of a century Macmillan has been in charge of an extraordinarily valuable property of mine which was developed, I do not say in spite of his exertions, but certainly with the minimum of attention and expenditure on his part. The same applies exactly to ——.[2] In both cases the profit of the business man was taken for granted and any lapse in a long established proposition was considered as a dispensation of Providence. If nothing is done now by these firms we shall have the sales steadily running down hill while we shall continue to be put off with figures which can be made to prove anything.

I have no doubt that, to keep up the sales, effort, expenditure and attention are required, but I wish it to be distinctly understood that I expect that effort to be made by the firms who have my property in charge.[3]

Notes

1. Sir Frederick Macmillan wrote to Watt on 17 October 1919 reporting the sales of RK's works in the uniform and pocket editions thus: 1918–19: 77,087 copies, as compared to 61,110 in 1912–13. Sir Frederick added: "In view of these figures I do not think there is anything to be unhappy about in the position of affairs" (Macmillan

Papers, British Library). On 22 October Sir Frederick again wrote to Watt to say that there had been a falling-off of sales in January–June 1919 as compared to 1918, but that this was the effect of the peace: the war had "stimulated sales", which would now return to earlier levels (Macmillan Papers, British Library).

2. Blank in copy. This letter appears in Simon Nowell-Smith, ed., *Letters to Macmillan*, 1967, pp. 279–80, where the blank is filled by "Methuens", no doubt correctly. I do not think that RK would have said this of Doubleday.

3. Macmillan replied on 4 November to say that he was sorry that his expression "'no reason to be unhappy about the position of affairs' … should have led Mr. Kipling to think that I was indifferent to the sale of his books. … There is no one in this house, from the Chairman to the smallest office boy, who does not consider it his duty to advance Mr. Kipling's interest in every way in his power." The only thing that Macmillan could think of that might have been neglected was newspaper advertising: "I have therefore arranged that between now and Christmas the standing advertisement of Mr. Kipling's editions should appear not at intervals as at present but in *every* list or general publications that we insert in the newspapers" (to Watt: Macmillan Papers, British Library).

To Monsignor Richard Barry-Doyle,[1] 8 November 1919

TLS: University of Texas

Bateman's / Burwash / Sussex / 8 November 1919

Private.

My dear Monsignor Doyle,

I am much honoured by the request in your letter but must entirely dissent from the opinions you have read into my writings regarding marriage. What I have in various ways woven into the fabric of my collected works is the view that too-early marriages were less apt to succeed than later ones. I have been a keen follower, over many years, of the careers of thousands of men who have come under my observation and I would reply to your questions about the best age for marrying by saying the happiest unions I know of are those entered into when the men were not less than thirty.

We are living in the disharmony of what is instinctive clashing with what the conventions of society permit, so the marriage age can not be as early as if we were living in a state of nature untrammelled by civilisation with its warping influences. So many varying human factors have to be taken into consideration when the age of marriage is the subject of discussion in these days. The budding impulse to mate naturally arises in a youth as his affections and their outlet in the feminine world outside the family circle and cravings for independence and position become dominant in his mind. It is, however, highly exceptional that the young can possibly foresee the course of their own development and their needs, or adequately gauge the personality and character of another.

It is certain that early marriages, in the majority of instances, are highly liable to lead to disaster, and, unless divorce is made much easier, there is every reason for their disapproval. Unless divorce is made easier, in fact the whole marriage ceremony is bound towards ultimate obsoleteness. It will not become obsolete in our lifetime but that is the goal rapidly taking form and towards which teeming unborn millions are plunging headlong even though they know it not.

With best wishes for the success of your work.

Believe me,
Yours sincerely,
Rudyard Kipling

Notes

1. Barry-Doyle (1878–1933), a second cousin of A. Conan Doyle, was an army chaplain, 1916–22. He built through his own efforts orphanages and other services for refugee Christian children from Asia Minor in Athens. I do not know what the occasion of this and the following letter is.

To Monsignor Richard Barry-Doyle, 8 November 1919
ALS: University of Texas

Bateman's / Burwash / Sussex / 8 November 1919

Private.

Dear Monsignor Doyle,

This is in the vein of a post-script amplifying a letter to you this morning in which I possibly did not reply fully enough to your question. My conclusion is that not before the age of thirty is a man likely to be equipped for the responsibility of choosing his mate and adapting himself subsequently to connubial life. Marriage leads to a still further development of character through the sacrifices which have to be met and the altruism that is needed, but this development can only take place when the foundations of the personality are sound. Among the immature the calls made on the higher sentiments are too great and the resulting strain provokes the man or woman to adopt some form of refuge – it may be alcohol, drugs, neurotic disease or distracting experiences. On the other hand marriage at an advanced age is apt to be a failure because the habits of thought and feeling of both parties are liable to be too rigid to render adaptability to such a changed form of life easy. There is far too much dogmatism about a conventional bond which is entered into by so many in a naive way without any consideration of the complex problems which sooner or later have to be faced. Education is much to the fore – and yet the potential husband and wife are ready to launch forth on the difficult course of matrimony more or less completely ignorant of its essential issues. Good maturity, stabilisation of character, knowledge of the world and experience should succeed[1] marriage and youth should wait.

Yours
R. K.

Note
1. Thus in MS: "precede"?

To André Chevrillon, 10 November 1919

Text: Copy, University of Sussex

Bateman's / Burwash / Sussex / Nov. 10. 1919

Dear Chevrillon,

I know that I wrote a reply to your most charming note acknowledging my "documentation" but whether, in the whirl in which I live just now, that letter ever went, by Allah I cannot tell, or recall.

But the sum and substance of it was that I do have confidence in you both as man and artist and therefore I sent you what I did for your background. But the [   ][1] of it are between ourselves and I don't see why the public need ever know the tale. As a matter of fact, they could (such as cared) find the facts more or less hinted at in various tales or in my books – the school influences in *Stalky & Co*; early France in the *Light that failed*; extreme youth in *Baa Baa Black Sheep* and so on. I expect every writer consciously or unconsciously gives the number and size and colour of the heifers that he plowed with to such as have time to look and eyes that see. In *Stalky* you'll find a list of books read by *Beetle* in his headmaster's study which strike me now as a very useful foundation for a child interested in letters. I think they occur in "The Last Term".[2]

I was trying to recall the other day what the deuce I ever made out of Pushkin and I Hermanstoff's[3] stories; but I do remember when I was a lad getting hold of the Contes Drolatiques[4] and a French Rabelais and the Father telling me that the Contes were a model of splendid parody. Then there was a life of Dumas in many volumes[5] that made my head spin with excitement and inchoate ideas and – as I think I once told you – a small, vilely printed Béranger that I had, and still have, which for some reason, took hold on me. Otherwise the French influences (excepting always Paris in '78) seem to have been few. *Nota*: my written French was only one degree worse than my Latin – which is saying something. But anyhow I was taught both and I hold that that at any rate, was a decent foundation in which to get knowledge. I praise Allah day and night that He preserved me from any knowledge whatever of the Boche tongue or literature or "thought", and that I have never numbered among my friends or even my acquaintances one member of those accursed tribes.[6]

Do you notice now how their insane psychology attempts to infect the Universe? There is one Einstein,[7] nominally a Swiss, certainly a Hebrew, who (the thing is so inevitable that it makes one laugh) comes forward, scientifically to show that, under certain conditions Space itself is warped and the instruments that measure it are warped also. There was a big discussion the other day before one of our learned societies[8] to show that Light has weight and therefore bends by its own weight like a shot from Big Bertha. Consequently, (I do not pretend to understand the mathematics of it) on the edges of the Universe there is no such thing as a straight line, parallel lines, or any of the accepted bases of measurement.

But the phrase that sticks in my mind is that "Space is warped". When you come to reflect on a race that made the world Hell, you see how just and right it is that they should decide that space *is* warped, and should make their own souls the measure of all Infinity. The more I see of the Boche's mental workings the more sure am I that he is Evil Incarnate, and, like all evil, a pathetic Beast. Einstein's pronouncement is only another little contribution to assisting the world towards flux and disintegration. If you notice how the Jew and pro-Boche papers deal with it, you will be enlightened.

Ever yours
RK

Notes
1. Blank in copy.
2. "The Last Term", *Stalky & Co.*, pp. 217–18. Chevrillon follows this lead in summarising RK's early reading in *Three Studies in English Literature*, p. 14.
3. Thus in copy, for "Lermontoff": "French translations of Muscovite authors called Pushkin and Lermontoff" ("The Last Term", p. 217).
4. By Balzac, 1832–7, in imitation of Rabelais.
5. Perhaps RK means Dumas' own *Mes Mémoires* (Paris, 20 vols, 1852–4).
6. One may note RK's admiration for Heine, acknowledged in his letter to Huret of 31 August 1905, and his friendship with Dr Fröhlich, as but two exceptions to this statement.

7. Einstein had just earned international fame when one of his predictions, based on the general theory of relativity, had been confirmed by the observations of a British expedition sent by the Royal Society to photograph a solar eclipse in May of this year. *The Times*, reporting on all this, identified Einstein as "a Swiss Jew" (8 November 1919).
8. At the Royal Society, 6 November: *The Times* account says that the report of the expedition to Brazil suggests that "space may acquire a twist or warp in certain circumstances" (7 November 1919).

To Frank N. Doubleday, 11 November 1919
ALS: Princeton University

Bateman's / Burwash / Sussex / Nov. 11. 1919.

Dear Old Man,

The *Atlantic Monthly* has just come in – about a week after your letter: our mail arrangements being, as usual, sketchy and irregular.

I've read the tale carefully.[1] Publish it by all means as propaganda, but the incident itself is too slight and too much a matter of common form to need any foreword. The fact of its being dwelt upon is unconscious testimony to the world's width of experience that divides our two countries. It happened all the time, for, obviously, one couldn't depart from one's engagements and what help one could give to other people just because a boy had been killed. If we had done that all life would have been paralyzed. We had to entertain a man two days after John was killed, and another man (he lost his son later) two days after that, and the matter was, naturally, not alluded to.[2] Lady Sherwood in the tale only tells the truth when she says that nothing is allowed to interfere with a man on leave having a good time.[3] That is the Law when one lives, as we all had to live, for four years next door to the cannon's mouth. It *is* a bit trying to take a boy to a music hall a week after his brother has been scuppered but it had to be done, and one had to sit in the same seats where one's own boy, a week before, was laughing at the same play. As I said, it is all common form but if your people don't realize it, by all means let 'em have the story as propaganda.[4]

We've just had our "two minutes' silence" in honour of the armistice and "all it freed us from." After a year's mucking about and deciding nothing we are in England beginning to realize a few of the things that we are now let in for; and, by all accounts, you seem to be realizing your share of trouble too. It's not a cheery outlook and it all came from not finishing the war; but leaving Germany capable of harm and making her a present of Russia.

So far as we, over here, can make out, the U.S.A. isn't going into the League and is not going to take any responsibilities for administering anything or any one (Ireland excepted!) outside her own borders. So the bottom is out of *that*! It doesn't seem much of a harvest for 12 months: and our Lloyd-George is rather inclined to recognize and make terms with the maniacs in Russia, whose principles of government your police seem to have unearthed at Baltimore, according to today's papers.[5] No. "Taking one consideration with another" the prospects ahead of us are in no way cheering for people who are paid by results and not because they are "organized."

For the moment our "Labour" situation is more easy but I think that is only a lull. It would be very funny if *"As easy as A.B.C."* all came true fifty years before the date given in the tale![6]

I'm very busy and so is C. but she is keeping well and we have servants – no small thing these days. We're wrestling with a leaky dam up the river which we are trying to mend with clay and concrete: also we are trying to get some cottages built but as there is no labour (it is easier to live on "unemployment doles" than to turn out and work) our chances are small. This is rather a lugubrious letter but yours was full of woes too.

We must just carry on as best we can and hope for things to mend; but there are times when l wish your great and good Mr Wilson and our equally great and good Lloyd-George were keeping each other company in the middle of the desert of Sahara. It is only the really earnest and uplifting man that makes earth a Hades.

All our love to you both.

Ever affectionately
Rud

Notes

1. Margaret Prescott Montague, "England to America", *Atlantic Monthly*, September 1919, pp. 322–31. The American hero, a Virginian with the Royal Flying Corps, visits the parents of his commanding officer in Devon; they entertain him without telling him that their son has been killed while the American has been away from the front on leave.
2. The Bateman's Visitors Book does not show any guests at this time.
3. "And in these days a boy's leave is so precious a thing that nothing must spoil it – *nothing*" (p. 331).
4. Doubleday published the story, which won the O. Henry Prize as "the best American story of 1919", in book form with an introductory note by John Drinkwater in place of the one that RK declined to write.
5. Under the direction of the Department of Justice scores of raids had been carried out on "nests of anarchists and Industrial Workers of the World" on 9 November (*The Times*, 10 November 1919). In Baltimore, six alleged "Bolsheviki" were arrested.
6. The story is set in AD 2065.

To George Parkin,[1] 16 November 1919
ALS: Public Archives of Canada

Bateman's / Burwash / Sussex / Nov. 16. 1919.

Dear Dr. Parkin

l was away when your wire came, about the O[range]. F[ree]. S[tate]. Scholarships but wired you, on my return that I could not agree with the idea of giving *Dixon*[2] the 1918 Scholarship.

My objections are (1) That the very pre-eminence of the boy who, his Committee assert, stands in a class by himself intellectually and athletically, is due to his having stood out of the war. This, in itself, would seem to be against Rhodes's requirement that a Rhodes Scholar should be a sportsman.

(2) As Oxford is constituted at present, such a boy as Dixon coming up unscathed and without war-experience into a society of young veterans is not likely to be well-received. Indeed the higher his scholastic and athletic achievements the more certainly will he attract to himself criticism of the means by which he reached that excellence. The chances are he might find himself more or less isolated; and, therefore, might be drawn to associate with the undesirable elements at Oxford of whom, as you know, there are an appreciable number. That, to my thinking, is a serious consideration.

The mere tacking of a rider of regret, that he had not war-service as well as scholarship, to his nomination would, it seems to me, show that the trustees were uneasy in their own minds on the matter – which would be no gain.

I could explain my views better verbally than in writing but l suggest that Dixon's name be dropped and that the 1918 scholarship be awarded to one or other of the two boys who did actual work in the war.

Very sincerely
Rudyard Kipling.

Notes
1. (Sir) George Parkin (1846–1922), the first secretary to the Rhodes Scholarship Trust. A Canadian, he had been a teacher and then an employee of the Imperial Federation League before becoming principal of Upper Canada College, Toronto, in 1895. He was appointed to the Rhodes secretaryship in 1902 and devoted the rest of his life to organising, directing, and publicising the work of the Trust.
    RK had been made a member of the Rhodes Trust in 1917, on the invitation of Dr Jameson (CK diary, 27 August 1917).
2. Peter Matthew Dixon (1895–1970), elected a Rhodes scholar from Grey University College, Bloemfontein. He was at University College, Oxford, 1920–2, and took a BA in Mathematics. He returned to South Africa and taught at the Grey College School. From the dates of his Oxford career it appears that he may have been refused election in 1918, but he did receive a Rhodes Scholarship.

To The Reverend James O. Hannay, 18 November 1919
TLS: Dalhousie University

Bateman's / Burwash / Sussex / 18th. Nov. 1919

Private

Dear Hannay,

I put in the whole of this morning reading your book on Ireland[1] – for which I expect you will be most impartially cursed by all parties. But it left me, personally, with a sense of confirmed hopelessness and despair – the sort of bored terror one has of a woman of 50 who explains that she has never been understood since she was born. This is a narrow and a Philistine view based, I suppose, on the fact that you put forward so searchingly, that the imaginative Irishry love non-competitive careers with nice small salaries from the Government.[2] I've hunted high and low, these many years, for any data that would present Ireland as a nation, and I have never come across any more than records of small caterans killing cattle and destroying their neighbours, and (this *must* be professional jealousy!) writing most dreary poems about it all. I've always looked on the land as the left flank of the long battle that Rome began to wage against England since the Reformation, and that's why I don't understand your dismissing the Religious question so lightly;[3] tho' I see that it couldn't be handled safely. Bless you for speaking up for Dean Swift (whose prose is Ithuriel's sword and whose verse is toilette-paper) and for your lightning phrase of dying "of excess of sanity".[4] None of our rulers will perish that way. But I'd like to tell you about your book by word of mouth some day.

Here's luck to your Boy across the water, and may he prosper! He has made the same discovery that, I fancy, Columbus did. But then Columbus lived before the League of Nations.

Ever sincerely,
Rudyard Kipling

Rev. James O. Hannay, M. A. etc.
  Carnalway,
    Kilcullen,
      Kildare.

Notes
1. *An Irishman Looks at His World*, 1919, published under Hannay's pseudonym of "George A. Birmingham".
2. In Dublin, Hannay writes, "the highest ambition of most men is a well-salaried post" (*An Irishman Looks at His World*, p. 238).
3. "We have attained a religious stability which would be simply impossible in a people deeply interested in religion" (p. 90).

4. "… that same cool sanity which gave their terrible force to the writings of Swift which turned him into a madman at last, if men can be made mad by excess of sanity" (pp. 194–5).

To General Sir Geoffrey Feilding,[1] 20 November 1919
ALS: Photocopy, University of Sussex

Bateman's / Burwash / Sussex / Nov 20. 1919.

Dear General Fielding
I enclose with this my draft of the proposed inscription for the Guards Memorial[2] and for the letter asking for subscriptions.[3]
On reflection 1 judged it better not to put in "and also" to the memory of the units etc. attached to the Guards Division as that word might convey the idea that the other arms were relegated to a secondary position.
Similarly, if one begins the inscription "to *all*" Guardsmen etc., it might look as if a point were made of including everyone: whereas of course all are included, as a matter of course, who have died.
I am a little doubtful as to the wording of the letter of appeal which seems to lump all officers and men in the Brigade as "Guardsmen"; but this I presume is the Committee's wish. Otherwise I should be inclined to use the phrase "Officers and men of His Majesty's Regiments of Foot Guards". I hope that some of these suggestions may at least form a basis for discussion.

Very sincerely
Rudyard Kipling

Notes
1. Feilding (1866–1932) commanded the Guards Division, 1916–18.
2. The Guards memorial stands on the west side of the Horse Guards Parade in Whitehall. According to a note accompanying the letter RK proposed the following inscription:

> To all members of His Majesty's Regiments
> of Foot Guards and of other units of the Guards
> Division who fell in the Great War.

The inscription actually used differs only in altering "all members of His Majesty's Regiments of" to "all Regiments of His Majesty's".
3. A note on the letter says that RK wrote: "Should sufficient funds be forthcoming the Committee will take into consideration other memorials that have or will be suggested."

To Sir Andrew Macphail, 22 November 1919

ALS: Photocopy, National Archives of Canada

Brown's Hotel, / London, W. 1. / Nov: 22: 1919.

Dear Macphail:

I forebore writing while the physical shadow was on you;[1] being altogether of Job's opinion in the matter of consolation. Now comes your sad letter of loss and another shadow[2] and there, I feel, I can without offence or intrusion reach out my hand to yours in sympathy. There is no comfort for these things – there never has been, and I don't pretend to pretend that I believe in any. Only, I am sorry – sorrier than any words can say – that it should have come to you, so wantonly to all appearance, and as an extra after these last five years.

We are all walking in a land of ghosts here – in a queerer world than the war made for us – a world with all props, hoops, screws and angle-irons removed and an irritated humanity stravaging[3] (there's no other word) in the middle of it all telling itself that it is "new" and "progressive" when it is only a shaken, disturbedly dreaming convalescent liable still to night-sweats, semi-hallucinations and spurts of rising temperature. It needs a doctor now to write of this world: but the only one I can think of is – his name was Thomas Browne[4] – is quite dead: and the sole clergyman whom I would have trusted for the job in default of him, died mad in Ireland quite a few years ago. I was reading Gulliver's Travels the other day and lamenting that he was not here to give us his rewritten version.

And atop of it all, comes the fantastic – but perfectly logical collapse of the U.S.A. and their wonderful spokesman[5] – a sort of Kopernick[6] *in excelsio.* D'you remember a German cobbler of that name, years before the war, who perceiving his countrymen's idolatry of uniforms, put on that of a general, invaded a small garrison town, had an inspection of troops, levied tribute of some sort, and then – went round the corner, took his uniform off and disappeared. The Huns, whose humour was never strong, caught and tried him later: and the simplicity of his explanation almost made even *them* laugh! But, at bottom, I confess I'm not altogether sorry, tho' it will throw fresh burdens on us within the Empire, to haul and push and kick this world into some sort of shape and consistency. But it's – in the long run – the worst thing that the U.S.A. ever did and all Europe is full of dry grins. *Apropos.* You know the theory that the gibberish of children's "counting-out" games is supposed to be remnants of the oldest speech in the world? And you remember of course the sacred rhyme of all the American children in our generation:–

> "Eeny, Meeny, Mainy, Mo –
> Catch a nigger by the toe.
> If he hollers let him go –

> Eeny, Meeny, Mainy, Mo!
> You're It!"[7]

(If you don't, Dorothy doubtless will have heard of it). And here's a nation that won't be "It" in the game – the nigger that hollered and had to be let go. Present the idea to Stephen Leacock for use in your University magazine. He can easily trace the connection between "Meeny, Mainy" back to "*Mene, Mene Tekel Upharsin*".[8]

Things on the farms here are looking up. We've got two woodcutters at work and these blistered hands have cut nearly two cords of wood along the river. (We're hard up for fuel). Also, one new calf has been born to our Guernsey cows a demobbed officer with a taste for fruit farming has hired one of the wife's farms; we've sold about twenty steers to what looks like profit till you reckon the cost of feeding; and our winter ploughing goes forward without hindrance from the weather. The wife (glory be), is very well and not too tired; and Elsie is enjoying herself in her youth. I've had (thanks to awful and potent Pills) a let-up in my pains for some months past and am busied with pens and ink – to no profit thank goodness but just stodgy work.

We came up to town yesterday, for the first time since summer and are here for a week doing social things; attending weddings among our kin and so forth.[9]

We had one glorious month in the Highlands – Glenartny was the place – and I found all the heather full of Macdonalds which is my mother's side and we united in thanking God for our Scotch blood and cursing all Campbells. But what a lovely land and what a portentous, granite-gutted, self-sufficient community: and *what* a system of education did John Knox give 'em! But I caught no salmon, though on the crest of Killin pass, (1500 feet) our car stole down a slope almost atop of a couple of stag in a wreath of mist: it was a sight to be remembered. They backed clean across the road and then walked into the tumbled hillside. We went also to Abbotsford[10] and were duly taken round Sir Walter's rooms which made me vehemently sick – and yet I had come for that purpose in pure love and worship. And his tomb in ruined Dryburgh made me sadder than all the rest. I think that when such as he have done their work they should be left with only their works for witness after them. The railway strike caught us up at St. Ronan's Well and we fled home – 400 miles in 2 days – through a land of straggling, wretched people trying to move about in lorries, busses and all sorts of wheeled things; rather like an evacuating back-area in France. The end of this procession of strange sights was an elephant on the Great North Road, pulling a Wombwell's menagerie car! Ours fairly shied at the sight of the black, sulky bulk of him padding his way into Grantham.

I don't suppose that any Papal interdict was ever as thorough as that Railway strike: and – it produced about the same effect, on the English, as an interdict. They began to question the Holiness of the Pope who had imposed it! Another year or two of this sort of thing and they will do more than question. 'Curious, how exactly the Papacy and Trades Unions follow the same path, in almost the same woods.

But, once more, I babble. Never mind. Forgive me and write us from time to time and take all our united affections for yourself and for Dorothy.

Ever
Rudyard

P.S. And still the pre-war whiskey holds out! Only there are dam few worthy to drink it.

Notes
1. Macphail, who was suffering from glaucoma, had had an eye operation in April 1919 and was prevented from reading until autumn of that year.
2. Macphail's close friend Julia Heinrich, a professional singer, died in a railway accident in the US in the summer of 1919; RK's reference may be to that event (information from Professor Ian Ross Robertson).
3. Wandering about aimlessly (Scottish dialect).
4. Sir Thomas Browne (1605–82), the great seventeenth century stylist, author of *Religio Medici, 1642, Vulgar Errors*, 1646, *Hydriotaphia*, 1658, and other tracts and treatises.
5. On 2 October, at the crisis of his struggle to persuade the nation to accept the peace treaty and the League of Nations, President Wilson suffered a stroke that put an end to his active life.
6. In 1906 Wilhelm Voigt, a cobbler, impersonated a Guards officer at Köpenick and made off with 4,000 marks from the municipal treasury. The story furnished the basis for *Der Hauptmann von Köpenick*, a comedy by Carl Zuckmayer, 1931.
7. Later used as the refrain of RK's "A Counting-Out Song" (*Land and Sea Tales*, 1923).
8. The handwriting on the wall at Belshazzar's feast: Daniel, 5.
9. I do not know whose weddings are meant.
10. Sir Walter Scott's home near Melrose; this was on 26 September (CK diary).

To the Editor, *Daily Telegraph*, [4 December 1919][1]
Text: Daily Telegraph, 5 December 1919

[Bateman's]

Sir –

A number of people from all parts of the world are visiting, and there is every sign that an immense number may be expected next year to visit, the French and Flanders fronts and the cemeteries behind. A proportion of these visitors will be relatives or next-of-kin to the dead, whose pilgrimages will be made with heavy hearts, but very many others will be drawn by curiosity and a natural interest in historical ground. But that ground, it should be remembered, is also holy – consecrated in every part by the freely-offered lives of men, and for that reason not to be overrun with levity.

It is inevitable that the handling of such multitudes of sightseers must be managed on ordinary tourist lines, so it rests with the individual tourist to have respect for the spirit that lies upon all that land of desolation and to walk through it with reverence. It is said that there is a tendency among some visitors to forget this obligation. Nothing would be gained by giving specific instances of what, after all, is more in the nature of unthinking carelessness than any intentional disrespect; but the Imperial War Graves Commission have asked me to express our most earnest hope that all who visit the battle areas will bear in mind that, at every step, they are in the presence of those dead through the merits of whose sacrifice they enjoy their present life and whatever measure of freedom is theirs today.

I am yours, etc.,
R.K.

Note
1. This letter appeared in other London papers on 5 December. In the *Morning Post* it is dated 4 December.

To H. A. Gwynne, 14 December 1919
ALS: Dalhousie University

Bateman's / Burwash / Sussex / Dec 14. 1919.

private.
Dear Old Man –
Some little time back in one of the papers, apropos of the outbreaks of cattle disease (foot and mouth) in England[1] was a statement that the attacks had been in some cases traced to the proximity of Hun prison camps where it was possible that the refuse of the food parcels which the Huns had been allowed to receive, had been thrown away where cattle could get at them and that the scraps of Hun beef etc. from infected cattle in Germany may have spread the trouble. I dare say that is true.[2] A little later there was announcement – in the *Times* I believe, of a new Bolshevik programme of

attack against the bourgeoisie which should include "the propagation of diseases and other methods of *Kultur*."

In the light of what you and I know* this isn't surprising and I expect there will be attempts at infection.

But it's the cattle trouble I'm thinking of mostly: and I have a sort of idea that we shall get some fresh foot and mouth or pleuro-pneumonia outbreaks. The trouble in Switzerland[3] may be a preliminary experiment.

But my point is this and I want the M.P. to point it out.[4] It might be worth while to watch people who have come in to little villages, whether as cobblers, small tradesmen and the like, within the past few months, who set up as Socialist or Bolshevik agitators. I can't make out where they get their stock and goods from or why it is worth their while to open shop. But if there *is* going to be any disease among the herds, it is the easiest thing in the world for unconnected strangers of that kind to spread it. As *we* know, we are up against creatures who are stopping at nothing whatever but if our people once got the idea that cattle infection was possibly spread by strangers in small villages, I fancy they might be very angry indeed. I want you to work out that line of thought, very carefully. No one took the trouble to comment on the first outbreaks of foot and mouth and the Hun prison camps: but you might dig up the note and you would see what it implied. The fact that I have a Guernsey herd and that last year there was an outbreak within a mile of me[5] doesn't make me exactly disinterested in the matter. Over and above that, I want a better watch kept on queer talkative Socio-Bolshio strangers in rural districts.

Ever thine
RK

* The spread of disease is one of the weapons.

Notes
1. There were outbreaks of foot-and-mouth disease all over England and elsewhere in Europe in this year, and a ban on imports of livestock had been imposed.
2. RK attempted to follow up this lead. On 17 December he wrote to Winston Churchill, then Secretary for War, asking for "a list of the places where German prisoners were confined during the war" (copy, Sussex); on the same day he wrote to Lord Lee, then president of the Board of Agriculture, for "a list of places where outbreaks of cattle diseases ... in England, Scotland and Wales – have occurred during the period of the war and a year afterwards" (copy, Sussex). I do not know what, if anything, came of these inquiries.
3. Where foot-and-mouth disease was then widespread.
4. I do not find that the subject was taken up in the *Morning Post*.
5. An outbreak of foot-and-mouth disease at Burwash was reported in September 1918 and cleared up by November (*The Times*, 27 September, 9 November 1918).

Register of Names and Correspondents

A full index will be published at the end of the final volume. For the convenience of the reader in the interim this list is provided of RK's correspondents and contemporaries identified in this volume. The page references are to the notes in which the identifications are made.

Aberdeen, Marchioness of, 61
Airey, Osmund, 565
  letter to: 21 August 1919
Aitken, Allen, 308
Aitken, Janet, 181
Aitken, John William Maxwell, 181
Aitken, Max, 1st Baron Beaverbrook, 48
  letters to: 6 September 1911; 15
    November 1911; 12 April 1912;
    9 April 1913; 29 July 1913; 14
    November 1913; 15 January 1914;
    15 May 1914; 3 September 1914;
    19 January 1915; [February 1915];
    6 December 1915; 9 November
    1916; 19 December 1916; 25
    February 1918; 11 April 1918
Aitken, Mrs Max, 88
Aitken, Peter Rudyard, 132
Alexander, Colonel Henry Lethbridge, 457
Alma-Tadema, Laurence, 298
  letter to: 21 April 1915
Alma-Tadema, Sir Lawrence, 7
Arran, 6th Earl of, 219
Ashmead-Bartlett, Ellis, 137
Asquith, Herbert Henry, 1st Earl of
  Oxford and Asquith, 25
Auriol, George
  letter to: [c. March 1911]

Baden-Powell, Sir Robert
  letter to: 29 July 1916
Bailey, Mrs Abe, 48
Baillie, Herbert, 356
  letter to: 12 January 1916
Baker, Herbert
  letters to: 24 January [1913]; 7 October
    1918
Baldwin, Arthur, 109
Baldwin, Diana Lucy, 88

Baldwin, Louisa
  letters to: 31 January 1911; 5 July
    [1916]; 19 [July] 1919
Baldwin, Margot, 113
Baldwin, Oliver
  letters to: 31 October 1914;
    20 November 1915; 3 October
    1916; 17 June 1918; 2 August 1918
Baldwin, Stanley
  letters to: 18 March 1911; [23 June 1911];
    6 May 1912; 23 October 1915; 20
    November 1915; 22 October 1916;
    29 January 1917; 1 December 1917;
    2 July 1918; 21 September 1918;
    [19? February 1919]; 13 June 1919;
    23 September 1919
Baldwin, Mrs Stanley
  letter to: [mid-September 1911]
Balestier, Anna Smith
  letters to: 25 December 1911; [9 July
    1912]; 24 September 1912;
    8 September 1916
Baring, Maurice, 320
Barnes, Ernest William, 360
Barry-Doyle, Monsignor Richard, 590
  letters to: 8 November 1919;
    8 November 1919
Bateson, Dr Vaughan
  letter to: 26 August 1919
Bathurst, Lady
  letter to: 15 June 1911
Bathurst, Ralph Henry, 46
Bathurst, William, 46
  letter to: 26 August 1911
Battenberg, Louis of, 1st Marquess of
  Milford Haven, 315
Beaverbrook, Lord: *see* Max Aitken
Beckett, Walter Napier, 387
Beit, Otto, 554
  letter to: 1 June 1919

603

Benedict XV, Pope, 454
Benson, A. C., 437
Berthillon, Alphonse, 320
Besant, Annie, 494
Billing, Noel Pemberton, 500
Birkenhead, 1st Earl of, 201
Bland-Sutton, Lady Edith, 303
    letter to: [9 May 1915]
Bland-Sutton, Sir John, 205
Blumenfeld, R. D., 123
    letters to: 18 June 1912; 12 June 1914;
        [4 August 1914]; 5 September
        1914; 6 October 1915
Bok, Edward
    letters to: 4 December 1911; 28 October
        1914; 5 December 1914
Booth, Frederick Handel, 195
Borden, Sir Robert, 125
Brade, Sir Reginald, 286
Brassey, Captain Cecil Henry, 320
Brassey, Thomas, 1st Earl Brassey, 118
Brett, George, 21
Briand, Aristide, 223
Bridges, Robert, 559
Brookfield, Charles H. E., 552
Brooking, J. H. C.
    letters to: 19 January 1918; 28
        November 1918
Brownrigg, Sir Douglas, 24 April 1916
Bruce, Herbert Alexander, 411
Buchanan, Brigadier-General K. J., 345
Buckle, George Earle
    letter to: 27 June [1911]
Bullen, Frank T., 236
    letter to: 20 May 1914
Burham, 1st Viscount, 475
Burke, Henry Morton, 302
Burne-Jones, Lady
    letter to: 28 February 1913
Burns, John, 123
Butler, Colonel L. J. P., 340
Butler, Montagu, 414
Byers, John Roddick, 74

Caclamanos, Demetrius, 514
    letter to: [8? October 1918]
Cadorna, General Luigi, 457
Caillaux, Joseph, 223
Cambon, Paul, 448
Campbell, Edward Fitzgerald, 118
Campbell, Lt-Col. Sir Guy, 3rd Baronet,
    118
Capello, General Luigi, 462

Carter, Ridgeley, 320
Casement, Sir Roger, 500
Cassell, Sir Ernest, 176
Castier, Jules, 533
Catherwood, Annie, 168
Cave, 1st Viscount, 513
Cecil, Lady Edward
    letters to: 16 March 1912; 3 December
        1914; 28 May 1916
Cecil, George, 270
Chamberlain, Mrs Joseph, 126
Chaplin, Henry, 126
Chapman, Robert William, 26
Chettle, Major Henry Francis, 537
Chevrillon, André
    letters to: 31 December 1915; 22 June
        1916; 22 July 1916; 7 August 1916;
        14 January 1919; 6 October 1919;
        11 October 1919; 22 October 1919;
        10 November 1919
Clifford, Sir Hugh, 521
    letter to: 18 November 1918
Colvin, Ian
    letter to: 5 October 1916
Cook, Frank Henry, 179
    letter to: 1 April 1913
Cook, General Henry Rex, 42
Cornford, Lawrence, 188
    letter to: 8 July 1913
Corning, Hanson Kelly, 16
Cowans, General Sir John, 315
Crasto, Colonel Shafto Longfield, 302
Crewe, Sir Charles P.
    letters to: 14–22 February 1912; 9 June
        1912; 22 December 1912; 14 July
        1914; 13 March 1915
Crewe, Ranulph, 140
Crichton-Stuart, Colum Edmund,
    176
Cromer, 1st Earl of, 175
Curteis, Dr Arthur William Statter, 144
Cuthbert, Captain James Harold, 284
Cuthbert, Mrs Harold, 469

Dalziel, James Henry, 1st Baron Dalziel,
    123
Dana, Henry Wadsworth Longfellow,
    534
Darmesteter, James, 577
Davidson, Randall Thomas, Archbishop
    of Canterbury, 115
Davis John W., 529
Dawson, Geoffrey, 38